Financial Technology

Financial Technology: A Comprehensive Introduction offers a comprehensive exploration of one of the most transformative forces in contemporary finance. This essential guide explains how FinTech is fundamentally reshaping financial transactions, institutional operations, and global financial engagement.

Blending theory with practical insights, the book traces FinTech's history and examines its influence across modern financial institutions, including banks, insurers, investment houses, and central banks. It introduces readers to the technologically driven evolution of financial markets, encompassing crypto-assets, algorithmic trading, and decentralised finance. The book further examines cutting-edge tools such as artificial intelligence, Regulatory Technology, advanced digital payment systems, and central bank digital currencies, all presented with clarity and analysis. Each chapter features learning objectives, practical case studies, and discussion questions to encourage deeper understanding and critical thinking.

Designed for students, financial professionals, policymakers, and investors, *Financial Technology: A Comprehensive Introduction* balances accessibility with depth. Serving as both an authoritative guide and a strategic framework, this book equips readers to navigate the rapidly evolving financial technology landscape and understand the complexities ahead.

Abdullah Al Mamoon is an academic, researcher, and author specialising in banking and finance, with over 20 years of professional and academic experience. His research focuses on financial economics, global capital allocation, ethical banking, and digital finance. He is a Certified Practicing Accountant (CPA), holds a PhD in International Finance and Banking, and is a Fellow of the Higher Education Academy, all of which reflect his commitment to research excellence and academic leadership.

Financial Technology

A Comprehensive Introduction

Abdullah Al Mamoon

Routledge
Taylor & Francis Group
LONDON AND NEW YORK

Designed cover image: metamorworks / Getty Images ©

First published 2027
by Routledge
4 Park Square, Milton Park, Abingdon, Oxon OX14 4RN

and by Routledge
605 Third Avenue, New York, NY 10158

Routledge is an imprint of the Taylor & Francis Group, an informa business

British Library Cataloguing-in-Publication Data
A catalogue record for this book is available from the British Library

ISBN: 978-1-041-30699-3 (hbk)
ISBN: 978-1-041-30698-6 (pbk)
ISBN: 978-1-003-77575-1 (ebk)

DOI: 10.4324/9781003775751

Typeset in Times New Roman
by SPi Technologies India Pvt Ltd (Straive)

Access the Support Material: www.routledge.com/9781041306986

To my wife, and my daughters, Monalisa and Annalisa, for their unwavering support and encouragement, for which I am deeply grateful.

And to my beloved aunt Gulnahar, whose prayers have always supported my success.

This work is especially dedicated to the cherished memory of my late parents, Abdul Monnan Ahmad and Sanowara Begum, whose guidance profoundly shaped my commitment to compassion, dignity, and meaningful contribution to society.

Contents

Figures

Tables

About the Author

Abdullah Al Mamoon is a distinguished academic, researcher, and author specialising in financial economics, banking, and international finance, with over 20 years of combined professional and scholarly experience. His work focuses on the intersection of monetary policy, financial markets, and digital finance, with particular emphasis on central banking, institutional transparency, and global capital allocation.

His research explores how institutional frameworks influence financial behaviour across international markets, contributing to the understanding of central bank independence and transparency, cross-border investment, and the integration of traditional finance with decentralised finance. His work is characterised by analytical rigour and significant policy relevance, bridging both theoretical and practical aspects of financial economics.

Beyond his research, Abdullah has developed a substantial profile in higher education, with extensive experience in curriculum development, innovative teaching, and academic leadership. He is widely recognised for a research-led, student-centred pedagogical approach that integrates real-world applications, robust quantitative methods, and technology-enhanced learning to enhance the overall learning experience and student outcomes.

He has held academic positions at several universities in the UK. His academic credentials include a PhD in International Finance and Banking, an MA in Islamic Banking and Finance, and an MBA specialising in Accounting and Finance. He is also a Fellow of the Higher Education Academy.

Preface

Finance and banking are rapidly evolving as digital technologies transform the global financial landscape. Innovations such as artificial intelligence, blockchain, big data, cloud computing, digital platforms, and algorithmic decision-making are changing how financial services are designed, delivered, and regulated, leading to major shifts across institutions, markets, and business models. As finance and technology become more integrated, it is crucial to understand both traditional principles and digital innovations. This book offers a comprehensive, future-oriented overview of the finance and banking ecosystem, covering financial fundamentals, institutions, markets, FinTech, digital transformation, regulatory changes, and emerging global trends.

Financial Technology: A Comprehensive Introduction provides a systematic, analytically based examination of this transformation. It combines core financial principles with the technological innovations shaping banking, payments, lending, investment management, regulation, and financial markets. The book traces the development of financial technology and locates FinTech within broader economic and institutional contexts, including financial ecosystems, globalisation, financial inclusion, risk management, and digital financial malfeasance.

The book adopts a balanced, critical view of technological progress, exploring both the opportunities of digital innovation—such as increased efficiency, accessibility, and financial inclusion—and the challenges to financial stability, regulation, governance, cybersecurity, and public trust. Using conceptual frameworks, historical analysis, and real-world scenarios, it underscores the complex trade-offs involved in technology-driven financial innovation.

This book, intended for advanced undergraduate and postgraduate students, educators, researchers, and industry professionals, blends accessibility with analytical precision. It offers the conceptual foundations and practical insights necessary to assess emerging financial technologies, promoting a deeper understanding of how digital innovation is transforming finance, banking, and the global financial system.

Introduction

The global financial system is undergoing a profound transformation driven by the rapid diffusion of digital technologies. Innovations such as mobile payments, digital lending platforms, artificial intelligence, big data analytics, distributed ledger technologies, and application programming interfaces are reshaping how financial services are produced, distributed, and regulated. Collectively described as *Financial Technology* (FinTech), these developments now sit at the centre of modern financial systems rather than at their margins. As a result, FinTech has become a core area of study for students and practitioners of finance, economics, business, and public policy.

Historically, financial services were dominated by large, vertically integrated institutions that controlled infrastructure, data, and customer relationships. Technological change occurred incrementally and was typically absorbed within existing organisational and regulatory frameworks. In contrast, the contemporary FinTech landscape is characterised by modularity, platform-based delivery, and ecosystem-level interaction. Financial services are increasingly embedded in non-financial digital environments, blurring traditional sectoral boundaries and reshaping the relationships among finance, technology, and society. These changes have expanded consumer choice and access while simultaneously introducing new risks, complexities, and regulatory challenges.

Financial Technology: A Comprehensive Introduction provides a structured and interdisciplinary framework for understanding this transformation. The book is designed for use across advanced undergraduate and postgraduate programmes, offering conceptual clarity for readers encountering FinTech for the first time while also supporting deeper analytical engagement with its systemic implications. Rather than presenting FinTech as a collection of isolated innovations, the text conceptualises it as an evolving ecosystem shaped by technological capabilities, institutional responses, regulatory frameworks, and broader economic and social forces.

A central premise of the book is that FinTech represents a structural transformation in financial intermediation rather than a purely technological upgrade. Technologies such as cloud computing, application programming Interfaces (APIs), artificial intelligence, and blockchain have enabled the unbundling of traditional financial services, the rise of platform-based business models, and the emergence of decentralised financial architectures. These developments challenge established theories of banking, market organisation, and regulation, requiring analytical perspectives that integrate finance with information systems, law, governance, and political economy.

At the same time, the book adopts a balanced and critical stance towards innovation. While FinTech has generated significant benefits, including efficiency gains, cost reductions, enhanced competition, and expanded financial inclusion, it has also produced new vulnerabilities. Issues such as cybersecurity risk, data concentration, algorithmic bias, regulatory fragmentation, financial crime, and ethical accountability are examined alongside technological advances. This dual focus reflects Routledge's emphasis on critical engagement and ensures that innovation is assessed within its broader institutional and societal context.

The book's structure progresses logically from foundational concepts to advanced applications. Early chapters establish the historical evolution of financial technology and the architectural foundations of FinTech ecosystems. Subsequent sections examine how digital innovation is reshaping core financial institutions, including banks, insurers, investment firms, and central banks, highlighting patterns of disruption, adaptation, and convergence. Later chapters address financial markets, regulatory technology, data analytics, artificial intelligence, cybersecurity, and emerging frontiers such as decentralised finance, sustainable finance, geopolitics, quantum finance, and human-centric innovation.

Pedagogically, the book is designed to support learning at multiple academic levels. Clear learning objectives, key terms, review questions, and applied case studies facilitate comprehension for undergraduate readers, while analytical questions, conceptual frameworks, and comparative regulatory analysis support postgraduate study and independent inquiry. Empirical examples are drawn from both advanced and emerging economies, reflecting the global and uneven development of FinTech and its implications for financial inclusion and economic development.

Finally, *Financial Technology: A Comprehensive Introduction* equips readers with the conceptual foundations, analytical tools, and critical perspective required to understand and evaluate the digital transformation of finance. In doing so, it aligns with Taylor & Francis' commitment to interdisciplinary scholarship, global relevance, and the integration of theory and practice in contemporary social science education.

Part 1

Foundations and Evolution of Technology in Finance and Banking

1 History and Evolution of Financial Technology (FinTech)

Chapter Overview

This chapter provides a comprehensive examination of the historical evolution and economic implications of Financial Technology (FinTech), tracing its development from rudimentary record-keeping systems to transformative innovations such as the credit card, the Automated Teller Machine (ATM), and the advent of Internet banking, which collectively laid the groundwork for modern digital finance. The 2008 Global Financial Crisis served as a pivotal catalyst, disrupting established market structures and fostering a competitive environment conducive to FinTech's accelerated growth. Enabled by advancements in blockchain, artificial intelligence (AI), and cloud computing, financial services have undergone a structural transformation, shifting from centralised, vertically integrated institutions towards decentralised, platform-based ecosystems that empower end users and enable greater service customisation. FinTech startups have played a critical role in unbundling traditional banking functions, enhancing consumer accessibility, choice, and specialisation across the financial value chain. The chapter further explores emergent trends such as embedded finance and open banking, which are reconfiguring the landscape of financial intermediation, while also addressing the regulatory challenges inherent in balancing innovation with systemic stability, consumer protection, and the imperative of advancing financial inclusion in an increasingly digitised global economy.

Learning Objectives

By the end of this chapter, you should be able to:

1. Analyse the evolution of FinTech, identifying the major technological innovations and regulatory interventions that have driven its transition from incremental innovation to systemic disruption.
2. Evaluate how the 2008 Global Financial Crisis reshaped the financial services landscape, particularly in weakening trust in traditional institutions and accelerating the adoption and investment in FinTech alternatives.
3. Explain the structural transformation of financial services, including the unbundling of vertically integrated banking models and the rise of embedded finance within non-financial digital ecosystems.

DOI: 10.4324/9781003775751-2

4. Assess the role of foundational enablers, such as Application Programming Interfaces (APIs), cloud computing, and open banking regulations, in supporting interoperability, scalability, and competition in modern financial services.
5. Critically examine the future direction of the financial ecosystem, considering strategic pressures on incumbent banks, the implications for financial inclusion and exclusion, and the emerging influence of technologies such as AI and decentralised finance (DeFi).

1.1 Introduction

The contemporary financial services sector is undergoing a structural transformation driven by the integration of advanced technologies into core banking and financial activities. This phenomenon, commonly referred to as FinTech, encompasses the application of digital innovation to enhance service delivery, operational efficiency, and user accessibility. By providing streamlined, technology-enabled solutions, FinTech firms increasingly challenge the market dominance, business models, and value propositions of traditional financial institutions, compelling incumbents to reassess their organisational structures and service architectures (Gimpel, Rau, & Röglinger, 2017).

Since its inception, the scope of FinTech has expanded significantly. Early implementations focused primarily on improving back-office functions, including process automation, data management, and transaction processing. Over time, however, the focus has shifted towards customer-facing applications. Contemporary FinTech now encompasses digital payments, alternative lending platforms, robo-advisory services, and data-driven wealth management solutions. This transition represents a critical inflexion point in the evolution of financial services, fundamentally altering how individuals and businesses access, manage, and interact with financial resources (Arner, Barberis, & Buckley, 2016).

Comprehending this rapid evolution is essential for interpreting the future trajectory of the global financial system. This chapter examines the historical development of FinTech alongside its present economic significance. By situating current innovations within a broader evolutionary framework, the analysis positions FinTech as a disruptive force that is reshaping competitive dynamics, accelerating digital transformation, and expanding financial inclusion, while also redefining its boundaries.

1.2 The Historical Evolution of FinTech

Many people think FinTech started in this century, but it really began with early computers and communication tools (Figure 1.1).

1.2.1 Early Foundations (1950s–1980s): The Automation Era

The mid-twentieth century marked the dawn of financial digitisation, a transformative period characterised by the systematic automation of previously manual, paper-based financial processes. A pivotal milestone in this evolution was the introduction of the credit card, beginning with the Diners Club in 1950, which initiated the transition towards cashless consumer payments and laid the groundwork for modern electronic transaction systems (Martin, 2020). This era also witnessed the deployment of mainframe computing in

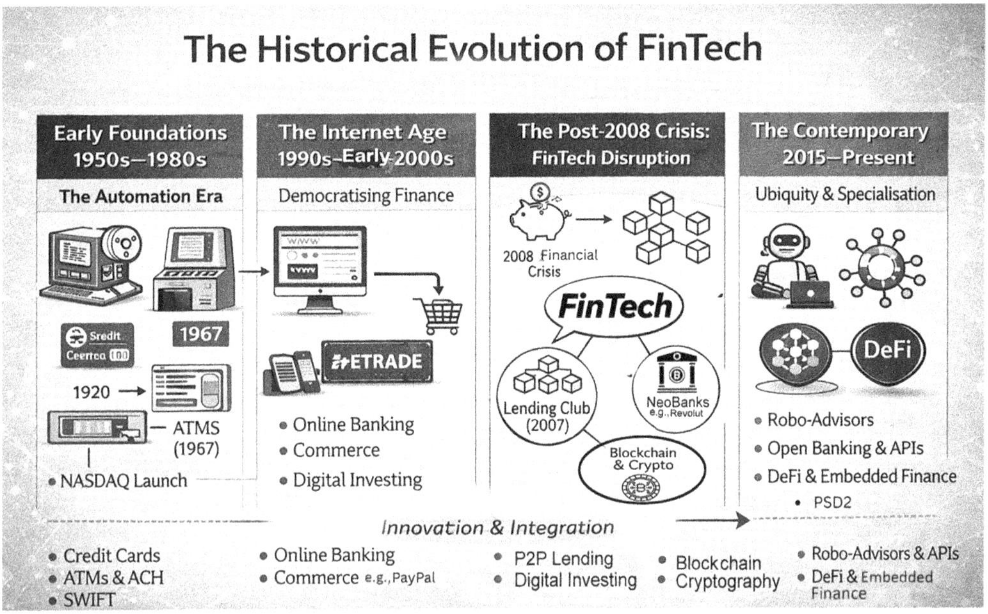

Figure 1.1 The Evolution of the FinTech Industry.

back-office banking operations, enabling early forms of digital data processing, account management, and transaction record-keeping. These technological advancements, though rudimentary by today's standards, significantly improved operational efficiency and set the stage for broader systemic change within the financial sector.

Institutional innovations further accelerated the momentum of digitisation. The introduction of ATMs, beginning with Barclays' launch in 1967, represented a paradigm shift in customer access to banking services, offering a new form of self-service banking beyond conventional branch hours (Batiz-Lazo, 2009). Concurrently, the 1970s saw the establishment of Automated Clearing House (ACH) systems, which reduced reliance on paper checks by enabling electronic interbank fund transfers. On the international front, the creation of the Society for Worldwide Interbank Financial Telecommunication in 1973 revolutionised cross-border payments by replacing error-prone telex systems with a secure, standardised messaging network (Scott & Zachariadis, 2014). In capital markets, the launch of NASDAQ as the world's first electronic stock exchange in the early 1970s, alongside the emergence of early algorithmic trading strategies, signalled a decisive shift towards screen-based, automated trading environments (Michie, 2008). Collectively, these developments established the institutional and technological foundations that would underpin the future digital transformation of global financial services.

1.2.2 The Internet Age (1990s–Early 2000s): Democratising Finance

The commercialisation of the Internet marked a pivotal shift in the trajectory of FinTech, transitioning innovation from back-end banking systems to direct, customer-facing digital services. The advent of the World Wide Web and the subsequent development of secure communication protocols such as Secure Sockets Layer by Netscape in 1994 laid the essential technical groundwork for the secure delivery of financial services online. Early pioneers in the financial sector, including Stanford Federal Credit Union in 1994 and Security First Network Bank in 1995, were among the first institutions to adopt Internet-based banking models, demonstrating the viability of remote account access and digital transaction processing. The integration of digital infrastructure into financial service delivery fundamentally altered the value proposition for consumers, enabling greater convenience and real-time interaction (Gomber et al., 2017). This period signified the beginning of a customer-centric approach in financial innovation, driven by the growing accessibility and reliability of online platforms.

Simultaneously, the rise of electronic commerce giants such as Amazon and eBay transformed consumer expectations around digital transactions. At the same time, the emergence of payment intermediaries like PayPal, founded in 1998, revolutionised the mechanics of online payments by enabling secure, P2P fund transfers. Online brokerage platforms, including eTRADE and Charles Schwab's digital offerings, have democratised access to capital markets by reducing entry barriers for retail investors. Concurrently, early personal finance management tools empowered individuals to track spending, manage budgets, and gain greater control over their financial lives. Collectively, these advancements expanded financial inclusion, enhanced transparency, and significantly reduced transaction costs. As a result, this era not only reshaped consumer behaviour but also established the foundational ecosystem for future, more sophisticated phases of FinTech, characterised by data analytics, platform economies, and seamless digital integration.

1.2.3 The Post-2008 Crisis: FinTech as a Disruptive Force

The 2008 Global Financial Crisis represents a critical inflexion point in the evolution of FinTech. The crisis significantly eroded public trust in established financial institutions. It exposed structural weaknesses in traditional banking models, thereby creating a conducive environment for new entrants offering alternative, technology-driven financial solutions (Philippon, 2016). During this period, the term *FinTech* gained widespread usage, referring to a new generation of firms characterised by agility, transparency, and a strong emphasis on user-centric design. Supported by the rapid diffusion of smartphones and substantial venture capital flows, these firms began to challenge incumbent institutions across multiple segments of the financial value chain.

One prominent area of innovation was P2P lending, also known as marketplace lending. Platforms like Lending Club (established in 2007) and Prosper provide a marketplace where individuals and small businesses can access financing directly from investors, bypassing traditional banks as intermediaries. This model constitutes a form of debt financing in which digital platforms connect borrowers with lenders, conduct credit evaluations, and manage loan servicing, all while functioning outside the conventional deposit-taking banking system.

A second major development involved the rise of mobile payments and digital-only banks. Services such as Venmo and Square (both established in 2009) were followed by later entrants, including Revolut and Chime, that delivered seamless, mobile-first financial experiences. Mobile payments, often referred to as mobile wallets or mobile money, enable transactions to be initiated and authorised on smartphones or other portable devices, reducing reliance on physical cash and cards. In parallel, neobanks, also known as challenger or digital banks, emerged as fully online institutions without branch networks, leveraging cloud infrastructure and data analytics to offer low-cost, user-friendly banking services.

Perhaps the most structurally transformative innovation of this period was the emergence of blockchain technology and cryptocurrencies. The publication of the Bitcoin whitepaper by Nakamoto in 2008 introduced a decentralised, P2P electronic cash system that operates without a central authority. The underlying blockchain architecture functions as a distributed digital ledger in which transactions are recorded across a network of computers and secured through cryptographic consensus mechanisms. This model laid the conceptual and technological foundation for a parallel, decentralised financial ecosystem that challenges conventional notions of intermediation, trust, and monetary sovereignty.

1.2.4 The Contemporary Ecosystem (2015–Present): Ubiquity and Specialisation

Since about 2015, the FinTech landscape has matured into a globally interconnected ecosystem characterised by increasing functional specialisation and strategic collaboration among incumbent financial institutions, technology firms, and startups. Rather than functioning solely as disruptors, FinTech players are now integral components of platform-based financial architectures, where modular services are interwoven through digital infrastructure and data-sharing frameworks. This evolution reflects a shift from isolated innovation to systemic integration, enabling greater efficiency, scalability, and customer-centricity across financial value chains. Banks or tech companies do not own the future of finance; it is orchestrated through ecosystems (McKinsey & Company, 2022). This collaborative model has laid the foundation for a series of transformative trends reshaping the delivery and consumption of financial services.

Among the most impactful developments is the rise of robo-advisory platforms such as Betterment and Wealthfront, which leverage algorithm-driven models rooted in modern portfolio theory and passive investment strategies to deliver low-cost, accessible wealth management services. These platforms utilise data analytics to personalise financial planning while significantly reducing the fees associated with traditional advisory services, thereby expanding access for retail investors who have been historically excluded from professional asset management. Concurrently, the institutionalisation of open banking, propelled by regulatory mandates such as the European Union's Revised Payment Services Directive (PSD2), has standardised secure data access via APIs. These structured protocols enable seamless interoperability between financial systems, fostering the emergence of third-party innovators and reinforcing a platform-oriented financial architecture grounded in data portability and user consent.

Parallel to these advancements, DeFi has emerged as a blockchain-native alternative to traditional financial intermediation. Platforms like Aave and Uniswap employ smart contracts, self-executing code on distributed ledgers, to facilitate lending, borrowing, and trading without centralised control, embodying principles of transparency, permissionless access, and programmability. While still experimental, DeFi represents a paradigm shift in how financial services can be structured and delivered. Complementing this, embedded finance has gained traction by integrating financial functionalities, such as payments, credit, and insurance, directly into non-financial platforms like Shopify and Uber. By embedding services at the point of need, this model transforms financial interactions into seamless, contextual experiences. Together, these trends underscore the growing convergence of finance with broader digital ecosystems, blurring sectoral boundaries and redefining the nature of financial service provision in the digital age.

1.3 The Evolving Economy of Finance and Banking: Disruption and Response

FinTech has fundamentally reshaped how financial institutions compete, deliver services, and generate revenue, introducing both opportunities and existential challenges for traditional banks.

1.3.1 The Unbundling of Traditional Banking

The radical unbundling of traditional banking services characterises modern financial markets. Historically, banks offered an integrated suite of services, deposits, payments, lending, investment, and insurance under a single institutional umbrella. FinTech, however, allows these services to be decoupled into modular, specialised offerings. Consumers can now assemble personalised financial ecosystems, using providers such as Robinhood or eToro for investments, Revolut for digital banking, and Wise for cross-border payments. This fragmentation challenges incumbents by eroding their historically integrated model, as FinTech firms often deliver superior efficiency, user experience, and lower costs.

APIs have become the linchpin of this transformation. Regulatory initiatives such as Open Banking in the UK and PSD2 in the EU mandate secure data sharing between banks and licensed third parties. This framework enables FinTech startups to access banking infrastructure and data while allowing incumbents to rebundle third-party services into their own platforms. For example, HSBC's Connected Money app aggregates multiple accounts and investment products from other providers, creating a mini financial app store. Banks must now decide whether to compete with agile innovators directly or leverage their scale and trust to become aggregators of these innovations.

1.3.2 The Shift in Consumer Trust and Behaviour

Trust, a foundational element of financial intermediation, has shifted from traditional banks to technology-driven platforms. The 2008 global financial crisis eroded confidence in legacy institutions, creating opportunities for digital alternatives that resonate with younger, tech-savvy consumers. A 2024 Deloitte survey reported that 62% of Gen Z and millennial consumers trust technology companies more than traditional banks for financial management. Platforms like PayPal, Venmo, and Chime illustrate this trend by offering real-time transactions, user-friendly interfaces, and transparent fee structures that legacy banks often struggle to match. As a result, traditional banks face pressure to modernise their digital infrastructure and adopt customer-centric approaches, or risk losing market share to more agile competitors.

1.3.3 Utility Risk: The Greatest Threat to Incumbent Banks

FinTech's rise introduces utility risk, the danger that traditional banks could be relegated to behind-the-scenes infrastructure providers. At the same time, customer relationships and value accrue to FinTech and Big Tech firms. Drasch, Schweizer, and Urbach (2018) note that this risk arises from unbundling and the migration of trust, leaving banks to handle commoditised back-end functions while losing brand relevance and profitability. Examples include Alibaba's Ant Group and Tencent's WeBank in China, which have captured substantial customer engagement and financial data while traditional banks provide only transactional support. The highly capital-intensive and regulated nature of banking exacerbates this vulnerability, as consumers increasingly prefer agile digital interfaces. To mitigate utility risk, banks must evolve from product-centric models to platform-based ecosystems, such as JPMorgan's Finn platform and Banco Bilbao Vizcaya Argentaria's (BBVA) Open Platform, which integrate innovative FinTech services to enhance the user experience, maintain relevance, and reclaim competitive advantage. Failure to adapt risks rendering traditional banks invisible utilities in an industry defined by digital agility, service personalisation, and seamless technological integration.

1.4 Key Practical Issues and Regulatory Enablers

The FinTech revolution is not occurring in a vacuum; it is shaped by practical technological challenges and a rapidly evolving regulatory landscape.

1.4.1 The Critical Role of Cloud Computing and Data Analytics

The FinTech revolution is not occurring in a vacuum; it is fundamentally shaped by practical technological enablers, primarily cloud computing and data analytics, which provide the backbone for innovation. The scalability and operational agility of contemporary firms are underpinned by these technologies, with cloud-native infrastructures from providers such as Amazon Web Services and Azure allowing startups to minimise capital expenditure, reduce operational overhead, and deploy services rapidly. Complementing this infrastructure, advanced data analytics and AI facilitate sophisticated capabilities, including AI-driven underwriting, real-time fraud detection, and highly personalised financial advice, that democratise services once exclusive to large institutions with vast resources. The cloud is the great equaliser, enabling smaller entities to compete effectively while generating the data necessary to drive a new era of intelligent, customer-centric finance. Consequently, these technological pillars are not merely operational tools but are critical regulatory enablers, as their secure and standardised implementation is a prerequisite for establishing the trust and robustness required by financial authorities.

1.4.2 The Regulatory Response: Sandboxes and Open Banking

Regulators have confronted the dual imperative of promoting financial innovation while maintaining systemic stability, as traditional regulatory processes frequently lag behind technological change. To address this, regulatory sandboxes and Open Banking frameworks have emerged as key mechanisms. Regulatory sandboxes, pioneered by the UK Financial Conduct Authority in 2015, offer FinTech firms a controlled environment to test new products and business models under temporary regulatory exemptions. Open Banking initiatives, including the EU's PSD2 and Australia's Consumer Data Right, require banks to provide secure, API-based access to customer data (with consent), enhancing consumer control and fostering competition. Collectively, these measures exemplify a proactive regulatory strategy that supports innovation while safeguarding financial oversight.

1.5 Conclusion

The evolution of FinTech is characterised by a pronounced shift from centralised, institution-driven systems towards decentralised, open-platform models. This evolution has redistributed power towards consumers, transforming financial services from exclusive, institutionally controlled offerings into widely accessible utilities. The global impact of initiatives such as M-Pesa in Kenya and Nubank in Brazil illustrates FinTech's capacity to enhance financial inclusion and empower individuals, reflecting a broader reorientation of the industry towards user-centred design and accessibility. This constitutes a permanent shift of power to consumers.

Future developments are likely to be shaped by the expansion of embedded finance, the continued evolution of DeFi, and the widespread integration of AI. Success in this environment will require firms to balance continuous innovation with cross-sector collaboration and adherence to increasingly complex regulatory frameworks. Organisations that adapt by evolving from traditional, product-oriented models into agile, transparent, and trusted intermediaries within the financial ecosystem will be best positioned to deliver inclusive and responsive services, thereby consolidating long-term industry influence and relevance.

Key Terms and Glossary

FinTech The integration of technology into offerings by financial services companies to improve their use and delivery to consumers.

Unbundling The process whereby specialised FinTech startups target specific functions of a traditional universal bank (e.g., payments, lending), breaking apart the integrated banking model.

Embedded Finance The integration of financial services (e.g., payments, lending, insurance) into non-financial platforms and user experiences, such as e-commerce sites or ride-sharing apps.

Utility Risk The threat that traditional banks are reduced to commoditised background infrastructure, merely processing transactions while FinTechs and tech giants own the customer relationship and interface.

Regulatory Sandbox A framework set up by a regulator that allows FinTech startups and other innovators to conduct live experiments in a controlled environment under a regulator's supervision.

Open Banking A banking practice that provides third-party financial service providers open access to consumer banking, transaction, and other economic data from banks and non-bank financial institutions through the use of APIs.

P2P Lending A method of debt financing that enables individuals to borrow and lend money without the use of an official financial institution as an intermediary.

Test Your Understanding

Multiple-Choice Questions

1 Which technological innovation in the 1950s marked the beginning of cashless consumer payments?

A ATM
B Diners Club Credit Card
C ACH
D NASDAQ electronic trading system

2 The 2008 Global Financial Crisis primarily contributed to the rise of FinTech by:

A Increasing trust in traditional banks
B Reducing the use of digital payments
C Highlighting weaknesses in traditional banking and enabling alternative financial solutions
D Eliminating the need for financial regulation

3 Peer-to-peer (P2P) lending platforms like Lending Club and Prosper:

A Function as traditional deposit-taking banks
B Allow direct financing from investors to borrowers outside conventional banks
C Only provide investment advisory services.
D Replace ATMs for consumer transactions

4 Which regulatory framework in the EU standardised secure data access via APIs to support Open Banking?

A GDPR
B PSD2
C Basel III
D MiFID II

5 Utility risk for incumbent banks refers to:

A The risk of losing operational infrastructure efficiency
B Being relegated to behind-the-scenes providers while digital platforms capture customer relationships and data
C Exposure to cybercrime through cloud computing
D The cost of regulatory compliance

Short Questions

1 Explain the concept of *unbundling* in modern banking and provide an example of a FinTech firm that exemplifies this trend.
2 How did the advent of blockchain and Bitcoin in 2008 transform traditional financial intermediation?
3 Describe two technological enablers that have allowed FinTech firms to compete effectively with traditional banks.

Analytical Questions

1 Evaluate how the 2008 Global Financial Crisis reshaped consumer trust and accelerated the adoption of FinTech solutions. Include examples of platforms that benefited.
2 Discuss the implications of Open Banking and API-based ecosystems on the competitive dynamics between incumbents and FinTech startups.
3 Analyse the potential risks and benefits for traditional banks in transitioning from product-centric models to platform-based ecosystems, citing examples such as JPMorgan's Finn or BBVA's Open Platform.

Case Study: The Rise and Fall of Wirecard

Wirecard AG, once celebrated as a leading European FinTech innovator, exemplifies both the promise and the perils of the digital finance era. Founded as a payment processor, Wirecard cultivated a reputation as an agile disruptor, challenging traditional banks and promoting itself as a high-growth technology firm. By 2020, the company achieved a market valuation exceeding $28 billion and was included in Germany's prestigious DAX 30 index. Its image as a fast-moving, innovative FinTech helped attract investors and maintain public confidence, even as questions emerged about its financial reporting.

However, this narrative concealed a complex and long-running accounting fraud. In 2024, Wirecard admitted that €1.9 billion reportedly held in trustee accounts in Asia likely did not exist, triggering insolvency and one of the largest post-war corporate collapses in Europe. The scandal highlighted critical failures in corporate governance, auditing, and regulatory oversight, revealing how the allure of innovation can mask systemic weaknesses. Wirecard's rise and fall underscores the dual nature of modern FinTech: while digital payment platforms offer significant efficiency and inclusion benefits, they also present substantial risks, including fraud and regulatory gaps, emphasising the need for more robust oversight and technological safeguards.

References

Heese, J., Wang, C. C. Y., & Labruyere, T. (2021). Wirecard: The Downfall of a German FinTech Star. Harvard Business School Case 121-058. Revised April 2021. Boston, MA: Harvard Business School Publishing. Available at: https://www.hbs.edu/faculty/Pages/item.aspx?num=59971

McCrum, D. (2021). *Money Men: A Hot Startup, a Billion-Dollar Fraud, a Fight for the Truth.* London: Bantam Press.

Case Study Questions

1. How did Wirecard's portrayal as an innovative, disruptive FinTech enable it to avoid scrutiny for an extended period, and what does this suggest about changing patterns of trust in financial services?
2. In what ways does Wirecard's collapse illustrate both the potential benefits of digital financial technologies, such as efficient payments, and the significant risks, including fraud and regulatory shortcomings, present in the modern FinTech landscape?
3. Drawing on the Wirecard case, what specific regulatory or technological interventions, such as RegTech or SupTech, could be introduced to enhance investor protection and uphold market integrity?

Further Reading

Arner, D. W., Barberis, J., & Buckley, R. P. (2016). The Evolution of FinTech: A New Post-Crisis Paradigm? *Georgetown Journal of International Law*, 47(4), 1271–1319

Gomber, P., Kauffman, R. J., Parker, C., & Weber, B. W. (2018). On the Fintech Revolution: Interpreting the Forces of Innovation, Disruption, and Transformation in Financial Services. *Journal of Management Information Systems*, 35(1), 220–265.

Philippon, T. (2016). The FinTech Opportunity. *NBER Working Paper No. 22476.*

References

Arner, D. W., Barberis, J., & Buckley, R. P. (2016). The Evolution of FinTech: A New Post-Crisis Paradigm? *Georgetown Journal of International Law*, 47(4), 1271–1319.

Batiz-Lazo, B. (2009). Emergence and Evolution of ATM Networks in the UK, 1967–2000. *Business History*, 51(1), 1–27. https://doi.org/10.1080/00076790802602164

Drasch, B. J., Schweizer, A., & Urbach, N. (2018). Integrating the 'Troublemakers': A Taxonomy for Cooperation Between Banks and FinTechs. *Journal of Economics and Business*, 100, 26–42.

Gimpel, H., Rau, D., & Röglinger, M. (2017). Understanding FinTech Start-ups – A Taxonomy of Consumer-oriented Service Offerings. *Electronic Markets*, 28(3), 245–264.
Gomber, P., Koch, J. A., & Siering, M. (2017). Digital Finance and FinTech: Current Research and Future Research Directions. *Journal of Business Economics*, 87(5), 537–580.
Martin, F. (2020). *Money: The Unauthorised Biography*. London: Vintage.
McKinsey & Company. (2022). *The Future of Banking: Ecosystems and Platforms*. McKinsey & Company. Available at: https://www.mckinsey.com
Michie, R. C. (2008). *The Global Securities Market: A History*. Oxford: Oxford University Press.
Nakamoto, S. (2008). *Bitcoin: A Peer-to-Peer Electronic Cash System*. [Online] Available at: https://bitcoin.org/bitcoin.pdf
Philippon, T. (2016). The FinTech Opportunity. *NBER Working Paper No. 22476*.
Scott, S. V., & Zachariadis, M. (2014). *The Society for Worldwide Interbank Financial Telecommunication (SWIFT): Cooperative Governance for Network Innovation, Standards, and Community*. Routledge.

2 The FinTech Ecosystem and Network Architecture

Chapter Overview

This chapter presents a detailed examination of the FinTech ecosystem, emphasising its principal components, key stakeholders, and the interactions that facilitate the provision of modern financial services. It systematically delineates the architectural frameworks that underpin FinTech networks, highlighting their critical role in ensuring efficiency, scalability, and interoperability. The analysis further explores foundational and emerging technologies, including Application Programming Interfaces (APIs), cloud computing, artificial intelligence (AI), and blockchain. It evaluates their transformative impact on domains such as payments, lending, and wealth management. In addition, the chapter considers major operational and strategic challenges, including regulatory heterogeneity and increasing cybersecurity risks. The concluding section identifies emerging trends, such as hyper-personalisation, quantum-resistant network protocols, and sustainable finance initiatives. It assesses their implications for financial inclusion and the broader trajectory of digital transformation.

Learning Objectives

By the end of this chapter, you should be able to:

1. Explain the FinTech ecosystem by identifying its core components, primary stakeholders, and the roles and interactions that drive modern financial services.
2. Analyse the multi-layered architecture of FinTech networks, detailing the functions and interdependencies of core infrastructure, middleware, APIs, and application layers.
3. Evaluate the role of enabling technologies, including APIs, AI, blockchain, and cloud computing, in fostering innovation and efficiency across payments, lending, wealth management, and other financial services.
4. Assess critical challenges and risks confronting the FinTech ecosystem, including regulatory uncertainty, cybersecurity threats, interoperability issues, and scalability constraints, and their implications for system resilience and trust.
5. Critically examine emerging trends and opportunities, such as embedded finance, hyper-personalisation, quantum-secure networks, and sustainable finance, and their potential to enhance financial inclusion, democratise access, and drive digital transformation.

DOI: 10.4324/9781003775751-3

2.1 Introduction

The FinTech ecosystem is a fast-changing environment composed of many interconnected groups and digital systems. This web of players leads the digital change in financial services and brings together startups, established financial firms, tech companies, regulators, and users. FinTech networks sit at the centre, serving as secure digital systems that allow real-time transactions and easy data sharing, adjusting quickly as the market changes.

Each member of this ecosystem has an important and linked role. Startups often introduce new technologies and business ideas, driving change and creativity. Established financial firms use FinTech to improve their services, operate more efficiently, or reach more customers, often by forming partnerships or acquiring other companies. Tech providers supply the tools and systems needed, such as AI, blockchain, and cloud computing. Regulators work to keep things stable, protect users, and support innovation within clear rules. Consumers are asking for faster, more open, and easier-to-use financial services, helping shape the ecosystem.

To fully understand the FinTech sector, we need to examine its structure and basic network architecture. This design is key and includes the rules, systems, and setup that allow secure communication, trusted transactions, and smooth data sharing across the network. These systems help launch new financial products quickly, support data-driven decision-making, and ensure operations are safe and reliable for a worldwide digital economy. Knowing these main technical parts is needed to see how the FinTech ecosystem works, changes, and gives value.

2.2 The FinTech Ecosystem: Core Components and Stakeholders

The FinTech ecosystem is sustained by dynamic interactions among a diverse array of stakeholders, each performing distinct and complementary roles that collectively drive innovation, efficiency, and growth within the financial services sector. Understanding these actors and their interrelationships is essential for appreciating how modern financial services are conceived, delivered, and regulated (Figure 2.1).

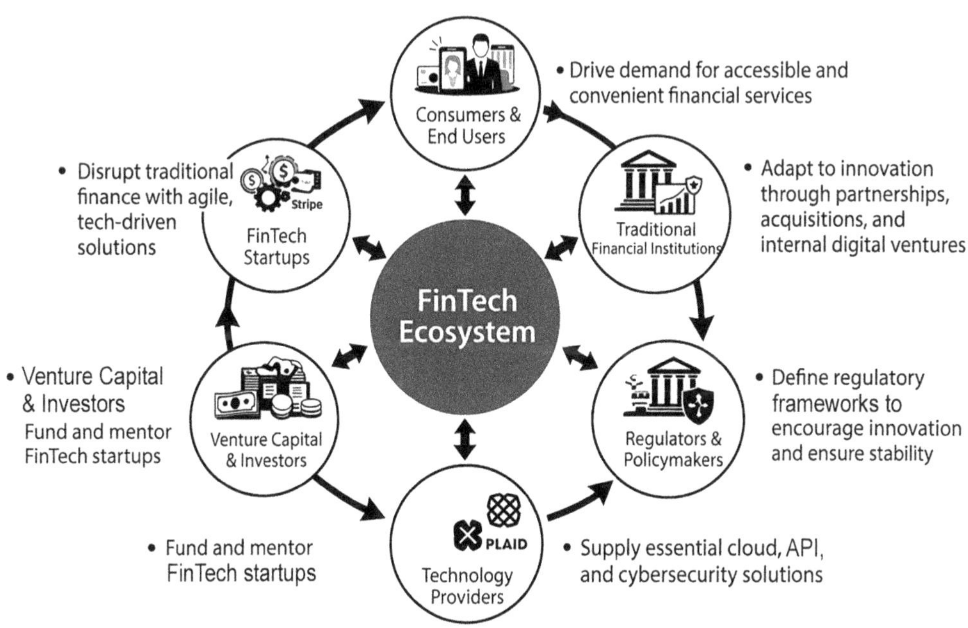

Figure 2.1 The FinTech Ecosystem: Core Components and Stakeholders.

2.2.1 Key Stakeholders

FinTech Startups: These are agile, digital-native firms that serve as primary agents of disruption within the financial sector. By leveraging advanced technologies such as AI, blockchain, and machine learning (ML), startups address specific financial challenges and create innovative, customer-centric solutions. Their offerings span a range of services, including digital payments (e.g., Stripe), peer-to-peer (P2P) and marketplace lending (e.g., LendingClub), and wealth management platforms (e.g., Betterment) (Gomber, Kauffman, Parker, & Weber, 2018). Startups often act as incubators of novel business models, pushing the boundaries of traditional financial practices.

Traditional Financial Institutions: Incumbent banks, insurance companies, and asset management firms are increasingly driven to innovate in response to both competitive pressures from startups and evolving customer expectations. These institutions adopt multiple strategies to maintain relevance, including strategic partnerships with FinTechs, acquisitions of innovative firms, and the development of internal digital ventures (e.g., Goldman Sachs' Marcus). Such initiatives aim to enhance operational efficiency, expand service offerings, and retain customer loyalty in a rapidly changing market (Vives, 2019).

Regulators and Policymakers: Regulatory bodies play a critical role in balancing the twin objectives of promoting innovation while safeguarding financial stability. They employ tools such as regulatory sandboxes (e.g., pioneered by the UK Financial Conduct Authority), open banking directives (e.g., PSD2 in Europe), and comprehensive frameworks for crypto-assets (e.g., MiCA). These measures establish the legal, operational, and compliance boundaries within which FinTech actors must operate, shaping both market behaviour and risk management practices.

Technology Providers: Companies offering cloud computing infrastructure (e.g., Amazon Web Services (AWS), Microsoft Azure), API middleware (e.g., Plaid), and cybersecurity solutions constitute the technological backbone of the FinTech ecosystem. They enable scalability, interoperability, and robust security, which are essential for supporting complex, high-volume financial operations. Their contributions ensure that both startups and established institutions can deliver seamless, reliable, and secure digital financial services (Gartner, 2023).

Venture Capital and Investors: Venture capital firms, angel investors, and corporate investment entities provide critical financial resources necessary for the growth and maturation of FinTech startups. Beyond capital, they often provide strategic guidance, industry expertise, and market access, thereby accelerating innovation and enabling the scaling of promising solutions in competitive markets.

Consumers and End Users: Individuals, households, and businesses constitute the ultimate drivers of innovation within the FinTech ecosystem. Their expectations for accessible, convenient, transparent, and personalised financial services continually shape product development, adoption patterns, and service delivery models. The feedback loop created by consumer demand incentivises ongoing innovation and ensures that financial services remain relevant, efficient, and inclusive.

2.2.2 Core Enablers of the FinTech Ecosystem

The growth, scalability, and sustained innovation of the FinTech ecosystem are underpinned by a set of critical enablers spanning technological infrastructure, data systems, capital markets, and regulatory frameworks. These enablers collectively establish the

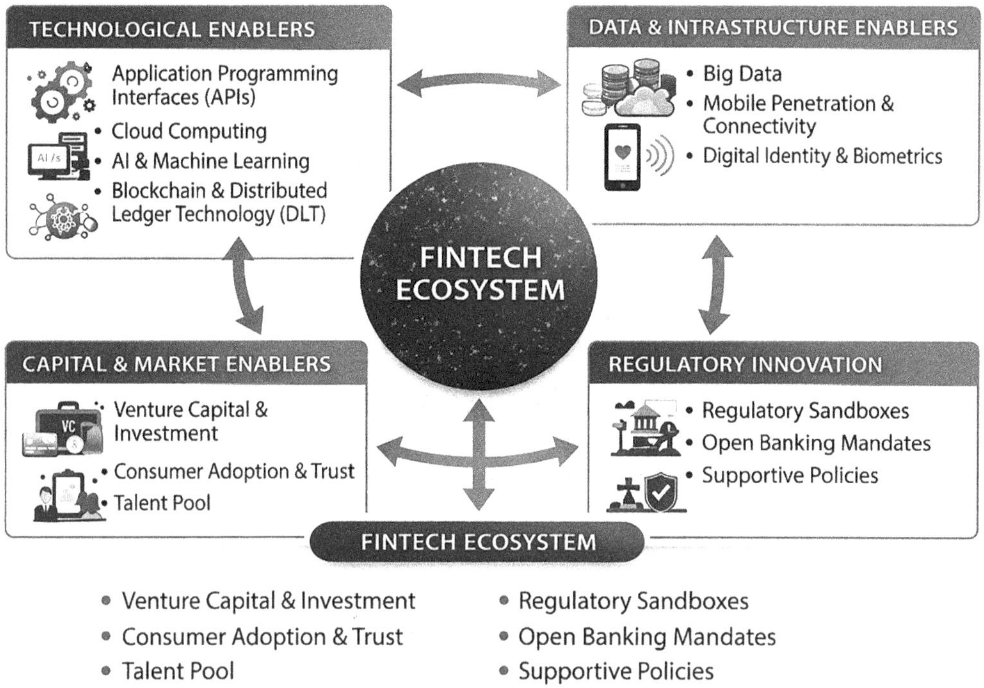

Figure 2.2 Core Enablers of the FinTech Ecosystem.

conditions necessary for startups, established financial institutions, and technology providers to deliver innovative, secure, and efficient financial services. By facilitating seamless integration, operational efficiency, and market expansion, they play a central role in shaping the evolution of the digital financial landscape (Figure 2.2).

2.2.2.1 *Technological Enablers*

Technological advancements constitute the foundational backbone of the FinTech ecosystem. They reduce operational costs, enhance system security, and create opportunities for novel business models that were previously infeasible:

APIs: APIs function as the connective infrastructure between disparate software systems, enabling interoperability and seamless communication. They are pivotal to Open Banking initiatives, enabling FinTech firms to access bank data, payment networks, and third-party services in a secure, standardised manner. This connectivity facilitates integrated, user-friendly financial services and promotes the creation of innovative, frictionless customer experiences.

Cloud Computing: Cloud-based platforms provide scalable, on-demand computing power and flexible data storage solutions. By leveraging services from providers such as AWS, Google Cloud, and Microsoft Azure, FinTech organisations can minimise capital expenditure on physical infrastructure, rapidly scale operations in response to demand fluctuations, and focus resources on product development and innovation.

AI and ML: AI and ML technologies drive sophisticated data analytics, automated decision-making, credit and risk assessment, fraud detection, and personalised customer engagement through tools such as chatbots and robo-advisors. These capabilities enable firms to optimise internal processes, reduce operational inefficiencies, and deliver tailored, data-driven financial solutions that enhance customer satisfaction and trust.

Blockchain and Distributed Ledger Technology: Blockchain provides a secure, transparent, and immutable record of transactions. Beyond underpinning cryptocurrencies, it enables smart contracts, cross-border payment solutions, and decentralised financial applications, thereby creating new models of trustless, tamper-proof financial interactions that expand the range of possible financial products and services.

2.2.2.2 *Data and Infrastructure Enablers*

Data and infrastructure form the critical inputs and connectivity pathways essential for FinTech innovation:

Big Data: The proliferation of structured and unstructured data from financial transactions, connected devices, and user behaviour allows FinTech firms to extract actionable insights, develop predictive models for risk and customer behaviour, and deliver highly personalised financial products and services.

Mobile Penetration and Connectivity: The global expansion of smartphone adoption and high-speed Internet connectivity serves as the primary channel through which most consumers access FinTech solutions. This connectivity has democratised access to financial tools, enabling broader financial inclusion and facilitating service delivery to previously underserved populations.

Digital Identity and Biometrics: Advanced identification technologies—including facial recognition, fingerprint scanning, and secure digital IDs—facilitate remote onboarding, authentication, and compliance with Know Your Customer (KYC) regulations. These innovations reduce reliance on physical branches, increase operational efficiency, and enhance security in digital financial services.

2.2.2.3 *Capital and Market Enablers*

Financial resources, market demand, and human capital are essential drivers of ecosystem growth and resilience:

Venture Capital and Investment: Venture capital and other strategic investments provide the funding for FinTech startups to evolve from conceptual ideas into scalable, high-impact enterprises. A robust investment ecosystem also offers strategic mentorship, market insights, and access to networks that accelerate growth and support sustainable innovation within competitive FinTech hubs.

Consumer Adoption and Trust: Individuals' and businesses' willingness to adopt digital financial solutions drives market demand, which sustains FinTech growth. Behavioural shifts, such as increased reliance on mobile banking and digital payments during the COVID-19 pandemic, have accelerated adoption rates and reinforced trust in these technologies as reliable, convenient alternatives to traditional financial services.

Talent Pool: A highly skilled workforce with combined expertise in finance, technology, data analytics, and regulatory compliance is essential for driving innovation. This includes software engineers, data scientists, quantitative analysts, and regulatory experts who enable FinTech firms to design sophisticated products, manage risks, and maintain operational excellence.

2.2.2.4 *Regulatory Innovation*

Adaptive and forward-looking regulatory frameworks provide the environment necessary for experimentation, responsible innovation, and sustainable ecosystem growth:

Regulatory Sandboxes: These controlled environments allow FinTech firms to pilot novel products and services with real customers under temporarily relaxed regulatory constraints. Sandboxes lower barriers to entry, encourage innovation, and provide regulators with opportunities to observe and assess emerging technologies in real-world conditions.

Open Banking Mandates: Policies such as the European Union's PSD2 require traditional banks to share customer data, with consent, with licensed third-party providers. This regulatory approach promotes competition, enhances transparency, and empowers FinTechs to develop innovative financial products and services that challenge traditional banking monopolies.

Supportive Government Policies: Initiatives promoting digital payments, financial inclusion, and competitive financial markets create a conducive environment for FinTech growth. These policies align innovation with broader societal and economic objectives, ensuring that technological advances benefit consumers, businesses, and the financial system as a whole.

2.3 The Architectural Layers of FinTech Networks

FinTech operates through a multi-layered network architecture. This structure ensures security, scalability, and interoperability among diverse systems (Figure 2.3).

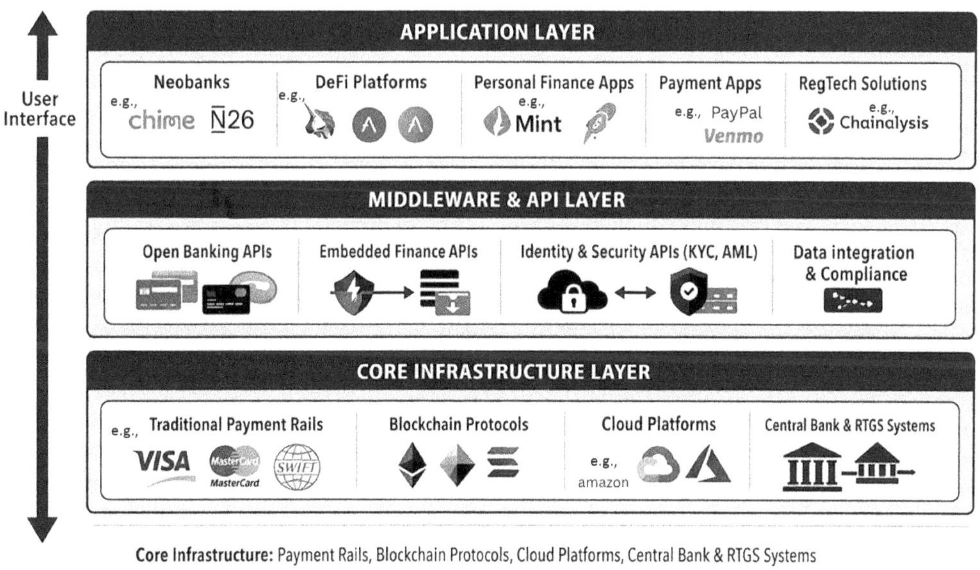

Figure 2.3 The Architectural Layers of FinTech Networks.

2.3.1 Core Infrastructure Layer (The Foundation)

The architectural layers of FinTech networks form a sophisticated, multi-tiered model that is essential for ensuring security, scalability, and interoperability. At the base lies the Core Infrastructure Layer, the fundamental plumbing of the financial world that processes, moves, and stores value and data. This foundational layer, largely invisible to end users, comprises critical components such as traditional payment rails like Visa, Mastercard, and the Society for Worldwide Interbank Financial Telecommunication, alongside emerging blockchain protocols such as Ethereum and Solana, which offer decentralised alternatives for value transfer and programmable money. Furthermore, this layer relies heavily on robust cloud platforms from providers such as AWS, Google Cloud, and Microsoft Azure, which provide the scalable computing power and data storage required for FinTech operations. The integration of modernised central bank infrastructures and real-time gross settlement systems also forms a crucial part of this underlying foundation, collectively enabling all subsequent financial activities.

2.3.2 Middleware and API Layer

The Middleware and API layer functions as the indispensable integration plane within FinTech networks, specifically engineered to abstract the inherent complexity of core infrastructure and translate often-disparate protocols into standardised, secure commands for application consumption. APIs are the crucial mechanism of this layer, enabling efficient data sharing and seamless connectivity across the ecosystem. This standardisation is vital for both regulatory compliance and innovation; mandated frameworks, such as PSD2, utilise Open Banking APIs to enable licensed third parties to securely access bank data with customer consent, thereby stimulating necessary competition (Zetzsche et al., 2020). Concurrently, Embedded Finance APIs are driving market evolution by enabling non-financial businesses to directly integrate services such as instant lending or payments into their user experiences, fundamentally blurring traditional industry boundaries. Finally, robust security and compliance are maintained through specialised APIs for Identity and Authentication Services, including KYC and fraud detection, underscoring this layer's pivotal role as the bridge supporting modern digital financial operations.

2.3.3 Application Layer

The Application Layer constitutes the uppermost stratum of FinTech networks, serving as the direct interface through which end users, both consumers and businesses, engage with and derive value from financial services. This pivotal layer is engineered to deliver specific, user-friendly solutions that address particular problems or meet distinct needs, functioning as the manifestation of underlying infrastructure. It encompasses a diverse array of platforms, including mobile-first Neobanks (e.g., Chime, N26) that offer streamlined banking experiences, and innovative Decentralised Finance (DeFi) platforms (e.g., Uniswap, Aave) that leverage smart contracts on blockchain infrastructure to provide services like lending and trading without traditional intermediaries. Additionally, this layer incorporates RegTech solutions such as Chainalysis, which automate critical regulatory compliance like KYC/AML and fraud detection, alongside popular Personal Finance Apps (e.g., Mint, Robinhood) and ubiquitous Payment Apps (e.g., PayPal, Venmo). Crucially, the Application Layer relies heavily on the underlying Middleware/API layer to seamlessly access and translate complex backend operations into intuitive, user-friendly experiences.

2.4 Key Practical Issues and Domain Applications

The FinTech ecosystem's architecture, while a powerful engine of innovation, inherently creates a dual reality: it enables novel financial applications while introducing significant operational, strategic, and regulatory challenges.

2.4.1 Domain Applications of FinTech

The transformative impact of FinTech is evident in its targeted disruption of traditional financial service verticals. These domain-specific applications leverage technology to enhance efficiency, accessibility, and user-centricity.

Payments (PayTech): This domain focuses on digitising and streamlining the movement of money. It encompasses digital wallets (e.g., Apple Pay, Google Pay) for seamless in-store and online transactions, P2P transfer platforms (e.g., Venmo, Cash App) for instant social payments, and cross-border solutions (e.g., Wise, Remitly) that utilise innovative networks to offer greater speed and transparency at lower costs than traditional correspondent banking (Cornelli et al., 2020).

Lending (LendTech): FinTech has reconfigured credit assessment and distribution. P2P and marketplace lending platforms (e.g., Funding Circle, LendingClub) directly connect borrowers with investors, while Buy Now, Pay Later providers (e.g., Klarna, Affirm) leverage alternative data and ML algorithms for instant, at-point-of-sale credit decisions, often serving segments overlooked by traditional banks (FSB, 2022).

Wealth Management (WealthTech): This domain democratises access to investment services. Robo-advisors (e.g., Betterment, Wealthfront) provide automated, algorithm-driven portfolio management at a low cost, and fractional investing platforms (e.g., Robinhood) lower the financial barriers to entering capital markets.

Insurance (InsurTech): Companies in this space (e.g., Lemonade, Root Insurance) utilise technologies like the Internet of Things for telematics and AI to create usage-based insurance models and automate the entire claims process, leading to more personalised policies and efficient operations (IAIS, 2022).

Regulatory Technology (RegTech): This application addresses the growing cost and complexity of compliance. RegTech solutions automate monitoring, reporting, identity verification (KYC/AML), and risk management processes, thereby enhancing the accuracy and efficiency of regulatory adherence for financial institutions (Arner et al., 2020).

2.4.2 Important Strategic Issues and Challenges

A central strategic dynamic shapes the FinTech ecosystem: the unbundling and subsequent rebundling of financial services. Initially, FinTech firms disrupted traditional banks by isolating high-margin services, such as payments, lending, and investing, and delivering them through specialised, user-centric digital solutions. However, the rise of APIs and platform-based models has enabled a rebundling phase, in which neobanks, super-apps, and even incumbents aggregate multiple financial services into unified digital ecosystems. This shift creates a strategic dilemma for established institutions, which must choose between in-house innovation, acquisitions, or platform strategies led by partnerships to remain competitive.

Despite rapid innovation, the ecosystem faces significant structural challenges. Regulatory fragmentation remains a major constraint, as nationally bounded legal frameworks struggle to govern borderless digital financial services, increasing compliance complexity and operational risk. Cybersecurity threats are also intensifying due to highly interconnected, API-driven infrastructures that expand vulnerability to data breaches, fraud, and smart contract exploits. Technical barriers persist in the form of scalability and interoperability limitations, particularly within blockchain networks and legacy banking integrations. Ultimately, FinTech risks deepening the digital divide, as effective access often depends on digital literacy, connectivity, and device availability. Ensuring sustainable and inclusive growth, therefore, requires coordinated regulation, stronger security frameworks, technical standardisation, and policies that promote equitable digital access.

2.4.3 Future Trends in the Ecosystem

The FinTech ecosystem and its underlying network architecture are undergoing a profound transformation, shaped by a confluence of technological innovation and shifting consumer demands. Central to this evolution is hyper-personalisation, where AI and advanced data analytics enable financial institutions to deliver real-time, context-aware services tailored to individual behaviours and preferences. The future of finance lies not in one-size-fits-all products, but in systems that anticipate needs before the customer even articulates them. This shift from standardised offerings to adaptive financial solutions is redefining customer engagement, driving efficiency, and enhancing risk assessment models across banking, insurance, and investment platforms.

Looking ahead, emerging trends such as quantum-secure networks, integration with Web3 and the metaverse, and the rise of Green FinTech are poised to further reshape the digital financial landscape. As quantum computing threatens the foundations of current cryptography, the financial sector is accelerating the adoption of post-quantum cryptography to safeguard data integrity and systemic resilience. Concurrently, the expansion into decentralised digital economies necessitates robust FinTech infrastructures capable of supporting tokenised assets, virtual property transactions, and new forms of digital ownership. Alongside these developments, sustainability is becoming a core design principle, as evidenced by energy-efficient blockchains and ESG-integrated financial platforms. Sustainable innovation is no longer a niche; it is the benchmark for long-term competitiveness in FinTech. Together, these trends underscore a future where financial technology is not only more intelligent and secure but also more inclusive and environmentally responsible.

2.5 Conclusion

The FinTech ecosystem is supported by a complex, multi-layered network architecture that integrates advanced technological infrastructures, including blockchain, AI, and cloud computing. This architectural foundation plays a central role in transforming the global financial system by enhancing operational efficiency, broadening access to financial services, and improving transactional transparency. The convergence of digital technologies with financial processes has not only driven product innovation but has also redefined the mechanisms through which financial value is generated, distributed, and managed. The ecosystem's dynamism stems from continuous interaction among diverse stakeholders, FinTech start-ups, incumbent financial institutions, technology providers, regulators, and investors, whose collective activities shape an increasingly interconnected and competitive marketplace.

Despite its transformative capacity, the long-term sustainability of the FinTech sector depends on effectively managing several structural and systemic challenges. Regulatory fragmentation, cybersecurity vulnerabilities, and the need for scalable, interoperable infrastructure present ongoing risks that require coordinated responses. Institutional resilience in digital finance, therefore, depends not solely on technological sophistication but also on collaborative governance, regulatory alignment, and shared security standards. Strategic engagement between industry participants and policymakers is essential to balance innovation with stability and consumer protection. By prioritising secure system design, inclusive access, and cross-sector cooperation, the FinTech ecosystem can better realise its potential to democratise financial services and contribute to a more equitable and accessible global financial environment.

Key Terms and Glossary

FinTech Ecosystem The complex, adaptive network of interconnected entities (startups, incumbents, regulators, tech providers) that collectively drive the digital transformation of financial services.

API (Application Programming Interface) A set of defined rules that enable different applications to communicate with each other. In FinTech, APIs are the backbone of Open Banking and embedded finance.

Neobank A type of direct bank that operates exclusively online without traditional physical branch networks.

RegTech The management of regulatory processes within the financial industry through technology, often to facilitate compliance, monitoring, and reporting.

DeFi (Decentralised Finance) An emerging financial technology based on secure distributed ledgers similar to those used by cryptocurrencies, which removes the control banks and institutions have on money and financial products.

Interoperability The ability of different systems, devices, applications, or products to connect and communicate in a coordinated way, without effort from the end user.

Test Your Understanding

Multiple-Choice Questions

1 Which of the following best describes the role of FinTech startups in the ecosystem?

A Primarily regulatory enforcement
B Incubators of innovation leveraging technologies like AI and blockchain
C Providers of cloud infrastructure
D Traditional asset managers

2 What is the primary function of the Middleware and API layer in FinTech networks?

A Directly managing customer transactions
B Ensuring connectivity, standardisation, and secure integration between core infrastructure and applications
C Storing transaction data in blockchain
D Regulating financial institutions

3 Which of the following is NOT considered a core technological enabler of the FinTech ecosystem?

A AI
B Blockchain
C Cloud Computing
D Physical branch networks

4 In the context of FinTech, "hyper-personalisation" refers to:

A Offering the same financial products to all customers
B Using AI and data analytics to provide services tailored to individual behaviours and preferences
C Integrating blockchain with national payment rails
D Mandating open banking across regions

5 What do FinTech's interconnected, API-driven networks pose as a key challenge?

A Reduced regulatory oversight
B Increased scalability
C Heightened cybersecurity risks and data breaches
D Limited innovation in payments

Short Questions

1 Explain how regulatory sandboxes support innovation within the FinTech ecosystem.
2 Identify three domain applications of FinTech and provide a brief example for each.
3 Describe the role of cloud computing in enhancing the scalability and efficiency of FinTech services.

Analytical Questions

1 Discuss the strategic dilemma faced by traditional financial institutions in the rebundling of financial services by FinTech firms, considering both competitive threats and partnership opportunities.
2 Evaluate the impact of emerging technologies such as blockchain, AI, and quantum-resistant networks on the security, efficiency, and inclusivity of financial services.
3 Assess how FinTech networks balance innovation and regulatory compliance, with reference to open banking initiatives and digital identity solutions.

Case Study: Plaid—The Connective Tissue of FinTech

Plaid operates as a core middleware provider within the FinTech ecosystem, enabling secure connectivity between consumer bank accounts and thousands of digital financial applications. Through a suite of standardised APIs, Plaid allows apps to access financial data such as account balances, transaction histories, and identity information, subject to user consent, without requiring each developer to build separate integrations with individual banks. This function significantly reduces technical complexity and accelerates innovation across the ecosystem. Popular services, including Venmo, Robinhood, and Chime, rely on Plaid's infrastructure to deliver payments, investing, and digital banking experiences.

By aggregating and normalising data from a fragmented banking landscape, Plaid acts as a translation and data-access layer that sits between traditional financial institutions and the application layer. Its strategic importance became widely visible in 2020 when Visa proposed acquiring the company for $5.3 billion, a deal later blocked by US regulators on antitrust grounds. The case drew attention to Plaid's growing influence over how financial data flows through the digital economy. As Plaid expanded globally and explored public listing plans, it also faced scrutiny over data privacy practices, user consent mechanisms, and its role as a highly centralised gateway to sensitive financial information, issues that highlight both the power and responsibility of infrastructure providers in modern FinTech.

References

CNBC (2020). *DOJ Files Antitrust Lawsuit to Block Visa's Plaid Acquisition*, 5 November. Available at: https://www.cnbc.com/2020/11/05/doj-files-antitrust-lawsuit-to-block-visas-plaid-acquisition-.html

Forbes (2021). *Visa, Fintech Startup Plaid Drop Merger Plans After DOJ Antitrust Lawsuit*, 12 January. Available at: https://www.forbes.com/sites/rachelsandler/2021/01/12/visa-drops-plans-to-acquire-fintech-startup-plaid-after-doj-antitrust-lawsuit

Case Study Questions

1 Analyse Plaid's role using the layered architecture model from the chapter. What would be the consequences for the Application Layer if a middleware provider like Plaid experienced a major, prolonged outage?

2 Plaid has faced scrutiny over data privacy and its access to users' banking credentials. Discuss the critical challenges (security, regulatory, trust) that such a central enabler in the ecosystem must navigate to be successful.

3 How does Plaid's business model exemplify the concept of *rebundling*, and what strategic value did large financial institutions like Visa see in acquiring it?

Further Reading

Arner, D.W., Barberis, J.N., & Buckley, R.P. (2016). The Evolution of FinTech: A New Post-Crisis Paradigm? *Georgetown Journal of International Law*, 47(4), 1271–1319.

Gomber, P., Kauffman, R.J., Parker, C., & Weber, B.W. (2018). On the FinTech Revolution: Interpreting the Forces of Innovation, Disruption, and Transformation in Financial Services. *Journal of Management Information Systems*, 35(1), 220–265.

Vives, X. (2019). Digital Disruption in Banking. *Annual Review of Financial Economics*, 11, 243–272.

References

Arner, D.W., Barberis, J., & Buckley, R.P. (2020). FinTech, RegTech and the Reconceptualization of Financial Regulation. *Northwestern Journal of International Law and Business*, 37, 371.

Cornelli, G., Doerr, S., & Gambacorta, L. (2020). FinTech and the Digital Transformation of Retail Banking. *BIS Bulletin*, 34. Basel: Bank for International Settlements.

FSB – Financial Stability Board (2022). *FinTech and Market Developments: 2022 Report*. Basel: FSB.

Gomber, P., Kauffman, R.J., Parker, C., & Weber, B.W. (2018). On the FinTech Revolution: Interpreting the Forces of Innovation, Disruption, and Transformation in Financial Services. *Journal of Management Information Systems*, 35(1), 220–265.

Gartner (2023). *Top Strategic Technology Trends for Financial Services*. Stamford: Gartner, Inc.
IAIS – International Association of Insurance Supervisors (2022). *InsurTech Developments and Implications for Insurance Regulation*. Basel: IAIS.
Vives, X. (2019). Digital Disruption in Banking. *Annual Review of Financial Economics*, 11, 243–272.
Zetzsche, D.A., Buckley, R.P., Arner, D.W., & Barberis, J.N. (2020). From FinTech to TechFin: The Regulatory Challenges of Data-Driven Finance. *New York University Journal of Law & Business*, 16(2), 393–446.

3 Financial Inclusion and Digital Transformation

Chapter Overview

This chapter examines the transformative synergy between digital innovation and the global advancement of financial inclusion, highlighting how technologies such as mobile connectivity, cloud computing, blockchain, and artificial intelligence are dismantling systemic barriers that have historically marginalised unbanked and underbanked populations (Demirgüç-Kunt et al., 2018). Central to this evolution are mobile money platforms, digital public infrastructure (DPI), and alternative credit scoring models that leverage non-traditional data to extend financial services to those without formal credit histories. These advancements are not only expanding access but also fostering broader socio-economic outcomes, including poverty reduction, women's economic empowerment, and more inclusive growth. However, persistent challenges, such as uneven digital access, low levels of financial and digital literacy, and inadequate consumer protection and data privacy frameworks, underscore the limitations of technology alone. As CGAP (2020) emphasises, digital transformation must move beyond simple access to digital tools and instead foster meaningful economic participation, resilience, and long-term empowerment. Achieving equitable and sustainable financial inclusion, therefore, requires a holistic approach that integrates technological innovation with robust policy, education, and regulatory safeguards.

Learning Objectives

By the end of this chapter, you should be able to:

1. Define financial inclusion and digital transformation and explain their interconnectedness.
2. Identify and analyse the key digital technologies and business models driving financial inclusion.
3. Evaluate the socio-economic impact of digital financial services on individuals, communities, and national economies.
4. Assess the critical challenges and risks, including digital exclusion and over-indebtedness, that accompany this transformation.
5. Discuss the role of policymakers, financial institutions, and technology providers in building an inclusive digital financial ecosystem.

DOI: 10.4324/9781003775751-4

3.1 Introduction

For decades, a significant proportion of the global adult population, estimated at around one-third, has remained excluded from formal financial services, effectively shutting billions of people out of the formal economy (World Bank, 2022). Barriers such as geographic remoteness from banking institutions, high transaction and account maintenance costs, lack of official identification, and limited or irregular income have historically constrained access to banking services. These challenges have disproportionately affected women, rural communities, and low-income populations, reinforcing structural inequalities and limiting opportunities for economic participation, social mobility, and poverty reduction. The resulting exclusion has created a persistent gap in global economic development, highlighting the urgent need for systemic interventions.

The current wave of digital transformation presents an unprecedented opportunity to address these historical constraints by introducing innovative channels for financial service delivery. Even basic mobile phones now enable unbanked and underbanked populations to access a range of financial services, including payments, savings, credit, and insurance (GSMA, 2023). This shift represents more than the digitisation of existing products; it constitutes a fundamental restructuring of financial systems, designed to enhance accessibility, affordability, and responsiveness while meeting the specific needs of marginalised populations.

This chapter critically examines the transformative potential of digital technologies in promoting financial inclusion. It analyses the economic, social, and developmental benefits of digital access, demonstrating how technology can expand economic participation, reduce inequality, and empower underserved communities. In addition, it evaluates the strategic, regulatory, and operational interventions necessary to ensure that digital financial transformation translates into meaningful empowerment, sustainable development, and equitable outcomes across diverse populations. By situating digital innovation within broader societal and economic objectives, the chapter underscores the potential for technology to drive inclusive, resilient, and adaptive financial ecosystems.

3.2 Understanding the Core Concepts

3.2.1 Financial Inclusion

Financial inclusion refers to the process by which individuals and businesses gain access to a broad range of financial products and services that are both useful and affordable, and that meet their specific needs. These services encompass payments, savings, credit, insurance, and other transactional instruments, and are delivered in a manner that is responsible, equitable, and sustainable (World Bank, 2022). The concept of financial inclusion is closely linked to economic development, as it facilitates poverty alleviation, promotes equitable access to economic opportunities, and supports inclusive growth by enabling individuals and enterprises to participate fully in the financial system.

3.2.2 Digital Transformation in Finance

Digital transformation in the financial sector involves integrating digital technologies across all operational, managerial, and customer-facing processes, resulting in fundamental changes in how financial institutions operate and deliver value. This transformation extends beyond the digitisation of conventional services, such as online banking, to

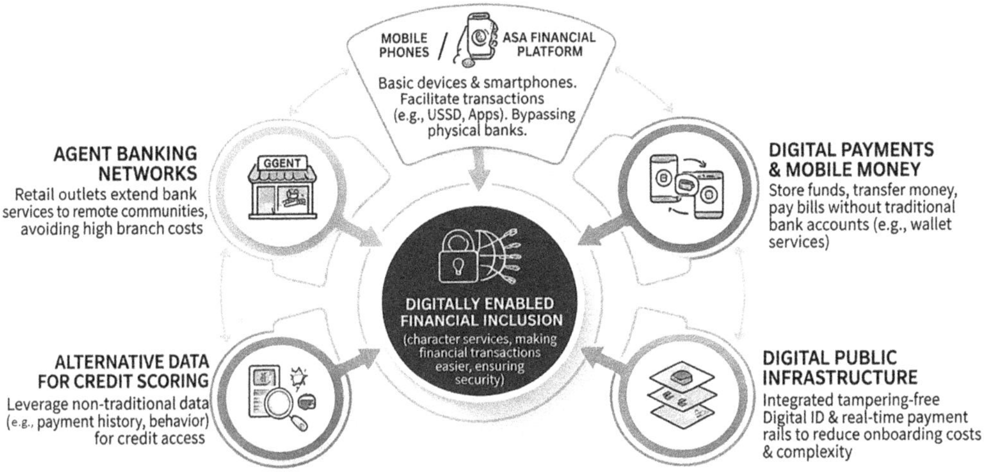

Figure 3.1 Key Drivers of Digitally Enabled Financial Inclusion.

encompass comprehensive restructuring of business models, operational frameworks, and service delivery mechanisms. Within this context, digital transformation functions as an enabler, providing the technological infrastructure, platforms, and innovative tools necessary to broaden financial access. Financial inclusion, in turn, represents the strategic objective of these efforts: leveraging digital technologies to ensure that financial services are accessible, affordable, and responsive to the diverse needs of underserved populations. The interrelationship is therefore complementary, with digital transformation supplying the mechanisms that facilitate the realisation of financial inclusion goals (Figure 3.1).

3.3 Key Drivers of Digitally Enabled Financial Inclusion

Several technological, infrastructural, and market forces are driving the expansion of financial inclusion by reducing barriers to access and enabling more efficient service delivery:

Mobile Phones as a Financial Platform: In regions where mobile phone penetration exceeds traditional bank account access, such as Nigeria and Bangladesh, even basic devices allow users to perform essential financial transactions. These include Unstructured Supplementary Service Data-based payments, airtime top-ups, and smartphone applications such as Paga in Nigeria or bKash in Bangladesh, which provide bill payments, transfers, and micro-savings, bypassing the need for physical banking infrastructure (Suri & Jack, 2016).

Digital Payment Systems and Mobile Money: Mobile money platforms, exemplified by M-Pesa in Kenya and Tigo Money in Tanzania, enable users to store funds, transfer money, and pay bills digitally through SMS or mobile apps. These systems reach broad populations, including those **without** formal bank accounts, providing a practical entry point into the formal financial system.

DPI (Digital Public Infrastructure.): Comprehensive digital frameworks such as India Stack integrate a **digital** identity system (Aadhaar), a real-time payments platform (UPI), and a consent-based data-sharing layer. These infrastructures significantly reduce onboarding costs and complexity while enabling scalable delivery of financial services to millions of users (Carrière-Swallow et al., 2021).

Alternative Data for Credit Scoring: FinTech firms leverage non-traditional data sources, such as mobile top-ups, utility payments, and social media activity, to generate credit scores for individuals without formal credit histories. Platforms such as Tala in Kenya and the **Philippines** use these methods to provide microloans to underserved populations, broadening access to credit (Berg et al., 2020).

Agent Banking Networks: **Retail** shops and local businesses serve as banking agents in countries such as Pakistan (EasyPaisa) and Brazil (Banco24Horas). These agents deliver essential services, deposits, withdrawals, and bill payments to remote communities, reducing the need for full-service bank branches while expanding financial access.

3.4 Impact and Opportunities on Financial Inclusion

Digitally driven financial inclusion produces measurable socio-economic outcomes by lowering barriers to financial participation, expanding access to services, and enabling new models of economic engagement. The impacts documented in recent research and empirical case studies span poverty alleviation, gender equity, government efficiency, transparency, and entrepreneurship.

3.4.1 *Poverty Reduction and Economic Resilience*

Empirical analyses confirm that the proliferation of digital financial services, particularly mobile money and electronic payments, correlates with expanded financial access and reduced income inequality. FinTech adoption significantly increases the share of adults with formal financial accounts and reduces income disparities by facilitating cheaper, more frequent transactions in developing economies. Technological adoption, as measured by mobile payment usage, is statistically associated with reductions in income inequality, indicating that digital financial inclusion supports broader poverty-reduction objectives.

3.4.2 *Women's Economic Empowerment*

Digital financial services have demonstrable effects on women's inclusion by enabling access to financial products and increasing economic participation. Globally, women are less likely than men to access or use digital technologies, constraining financial inclusion; closing this digital divide is central to inclusive growth. Evidence from sub-Saharan Africa shows that the share of women owning financial accounts has more than doubled over a decade, driven by mobile money adoption that simplifies account access. Targeted initiatives, such as rural empowerment programmes that provide digital tools and financial literacy (e.g., India's Digital Nari), demonstrate scalable models for integrating women as users and providers of digital financial services.

3.4.3 *Efficiency in Government Transfers and Social Protection*

Digital Government-to-Person (G2P) payment systems significantly enhance the distribution of social benefits by reducing leakage through corruption and lowering administrative costs. Digital disbursement of wages and social benefits rapidly scales financial inclusion, as exemplified by Bangladesh's digital wage payments to garment workers: millions of digital accounts were opened within weeks for direct transfers during the COVID-19 lockdown. Cross-border remittances similarly benefit from digitisation; converting remittance flows from traditional to digital channels can reduce transfer costs and increase liquidity.

3.4.4 Enhanced Transparency and Formalisation

The transition from cash to digital transactions generates comprehensive, traceable economic records that can improve tax compliance and integrate informal businesses into formal financial systems. Digital financial data streams expand the tax base and facilitate enforcement, thereby strengthening financial governance. Research in emerging economies links digital financial market participation with broader economic development outcomes, including infrastructure investment and technological adoption that contribute to sustainable growth.

3.4.5 Promotion of Entrepreneurship and Small Business Growth

Access to digital savings, payment, and credit platforms creates productive opportunities for micro-entrepreneurs and small enterprises. FinTech services enable improved cash-flow management, access to microcredit, and participation in digital marketplaces. E-wallet and mobile money platforms such as M-Pesa in Kenya, PhonePe in India, and GoPay in Indonesia illustrate how digital financial tools have expanded user bases into tens of millions, facilitating transactions worth billions of dollars annually and enabling micro-enterprises to increase revenues. Furthermore, digital finance contributes to firm innovation by enabling investment in human capital and long-term strategic capabilities among micro and small enterprises in developing countries.

3.5 Challenges and Risks to Financial Inclusion

Although digital financial services have the potential to accelerate financial inclusion, they also introduce significant structural constraints and systemic risks that can undermine the integrity and sustainability of inclusive financial systems. These challenges are multidimensional, spanning infrastructure deficits, literacy gaps, regulatory shortcomings, consumer protection vulnerabilities, and socio-economic bias.

3.5.1 Digital Divide and Infrastructure Barriers

Persistent inequalities in digital infrastructure, such as limited broadband connectivity, unreliable electricity supply, and low smartphone penetration, continue to restrict access to digital financial services for the poorest and most rural populations. These infrastructure deficits not only limit adoption but also reduce the reliability and continuity of digital financial engagements, thereby perpetuating a new form of exclusion even as services proliferate. Without substantial investment in telecommunications and last-mile delivery models, the digital divide will remain a principal barrier to inclusive finance.

3.5.2 Digital and Financial Literacy Gaps

Inadequate digital financial literacy impedes users' ability to understand and use financial products effectively, increasing their susceptibility to suboptimal decision-making and fraudulent schemes. Populations with limited education or low familiarity with digital tools often misunderstand terms, misinterpret privacy disclosures, or lack the skills to evaluate risks, which exacerbates vulnerability to predatory practices. Studies show that a substantial share of users do not comprehend basic application permissions and financial terms, undermining meaningful informed consent.

3.5.3 *Consumer Protection and Predatory Practices*

The rapid proliferation of digital credit platforms has heightened consumer protection risks. Digital lenders frequently operate outside traditional regulatory oversight, offering rapid, minimal-screening loans that can precipitate over-indebtedness, loan stacking, and financial distress. Evidence from multiple jurisdictions shows aggressive lending and collection practices, including mass marketing to vulnerable users without adequate assessment of repayment capacity and harassment via mobile and social media channels. These practices can erode welfare and trust in financial systems.

3.5.4 *Fraud, Data Privacy, and Cybersecurity Risks*

The digitalisation of financial services increases exposure to fraud, identity theft, and cybersecurity breaches. Financial service providers and users both face risks from phishing schemes, fraudulent applications, and unauthorised access to personal data. Studies indicate that a significant portion of digital lending applications transmit sensitive information without robust consent mechanisms and that fraud incidents are prevalent in several markets. The average cost of data breaches in the financial sector continues to rise, highlighting the material risk to both institutions and consumers.

3.5.5 *Regulatory Gaps and Compliance Challenges*

Regulatory frameworks in many countries struggle to keep pace with digital innovation. Gaps in supervision, unclear licensing requirements, and jurisdictional inconsistencies create environments where unregulated or unauthorised providers can exploit legal ambiguities. This regulatory lag exposes consumers to the risks of predatory lending, inadequate dispute-resolution mechanisms, and insufficient privacy safeguards. Effective regulatory responses require coordination across multiple authorities and harmonisation of FinTech oversight to balance innovation with consumer protection.

3.5.6 *Algorithmic Bias and Inclusion Risks*

Automated decision-making systems deployed in credit scoring and customer targeting can embed and amplify socio-economic biases. Algorithmic models that rely on limited or non-representative data can exclude underserved groups, such as women, informal workers, or rural populations, thereby perpetuating existing disparities rather than alleviating them. The lack of explainability and transparency in these models reinforces trust deficits and complicates regulatory oversight.

3.5.7 *Trust Deficits and Adoption Barriers*

Widespread concerns regarding data security, unclear terms and conditions, and negative experiences with unregulated providers undermine confidence in digital financial services. Trust is essential for sustained engagement, where users perceive platforms as opaque or risky, adoption rates stagnate, and long-term inclusion objectives are jeopardised. Socio-cultural factors, including scepticism towards formal financial systems and cultural norms that restrict access for certain groups, further compound these trust challenges.

3.5.8 Financial Stability and Systemic Risk

Beyond individual consumer harm, unchecked digital credit growth poses broader risks to financial stability. Widespread over-indebtedness, weak underwriting standards, and poorly supervised digital credit markets can contribute to credit cycles that amplify systemic vulnerabilities. Without robust risk management frameworks, the digitalisation of finance risks replicating or exacerbating structural instabilities seen in other credit markets.

3.6 Key Implications for the Future of Financial Inclusion

The future of financial inclusion is shifting from basic access, such as account ownership, towards enhancing users' financial well-being through digitally enabled, hyper-personalised services. Artificial intelligence (AI) and machine learning are revolutionising financial ecosystems by enabling dynamic segmentation and tailored solutions, such as savings plans or credit products, based on real-time cash-flow patterns rather than traditional credit histories. Hyper-personalised financial guidance, including AI-driven coaching and behavioural nudges, represents the next frontier in aligning financial tools with users' economic realities. This evolution not only broadens participation but also ensures financial resilience, particularly for underserved populations.

Beyond personalisation, technology is dismantling long-standing barriers to inclusion. AI-driven alternative data, such as mobile usage or digital transaction histories, is creating financial identities for the unbanked, reducing reliance on conventional documentation. Simultaneously, multilingual conversational AI and voice-based interfaces are bridging linguistic and literacy gaps, making services accessible across diverse demographics. Interoperable payment infrastructures, like Mojaloop, further lower entry barriers by enabling seamless transactions across providers, particularly for last-mile users. Interoperability does not just reduce friction; it democratises access, ensuring digital finance reaches those previously excluded.

However, this transformation demands responsible governance. Public-private partnerships (PPPs) and blended finance models are crucial to scaling infrastructure in underserved regions, while ethical AI frameworks must safeguard against bias and misuse of data. Strengthened hybrid delivery models that combine digital efficiency with human-centric engagement will ensure sustainable inclusion, especially in rural areas. Ultimately, financial inclusion is converging with broader development goals, such as climate resilience, where data-driven solutions like satellite-based credit empower smallholder farmers. As the sector evolves, balancing innovation with equity will define its success in fostering inclusive, resilient economies.

3.7 Conclusion

In conclusion, digital transformation has fundamentally reshaped the global pursuit of financial inclusion, presenting an unprecedented opportunity to achieve universal financial access. By leveraging innovative technologies to bridge historical gaps, notable successes, from the widespread adoption of mobile money in Africa to the implementation of robust DPI in Asia, illustrate how scalable digital solutions are demonstrably advancing meaningful financial inclusion worldwide. However, it is critical to recognise that true inclusion requires more than the mere deployment of technology; it demands a proactive and strategic effort to ensure its benefits are universally shared. As the World Bank emphasises, Digital technologies help accelerate financial inclusion. Still, they are not a silver bullet, underscoring the need to address the persistent digital divide, strengthen consumer protection frameworks, and promote essential digital literacy.

Ultimately, the success of this digital revolution should not be measured by the simplistic metric of the number of accounts created, but by tangible improvements in the economic well-being and security of the most vulnerable populations. Building trust and enabling these groups to access and leverage digital financial tools safely is paramount. Therefore, a balanced approach that harmonises rapid technological innovation with thoughtful, human-centred policies is indispensable. This strategic equilibrium is the cornerstone for ensuring that digital progress genuinely translates into more inclusive, resilient, and sustainable economic development for all.

Key Terms and Glossary

Financial Inclusion The availability and equality of opportunities to access affordable and appropriate financial products and services.

Unbanked Adults who do not have an account at a formal financial institution.

Underbanked Individuals who have a bank account but lack access to, or do not use, a full suite of financial services like credit, insurance, and savings products.

Mobile Money A service that allows users to store, send, and receive money using a mobile phone.

Digital Identity A unique electronic representation of an individual used for authentication in online transactions.

Agent Banking A service that allows a retail agent (e.g., a corner shop) to conduct basic banking transactions on behalf of a financial institution.

Alternative Data Information not found in traditional credit reports used to assess a borrower's creditworthiness (e.g., mobile phone usage, utility payments).

G2P (Government-to-Person) Payments Digital transfers of social benefits, subsidies, or pensions from a government directly to a citizen's account.

Test Your Understanding

Multiple-Choice Questions

1 Which of the following best defines financial inclusion?

A Access to luxury financial products for high-income individuals
B The process of providing individuals and businesses with affordable, useful financial services that meet their needs
C Mandatory digital payments in all countries
D Exclusive focus on credit provision by banks

2 Mobile money platforms such as M-Pesa primarily contribute to financial inclusion by:

A Replacing banks entirely in urban areas
B Enabling users without formal bank accounts to store, transfer, and pay digitally
C Reducing smartphone penetration in rural areas
D Providing only large-scale corporate financial services

3 A major challenge limiting the effectiveness of digital financial inclusion is:

A Excessive mobile phone penetration
B Algorithmic bias, digital literacy gaps, and uneven digital infrastructure
C Over-regulation of fintech startups in developed markets
D Abundance of government subsidies for digital adoption

4 How does DPI like India Stack enhance financial inclusion?

A By providing physical bank branches in rural areas
B By integrating digital identity, payments, and consent-based data sharing to reduce onboarding costs and scale services
C By offering only microloans to select populations
D By replacing traditional banks with government-only financial services

5 Hyper-personalisation in digital financial services refers to:

A Providing generic financial advice to all users
B Using AI and real-time data to tailor financial products and guidance to individual behaviours and cash flows
C Requiring all users to have a formal credit history before accessing services
D Restricting digital services to urban populations

Short Questions

1 Explain how mobile money platforms reduce structural barriers to financial inclusion in rural or low-income communities.
2 Define alternative data in digital credit scoring and describe one benefit and one risk associated with its use.
3 Why are consumer protection and data privacy frameworks considered essential for sustainable digital financial inclusion?

Analytical Questions

1 Critically evaluate the argument that digital transformation alone is insufficient to achieve meaningful financial inclusion without complementary policy and educational interventions.
2 Analyse how digital financial services can simultaneously promote financial inclusion and introduce new forms of exclusion or inequality.
3 Assess the long-term implications of AI-driven hyper-personalised financial services for both financial resilience and ethical risk in emerging markets.

Case Study: M-Pesa and the Financial Transformation of Kenya

Launched in 2007 by Safaricom, M-Pesa is an SMS-based mobile money service that transformed Kenya's financial landscape by enabling users to deposit, transfer, and withdraw funds through a widespread network of retail agents. Initially designed to facilitate microfinance loan repayments, it quickly became a mainstream remittance platform, particularly for connecting urban earners with rural family members.

M-Pesa's rapid adoption, exceeding 80% of Kenya's adult population by 2021, was underpinned by several critical factors: simple technology accessible on basic mobile phones, a culturally aligned service addressing the need for secure, convenient financial transactions, and supportive regulatory policies that enabled mobile money to operate with minimal friction.

A key innovation was the agent network, which effectively solved the *last-mile* problem that had limited traditional banks' reach in rural areas. By decentralising cash-in and cash-out points, M-Pesa made financial services accessible even in low-density regions. However, challenges remain in ensuring agent liquidity, network sustainability, and consumer protection.

Beyond enabling everyday transactions, M-Pesa contributed to poverty reduction, financial resilience, and occupational diversification, while spurring complementary services like M-Shwari for savings and credit. The Kenyan experience illustrates how the convergence of technology, social context, and regulation can catalyse widespread financial inclusion, offering lessons for replication in other markets.

Reference

Lal, R., Cox, L., & McAra, S. (2016) *M-Pesa: Financial Inclusion in Kenya*. Harvard Business School Case 516-011. Available at: https://www.hbs.edu/faculty/Pages/item.aspx?num=50788 [Accessed 1 March 2026].

Case Study Questions

1 What were the primary technological, social, and regulatory factors that contributed to the rapid adoption and success of M-Pesa in Kenya?
2 In what ways did M-Pesa's agent network address the *last-mile* challenge that traditional banks struggled with, and what are the potential limitations of relying on this model?
3 If a mobile network operator in a neighbouring country aims to replicate M-Pesa's success, what two key strategies would you recommend to ensure widespread adoption and meaningful financial inclusion?

Further Reading

Carrière-Swallow, Y., Haksar, V., & Patnam, M. (2021). India's Digital Revolution: The Promise of a New Financial Architecture. *BIS Papers No. 123*.

Demirgüç-Kunt, A., Klapper, L., Singer, D., & Ansar, S. (2021). *The Global Findex Database 2021: Financial Inclusion, Digital Payments, and Resilience in the Age of COVID-19*. Washington, DC: World Bank.

World Economic Forum. (2023). *The Future of Global Financial Inclusion*. Geneva: WEF.

References

Berg, T., Burg, V., Gombović, A., & Puri, M. (2020). On the Rise of FinTechs: Credit Scoring Using Digital Footprints. *The Review of Financial Studies*, 33(7), 2845–2897.

Carrière-Swallow, Y., Haksar, V., & Patnam, M. (2021). India's Digital Revolution: A Look at the Potential for Digital Finance. *IMF Departmental Paper*.

CGAP. (2020). The New Age of Digital Financial Inclusion: Managing the Opportunities and Risks. *CGAP Annual Report*.

Demirgüç-Kunt, A., Klapper, L., Singer, D., & Ansar, S. (2018). *The Global Findex Database 2017: Measuring Financial Inclusion and the FinTech Revolution*. World Bank.

GSMA. (2023). *The Mobile Economy 2023*. London: GSMA Intelligence.

Suri, T., & Jack, W. (2016). The Long-Run Poverty and Gender Impacts of Mobile Money. *A Review of the Literature Science*, 354(6317), 1288–1292.

World Bank. (2022). *Global Findex Database 2021: Financial Inclusion, Digital Payments, and Resilience in the Age of COVID-19*. Washington, DC: World Bank Group.

4 FinTech and Globalisation

Reshaping Global Economics, Finance, and Banking

Chapter Overview

This chapter provides a comprehensive analysis of how Financial Technology (FinTech) is fundamentally reshaping the global landscape of economics, finance, and banking. It first examines how FinTech advances global economic integration by reducing barriers to cross-border payments, enhancing financial inclusion, and facilitating more efficient international trade (World Bank, 2023). The analysis then explores how FinTech disrupts traditional banking by challenging incumbent monopolies, promoting open banking and Application Programming Interface (API)-driven finance, and transforming global capital markets through innovations like tokenisation and decentralised finance (DeFi) (BCG, 2023). Furthermore, the chapter addresses the critical regulatory and geopolitical challenges in this evolution, including significant cybersecurity risks and complex, divergent global regulations (Financial Stability Board, 2023). It concludes with a forward-looking outlook on the future of a hyper-globalised FinTech economy, shaped by Central Bank Digital Currencies (CBDCs), Artificial Intelligence (AI), and the rising demand for sustainable FinTech solutions.

Learning Objectives

By the end of this chapter, you should be able to:

1. Explain the mechanisms through which FinTech accelerates cross-border economic integration and expands access to financial services for underserved populations.
2. Analyse how FinTech business models disrupt incumbent banking structures, weaken traditional monopolistic advantages, and alter competitive dynamics in financial services.
3. Evaluate the role of open banking frameworks and API-driven ecosystems in transforming data portability, service interoperability, and end-user financial experiences.
4. Assess the impact of tokenisation, DeFi, and digital assets on the structure, efficiency, and accessibility of global capital markets.
5. Examine the principal regulatory, geopolitical, technological, and sustainability challenges shaping the evolution of FinTech, including the influence of CBDCs and AI on the future financial system.

DOI: 10.4324/9781003775751-5

4.1 Introduction

FinTech drives the contemporary wave of globalisation by systematically dismantling conventional obstacles in the financial sector. FinTech facilitates frictionless cross-border transactions and significantly broadens access to essential banking services for previously underserved populations, thereby fostering financial inclusion on a global scale (IMF, 2022).

At its core, FinTech uses cutting-edge technologies such as blockchain to enhance transparency and security, AI to deliver sophisticated data analysis and personalised services, and DeFi protocols to empower peer-to-peer economic interactions. Together, these technologies re-architect financial operations and set new paradigms for capital flow, business models, and international economic relations (Zetzsche et al., 2020).

This transformative shift extends beyond operational efficiencies and fundamentally alters global economics, the structure of financial markets, and the competitive landscape of banking. A thorough understanding of these changes, supported by empirical examples, regulatory developments, and future trends, is essential for navigating the complexities of the modern global economy. This chapter provides a comprehensive analysis of these critical developments.

4.2 FinTech's Role in Global Economic Integration

FinTech is fundamentally reshaping the processes that underpin global economic integration by reducing frictions in cross-border financial activity and expanding participation in the international economy. Digital payment infrastructures and distributed ledger technologies have significantly increased the speed, security, and cost-efficiency of international transactions. By lowering reliance on traditional intermediaries, these systems enable firms, including small- and medium-sized enterprises, to participate more effectively in global trade and financial networks, thereby intensifying economic interdependence.

FinTech also serves as a major driver of global financial inclusion. Mobile financial services, peer-to-peer lending platforms, and data-driven credit assessment models extend formal financial access to underserved populations, particularly in emerging and developing economies. This inclusion facilitates access to savings, credit, and investment tools, integrating previously excluded groups into formal economic systems and supporting local growth.

In addition, FinTech enhances data transparency, and information flows across markets, improving risk assessment and decision-making for investors and regulators and contributing to a more resilient and interconnected global financial architecture.

4.2.1 Cross-Border Payments and Remittances

FinTech is reshaping global economic integration by addressing enduring inefficiencies in cross-border payments and remittances. Traditional systems have long been constrained by high costs and slow processing, with average remittance fees reported at 6–7%, disproportionately burdening migrant workers and limiting essential capital flows (World Bank, 2023). Emerging FinTech solutions mitigate these constraints by leveraging distributed ledger technologies and digital architectures. For example, blockchain-enabled platforms significantly lower transaction costs and enable near-real-time settlement. At the same time, digital-first money transfer services reduce foreign exchange (FX) and transfer fees substantially compared with conventional banking networks.

The broader economic implications of these innovations underscore FinTech's integrative potential. Mobile money systems have facilitated substantial financial activity in contexts where formal banking is limited, contributing measurably to national economic performance. Macro-level analyses suggest that widespread FinTech adoption could generate significant global cost savings in remittances. By reducing transactional frictions and accelerating fund transfers, FinTech enhances liquidity, expands access to financial services, and supports deeper integration of global financial flows.

4.2.2 Financial Inclusion

FinTech is playing a pivotal role in advancing financial inclusion in emerging markets, directly addressing the World Bank's (2023) finding that approximately 2 billion adults remain unbanked. By deploying accessible and low-cost digital alternatives, FinTech innovations are effectively integrating previously excluded populations into the formal financial system. This is exemplified by the rise of neobanks like Nubank in Brazil and Kuda Bank in Nigeria, which have provided millions with their first formal banking experience through fully digital operations. At the same time, Buy Now, Pay Later platforms have expanded credit access across regions like Southeast Asia. The monumental scale of this adoption is evident in the success of national infrastructures; India's Unified Payments Interface processed over 10 billion monthly transactions in 2023, and Brazil's Pix system is used by 75% of the adult population. These developments not only democratise access to financial services but also, as the IMF (2022) affirms, drive broader economic growth and integration by creating a more inclusive and interconnected global economy.

4.3 FinTech's Disruption of Global Banking

The rise of FinTech has generated a structural transformation in the global banking sector, challenging entrenched operating models and compelling incumbent institutions to reassess their strategic roles within an increasingly digital financial environment. By deploying technologies such as AI, distributed ledger systems, and cloud computing, FinTech firms have improved process efficiency, reduced intermediation costs, and enhanced transparency, thereby lowering barriers to financial service access. This technological shift has reconfigured segments of the traditional banking value chain and intensified competition across payments, lending, wealth management, and advisory services.

Simultaneously, consumer expectations have evolved, shaped by seamless digital interfaces, real-time services, and personalised financial products offered through mobile-first platforms. Legacy banks, often constrained by complex infrastructures and regulatory burdens, face growing pressure to modernise their systems and adopt more agile, customer-centric approaches. The expansion of neobanks and large technology firms into financial services has further intensified this competitive landscape. In response, established institutions are increasingly pursuing digital transformation strategies, strategic partnerships, and targeted acquisitions to sustain market relevance and operational competitiveness.

4.3.1 Decline of Traditional Banking Monopolies

Historically, traditional banks held near-exclusive dominance over financial services, fostering high entry barriers that enabled inflated fees, sluggish processes, and impersonal customer experiences. FinTech's rapid ascent has dismantled this monopoly by introducing nimble digital solutions, such as neobanks, peer-to-peer lending, and blockchain-based payments, that prioritise efficiency, affordability, and inclusivity. As tech-driven firms like

Table 4.1 Traditional Banks vs FinTech Disruptors

Dimension	*Traditional bank*	*FinTech disruptions*
Speed	Days for loans	Minutes (e.g., Klarna, Affirm)
Fees	High cross-border costs	Low-cost (e.g., Revolut, Wise)
Accessibility	Branch-dependent	Mobile-first (e.g., Chime, N26)

Stripe and Revolut redefine expectations, customers increasingly bypass legacy institutions, eroding their market share. FinTech isn't just competing with banks; it's redefining what banking means. This paradigm shift compels traditional banks to innovate or face obsolescence, fragmenting the financial landscape into a dynamic, consumer-centric ecosystem. Table 4.1 shows the key distinctions between traditional and fintech banking.

4.3.2 *Open Banking and API-Driven Finance*

Open Banking and API-driven finance signify a fundamental transition from closed, institution-centric banking models to a more integrated digital financial ecosystem. Under Open Banking frameworks, regulated banks are required to share customer financial data with authorised third parties upon explicit customer consent, using APIs as standardised conduits for secure data exchange (European Banking Authority, 2023). Regulatory initiatives such as the Revised Payment Services Directive (PSD2) in Europe and the UK's Open Banking regime illustrate this shift. At the same time, efforts in the United States, including the Financial Data Exchange coalition, aim to establish industry-wide data sharing standards.

These developments are reshaping financial intermediation by enabling third-party providers to deliver enhanced services. Platforms such as Plaid and Tink enable consumers to access aggregated account information, budgeting tools, and integrated financial dashboards. Strategic collaborations, exemplified by Goldman Sachs' partnership with Apple for the Apple Card, further demonstrate how APIs are enabling incumbent banks to innovate and broaden their product offerings.

4.4 FinTech and Global Capital Markets

FinTech is exerting a transformative influence on global capital markets by improving efficiency, widening participation, and strengthening transparency across the financial value chain. Its impact extends across the trading lifecycle, reshaping processes for capital formation, execution, clearing, and settlement. Technological advancements such as AI-driven algorithmic trading have accelerated transaction speeds and enhanced price discovery. Simultaneously, distributed ledger technology is modernising post-trade infrastructure by enabling secure, immutable record-keeping and the potential for near-real-time settlement, which may reduce counterparty and operational risk. FinTech innovations also promote broader market access through tokenisation and fractional ownership models, while data analytics tools enhance risk assessment and portfolio management.

4.4.1 *Tokenisation of Assets*

Tokenisation involves representing ownership rights to real-world assets as digital tokens recorded on a blockchain, enabling divisibility, transferability, and broader investor participation. This model is expected to unlock market potential exceeding $5 trillion by 2030 (BCG, 2023). Applications span multiple asset classes: in real estate, platforms such as Propy support fractional ownership, while BlackRock USD Institutional Digital Liquidity Fund tokenised money-market fund illustrates growing institutional adoption of tokenised financial instruments.

4.4.2 DeFi and Global Liquidity

DeFi is transforming global capital markets by establishing an open, permissionless financial ecosystem that enables direct peer-to-peer transactions and lending without traditional intermediaries, thereby augmenting global liquidity. Total Value Locked in DeFi protocols surpassed $100 billion in 2024 (DeFi Llama, 2024). Despite its growth, DeFi faces substantive challenges, including regulatory ambiguity across jurisdictions (Financial Stability Board, 2023) and smart contract vulnerabilities, which contributed to over $3 billion in protocol exploits in 2023 (Chainalysis, 2024).

4.5 Regulatory and Geopolitical Challenges

The international expansion of FinTech is constrained by regulatory fragmentation and geopolitical tensions. Innovation frequently outpaces supervisory frameworks, creating risks of regulatory arbitrage, inconsistent compliance standards, and uneven enforcement of consumer protection and anti-money laundering (AML)/Counter-Terrorist Financing requirements across jurisdictions (Zetzsche et al., 2020). Geopolitical considerations, including digital sovereignty and data localisation policies, further complicate cross-border operations. In addition, strategic competition surrounding CBDC development is introducing new power dynamics into the global financial system (Figure 4.1).

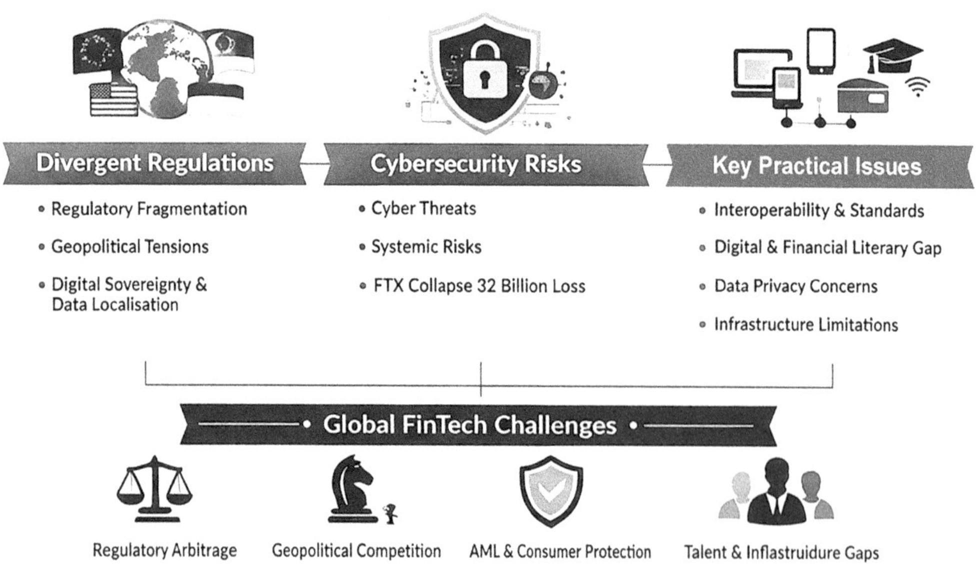

Figure 4.1 Regulatory and Geopolitical Challenges in FinTech.

Table 4.2 Divergent Regulatory Approaches to FinTech

Jurisdiction	*Regulatory stance*	*Policy approach*
EU	Strict	Crypto licensing frameworks (Markets in Crypto-Assets Regulation, Digital Operational Resilience Act)
USA	Fragmented	Securities and Exchange Commission vs U.S. Commodity Futures Trading Commission crackdown on unregistered securities
Singapore	Pro-innovation	CBDC and stablecoin pilots (Monetary Authority of Singapore Sandbox)

4.5.1 *Divergent Global Regulations*

The patchwork of divergent regulatory frameworks across jurisdictions presents a substantial hurdle for globally ambitious FinTech firms. The lack of harmonisation can stifle cross-border innovation, increase operational costs, and create market fragmentation. Table 4.2 shows the global regulatory approach to FinTech.

4.5.2 *Cybersecurity and Systemic Risks*

The rapid expansion of FinTech heightens exposure to cybersecurity threats and systemic risks, as increasingly digital and interconnected platforms expand potential attack surfaces. The 2023 collapse of Futures Exchange or Futures and Spot Exchange, resulting in approximately $8 billion in customer losses, illustrates the systemic contagion such failures can generate (Chainalysis, 2024). To mitigate these risks, firms are deploying AI and machine learning; platforms such as Feedzai and Darktrace monitor large datasets in real time to detect suspicious activity and safeguard transactional integrity.

4.5.3 *Key Practical Issues*

The globalisation of FinTech faces several practical challenges that impede its full potential. Interoperability and standardisation remain central issues, as diverse FinTech platforms, legacy banking systems, and national payment infrastructures often operate under incompatible protocols, limiting the creation of a seamless, hyper-connected financial ecosystem. For example, cross-border payment platforms such as Ripple must navigate disparate regulatory and technical standards to facilitate efficient transactions.

Digital literacy and user adoption also constrain FinTech's impact, as uneven levels of digital and financial literacy across regions can exclude vulnerable populations, reinforcing a digital divide. Data privacy and ownership are critical concerns, particularly under Open Banking frameworks, where consumers must be able to understand and control third-party access to their financial data.

In emerging markets, infrastructure limitations, including limited internet connectivity and smartphone penetration, restrict scalability, as seen in certain rural areas of Sub-Saharan Africa. Furthermore, the sector faces a significant talent gap; the shortage of professionals skilled in both finance and technology can slow innovation and hinder the effective deployment of new solutions within traditional financial institutions.

4.6 The Future: A Hyper-Globalised FinTech Economy

The evolution of FinTech points towards a hyper-globalised financial ecosystem, where blockchain, AI, and IoT enable rapid, transparent, and cost-efficient cross-border transactions. This environment promises enhanced financial inclusion by providing seamless access to diverse services globally, contingent on coordinated international regulation, robust cybersecurity measures, and effective data governance.

4.6.1 Central Bank Digital Currencies

CBDCs are emerging as a foundational element of a hyper-globalised FinTech ecosystem, with active initiatives including China's Digital Yuan, Nigeria's e-Naira, and the European Central Bank's Digital Euro project (IMF, 2022). CBDCs have the potential to gradually replace physical cash, offering secure, traceable transactions. Moreover, programmable features embedded within CBDCs could enable automated tax collection and smart contract-based payments, fundamentally transforming financial interactions and the efficiency of monetary systems.

4.6.2 AI and Autonomous Finance

Advancements in AI are driving the emergence of autonomous finance, reshaping global FinTech. AI-driven hedge funds, exemplified by Numerai, analyse large datasets and execute trades across international markets with minimal human oversight, enhancing liquidity (CB Insights, 2023). Concurrently, generative AI is transforming client-facing services; for instance, Morgan Stanley's collaboration with OpenAI delivers personalised financial advice, broadening access to advanced wealth management strategies and promoting more inclusive global financial participation.

4.6.3 Sustainable FinTech

Sustainable FinTech, or Green FinTech, leverages digital technologies to advance climate finance and responsible investment, supporting both ecological sustainability and financial stability. Blockchain-based platforms like KlimaDAO facilitate the tokenisation of Verified Carbon Units, enhancing accessibility and transparency in carbon markets (BCG, 2023). Similarly, the tokenisation of Green Bonds improves traceability of fund allocation and environmental impact, fostering investor confidence and accelerating the transition towards a low-carbon, sustainable global financial ecosystem.

4.7 Conclusion

FinTech has emerged as a pivotal driver of globalisation, fundamentally reshaping the structure and functioning of international finance and banking. By harnessing technological innovation, FinTech has reduced traditional barriers, enabling faster, more cost-efficient, and inclusive cross-border financial services. Digital financial platforms, including instant payments and online lending systems, have expanded access to previously underserved populations; the World Bank estimates that digital financial services could reach 1.7 billion unbanked adults worldwide, highlighting FinTech's role in promoting financial inclusion and economic interdependence.

However, the rapid expansion of FinTech also generates significant challenges, including regulatory fragmentation, cybersecurity risks, and the potential exacerbation of financial inequality. Addressing these issues necessitates coordinated international regulatory frameworks and robust governance mechanisms. Looking ahead, the deployment of advanced technologies such as AI, blockchain, and CBDCs is expected to further diminish geographical constraints, consolidating FinTech's role in fostering a more integrated, efficient, and resilient global financial system.

Key Terms and Glossary

Cross-border payments Transactions where the payer and the recipient are situated in different countries.

Financial Inclusion The effort to make financial products and services accessible and affordable to all individuals and businesses, particularly those excluded from the traditional banking system.

Tokenisation The process of converting rights to an asset into a digital token on a blockchain.

CBDC A digital form of a country's fiat currency that is a direct liability of the central bank.

Regulatory Arbitrage The practice of capitalising on a regulatory difference between two or more markets, often by operating in the jurisdiction with the most favourable laws.

Programmable Money Digital money that can be designed with rules governing its use, such as expiration dates or specific spending conditions.

Test Your Understanding

Multiple-Choice Questions

1 Which mechanism best explains how FinTech accelerates global economic integration?

A Increasing reliance on cash-based informal trade
B Reducing cross-border transaction frictions through digital payment and settlement technologies
C Expanding physical bank branch networks internationally
D Restricting financial data flows between countries

2 A core competitive advantage of FinTech firms over traditional banks is their ability to:

A Operate without any regulatory oversight
B Maintain higher capital reserves
C Deliver low-cost, mobile-first, and API-enabled financial services
D Control national monetary policy

3 What is the primary function of Open Banking frameworks?

A Allow central banks to access all private bank data
B Require banks to share customer-permitted data with licensed third parties via secure APIs

C Eliminate traditional banks from the financial system
D Replace payment systems with cryptocurrencies

4 Tokenisation in capital markets primarily contributes to:

A Eliminating the need for financial intermediaries entirely
B Restricting asset ownership to institutional investors
C Enabling fractional ownership and improving asset liquidity through blockchain-based representation
D Fixing exchange rates across global markets

5 A major regulatory challenge associated with the global expansion of FinTech is:

A Uniform global supervision of digital finance
B The absence of technological innovation
C Divergent national regulations that create compliance complexity and regulatory arbitrage risks
D Excessive standardisation of financial rules

Short Questions

1 Explain how FinTech innovations have reduced the cost and increased the speed of cross-border remittances.
2 What role do APIs play in the development of Open Banking ecosystems?
3 Identify two systemic risks linked to the growth of DeFi.

Analytical Questions

1 Critically assess how FinTech both challenges and collaborates with traditional banks in the evolving global financial ecosystem.
2 Analyse the geopolitical implications of CBDC development for international monetary power dynamics.
3 Evaluate whether regulatory fragmentation is a greater obstacle to global FinTech expansion than technological limitations. Justify your position with examples.

Case Study: Revolut—Disrupting Cross-Border Banking

Revolut, founded in 2015, exemplifies how fintech companies are transforming global finance by addressing inefficiencies in traditional banking and cross-border payment systems. Conventional banks have historically imposed high FX markups, opaque fee structures, and slow settlement times for international transactions, constraining both individual consumers and small enterprises engaged in global commerce. Revolut leveraged these gaps by providing a mobile-first platform with multi-currency accounts, real-time interbank FX rates (subject to fair usage), and low-cost international transfers. By integrating with local banking infrastructures and payment networks, Revolut reduces reliance on intermediaries, accelerates transaction speeds, and lowers costs, enabling seamless cross-border financial activity that supports global economic integration.

From an operational perspective, Revolut employs a hybrid model that combines electronic money institution (EMI) licences, selective banking licences, and strategic partnerships with regulated financial entities. This structure allows near-instant transfers within its ecosystem and competitive FX rates compared with traditional banks, which often charge 3–5% above mid-market rates. The platform's digital-first architecture also facilitates rapid expansion across more than 30 countries, demonstrating the scalability of fintech solutions for efficiently connecting global financial networks.

Globalisation and the expansion of FinTech have required Revolut to navigate diverse regulatory frameworks. The firm has faced scrutiny concerning AML and know-your-customer compliance, particularly given its automated onboarding and rapid user growth. Key challenges included compliance with the European Union's PSD2 directives, securing a full banking licence in Lithuania for European Economic Area (EEA) operations, and adapting to post-Brexit regulatory divergence in the United Kingdom. Initial operations under EMI licences drew regulatory arbitrage criticism, but Revolut addressed these concerns by investing in compliance infrastructure, enhancing transaction monitoring, expanding risk and compliance teams, and increasing transparency.

Revolut's contribution to financial inclusion and globalisation is significant. Its low-cost FX services and multi-currency accounts reduce barriers for digitally literate users, freelancers, and small businesses, enabling efficient participation in global trade and international finance. By lowering remittance costs and improving access to cross-border transactions, Revolut accelerates financial integration and economic participation. World Bank data (2023) indicate a downward trend in global remittance fees, with fintech providers like Revolut increasing competition and reducing costs in major currency corridors, demonstrating the tangible impact of digital-first financial services on global economic networks.

References

Revolut (2025) *Annual Report and Financial Statements*. Available at: https://www.revolut.com/ (Accessed: 1 March 2026).

World Bank (2023) *Remittance Prices Worldwide Database*. Available at: https://remittanceprices.worldbank.org/ (Accessed: 1 March 2026).

Case Study Questions

1. How has Revolut leveraged fintech innovation to reshape global finance, particularly by improving cross-border payments and reducing traditional banking inefficiencies?
2. What regulatory and compliance challenges has Revolut faced in different jurisdictions, and how has its licensing strategy enabled it to operate globally while managing risks associated with regulatory arbitrage?
3. In what ways has Revolut advanced financial inclusion and facilitated global economic participation for consumers and small businesses, and how does World Bank data support its role in lowering remittance costs and enhancing access to international financial systems?

Further Reading

Bank for International Settlements (2023) *Annual Economic Report 2023*. Basel: BIS. Available at: https://www.bis.org/publ/arpdf/ar2023e.htm (Accessed: 1 March 2026).
IMF (2022). *FinTech and Financial Inclusion in Emerging Markets*. Washington, D.C, International Monetary Fund.
Zetzsche, D. A., Buckley, R. P., Arner, D. W., & Barberis, J. N. (2020). FinTech and the Future of Finance. *European Banking Institute Working Paper Series*.

References

Boston Consulting Group (2023). *The Tokenisation of Assets: A $5T Opportunity*. Boston: Boston Consulting Group.
CB Insights (2023) State of AI Q1'23 Report: Generative AI momentum isn't enough to save AI funding from a steep fall in Q1'23. Available at: https://www.cbinsights.com/research/report/ai-trends-q1-2023
Chainalysis (2024). *The 2024 Crypto Crime Report*. New York: Chainalysis.
DeFi Llama (2024). *Total Value Locked (TVL) Dashboard*. Available at: https://defillama.com (Accessed: 15 May 2024).
European Banking Authority (2023). *PSD2 Impact Report*. London: EBA.
Financial Stability Board (FSB) (2023). *Global Monitoring Report on FinTech Risks*. Basel: FSB.
IMF (2022). *FinTech and Financial Inclusion in Emerging Markets*. Washington, DC: International Monetary Fund.
World Bank (2023) *Remittance Prices Worldwide*. Quarterly Report, Issue 41. Washington, DC: World Bank.
Zetzsche, D. A., Buckley, R. P., Arner, D. W., & Barberis, J. N. (2020). FinTech and the Future of Finance. *European Banking Institute Working Paper Series*.

5 Fraud, Identity and Financial Crime Evolving with FinTech

Chapter Overview

This chapter provides a critical analysis of the evolving landscape of financial crime within the FinTech ecosystem. The same characteristics that drive FinTech innovation, namely speed, accessibility, and digitalisation, also create opportunities for sophisticated fraud and exploitation. The discussion outlines the principal types of FinTech crime, including payment fraud, identity theft, and specific vulnerabilities in decentralised finance (DeFi). It further explores technology's dual role as both a facilitator of malicious activity and a means of robust defence. Attention is given to advancements in biometrics, artificial intelligence (AI)–driven monitoring, and blockchain analytics. The chapter also addresses regulatory and compliance challenges, with emphasis on the need for Anti-Money Laundering (AML) and Counter-Financing of Terrorism (CFT) frameworks to adapt to emerging models. Finally, it evaluates current trends and strategies critical to protecting the future of the digital financial system.

Learning Objectives

By the end of this chapter, you should be able to:

1. Identify and classify the major forms of fraud, identity abuse, and financial crime prevalent in FinTech ecosystems.
2. Explain identity-related crime mechanisms, including identity theft and synthetic identity fraud (SIF), and how they are exploited within digital financial services.
3. Analyse financial crime and money laundering risks associated with cryptocurrencies, DeFi, and other emerging financial technologies.
4. Evaluate the effectiveness of technological controls, including AI, machine learning, biometrics, and transaction monitoring, in preventing and detecting financial crime.
5. Assess regulatory and operational challenges, including AML/CFT obligations (e.g., the 6th Anti-Money Laundering Directive (AMLD6) and the US Bank Secrecy Act (BSA)), and propose a multi-layered, risk-based financial crime management strategy that balances security, user experience (UX), and financial inclusion.

DOI: 10.4324/9781003775751-6

5.1 Introduction

The digital transformation of financial services has significantly enhanced efficiency, accessibility, and financial inclusion. However, it has simultaneously given rise to a fundamentally altered financial crime landscape. Core characteristics of FinTech innovation, such as remote digital onboarding, near-instantaneous transaction processing, and cross-border scalability, have expanded the attack surface available to fraudsters and other illicit actors (Levi, 2017). As a result, long-established criminal activities, including fraud and money laundering, have evolved to exploit technological vulnerabilities and the diminished reliance on physical interactions that characterise digital finance.

The rapid growth of cryptocurrencies and DeFi has further intensified these challenges. Pseudo-anonymity, disintermediation, and the absence of centralised control mechanisms complicate traditional approaches to customer due diligence (CDD), transaction monitoring, and regulatory enforcement (Zetzsche et al., 2020). These features not only facilitate novel forms of financial crime but also strain existing legal and supervisory frameworks that were designed for conventional financial institutions.

This chapter argues that mitigating financial crime risks in FinTech environments requires a nuanced, technology-enabled, and risk-based approach. Rather than providing a descriptive taxonomy of illicit activities, the analysis foregrounds the structural and operational vulnerabilities embedded within FinTech business models. The chapter first outlines the principal forms of fraud and identity-related crime affecting FinTech firms, before examining the specific risks associated with cryptocurrencies and DeFi protocols. It then evaluates the technological and regulatory mechanisms available for financial crime prevention and detection. The overarching aim is to develop an integrated framework for understanding how FinTechs can effectively combat illicit activity while continuing to promote innovation and financial inclusion.

5.2 The Landscape of Financial Crime in FinTech

The FinTech ecosystem has significantly advanced financial innovation and inclusion. Yet it is inherently exposed to elevated financial crime risk due to a persistent gap between rapid technological innovation and the maturity of risk and compliance controls. Accelerated product development, digital onboarding, and global scalability often outpace the implementation of robust anti-financial crime frameworks, placing FinTech firms under heightened pressure to balance growth with regulatory compliance (Arner, Barberis, & Buckley, 2017). The scale of this challenge is reflected in global compliance expenditure, which reached an estimated USD 274 billion in 2024, underscoring the substantial resources required to manage financial crime risk effectively (LexisNexis Risk, 2024).

The contemporary threat landscape is characterised by both the adaptation of traditional crimes and the emergence of technology-enabled illicit activity. Established schemes such as fraud and money laundering have evolved into digital forms, including SIF, credential stuffing leading to account takeover (ATO), and the misuse of peer-to-peer (P2P) payment platforms for laundering purposes (Europol, 2023). At the same time, novel risks have emerged from FinTech infrastructures themselves. These include the exploitation of vulnerabilities in DeFi protocols through smart contract attacks and the abuse of Application Programming Interfaces (APIs) to facilitate unauthorised access or transaction manipulation (Chainalysis, 2024).

Addressing this complex environment requires a shift from manual, reactive compliance processes to agile, technology-driven approaches, including RegTech, AI, and advanced data analytics to enhance financial crime prevention and detection.

5.3 Primary Typologies of FinTech-Facilitated Fraud

The digital nature of FinTech creates a dynamic and complex fraud landscape. Criminal actors exploit vulnerabilities across the entire customer journey, from onboarding to transactions, employing a range of sophisticated and evolving techniques. These fraud typologies can be categorised by their primary attack vector (Figure 5.1).

5.3.1 Payment Fraud

This category involves the direct theft of funds through the manipulation of payment systems and accounts, representing the most immediate financial loss for consumers.

Authorised Push Payment (APP) Fraud: APP Fraud occurs when victims are deceived through social engineering into authorising real-time payments to accounts controlled by criminals. Common methods include impersonation of banks or public authorities, as well as investment and romance scams. For example, fraudsters may pose as a bank's fraud team to induce urgent transfers. The near irreversibility of systems such as the UK's Faster Payments significantly amplifies consumer harm (UK Finance, 2023).

Card-Not-Present (CNP) Fraud: CNP Fraud represents the predominant form of payment card fraud in digital commerce. It occurs when criminals use compromised card credentials, often obtained through data breaches or phishing, to conduct unauthorised online transactions. For example, stolen card details may be used to purchase goods via e-commerce platforms without physical card verification.

ATO (Account Takeover): ATO Fraud occurs when criminals obtain unauthorised access to a legitimate user's financial account using compromised credentials acquired through phishing, data breaches, or credential stuffing attacks. For example, attackers may exploit reused passwords to access digital wallets, modify account details, and initiate fraudulent transfers without the account holder's knowledge (ACFE, 2023).

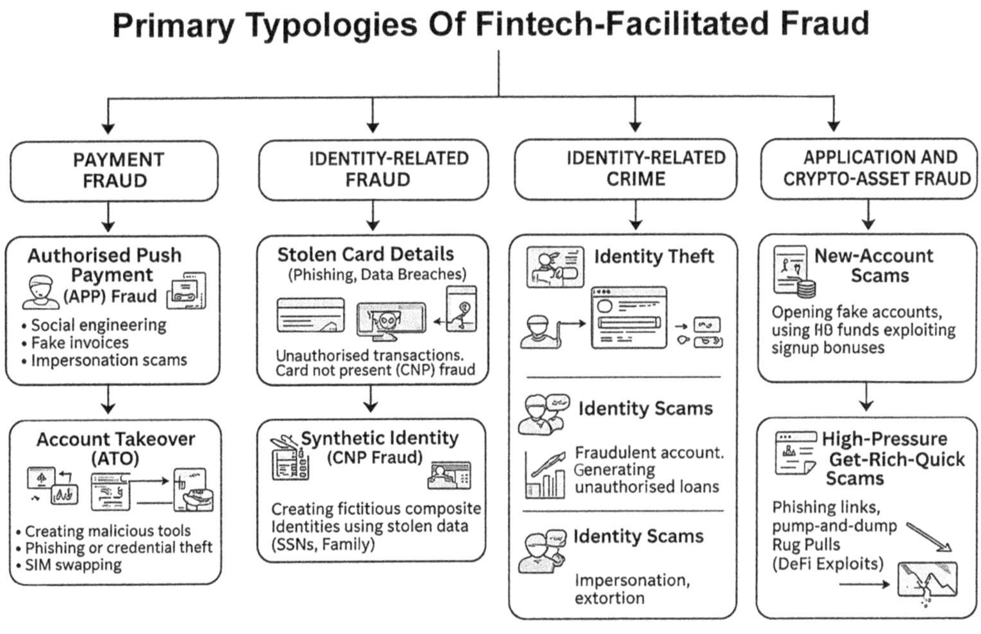

Figure 5.1 Primary Typologies of FinTech-Facilitated Fraud.

5.3.2 Identity-Related Crime

Digital identity is the key to accessing financial services, making it a prime target for compromise. This category underpins many other forms of fraud.

Identity Theft: Identity Theft involves the unlawful acquisition and misuse of an individual's personally identifiable information, such as name, address, or national identification number, to impersonate the victim. For example, stolen identity data may be used to open digital bank accounts or apply for credit facilities without the individual's consent.

SIF (Synthetic Identity Fraud): SIF is an advanced form of identity abuse in which criminals construct fictitious identities by combining genuine personal data with fabricated information. For example, a real national identification number may be paired with a false name and address. These identities are often cultivated through "credit grooming" before being exploited in large-scale credit default schemes, making detection particularly challenging for traditional verification systems (FTC, 2022).

5.3.3 Application and Onboarding Fraud

This occurs at the initial point of customer acquisition, exploiting digital onboarding processes to infiltrate the financial system.

New Account Fraud: New Account Fraud occurs when criminals exploit stolen or synthetic identities to open financial accounts for illicit purposes. For example, such accounts may be used as mule accounts to receive and transfer criminal proceeds or to obtain credit products that are deliberately defaulted on, resulting in direct financial losses to institutions.

5.3.4 Investment and Crypto-Asset Fraud

The promise of high returns and the complex, often unregulated nature of new asset classes create fertile ground for sophisticated scams.

Investment Scams: Fraudulent schemes in the fintech and cryptocurrency sector often exploit digital platforms to lure investors with promises of guaranteed, high-yield returns. Perpetrators employ high-pressure tactics through social media campaigns, phishing emails, or counterfeit websites. For instance, "crypto-rocketing" scams mimic legitimate trading platforms but operate as Ponzi or pyramid schemes, defrauding participants by redistributing new investments to earlier investors.

Rug Pulls: Rug pulls are a DeFi-specific form of fraud in which developers launch a new token to attract investor liquidity. After artificially inflating the token's value, they abruptly withdraw all funds from the associated liquidity pool, causing a collapse and rendering investments worthless. For example, the 2021 Squid Game token incident resulted in total investor losses (Chainalysis, 2024).

5.4 Money Laundering and the FinTech Ecosystem

The innovative features of FinTech services, namely speed, accessibility, and global reach, also increase their susceptibility to money laundering. Criminal actors exploit the high volume and rapidity of digital transactions to conceal the origins of illicit funds. The

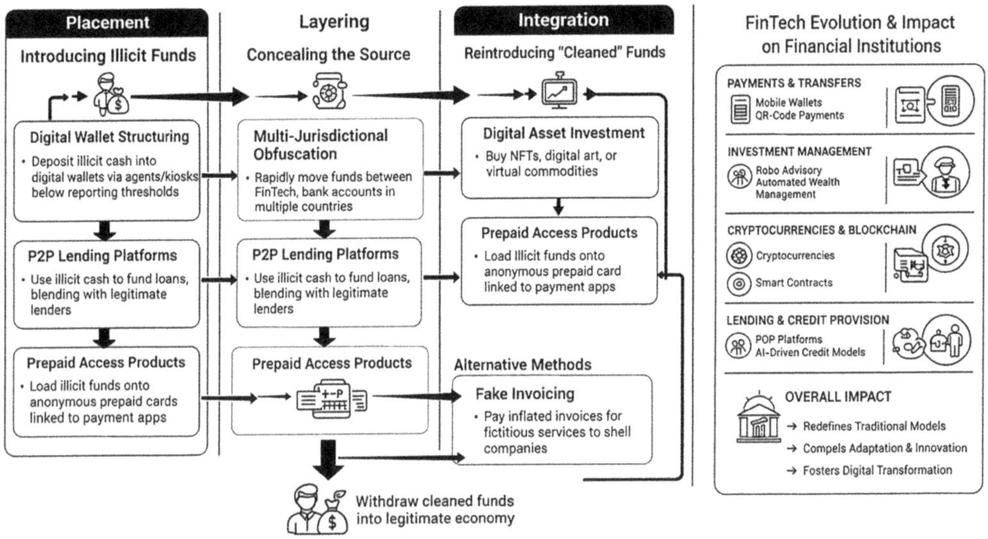

Figure 5.2 Money Laundering in the FinTech Ecosystem.

conventional three-stage model of money laundering, placement, layering, and integration, has been readily adapted to these digital channels, creating distinctive challenges for detection and regulatory compliance (Figure 5.2).

5.4.1 *Placement: Introducing Illicit Funds*

The placement stage involves introducing proceeds of crime into the formal financial system, often exploiting FinTech channels to evade detection.

Digital Wallet Structuring: Illicit funds are deposited into digital wallets in small increments below regulatory reporting thresholds, a practice known as structuring or smurfing (Levi & Reuter, 2006). For example, criminals have used multiple small deposits into PayPal and cryptocurrency wallets to avoid detection by regulatory authorities.

P2P Lending Platforms: Criminals may inject illicit capital into P2P lending platforms, commingling illegal proceeds with legitimate investor funds (Zdanowicz, 2022). In 2022, authorities identified schemes where fraudulent identities funded loans on platforms like LendingClub, concealing the origin of the proceeds.

Prepaid Access Products: Anonymous or semi-anonymous prepaid cards connected to digital payment applications are used to mask the source of illicit funds. In 2021, law enforcement uncovered cases where prepaid cards facilitated the transfer of drug-related proceeds into mobile wallets (FATF, 2021).

5.4.2 *Layering: Concealing the Source*

Layering seeks to obscure the criminal origin of funds through complex and repeated transactions across jurisdictions and platforms.

Multi-Jurisdictional Obfuscation: Illicit funds are rapidly moved across multiple accounts held at both FinTech and traditional banks in different countries, exploiting regulatory gaps (Ferwerda & de Weijer, 2019). For instance, the 2020 "Troika Laundromat" case involved a network of cross-border transfers designed to conceal the source of criminal proceeds.

Cryptocurrency Conversion: Criminals convert fiat currency into cryptocurrencies, route funds through mixers or multiple wallets (tumbling), and reconvert them into other fiat currencies to obscure their origins. The 2019 PlusToken scam exemplified this, concealing over $2 billion in illicit crypto assets (Foley, Karlsen, & Putniņš, 2019).

Micro-Transactions: Small-scale transactions, such as minor e-commerce payments or utility bills, are used to layer funds and complicate forensic tracing. In 2021, investigators identified schemes that used micro-payments on platforms such as Amazon and PayPal to launder stolen assets (Europol, 2021).

5.4.3 Integration: Reintroducing "Cleaned" Funds

In the integration phase, laundered funds are reintroduced into the legitimate economy, appearing as lawful income.

Digital Asset Investment: Illicit proceeds are invested in high-value digital assets, such as non-fungible tokens (NFTs) or virtual art, to enter legitimate markets. In 2022, authorities investigated schemes where NFTs on OpenSea were purchased to launder cryptocurrency proceeds (Europol, 2022).

High-Value E-Commerce: Criminals acquire luxury goods, electronics, or precious metals via online platforms and later resell them to establish a legitimate financial trail. In 2020, eBay and Alibaba were implicated in laundering schemes involving high-value purchases (FATF, 2023).

Fake Invoicing: Previously layered funds are used to pay fictitious or inflated invoices issued by shell companies, simulating legitimate business revenue. The 2019 Danske Bank case highlighted fraudulent invoicing methods to integrate illicit funds into corporate accounts (Danske Bank, 2019).

5.5 The DeFi and Crypto-Asset Conundrum

DeFi represents a transformative shift in the financial sector; however, its foundational principles, disintermediation, permissionless access, and pseudo-anonymity, pose significant challenges for preventing financial crime. Although blockchain ledgers are transparent and immutable, the absence of central intermediaries to implement AML/CFT measures creates regulatory gaps. For example, the 2021 Poly Network exploit highlighted how large-scale DeFi thefts can occur with minimal oversight, resulting in the temporary misappropriation of over $600 million in digital assets (Zetzsche et al., 2020).

Key Financial Crime Vulnerabilities in DeFi

Pseudo-Anonymity and Illicit Finance: DeFi protocols often forgo user identity verification, allowing wallet addresses to remain pseudonymous. While transactions are publicly recorded, tracing them to real-world actors is challenging, enabling money laundering and sanctions evasion. For example, the 2022 Tornado Cash case involved illicit fund transfers facilitated by crypto mixers (Foley et al., 2019).

Smart Contract Exploits and Theft: DeFi protocol security relies entirely on the integrity of smart contract code. Code vulnerabilities are frequently exploited, allowing hackers to drain liquidity pools. For instance, the 2023 Wormhole exploit resulted in $325 million in stolen funds, which were subsequently laundered through multiple crypto platforms (Chainalysis, 2024).

Obfuscation Services—Mixers and Tumblers: Mixers and tumblers disrupt the traceability of blockchain transactions by pooling and redistributing funds, severing links between source and destination addresses. For example, the 2022 Tornado Cash platform was used to launder millions in cryptocurrency, complicating regulatory oversight and forensic investigations (Foley et al., 2019).

Regulatory Arbitrage in a Borderless System: DeFi's decentralised and global nature enables developers and users to exploit jurisdictions with weak or absent AML/CFT regulations, undermining international financial crime controls. For example, the 2021 Poly Network hack highlighted how cross-border DeFi operations complicated recovery and enforcement efforts (Zetzsche et al., 2020).

5.6 Regulatory Framework and Compliance Challenges

FinTech firms operate within a complex and often fragmented global regulatory environment governing AML/CFT. They are required to interpret and implement international standards, such as the Financial Action Task Force (FATF) recommendations, into domestic legislation, including the European Union's AMLD and the US BSA. This multifaceted regulatory landscape imposes substantial operational and compliance burdens, particularly for entities providing cross-border financial services (Arner et al., 2020). As regulated financial institutions, FinTechs must adhere to several fundamental compliance pillars outlined below.

5.6.1 Know Your Customer (KYC)/CDD

As a primary control in the first line of defence, KYC/CDD mandates that financial institutions verify customer identities during onboarding and at regular intervals. This process evaluates risk factors, including geographic location, industry sector, and transaction behaviour, to implement a risk-based approach. For example, a fintech may apply enhanced scrutiny to clients in high-risk jurisdictions.

5.6.2 Transaction Monitoring

Financial institutions are required to implement ongoing monitoring of customer transactions to detect patterns indicative of money laundering, terrorist financing, or fraud. This entails using rule-based systems and, increasingly, machine learning algorithms to identify anomalies in real time. For instance, a sudden high-value transfer from a low-activity account may trigger an alert for investigation.

5.6.3 Suspicious Activity Reporting (SARs)

Upon detecting potentially illicit activity, fintech firms are legally obligated to submit an SAR to the relevant Financial Intelligence Unit, such as the Financial Crimes Enforcement Network in the United States. For example, repeated structuring of deposits below reporting thresholds by a single customer may prompt an SAR submission to support law enforcement investigations.

5.6.4 *The Travel Rule*

The Travel Rule, a core FATF standard extended to Virtual Asset Service Providers (VASPs), requires that identifying information for both the originator and beneficiary accompany cryptocurrency transfers exceeding defined thresholds (e.g., $3,000 or €1,000). For example, a VASP processing a high-value Bitcoin transfer must collect and transmit the sender's and recipient's identifying details to comply with AML obligations.

5.6.5 *The Central Compliance Conundrum*

A persistent challenge for FinTechs is reconciling stringent regulatory compliance with cost efficiency and financial inclusion. Implementing comprehensive KYC, CDD, and transaction monitoring systems is resource-intensive, particularly for startups. Moreover, strict identity verification may unintentionally exclude legitimate yet under-documented customers, such as refugees or migrant workers, thereby highlighting the inherent tension between safeguarding the financial system and promoting equitable access to digital financial services.

5.7 Key Practical Issues in FinTech Financial Crime Compliance

Navigating the financial crime landscape requires FinTechs to address several critical, interconnected challenges that sit at the intersection of technology, regulation, and business strategy.

5.7.1 *The Security vs UX Trade-Off*

FinTechs face a fundamental tension between enforcing robust security measures and ensuring a seamless UX. Mandatory procedures such as multi-factor authentication, comprehensive KYC forms, and manual document verification enhance compliance but may increase onboarding attrition. For instance, stringent identity verification requirements imposed on new mobile banking customers may increase onboarding friction, resulting in elevated drop-off rates during account creation and, consequently, constraining customer acquisition and platform growth. The User Friction–Security Provision Matrix provides a structured analytical framework for assessing this trade-off, enabling the systematic alignment of product design with an optimal ideal zone in which security controls are calibrated against usability considerations (Figure 5.3).

The matrix categorises product security and UX into four quadrants. The Ideal Zone (Top-Left) represents optimal solutions where robust security is seamlessly integrated (e.g., biometrics), minimising user friction. The Compliance Zone (Top-Right) accepts high friction in regulated environments, prioritising compliance. The Legacy Zone (Bottom-Left) reflects outdated systems favouring usability over security, such as password reuse. The Inefficient Zone (Bottom-Right) epitomises poor design, offering minimal security while wasting effort. This framework guides development towards the Ideal Zone, balancing security and intuitive UX.

5.7.2 *The Synthetic Identity Detection Gap*

SIF is challenging to detect, as it combines genuine and fabricated information, often bypassing standard KYC and database verification. For example, a legitimate Social Security Number (SSN) paired with a fictitious name and address can be "credit groomed" over months, creating a credible history before executing a large-scale bust-out.

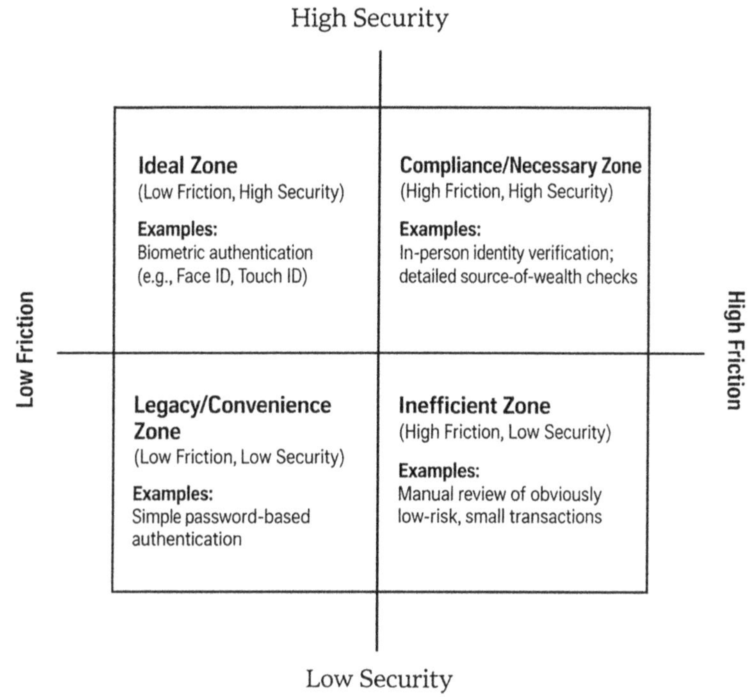

Figure 5.3 Security–Friction Matrix for UX.

5.7.3 Navigating the Complex Web of Global AML/CFT Regulations

FinTechs operating internationally face a complex regulatory landscape that requires simultaneous compliance with overlapping and evolving AML/CFT frameworks. For instance, a firm processing cross-border payments must reconcile the EU's AMLD, the US BSA, FATF guidelines, and local data privacy laws, increasing operational complexity and the risk of inadvertent non-compliance.

5.8 Future Trends and Strategic Defences

The future of financial crime prevention will depend on adopting proactive, data-driven, and collaborative strategies.

AI-Powered Predictive Analytics: FinTechs are increasingly leveraging AI-driven predictive analytics to shift from reactive detection to proactive prevention of financial crime. For example, machine learning models can analyse transaction patterns to identify emerging fraud rings or money laundering networks, enabling early intervention before significant financial or reputational harm occurs.

Industry-Wide Collaboration: FinTechs are increasingly engaging in secure, cross-industry collaboration to combat financial crime. By sharing intelligence on fraud and suspicious activity through consortia or information-sharing platforms, firms can strengthen collective defences. For example, multiple banks and FinTechs may exchange anonymised transaction data to identify emerging cybercrime networks before they escalate.

Quantum-Resistant Cryptography: FinTechs are exploring quantum-resistant cryptographic methods to safeguard financial data and blockchain systems against the potential threat posed by quantum computing, which could compromise existing encryption. For example, post-quantum algorithms can secure transaction ledgers and digital wallets, ensuring long-term integrity and resilience of critical financial infrastructures.

Behavioural Biometrics and Continuous Authentication: FinTechs are adopting continuous, behaviour-based authentication to complement point-in-time verification, enhancing fraud detection and financial crime prevention. For example, systems may monitor typing patterns or device interactions to identify anomalies, enabling real-time intervention. Effective risk management requires integrating AI, biometrics, and a multi-layered compliance strategy to safeguard the digital financial ecosystem.

5.9 Conclusion

The rapid evolution of financial technology has introduced significant advancements in accessibility, efficiency, and the digitalisation of financial services. However, these innovations are accompanied by increased exposure to financial crime, including payment fraud, identity theft, and emerging threats within DeFi. As technological innovation outpaces traditional regulatory frameworks, malicious actors exploit vulnerabilities in digital systems, often leveraging the very tools intended to enhance financial inclusion. This duality highlights a fundamental insight: technology functions simultaneously as an enabler of crime and a critical instrument for its prevention. Advanced tools, such as AI-driven transaction monitoring, biometric authentication, and blockchain analytics, have therefore become essential for detecting suspicious activity and safeguarding digital identities in real time.

Yet technological solutions alone are insufficient to mitigate financial crime risks. A coordinated, cross-sector response is necessary to maintain the efficacy of AML and CFT frameworks in a rapidly evolving environment. Regulatory agility, combined with industry-wide collaboration, is essential to address gaps created by novel business models and decentralised platforms. Consequently, compliance strategies must shift from reactive measures to proactive, risk-based approaches. The integrity of the digital financial ecosystem depends on continuous vigilance and cooperation among regulators, financial institutions, and technology providers, ensuring that innovation proceeds alongside robust safeguards that maintain security, resilience, and public trust.

Key Terms and Glossary

SIF (Synthetic Identity Fraud) A type of fraud in which criminals combine real (e.g., a stolen SSN) and fabricated information to create a new, fictitious identity.

APP Fraud A scam where the victim is tricked into voluntarily sending a payment to a fraudster.

AML (Anti-Money Laundering) A set of laws, regulations, and procedures intended to prevent criminals from disguising illegally obtained funds as legitimate income.

KYC (Know Your Customer) The process of a business verifying the identity of its clients to assess risk and ensure legitimacy.

Smart Contract Exploit A security breach that takes advantage of a vulnerability in a smart contract's code to steal funds or disrupt a DeFi protocol.

Behavioural Biometrics A security measure that authenticates users based on their unique patterns of interaction with a device, such as keystroke dynamics or mouse movements.

Test Your Understanding

Multiple-Choice Questions

1 Which of the following best describes SIF in FinTech?

A Using stolen credit card information for online purchases
B Constructing a fictitious identity using a combination of real and fabricated information
C Impersonating a bank official to trick customers into making payments
D Exploiting vulnerabilities in smart contracts to steal crypto assets

2 What is the primary purpose of AI-powered predictive analytics in financial crime prevention?

A To automate onboarding processes for new customers
B To replace human compliance teams entirely
C To identify emerging fraud rings or money laundering patterns before significant harm occurs
D To monitor employee productivity in FinTech firms

3 The Travel Rule requires VASPs to:

A Track all cryptocurrency transactions without exception
B Collect and transmit originator and beneficiary information for transfers above a threshold
C Monitor only fiat currency transfers across borders
D Implement biometric authentication for all users

4 In the Security vs UX matrix, which quadrant represents solutions that combine robust security with minimal user friction?

A Compliance Zone
B Legacy Zone
C Inefficient Zone
D. Ideal Zone

5 Which DeFi-specific vulnerability was exemplified by the 2021 Poly Network exploit?

A Identity theft through phishing attacks
B Theft due to smart contract vulnerabilities
C Structuring of funds through digital wallets
D Misuse of prepaid access products

Short Questions

1 Explain the three stages of money laundering and provide one FinTech-specific example for each stage.
2 What are the key challenges for FinTechs in complying with global AML/CFT regulations?
3 Describe the difference between APP fraud and CNP fraud.

Analytical Question

1 Evaluate the tension between regulatory compliance, cost efficiency, and financial inclusion in FinTechs, and propose strategies to mitigate the associated risks.
2 Analyse the role of emerging technologies, such as AI, behavioural biometrics, and blockchain analytics, in balancing the dual function of technology as both a facilitator of and a defence against financial crime.
3 Considering the decentralised and pseudo-anonymous nature of DeFi, critically assess how traditional AML/CFT frameworks may be adapted or reimagined to prevent illicit activity effectively.

Case Study: The SIF (Synthetic Identity Fraud) Epidemic

SIF has emerged as one of the fastest-growing and most costly financial crimes, resulting in billions of dollars in annual losses. Unlike conventional identity theft, SIF involves the creation of entirely new identities by combining genuine, often stolen elements, such as SSNs, with fabricated information, including names, addresses, and dates of birth. These Frankenstein identities are carefully engineered to bypass automated verification and digital onboarding systems, exploiting the very efficiency that FinTechs and neobanks provide.

SIF typically unfolds in two stages. The first is a prolonged credit grooming period, during which the synthetic identity is gradually used to establish a credible financial history. This may include opening small accounts, making timely payments, or transacting through P2P platforms, creating a semblance of legitimacy. Once the identity achieves sufficient trustworthiness, perpetrators initiate the bust-out phase, maxing out credit lines, withdrawing funds, or defaulting on loans, often resulting in significant losses for the institution.

Digital-native financial services are particularly susceptible due to their reliance on automated systems, rapid onboarding processes, and limited manual oversight. The scale and speed of transactions in these environments allow synthetic identities to proliferate undetected. Addressing SIF requires proactive, multi-layered strategies that integrate advanced technologies, continuous monitoring, and risk-based compliance practices while balancing UX and regulatory obligations (Federal Reserve Bank of Boston, 2019).

Reference

Federal Reserve Bank of Boston. (2019). *Synthetic Identity Fraud in the U.S. Payment*. https://fedpaymentsimprovement.org/wp-content/uploads/frs-synthetic-identity-payments-fraud-white-paper-july-2019.pdf

Case Study Questions

1 Explain why digital-native FinTechs and neobanks are more susceptible to SIF than traditional banks that rely on more manual verification processes.
2 Design a multi-layered approach that a FinTech lender could implement to detect and prevent SIF. Your answer should integrate technological solutions (e.g., AI, machine learning, biometric verification) and procedural controls across the customer onboarding process and ongoing account management.
3 Evaluate the trade-offs between implementing comprehensive fraud prevention measures and maintaining a seamless, low-friction UX. How can FinTechs balance security requirements with customer convenience and satisfaction?

Further Reading

Demetis, D. S. (2018). *Technology and Anti-Money Laundering: A Systems Theory and Risk-Based Approach*. Cheltenham: Edward Elgar Publishing.
Financial Action Task Force (FATF) (2023) *Virtual Assets and Virtual Asset Service Providers: Updated Guidance for a Risk-Based Approach*. Paris: FATF.
Levi, M. (2017). Fraud and Financial Crime. In S.S. Simpson & D. Weisburd (Eds.), *The Oxford Handbook of White-Collar Crime*. Oxford: Oxford University Press.

References

Arner, D. W., Barberis, J., & Buckley, R. P. (2017). FinTech and RegTech in a Nutshell, and the Future in a Sandbox. *Research Handbook on Digital Transformations*, 362–388.
Arner, D.W., Barberis, J. and Buckley, R.P. (2020) The Evolution of Fintech: A New Post-Crisis Paradigm? *Georgetown Journal of International Law*, 48(4), pp. 1271–1319.
Association of Certified Fraud Examiners (2023) *Occupational Fraud 2022: A Report to the Nations*. Austin, TX: Association of Certified Fraud Examiners.
Chainalysis (2024) *The 2024 Crypto Crime Report*. New York: Chainalysis.
Danske Bank (2019) *Report on the Estonian Branch Investigation and Anti-Money Laundering Failures*. Copenhagen: Danske Bank.
Europol (2021) *Internet Organised Crime Threat Assessment (IOCTA) 2021*. The Hague: European Union Agency for Law Enforcement Cooperation
Europol (2022) *Cryptocurrencies and Non-Fungible Tokens: Emerging Threats in Money Laundering Typologies*. The Hague: European Union Agency for Law Enforcement Cooperation.
Europol. (2023). *The Other Side of the Coin: An Analysis of Financial and Economic Crime*. Luxembourg: Publications Office of the European Union.
Federal Reserve Bank of Boston (2019) *Synthetic Identity Fraud: A Guide for Financial Institutions*. Boston, MA: Federal Reserve Bank of Boston
Federal Trade Commission (FTC). (2022). *Consumer Sentinel Network Data Book 2021*.
Ferwerda, J. and de Weijer, F. (2019) *The Economics of Money Laundering: Policy Analysis and Implications*. The Hague: Clingendael Institute.
Financial Action Task Force (FATF) (2021) *Virtual Assets Red Flag Indicators of Money Laundering and Terrorist Financing*. Paris: FATF.
Foley, S., Karlsen, J.R. and Putniņš, T.J. (2019) 'Sex, Drugs, and Bitcoin: How Much Illegal Activity Is Financed through Cryptocurrencies?', *Review of Financial Studies*, 32(5), pp. 1798–1853
Financial Action Task Force (FATF). (2023). *Updated Guidance for a Risk-Based Approach to Virtual Assets and Virtual Asset Service Providers*.
Levi, M. (2017). Fraud and Financial Crime. In *The Oxford Handbook of White-Collar Crime*. Oxford University Press.
Levi, M. and Reuter, P. (2006). Money Laundering. *Crime and Justice: A Review of Research*, 34, 289–375.
LexisNexis Risk Solutions. (2024). *The True Cost of Financial Crime Compliance Study*.
UK Finance. (2023). *Fraud – The Facts 2023: The Definitive Overview of Payment Industry Fraud*.
Zdanowicz, J.S. (2022) *Money Laundering and Financial Crimes: A Comprehensive Guide for Financial Institutions*. Hoboken, NJ: John Wiley & Sons.
Zetzsche, D. A., Buckley, R. P., Arner, D. W., & Föhr, L. (2020). The Decentralised Financial System (DeFi): A New FinTech Paradigm. In *The Future of Financial Systems*. Berlin: De Gruyter.

6 FinTech

Risk, Governance, and Ethical Challenges

Chapter Overview

The rapid expansion of Financial Technology (FinTech) has significantly enhanced operational efficiency and broadened access to financial services. However, this growth has simultaneously introduced novel risks, governance complexities, and ethical challenges that test the sufficiency of existing regulatory frameworks and accountability structures (Arner et al., 2020). This chapter moves beyond an examination of FinTech's operational advantages to provide a systematic analysis of its associated adverse impacts. It identifies and evaluates the sector's primary risk domains, including cybersecurity vulnerabilities, operational disruptions, and regulatory compliance threats. The discussion further addresses governance challenges, particularly those arising from algorithmic decision-making and the outsourcing of critical functions to third-party providers (TPPs). Ethical considerations, such as the protection of personal data, mitigating algorithmic bias, and the potential exacerbation of financial exclusion, are also examined. The chapter concludes by assessing emerging frameworks and best practices designed to promote responsible innovation, emphasising the need to balance technological advancement with rigorous ethical oversight and sustainable governance mechanisms.

Learning Objectives

By the end of this chapter, you should be able to:

1 Identify and categorise the principal risks associated with FinTech operations, including cybersecurity threats, operational vulnerabilities, and regulatory compliance challenges.
2 Explain governance challenges arising from algorithmic decision-making and the management of complex third-party service provider networks.
3 Analyse the ethical implications of FinTech adoption, with particular focus on data privacy, algorithmic bias, and the potential for financial exclusion.
4 Evaluate the strengths and limitations of different regulatory approaches, including regulatory sandboxes and principle-based governance frameworks.
5 Discuss strategies for integrating effective risk management and ethical artificial intelligence (AI) practices within FinTech organisations, balancing operational efficiency, compliance, and societal responsibility.

DOI: 10.4324/9781003775751-7

6.1 Introduction

The FinTech revolution has fundamentally transformed the global financial services landscape, enhancing accessibility and intensifying competition across established markets. However, this accelerated pace of innovation, characterised by rapid product deployments, extensive reliance on algorithms, and disruptive business models, often surpasses the capacity of traditional institutions and regulatory bodies to implement commensurate risk management, governance, and ethical frameworks (Zetzsche et al., 2020). This structural lag creates a critical tension: the benefits of financial democratisation are counterbalanced by heightened systemic vulnerabilities and consumer protection risks, demanding strategic attention from industry stakeholders.

Modern FinTech operations are digitally native, highly automated, and dependent on complex data modelling. These characteristics introduce novel risks that extend beyond traditional financial threats, necessitating a comprehensive re-evaluation of control structures and ethical standards suitable for agile, technology-driven environments (World Economic Forum, 2021). Key vulnerabilities include algorithmic bias, large-scale data privacy breaches, systemic interconnectedness via shared Application Programming Interfaces (APIs), and opaque automated decision-making processes. Such challenges directly test foundational principles of accountability and transparency.

The long-term resilience and success of the FinTech ecosystem hinge on addressing these core risk, governance, and ethical challenges with the same innovation applied to product development and market expansion. Sustainable performance requires organisations to move beyond reactive compliance, embedding robust internal controls, ethical oversight, and resilient risk management structures at the heart of their operations. This approach is essential for maintaining consumer trust and establishing FinTech firms as responsible and stable actors within the modern financial system.

6.2 The FinTech Risk Landscape

A FinTech firm's risk profile encompasses both traditional financial risks and technology-driven threats, which are often exacerbated by rapid growth and operational velocity (Figure 6.1).

6.2.1 Cybersecurity and Data Integrity Risks

FinTech companies hold significant amounts of valuable financial and personal data, making them attractive targets for cyberattacks. The risks involved go beyond typical data breaches and include the following:

API Vulnerabilities: Open banking and embedded finance models rely extensively on APIs to enable secure communication between disparate software systems. Insufficiently protected APIs can make them attractive targets for cybercriminals, leading to data breaches or service disruptions. For instance, in 2021, the Tink API was exploited, exposing sensitive customer financial information and demonstrating the systemic risk posed by inadequately secured integration points (FSB, 2022).

Cloud Concentration Risk: The FinTech sector's dependence on a limited number of major cloud service providers, including Amazon Web Services (AWS), Microsoft Azure, and Google Cloud, generates systemic vulnerabilities. A service outage or security breach at

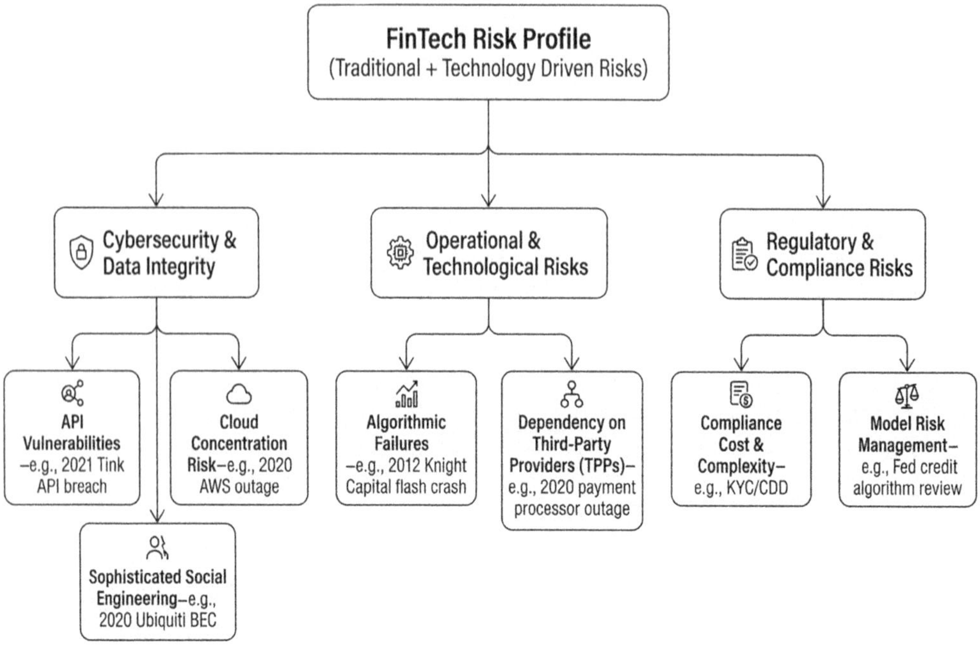

Figure 6.1 FinTech Risk Profile.

a single provider can simultaneously disrupt operations across multiple FinTech platforms, affecting both institutions and customers. For example, the 2020 AWS outage caused widespread service interruptions for numerous digital banking and payment platforms, highlighting the risks of cloud concentration (KPMG, 2023).

Sophisticated Social Engineering: Phishing and Business Email Compromise (BEC) attacks increasingly exploit human vulnerabilities, circumventing technological safeguards through highly targeted and convincing deception. Phishing involves deceiving individuals into disclosing sensitive information, while BEC involves impersonating senior executives to defraud organisations. For example, the 2020 BEC attack on Ubiquiti Networks resulted in fraudulent wire transfers exceeding $46 million, illustrating the substantial financial and operational risks posed by social engineering tactics (FBI, 2021).

6.2.2 Operational and Technological Risks

These risks originate from failures in internal processes, personnel, and technological systems.

Algorithmic Failures: Errors or biases in AI and Machine Learning (ML) models can produce significant operational and financial consequences. For instance, flawed trading algorithms have triggered "lash crashes", while defective credit-scoring models may systematically reject creditworthy applicants. A notable example is the 2012 Knight Capital incident, in which a software malfunction in automated trading systems resulted in a $440 million loss, demonstrating the systemic risks posed by algorithmic failures (Bailey et al., 2021).

Dependency on TPPs: FinTech firms increasingly rely on multiple TPPs to deliver critical services, creating vulnerabilities if these partners fail. Coupled with the expectation of continuous, 24/7 service availability, any system downtime can result in immediate financial losses and reputational damage. For example, the 2020 outage of a major payment processor disrupted multiple FinTech platforms worldwide, underscoring the operational and systemic risks of third-party dependencies (KPMG, 2023).

6.2.3 *Regulatory and Compliance Risks*

FinTech's global and innovative nature poses complex regulatory challenges. Some FinTechs operate in jurisdictional grey areas, possibly exploiting gaps between national regulatory regimes. This results in legal uncertainty and increases the risk of future regulatory action (Zetzsche et al., 2020).

Compliance Cost and Complexity: FinTech start-ups face substantial financial and operational pressures in adhering to complex regulatory frameworks, including Anti-Money Laundering/Combating the Financing of Terrorism obligations and data protection requirements such as the General Data Protection Regulation. The high cost of compliance can constrain innovation and market entry. For example, small digital lenders often struggle to implement robust KYC/CDD systems due to limited resources, creating both operational and regulatory challenges (Arner et al., 2020).

Model Risk Management (MRM): Regulators are increasingly focusing on the use of AI and predictive models in critical FinTech functions, such as credit underwriting and fraud detection. MRM encompasses processes for assessing, validating, and mitigating risks arising from models, ensuring fairness, accuracy, and robustness. For example, the U.S. Federal Reserve has emphasised rigorous validation of credit-scoring algorithms to prevent discriminatory outcomes and systemic risk (FD, 2021).

6.3 Governance Challenges in FinTech: Ensuring Accountability and Oversight

6.3.1 *Algorithmic Oversight and Explainable AI (XAI)*

The rapid integration of AI and ML in FinTech introduces the "black box" problem, wherein decision-making processes are opaque and difficult for humans to interpret. Algorithmic governance involves establishing oversight, accountability, and transparency for these automated systems. For example, if a lending algorithm denies credit or flags a transaction as fraudulent, regulators, auditors, and customers require clear explanations for the decision. XAI frameworks aim to make these processes interpretable, thereby enhancing trust, supporting regulatory compliance (e.g., fair lending requirements under the Equal Credit Opportunity Act), and enabling effective audit trails (Arner et al., 2020).

6.3.2 *Third-Party Risk Governance*

FinTech firms increasingly rely on TPPs for critical services, creating complex operational and regulatory dependencies. Traditional Third-Party Risk Management (TPRM) approaches are often insufficient for dynamic, integrated FinTech ecosystems. Effective governance requires continuous evaluation of TPPs' cybersecurity posture, financial stability, and compliance with regulatory obligations. For instance, a cloud service outage or breach at a provider such as AWS or Google Cloud can disrupt multiple FinTech operations simultaneously, highlighting the importance of robust oversight throughout the supply chain (Deloitte, 2022).

6.3.3 Data Governance and Control Frameworks

Given FinTech's reliance on vast volumes of sensitive data, strong data governance is essential. This includes defining data ownership, ensuring accuracy and consistency, managing data lifecycles, and implementing strict access controls to prevent unauthorised use. For example, monitoring access to customer account information shared with payment processors or lending platforms mitigates risks of data leakage or misuse (World Economic Forum, 2021).

6.4 Ethical Challenges in the FinTech Ecosystem

6.4.1 Data Privacy and User Consent

FinTech business models often rely on extensive collection and analysis of user data, raising ethical concerns that extend beyond mere regulatory compliance. The distinction between personalisation and surveillance is subtle. Key issues include obtaining meaningful user consent, limiting the use of data to its original purpose, and preventing the creation of detailed behavioural profiles without users' informed awareness. For example, certain mobile payment platforms collect transaction histories and location data to personalise offers, potentially exposing sensitive financial behaviour without the user's explicit consent (Mittelstadt, 2019).

6.4.2 Algorithmic Bias and Fairness

The use of AI and ML in FinTech carries the risk of amplifying existing societal biases present in training datasets. For instance, credit-scoring algorithms trained on historical lending data may systematically disadvantage minority or low-income applicants, resulting in digital redlining. Addressing these biases requires both technical interventions, such as bias mitigation algorithms, and ethical oversight to ensure equitable access to financial services (Balyuk & Davydenko, 2021).

6.4.3 Financial Inclusion and Digital Exclusion

While FinTech innovations have the potential to broaden financial access, digital-only platforms may inadvertently exacerbate exclusion. Populations such as older people, low-income individuals, or those with limited internet access may be marginalised, creating gaps in access to essential financial services. For example, fully digital banking services in rural regions of developing countries have left certain communities reliant on informal financial channels (World Bank, 2021).

6.5 Future Frameworks: Towards Responsible Innovation

Addressing these challenges requires a proactive, collaborative approach.

6.5.1 *Emerging Frameworks for Responsible FinTech Innovation*

Emerging frameworks for responsible FinTech innovation reflect a shift from reactive compliance towards proactive, collaborative governance involving regulators, industry participants, and technology providers. Regulatory sandboxes enable FinTech firms to test novel products in controlled environments under supervisory oversight, while Supervisory Technology enhances regulators' ability to monitor risks through advanced data analytics; for example, the UK Financial Conduct Authority's sandbox has supported the testing of AI-driven lending models alongside regulatory learning (Buckley et al., 2020). In parallel, principle-based ethical AI frameworks have become governance benchmarks, emphasising fairness, transparency, accountability, and contestability in automated decision-making, with digital lenders increasingly conducting algorithmic audits and bias testing to prevent discriminatory outcomes (Floridi et al., 2018). Complementing these approaches, the principle of privacy by design embeds data protection measures, such as encryption, data minimisation, and access controls, into system architecture from inception, as illustrated by mobile payment platforms that restrict data retention to reduce breach exposure and strengthen consumer trust.

6.5.2 *Practical Challenges in Implementing FinTech Risk and Governance*

Implementing effective FinTech risk and governance frameworks is complicated by the difficulty of translating high-level ethical and regulatory principles into day-to-day operations, particularly in fast-growing firms facing skills shortages at the intersection of finance, regulation, AI, and cybersecurity. Non-financial risks, such as reputational harm arising from ethical lapses or algorithmic bias, are inherently difficult to quantify, despite their potential to trigger long-term customer attrition and regulatory scrutiny. These challenges are compounded for globally active FinTechs operating in fragmented, evolving regulatory environments, where divergent requirements for data protection and AI governance increase compliance complexity and risk (Zetzsche et al., 2020). Additionally, firms must navigate the trade-off between the predictive performance of advanced AI models and the need for explainability and accountability, particularly in high-impact applications such as credit decision-making and fraud detection.

6.5.3 *The FinTech Risk and Governance Lifecycle*

Risk and ethical management in FinTech is most effectively conceptualised as a continuous lifecycle rather than a discrete compliance exercise, with a central Governance and Oversight Core guiding all stages of activity (Figure 6.2). During the design and development phase, ethical principles and risk considerations are embedded from the outset through practices such as bias testing, data minimisation, and privacy-by-design. In deployment and operations, the emphasis shifts to real-time risk controls, robust third-party management, and transparent user engagement. The monitoring and review phase involves continuous oversight of AI systems to identify performance drift or emerging bias, as well as post-incident analysis that informs iterative improvements. This lifecycle perspective highlights that responsible FinTech innovation depends on sustained vigilance, adaptive governance, and ongoing refinement to preserve the integrity and resilience of the digital financial ecosystem.

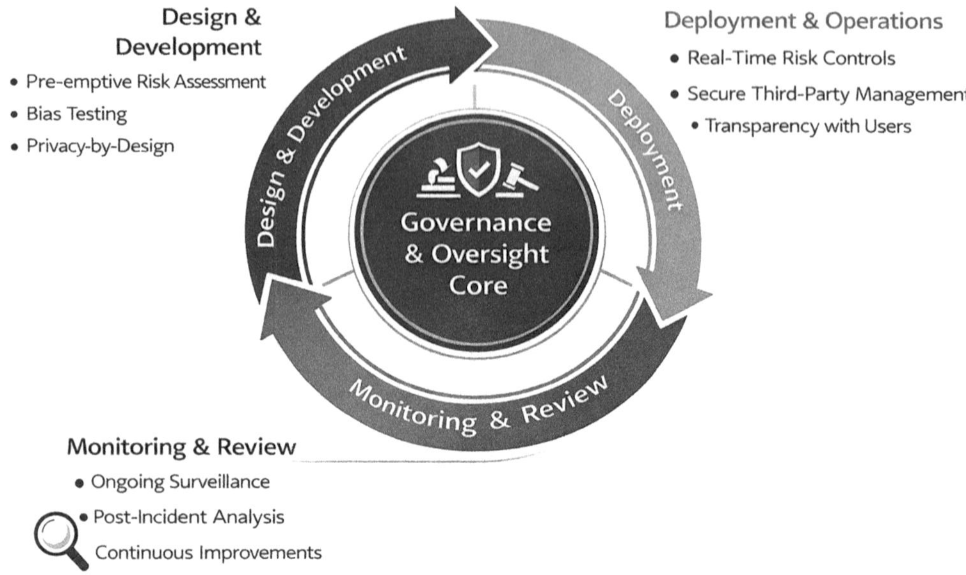

Figure 6.2 The FinTech Risk and Governance Lifecycle.

6.6 Conclusion

In conclusion, the FinTech sector has reached a pivotal stage in its development, transitioning from an era of rapid disruption to one that increasingly demands institutional maturity. The long-term sustainability of the industry will be determined not solely by the speed of technological advancement, but by the strength of its risk management practices, governance structures, and commitment to ethical conduct. As FinTech continues to integrate more deeply into the global financial system, the prioritisation of these foundational elements is essential to ensure resilience, credibility, and sustainable growth.

Addressing risk, governance, and ethical considerations is therefore integral to the future of responsible financial innovation. These dimensions underpin systemic stability, safeguard market integrity, and enhance consumer protection, thereby fostering the trust necessary for FinTech firms to evolve from niche innovators into established financial institutions. Organisations that embed robust governance and ethical principles within their operational culture will be better equipped to mitigate operational and reputational risks, gaining durable strategic advantages. Ultimately, responsible innovation will be a defining factor in achieving long-term competitiveness and leadership in the financial services industry.

Key Terms and Glossary

Algorithmic Bias Systematic and repeatable errors in a computer system that create unfair outcomes, such as privileging one arbitrary group of users over others.

XAI (Explainable Artificial Intelligence) Methods and techniques in the application of AI technology, such that human experts can understand the results of the solution.

TPRM (Third-Party Risk Management) The process of identifying, assessing, and mitigating risks presented by using external vendors and service providers.

Digital Exclusion The inability of a portion of the population to access digital technologies, leading to disadvantages in accessing services like digital finance.

Cloud Concentration Risk The systemic risk that arises from the financial system's widespread reliance on a small number of critical cloud service providers.

Responsible Innovation A framework for developing and deploying new technologies in a way that considers ethical, social, and environmental impacts.

Test Your Understanding

Multiple-Choice Questions

1 Which factor most clearly distinguishes FinTech risk profiles from those of traditional financial institutions?

A Greater exposure to interest rate volatility
B Reliance on physical branch infrastructure
C High dependence on digital automation and data-driven systems
D Lower regulatory scrutiny

2 The *black box* problem in FinTech primarily refers to:

A Inadequate cybersecurity controls in cloud computing
B The opacity of complex AI and ML decision-making processes
C The absence of financial disclosures by FinTech firms
D Regulatory arbitrage across jurisdictions

3 Which of the following best describes cloud concentration risk?

A Excessive storage of customer data in decentralised databases
B Dependence on multiple competing cloud providers
C Over-reliance on a small number of dominant cloud service providers
D Inefficient data encryption practices

4 What is the primary purpose of regulatory sandboxes in the FinTech ecosystem?

A To replace traditional licensing requirements
B To allow unrestricted innovation without oversight
C To enable controlled testing of innovations under regulatory supervision
D To reduce cybersecurity standards for start-ups

5 Which ethical risk arises when AI systems replicate historical discrimination in financial decision-making?

A Data minimisation failure
B Digital redlining
C Cloud vendor lock-in
D Model overfitting

Short Questions

1 What is TPRM, and why is it particularly important for FinTechs?
2 Explain the ethical concern of data privacy and surveillance in the context of FinTech business models.
3 Define MRM and explain why it is increasingly important in FinTech.

Analytical Questions

1 Critically evaluate why digital-native FinTech firms face heightened cybersecurity and operational risks compared to traditional banks. In your answer, refer to APIs, cloud concentration, and automation.
2 Discuss the governance challenges associated with algorithmic decision-making in FinTech. How do XAI frameworks contribute to regulatory compliance and ethical accountability?
3 Assess the extent to which responsible innovation frameworks, such as regulatory sandboxes, ethical AI principles, and lifecycle-based governance, can reconcile rapid technological innovation with consumer protection and systemic stability.

Case Study: Algorithmic Bias in Lending

In 2019, Apple Card, a digital credit card developed by Apple and issued by Goldman Sachs, became the subject of intense public scrutiny following allegations of gender-based discrimination in its credit-limit decisions. Several customers reported that women were routinely offered credit limits significantly lower than those of their male counterparts with comparable or stronger financial profiles. The controversy gained prominence when entrepreneur David Heinemeier Hansson publicly disclosed that his wife had received a credit limit substantially lower than his own, despite having a higher credit score and shared household assets.

These complaints triggered an investigation by the New York State Department of Financial Services (NYDFS) into whether Apple Card's credit-assessment model violated fair lending principles. Although the issuer denied intentional discrimination, the case exposed critical weaknesses in algorithmic decision-making systems that rely heavily on historical data and complex ML models. In particular, the opaque nature of the model, commonly referred to as the *black box* problem, made it difficult for consumers, regulators, and auditors to understand how credit decisions were reached.

The Apple Card case became a landmark example of how AI-driven lending systems can unintentionally replicate structural inequalities embedded in historical financial data. It underscored the ethical, governance, and reputational risks associated with automated credit scoring, highlighting the necessity for transparency, explainability, and robust oversight in FinTech lending models (BBC, 2019; NYDFS, 2019).

References

BBC (2019). Apple Card Investigated After Gender Discrimination Complaints. *BBC News*, 11 November. Available at: https://www.bbc.co.uk/news/business-50365609 (Accessed: 1 March 2026).

New York State Department of Financial Services (NYDFS) (2019). *Report on the New York State Department of Financial Services Investigation into Goldman Sachs' Credit Card Practices*. Available at: https://www.dfs.ny.gov/reports_and_publications/press_releases/pr202103251 (Accessed: 1 March 2026).

Case Study Questions

1 In what ways can credit-scoring algorithms train on historical lending data unintentionally absorb and reinforce existing societal biases, and how might these biases manifest in automated credit decisions?
2 Which governance mechanisms and technical controls, such as XAI, model validation, and bias detection or auditing tools, should FinTech firms adopt to mitigate algorithmic bias and promote fairness in credit assessment?
3 Why does addressing algorithmic bias constitute a strategic business priority for FinTech firms beyond regulatory compliance, particularly in relation to consumer trust, reputational resilience, and long-term market sustainability?

Further Reading

Arner, D.W., Buckley, R.P., Zetzsche, D.A. & Veidt, R. (2020). Sustainability, FinTech and Financial Inclusion. *European Business Organisation Law Review*, 21, pp. 7–35.

Floridi, L., Cowls, J., Beltrametti, M., et al. (2018). AI4People—An Ethical Framework for a Good AI Society. *Minds and Machines*, 28(4), pp. 689–707.

World Economic Forum (2021). *The Global Risks Report 2021*, Geneva: World Economic Forum.

References

Arner, D.W., Buckley, R.P., Zetzsche, D.A., & Veidt, R. (2020). Sustainability, FinTech and Financial Inclusion. *European Business Organisation Law Review* 21, 7–35.

Bailey, D., Kuang, P., & Zhang, D. (2021). The Ethics of Algorithmic Trading. *Journal of Business Ethics.* 171, 519–535.

Balyuk, T., & Davydenko, S. (2021). AI in Credit Scoring: Evidence from Commercial Lending. *Review of Financial Studies.* 34(5), 2401–2440.

Buckley, R.P., Arner, D.W., Zetzsche, D.A., & Didenko, A. (2020) The future of FinTech and financial regulation', in N.M. Davidson, M. Finck & J.J. Infranca (Eds.), *The Cambridge Handbook of the Law of the Sharing Economy*. Cambridge: Cambridge University Press.

Deloitte (2022) *Global third-party risk management survey 2022*. Available at: Deloitte Insights (Accessed: 23 May 2026). https://www.deloitte.com/global/en/services/consulting-risk/research/2022-third-party-risk-management-survey.html

Federal Bureau of Investigation (FBI) (2021) *Business Email Compromise (BEC): Crime Trends and Advisory*. Washington, DC: FBI Internet Crime Complaint Center (IC3)

Federal Reserve (FD) (2021). *Supervisory Guidance on Model Risk Management*. SR Letter 11–17.

Financial Stability Board (FSB) (2022). *FinTech and Market Structure in Financial Services: Market Developments and Potential Financial Stability Implications*. Available at: https://www.fsb.org/

Floridi, L., Cowls, J., Beltrametti, M., et al. (2018). AI4People—An Ethical Framework for a Good AI Society: Opportunities, Risks, Principles, and Recommendations. *Minds and Machines* 28, 689–707.

KPMG (2023). *The Evolving Cybersecurity Landscape in Financial Services*. Available at: https://kpmg.com/xx/en/home/insights/2023/02/evolving-cybersecurity-landscape-financial-services.html
Mittelstadt, B. (2019). Principles Alone Cannot Guarantee Ethical AI. *Nature Machine Intelligence* 1, 501–507.
World Bank (2021). *Global Findex Database 2021*. Available at: https://www.worldbank.org/en/publication/globalfindex
World Economic Forum (2021). *The Global Risks Report 2021*. Available at: https://www.weforum.org/reports/the-global-risks-report-2021/
Zetzsche, D.A., Buckley, R.P., Arner, D.W., & Barberis, J.N. (2020). Regulating Artificial Intelligence in Finance: Putting the Human in the Loop. *Sydney Law Review*, 43(1), 43–81.

Part 2

The Institutions and Financial Technology

7 The Development of Technology and Financial Institutions

Chapter Overview

This chapter examines the evolving relationship between traditional financial institutions, such as banks, insurance companies, credit unions, and investment firms, and emerging Financial Technology (FinTech), analysing their roles and classifications within a rapidly digitalising financial system. It explores how innovations, including artificial intelligence (AI), blockchain technology, digital banking, and regulatory technology (RegTech), are transforming operational processes, service delivery, and business models (Arner et al., 2016), while also addressing the associated risks and regulatory challenges. Furthermore, the chapter considers future developments, including decentralised finance (DeFi), embedded finance, central bank digital currencies (CBDCs), and green FinTech. It evaluates how their integration is reshaping the financial ecosystem by enhancing efficiency, promoting customer-centric services, and supporting inclusive and sustainable economic growth.

Learning Objectives

By the end of this chapter, you should be able to:

1. Explain the fundamental functions of financial institutions, including financial intermediation, risk management, and payment systems, within a technology-driven environment.
2. Analyse the transformative impact of FinTech innovations, such as AI, blockchain, digital platforms, and robo-advisory services, on traditional banking, insurance, lending, and investment activities.
3. Evaluate the role of RegTech in enhancing regulatory compliance, governance, and operational efficiency in financial institutions.
4. Compare traditional financial models with FinTech-enabled and decentralised alternatives, including embedded finance and DeFi.
5. Assess key challenges and future directions in FinTech adoption, including regulatory constraints, cybersecurity risks, financial inclusion, and sustainability initiatives such as green finance.

DOI: 10.4324/9781003775751-9

7.1 Introduction

Traditional financial institutions, including banks, credit unions, and investment firms, have historically played a central role in supporting the global economy by delivering core financial services such as deposit-taking, lending, and asset management (Mishkin & Eakins, 2018). Through these functions, they have shaped how individuals and businesses interact with and utilise the financial system. In parallel, FinTech has emerged as a transformative force within the industry, leveraging advanced digital technologies to enhance, automate, and reconfigure the provision of financial services (Gomber et al., 2018).

The convergence of traditional finance and technological innovation has accelerated the evolution of the financial sector, challenging established business models and operational practices. FinTech-driven solutions prioritise speed, accessibility, and customer-centric service delivery, thereby redefining competitive dynamics and reshaping user expectations. This shift has facilitated the emergence of new financial intermediaries, platforms, and service models that extend beyond the constraints of conventional financial structures.

Integrating technology with traditional financial systems is increasingly recognised as essential for fostering a more efficient, inclusive, and resilient financial ecosystem. By automating complex processes, reducing transaction costs, and expanding access to financial services, FinTech enhances the capabilities of incumbent institutions while promoting broader financial inclusion. Consequently, an understanding of this evolving relationship is critical for financial professionals seeking to navigate contemporary financial markets, adopt technological innovations, and support sustainable economic participation on a global scale.

7.2 Definition and Classification of Financial Institutions

Financial institutions are organisations that provide financial services to individuals, firms, and governments and act as intermediaries between surplus and deficit economic units by efficiently allocating financial resources within the economy (Mishkin & Eakins, 2018). Their core activities include deposit-taking, lending, investment facilitation, insurance provision, and payment services. Historically, these institutions have dominated the financial system by performing key functions such as financial intermediation, risk transformation, and liquidity provision (Merton & Bodie, 1995). However, the emergence of FinTech has disrupted traditional institutional models by introducing digital innovations such as mobile payment systems, peer-to-peer (P2P) lending platforms, and DeFi, which reduce reliance on conventional intermediaries (Arner et al., 2016). For example, P2P platforms such as LendingClub directly connect borrowers and lenders, bypassing traditional banking structures.

7.2.1 Key Financial Institutions

Commercial Banks: Commercial banks play a pivotal role in maintaining economic stability by mobilising deposits and extending credit to households and businesses. Their core services include deposit-taking, loan provision, and the management of payment and settlement systems, all of which support financial inclusion and facilitate the effective transmission of monetary policy (Mishkin & Eakins, 2018). By evaluating credit risk and allocating funds to productive activities, commercial banks contribute to economic growth and financial system stability. For example, international banks such as Hongkong and Shanghai Banking Corporation and Barclays support small- and medium-sized enterprises through business lending, trade finance, and transaction services, thereby fostering entrepreneurship and employment.

Investment Banks: Investment banks specialise in capital markets activities and provide advisory services for securities underwriting, mergers and acquisitions, corporate restructuring, and risk management. These institutions play a crucial role in enhancing market efficiency and liquidity by helping corporations and governments raise long-term capital through equity and debt markets. In addition, investment banks act as intermediaries between issuers and investors, helping to price and distribute securities effectively. For instance, firms such as Goldman Sachs advise corporations on initial public offerings and large-scale mergers, supporting capital formation and market development.

Insurance Companies: Insurance companies operate primarily as risk management institutions by underwriting policies that protect individuals and organisations against financial losses arising from uncertain events. By pooling and diversifying risks, insurance firms reduce the financial impact of adverse outcomes on policyholders. Furthermore, by investing collected premiums in financial markets, insurance companies contribute to long-term capital accumulation and economic growth (Saunders & Cornett, 2021). Examples include life, health, and property insurance providers such as Allianz, which play an important role in promoting financial security and stability.

Credit Unions: Credit unions are member-owned financial cooperatives that provide essential banking services, including savings accounts and personal loans, often at lower costs and with more favourable interest rates than commercial banks. Their not-for-profit and community-oriented structure allows them to prioritise member welfare over profit maximisation. As a result, credit unions promote financial inclusion by serving individuals and communities that may be underserved by traditional banks (Mishkin & Eakins, 2018). For example, local credit unions frequently provide affordable credit to low-income households and small local businesses, supporting community development.

Pension and Mutual Funds: Pension and mutual funds are institutional investors that pool savings from individuals and invest them in diversified portfolios of financial assets, such as equities, bonds, and real estate. These institutions play a critical role in retirement planning and long-term wealth accumulation while also enhancing capital market liquidity and stability (Allen & Gale, 2000). By allocating funds across a wide range of assets, pension and mutual funds help mitigate investment risk and support efficient capital allocation. Examples include pension funds investing in government bonds to ensure stable returns for retirees.

Asset Management Firms: Asset management firms professionally manage investment portfolios on behalf of individual and institutional clients using advanced portfolio diversification and risk management strategies. Their objective is to optimise returns in line with clients' risk preferences and investment horizons. By directing capital into productive sectors of the economy, asset management firms enhance market efficiency and support economic growth. For instance, BlackRock manages assets across global equity and fixed-income markets, influencing capital flows and investment trends worldwide.

7.2.2 Core Functions of Financial Institutions

Financial institutions perform several essential and interrelated functions that underpin the functioning of the financial system:

Financial Intermediation: Financial institutions act as intermediaries by channelling funds from savers to borrowers, assessing creditworthiness, and allocating capital efficiently. This process reduces information asymmetries and transaction costs, thereby supporting economic growth and productive investment (Mishkin & Eakins, 2018). For example, banks transform household savings into business loans that finance expansion and innovation.

Risk Management: Institutions identify, measure, and manage a wide range of financial risks, including credit, market, liquidity, and operational risks. They employ tools such as diversification, hedging instruments, and regulatory capital frameworks to mitigate potential losses and ensure financial stability (Saunders & Cornett, 2021). Insurance firms spreading risk across large pools of policyholders provide a clear illustration of effective risk management.

Liquidity Provision: By offering deposit accounts and participating in financial markets, financial institutions ensure that economic agents have timely access to liquid funds. This liquidity provision supports confidence in the financial system and facilitates smooth economic activity. Demand deposits, for example, allow customers immediate access to cash for transactions and emergencies.

Payment Services: Financial institutions provide the infrastructure necessary for secure and efficient transactions, including electronic funds transfers, debit and credit cards, and mobile payment systems. As cash usage declines, the development of digital payment solutions has become increasingly important. Technologies such as mobile banking apps and digital wallets, including Apple Pay, exemplify this evolving role.

Wealth Management: Wealth management involves the comprehensive administration of clients' financial assets through investment planning, tax optimisation, retirement planning, and estate management. Financial institutions tailor these services to individual needs and risk profiles, particularly for high-net-worth individuals. Private banking services are a prominent example of personalised wealth management.

Capital Formation: Financial institutions mobilise savings and channel them into investments in infrastructure, technology, and entrepreneurial ventures, thereby supporting long-term economic development (Merton & Bodie, 1995). Venture capital funds financing start-ups illustrate how financial institutions contribute to innovation, productivity growth, and job creation.

7.3 The Evolution of FinTech and Its Impact on Financial Institutions

FinTech has evolved from the early adoption of basic online banking services to sophisticated digital platforms that leverage AI, machine learning (ML), big data analytics, and distributed ledger technology (DLT). This technological progression has fundamentally transformed the structure, efficiency, and competitive dynamics of the financial services industry (Arner et al., 2016). As FinTech innovations continue to mature, they increasingly challenge traditional financial institutions by reshaping service delivery, customer engagement, and operational models across key financial activities (Figure 7.1).

Payments and Transfers: FinTech innovations have significantly enhanced the efficiency and accessibility of payment and transfer systems. Technologies such as mobile wallets, QR-code-based payments, and blockchain-enabled transfer networks facilitate real-time, low-cost transactions, reducing dependence on cash and conventional banking channels (Gomber et al., 2018). For example, mobile payment platforms such as M-Pesa have expanded financial access in developing economies by enabling users to conduct transactions without traditional bank accounts, thereby promoting financial inclusion.

Lending and Credit Provision: The lending landscape has been transformed by P2P lending platforms and AI-driven credit assessment models. Digital platforms such as LendingClub directly connect borrowers and lenders, bypassing traditional banking intermediaries and lowering transaction costs. Furthermore, AI-based credit scoring

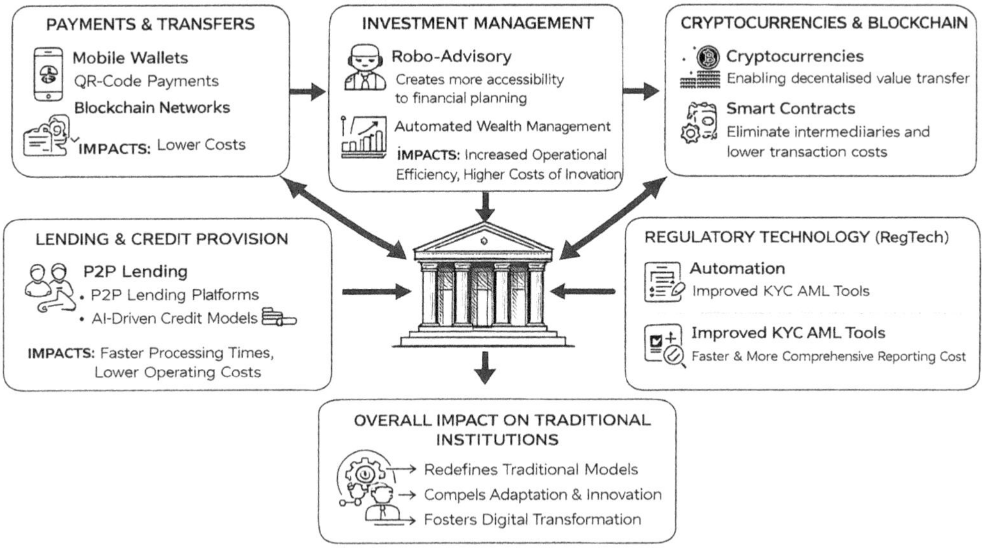

Figure 7.1 FinTech Evolution and Impact on Financial Institutions.

systems utilise alternative data sources to assess borrower risk, increasing credit access for underserved individuals and small businesses. These innovations challenge conventional lending models that rely heavily on collateral and historical credit records (Philippon, 2016).

Investment Management: FinTech has also disrupted investment management with the introduction of robo-advisory services that provide automated, algorithm-driven portfolio management and financial planning. Platforms such as Betterment offer low-cost, scalable investment solutions that were previously accessible primarily to high-net-worth individuals. By reducing fees and minimising human intervention, robo-advisors enhance accessibility and efficiency within the investment management sector.

Cryptocurrencies and Blockchain Technology: The emergence of cryptocurrencies and blockchain-based platforms has introduced decentralised alternatives to traditional financial systems. Cryptocurrencies such as Bitcoin enable P2P value transfers without reliance on centralised intermediaries, while smart contract platforms like Ethereum automate and enforce contractual agreements through code. These innovations challenge the traditional roles of banks and clearing institutions by offering transparent, secure, and decentralised transaction mechanisms (Tapscott & Tapscott, 2016).

RegTech: RegTech has gained prominence as financial institutions face increasing regulatory complexity and compliance costs. RegTech solutions utilise automation, data analytics, and AI to streamline compliance processes such as Anti-Money Laundering (AML) monitoring and Know Your Customer (KYC) verification. By improving accuracy and reducing manual intervention, these technologies enhance regulatory effectiveness while lowering operational costs (Butler et al., 2019). For example, automated transaction monitoring systems enable real-time detection of suspicious activities, strengthening risk management frameworks. Table 7.1 represents the distinction between traditional and FinTech-enabled financial institutions.

Table 7.1 Traditional vs FinTech-Enabled Financial Institutions

Characteristic	*Traditional Financial Institutions*	*FinTech-Enabled Financial Institutions*
Business Model	Branch-based, physical presence	Digital-first, mobile-centric
Technology	Legacy systems (e.g., mainframes)	Cloud-native, AI/ML-driven
Onboarding	Days/weeks (paper-intensive)	Minutes (digital KYC)
Transaction Speed	1–3 business days (wires)	Real-time/instant payments
Fees	Higher (account, wire, overdraft fees)	Lower/zero fees
Interest Rates	Low savings rates (~0.01% APY)	Competitive rates (~2–4% APY)
Innovation	Slow adoption (regulatory constraints)	Rapid iteration (API-driven)
Global Reach	Limited by correspondent banking	Borderless (crypto/stablecoins)
Regulation	Heavy (e.g., Basel III, Dodd-Frank)	Lighter (varies by jurisdiction)
Risk Management	Manual processes	AI-powered fraud detection
Examples	JPMorgan, HSBC, Citibank	Revolut, Chime, Nubank, Stripe

7.4 Integration of FinTech with Traditional Financial Institutions

The interaction between FinTech and traditional financial institutions has evolved from initial disruption to increasingly collaborative relationships. Partnerships, strategic alliances, and acquisitions have become common, enabling traditional institutions to leverage technological innovations while FinTech firms gain broader market reach and credibility. This integration delivers multiple strategic benefits and is driven by several key technological innovations.

7.4.1 Key Benefits of FinTech Integration

Enhanced Customer Experience: Digital platforms, AI-powered chatbots, and mobile applications provide personalised, on-demand services, improving accessibility, convenience, and overall client satisfaction. For example, Bank of America's virtual assistant, *Erica*, offers 24/7 financial guidance and account management, significantly enhancing user engagement and support efficiency (Begenau et al., 2018).

Operational Efficiency: Automation of processes such as loan origination, compliance monitoring, and transaction processing reduces operational costs, minimises human error, and accelerates service delivery. AI-based loan approval systems, for instance, shorten decision-making times and reduce administrative overhead, allowing institutions to allocate resources more effectively.

Data-Driven Insights: Advanced analytics and ML enable financial institutions to analyse customer behaviour, optimise product offerings, and assess risk with greater accuracy. This supports the development of hyper-personalised financial products, targeted marketing strategies, and improved strategic decision-making.

7.4.2 Key FinTech Innovations Driving Integration

Blockchain and DLT: Blockchain and DLT provide secure, transparent, and tamper-resistant transaction records, reducing reliance on intermediaries and enabling near real-time settlement. Smart contracts allow automated execution of agreements without manual intervention (Crosby et al., 2016). For instance, J.P. Morgan's *JPM Coin* utilises DLT for intra-bank transfers, improving transaction speed while reducing operational risk.

AI and ML: AI and ML enhance multiple facets of financial services, including customer support, fraud detection, credit scoring, and compliance monitoring. These technologies enable faster, more informed decision-making and more efficient operations (Begenau et al., 2018). Practical applications include Bank of America's *Erica* and AI-driven fraud detection systems.

Digital-Only Banks (Neobanks): Neobanks operate entirely online, without physical branches, offering lower fees, greater accessibility, and streamlined user experiences, thereby pressuring traditional banks to accelerate their digital transformation. Examples include *Revolut* and *N26*, which provide seamless international payments, budgeting tools, and real-time financial insights (Feyen et al., 2021).

RegTech: RegTech automates regulatory compliance processes, including AML and KYC procedures. By improving accuracy, reducing manual workload, and cutting compliance costs, RegTech enhances institutional efficiency and mitigates regulatory risk (Butler et al., 2019). Automated transaction monitoring and reporting systems exemplify RegTech applications in modern financial institutions.

7.5 Future Trends Shaping Financial Services

The convergence of traditional financial institutions and FinTech is accelerating, driven by several transformative trends that are poised to reshape the financial services landscape. These trends not only introduce technological innovations but also present strategic, regulatory, and operational considerations for established financial players.

DeFi: DeFi seeks to replicate conventional financial systems, including lending, trading, and asset management, on open blockchain networks. Operating without central intermediaries, DeFi has the potential to reduce transaction costs, increase transparency, and expand access to financial services. For traditional financial institutions, this trend represents both a challenge and an opportunity: while DeFi can disrupt conventional revenue streams and intermediated processes, banks can leverage blockchain expertise to develop hybrid models that combine decentralised infrastructure with institutional trust and compliance frameworks. The integration of DeFi mechanisms may also necessitate new regulatory approaches to mitigate systemic risk and protect consumers.

Embedded Finance: Embedded finance involves the integration of financial services, such as payments, lending, and insurance, directly into non-financial digital platforms, including e-commerce marketplaces and ride-sharing applications. This trend enhances customer convenience, increases engagement, and creates additional revenue streams. For incumbent banks, embedded finance requires rethinking traditional distribution channels and adopting Application Programming Interface–driven partnerships with platform providers. Strategically, it offers opportunities to capture previously inaccessible customer segments; however, it also increases dependency on third-party ecosystems and raises operational risks related to data security and compliance (McKinsey, 2022).

CBDCs: CBDCs are digital representations of sovereign money issued and regulated by central banks. CBDCs have the potential to modernise payment systems, increase settlement efficiency, and expand financial inclusion. For traditional banks, the introduction of CBDCs presents complex implications. While they may reduce cash-handling costs and improve transaction transparency, CBDCs could also shift deposits away from commercial banks, affecting liquidity and lending capacities. Additionally, banks must adapt to potential regulatory and technological frameworks imposed by central banks to ensure interoperability and secure integration into existing financial infrastructures (BIS, 2020).

Green FinTech: Green FinTech refers to technological innovations that promote sustainable finance and support Environmental, Social, and Governance (ESG) objectives. Examples include platforms facilitating green bond issuance, carbon credit trading, and ESG-focused investment analytics. Green FinTech enables financial institutions to integrate sustainability considerations into core operations, attract ESG-conscious investors, and comply with increasingly stringent regulatory requirements. For traditional banks, this trend represents both a strategic opportunity to differentiate services and a compliance imperative, as global regulatory frameworks increasingly mandate transparency in environmental and social impact reporting (Dorfleitner et al., 2021).

Implications for the Financial Services Sector: Collectively, these trends indicate a fundamental transformation in financial services, shifting from product-centric to platform-centric and technology-enabled models. Traditional institutions must adopt agile strategies that balance innovation adoption with regulatory compliance, risk management, and customer trust. Strategic collaborations with FinTech firms, investments in digital infrastructure, and proactive engagement with regulators will be essential to remain competitive in an increasingly decentralised, embedded, and sustainable financial ecosystem.

7.6 Key Practical Issues of FinTech in Financial Institutions

While integrating FinTech with traditional financial institutions offers significant advantages, it also introduces several critical practical challenges that must be carefully managed. Addressing these issues is essential to ensure sustainable adoption, operational efficiency, and the protection of customer interests.

Regulatory Fragmentation and Compliance: FinTech firms operating across multiple jurisdictions face a complex, fragmented regulatory landscape. National variations in data privacy, AML, KYC, and consumer protection laws significantly increase compliance costs and introduce legal uncertainty. Financial institutions must therefore implement robust regulatory frameworks and continuously monitor evolving legislation to mitigate legal and reputational risks.

Cybersecurity and Data Privacy: The growing digitisation of financial services and the collection of sensitive customer data expand the attack surface for cyber threats. Ensuring comprehensive cybersecurity measures, including encryption, multi-factor authentication, and real-time threat detection, is critical. Maintaining customer trust through transparent data handling practices and compliance with data protection regulations is equally essential.

Legacy System Integration: Traditional financial institutions often struggle to integrate agile FinTech solutions with their legacy IT infrastructures. These monolithic systems are typically rigid, costly to maintain, and resistant to rapid change, making integration time-consuming and operationally risky. Strategic planning, modular system upgrades, and the adoption of middleware solutions are often necessary to enable seamless interoperability.

Digital Literacy and Inclusion: Although FinTech has the potential to enhance financial inclusion, disparities in digital literacy and access persist. Vulnerable populations, including older people, low-income households, and rural communities, may face barriers to adopting digital financial services. Institutions must therefore invest in education, user-friendly design, and accessible delivery channels to ensure that technological innovations do not exacerbate inequality.

Operational Resilience: The reliance on complex, interconnected digital platforms and third-party service providers introduces new operational risks. System failures, service interruptions, and dependency on external vendors can significantly impact service continuity. Strengthening business continuity planning, disaster recovery protocols, and third-party risk management frameworks is crucial to maintaining operational resilience.

7.7 Conclusion

The integration of technological innovation with traditional financial institutions represents a transformative evolution in the global financial landscape. FinTech has driven significant operational efficiencies while reshaping customer expectations by enabling faster, more accessible, and user-centric financial services. Digital platforms are increasingly embedded in core banking functions, including real-time payments, algorithmic lending, and automated wealth management, enhancing financial institutions' responsiveness and adaptability to dynamic market conditions. This technological integration has also extended financial inclusion to underbanked and unbanked populations, particularly in emerging economies, thereby broadening economic participation. According to the Financial Stability Board (FSB, 2023), the convergence of finance and technology holds immense promise for enhancing the resilience and reach of financial systems, provided it is guided by sound regulatory oversight.

At the same time, the rapid adoption of digital FinTech introduces heightened regulatory and systemic challenges that demand coordinated, forward-looking governance. Ensuring data privacy, mitigating cyber threats, and maintaining operational resilience are critical to preserving trust and stability in an increasingly digitised environment. The FSB (2023) highlights that the ethical deployment of AI and the harmonisation of cross-border regulatory standards are essential to mitigating risks associated with technological dependence. Collaboration between traditional financial institutions and FinTech innovators has therefore become imperative: banks contribute regulatory experience and robust infrastructure, while FinTechs provide agility and technological expertise. Together, these partnerships cultivate a financial system that is more efficient, inclusive, and resilient, supporting sustainable global economic growth.

Key Terms and Glossary

Financial Intermediation The process performed by banks of taking in funds from a depositor and then lending them out to a borrower.

Digital Banking The comprehensive digitisation of all traditional banking activities and services that were historically accessible only through in-person visits to physical bank branches.

Banking-as-a-Service (BaaS) A model where licensed banks integrate their digital banking services directly into the products of non-bank third parties.

Green FinTech The use of technology to develop financial products and services that promote environmental sustainability and support ESG goals.

Liquidity Provision The function of financial institutions is to ensure that economic agents have access to liquid funds, maintaining the smooth functioning of the financial system.

Test Your Understanding

Multiple-Choice Questions

1 Which of the following best describes the primary function of financial institutions in a traditional economy?

A Creating cryptocurrencies for digital transactions
B Acting as intermediaries between surplus and deficit economic units
C Providing only insurance services
D Eliminating the need for regulatory oversight

2 Which FinTech innovation specifically enables automated compliance processes such as AML and KYC?

A Blockchain
B RegTech
C Robo-advisors
D Mobile wallets

3 A key benefit of integrating FinTech with traditional financial institutions is:

A Increased manual processing of transactions
B Reduced accessibility for customers
C Enhanced operational efficiency and data-driven insights
D Elimination of all regulatory requirements

4 Embedded finance refers to:

A Integrating financial services directly into non-financial platforms
B Central banks issuing digital currencies
C P2P lending platforms
D Insurance companies offering only online policies

5 Which of the following challenges is most closely associated with legacy system integration in banks?

A Rapid technological adoption
B Incompatibility between monolithic systems and agile FinTech solutions
C Expansion of financial inclusion
D Automated fraud detection

Short Questions

1. Explain how P2P lending platforms challenge traditional banking models.
2. Identify two ways in which AI and ML enhance financial services within banks.
3. Briefly describe one potential benefit and one potential risk of CBDCs for traditional banks.

Analytical Questions

1. Evaluate the impact of FinTech integration on financial inclusion in emerging economies. Discuss specific technologies and their role in extending services to underbanked populations.
2. Discuss the regulatory and operational challenges that traditional financial institutions face when collaborating with FinTech firms. Include examples of strategies that banks can adopt to mitigate these risks.
3. Compare and contrast traditional financial institutions with FinTech-enabled institutions in terms of business models, service delivery, and risk management. How does this transformation affect competitiveness in the financial sector?

Case Study: Goldman Sachs' Marcus—A Traditional Giant's Digital Foray

In 2016, Goldman Sachs, a global investment banking leader, launched *Marcus*, its direct-to-consumer digital banking platform, marking a strategic move beyond its traditional wholesale and investment-focused business model. The initiative aimed to diversify revenue streams and respond to emerging FinTech trends, including the unbundling of financial services and the growing utility risk posed by agile, technology-driven competitors. Marcus initially offered high-yield savings accounts and unsecured personal loans, leveraging Goldman Sachs' expertise in risk management, capital allocation, and financial analytics. Within a few years, it successfully amassed over $100 billion in deposits, demonstrating strong customer interest in digital-first banking services.

Despite early growth, Marcus encountered challenges typical of established institutions entering retail banking. High customer acquisition costs, competition from low-cost digital-native banks, and the need to develop user-friendly digital interfaces created operational and strategic pressures. Additionally, cultural differences between Goldman Sachs' investment banking ethos and the customer-focused demands of retail banking complicated internal alignment and slowed innovation. By scaling back its ambitions, the firm highlighted the difficulty of sustaining a standalone retail FinTech venture, even with deep financial expertise and ample capital. The Marcus experience underscores the importance of strategic partnerships, technological integration, and adaptive business models in navigating the evolving interface between traditional banking and FinTech innovation.

References

Goldman Sachs (2016) *Marcus by Goldman Sachs Launches as the Firm's First Consumer Banking Platform*. Available at: https://www.goldmansachs.com/our-firm/history/moments/2016-marcus (Accessed: 1 March 2026).

Murray, S. (2023) Marcus Ceases its Lending Business and Admits it Tried to Do Too Much too Quickly. *deBanked*, 23 January. Available at: https://debanked.com (Accessed: 1 March 2026).

Case Study Questions

1 Evaluate Marcus as Goldman Sachs' response to unbundling and utility risk. What were its key strengths and weaknesses?
2 Why did Marcus struggle as a standalone retail business despite Goldman Sachs' expertise? Consider costs and cultural challenges.
3 What does Marcus reveal about the future of collaboration versus competition between traditional banks and FinTechs?

Further Reading

Arner, D.W., Barberis, J.N., & Buckley, R.P. (2016). The Evolution of Fintech: A New Post-Crisis Paradigm?. *Georgetown Journal of International Law*, 47(4), 1271–1319.
BIS (2020). *Central Bank Digital Currencies: Foundational Principles and Core Features*. Basel, Switzerland: Bank for International Settlements.
Gomber, P., Koch, J.-A., & Siering, M. (2018) 'Digital Finance and FinTech: Current Research and Future Research Directions. *Journal of Business Economics*, 87(5), 537–580.

References

Allen, F., & Gale, D. (2000). *Comparing Financial Systems*. Cambridge, MA: MIT Press.
Arner, D. W., Barberis, J., & Buckley, R. P. (2016). The Evolution of FinTech: A New Post-Crisis Paradigm? *University of Hong Kong Faculty of Law Research Paper, No. 2016/012*.
Begenau, J., Farboodi, M., & Veldkamp, L. (2018). Big Data in Finance and the Growth of Large Firms. *Journal of Monetary Economics*, 97, 1–19.
BIS (Bank for International Settlements). (2020). *Central Bank Digital Currencies: Foundational Principles and Core Features*. Report by the BIS Innovation Hub.
Butler, T., O'Brien, L., & McGovern, D. (2019). A Framework for RegTech: Leveraging Technology to Navigate Regulatory Complexity. *Journal of Financial Transformation*, 50, 15–25.
Crosby, M., Pattanayak, P., Verma, S., & Kalyanaraman, V. (2016). Blockchain Technology: Beyond Bitcoin. *Applied Innovation Review*, 2, 6–19.
Dorfleitner, G., Braun, D., & Utz, S. (2021). The Impact of Green FinTech on Sustainability Performance: A Conceptual Framework. *Journal of Sustainable Finance & Investment*, 11(1), 1–22.
Feyen, E., Frost, J., Gambacorta, L., Natarajan, H., & Saal, M. (2021). FinTech and the Digital Transformation of Financial Services: Implications for Market Structure and Public Policy. *BIS Papers, No. 117*.
Financial Stability Board (FSB). (2023). *Global Monitoring Report on FinTech Risks*. Basel: FSB.
Gomber, P., Kauffman, R. J., Parker, C., & Weber, B. W. (2018). On the FinTech Revolution: Interpreting the Forces of Innovation, Disruption, and Transformation in Financial Services. *Journal of Management Information Systems*, 35(1), 220–265.
McKinsey & Company. (2022). *The Rise of Embedded Finance*. McKinsey Global Payments Report.
Merton, R. C., & Bodie, Z. (1995). A Conceptual Framework for Analysing the Financial Environment. In *The Global Financial System: A Functional Perspective*. Boston, MA: Harvard Business School Press.
Mishkin, F. S., & Eakins, S. G. (2018). *Financial Markets and Institutions* (9th ed.). Boston, MA: Pearson.
Philippon, T. (2016). The FinTech Opportunity. *NBER Working Paper, No. 22476*.
Saunders, A., & Cornett, M. M. (2021). *Financial Institutions Management: A Risk Management Approach* (11th ed.). New York: McGraw-Hill Education.
Tapscott, D., & Tapscott, A. (2016). *Blockchain Revolution: How the Technology Behind Bitcoin Is Changing Money, Business, and the World*. New York: Penguin.

8 The Digital Transformation of Banking

Integrating Traditional Functions with Financial Technology

Chapter Overview

This chapter provides a comprehensive examination of the evolution of the banking sector as it converges with traditional financial practices and technological innovation. It synthesises the fundamental principles underpinning retail, personal, and commercial banking, highlighting their essential functions in deposit-taking, lending, and payment processing. The chapter further offers a critical analysis of the disruptive and complementary dynamics introduced by Financial Technology (FinTech). Key innovations, including digital banking platforms, artificial intelligence (AI)-driven services, blockchain applications, and open banking APIs, are explored in detail. A comparative assessment of traditional banking models versus FinTech-enabled frameworks is undertaken, elucidating differences in operational efficiency, customer engagement, and service delivery. The chapter also rigorously addresses the risks inherent in digital banking, including cybersecurity threats, regulatory complexities, and challenges posed by the digital divide. Finally, it projects emerging trends such as embedded finance, hyper-personalised banking solutions, and sustainable finance, situating these developments within an increasingly competitive and collaborative financial ecosystem.

Learning Objectives

By the end of this chapter, you should be able to:

1. Analyse the core functions, services, and operational structures of retail, personal, and commercial banking.
2. Identify and evaluate key FinTech innovations and their effects on the banking value chain and customer experience.
3. Compare and contrast traditional and FinTech-driven banking models in terms of efficiency, cost structures, and service delivery.
4. Assess the major risks and regulatory challenges in digital banking, including cybersecurity, data privacy, and compliance complexities.
5. Examine and predict the impact of emerging trends such as embedded finance, AI-powered services, and sustainable banking on the sector's future.

DOI: 10.4324/9781003775751-10

8.1 Introduction

Banking has long functioned as a cornerstone of the financial system, serving as a trusted intermediary between savers and borrowers (Mishkin & Eakins, 2018). Its primary functions, accepting deposits, extending credit, and facilitating payments, have historically provided stability, supporting both individual financial management and commercial activity. These enduring roles have shaped the operational principles and institutional frameworks of traditional financial institutions.

In recent years, however, the financial sector has experienced a profound transformation driven by the emergence of Financial Technology (FinTech). This technological paradigm shift manifests in innovations such as digital payments, peer-to-peer lending, and crowdfunding platforms, which challenge conventional banking practices and redefine the mechanisms of financial intermediation (Arner, Barberis, & Buckley, 2016). FinTech extends beyond simple process automation, fundamentally altering customer engagement, credit assessment, and transaction processing. Consequently, it necessitates a critical reassessment of traditional operational models and the delivery of financial services.

This chapter examines the ongoing digital transformation of banking. It begins by reviewing the foundational principles of banking, distinguishing between retail/personal and commercial sectors, before analysing the technological forces driving innovation. Key themes include automation, novel financial products, personalised service offerings, and heightened competition introduced by FinTech. The chapter further evaluates the implications of these developments for banking business models, customer expectations, and the competitive landscape, emphasising the emergence of a new financial ecosystem in which agility, data-driven decision-making, and customer-centricity are essential for sustained success.

8.2 The Foundations of Banking: Roles and Functions

Banking constitutes a central pillar of the financial system, providing critical intermediation between savers and borrowers and facilitating economic stability and growth (Mishkin & Eakins, 2018).

8.2.1 Definition and Types of Banking Institutions

Banking institutions constitute a foundational component of the financial system, performing the critical role of intermediating between savers and borrowers while providing essential financial services that support economic activity and stability (Mishkin & Eakins, 2018). These institutions facilitate capital allocation, enable payments, manage risk, and contribute to wealth creation across both the individual and business sectors. While retail and commercial banks form the core of the banking industry, the contemporary banking ecosystem is highly diverse, encompassing specialised institutions designed to meet distinct market needs, regulatory frameworks, and technological innovations.

Retail Banks: Retail banks primarily serve individual customers, offering deposit accounts, personal loans, mortgages, and payment services (Rose & Hudgins, 2020). They provide households with foundational financial access and security, enabling day-to-day transactions, savings accumulation, and borrowing. For example, Wells Fargo and Barclays provide a range of retail banking products, including online savings accounts, mobile banking applications, and home mortgages, thereby facilitating both financial inclusion and personal wealth management.

Commercial Banks: Commercial banks focus on business clients, providing financing, treasury management, trade finance, and cash management services (Saunders & Cornett, 2021). These banks support businesses in managing operational liquidity, raising capital for expansion, and mitigating financial risks. For instance, JPMorgan Chase's commercial banking division assists corporations in securing working capital loans, structuring syndicated financing for large projects, and implementing automated cash management systems to optimise corporate liquidity.

Investment Banks: Investment banks specialise in capital markets, underwriting securities, facilitating mergers and acquisitions (M&A), and offering advisory services (Fabozzi, Modigliani, & Jones, 2016). They enable firms to raise equity and debt capital, support corporate restructuring, and provide market-making services. Goldman Sachs, for example, advises startups on initial public offerings (IPOs) and guides multinational corporations through complex M&A transactions, demonstrating the strategic role of investment banks in large-scale financial intermediation.

Credit Unions: Credit unions are member-owned cooperatives that provide retail banking services with a community-oriented focus and preferential rates (Burritt & Christ, 2016). They often emphasise financial literacy, community development, and low-cost borrowing. The Navy Federal Credit Union in the U.S., for example, serves military personnel and their families, offering favourable mortgage and loan products while reinvesting profits to benefit members.

Savings and Loan Banks: Savings and loan banks primarily accept deposits and provide mortgage financing, promoting homeownership and financial stability (Mishkin & Eakins, 2018). In the United States, Savings and Loan associations historically played a central role in funding residential real estate, offering long-term loans at favourable rates.

8.2.2 *Products and Services Provided by Banking Institutions*

Banking institutions provide a wide range of products and services tailored to the diverse needs of their clients, from individual consumers to large corporations and specialised market segments. These services are designed to ensure financial security, facilitate transactions, enable investment, and support economic growth. For analytical clarity, these services can be grouped according to the type of banking institution.

8.2.2.1 *Retail and Personal Banking Services*

Retail banks focus primarily on individual customers, addressing their financial needs through services that enhance liquidity, security, and wealth accumulation (Rose & Hudgins, 2020). The core services include:

Deposit Accounts: Retail banks offer a range of deposit products, including savings, current, and fixed-term accounts. These accounts provide a secure means to store funds while maintaining liquidity for everyday use or long-term savings goals. For example, a client may maintain a savings account to gradually accumulate wealth while using a current account for daily transactions, such as bill payments and retail purchases. Fixed-term deposits, on the other hand, allow clients to earn higher interest rates for funds locked in for a defined period, often used to achieve targeted financial goals.

Lending and Credit Facilities: Personal loans, mortgages, and credit cards are designed to meet individual financial needs. These products enable consumers to finance major purchases, such as homes or vehicles, and manage short-term liquidity requirements. Mortgages allow clients to invest in real estate while spreading repayments over extended periods, whereas revolving credit lines, such as credit cards, offer flexible liquidity management for everyday expenses.

Payments and Settlements: Modern retail banking increasingly relies on digital platforms to facilitate payments and settlements. Services include debit and credit card networks, mobile and internet banking, and real-time payment systems that enhance transaction speed, transparency, and security. For instance, clients can make instant peer-to-peer transfers or pay utility bills online, minimising reliance on traditional paper-based methods and physical branch visits.

Wealth Management and Financial Planning: Retail banks often provide comprehensive advisory services to help clients optimise their financial position. Services may include investment advisory, retirement planning, and tax-optimised financial strategies. For example, private banking divisions within retail banks may assist clients in diversifying their investment portfolios following a significant inheritance or business exit, thereby ensuring long-term financial goals are met.

8.2.2.2 Commercial Banking Services

Commercial banks cater to business clients of all sizes, offering products and services that enhance operational efficiency, support growth, and manage financial risks (Saunders & Cornett, 2021). Key services include:

Business Lending: Commercial banks provide loans and credit facilities to support working capital needs, capital expenditures, equipment financing, and business expansion. For example, a manufacturing company might secure a commercial loan to acquire new production machinery while using a revolving line of credit to meet short-term payroll and supplier obligations.

Treasury and Cash Management: Businesses require solutions to efficiently manage cash flows, optimise liquidity, and control the timing of receivables and payables. Services such as integrated cash management platforms, automated sweeps, and concentration account structures help firms consolidate multiple accounts, minimise idle cash, and maximise returns on available funds.

Trade Finance: Commercial banks play a critical role in facilitating domestic and international trade by providing Letters of Credit (L/Cs), bank guarantees, and import/export financing. For instance, an exporter can use an L/C to guarantee payment upon shipment confirmation, reducing the counterparty risk inherent in cross-border transactions.

Foreign Exchange (FX) and Hedging Services: Global operations expose firms to currency and interest rate fluctuations. Commercial banks provide instruments such as forward contracts, currency options, and interest rate swaps, enabling firms to hedge against market volatility. For example, a multinational company importing raw materials can secure a forward FX contract to lock in a future exchange rate, stabilising input costs and protecting profit margins.

8.2.2.3 Other Banking Services

Beyond retail and commercial banking, other types of financial institutions offer niche products to meet the requirements of specific market segments:

Investment Banks: These institutions focus on capital markets, underwriting, M&A advisory, and structured finance. For example, an investment bank may guide a technology startup through a private equity funding round or an IPO, enabling access to substantial capital for expansion.

Credit Unions: Member-owned cooperatives focus on community-oriented savings and lending products, often providing lower interest rates and financial education programmes to members.

Savings and Loan Banks: These banks focus primarily on mortgage financing and deposit-taking services, historically promoting home ownership and personal savings.

Islamic Banks: Operating under Sharia-compliant principles, Islamic banks provide interest-free loans and profit-sharing investment accounts. For example, Al Rajhi Bank offers home financing through Murabaha (cost-plus) contracts, allowing clients to access financial services in accordance with religious law (Usmani, 2002).

Green Banks: Specialised institutions financing environmentally sustainable projects, such as renewable energy initiatives, energy-efficient infrastructure, and climate mitigation programmes. For example, Connecticut Green Bank supports solar energy installations and green infrastructure financing (Bird, Mandell, & Ye, 2019).

8.2.3 Economic and Strategic Significance

The wide range of products and services offered by banking institutions supports both individual financial security and broader economic growth. Retail banking enhances personal wealth and liquidity management, commercial banking enables business expansion and efficient capital allocation, and specialised institutions, such as green banks and neobanks, promote innovation, sustainability, and inclusion in the financial system (Mishkin & Eakins, 2018; Rose & Hudgins, 2020; Saunders & Cornett, 2021). Collectively, these offerings ensure a dynamic and resilient financial ecosystem that can meet the needs of diverse client segments.

8.3 The Rise of FinTech in Banking

The emergence of Financial Technology (FinTech) has profoundly reshaped the banking sector, driving digital transformation across traditional and specialised financial institutions. By streamlining operational processes, enhancing accessibility, and enabling highly personalised services, FinTech has redefined customer expectations and competitive dynamics (Gomber, Koch, & Siering, 2017). Financial institutions are increasingly adopting FinTech innovations not only to improve efficiency but also to respond to evolving regulatory environments and digitally savvy clientele. The following sections examine key innovations, their applications across different banking types, and the resulting transformation in operational models and service delivery (Figure 8.1).

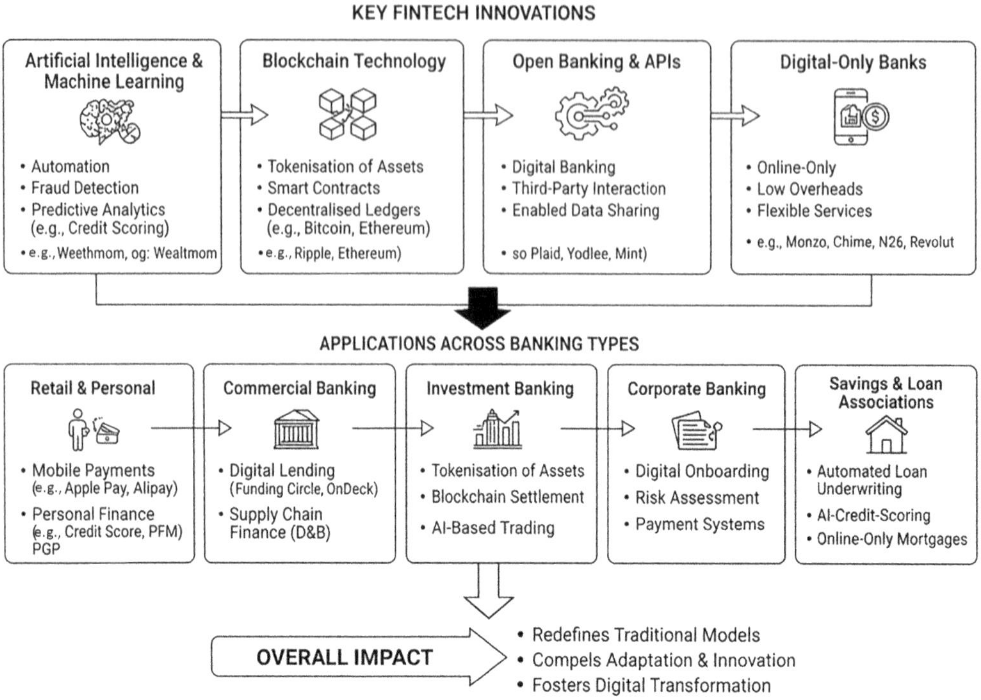

Figure 8.1 Key FinTech Innovations and Sectoral Applications.

8.3.1 *Key FinTech Innovations*

8.3.1.1 *AI and Machine Learning (ML)*

AI and ML are driving automation, predictive analytics, and enhanced decision-making across the banking industry. Algorithms analyse large datasets to improve credit scoring, detect fraud, and provide personalised financial advice (Balyuk & Davydenko, 2021; Nguyen, Nguyen, & Ho, 2020). For example, in retail banking, AI-powered chatbots such as Erica by Bank of America provide real-time customer support and account management, while robo-advisors like Betterment automate investment portfolios for personal banking clients.

8.3.1.2 *Blockchain Technology*

Blockchain provides a secure, immutable, and decentralised ledger, offering applications across payment systems, trade finance, and regulatory compliance (Tapscott & Tapscott, 2016). In commercial banking, blockchain-based platforms such as Marco Polo streamline trade finance, reduce paperwork, and accelerate cross-border settlement. Similarly, credit unions are experimenting with blockchain to enhance transparency and reduce transaction costs for members.

8.3.1.3 *Open Banking and APIs*

Open Banking initiatives, including Europe's PSD2 regulation, require banks to share customer data via secure APIs (Zetzsche, Buckley, & Arner, 2020). This facilitates collaboration with third-party FinTech providers, enabling innovations in payments, lending, and financial management. For example, digital wallets and budgeting tools can now access customer banking data to provide real-time financial insights. Retail and challenger banks benefit from Open Banking by offering personalised products without the need for extensive legacy infrastructure.

8.3.1.4 Digital-Only Banks: Neobanks and Challenger Banks

Neobanks and challenger banks operate primarily online, leveraging technology to reduce overheads and enhance customer experience (McKinsey & Company, 2023). They offer features such as instant account opening, real-time payments, and AI-driven insights. For instance, Monzo and Chime target retail banking clients with mobile-first, low-cost solutions, while Asian nano banks provide ultra-lightweight banking services for underbanked populations.

8.3.2 FinTech Applications Across Banking Types

8.3.2.1 Retail and Personal Banking

Retail and personal banking have been significantly transformed by FinTech, with technological solutions automating core processes, improving accessibility, and delivering highly personalised services to clients (Thakor, 2020). Key applications include:

Robo-Advisors: Platforms such as Betterment and Wealthfront automate investment portfolio management and financial planning. Using algorithms and AI, robo-advisors tailor investment strategies to individual risk preferences and financial goals, providing cost-effective solutions that were previously accessible only to high-net-worth clients.

Digital Wallets and Peer-to-Peer (P2P) Payments: Services such as Apple Pay, Google Pay, and Venmo enable instantaneous money transfers and mobile payments, reducing dependence on traditional bank branches. These innovations also support contactless payments and real-time fund settlement, significantly improving customer convenience.

AI-Powered Customer Support: Chatbots and virtual assistants, such as Erica by Bank of America, provide 24/7 support for account inquiries, transaction monitoring, and personalised financial advice. This improves responsiveness, reduces operational costs, and enhances the customer experience.

Personal Finance Management Tools: FinTech apps integrate with bank accounts to offer budgeting, automated savings, and spending analysis. For example, platforms like Mint and Yolt analyse transaction data to provide actionable insights, helping customers optimise financial decisions.

8.3.2.2 Commercial Banking

In commercial banking, FinTech solutions focus on enhancing operational efficiency, risk management, and transparency for business clients (Davenport & Ronanki, 2018). Examples of sector-specific innovations include:

Digital Lending Platforms: Platforms such as Kabbage and Fundbox digitise and automate the credit approval process for small and medium-sized enterprises. These systems use real-time data, alternative credit scoring models, and AI to expedite loan decisions, reducing the traditional delays associated with manual underwriting.

Treasury and Cash Management Systems: Advanced platforms, such as HighRadius, provide commercial clients with real-time visibility into cash positions, receivables, and payables. Automation of cash flow monitoring and reconciliation enables businesses to optimise liquidity, reduce idle cash, and improve working capital efficiency.

Blockchain in Trade Finance: Blockchain-based networks, such as Marco Polo, improve transparency and security in trade finance. Smart contracts automate payment release upon verification of shipping documentation, reducing settlement times, minimising paperwork, and mitigating counterparty risk in cross-border transactions.

Risk Management Tools: AI-powered predictive analytics allow commercial banks to monitor credit exposure, detect fraudulent transactions, and assess market risks in real time, thereby improving portfolio resilience and operational decision-making.

8.3.2.3 Investment Banking

Investment banking has leveraged FinTech primarily for analytics, risk management, and transaction efficiency (Gomber, Koch, & Siering, 2017):

AI-Based Market Analytics: ML algorithms analyse vast market datasets to enhance trading strategies, perform equity research, and support M&A advisory. These predictive models enable faster, data-driven decision-making.

Blockchain for Securities and Compliance: Blockchain facilitates digital asset issuance, securitisation, and compliance tracking. For instance, tokenised securities can be traded more efficiently, while distributed ledgers provide transparent audit trails for regulators.

Automated Deal Execution: AI-driven tools streamline the structuring and execution of complex financial transactions, reducing human error and operational risk while accelerating transaction timelines.

8.3.2.4 Credit Unions

Credit unions, as member-focused institutions, adopt FinTech to improve accessibility, reduce costs, and expand service offerings (Burritt & Christ, 2016):

Mobile Banking Solutions: Mobile apps enable members, particularly in underserved or rural areas, to access accounts, make payments, and monitor balances without visiting a branch.

Peer-to-Peer Lending and Microfinance Platforms: These platforms allow members to access low-cost microloans, facilitate community lending, and strengthen financial inclusion. For example, credit unions may partner with digital lending platforms to provide members with alternative credit options.

Automated Member Services: AI and chatbots assist with account inquiries, loan applications, and financial guidance, improving efficiency and enhancing the member experience.

8.3.2.5 Savings and Loan Banks

Savings and loan banks, historically focused on mortgage lending and deposit-taking, are increasingly leveraging FinTech to digitise core operations and enhance efficiency:

Automated Underwriting: Platforms using AI and ML streamline mortgage approvals, evaluating applicant risk profiles quickly while ensuring compliance with lending regulations.

Table 8.1 Traditional vs Digital Banking Comparison

Feature	*Traditional Banking*	*Digital Banking*
Access and Onboarding	Branch-dependent, slow know-your-customer (KYC) process (days/weeks)	Digital-first, instant sign-up with eKYC (minutes)
Transaction Speed	Slow transfers (1–3 business days for wires/ACH)	Real-time/instant payments (24/7 processing)
Cost Structure	High fees (monthly maintenance, overdraft, wire fees)	Low/no fees, freemium models, subscription-based pricing
Customer Service	In-person call centres with limited hours	AI chatbots, 24/7 in-app support, omnichannel assistance
Innovation Cycle	Slow, legacy system-dependent, annual updates	Rapid, agile development, cloud-native, continuous deployment
Credit Assessment	Rigid criteria (Fair Isaac Corporation scores, collateral, income verification)	Algorithmic, using alternative data (cash flow, transaction history, digital footprint)

Digital Deposit Management: Cloud-based systems enable real-time account monitoring, mobile deposits, and automated reconciliation, reducing operational overhead and improving service quality.

Enhanced Customer Engagement: Personalised financial advice and automated reminders for savings plans or mortgage payments increase client engagement and retention.

Table 8.1 below compares Traditional and Digital Banking.

8.4 Key Practical Issues in Implementation

The transformation to a fully digitised banking ecosystem presents complex challenges that institutions must address to maintain operational efficiency, regulatory compliance, and customer satisfaction. Three critical issues are legacy system integration, regulatory compliance, and balancing security with user experience.

8.4.1 Legacy System Integration

Integrating modern FinTech solutions with decades-old core banking systems poses a significant challenge due to the rigidity and complexity of legacy infrastructure, often referred to as 'technical debt' (Gartner, 2023). A complete system replacement is costly and risky, leading many banks to adopt hybrid solutions, such as middleware or phased modernisation. This often creates a 'two-speed IT' environment, where legacy systems support traditional operations while digital platforms handle new services, increasing complexity and slowing innovation. For example, integrating real-time mobile payments into an older core system can delay rollout and raise maintenance costs.

8.4.2 Navigating the Regulatory Landscape

Banks and FinTechs operate in a fragmented regulatory environment covering data privacy (e.g., General Data Protection Regulation), anti-money laundering, open banking mandates (e.g., PSD2), and consumer protection (Zetzsche, Buckley, & Arner, 2020). Variations across jurisdictions create uncertainty, increase compliance costs, and can delay product launches. For instance, a neobank expanding across Europe must reconcile differing privacy and licensing rules, complicating market entry and innovation.

8.4.3 Balancing Security with Customer Experience

Digital banking requires robust security measures, multi-factor authentication (MFA), AI-driven fraud detection, and real-time monitoring to protect data and assets (Kshetri, 2013). However, excessive security can introduce friction, undermining the user experience. For example, requiring multiple verification steps for each transaction may deter mobile app usage. Banks must therefore optimise security while maintaining seamless, convenient service.

8.5 Risks and Challenges in Digital Banking

The transformation of banking through digital and FinTech solutions introduces substantial risks that require careful management.

8.5.1 Cybersecurity Threats

Interconnected digital platforms, API-based services, and cloud infrastructure expand the attack surface for cyber threats. Banks face sophisticated phishing campaigns, ransomware attacks, and business email compromise schemes, all of which can disrupt operations and cause financial losses. According to the FBI IC3 (2021), cybercrime results in billions of dollars in annual losses to financial institutions globally.

8.5.2 Data Privacy and Integrity

Data-driven FinTech models raise heightened concerns about privacy and ethical data use. Ensuring data integrity and compliance with regulations such as GDPR is essential. Violations can lead to significant financial penalties, reputational damage, and erosion of customer trust. For instance, breaches of customer financial data in digital wallets or neobank platforms can undermine confidence and impede adoption.

8.5.3 Regulatory Ambiguity

Many FinTech innovations operate in regulatory grey zones, particularly in emerging markets or cross-border operations. Inconsistent standards across jurisdictions complicate compliance and increase operational costs. For example, cryptocurrency-based payment services may be regulated differently in the U.S., EU, and Asia, necessitating customised governance frameworks. Regulatory ambiguity, therefore, remains a critical barrier to scaling FinTech solutions (WTO, 2022).

8.5.4 The Digital Divide

The shift towards digital-first banking risks marginalising vulnerable populations, including older people, low-income households, and rural communities lacking internet access or digital literacy (OECD, 2021). Failure to address this divide may exacerbate financial inequality, highlighting the need for inclusive digital banking strategies such as simplified mobile interfaces and community-based digital education programmes.

8.6 The Future of Banking: Collaborative Models and Emerging Trends

The future of banking is increasingly defined by collaboration and technological integration, rather than purely competitive dynamics. Traditional banks are partnering with FinTechs, while neobanks are acquiring full licences, creating a hybrid, interconnected financial ecosystem.

8.6.1 Convergence and Collaboration

The financial landscape now reflects a blend of cooperation and competition. Traditional banks are launching digital sub-brands (e.g., Bank of America's Erica) and partnering with FinTech firms, such as JPMorgan Chase's collaboration with OnDeck. Banking-as-a-Service (BaaS) models enable regulated banks to provide infrastructure to non-bank entities via APIs, exemplified by Goldman Sachs' Marcus platform powering the Apple Card (Gomber et al., 2017). This integration facilitates agility, scalability, and access to innovative services while leveraging regulatory compliance capabilities.

8.6.2 Embedded Finance

Embedded finance integrates banking functionalities, payments, lending, and insurance directly into non-financial platforms (McKinsey & Company, 2022). Examples include Shopify Balance for merchants and Uber Wallet for rideshare payments, which embed financial services into operational flows. This trend shifts banking from traditional institutional interfaces to contextual, real-time delivery, enhancing convenience and relevance for consumers while compelling incumbent banks to prioritise collaborative, API-driven models.

8.6.3 Hyper-Personalisation with AI

Advanced AI and big data analytics enable hyper-personalisation in banking. Institutions can provide tailored product recommendations, dynamic pricing, and proactive financial advice based on customer behaviour and life events. For instance, AI may suggest a mortgage refinancing option when a client's financial profile changes or automatically adjust investment allocations based on market conditions and individual risk preferences (Thakor, 2020).

8.6.4 Sustainable and Environmental, Social, and Governance (ESG)–Focused Banking

Growing demand for ESG integration has driven banks to adopt sustainable finance practices. Using data analytics, institutions assess ESG performance for credit decisions, risk management, and investment strategies. Green lending initiatives, such as financing renewable energy projects, illustrate how sustainability is becoming integral to banking operations and product offerings (World Economic Forum, 2023).

8.6.5 Decentralised Finance (DeFi)

Decentralised Finance (DeFi), built on blockchain protocols, is emerging as a potential disruptor to traditional banking. DeFi applications explore peer-to-peer lending, decentralised trading, and smart contract-based finance, potentially reducing reliance on centralised intermediaries. While still in early adoption stages, platforms leveraging DeFi could fundamentally reconfigure capital allocation and transactional processes in the future (Chen & Bellavitis, 2019).

8.7 Conclusion

The banking industry is currently at a critical inflexion point, driven by the rapid proliferation of Financial Technology (FinTech), which is fundamentally reshaping traditional service delivery models and customer expectations. FinTech firms, leveraging agile methodologies, data-driven decision-making, and highly personalised solutions, are challenging incumbent institutions to reassess and adapt their operational frameworks. To maintain competitiveness and relevance, banks must develop hybrid operating models that integrate their core strengths, such as financial stability, regulatory expertise, and established customer trust, with the speed, innovation, and customer-centric design principles characteristic of FinTech (Gomber, Koch, & Siering, 2017). As one industry analyst observes, the future of banking is not about choosing between tradition and technology, but about harmonising the two to create superior value. This integration is not merely strategic; it is essential for sustaining long-term viability in an increasingly digital financial ecosystem.

Achieving success in this transformed environment requires alignment between strategic vision and effective technological implementation. Banks must navigate systemic challenges, including integrating legacy IT infrastructure, safeguarding data security, and instituting comprehensive governance frameworks to manage emerging digital risks (Kshetri, 2013; Gartner, 2023). Collaboration, both internally across business units and externally with FinTech partners, regulators, and technology providers, is pivotal for accelerating innovation while ensuring regulatory compliance and operational resilience. Institutions that cultivate agility, technological literacy, and customer-centricity will emerge as market leaders. By balancing innovation with stability, banks can deliver secure, accessible, and highly personalised financial services, thereby positioning themselves for sustainable growth and leadership in the digital-first era.

Key Terms and Glossary

Commercial Banking Banking that provides services such as accepting deposits, making business loans, and offering basic investment products to businesses.

Challenger Banks A new, small retail bank set up with the intention of competing for business with large, long-established national banks.

Legacy System Integration The challenge of connecting new, agile FinTech solutions with outdated, monolithic core banking IT systems.

Hyper-Personalisation The use of AI and real-time data to deliver financial products, advice, and marketing messages tailored to an individual's specific context and behaviour.

ESG Lending The practice of incorporating ESG criteria into loan underwriting and pricing.

Test Your Understanding

Multiple-Choice Questions

1 Which of the following best describes the primary function of retail banks?

A Underwriting securities and facilitating M&A
B Providing deposit accounts, personal loans, and payment services to individuals
C Offering trade finance and treasury management exclusively to large corporations
D Issuing cryptocurrencies and managing decentralised finance platforms

2 Which FinTech innovation primarily enables banks to share customer data securely with third-party providers?

A AI
B Blockchain
C Open Banking APIs
D Robo-advisors

3 Which of the following is an example of a neobank or challenger bank?

A JPMorgan Chase
B Goldman Sachs
C Monzo
D Navy Federal Credit Union

4 What is a key practical challenge when integrating FinTech solutions with legacy banking systems?

A Customer adoption of digital wallets
B Technical debt and the rigidity of monolithic core systems
C Excess liquidity in financial markets
D Insufficient fintech startup funding

5 Which emerging trend involves embedding financial services such as payments and lending directly into non-financial platforms?

A Sustainable finance
B Hyper-personalisation
C Embedded finance
D Decentralised finance (DeFi)

Short Questions

1 Explain how AI and ML are applied in retail banking to improve customer service and investment advice.
2 Identify two risks associated with digital banking and describe why they are significant for financial institutions.
3 What is BaaS, and how does it facilitate collaboration between traditional banks and FinTech companies?

Analytical Questions

1 Compare and contrast traditional banking models with FinTech-driven banking in terms of operational efficiency, customer experience, and risk management. Provide examples from retail, commercial, and investment banking.
2 Evaluate the impact of FinTech innovations such as digital wallets, robo-advisors, and blockchain on financial inclusion and accessibility. What challenges remain in addressing the digital divide?
3 Discuss how banks can balance cybersecurity requirements with delivering a seamless customer experience in a digital-first ecosystem. Include examples of potential trade-offs and strategies to optimise both security and convenience.

Case Study: JPMorgan Chase's Digital Transformation

JPMorgan Chase, the largest U.S. bank by assets, has aggressively embraced digital transformation to maintain its competitive position in an evolving financial landscape. Recognising the threat posed by agile FinTechs and digital-first challengers, the bank has invested heavily in technology, committing billions of dollars annually to modernising infrastructure, enhancing digital capabilities, and improving the customer experience.

In retail banking, JPMorgan experimented with Finn, a neobank designed to attract digitally native customers with mobile-first solutions and low fees, demonstrating a build strategy to innovate internally. The bank has also deployed AI-powered virtual assistant Erica, which provides account insights, fraud alerts, and financial guidance, exemplifying the use of AI to personalise customer services.

Beyond retail, JPMorgan has pioneered the JPM Coin, a blockchain-based digital currency designed for instantaneous institutional payments and settlement. This initiative illustrates the bank's dual approach: leveraging FinTech not only to defend market share but also to create operational efficiencies and new revenue opportunities in wholesale banking.

These innovations coexist alongside JPMorgan's legacy core banking systems, creating a hybrid operating model. While this approach allows the bank to modernise services and explore emerging technologies, integrating agile digital solutions with decades-old infrastructure introduces significant operational, technical, and governance challenges.

References

JPMorgan Chase & Co. (2023) *Annual Report 2023*. Available at: https://www.jpmorganchase.com/ir/annual-report (Accessed: 1 March 2026).

JPMorgan Chase & Co. (2023) *Investor Day Presentations and Technology Investment Reports*. Available at: https://www.jpmorganchase.com/ir/annual-report (Accessed: 1 March 2026).

Case Study Questions

1 Compare JPMorgan's 'build and acquire' approach to partnering with FinTechs. What are the main benefits and drawbacks of each for a legacy bank?
2 How does JPM Coin demonstrate JPMorgan using FinTech to create new revenue streams and improve operational efficiency?
3 What challenges arise when integrating AI and blockchain solutions with JPMorgan's legacy core banking systems?

Further Reading

Arner, D.W., Barberis, J.N., & Buckley, R.P. (2016). The Evolution of Fintech: A New Post-Crisis Paradigm? *Georgetown Journal of International Law*, 47(4), 1271–1319.

Gomber, P., Koch, J.-A., & Siering, M. (2017). Digital Finance and FinTech: Current Research and Future Research Directions. *Journal of Business Economics*, 87(5), 537–580.

Thakor, A.V. (2020). Fintech and Banking: What Do We Know? *Journal of Financial Intermediation*, 41, 100833.

References

Arner, D.W., Barberis, J., & Buckley, R.P. (2016) The Evolution of FinTech: A New Post-Crisis Paradigm? *Georgetown Journal of International Law*, 47, 1271–1319.

Balyuk, T., & Davydenko, S. (2021) AI in Credit Scoring: Evidence from Commercial Lending. *Review of Financial Studies*, 34(5), 2401–2440.

Bird, L., Mandell, S., & Ye, E. (2019) *State Green Banks: A Summary of Models and Lessons Learned.* Golden, CO: National Renewable Energy Laboratory (NREL)

Burritt, R.L., & Christ, K.L. (2016) *Accounting, Accountability and Society: Credit Unions and Cooperative Financial Institutions*. Abingdon: Routledge.

Chen, Y., & Bellavitis, C. (2019) Decentralised Finance: Blockchain Technology and the Quest for an Open Financial System. *SSRN Electronic Journal* Available at https://papers.ssrn.com/sol3/papers.cfm?abstract_id=3418557

Davenport, T.H., & Ronanki, R. (2018) Artificial Intelligence for the Real World. *Harvard Business Review*, 96(1), 108–116.

Fabozzi, F.J., Modigliani, F., & Jones, F.J. (2016). *Foundations of Financial Markets and Institutions.* 4th edn. Boston, MA: Pearson.

Gartner (2023). *Technical Debt and Legacy System Modernisation in Financial Services.* Stamford, CT: Gartner Research. Available at: Gartner Research (Accessed: 23 May 2026).

Gomber, P., Koch, J.A., & Siering, M. (2017). Digital Finance and FinTech: Current Research and Future Research Directions. *Journal of Business Economics*, 87(5), 537–580.

Kshetri, N. (2013). Privacy and Security Issues in Cloud Computing: The Role of Institutions and Institutional Evolution. *Telecommunications Policy*, 37(4–5), 372–386.

McKinsey & Company (2022). *Embedded Finance: A $7 Trillion Opportunity*. Available at: https://www.mckinsey.com (Accessed: 15 October 2023).

McKinsey & Company (2023) *Global Retail Banking Report: Digital, Personal, and Profitable*. New York: McKinsey & Company.

Mishkin, F.S., & Eakins, S.G. (2018). *Financial Markets and Institutions* (9th ed.). Boston, MA: Pearson.

Nguyen, Q., Nguyen, N.P., & Ho, C. (2020). The Role of AI in Customer Service: A Systematic Review. *Journal of Service Theory and Practice*, 30(1), 1–24.

Organisation for Economic Co-operation and Development (OECD) (2021) *Bridging Digital Divides in G20 Countries*. Paris: OECD Publishing.

Rose, P.S., & Hudgins, S.C. (2020) *Bank Management & Financial Services* (10th ed.). New York: McGraw-Hill.

Saunders, A., & Cornett, M.M. (2021). *Financial Institutions Management: A Risk Management Approach* (10th ed.). New York: McGraw-Hill.

Tapscott, D., & Tapscott, A. (2016) *Blockchain Revolution: How the Technology Behind Bitcoin is Changing Money, Business, and the World.* New York: Penguin.

Thakor, A.V. (2020) FinTech and Banking: What Do We Know? *Journal of Financial Intermediation*, 41, 100833.

Usmani, M.T. (2002) *An Introduction to Islamic Finance*. Karachi: Maktaba Ma'ariful Qur'an.

World Economic Forum (2023) *ESG and FinTech: Driving Sustainable Finance*. Available at: https://www.weforum.org/ (Accessed: 15 October 2023).

World Trade Organization (WTO) (2022) *Financial Technology and Trade in Financial Services.* Geneva: World Trade Organisation.

Zetzsche, D.A., Buckley, R.P., & Arner, D.W. (2020) The Evolution of FinTech: A New Post-Crisis Paradigm? *University of New South Wales Law Research Paper* (2020-65).

9 Investment Banking and Brokerage

Chapter Overview

This chapter analyses the impact of Financial Technology (FinTech) on investment banking and brokerage, two core components of capital markets that were traditionally distinct in function and scope. While investment banks historically focused on capital raising, mergers and acquisitions (M&A), and strategic advisory services, brokerages primarily facilitated securities trading; however, digitalisation has increasingly driven their convergence. The chapter outlines their foundational structures before examining how technologies such as artificial intelligence (AI), blockchain, and advanced data analytics are transforming deal-making, trading, advisory functions, and risk management. It critically compares traditional and FinTech-driven models, highlighting emerging synergies alongside key challenges, including cybersecurity risks, regulatory constraints, and technological dependence. The discussion concludes by identifying future industry trends, notably decentralised finance (DeFi), hyper-personalised financial services, and the early potential of quantum computing.

Learning Objectives

By the end of this chapter, you should be able to:

1. Explain and differentiate the fundamental functions, organisational structures, and business models of investment banks and brokerage firms.
2. Analyse how FinTech innovations are reshaping traditional activities such as underwriting, trading, advisory services, and risk management.
3. Evaluate the application and significance of AI, blockchain technology, and algorithmic trading within contemporary capital markets.
4. Compare and assess traditional versus FinTech-driven models with respect to operational efficiency, cost structures, market accessibility, and risk profiles.
5. Critically appraise regulatory, cybersecurity, and operational challenges arising from digital transformation, and discuss the implications of emerging trends such as tokenised securities, DeFi, and AI-enabled analytics.

DOI: 10.4324/9781003775751-11

9.1 Introduction

Investment banking and brokerage constitute essential pillars of the global financial system, underpinning capital formation and ensuring market liquidity. Investment banks operate primarily as strategic intermediaries and advisors, delivering specialised services such as capital raising through initial public offerings (IPOs), M&A advisory, and sales and trading for corporate, governmental, and institutional clients (Arner, Barberis, & Buckley, 2017). Brokerage firms, by contrast, focus on facilitating market participation and trade execution, serving both retail and institutional investors through services ranging from basic transaction execution to integrated wealth management solutions (Bodie, Kane, & Marcus, 2021).

The rapid emergence of FinTech has substantially reshaped both sectors. Technologies such as AI, blockchain, and cloud computing are increasingly embedded within operational and strategic frameworks to enhance efficiency, improve transparency, and expand access to financial markets. However, this technological integration also introduces new sources of risk and heightens competitive pressures in an already complex and dynamic environment.

FinTech-driven disruption is fundamentally altering the core activities and competitive landscape of investment banks and brokerage firms. The interaction between technological innovation and evolving client expectations has accelerated the convergence of business models and service offerings across institutions that were once clearly differentiated. Accordingly, this chapter examines the evolution of investment banking and brokerage, with particular emphasis on the role of FinTech in driving strategic transformation within these sectors.

9.2 The Institutional Landscape of Investment Banking and Brokerage

9.2.1 Defining Investment Banking and Brokerage

Investment banking and brokerage represent two distinct yet interrelated institutional pillars of capital markets. Investment banking refers to a set of specialised financial services focused on capital formation, corporate restructuring, and strategic advisory activities. Investment banks act as intermediaries between issuers and investors, assisting corporations, governments, and institutions in raising capital through equity and debt instruments, advising on M&A, and providing valuation, risk management, and trading services (Arner, Barberis, & Buckley, 2017).

Brokerage, by contrast, centres on facilitating market participation and liquidity by executing securities transactions for clients. Brokerage firms provide investors, both retail and institutional, with access to financial markets, trade execution, investment advice, research, and portfolio management services. While historically transactional, modern brokerage has expanded to encompass wealth management and technology-driven investment platforms (Bodie, Kane, & Marcus, 2021).

9.2.2 Types of Investment Banks and Their Core Functions

The investment banking industry is organised into distinct categories based on client size, geographic scope, and the breadth of services offered. This stratification allows institutions to specialise and efficiently meet the financing and advisory needs of different market segments.

Bulge Bracket Investment Bank: A Bulge Bracket Investment Bank is a large, globally integrated financial institution that provides a full spectrum of investment banking services across equity, debt, advisory, and trading. Their core activities include underwriting large-scale equity and debt issuances, advising on complex and cross-border M&A, market-making, and risk management for multinational corporations and sovereign entities. Prominent examples include Goldman Sachs and JPMorgan Chase, which routinely lead high-value IPOs and major international M&A transactions.

Middle-Market Investment Bank: Middle-Market Investment Banks specialise in serving mid-sized companies that require tailored financial solutions but do not operate at the scale of multinational corporations. These banks focus on capital raising, M&A advisory, restructuring, and private placements, often emphasising sector-specific expertise and close client relationships. Firms such as Jefferies and Houlihan Lokey exemplify this category by advising medium-sized enterprises on growth financing and strategic transactions.

Boutique Investment Bank: Boutique Investment Banks are specialised advisory firms that concentrate on niche areas, most commonly M&A advisory, restructuring, or sector-focused consulting. Unlike bulge bracket banks, boutiques generally do not engage in large-scale underwriting or trading. Instead, firms such as Evercore and Lazard compete on high-profile transactions by offering independent advice, deep industry knowledge, and conflict-free advisory services.

Captive Investment Bank: A captive investment bank is an in-house investment banking division within a larger financial institution or corporate group. Their primary role is to support the strategic, financing, and risk management needs of the parent organisation rather than external clients. An example is Royal Bank of Canada (RBC) Capital Markets, which operates within the Royal Bank of Canada group and provides integrated advisory and capital markets services aligned with the bank's broader corporate strategy.

9.2.3 Types of Brokerage Firms and Their Core Functions

Brokerage firms facilitate access to financial markets by executing securities transactions and providing investment-related services. Over time, brokerage models have evolved from relationship-based advisory services to technology-driven platforms that prioritise efficiency, accessibility, and cost reduction.

Full-Service Brokerage: Full-Service Brokerages offer comprehensive investment services, including personalised financial advice, portfolio management, estate planning, and proprietary investment research. These firms typically serve high-net-worth individuals (HNWIs) and institutional investors who require customised solutions and ongoing advisory support. Examples include Merrill Lynch and Morgan Stanley, which combine traditional brokerage services with integrated wealth management offerings.

Discount Brokerage: Discount Brokerages focus primarily on efficient and low-cost trade execution, offering limited or no personalised investment advice. Their core function is to enable self-directed investors to execute trades independently using online platforms, supported by basic research tools and market data. Firms such as Charles Schwab exemplify this model by providing affordable access to equity, bond, and fund markets.

Table 9.1 Core Services Comparison: Investment Banking vs Brokerage

Functions	*Investment Banking Focus*	*Brokerage Focus*
Capital Raising	Underwriting equity/debt (IPOs, bonds) for corporations	Facilitating access to these securities for investors
Advisory	Strategic M&A, restructuring, and valuation for corporations	Investment advice and portfolio management for individuals/institutions
Trading and Execution	Proprietary trading, market-making for institutional clients	Executing buy/sell orders on behalf of retail and institutional clients
Research	In-depth analysis of companies, industries, and M&A targets	Market commentary, stock recommendations, and portfolio strategy for investors
Asset Management	Managing large institutional portfolios and alternative assets	Managing discretionary and advisory portfolios for retail and HNW clients

Online and Digital Brokerage: Online and Digital Brokerages are FinTech-enabled platforms that enhance market accessibility through mobile-first interfaces, commission-free trading, and innovative features such as fractional share investing and social trading. Platforms such as Robinhood and eToro have significantly lowered entry barriers for retail investors, particularly younger and first-time participants, by simplifying trading processes and reducing transaction costs (Zheng et al., 2020).

Institutional Brokerage: Institutional Brokerages cater exclusively to professional investors, including hedge funds, pension funds, mutual funds, and asset managers. These firms provide advanced trade execution, liquidity provision, market-making services, and sophisticated research and analytics. Institutional brokerages play a critical role in maintaining market liquidity and price efficiency, particularly in high-volume, complex trading environments.

Table 9.1 compares Investment Banking and Brokerage activities.

9.2.4 Comparative Services and Significance in Capital Markets

Investment banks and brokerage firms occupy complementary yet distinct roles within capital markets, with investment banks primarily engaged in underwriting securities, providing strategic corporate advisory, conducting proprietary trading, and managing institutional and alternative asset portfolios. In contrast, brokerages focus on facilitating investor access, executing trades, offering portfolio management and advisory services, and supporting both retail and high-net-worth clients (Bodie, Kane, & Marcus, 2021; Arner, Barberis, & Buckley, 2017). Together, these institutions underpin market efficiency, with investment banks driving capital formation, corporate growth, and financial innovation, and brokerages enhancing liquidity, price discovery, and broad investor participation. The growing adoption of FinTech, including AI, blockchain, and algorithmic trading, has blurred traditional boundaries, fostering greater convergence and interdependence in service delivery and operational models across the financial ecosystem (Davenport & Ronanki, 2018; Tapscott & Tapscott, 2016).

9.3 The FinTech Disruption: Investment Banking and Brokerage

FinTech is fundamentally reshaping the operational and strategic landscape of investment banking and brokerage. Rather than simply automating existing processes, these innovations are transforming traditional business models, altering client interactions, and redefining competitive dynamics across the financial ecosystem (Arner, Barberis, & Buckley, 2017) (Figure 9.1).

9.3.1 Investment Banks and FinTech-Enhanced Transformation

In investment banking, FinTech is driving a shift from traditional, relationship-driven models towards hybrid, technology-enabled platforms. Bulge bracket banks, such as Goldman Sachs and JPMorgan Chase, are increasingly integrating AI and predictive analytics into M&A advisory, deal origination, and market forecasting. Blockchain applications, exemplified by JPM Coin, are streamlining settlements and reducing the operational frictions historically associated with cross-border transactions. Algorithmic trading and advanced data analytics are also enhancing market-making operations, enabling banks to execute large-scale trades faster and more accurately while reducing human error and costs.

Middle-market and boutique banks are leveraging similar technologies to compete more effectively. AI-driven tools, natural language processing, and machine learning allow these banks to identify potential deals, analyse market trends, and optimise valuations more efficiently than traditional manual processes. Tokenisation and blockchain-based platforms are also enabling fractional ownership of complex assets, expanding investment opportunities for clients and introducing new revenue streams. Captive banks are adopting automation and predictive analytics internally, improving strategic decision-making and treasury management while reducing dependency on external advisory inputs.

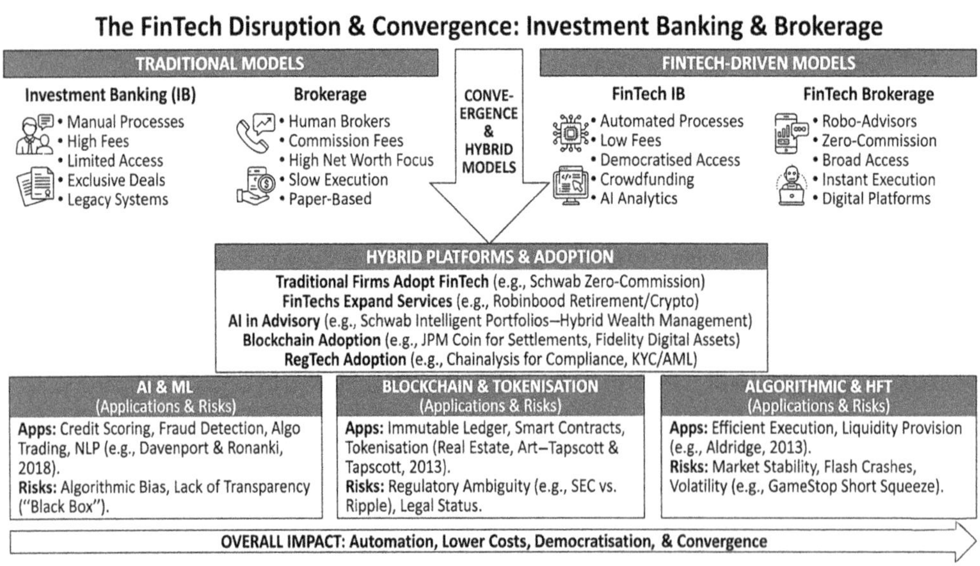

Figure 9.1 FinTech Innovation in Investment Banking and Brokerage.

9.3.2 Brokerage Firms and FinTech-Enabled Transformation

Brokerage firms have undergone a similar transformation, with FinTech disrupting the traditional trade execution and advisory model. Full-service brokerages, such as Merrill Lynch and Morgan Stanley, now combine AI-driven robo-advisory platforms with human expertise, enabling hybrid wealth management solutions that were not feasible under traditional models. Blockchain-enabled custody and digital asset platforms are also expanding the investment options available to high-net-worth clients, creating new avenues for asset management beyond conventional securities.

Discounts and online brokerages have seen the most dramatic disruption. Platforms like Charles Schwab, Robinhood, and eToro leverage mobile-first interfaces, commission-free trading, fractional investing, and gamified experiences to democratise market access. Algorithmic trading, AI-driven analytics, and predictive recommendation engines enable retail investors to make more informed decisions and execute trades with speed and precision that traditional brokerage models cannot.

Institutional brokerages have adopted high-frequency trading (HFT) and algorithmic execution to enhance liquidity and improve pricing efficiency. At the same time, AI and blockchain tools support compliance monitoring, risk management, and transaction transparency. These innovations challenge the traditional brokerage model by blending execution, analytics, and advisory into a technology-driven, scalable infrastructure.

9.3.3 Implications of FinTech Disruption

The integration of FinTech across investment banking and brokerage has given rise to hybrid models that blur traditional distinctions between advisory, trading, and market access services. This transformation has generated multiple strategic effects: operational efficiency has improved through automation, AI, and algorithmic trading, which accelerate deal execution, optimise workflows, and reduce costs; market access has expanded as tokenisation and digital platforms enable both retail and institutional clients to engage with previously illiquid or complex assets; strategic innovation has emerged from hybrid models that combine human expertise with AI analytics, facilitating personalised advisory services and data-driven decision-making; and risk and compliance considerations have become more complex, as blockchain, AI, and RegTech introduce new regulatory, cybersecurity, and ethical challenges, including algorithmic bias and system vulnerabilities. Overall, FinTech is not merely an efficiency-enhancing tool but a transformative force, reshaping the strategic operations of investment banks and brokerage firms to create more agile, client-centric, and technology-enabled business models than traditional approaches previously allowed (Arner et al., 2017; Tapscott & Tapscott, 2016; Davenport & Ronanki, 2018).

Table 9.2 shows the distinction between traditional and fintech-driven brokerage models.

9.4 Risks and Challenges in the Digital Era

The adoption of FinTech in investment banking and brokerage has introduced significant risks alongside operational efficiencies. Cybersecurity threats represent a primary concern, as malicious actors increasingly target digital platforms. Data breaches, phishing attacks, and exchange hacks can lead to substantial financial and reputational losses; for instance, approximately $3 billion was reported stolen from cryptocurrency platforms in 2022, highlighting vulnerabilities in digital asset management and transaction infrastructure

Table 9.2 The Distinction Between Traditional and Fintech-Driven Models

Feature	*Traditional Model*	*FinTech-Driven Model*
Deal Origination/Client Onboarding	Relationship-driven, manual, slow	AI-powered matchmaking, instant digital onboarding
Capital Raising	IPO-heavy, slow (6–12 months), high fees	Security Token Offerings (STOs), crowdfunding, faster, lower cost
Trading and Execution	Manual order routing, OTC markets	Algorithmic and HFT, dark pools
Advisory and Research	Human-intensive, premium for HNWIs	Robo-advisors, AI-powered analytics, accessible to retail
Cost Structure	High fees (e.g., 5–7% on IPOs)	Zero-commission trading and lower advisory fees
Investor Access	Restricted to institutional and HNW clients	Democratised via fractional shares and digital platforms
Settlement and Custody	T+2 settlement, centralised custody	Instant settlement via Distributed Ledger Technology, self-custody options (e.g., DeFi wallets)

(Chainalysis, 2023). To mitigate these threats, firms are deploying AI-driven fraud detection systems, biometric authentication, and advanced encryption protocols.

Regulatory and compliance risks have also intensified, as technological innovation frequently outpaces the development of legal frameworks. Investment banks and brokerages must navigate evolving regulations concerning data privacy (e.g., GDPR, MiFID II), cryptocurrency, and algorithmic trading. Non-compliance can result in significant fines, legal liability, and reputational damage (Arner et al., 2017).

Operational and platform dependence is another challenge, as financial institutions increasingly rely on complex technology stacks. System outages, software bugs, and AI model errors can disrupt trading, settlement, and advisory functions, potentially causing financial loss and reputational harm. Similarly, market conduct and ethical considerations have emerged as pressing concerns. The gamification of retail trading platforms can encourage impulsive investing, while AI-driven advisory services raise issues of accountability, transparency, and algorithmic bias (Davenport & Ronanki, 2018).

9.5 The Future Trajectory of FinTech in Capital Markets

The convergence of FinTech with investment banking and brokerage is expected to accelerate, driven by emerging technologies and evolving client demands. Hyper-personalisation will allow AI to deliver fully customised investment strategies and dynamically optimise portfolios for both retail and institutional clients, leveraging granular behavioural and financial data to tailor recommendations in real time (PwC, 2023).

DeFi presents the potential to further disintermediate traditional intermediaries by enabling peer-to-peer capital raising, trading, and settlement through blockchain protocols. While promising, DeFi adoption remains constrained by regulatory uncertainty and security considerations (World Economic Forum, 2023).

AI-powered capital markets will increasingly inform IPO pricing, risk assessment, and investment allocation. Advanced machine learning models can process large-scale market and sentiment data to generate real-time valuations and predictive insights. In contrast, experimental applications such as virtual or Metaverse capital markets may emerge, creating new platforms for digital asset trading (PwC, 2023).

Finally, though in its early stages, quantum computing has the potential to revolutionise financial modelling, portfolio optimisation, and risk analysis by performing computations beyond the capacity of classical systems. However, it simultaneously poses systemic risks, as quantum capabilities could compromise current cryptographic standards and financial security protocols (Arute et al., 2019).

9.6 Conclusion

The investment banking and brokerage landscape is experiencing a profound and enduring transformation, driven by the emergence of FinTech as a central operational driver rather than a peripheral innovation. This paradigm shift represents a decisive departure from legacy systems, compelling established institutions to reconceptualise value creation and delivery within an increasingly complex financial ecosystem. Digital proficiency is becoming a core competency, as the industry moves from traditional, relationship-based models towards automated, data-driven frameworks. In this environment, platform accessibility, algorithmic efficiency, and data integrity have emerged as critical determinants of competitive advantage, supplanting manual processes in capital markets, trading, and advisory functions. Consequently, the historical boundaries separating investment banks, brokerages, and technology providers are becoming increasingly fluid, fostering a more integrated and dynamic ecosystem in which technical expertise and scalable infrastructure serve as primary differentiators.

Future leadership in investment banking and brokerage will depend on the capacity to develop smarter, faster, and more secure financial solutions underpinned by advanced technologies such as AI, blockchain, and cloud computing. At the same time, the acceleration of innovation heightens the importance of robust governance and risk management frameworks. Firms must ensure regulatory compliance, protect against cyber threats, and uphold ethical standards in data usage. As highlighted by industry analysts, the principal challenge lies in innovating at speed while maintaining fiduciary trust, emphasising the need to balance technological agility with stringent regulatory and ethical oversight. This balance will be critical in sustaining the resilience, credibility, and long-term competitiveness of financial institutions.

Key Terms and Glossary

Capital Raising The process by which a company raises funds from external sources to finance its activities, such as through an IPO.

Algorithmic Trading The use of computer algorithms to automatically make trading decisions, submit orders, and manage those orders after submission.

Robo-Advisors Digital platforms that provide automated, algorithm-driven financial planning services with minimal human supervision.

STOs (Security Token Offering) A type of public offering in which tokenised digital securities, known as security tokens, are sold in cryptocurrency exchanges.

Dark Pools Private financial forums or exchanges for trading securities not accessible by the investing public.

Test Your Understanding

Multiple-Choice Questions

1 Which of the following best describes the primary distinction between investment banks and brokerage firms?

A Investment banks focus on trade execution, while brokerages underwrite securities.
B Investment banks provide strategic advisory and capital raising, while brokerages facilitate market access and trade execution.
C Investment banks only serve retail clients, while brokerages serve institutional clients.
D Investment banks and brokerages provide identical services, but brokerages use digital platforms.

2 Which FinTech innovation is primarily used by investment banks to enable real-time settlements and improve transaction efficiency?

A Robo-advisors
B Blockchain (e.g., JPM Coin)
C HFT
D Crowdfunding platforms

3 Which type of brokerage is characterised by low-cost trade execution with limited advisory services for self-directed investors?

A Full-service brokerage
B Institutional brokerage
C Discount brokerage
D Boutique brokerage

4 One major risk associated with FinTech adoption in investment banking and brokerage is:

A Reduced market access for retail investors
B Lower efficiency in trading operations
C Cybersecurity threats and operational platform dependence
D Overreliance on manual advisory services

5 Hyper-personalisation in capital markets refers to:

A Standardised portfolio recommendations for institutional investors
B AI-driven customised investment strategies tailored to individual client profiles
C Faster trade execution using algorithmic trading
D DeFi platforms for peer-to-peer trading

Short Questions

1 Explain how FinTech is blurring the traditional boundaries between investment banks and brokerage firms.
2 Identify and briefly describe two major regulatory or ethical challenges arising from the adoption of AI and blockchain in financial services.
3 Describe one example of how FinTech has enhanced market accessibility for retail investors.

Analytical Questions

1 Compare and contrast the operational efficiency and client accessibility of traditional investment banking and FinTech-enabled models. Discuss the implications for competitive advantage.
2 Evaluate the potential risks and benefits of adopting DeFi protocols for capital raising within investment banks. Consider both regulatory and technological perspectives.
3 Suppose a mid-sized investment bank adopts AI-powered predictive analytics for M&A advisory. Analyse how this might impact deal origination, client relationships, and internal decision-making compared to a traditional approach.

Case Study: The GameStop Saga and the Role of Robinhood

In January 2021, GameStop, a struggling video game retailer, became the focus of an unprecedented market event when a coordinated group of retail investors on the Reddit forum r/WallStreetBets drove its share price to extraordinary levels. The resulting short squeeze inflicted substantial losses on hedge funds that had bet against the stock. Central to the episode was Robinhood, a digital-first brokerage known for its gamified, mobile-centric interface and zero-commission trading model, which had facilitated rapid access for a large number of retail investors. At the height of the frenzy, Robinhood temporarily restricted the purchase of GameStop and other highly shorted stocks, citing liquidity and regulatory requirements. This action sparked widespread criticism, accusations of market manipulation, and prompted a congressional inquiry into the company's business practices, particularly its reliance on payment-for-order-flow to generate revenue. The episode highlighted how FinTech platforms can amplify retail investor influence while also exposing vulnerabilities in operational risk, platform design, and the alignment of financial incentives with client interests. It also underscored the shifting power dynamics in modern capital markets, where coordinated retail investors, enabled by technology, can challenge institutional positions and disrupt traditional trading norms (U.S. House Committee on Financial Services, 2021).

References

Cato Institute, 2021. The GameStop episode: What Happened and What Does it Mean? *Cato Journal*, 41(3). Available at: https://www.cato.org/cato-journal/fall-2021/gamestop-episode-what-happened-what-does-it-mean (Accessed: 1 March 2026).

U.S. House Committee on Financial Services (2021). GameStop Stock Manipulation: Hearing Before the Committee on Financial Services, U.S. House of Representatives. *117th Congress*. Washington, DC: U.S. Government Publishing Office.

Case Study Questions

1 How did Robinhood's zero-commission, mobile-first platform and gamified features contribute to the rapid participation of retail investors in the GameStop short squeeze?
2 What ethical and operational issues does the event highlight, particularly regarding Robinhood's payment-for-order-flow model and its responsibilities to clients?
3 What does this case illustrate about the changing power dynamics in capital markets when technology empowers retail investors to influence market outcomes collectively?

Further Reading

Arner, D.W., Barberis, J.N., & Buckley, R.P. (2017). FinTech and Regtech in a Nutshell, and the Future in a Sandbox. *Research Foundation Briefs*, 3(4), 1–20.

Tapscott, D., & Tapscott, A. (2016). *Blockchain Revolution: How the Technology Behind Bitcoin Is Changing Money, Business, and the World.* New York: Portfolio.

World Economic Forum. (2023). *The Future of Capital Markets: Opportunities and Risks of Decentralised Finance.* Geneva: World Economic Forum.

References

Arner, D. W., Barberis, J., & Buckley, R. P. (2017). FinTech and RegTech in a Nutshell, and the Future in a Sandbox. *Journal of Financial Perspectives*, 3(3), 1–20.

Arute, F. et al. (2019) 'Quantum supremacy using a programmable superconducting processor', *Nature*, 574(7779), 505–510.

Bodie, Z., Kane, A., & Marcus, A. J. (2021). *Investments* (12th ed.). New York: McGraw-Hill Education.

Chainalysis (2023) *The 2023 Crypto Crime Report*. New York: Chainalysis.

Davenport, T. H., & Ronanki, R. (2018). Artificial Intelligence for the Real World. *Harvard Business Review*, 96(1), 108–116.

PwC (2023) *Asset and Wealth Management Revolution 2023: The Power to Shape the Future*. London: PwC

Tapscott, D., & Tapscott, A. (2016). *Blockchain Revolution: How the Technology Behind Bitcoin Is Changing Money, Business, and the World.* New York: Penguin.

World Economic Forum. (2023). *The Future of Global Financial Services*. WEF Reports.

Zheng, X., Wang, W., & Wang, H. (2020). The Rise of Social Trading Platforms: A New Paradigm for Investment? *Journal of Behavioural and Experimental Finance*, 28, 100400.

10 Insurance and Financial Technology (InsurTech)

Chapter Overview

This chapter explores insurance technology (InsurTech) as the convergence of insurance and financial technology, positioning insurance as a core mechanism of financial intermediation that facilitates risk pooling, capital formation, and loss compensation, thereby underpinning broader economic stability (Rejda & McNamara, 2017). It examines how advanced technologies, including artificial intelligence (AI), blockchain, the Internet of Things (IoT), and digital platform ecosystems, are reshaping insurance value chains across distribution, underwriting, pricing, claims management, and customer engagement. A comparative analysis is presented between traditional insurance operating models and technology-enabled approaches, emphasising shifts in data utilisation, operational efficiency, and customer-centric design. The chapter further addresses emerging challenges associated with digital transformation, including cybersecurity vulnerabilities, evolving regulatory and compliance requirements, and issues of digital exclusion. It concludes by evaluating prospective industry trajectories, including the rise of parametric insurance products, the integration of embedded insurance within non-insurance platforms, and the development of AI-driven insurers characterised by automation, real-time analytics, and highly personalised risk assessment.

Learning Objectives

By the end of this chapter, you should be able to:

1. Analyse the economic functions of insurance institutions and their role in financial intermediation, risk transfer, and economic stability.
2. Examine how InsurTech innovations are transforming core insurance operations, including underwriting, pricing, distribution, and claims management.
3. Evaluate the application of key financial technologies in insurance, such as AI, automation, and IoT-enabled data collection.
4. Compare traditional insurance models with technology-enabled alternatives in terms of efficiency, accessibility, personalisation, and consumer trust.
5. Assess emerging risks, regulatory considerations, and future industry developments, including parametric insurance, embedded coverage, and AI-driven business models.

DOI: 10.4324/9781003775751-12

10.1 Introduction

Insurance is a foundational component of the global financial system, providing a formal mechanism for individuals and firms to manage exposure to risk and uncertainty. Its central function is to pool policyholder contributions to compensate for insured losses, thereby facilitating risk transfer, enhancing financial security, and supporting macroeconomic stability (Rejda & McNamara, 2017). This institutional framework of collective risk sharing has historically played a critical role in promoting economic resilience, investment continuity, and long-term growth.

In the contemporary period, the insurance industry is undergoing a structural transformation driven by advances in financial technology, particularly in InsurTech. InsurTech refers to the application of digital technologies, such as AI, blockchain, and the IoT, to insurance processes and business models. These technologies improve data acquisition and analytics, refine underwriting precision, accelerate claims settlement, and enhance customer interaction, thereby increasing operational efficiency and expanding the scope of risk management capabilities (Eling & Lehmann, 2018).

This chapter provides an integrated analysis of the modern insurance landscape by examining both the foundational principles of insurance and the technological innovations reshaping the sector. Through this dual perspective, it highlights how digital transformation is redefining risk assessment, product design and distribution, and customer engagement, offering a comprehensive understanding of the evolving role of insurance within the broader financial ecosystem.

10.2 The Role and Functions of Insurance

10.2.1 Definition and Purpose of Insurance

Insurance is a formal financial arrangement in which an insurer agrees to compensate an individual or organisation for specified losses in exchange for a premium. At its core, insurance facilitates risk transfer from policyholders to a risk-bearing institution that manages uncertainty through actuarial assessment and exposure diversification (Rejda & McNamara, 2017). By pooling contributions from many policyholders, insurers can spread risk and make financial protection affordable and predictable. This mechanism enables households and firms to undertake productive activities, such as home ownership, business investment, or infrastructure development, that might otherwise be considered excessively risky.

10.2.2 Functions of Insurance

Risk Pooling: Insurers aggregate premiums from a large number of policyholders to cover the losses of the relatively small proportion who experience insured events. This diversification reduces individual financial volatility and enables households and firms to undertake productive but uncertain activities (Cummins & Weiss, 2020). For instance, thousands of homeowners pay annual premiums, allowing the insurer to compensate the few whose properties suffer fire damage in a given year.

Capital Accumulation and Investment: Insurance companies collect premiums in advance of claims and invest these funds in financial markets, government securities, and long-term projects. This process ensures liquidity for future claims while also contributing to capital formation and economic development (Dorfman & Cather, 2021). For instance, life insurers invest premium income in infrastructure bonds that finance transportation or energy projects.

Loss Compensation: A central function of insurance is indemnification, restoring policyholders to their approximate financial position prior to a covered loss. Timely compensation supports consumption stability and business continuity (Rejda & McNamara, 2017). For instance, a health insurer reimbursing hospital expenses following a policyholder's surgery.

Promotion of Economic Stability: Insurance acts as a financial shock absorber by providing resources for recovery after adverse events. This reduces the long-term economic disruption caused by accidents, natural disasters, or health crises and encourages entrepreneurial risk-taking (Swiss Re Institute, 2022). For instance, business interruption insurance enables a firm to continue paying employees and fixed costs after flood damage.

Support for Credit, Savings, and Investment: Insurance underpins lending and investment by protecting assets used as collateral and by offering savings-oriented products, particularly in life and pension insurance. These mechanisms strengthen financial systems and support sustained economic growth (Dorfman & Cather, 2021). For instance, mortgage lenders require property insurance to safeguard the value of homes used as loan collateral.

10.2.3 Types of Insurance and Their Services

Life Insurance Companies: Life insurers protect against the financial consequences of death and, in many cases, longevity risk. Their products often combine risk coverage with long-term savings or investment elements, supporting household financial planning and retirement security (Dorfman & Cather, 2021). Benefits may be paid as lump sums or structured income streams to beneficiaries. For instance, a 20-year term life insurance policy that pays a fixed amount to the policyholder's family if the insured dies within the coverage period, helping replace lost income and cover living expenses.

General Insurance (Property and Casualty (P&C)) Providers: General insurers, also known as P&C insurers, cover non-life risks, including property damage and legal liability. Their services protect individuals and businesses against financial losses arising from accidents, theft, fire, natural disasters, and third-party claims for injury or property damage. These policies are typically short-term and renewable annually. For Instance, homeowners' insurance that compensates for repair or rebuilding costs after fire or storm damage, and motor insurance that covers both vehicle damage and third-party liability.

Health Insurance Companies: Health insurers specialise in financing healthcare expenditures by covering medical and surgical costs incurred by policyholders. Coverage may include hospitalisation, physician consultations, prescription drugs, maternity care, and preventive services. By spreading healthcare costs across a risk pool, health insurance reduces financial barriers to treatment and protects households from catastrophic medical expenses. For instance, a comprehensive health plan that covers hospital stays, diagnostic tests, and specialist visits following a serious illness.

Reinsurance Companies: Reinsurers ensure insurance companies by assuming portions of their risk portfolios through contractual arrangements such as treaty or facultative reinsurance. This risk-sharing mechanism increases the underwriting capacity of primary insurers, protects them against severe or unexpected losses, and contributes to overall market stability (Cummins & Weiss, 2020). For instance, catastrophe reinsurance that reimburses a primary insurer when total claims from a major earthquake exceed a predefined threshold.

10.2.4 Economic Significance of Insurance

Insurance holds substantial macroeconomic significance beyond its immediate role in individual risk protection. By pooling risks across large populations, insurers reduce income and wealth volatility for households and firms, thereby enabling greater participation in economic activity and long-term planning (Cummins & Weiss, 2020). At the same time, insurance companies function as major institutional investors, channelling accumulated premiums into financial markets, government securities, and infrastructure projects, which support capital formation and sustained economic development (Dorfman & Cather, 2021). By providing loss compensation, insurers restore policyholders' financial positions after adverse events, ensuring the continuity of consumption and business operations (Rejda & McNamara, 2017). More broadly, insurance systems enhance economic stability by acting as financial shock absorbers: they strengthen credit markets by protecting collateral, encourage entrepreneurship by mitigating downside risk, and facilitate post-disaster recovery through timely claims payments. For example, catastrophe insurance payouts following natural disasters provide critical liquidity, enabling affected communities and businesses to rebuild more rapidly and reducing prolonged economic disruption (Swiss Re Institute, 2022). Collectively, these functions underscore insurance's role as a central pillar of financial intermediation and economic resilience.

10.3 A Comparison of Traditional and FinTech Insurance

Table 10.1 delineates the principal similarities and differences between traditional insurance models and those facilitated by FinTech. It highlights concrete distinctions in cost, accessibility, customisation, and trust, providing a clear basis for understanding the divergence and convergence of these approaches across key aspects of insurance provision.

Table 10.1 compares traditional insurance and FinTech insurance.

Table 10.1 A Comparison Between Traditional Insurance and FinTech Insurance

Characteristics	*Traditional Insurance*	*FinTech Insurance*
Business Model	Agent/broker-dependent	Direct-to-Consumer (D2C) Digital Platforms
Underwriting	Manual, actuarial table-based	AI-driven, dynamic pricing models
Policy Purchase	Weeks (medical checks, paperwork)	Minutes (instant digital approval)
Claims Processing	30–90 days (manual review)	<24 hours (AI/blockchain automation)
Customer Interaction	Call Centres, Physical Offices	Chatbots, Mobile Apps, Self-Service Platforms
Data Usage	Limited historical data	IoT/Telematics real-time data
Product Types	Standardised packages	Micro-insurance, on-demand, parametric coverage
Pricing	Fixed premiums	Usage-based (e.g., pay-per-mile, pay-per-trip)
Innovation Cycle	3–5 years for new products	Quarterly feature and product updates
Fraud Detection	Post-claim investigations	Predictive AI models, real-time monitoring
Global Reach	Limited by local licensing and regulations	Digital-first, cross-border potential with regulatory tech
Examples	Allstate, AXA, Prudential	Lemonade, Oscar Health, ZhongAn, Root Insurance

10.4 Key FinTech Innovations in Insurance (InsurTech)

Digital Onboarding and Distribution: Mobile applications, web-based interfaces, and digital marketplaces enable rapid policy issuance without reliance on traditional agents or brokers (Figure 10.1). AI chatbots and robo-advisory tools improve customer engagement and responsiveness to service (McKinsey & Company, 2023). Applications include instant online term life policies, app-based motor and travel insurance sales, digital health enrolment integrated with telemedicine, and electronic treaty placement platforms in reinsurance.

AI-Powered Underwriting and Dynamic Pricing: Machine learning models analyse large, heterogeneous datasets to refine risk assessments and improve premium accuracy (Nguyen et al., 2021). Telematics facilitate usage-based motor insurance; wearable devices inform wellness-linked health pricing; predictive analytics enhance mortality modelling in life insurance; and AI-driven catastrophe models strengthen reinsurance portfolio management.

Claims Automation: AI, image recognition, and robotic process automation reduce settlement times, operational costs, and fraud exposure (Chen et al., 2020). Property and motor claims are assessed through digital image analysis, medical claims are automatically verified, life benefits are processed via digital documentation, and reinsurers deploy automated loss-reporting systems following catastrophic events.

IoT Integration: Real-time data from connected devices supports preventive and behaviour-based insurance models (Bhattacharya et al., 2019). Telematics reward safe driving, smart home sensors mitigate property risk, wearable devices support health monitoring, and satellite data assist reinsurers in tracking catastrophe exposure.

Parametric Insurance: Predefined payouts are triggered by objective indices rather than assessed losses, enabling rapid and transparent compensation (Cummins & Weiss, 2020). Examples include rainfall-index crop insurance, flight-delay travel cover, fixed-diagnosis health benefits, and catastrophe-index reinsurance agreements.

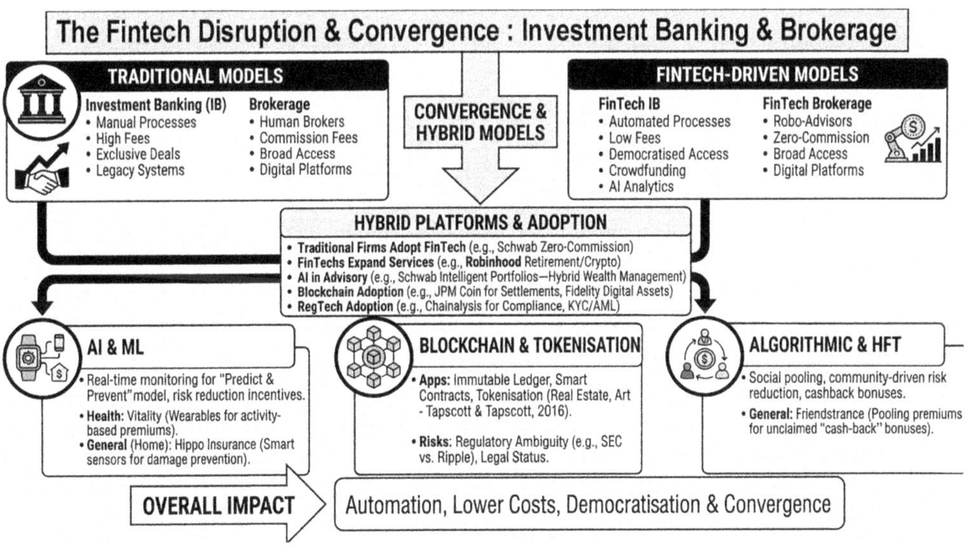

Figure 10.1 InsurTech: FinTech Innovations Transforming Insurance.

On-Demand Insurance: Short-term, usage-based policies are activated through digital platforms to align coverage with temporary risk exposure (Gatteschi et al., 2018). Applications include gadgets, vehicles, and travel protection designed for time-specific use.

Peer-to-Peer (P2P) Insurance: Digital platforms facilitate member-based risk pools that enhance transparency and reduce fraud by aligning incentives (Schwarcz & Schwarcz, 2021). Examples include community property schemes, digital health cost-sharing arrangements, mutual-style life protection, and reinsurance structures safeguarding pooled risks against aggregate losses.

10.5 Risks and Challenges of FinTech in Insurance

The integration of FinTech into the insurance sector presents substantial benefits but also introduces significant risks and operational challenges. Regulatory uncertainty is a primary concern, as many InsurTech models operate in areas where existing legal frameworks are unclear or evolving. This can create compliance risks and inhibit investment, prompting regulators to adopt adaptive mechanisms such as regulatory sandboxes to test innovations safely (Zetzsche et al., 2020). Cybersecurity threats are amplified by increased digitalisation and extensive data collection, exposing insurers to potential breaches that can result in financial loss and erosion of consumer trust (Financial Stability Board, 2021). Closely linked are data privacy concerns, particularly regarding the use of sensitive health, behavioural, and financial information. Insurers must comply with stringent regulations, including the General Data Protection Regulation, while maintaining ethical data practices to protect customer confidence (Romanova et al., 2020).

Operationally, integrating FinTech solutions with legacy systems remains challenging. Incumbent insurers often rely on outdated Information Technology (IT) infrastructure, making the adoption of agile, Application Programming Interface (API)–driven technologies complex, costly, and prone to technical issues (McKinsey & Company, 2022). Additionally, the digital divide can exclude vulnerable populations, such as older people or those without digital skills, potentially exacerbating inequities in insurance access. Consumer trust is also critical, as hyper-personalised, AI-driven offerings must balance privacy, transparency, and algorithmic fairness to maintain credibility (EY, 2020).

10.6 Key Practical Issues of InsurTech

The practical deployment of InsurTech raises several operational concerns. Data standardisation and interoperability are essential, as InsurTech depends on heterogeneous data sources, including IoT devices, wearables, and third-party APIs. Yet inconsistent formats and limited integration can reduce the effectiveness of data-driven insights. Technical debt and scalability pose additional challenges; early-stage InsurTech platforms often rely on fragile Minimum Viable Product architectures that may compromise system stability and hinder future development as the business scales.

Claims fraud in digital channels is another emerging issue. While AI enhances fraud detection, automated onboarding and claims processing also enable sophisticated fraudulent activities, such as manipulated images or synthetic identities. Insurers must continuously update algorithms to mitigate these risks. The talent gap is a persistent challenge, as skilled professionals with combined expertise in insurance, AI, blockchain, and data analytics are in high demand and short supply.

Effective customer education and onboarding are critical, particularly for complex products like parametric insurance or for clients unfamiliar with digital platforms. Similarly, legacy system integration debt requires substantial investment to modernise IT infrastructure without disrupting ongoing operations. Insurers must also devote resources to regulatory compliance and sandbox navigation, ensuring adherence to disparate international rules while testing innovative products. Finally, data privacy and ethical AI governance are essential, encompassing transparent data usage, bias detection in algorithms, and responsible decision-making. Addressing the digital divide through hybrid service models and user-friendly interfaces remains a key operational priority.

10.7 Future Trends in FinTech Insurance

Looking forward, several trends are expected to shape the InsurTech landscape. Parametric insurance is likely to expand, particularly for climate-related risks and natural disasters, offering rapid, transparent payouts that enhance financial resilience for policyholders (Cummins & Weiss, 2020). Embedded insurance will become increasingly prevalent, integrating coverage directly into non-insurance platforms and transactions, such as electronics purchases or travel bookings, facilitated by API-driven connections (Deloitte, 2023). Finally, the rise of AI-first insurers, exemplified by companies such as ZhongAn in China, will accelerate. These fully digital, AI-native entities utilise machine learning and automation across underwriting, pricing, claims, and customer service, delivering greater efficiency, operational agility, and highly personalised insurance experiences (Lee & Teo, 2021).

10.8 Conclusion

In conclusion, InsurTech represents a transformative evolution of the insurance sector, shifting it from a predominantly reactive industry to an active facilitator of risk management. The adoption of predictive analytics, AI, and real-time data enables insurers to develop highly personalised, usage-based products that align coverage with the diverse and dynamic risk profiles of contemporary households and businesses. This technological integration extends beyond operational efficiency, redefining the insurer's role from a traditional financial indemnifier to a strategic contributor to economic resilience and stability. Consequently, the deliberate adoption of digital tools has become essential for insurers seeking to maintain relevance in an increasingly competitive, data-driven market.

The long-term sustainability of this evolving ecosystem depends on the careful management of associated risks. Effective InsurTech deployment requires a shift from reactive claims settlement towards proactive risk mitigation, supported by rigorous frameworks for data privacy, ethical AI governance, and regulatory compliance. Balancing innovation with consumer protection is critical to preserving trust and credibility. Insurers that demonstrate transparency in data management, operational agility, and adherence to ethical standards will be best positioned to maintain stakeholder confidence, enhance resilience, and ensure that insurance remains a vital pillar of global financial stability.

Key Terms and Glossary

Risk Pooling The fundamental principle of insurance, where premiums from many policyholders are collected to pay for the losses of a few.

Underwriting The process an insurer uses to evaluate the risk and exposures of potential clients and to determine the premium to be charged for insurance.

Usage-Based Insurance (UBI) A type of vehicle insurance that calculates premiums based primarily on the driving behaviour of the insured, often monitored via telematics.

Parametric Insurance A type of insurance that offers a pre-agreed payout upon the occurrence of a predefined event (e.g., an earthquake of a specific magnitude), rather than indemnifying actual losses.

AI-First Insurers Insurance companies built from the ground up with AI at the core of all operations, from underwriting to claims processing.

Test Your Understanding

Multiple-Choice Questions

1 Which of the following best describes the primary economic function of insurance?

A Generating profits through high-risk investments
B Pooling risk and providing financial protection to policyholders
C Offering only long-term savings and investment products
D Eliminating all types of financial uncertainty for households and firms

2 In FinTech-enabled insurance, which technology is most commonly used for dynamic pricing and risk assessment?

A Manual actuarial tables
B AI and machine learning
C Traditional customer surveys
D Fixed premium schedules

3 Which of the following is an example of parametric insurance?

A Home insurance that reimburses repair costs after a fire
B Health insurance covering hospital bills
C Crop insurance that pays out automatically if rainfall falls below a set threshold
D Auto insurance based on annual mileage

4 What is a primary challenge associated with InsurTech adoption?

A Reduction in data availability
B Limited technological applications
C Cybersecurity vulnerabilities and regulatory uncertainty
D Increased manual underwriting

5 Embedded insurance refers to:

A Insurance purchased only through traditional agents
B Coverage integrated directly into non-insurance products or platforms
C Life insurance with long-term savings components
D Reinsurance for catastrophic events

Short Questions

1 Explain how insurance contributes to macroeconomic stability.
2 Identify two ways in which IoT devices are used to enhance insurance services.
3 What distinguishes AI-first insurers from traditional insurance companies?

Analytical Questions

1 Compare and contrast traditional insurance underwriting with AI-driven underwriting in terms of efficiency, accuracy, and consumer impact.
2 Assess the potential risks and ethical considerations of using real-time consumer data for UBI pricing.
3 Evaluate the implications of embedded insurance for both consumers and traditional insurers, considering accessibility, competition, and regulatory challenges.

Case Study: Lemonade—Innovating Insurance Through Technology and Social Responsibility

Lemonade is a digital-first insurance company that offers renters' and homeowners' coverage using a disruptive business model based on P2P principles. Unlike traditional insurers, Lemonade separates its operational revenue from claims payments: it charges a flat fee to cover operating costs and pays claims from pooled policyholder premiums. Any leftover funds at the end of the year are donated to charities selected by policyholders, aligning the company's incentives with customers rather than denying claims. This model is designed to reduce the common conflict of interest in traditional insurance, where companies profit by minimising payouts.

Technology plays a central role in Lemonade's operations. AI and machine learning automate underwriting, policy issuance, and claims processing, enabling most claims to be approved instantly. Behavioural economics is embedded into the platform to encourage honesty and transparency from policyholders, further supporting trust. Digital interfaces and chatbots simplify the customer experience, reducing complexity compared to conventional insurance processes that often require extensive paperwork and agent interactions.

While innovative, Lemonade's reliance on AI and automated decision-making introduces potential operational and reputational risks, particularly if algorithms misjudge claims or fail to detect fraud. Additionally, scaling the P2P and social-good aspects may challenge profitability as the company faces investor pressure and a growing policyholder base.

References

Lemonade, Inc. (2020). Registration Statement on Form S-1 filed with the U.S. Securities and Exchange Commission, 8 June 2020. Available at: https://www.lemonade.com/investor/filings (Accessed: 1 March 2026).

Lemonade, Inc. (2025). Lemonade, Inc. Form 8-K Current Report filed with the U.S. Securities and Exchange Commission, 5 November 2025. Available at: https://www.lemonade.com/investor/filings (Accessed: 1 March 2026).

Case Study Questions

1 In what ways does Lemonade's business model and use of AI and digital platforms tackle the common consumer concerns of trust and complexity in traditional insurance?
2 What are the potential risks and limitations of Lemonade's heavy reliance on AI for underwriting, policy issuance, and instant claims processing? How might errors or system failures impact the company and its policyholders?
3 As Lemonade grows and faces investor pressure to generate profits, to what extent can its socially responsible, anti-conflict-of-interest branding be maintained? What challenges might arise in sustaining this model at scale?

Further Reading

Cummins, J.D., & Weiss, M.A. (2020). Risk-based Capital and Systemic Risk in the Global Insurance Industry. *Journal of Risk and Insurance*, 87(3), 561–608.
Deloitte. (2023). *The Future of Embedded Insurance*. New York: Deloitte.
Eling, M., & Lehmann, M. (2018). The Impact of Digitalisation on the Insurance Value Chain and the Insurability of Risks. *The Geneva Papers on Risk and Insurance – Issues and Practice*, 43(3), 359–396.
Zetzsche, D.A., Buckley, R.P., Arner, D.W., & Barberis, J.N. (2020). Regulating a Revolution: From Regulatory Sandboxes to Smart Regulation. *Fordham Journal of Corporate & Financial Law*, 23(1), 31–103.

References

Bhattacharya, S., Ranganathan, P., & Singh, S. (2019). Leveraging IoT for Usage-Based Insurance: A Study of Auto Telematics. *Journal of Risk and Insurance*, 86(4), 1021–1045.
Chen, Y., Wang, L., & Li, P. (2020). Blockchain in Insurance: Opportunities and Challenges. *Journal of Financial Transformation*, 51, 15–29.
Cummins, J. D., & Weiss, M. A. (2020). Convergence of Insurance and Financial Markets: Hybrid and Securitised Risk Transfer Solutions. *Journal of Risk and Insurance*, 87(1), 5–36.
Deloitte. (2023). *The Future of Embedded Insurance*. New York: Deloitte Centre for Financial Services.
Dorfman, M. S., & Cather, D. A. (2021). *Introduction to Risk Management and Insurance* (11th ed.). Boston, MA: Pearson.
Eling, M., & Lehmann, M. (2018). The Impact of Digitalisation on the Insurance Industry: A Review of the Literature. *Geneva Papers on Risk and Insurance - Issues and Practice*, 43(2), 269–307.
EY. (2020). *Global Insurance Outlook: Balancing Innovation and Trust*. London: Ernst & Young.
Financial Stability Board (FSB). (2021). *Cyber Resilience in Financial Institutions*. Basel, Switzerland: Financial Stability Board..
Gatteschi, V., Lamberti, F., Demartini, C., & Santamaria, V. (2018). Blockchain and Smart Contracts for Insurance: Is the Technology Mature Enough? *Future Internet*, 10(2), 20.
Lee, C., & Teo, E. G. (2021). The Rise of AI-First Insurers: The Case of ZhongAn. *Journal of Digital Banking*, 5(3), 234–247.
McKinsey & Company. (2022). *Insurance Technology: The $1 Trillion Opportunity*. New York: McKinsey & Company.
McKinsey & Company. (2023). *Global Insurance Report: Closing the Profitability Gap*. New York: McKinsey & Company.
Nguyen, T., Zhou, L., & Spiegler, V. (2021). Artificial Intelligence in Insurance Underwriting: A Review and Research Agenda. *British Actuarial Journal*, 26, E15.

Rejda, G. E., & McNamara, M. J. (2017). *Principles of Risk Management and Insurance* (13th ed.). Boston, MA, Pearson Education.

Romanova, I., Kudinska, M., & Lāce, N. (2020). Data Privacy and Protection in the Age of FinTech and InsurTech. *Journal of Financial Regulation and Compliance*, 28(3), 405–421.

Schwarcz, D., & Schwarcz, S. L. (2021). Peer-to-Peer Insurance and the Future of Risk Pooling. *University of Pennsylvania Law Review*, 169, 151–202.

Swiss Re Institute. (2022). *Digital Transformation in Insurance: Opportunities and Risks*. Sigma Report No. 4/2022.

Zetzsche, D.A., Buckley, R.P. and Arner, D.W. (2020) Regulating InsurTech: From Sandboxes to Smart Contracts. In J. Chen, D. Gozman, & J. Bruckner (Eds.), *The Cambridge Handbook of FinTech*. Cambridge: Cambridge University Press.

11 Central Banks, Monetary Policy, and Digital Currencies

Chapter Overview

This chapter explores how central banks are adapting to the challenges posed by Financial Technology (FinTech) within the context of their core mandates. Historically, central banks have focused on implementing monetary policy, issuing currency, and ensuring financial stability (Mishkin, 2018). However, the rapid evolution of digital technologies is reshaping these traditional functions. The expansion of digital payment systems, alternative lending platforms, automated financial advisory services, and decentralised technologies has necessitated a reassessment of central bank strategies and supervisory frameworks. In response, central banks are examining the implementation of Central Bank Digital Currencies (CBDCs), adopting regulatory technology (RegTech), and upgrading payment infrastructures to preserve operational effectiveness and institutional relevance (BIS, 2020). The chapter further evaluates the incorporation of emerging technologies, including blockchain and artificial intelligence (AI), highlighting their potential to enable data-driven policy formulation while simultaneously presenting regulatory and economic challenges (Carstens, 2021).

Learning Objectives

By the end of this chapter, you should be able to:

1. Explain the evolving role of central banks in the context of FinTech innovations.
2. Describe the core functions of central banks and how they are affected by digital technologies.
3. Analyse the design, types, benefits, and risks of CBDCs.
4. Assess the implications of blockchain, AI, and machine learning (ML) on monetary policy, payment systems, and financial stability.
5. Critically evaluate the Policy Trilemma of Digital Currency and its impact on central bank decision-making.

DOI: 10.4324/9781003775751-13

11.1 Introduction

Central banks play a pivotal role in the global financial system, with primary responsibilities including maintaining macroeconomic stability through money supply management, setting interest rates, and controlling inflation. Recent advancements in FinTech are fundamentally challenging traditional approaches to these mandates. As Prasad (2021) notes, innovations such as faster payment systems, alternative lending platforms, and digital assets are compelling monetary authorities to reconsider their operational strategies. This shift also necessitates a reassessment of the regulatory frameworks governing financial markets.

FinTech developments have a direct impact on the transmission mechanisms of monetary policy. Whereas conventional policy tools primarily operate through commercial banking channels, the growing significance of non-bank financial intermediaries and decentralised technologies introduces new complexities. This transformation may constrain central banks' ability to manage liquidity effectively and to influence credit conditions. Accordingly, central banks are required to adapt their supervisory frameworks to efficiently regulate digital asset markets and alternative payment systems. Such interventions are critical to preserving financial stability, ensuring market integrity, and maintaining the centrality of sovereign currency in commercial transactions.

In response to these challenges, central banks are investigating the potential issuance of CBDCs. CBDCs represent a strategic modernisation of central bank money, providing a secure, risk-free public payment option in a digital economy. Additionally, central banks are assessing the adoption of technologies such as blockchain and distributed ledger platforms to enhance the efficiency and resilience of wholesale interbank settlement systems. Through these technological innovations, central authorities seek to uphold operational effectiveness while retaining regulatory oversight within an increasingly digital financial landscape.

11.2 Functions of Central Banks and Their Role in the Financial System and Economy

Central banks are pivotal institutions within national and global financial systems, tasked with managing a country's monetary framework and ensuring economic stability. Unlike profit-oriented commercial banks, central banks are typically government-owned or operate with substantial independence, with mandates that prioritise macroeconomic stability, inflation control, and the regulation of financial markets. Prominent examples include the Federal Reserve System (United States), the European Central Bank (ECB), and the Bank of England (BoE).

11.2.1 Definition and Conceptual Understanding

A central bank is a public, often independent, institution responsible for regulating a nation's money supply, managing credit availability and cost, and overseeing the foreign exchange (FX) value of its currency (Mishkin, 2018). Its regulatory interventions may be nonselective or designed to influence credit allocation across competing sectors. The primary objectives of a modern central bank include maintaining monetary and credit conditions conducive to high levels of employment and production, achieving price stability, and ensuring sufficient international reserves to support external trade and financial obligations.

11.2.2 Core Functions of Central Banks

Central banks perform a range of interrelated functions aimed at preserving financial stability and supporting sustainable economic growth (Figure 11.1).

Monetary Policy Implementation: Central banks formulate and execute monetary policy by regulating the money supply, interest rates, and credit conditions to achieve macroeconomic objectives such as price stability, full employment, and sustainable growth. Tools employed include open market operations, reserve requirements, and benchmark interest rate adjustments (Mishkin, 2018). For example, the Federal Reserve uses the federal funds rate to influence borrowing costs and liquidity in the US economy.

Currency Issuance and Management: Central banks have exclusive authority to issue legal tender, including banknotes and coins, while ensuring adequate circulation and maintaining public confidence in the currency. They also manage currency reserves to stabilise domestic and FX markets. The BoE's issuance of banknotes is an example of this function in practice.

Banker to Banks and Government: Central banks provide essential services to commercial banks, such as account management, payment processing, and liquidity support as a lender of last resort during financial stress. They also manage government accounts, conduct debt auctions, and facilitate public borrowing. For instance, the ECB manages euro-denominated accounts for European Union (EU) member states and intervenes in bond markets to maintain liquidity.

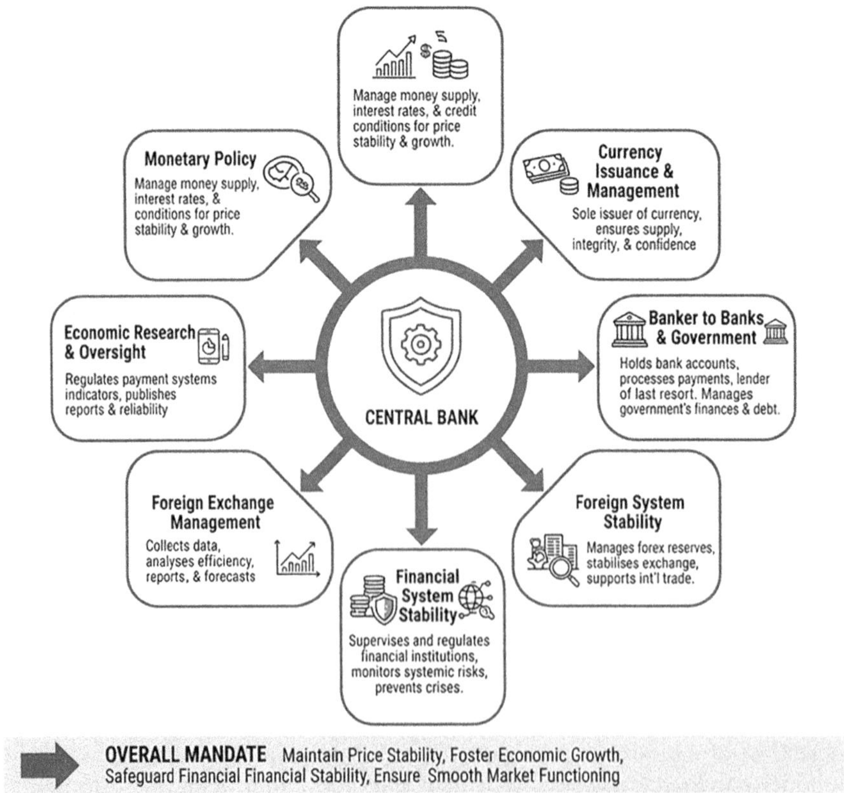

Figure 11.1 Core Functions of a Central Bank.

Financial System Stability: Central banks supervise and regulate financial institutions to prevent systemic risks and ensure solvency. They monitor vulnerabilities in the banking sector, conduct stress tests, and implement macroprudential policies to mitigate financial crises (Carstens, 2021). The 2008 global financial crisis highlighted the importance of central banks as stabilisers, with coordinated interventions by the Federal Reserve and the ECB preventing systemic collapse.

FX Management: Central banks maintain and regulate FX reserves to ensure exchange rate stability, support international trade, and intervene in currency markets as necessary. For example, the Bank of Japan has historically intervened to prevent excessive yen appreciation that could harm export competitiveness.

Payment System Oversight: Central banks regulate and supervise national payment infrastructures to ensure efficiency, security, and reliability. This includes setting standards for electronic payments and promoting interoperability. The Bank for International Settlements (BIS) (2020) notes that robust oversight of payment systems reduces transaction costs and strengthens trust in digital financial transactions.

Economic Research and Analysis: Central banks conduct extensive economic research and collect data to inform policy decisions. They provide forecasts, policy guidance, and analysis to financial markets, the public, and government policymakers, thereby supporting transparency and credibility. For instance, the ECB publishes its Economic Bulletin and Monetary Policy Accounts to communicate policy rationale and economic outlook.

Lender of Last Resort: Central banks provide emergency liquidity to solvent but temporarily illiquid financial institutions to prevent systemic failure. This function is essential for maintaining confidence in the banking system and ensuring uninterrupted credit flow during crises (Mishkin, 2018).

Inflation Management: By controlling interest rates and the money supply, central banks aim to maintain price stability, typically targeting an inflation rate of around 2%. Stable inflation preserves the currency's purchasing power and supports long-term economic growth.

11.2.3 Significance of Central Banks in the Financial System

The independence of central banks from political pressures is critical for effective monetary policy, allowing decisions to be based on economic data rather than short-term political considerations. Central banks underpin economic stability by managing inflation, supervising financial institutions, and supporting payment systems. Their evolving role reflects changes in the global financial environment, including the emergence of digital payment systems, non-bank financial intermediaries, and new financial instruments (BIS, 2020).

11.3 FinTech Innovation in Central Banking

The adoption of FinTech is reshaping central banks' operational landscape, affecting both traditional functions and strategic priorities. The rapid proliferation of digital payment systems, including mobile wallets, online platforms such as PayPal and Stripe, and real-time settlement systems, has necessitated a reassessment of regulatory frameworks and monetary oversight. Central banks now play an essential role in ensuring the security, efficiency, and stability of these emerging financial technologies while maintaining confidence in the broader monetary system (BIS, 2020). FinTech innovations have implications across

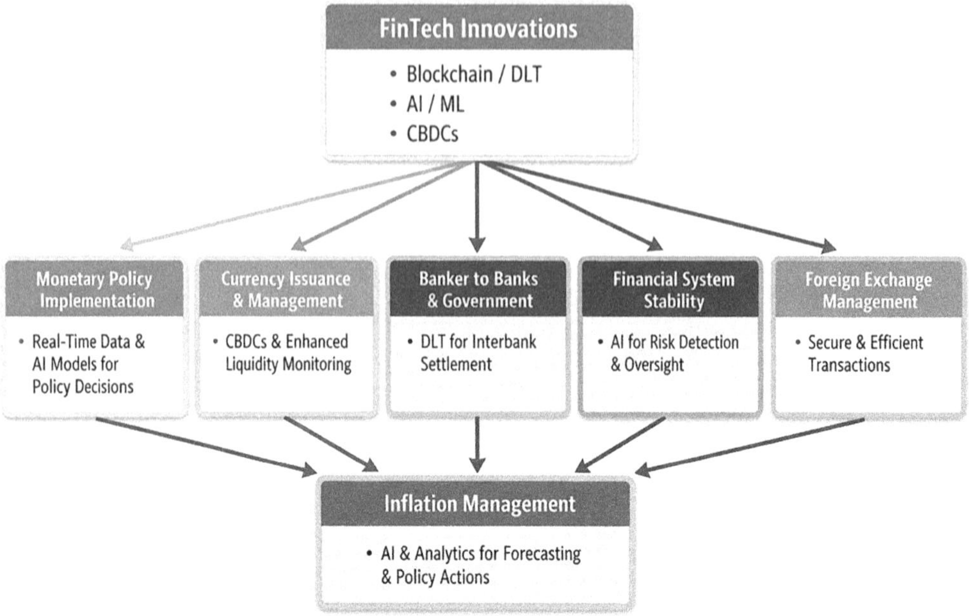

Figure 11.2 Implications of FinTech in Central Bank Functions.

the core functions of central banks, influencing monetary policy implementation, currency management, financial stability, and payment system oversight (Figure 11.2).

11.3.1 Blockchain and Distributed Ledger Technology (DLT)

Central banks are exploring blockchain and distributed ledger technologies to enhance transparency, security, and operational efficiency. DLT enables near real-time settlement, reduces reliance on intermediaries, and minimises operational risk in payment and settlement systems. For instance, the Bank of Canada's Project Jasper has demonstrated the feasibility of using DLT for interbank clearing and settlement, including cross-border transactions (Boar et al., 2020). Applications of DLT extend to the infrastructure of wholesale CBDCs, which can streamline monetary operations, support more accurate liquidity management, and improve monitoring of systemic risks. By integrating DLT, central banks enhance their capacity to maintain financial stability and reinforce the resilience of currency issuance and settlement systems.

11.3.2 AI and ML

AI and ML technologies are increasingly deployed to improve economic modelling, forecasting, and supervisory processes. These technologies enable central banks to detect anomalies in financial transactions, identify fraud, and automate regulatory compliance through supervisory technology (SupTech) applications (Carstens, 2021). AI-driven predictive models allow more precise estimation of inflation trends, gross domestic product growth, and credit conditions, thereby improving the effectiveness of monetary policy implementation. For example, the BoE has applied ML algorithms to enhance stress-testing models, providing more granular assessments of banking sector vulnerabilities and systemic risks. These innovations allow central banks to respond more quickly and accurately to emerging economic and financial conditions, reinforcing their role in financial system oversight and inflation management.

11.3.3 Central Bank Digital Currencies

CBDCs represent a transformative FinTech innovation with direct implications for core central bank functions. CBDCs are digital forms of sovereign currency issued by central banks, providing secure, risk-free public payment options. They facilitate faster, cheaper, and more inclusive payment mechanisms while enabling authorities to implement monetary policy more directly by influencing digital liquidity conditions (BIS, 2020). For example, the People's Bank of China's digital yuan initiative has enhanced transaction efficiency and broadened access to digital payments. CBDCs can also strengthen the central bank's ability to act as the government's banker, manage currency circulation, and oversee financial system stability, while improving FX operations by providing a secure, traceable form of digital money for cross-border settlements.

11.3.4 Implications of FinTech for Core Central Bank Functions

FinTech is fundamentally transforming central banking, influencing traditional functions while enhancing operational capabilities:

Monetary Policy Implementation: FinTech advances, particularly real-time digital payment data and AI-driven models, enhance central banks' ability to monitor liquidity conditions, credit flows, and spending patterns with higher frequency and granularity than traditional indicators. These capabilities support more timely policy adjustments, such as interest rate changes or changes to reserve requirements (Das et al., 2023).

Currency Issuance and Management: CBDCs act as digital legal tender that complements physical cash, offering secure, traceable, and efficient forms of central bank money. CBDC design features influence monetary operations and liquidity conditions, with research indicating that careful design can mitigate adverse effects on monetary forecasting and policy implementation (Kunaratskul, Reslow & Singh, 2024).

Banker to Banks and Government (Settlement Infrastructure): DLT and modern digital settlement infrastructures are being explored to improve interbank settlement and government account operations. Trials involving programmable ledgers demonstrate potential improvements in settlement speed and transparency while preserving central bank money as the settlement asset (Patel, Kasiyanto & Reslow, 2024).

Financial System Stability and Supervisory Oversight: AI and predictive analytics strengthen central banks' surveillance capacity by processing large datasets to detect emerging systemic vulnerabilities. These tools augment traditional prudential frameworks and can inform macroprudential interventions, although governance and model risk remain important considerations (Gross et al., 2025).

FX Management and Cross-Border Transactions: FinTech-enabled digital platforms and tokenised reserves can reduce settlement latency and increase transparency in cross-border transactions. Multiple CBDC experiments, such as multi-CBDC bridges, illustrate how distributed ledger platforms might support real-time, peer-to-peer settlement of payments and FX transactions (BIS, 2024).

Payment System Oversight: Innovations in APIs, programmable payments, and tokenisation improve the security, interoperability, and efficiency of payment systems. Central banks are adapting oversight frameworks to integrate such technologies while maintaining resilience against operational and cyber risks (Patel, Kasiyanto & Reslow, 2024).

Inflation Management: Advanced analytics that incorporate high-frequency digital payment indicators support more accurate and timely inflation forecasting, enabling central banks to make more proactive monetary policy decisions in pursuit of price stability (Das et al., 2023).

11.4 Central Bank Digital Currencies

The development of CBDCs represents a significant innovation at the intersection of central banking and FinTech. Shifts in payment behaviour drive this evolution, the emergence of private digital currencies, and rising public expectations for fast, secure, and convenient digital transactions. Consequently, central banks worldwide are evaluating the issuance of digital forms of sovereign currency to maintain monetary sovereignty and enhance the efficiency of payment systems (BIS, 2020).

11.4.1 Characteristics of CBDCs

A CBDC is a digital representation of a country's sovereign currency, issued and regulated directly by the central bank. Unlike decentralised cryptocurrencies, CBDCs are centralised, constitute a liability of the issuing authority, and combine the efficiency of digital payments with the stability of state-backed money (BIS, 2020). Table 11.1 summarises notable CBDC initiatives globally.

Table 11.1 Central Bank Digital Currency (CBDC) Projects Worldwide

Country/Region	*CBDC Name*	*Type*	*Current Status*
China	Digital Yuan (e-CNY)	Retail	The e-CNY issued by the People's Bank of China remains in large-scale pilot deployment across multiple cities. It is not yet fully nationwide legal tender in the same operational sense as cash, although it is widely tested
Nigeria	eNaira	Retail	The eNaira was launched in October 2021 by the Central Bank of Nigeria and is officially in circulation, though adoption rates have been mixed
The Bahamas	Sand Dollar	Retail	The Sand Dollar was fully launched nationwide by the Central Bank of The Bahamas in 2020. It is one of the first fully operational retail CBDCs
Eurozone	Digital Euro	Retail	The ECB completed the investigation phase in 2023 and moved into a preparation phase (design and rulebook development). It has not yet been launched
Canada	Project Jasper	Wholesale	Project Jasper was a wholesale DLT experiment conducted by the Bank of Canada in collaboration with industry partners. It was a research project rather than a live CBDC pilot and has concluded

11.4.2 Types of CBDCs

CBDCs are generally classified into two categories:

Retail CBDCs: Intended for general public use in everyday transactions, functioning similarly to digital cash. Retail CBDCs aim to enhance payment efficiency, expand financial inclusion, and provide secure access to digital money. Examples include China's e-CNY, which has been piloted in cities such as Shenzhen and Shanghai for everyday payments at retail outlets, on public transport, and on online platforms. Another example is The Bahamas' Sand Dollar, which has been implemented nationwide to provide residents, including those in remote areas, with access to digital financial services.

Wholesale CBDCs: These are restricted to financial institutions and are designed for interbank settlements, large-value payments, and high-volume transactions. Wholesale CBDCs improve the speed, transparency, and security of financial operations. Canada's Project Jasper tested a DLT-based wholesale CBDC for real-time interbank settlement. At the same time, Singapore's Project Ubin explored a blockchain-based system for high-value cross-border payments between banks, demonstrating reductions in settlement time and operational risk.

11.4.3 Benefits of CBDCs

CBDCs provide several potential advantages, each illustrated with practical examples:

Enhanced Payment Systems: CBDCs can enable faster, cheaper, and more secure domestic and cross-border payments (IMF, 2021). For instance, China's digital yuan pilot has enabled instantaneous retail transactions and cross-border remittances between select Chinese and Hong Kong financial institutions.

Financial Inclusion: CBDCs can provide digital financial services to unbanked or underbanked populations (World Bank, 2022). Nigeria's eNaira was introduced to expand access to secure digital payments, particularly for rural populations who previously had limited access to banking services.

Monetary Policy Implementation: By providing central banks with greater visibility into digital liquidity and transaction flows, CBDCs can improve the effectiveness of monetary policy (Bank of England, 2020). The BoE's ongoing CBDC research suggests that digital currency can facilitate more precise adjustments to money supply and credit conditions.

Control of Illicit Activity: CBDCs' traceability enables improved Anti-Money Laundering and Countering the Financing of Terrorism measures (FATF, 2021). For example, eNaira transactions are fully traceable, allowing regulators to monitor large transfers and detect suspicious activities.

11.4.4 Risks and Challenges of CBDCs

Despite their advantages, CBDCs pose notable challenges, often illustrated through real-world concerns:

Privacy and Surveillance Risks: The capacity to monitor transactions in real time raises concerns about financial privacy and mass surveillance (BIS, 2022). For example, critics of China's e-CNY pilot have highlighted the potential for authorities to track individual spending habits.

Threats to Financial Stability: In times of financial stress, CBDCs may be seen as safer than commercial bank deposits, potentially causing rapid withdrawals and bank disintermediation (IMF, 2021). Hypothetically, widespread adoption of a CBDC could prompt deposit outflows during a banking crisis.

Cybersecurity Vulnerabilities: As centralised digital systems, CBDCs are attractive targets for cyberattacks, and technical failures could disrupt financial operations (FSB, 2022; World Economic Forum, 2023). The BoE and BIS have highlighted the need for robust security protocols to prevent breaches in wholesale and retail CBDC systems.

Implementation and Adoption Challenges: Developing CBDC infrastructure requires substantial investment, and segments of the population without digital literacy or access may be excluded (World Bank, 2022). For example, while the Sand Dollar is available across the Bahamas, uptake in remote islands depends on smartphone access and network coverage.

Legal and Regulatory Uncertainties: The legal frameworks for CBDCs and cross-border transactions are often unclear, creating potential conflicts across jurisdictions (BIS, 2023; IMF, 2023). The Digital Euro is still under investigation, partly due to concerns over harmonising regulations across EU member states.

11.5 Key Practical Issues of CBDC

The integration of FinTech into central banking presents both opportunities and challenges. Central banks must reconcile their core mandates of monetary stability, financial integrity, and public trust with the operational and technological changes driven by innovations such as blockchain, DLT, AI, ML, and CBDCs (BIS, 2020; Carstens, 2021). One of the most significant conceptual frameworks for central banks in the digital currency space is the Policy Trilemma of Digital Currency, which highlights the inherent tension between three competing objectives: financial stability, individual privacy, and operational efficiency and control.

11.5.1 Policy Trilemma and Design Implications

Central banks face a design *trilemma* when implementing CBDCs because enhancing one objective can compromise others. For example, maximising user privacy through fully anonymous digital cash may weaken regulatory oversight and facilitate illicit financial activity, challenging the stability and integrity of the financial system. Conversely, highly controlled systems that require detailed transaction monitoring improve compliance but reduce privacy (Murphy et al., 2024). Policymakers, therefore, seek balanced design frameworks:

Stability vs Privacy: Tiered privacy approaches permit small-value transactions to retain higher privacy, while larger transactions require identity verification, balancing regulatory oversight with user confidentiality. Such privacy-by-design models help align CBDC data use with transparency and accountability (Murphy et al., 2024).

Efficiency vs Privacy: Emerging cryptographic techniques, such as zero-knowledge proofs, enable verifying transaction validity without exposing underlying personal data, supporting efficient compliance without full disclosure of sensitive information (Murphy et al., 2024).

Stability vs Efficiency: Two-tiered CBDC models, in which central banks issue digital currency to intermediaries (e.g., commercial banks) for distribution, help preserve financial intermediation while leveraging private-sector efficiency in payment processing (IMF, 2024). By maintaining intermediation, central banks can mitigate direct disintermediation risk while ensuring broad access.

11.5.2 Operational and Regulatory Challenges

FinTech adoption presents multiple operational and legal challenges for central banks:

Regulatory and Legal Adaptation: Rapid innovation often outpaces existing legal frameworks, requiring continuous legislative and supervisory adaptation to ensure effective oversight and legal certainty for digital currency systems (Bechara et al., 2025).

Cybersecurity Risks: CBDC ecosystems expand the attack surface of national payment infrastructure. Breaches could disrupt critical financial services and expose sensitive transaction data, necessitating robust cyber-resilience protocols and coordinated security frameworks (Bharath, Paduraru & Gaidosch, 2024; Fanti, Lipsky & Moehr, 2022).

Monetary Policy Transmission: The emergence of private digital currencies and decentralised finance platforms can weaken central banks' influence over liquidity and credit conditions, complicating the transmission of policy decisions (Gross et al., 2025). Well-designed CBDCs are intended to mitigate this risk by aligning with monetary policy instruments.

Digital Divide: Unequal access to technology infrastructure may exacerbate financial exclusion, hindering CBDC adoption among underbanked groups unless inclusive design and outreach strategies are incorporated (IMF, 2024).

Financial Stability Risks: Distributed ledger platforms, crypto-assets, and programmable financial products introduce novel systemic risks. Central banks must develop real-time supervisory mechanisms and risk assessment tools to monitor and respond to such dynamics (Gross et al., 2025).

11.5.3 Strategic Convergence and Innovation of CBDC

To address these challenges and modernise monetary frameworks, central banks are adopting convergent strategies:

Development of CBDCs: Many central banks are researching and piloting both retail and wholesale CBDCs to improve payment efficiency, financial inclusion, and policy transmission. Examples include China's digital yuan pilots and the Bahamas' Sand Dollar project, which are operational experiments in broad-based deployment of digital currencies. Additionally, Canada's Project Jasper explored wholesale DLT-based settlement mechanisms (BIS, 2025).

Adoption of RegTech and SupTech: RegTech and SupTech, including AI and ML, are used to automate compliance processes, detect anomalous financial activity, improve forecasting, and enhance practices such as stress testing and risk modelling. These tools help supervisors manage complex, high-volume data environments (IMF, 2025).

Collaboration with FinTech Firms: Innovation hubs and regulatory sandboxes enable central banks to test emerging technologies in controlled environments, fostering collaboration with private-sector innovators while maintaining regulatory oversight and mitigating risk (BIS Innovation Hub reports).

Modernisation of Payment Systems: Integrating DLT into real-time gross settlement systems can enhance transaction speed, transparency, and operational resilience. Singapore's Project Ubin, for instance, tested blockchain-based interbank settlement to reduce operational risk and improve liquidity efficiency.

Promotion of Financial Inclusion and Literacy: Digital platforms and outreach initiatives are used to extend financial services to underbanked populations and increase public understanding and safe use of digital financial products. Strategic education campaigns are critical to broad CBDC adoption (IMF, 2024).

11.5.4 Emerging Trends in FinTech and Central Banking

Central banks are exploring forward-looking technologies to strengthen resilience and prepare for future challenges:

Interoperable CBDCs: Cross-border CBDC frameworks aim to facilitate faster, cheaper, and more transparent international payments. Multi-CBDC platforms, such as the *mBridge* project involving several central banks, illustrate efforts to develop shared ledgers that support peer-to-peer cross-border payments and FX transactions. Such interoperability initiatives aim to reduce fragmentation and enhance global integration of digital payments (mBridge, 2024; IMF interoperability principles).

Quantum-Resistant Cryptography: As quantum computing evolves, existing cryptographic methods may become vulnerable to attacks. Central banks are investigating quantum-resistant cryptographic protocols to secure CBDCs and the broader financial infrastructure against emerging threats, recognising that traditional encryption may not suffice in post-quantum environments (World Economic Forum interoperability principles).

Green FinTech Initiatives: FinTech is being leveraged to support sustainable finance objectives, including the use of blockchain for tracking green investment flows and carbon credit markets, and AI for climate-related risk modelling. These applications can help central banks integrate environmental sustainability into financial policy frameworks (IMF, 2024).

11.6 Conclusion

In conclusion, the rapid advancement of FinTech compels central banks to adopt proactive strategies to maintain their core mandates of economic and financial stability. The emergence of CBDCs, alongside enabling technologies such as blockchain and AI, signals a fundamental transformation in the conduct of monetary policy and the oversight of financial systems. Central banks are therefore tasked with simultaneously promoting innovation and ensuring the security, stability, and inclusivity of the financial ecosystem. Their capacity to navigate this evolving digital landscape, where advanced technologies enhance operational efficiency and introduce new policy instruments, while also introducing cyber risks and systemic vulnerabilities, will be critical to sustaining institutional effectiveness.

A central challenge in this context is resolving the inherent Policy Trilemma of Digital Currency, which requires balancing monetary sovereignty, financial stability, and widespread accessibility. The ability of central banks to manage these competing priorities will shape the future architecture of the financial system, determining whether it is both resilient and adaptable while remaining credible and inclusive for all stakeholders. Consequently, the integration of digital currencies represents not merely a technological upgrade but a strategic recalibration of central banking, redefining operational frameworks, policy tools, and institutional responsibilities for the digital age.

Key Terms and Glossary

Monetary Policy The measures by which the monetary authority of a country, such as the central bank, controls the supply of money, often targeting an inflation rate or interest rate to ensure price stability, and supporting economic growth and confidence in the currency.

Lender of Last Resort The function of a central bank is to provide emergency liquidity to financial institutions experiencing financial distress or facing the risk of failure, thereby promoting stability within the financial system.

Wholesale CBDC A CBDC designed for use by financial institutions for interbank payments and settlement processes.

SupTech The use of technology by regulatory bodies to supervise and monitor the financial industry more effectively and efficiently.

Policy Trilemma of Digital Currency The challenge of simultaneously achieving Financial Stability, Individual Privacy, and Operational Efficiency and Control in the design of a CBDC.

Test Your Understanding

Multiple-Choice Questions

1 Which of the following best defines a CBDC?

A A decentralised cryptocurrency managed by private entities
B A digital version of sovereign currency issued by a central bank
C A commercial bank digital account
D A blockchain token for cross-border trade

2 What is one key benefit of CBDCs for central banks?

A Elimination of commercial banks
B Enhanced control over digital liquidity and monetary policy transmission
C Complete anonymity for all transactions
D Unlimited issuance of currency without regulation

3 Which FinTech innovation allows central banks to conduct real-time monitoring and predictive risk assessments?

A Mobile banking
B Blockchain and DLT
C AI and ML
D Contactless payment cards

4 The Policy Trilemma of Digital Currency involves a trade-off between:

A Speed, cost, and adoption
B Financial stability, individual privacy, and operational efficiency
C Inflation, deflation, and unemployment
D Interest rates, currency issuance, and credit availability

5 Which of the following is an example of a wholesale CBDC initiative?

A China's e-CNY
B The Bahamas' Sand Dollar
C Canada's Project Jasper
D Nigeria's eNaira

Short Questions

1 Explain how blockchain and DLT can improve central bank operations.
2 Identify two operational risks associated with the implementation of CBDCs.
3 Briefly describe the impact of AI and ML on monetary policy and financial system stability.

Analytical Questions

1 Evaluate the potential advantages and disadvantages of retail versus wholesale CBDCs, using examples from existing pilot projects.
2 Discuss how central banks can manage the Policy Trilemma of Digital Currency while maintaining financial stability and public trust.
3 Analyse the role of FinTech innovations (blockchain, AI, and CBDCs) in reshaping the traditional functions of central banks, particularly in monetary policy implementation and payment system oversight.

Case Study: The Digital Yuan (e-CNY)—China's CBDC Pilot

China has emerged as a global frontrunner in CBDC development with the launch of the digital Yuan, or e-CNY. The People's Bank of China (PBOC) has conducted extensive pilots involving millions of citizens and businesses, integrating the digital currency into retail payments, government disbursements, and municipal services. Domestically, the e-CNY aims to enhance financial inclusion by providing digital payment access to underbanked populations and regions with limited banking infrastructure. Simultaneously, it offers the Chinese government greater oversight of the financial system, allowing authorities to monitor transaction flows, limit illicit financial activities, and moderate the dominance of private payment platforms such as Alipay and WeChat Pay.

From an international perspective, the digital Yuan reflects China's ambition to increase the global use of its currency, potentially challenging the pre-eminence of the US dollar in cross-border trade and financial markets. The design of the e-CNY reflects careful consideration of the Policy Trilemma of Digital Currency: operational efficiency is prioritised through real-time settlement and integration with mobile wallets, privacy is partially preserved for small-value transactions, and systemic stability is reinforced through two-tiered distribution via commercial banks. These choices illustrate the balancing act between technological innovation, regulatory control, and public trust. The e-CNY pilot provides insights into both the domestic transformation of payment systems and the broader strategic implications for the international monetary landscape (PBOC, 2023; BIS, 2021).

References

Bank for International Settlements (BIS). (2021). *Central Bank Digital Currencies: Foundational Principles and Core Features* [online]. Bank for International Settlements. Available at: https://www.bis.org/publ/othp59.pdf (Accessed: 1 March 2026).

People's Bank of China (PBOC). (2023). *Progress of Research and Development of e-CNY in China* [online]. People's Bank of China. Available at: http://www.pbc.gov.cn/en/3688110/3688172/5188125/5557187/index.html (Accessed: 1 March 2026).

Case Study Questions

1 Why is China developing a digital Yuan? Consider both domestic goals, such as controlling Big Tech and promoting financial inclusion, and international goals, such as increasing the global use of the Yuan.
2 Using the Policy Trilemma of Digital Currency, explain the trade-offs the PBOC is making between operational efficiency, individual privacy, and financial stability in the design of the e-CNY. How does the two-tier distribution system address these trade-offs?
3 If the digital Yuan is widely adopted for international trade and payments, what potential effects could this have on global finance and the dominance of the US dollar?

Further Reading

BIS. (2020). *Central Bank Digital Currencies: Foundational Principles and Core Features*. Basel: Bank for International Settlements.

Carstens, A. (2021). *Digital Currencies and the Future of the Monetary System*. Speech presented at the International Monetary Fund, Washington, DC.

Prasad, E. (2021). *The Future of Money: How the Digital Revolution Is Transforming Currencies and Finance*. Cambridge, MA: Harvard University Press.

References

Bank for International Settlements (BIS). (2020). *Central Bank Digital Currencies: Foundational Principles and Core Features*. Available at: https://www.bis.org/publ/othp33.htm (Accessed: 18 October 2023).

Bank for International Settlements (BIS). (2022). *CBDCs in the Digital Age: Privacy and Trust*. Available at: https://www.bis.org (Accessed: 18 October 2023).

Bank for International Settlements (BIS). (2023). *Cross-Border CBDCs: Regulatory Challenges*. Available at: https://www.bis.org (Accessed: 18 October 2023).

Bank for International Settlements (BIS) (2024) *mBridge: Enabling Cross-Border Payments and FX Settlement Using CBDCs*. Basel: Bank for International Settlements.

Bank for International Settlements (BIS) (2025) *Project Jasper and distributed ledger technology in wholesale settlement systems*. Basel: Bank for International Settlements.

Bank of England (BoE). (2020). *Central Bank Digital Currency: Opportunities, Challenges and Design*. Available at: https://www.bankofengland.co.uk/paper/2020/central-bank-digital-currency-opportunities-challenges-and-design-discussion-paper (Accessed: 18 October 2023).

Bechara, M., Frost, J. and Wierts, P. (2025) *Regulating Digital Currencies: Legal Uncertainty and Supervisory Adaptation*. Basel: Bank for International Settlements.

Bharath, S., Paduraru, C. and Gaidosch, T. (2024) *Cyber Resilience in Central Bank Digital Currency Systems*. Washington, DC: International Monetary Fund.

Boar, C., Holden, H. & Wadsworth, A. (2020). Impending Arrival – A Sequel to the Survey on Central Bank Digital Currency. *BIS Papers. No. 107*.

Carstens, A. (2021). *Digital Currencies and the Future of the Monetary System*. Available at: https://www.imf.org (Accessed: 18 October 2023).

Das, S., Auer, R. and Frost, J. (2023) *Central Bank Digital Currencies and the Future of Monetary Policy*. Basel: Bank for International Settlements.

Fanti, R., Lipsky, J. and Moehr, N. (2022) *Cybersecurity Risks in Digital Payment Infrastructures and CBDCs*. Basel: Bank for International Settlements.

Financial Action Task Force (FATF). (2021). *Updated Guidance for a Risk-Based Approach to Virtual Assets and Virtual Asset Service Providers*. Available at: https://www.fatf-gafi.org/ (Accessed: 18 October 2023).

Financial Stability Board (FSB). (2022). *Assessment of Risks to Financial Stability from Crypto Assets*. Available at: https://www.fsb.org/ (Accessed: 18 October 2023).

Gross, J., Turner, A. and Vuillemey, G. (2025) *AI, Data Analytics and Macroprudential Policy: Emerging Tools for Financial Stability*. Basel: Bank for International Settlements.

International Monetary Fund (IMF). (2021). *The Rise of Public and Private Digital Money*. Available at: https://www.imf.org/en/Publications/FinTech-Notes/Issues/2021/07/29/The-Rise-of-Public-and-Private-Digital-Money-460266 (Accessed: 18 October 2023).

International Monetary Fund (IMF). (2023). *Legal and Regulatory Considerations for CBDCs*. Available at: https://www.imf.org (Accessed: 18 October 2023).

International Monetary Fund (IMF) (2024) *Central Bank Digital Currencies and the Two-tier Financial System*. Washington, DC: International Monetary Fund.

International Monetary Fund (IMF) (2025) *RegTech and SupTech: Artificial Intelligence and Machine Learning in Financial Supervision*. Washington, DC: International Monetary Fund.

Kunaratskul, T., Reslow, A. and Singh, S. (2024) *Central Bank Digital Currency Design and Implications for Monetary Policy and Financial Stability*. Basel: Bank for International Settlements.

Mishkin, F. S. (2018). *The Economics of Money, Banking and Financial Markets* (12th ed.). New York: Pearson.

Murphy, R., Turner, A. and Vives, X. (2024) *Digital Surveillance, Privacy and Financial Compliance in Modern Payment Systems*. Basel: Bank for International Settlements

Patel, K., Kasiyanto, S. and Reslow, A. (2024) *Programmable Ledgers, CBDCs and the Future of Interbank Settlement*. Basel: Bank for International Settlements.

Prasad, E. (2021). *The Future of Money: How the Digital Revolution Is Transforming Currencies and Finance*. Cambridge: Harvard University Press.

World Bank. (2022). *Financial Inclusion and the Role of CBDCs*. Available at: https://www.worldbank.org (Accessed: 18 October 2023).

World Economic Forum (WEF). (2023). *Cybersecurity Risks in CBDC Systems*. Available at: https://www.weforum.org/ (Accessed: 18 October 2023).

Part 3

Market and Digital Innovation

12 Digital Innovation in the Financial Market

Chapter Overview

This chapter explores the structure and functional dynamics of financial markets, with a particular focus on the transformative effects of Financial Technology (FinTech) on traditional market operations. It begins by establishing the essential roles financial markets play in the economy, including the efficient allocation of capital, liquidity provision, risk transfer and management, and accurate price discovery. The chapter further categorises financial markets into key types: capital, commodity, derivatives, money, and foreign exchange (Forex) markets, highlighting their distinct functions and interrelationships (Mishkin, 2021). Building on this conceptual foundation, the analysis examines the disruptive potential of emerging FinTech innovations, including blockchain technology, artificial intelligence (AI), algorithmic trading, decentralised finance (DeFi), and asset tokenisation. It illustrates how these developments are reshaping market efficiency, transparency, and accessibility. In addition, the chapter critically addresses the regulatory challenges posed by these innovations, the heightened cybersecurity risks associated with digital platforms, and the ongoing tension between the drive for technological advancement and the imperative of promoting inclusive access to financial services, ultimately situating FinTech as both an opportunity and a source of systemic complexity within contemporary financial markets.

Learning Objectives:

By the end of this chapter, you should be able to:

1. Explain the structure, functions, and classifications of financial markets.
2. Analyse the transformative role of FinTech innovations, including blockchain, AI, and DeFi, in enhancing market efficiency, liquidity, and transparency.
3. Evaluate the practical challenges and systemic risks associated with FinTech integration, such as interoperability gaps, algorithmic risk, and data governance issues.
4. Assess regulatory, compliance, and cybersecurity challenges in digital financial markets and discuss potential strategies for risk mitigation.
5. Examine the implications of FinTech for financial inclusion and the digital divide and propose approaches to promote equitable access to financial services.

DOI: 10.4324/9781003775751-15

12.1 Introduction

Contemporary financial markets are experiencing a profound transformation driven by technological advancement. Historically, these markets have been characterised by their functions in price discovery, efficient capital allocation, and risk management, encompassing the trading of equities, bonds, currencies, and derivatives. Established market frameworks have traditionally provided liquidity, stability, and investor confidence (Bodie, Kane, & Marcus, 2021). In recent years, the emergence of FinTech has accelerated the shift from manual, segmented processes to automated, globally interconnected systems, reshaping operational standards in terms of speed, cost efficiency, and accessibility.

The application of advanced technologies to core financial operations largely facilitates this transformation. AI and Machine Learning (ML) are increasingly used to optimise trading strategies, enhance quantitative risk modelling, and strengthen compliance monitoring, enabling instantaneous decision-making and reduced operational latency. Similarly, Distributed Ledger Technology, particularly blockchain, introduces real-time, immutable record-keeping that can potentially replace traditional settlement and clearing mechanisms. Collectively, these innovations mitigate long-standing inefficiencies and frictions in financial markets, thereby promoting greater transparency, efficiency, and accessibility across the financial system (Arner, Barberis, & Buckley, 2016).

The digitalisation of financial markets also poses significant challenges for market intermediation and regulation. While automated platforms and digital processes improve liquidity and expand access, they simultaneously introduce new operational complexities and systemic risks, particularly regarding data integrity and cybersecurity. Financial professionals must therefore acquire technological expertise and adapt their strategies to remain effective in this evolving landscape. Regulatory authorities are similarly required to update oversight frameworks to supervise emerging asset classes and algorithmic trading practices, ensuring that innovation proceeds without compromising market stability, integrity, or resilience.

12.2 Overview of Financial Markets

Financial markets function as structured platforms for the exchange of financial assets, enabling participants to mobilise funds, manage risk, and facilitate economic growth. They can be classified into distinct types based on their roles, the instruments traded, and the maturity of financial products. Understanding the objectives and key components of these markets is essential for analysing their contribution to the broader financial system.

12.2.1 Definition, Objectives, and Key Functions of Financial Markets

Financial markets are defined as institutional arrangements through which savings are channelled from surplus units, such as households, to deficit units, including corporations and governments, to fund productive investments and support economic development (Mishkin, 2021). They perform several critical functions:

Capital Allocation: Financial markets allocate capital efficiently by directing funds to the most productive uses. For example, a technology start-up may raise equity capital in a capital market to finance research and expansion, while investors evaluate the associated risks and expected returns (Mishkin, 2021).

Liquidity Provision: Markets offer liquidity, allowing participants to convert assets into cash quickly with minimal price impact. Highly liquid markets, such as the New York Stock Exchange, feature narrow bid-ask spreads and high trading volumes, which enhance investor confidence and operational efficiency (Bodie, Kane, & Marcus, 2021).

Price Discovery: The interaction of supply and demand in financial markets determines asset prices, reflecting the aggregate information and expectations of market participants. For instance, the price of a publicly traded stock, like Apple Inc., adjusts continuously in response to earnings announcements and macroeconomic news.

Risk Transfer: Through derivative instruments such as futures, options, and swaps, participants can hedge against financial risks, including fluctuations in commodity prices, interest rates, or credit exposure. For example, an airline company may use fuel futures to manage the risk of volatile oil prices (Hull, 2022).

12.2.2 Types of Financial Markets

Capital Markets: These markets facilitate long-term funding by issuing and trading equity (stocks) and debt (bonds). The primary market involves the original issuance of securities, such as a corporate Initial Public Offering (IPO). In contrast, the secondary market enables trading among investors, as seen on exchanges such as the London Stock Exchange (Mishkin, 2021).

Commodity Markets: Commodity markets provide platforms for trading raw materials. They are categorised as hard commodities, such as gold, crude oil, and metals, and soft commodities, including wheat, coffee, and cocoa. These markets are crucial for global trade and are sensitive to supply chain disruptions, geopolitical tensions, and seasonal factors. For example, the Chicago Mercantile Exchange facilitates trading in agricultural futures.

Derivatives Markets: Derivatives derive their value from an underlying asset, such as commodities, equities, or interest rates. Futures, options, and swaps allow participants to hedge risk or engage in speculative trading. For instance, a portfolio manager may purchase options to protect against potential declines in stock prices (Hull, 2022).

Money Markets: Money markets deal in short-term debt instruments with maturities of one year or less, such as Treasury bills, commercial paper, and certificates of deposit. They serve as a mechanism for managing short-term liquidity needs for both financial institutions and corporations. For example, companies often issue commercial paper to cover operational expenses.

Forex Markets: The Forex market is a decentralised global marketplace for currency trading. Operating continuously across different time zones, it is the largest financial market by trading volume, supporting international trade and investment. For example, multinational corporations use the Forex market to hedge foreign currency exposure or facilitate cross-border payments.

12.3 Stakeholder in the Financial Market

Financial markets function as structured ecosystems comprising diverse participants whose interactions enable capital formation, liquidity provision, price discovery, and risk transfer. These participants include individual investors, institutional investors, intermediaries, and regulators. Each group performs distinct but interdependent roles that collectively maintain market efficiency and stability. Understanding these roles is crucial for analysing how financial markets allocate resources and respond to economic shocks.

Individual investors, also known as retail investors, allocate personal savings to financial instruments such as equities, bonds, exchange-traded funds, and mutual funds via brokerage platforms. Although limited individually in financial capacity, their aggregated trading activity significantly contributes to liquidity and decentralised price discovery. Retail participation can affect short-term volatility, especially during periods of speculative enthusiasm or coordinated trading behaviour.

Institutional investors, including pension funds, insurance companies, mutual funds, hedge funds, and sovereign wealth funds, manage substantial capital pools on behalf of beneficiaries. Portfolio optimisation, risk management, regulatory requirements, and long-term return objectives generally guide their investment strategies. Due to their scale and expertise, institutional investors significantly influence asset prices, capital flows, and overall market sentiment, thereby shaping liquidity conditions and sectoral development.

Intermediaries, including brokers, dealers, investment banks, exchanges, and clearing institutions, facilitate transactions between buyers and sellers. They offer services including trade execution, underwriting, market-making, settlement, and advisory support. By reducing transaction costs, efficiently matching counterparties, and maintaining orderly trading mechanisms, intermediaries improve market transparency and operational efficiency.

Regulators supervise financial markets to ensure integrity, transparency, and systemic stability. By enforcing disclosure standards, prudential regulations, and anti-fraud measures, regulatory authorities protect investors and reduce systemic risk. The interactions among investors, intermediaries, and regulators create a dynamic financial system in which capital is continuously allocated, risks are redistributed, and market discipline is upheld.

12.4 The Role of FinTech in the Financial Market

FinTech refers to the application of advanced technological solutions to the provision of financial services, aiming to enhance efficiency, security, and accessibility while reducing operational costs. In recent years, FinTech has emerged as a transformative force, reshaping the structure, operations, and accessibility of financial markets. Key innovations include blockchain and distributed ledger technologies, AI and ML, DeFi platforms, algorithmic trading systems, tokenisation of assets, and digital payment and crowdfunding platforms (Arner, Barberis, & Buckley, 2016; Tapscott & Tapscott, 2016) (Figure 12.1).

12.4.1 Innovations and Their Impact on Financial Market Functions

FinTech innovations significantly influence the core functions of financial markets. First, they enhance capital allocation by widening access to financial instruments, enabling broader participation from retail investors and non-traditional funding sources. For instance, mobile trading applications like Robinhood and crowdfunding platforms like Kickstarter allow smaller investors to participate in equity and debt markets, thereby improving the flow of capital to productive ventures (Zheng et al., 2020). Second, FinTech improves liquidity provision. Blockchain-based settlement systems enable near-instantaneous trade clearing, reducing counterparty risk and transaction costs, thereby increasing market depth and enabling the quick conversion of assets to cash (Tapscott & Tapscott, 2016). Third, price discovery is enhanced through AI and big data analytics, which integrate vast datasets into market pricing models, enabling a more accurate real-time reflection of asset values (Davenport & Ronanki, 2018). Finally, FinTech facilitates risk transfer and management through derivatives, smart contracts, and predictive analytics, enabling

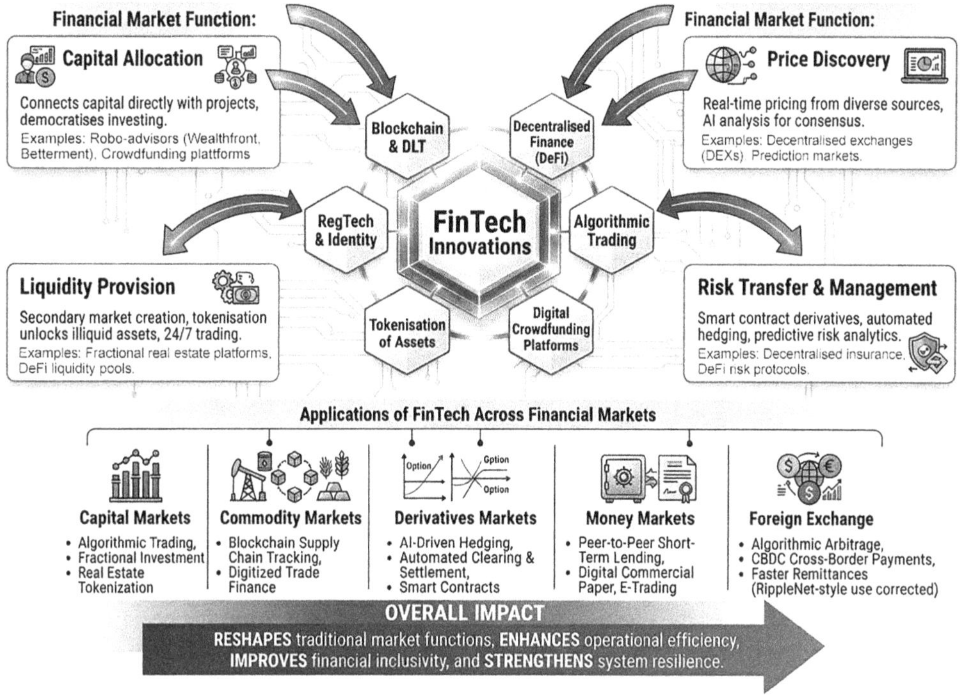

Figure 12.1 FinTech Innovations in Financial Markets.

participants to hedge against market, credit, and operational risks more effectively. DeFi platforms, for example, allow peer-to-peer lending and borrowing while offering transparent mechanisms for risk assessment (World Bank, 2022).

12.4.2 Application of FinTech Across Financial Markets

FinTech applications are increasingly integrated across all major financial market types. In capital markets, AI-driven algorithmic trading platforms enhance the speed and efficiency of trade execution. At the same time, tokenisation enables fractional ownership of high-value assets such as real estate or art, increasing market accessibility and liquidity (Arner et al., 2016). In commodity markets, blockchain and smart contracts streamline supply chain finance and trade settlement, ensuring transparency and reducing the operational risks of futures and spot transactions (Tapscott & Tapscott, 2016). Derivatives markets benefit from automated risk management and algorithmic execution, where AI models predict price movements and execute hedging strategies with minimal human intervention (Hull, 2022). In money markets, digital platforms facilitate real-time trading in short-term debt instruments, such as Treasury bills and commercial paper, thereby improving liquidity management for institutions and corporations (Mishkin, 2021). Finally, in the Forex market, algorithmic trading and AI-based forecasting tools enhance trade efficiency. At the same time, blockchain-enabled cross-border settlement systems reduce transaction costs and settlement delays, exemplified by platforms such as RippleNet. Collectively, these applications demonstrate how FinTech innovations are reshaping traditional financial functions, enhancing efficiency, inclusivity, and operational resilience across global financial markets.

12.5 Key Practical Issues in FinTech-Driven Financial Markets

The integration of FinTech into modern markets offers substantial efficiency and accessibility benefits, yet it also introduces complex operational and systemic challenges. These challenges have significant implications for market participants, policymakers, and regulators.

12.5.1 Interoperability and System Fragmentation

The proliferation of DeFi protocols, blockchain networks, and traditional financial infrastructures has exposed a critical interoperability gap. Seamless transfer of digital assets and information across these heterogeneous systems remains technically demanding, often resulting in market segmentation and reduced operational efficiency. For instance, bridging assets between Ethereum-based platforms and legacy banking systems requires sophisticated smart contracts and custodial arrangements, which may introduce latency, errors, or security vulnerabilities (Harz et al., 2019).

12.5.2 Algorithmic Trading Risks and Market Stability

The growing prevalence of algorithmic and high-frequency trading (HFT) has amplified systemic vulnerabilities. Algorithmic strategies may exhibit correlated behaviour, potentially triggering sudden market disruptions such as flash crashes. Moreover, the opaque nature of some algorithmic models, often referred to as *black boxes*, raises concerns about undetected errors or manipulative strategies that could undermine market stability. The 2010 Flash Crash, where the U.S. equity market lost nearly 9% of its value within minutes, exemplifies the systemic risks posed by high-speed algorithmic trading (Budish, Cramton, & Shim, 2015).

12.5.3 Data Governance and Algorithmic Bias

The deployment of AI in financial decision-making requires vast datasets, which pose challenges related to data privacy, ownership, and quality. Ensuring that AI models are trained on representative and unbiased datasets is essential to prevent discriminatory or erroneous outcomes. For example, lending algorithms that rely on skewed historical credit data may inadvertently perpetuate socioeconomic disparities, emphasising the importance of robust data governance frameworks (Raghavan et al., 2020).

12.5.4 Regulatory Arbitrage and Shadow Finance

The cross-border nature of many FinTech applications facilitates regulatory arbitrage. Entities can exploit jurisdictions with weaker oversight, effectively creating a parallel shadow financial system that may circumvent consumer protection and anti-money laundering standards. The rapid expansion of unregulated DeFi platforms illustrates this risk, as participants can trade large volumes of digital assets outside traditional regulatory supervision (U.S. Securities and Exchange Commission, 2023).

12.6 Regulatory Challenges in FinTech Innovation

The rapid evolution of FinTech necessitates adaptive regulatory frameworks that balance innovation with market stability and consumer protection.

12.6.1 Cybersecurity Vulnerabilities

The digital infrastructure underlying FinTech is inherently susceptible to cyber threats. High-profile incidents, such as the 2014 collapse of Mt. Gox, where hackers stole approximately 850,000 bitcoins, highlight the catastrophic consequences of security breaches. Such events undermine investor confidence and can destabilise markets, underscoring the need for robust cybersecurity measures and continuous monitoring (Moore & Christin, 2013).

12.6.2 Compliance Complexity and Regulatory Adaptation

Regulators face the dual challenge of enforcing existing financial laws while accommodating novel FinTech innovations. The classification of emerging digital assets, particularly cryptocurrencies, remains contentious, complicating taxation, disclosure, and investor protection obligations. For example, the Securities and Exchange Commission (SEC) has consistently struggled to distinguish between utility tokens, security tokens, and other digital assets, underscoring the need for flexible yet enforceable regulatory guidelines (U.S. Securities and Exchange Commission, 2023).

12.6.3 Financial Inclusion and Digital Divide

While FinTech has the potential to promote financial inclusion through mobile banking and digital wallets, it may inadvertently exacerbate exclusion among populations lacking digital literacy or access to technology. In developing regions, initiatives such as M-Pesa in Kenya demonstrate how mobile money can bridge financial gaps, yet gaps remain for marginalised groups unable to engage with digital platforms (World Bank, 2022). Policymakers must therefore design interventions that balance technological innovation with equitable access.

12.7 Conclusion

Global financial markets, as the foundation of economic stability, are undergoing a transformative shift driven by digital technologies such as blockchain, AI, and DeFi. These innovations enhance efficiency, transparency, and accessibility, fundamentally reshaping traditional financial ecosystems. However, the rapid integration of such technologies introduces significant challenges, including cybersecurity vulnerabilities, regulatory gaps, and systemic risks arising from interconnected digital infrastructures. Effective risk management and adaptive oversight are therefore essential to mitigate these threats while enabling sustainable market growth (World Economic Forum, 2023).

Looking forward, the financial sector must balance technological innovation with robust governance to ensure long-term stability and inclusivity. Strategic planning, informed by collaboration among regulators, industry stakeholders, and technology innovators, will be critical in fostering resilient financial systems. The ability to harmonise technological progress with systemic safeguards will determine whether digital advancements translate into equitable and sustainable economic outcomes, shaping the future trajectory of global financial markets (Gates, 1995).

Key Terms and Glossary

Price Discovery The process through which market prices are determined, typically by the interaction of buyers and sellers in a marketplace.

Capital Markets Financial markets for the buying and selling of long-term debt or equity-backed securities.

Derivatives Market The financial market for derivatives, which are financial contracts whose value is derived from an underlying asset.

Money Market The segment of the financial market in which financial instruments with high liquidity and very short maturities are traded.

Market Fragmentation A situation where a financial market is split into various segments or venues, potentially leading to inefficiencies.

Test Your Understanding

Multiple-Choice Questions

1 Which of the following best describes the primary function of financial markets?

A To generate profits for regulators
B To allocate capital efficiently, provide liquidity, facilitate price discovery, and enable risk transfer
C To enforce tax regulations
D To standardise financial reporting

2 Which FinTech innovation allows for peer-to-peer lending and transparent automated risk assessment?

A Algorithmic trading
B DeFi
C Money market instruments
D Futures and options

3 The 2010 Flash Crash in the U.S. equity market primarily highlighted risks associated with:

A DeFi protocols
B High-frequency and algorithmic trading
C Blockchain immutability
D Mobile banking platforms

4 Which of the following is a major cybersecurity incident in FinTech history?

A Mt. Gox collapse
B IPO of Apple Inc.
C Launch of RippleNet
D Kickstarter crowdfunding campaigns

5 Financial inclusion challenges in FinTech are primarily caused by:

A Lack of blockchain technology
B Digital divide and limited access to technology or literacy
C Over-regulation in capital markets
D. Excessive algorithmic trading

Short Questions

1 Define FinTech and explain its impact on traditional financial market operations.
2 Identify two key risks introduced by algorithmic trading and explain their potential effects on market stability.
3 Explain the concept of regulatory arbitrage in the context of digital financial markets.

Analytical Questions

1 Discuss how blockchain and tokenisation can improve capital allocation and market liquidity. Provide examples from capital or commodity markets.
2 Evaluate the trade-off between financial innovation and regulatory oversight in the context of DeFi platforms. How can regulators balance innovation with consumer protection?
3 Analyse the role of AI and big data analytics in price discovery. How can biased datasets affect market fairness, and what governance measures can mitigate these risks?

Case Study: The Flash Crash of 2010 and Algorithmic Interdependence

On May 6, 2010, U.S. equity markets experienced an extreme and rapid disruption widely known as the *Flash Crash*. Within a matter of minutes, major equity indices plunged sharply, with the Dow Jones Industrial Average falling nearly 1,000 points before rebounding almost as quickly. According to the joint report by the U.S. SEC and the Commodity Futures Trading Commission (CFTC), the episode was not triggered by a single technical failure but by the interaction of automated trading systems operating at very high speeds.

The event began with a large sell order in the futures market, executed by an automated algorithm that traded based on volume rather than price or time. This order interacted with HFT firms that rapidly bought and sold contracts among themselves, generating intense trading volume but little genuine liquidity. As market conditions deteriorated, many algorithms withdrew from providing liquidity or switched to aggressive selling strategies. The resulting feedback loop between equity and futures markets amplified price declines across multiple asset classes. The highly interconnected structure of modern electronic markets, combined with the speed and autonomy of algorithmic systems, allowed localised stress to escalate into a broad market disruption within minutes, exposing structural vulnerabilities in automated financial ecosystems.

Reference

U.S. Securities and Exchange Commission (SEC) and U.S. Commodity Futures Trading Commission (CFTC). (2010). *Findings Regarding the Market Events of May 6, 2010* [online]. Washington, DC: U.S. Securities and Exchange Commission and U.S. Commodity Futures Trading Commission. Available at: https://www.sec.gov/news/studies/2010/marketevents-report.pdf (Accessed: 2 March 2026).

Case Study Questions

1 In what ways did the high level of interconnectivity and automation in contemporary financial markets accelerate both the transmission and the intensity of price declines during the Flash Crash?
2 Which specific challenge associated with algorithmic integrity and market stability is illustrated by the events of the Flash Crash, and why does it represent a systemic risk?
3 What regulatory reforms and technological risk controls have been introduced since 2010, such as circuit breakers and stricter algorithm testing requirements, to reduce the likelihood of similar disruptions, and to what extent do these measures adequately address the underlying vulnerabilities?

Further Reading

Bodie, Z., Kane, A., & Marcus, A.J. (2021). *Investments*. 12th ed. New York: McGraw-Hill Education.
Hull, J. C. (2022). *Options, Futures, and Other Derivatives*. Boston, MA: Pearson.
World Economic Forum. (2023). *The Future of Global Financial and Monetary Systems*. Geneva: World Economic Forum.

References

Arner, D. W., Barberis, J., & Buckley, R. P. (2016). The Evolution of FinTech: A New Post-Crisis Paradigm? *Georgetown Journal of International Law*, 47(4), 1271–1320.
Bodie, Z., Kane, A., & Marcus, A. J. (2021). *Investments* (12th ed.). New York: McGraw-Hill Education.
Budish, E., Cramton, P., & Shim, J. (2015). The High-Frequency Trading Arms Race: Frequent Batch Auctions as a Market Design Response. *The Quarterly Journal of Economics*, 130(4), 1547–1621.
Davenport, T. H., & Ronanki, R. (2018). Artificial Intelligence for the Real World. *Harvard Business Review*, 96(1), 108–116.
Gates, B. (1995) *The Road Ahead*. New York: Viking.
Harz, D., Gudgeon, L., Gervais, A. and Knottenbelt, W.J. (2019) Balance: Dynamic Adjustment of Cryptocurrency Deposits. In *Proceedings of the 2019 ACM SIGSAC Conference on Computer and Communications Security (CCS '19)*, pp. 1485–1502
Hull, J. C. (2022). *Options, Futures, and Other Derivatives* (11th ed.). Boston, MA: Pearson.
Mishkin, F. S. (2021). *The Economics of Money, Banking, and Financial Markets* (13th ed.). Boston, MA: Pearson.
Moore, T. and Christin, N. (2013) Beware The Middleman: Empirical Analysis of Bitcoin-Exchange Risk. In *Financial Cryptography and Data Security (FC 2013)*, Lecture Notes in Computer Science, vol. 7859. Berlin: Springer, pp. 25–33.
Raghavan, M., Barocas, S., Kleinberg, J. and Levy, K. (2020) Mitigating Bias in Algorithmic Lending: a Framework for Understanding Fairness in Credit Decisioning. In *Proceedings of the 2020 Conference on Fairness, Accountability, and Transparency (FAccT '20)*, pp. 469–481.

Securities and Exchange Commission (SEC). (2023). *Spotlight on Crypto Assets*. Washington, DC: U.S. Securities and Exchange Commission.

Tapscott, D., & Tapscott, A. (2016). *Blockchain Revolution: How the Technology Behind Bitcoin Is Changing Money, Business, and the World*. New York : Penguin.

World Bank. (2022). *FinTech and the Future of Finance: Market and Policy Implications*. Washington, DC: World Bank Group.

Zheng, X., Chen, Y., Li, J. and Wang, H. (2020) The Rise of Social Trading Platforms: A Study of Investor Behaviour, *Journal of Financial Technology Studies*, 1(1), 45–59.

13 Capital Markets and Financial Technology

Chapter Overview

This chapter provides an academic examination of the transformative role of Financial Technology (FinTech) in global capital markets, encompassing both equity and debt instruments. It explores how technologies such as blockchain, artificial intelligence (AI), and algorithmic trading are restructuring core market functions, including securities issuance, trading, settlement, and regulatory compliance (Arner, Barberis, & Buckley, 2020; World Economic Forum, 2022). After outlining the foundational structures of equity and bond markets, the chapter analyses key FinTech innovations, including tokenised securities, robo-advisory platforms, AI-driven credit and sentiment analysis, and advanced electronic trading systems. It then compares traditional and technology-enabled market models to identify areas of convergence and divergence in intermediation, cost efficiency, and market access. The chapter concludes by evaluating emerging risks and regulatory challenges, particularly those related to financial stability (FSB, 2023), while considering the longer-term evolution towards a more efficient, inclusive, and digitally integrated capital market ecosystem.

Learning Objectives

By the end of this chapter, you should be able to:

1. Define the core components, participants, and functions of traditional equity and bond markets.
2. Explain how FinTech innovations, including blockchain, AI, and algorithmic trading, are transforming the issuance, trading, and settlement of capital market instruments.
3. Compare traditional capital market structures with FinTech-enabled markets, highlighting differences in efficiency, accessibility, and participant roles.
4. Analyse the key risks, regulatory challenges, and practical issues associated with integrating FinTech into capital markets.
5. Evaluate case studies and emerging trends, including hyper-personalisation and DeFi applications, to assess the benefits, limitations, and future trajectory of capital markets.

DOI: 10.4324/9781003775751-16

13.1 Introduction

Capital markets serve as the primary drivers of the global economy by providing mechanisms for corporations and governments to secure long-term funding. Investors benefit through opportunities for capital appreciation and income generation. These markets are typically divided into two main segments: equity markets, which facilitate the exchange of ownership shares, and debt markets, which focus on bonds and structured loans. Historically, institutional dominance, complex processing, and significant opacity, particularly in the over-the-counter (OTC) sector, characterised these markets (Mishkin & Eakins, 2018). Such complexity and friction limited direct participation, resulting in widespread reliance on established intermediaries and the development of a centralised, often cumbersome infrastructure.

The emergence of FinTech represents a significant paradigm shift that fundamentally challenges the traditional architecture of capital allocation. FinTech introduces not only incremental improvements but also a systemic overhaul that affects nearly every aspect of market operations, including trading infrastructure and the end-user experience. Disruptions encompass the automation of high-frequency trading (HFT), the democratisation of retail access through user-friendly platforms, the enhancement of regulatory oversight via advanced RegTech tools, and the transformation of data analytics (Claessens, Frost, Turner, & Zhu, 2018). The digital revolution necessitates a comprehensive re-evaluation of market structures to maintain efficiency and security in an increasingly rapid, decentralised environment.

This chapter examines the dual evolution of capital markets, focusing on how FinTech innovations are reshaping both public equity and fixed-income markets. The analysis includes an in-depth review of digital trading platforms, distributed ledger technology (DLT), and advanced predictive analytics to clarify the comprehensive impact of digital transformation. Additionally, the chapter identifies new strategic opportunities arising from digitalisation and addresses critical regulatory and operational challenges faced by issuers, investors, and regulators in the current rapidly evolving landscape.

13.2 An Overview of Capital Markets

13.2.1 Concept, Purpose, and Objectives of the Capital Market

A capital market is a financial system in which long-term funds are raised and traded through equity and debt securities with maturities exceeding one year. It enables the transfer of savings from surplus economic units, such as households and institutions, to deficit units, including corporations and governments, for productive investment. The primary purpose of the capital market is to facilitate capital formation and promote sustainable economic growth. Its core objectives include efficient resource allocation, liquidity provision, price discovery, and risk diversification. For example, when a government issues long-term bonds to finance highway infrastructure, it uses the capital market to convert private savings into public investment that supports national productivity (Bodie, Kane, & Marcus, 2021).

13.2.2 Sources of Funds in the Capital Market

13.2.2.1 Individual and Institutional Savings

Individual savings form a foundational source of capital. These funds enter markets directly through personal investments in shares and bonds or indirectly via institutional vehicles such as pension funds, insurance companies, and mutual funds. Institutional investors are particularly influential due to their scale and long-term investment orientation. For instance, pension funds often invest heavily in government and corporate bonds to match long-term liabilities.

13.2.2.2 Foreign Capital Flows

Foreign investors provide additional funding through cross-border portfolio and direct investment. These flows are especially significant in emerging economies and in capital-intensive sectors such as energy and infrastructure. However, regulatory policies may limit foreign participation in strategic industries. For example, foreign investment in telecommunications or defence sectors is often restricted for national security reasons.

13.2.3 Debt Financing: Characteristics and Types

Debt financing involves raising capital by borrowing, in which the issuer is obligated to repay the principal and periodic interest. Debt securities are characterised by predetermined income payments (fixed or floating interest), defined maturity dates, and seniority over equity in the event of liquidation. Holders of debt instruments are creditors and do not possess ownership rights or voting control. Because of their contractual income structure and priority claims, debt instruments generally carry lower risk and lower expected returns than equity securities.

Types of Debt Instruments

Government Bonds: These are long-term securities issued by national governments to finance public expenditure. They are considered low risk because they are backed by the government's taxation and monetary authority. For example, a government may issue a 10-year bond with a face value of $1,000 and an annual coupon rate of 4%, meaning the investor receives $40 in annual coupons and the $1,000 principal at maturity.

Corporate Bonds: Corporations issue bonds to finance expansion, acquisitions, or capital projects. These bonds carry higher risk than government bonds and therefore offer higher interest rates. For instance, if a firm issues a 5-year bond with a face value of $1,000 at a 6% coupon rate, investors receive $60 annually and $1,000 at maturity.

Municipal Bonds: Issued by local or regional governments, these bonds finance infrastructure such as schools or highways. They often provide tax advantages to investors. A city issuing a $5,000 bond at 3% interest would pay $150 in annual interest until maturity.

Debentures: These are unsecured corporate bonds not backed by specific collateral but supported by the issuer's creditworthiness. Because they lack asset backing, they usually offer higher yields.

Convertible Bonds: These hybrid instruments allow investors to convert bonds into a predetermined number of shares. For example, a $1,000 convertible bond with a 5% coupon may be convertible into 50 shares of the issuing company, allowing the investor to benefit if the company's share price rises.

13.2.4 Equity Financing: Characteristics and Types

Equity financing involves raising capital by selling ownership stakes in a company. Equity instruments confer partial ownership to investors, who may benefit from dividends and capital gains as the company grows. Unlike debt, equity does not obligate the company to fixed payments, making it a flexible source of long-term funding. Equity holders assume higher risk than debt investors because they are residual claimants, receiving dividends only after all obligations to creditors are met. Consequently, equity markets are characterised by higher potential returns, price volatility, and exposure to company performance and market conditions (Bodie, Kane, & Marcus, 2021).

Types of Equity Instruments

Common Shares: Common shares represent basic ownership in a company and typically provide voting rights on corporate matters, such as electing the board of directors. Dividends on common shares are variable, depending on profitability and board decisions. For example, if a technology company issues one million common shares at $20 each during an Initial Public Offering (IPO), it raises $20 million. If the company declares a $1-per-share dividend, investors receive $1 million in total dividends, in addition to any capital gains if the share price rises to $30.

Preferred Shares: Preferred shares provide fixed dividends and priority over common shareholders in dividend payments and asset distribution during liquidation. However, preferred shareholders usually do not have voting rights. For instance, a company issues 100,000 preferred shares at $100 each with a fixed annual dividend of 6%. Investors receive $6 per share annually, resulting in total annual dividend payments of $600,000, and have priority over common shareholders in dividend distribution.

Participating Preferred Shares: These shares provide fixed dividends like standard preferred shares but also allow shareholders to participate in additional profits beyond the fixed amount, often linked to common share performance. For example, a participating preferred share with a $5 fixed dividend may also entitle the investor to an additional $2 per share if the company exceeds certain profit targets.

Convertible Preferred Shares: These shares can be converted into a predetermined number of common shares at the shareholder's discretion. For example, a convertible preferred share with a $100 par value may be convertible into ten common shares. If the company's common share price rises to $15, the investor benefits by converting and gaining $50 in capital appreciation per preferred share {(10x15)–100}, in addition to any dividends received before conversion.

13.2.5 Key Participants and Market Mechanisms

13.2.5.1 Market Participants

Capital markets involve issuers, investors, and intermediaries. Issuers include corporations and governments that raise funds by offering securities. Investors include retail and institutional participants seeking returns through dividends, interest, or capital gains. Intermediaries, such as investment banks, brokers, dealers, and market makers, facilitate issuance and trading. Investment banks underwrite new securities issues, brokers execute trades for clients, and market makers provide liquidity by quoting continuous buy and sell prices.

13.2.5.2 Trading Mechanisms

Trading mechanisms differ across asset classes. Equity securities are primarily traded on centralised exchanges that enhance transparency and price discovery. For example, shares of multinational corporations trade on organised exchanges like the New York Stock Exchange (NYSE). In contrast, bond markets have traditionally operated through decentralised OTC systems, where transactions occur through dealer networks. However, technological innovation and regulatory reforms are increasingly shifting bond trading towards electronic platforms, improving transparency and efficiency (Bank for International Settlements, 2019).

13.2.6 Capital Market Efficiency

Capital market efficiency refers to how fully and quickly asset prices incorporate available information, as described by Efficient Market Hypothesis. In the weak form, prices reflect all past trading data, meaning investors cannot consistently earn abnormal returns using only historical price patterns; for example, a trader relying solely on chart trends or moving averages should not systematically outperform the market. The semi-strong-form states that prices adjust rapidly to all publicly available information, such as earnings announcements or economic reports; for instance, when a company releases unexpectedly strong quarterly profits, its share price typically rises almost immediately, leaving little opportunity to profit once the news is public. The strong form holds that prices incorporate all information, public and private, implying that even insiders with confidential knowledge cannot consistently achieve excess returns. This extreme scenario is largely theoretical, though it serves as a benchmark for understanding the limits of market efficiency.

13.3 The Role of FinTech in Capital Markets

FinTech has become a structural force in capital markets by digitising infrastructure, automating intermediation, and embedding advanced analytics into core financial processes. Technologies such as DLT, cloud computing, APIs, AI, and regulatory technology (RegTech) are transforming how securities are issued, traded, settled, and supervised. These changes go beyond incremental efficiency gains, reconfiguring the traditional roles of exchanges, brokers, custodians, and rating agencies while lowering barriers to participation (Arner, Barberis, & Buckley, 2016; McWaters, Galaski, & Chatterjee, 2017) (Figure 13.1).

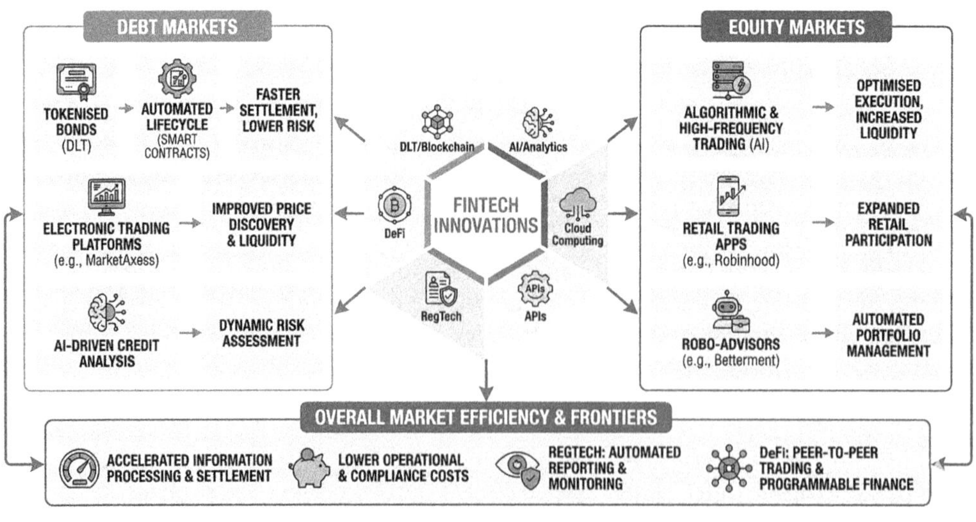

Figure 13.1 FinTech's Transformative Role in Capital Markets.

In debt markets, FinTech is reshaping bond issuance, trading, and credit assessment. DLT enables tokenised bonds with automated lifecycle management through smart contracts, supporting faster settlement, reduced counterparty risk, and greater transparency (Tapscott & Tapscott, 2016; Chen, Pelger, & Zhu, 2023). The European Investment Bank's blockchain-based 'bond-I' illustrates the practical use of DLT in primary debt markets (EIB, 2021). In secondary trading, electronic all-to-all platforms such as MarketAxess and Tradeweb improve price discovery and liquidity in traditionally opaque OTC bond markets (Mazzocchi, 2021). AI-driven models further enhance credit risk analysis by incorporating large, unstructured datasets into dynamic default probability assessments (Jagtiani & Lemieux, 2021).

In equity markets, automation and digital platforms dominate FinTech innovation. Algorithmic and HFT systems use AI to optimise execution across fragmented venues, narrowing bid-ask spreads and increasing liquidity, though they also raise concerns about volatility and systemic risk (Lewis, 2014; SEC, 2023). Retail participation has expanded through commission-free trading apps and fractional share ownership offered by platforms such as Robinhood and Zerodha, contributing to phenomena such as "meme stock" trading episodes (Foley & Putniņš, 2022). Robo-advisors like Betterment and Wealthfront extend algorithmic decision-making to portfolio management, providing low-cost, diversified investment strategies to retail investors (Kaplan & Sauer, 2017; D'Acunto, Prabhala, & Rossi, 2019).

Across both debt and equity markets, FinTech improves overall market efficiency by accelerating information processing, shortening settlement cycles, and lowering operational and compliance costs. Cloud-based systems and APIs enable real-time data integration and scalable analytics, while RegTech automates reporting, monitoring, and surveillance functions (McWaters, Galaski, & Chatterjee, 2017; Arner, Barberis, & Buckley, 2016). At the frontier, decentralised finance (DeFi) platforms use smart contracts to facilitate peer-to-peer trading of tokenised securities and automated financial flows. Protocols such as Maple Finance demonstrate how DeFi structures are beginning to intersect with traditional capital market activities, pointing towards more programmable and disintermediated market models (Schär, 2021).

13.4 A Comparison of Traditional and FinTech Capital Markets

Table 13.1 highlights the fundamental shifts that FinTech has driven across both equity and bond markets and compares traditional and FinTech-enabled capital markets.

Table 13.1 The Fundamental Shifts that FinTech has Driven Across Both Equity and Bond Markets

Feature	*Traditional Capital Markets*	*FinTech Capital Markets*
Market Access	Institutional dominance: high costs limit retail access (Mishkin & Eakins, 2018)	Democratised via zero-commission brokers, fractional shares, and P2P bond platforms (Bavoso, 2020)
Trading and Settlement Speed	Equity: Near-real-time; Bond: Slow T+2 settlement (BIS, 2019)	Near-instant execution and settlement (T+0/T+1) via HFT, blockchain, and central bank digital currencies (CBDCs) (BIS, 2023)

(*Continued*)

Table 13.1 (Continued)

Feature	*Traditional Capital Markets*	*FinTech Capital Markets*
Intermediaries	Heavy reliance on brokers, clearinghouses, and custodians	Disintermediated via P2P platforms, DeFi, and smart contracts (Schär, 2021)
Transparency	Limited (e.g., dark pools in equities, opaque OTC bond dealings)	Enhanced via real-time analytics, A2A platforms, and transparent blockchain ledgers (Mazzocchi, 2021)
Cost Structure	High fees (brokerage, underwriting, custody)	Lower costs through automation and reduced intermediary layers (Claessens et al., 2018)
Innovation and Products	Dominated by plain vanilla stocks and bonds	Rapid innovation with tokenised securities, dynamic coupon structures, and Environmental, Social, and Governance (ESG)-linked products (WEF, 2022)

13.5 Opportunities and Challenges

The integration of FinTech into capital markets brings both opportunities and challenges. Market volatility and manipulation have become prominent concerns, as seen in the 2021 GameStop short squeeze, where social media and commission-free trading drove prices away from fundamentals (Foley & Putniņš, 2022). High-frequency and algorithmic trading can also trigger flash crashes (Lewis, 2014). Cybersecurity and data privacy risks are significant, with digital platforms and DeFi protocols vulnerable to hacks and fraudulent digital assets (FSB, 2022). Regulatory frameworks often lag behind innovation, creating legal uncertainty around smart contracts and tokenised securities (Arner et al., 2020), while digital exclusion can limit access for populations with low technological literacy (Demirgüç-Kunt, Klapper, & Singer, 2017).

At the same time, convergence between traditional and digital models is evident. Hybrid platforms, such as Charles Schwab's zero-commission trading and JPMorgan's blockchain-based bond issuance, illustrate the blending of conventional and FinTech practices (J.P. Morgan, 2020). Institutional investors increasingly use AI and big data for equity and bond strategies (Bodie et al., 2021), while regulators adopt sandboxes and approve products like Bitcoin ETFs, signalling the mainstreaming of digital assets (Zetzsche et al., 2020). Emerging models, including fractional shares, social trading, and DeFi protocols like synthetic stocks on Mirror or tokenised bonds on Maple Finance, create new avenues for market participation.

Overall, FinTech enhances liquidity, transparency, and efficiency in capital markets. However, it also introduces risks related to volatility, cybersecurity, regulatory uncertainty, and financial inclusion, underscoring the need for careful oversight and risk management.

13.6 Key Practical Issues in FinTech-Driven Capital Markets

Systemic Risk from Technological Interdependence: The widespread use of algorithmic trading strategies can amplify market volatility, as seen in flash crashes where highly correlated algorithms trigger rapid price swings. Dependence on common cloud infrastructures and APIs creates single points of failure, increasing systemic vulnerability (FSB, 2023; SEC, 2023). For example, the 2010 *Flash Crash* demonstrated how algorithmic interconnections can destabilise equity markets within minutes.

Legacy System Integration Challenges: Integrating agile FinTech solutions with legacy core banking and T+2 settlement systems can create operational friction, increase costs, and heighten the risk of failures (Gomber, Kauffman, Parker, & Weber, 2018). For instance, implementing blockchain-based bond settlement alongside traditional clearing systems requires complex reconciliation processes and can delay execution.

Data Integrity, Standardisation, and AI Bias: AI and machine learning models are only as reliable as the data they use. Poor-quality, biased, or non-standardised datasets, particularly for ESG metrics, can result in inaccurate outputs or discriminatory outcomes, such as mispriced ESG-linked securities (Jagtiani & Lemieux, 2021).

Regulatory Arbitrage in a Borderless Market: Decentralised finance (DeFi) platforms and global FinTech brokers often operate across jurisdictions with inconsistent oversight, creating regulatory gaps that may compromise investor protection and market integrity (Zetzsche et al., 2020). For example, certain DeFi lending protocols provide tokenised credit globally without adhering to local securities laws.

Market Fragmentation and Liquidity Silos: The growth of multiple electronic trading platforms and blockchain networks can fragment liquidity across non-interoperable venues, reducing price transparency and harming market efficiency (BIS, 2019). For example, fragmented OTC bond trading across different electronic platforms can make price discovery more difficult for institutional investors.

13.7 The Future of Capital Markets in the FinTech Era

The evolution of capital markets in the FinTech era is expected to be shaped by several transformative trends. Increased decentralisation is likely, with broader adoption of tokenised equities and bonds traded on Decentralised Exchanges (DEXs), enabling peer-to-peer transactions and reduced reliance on traditional intermediaries (Schär, 2021). Hyper-personalisation will emerge through AI-driven investment solutions, offering fully tailored portfolios that align with individual investor goals, risk preferences, and values (D'Acunto et al., 2019). Global market integration is anticipated, supported by interoperable trading systems and CBDCs, facilitating seamless, real-time cross-border transactions (BIS, 2023).

The growth of sustainable finance is also expected, as AI-powered analytics enhance the development and pricing of green bonds and ESG-linked equity products, improving transparency and supporting responsible investment (International Capital Market Association, 2021). Finally, the advent of quantum computing has the potential to transform capital markets by enabling rapid, highly complex pricing, risk modelling, and portfolio optimisation across all asset classes, offering unprecedented computational capacity for decision-making (World Economic Forum, 2022). Collectively, these developments suggest a future capital market ecosystem that is more decentralised, personalised, integrated, sustainable, and technologically advanced.

13.8 Conclusion

In conclusion, global capital markets are experiencing a profound transformation driven by the rapid integration of FinTech. Innovations such as DLT (blockchain), AI, and advanced digital platforms have expanded market access, improved operational efficiency, and introduced new mechanisms for capital formation across both equity and fixed-income markets. While these technological advancements enhance efficiency and inclusivity, their accelerated adoption also generates significant systemic risks. As highlighted by the

Financial Stability Board (FSB, 2023), effective risk management is essential to address challenges related to data integrity, cyber resilience, and market liquidity within increasingly decentralised financial environments.

The future trajectory of capital markets will depend on the successful convergence of traditional financial infrastructure with emerging digital technologies. However, this evolution often exceeds the pace at which legal and regulatory frameworks can adapt, resulting in operational and compliance challenges for incumbent institutions. Addressing these complexities requires coordinated engagement among technology developers, established financial institutions, and regulatory authorities, as emphasised by Arner et al. (2020). Such collaboration is critical to achieving a sustainable and secure capital market ecosystem that simultaneously promotes innovation while safeguarding stability and protecting the interests of all market participants.

Key Terms and Glossary

Primary Market The financial market where new securities are issued for the first time (e.g., through an IPO).

Secondary Market The market where previously issued securities (e.g., stocks, bonds) are traded among investors, without the involvement of the issuing company.

Tokenisation The process of converting rights to a real-world asset (like a stock or bond) into a digital token on a blockchain.

HFT A subset of algorithmic trading characterised by extremely high speed, high turnover rates, and high order-to-trade ratios, often leveraging co-location services.

Smart Contract Self-executing contracts with the terms of the agreement directly written into code, which automatically execute when predetermined conditions are met.

Fixed-Income Security An investment that provides a return in the form of fixed periodic payments and the eventual return of principal at maturity (e.g., a bond).

All-to-All (A2A) Trading A market structure, often electronic, where all participants (including buy-side and sell-side firms) can trade directly with one another, enhancing liquidity and price transparency.

Democratisation of Access The process of lowering barriers (like cost, minimum investment, and complexity) to allow retail investors to participate in financial markets on a more level playing field with institutions.

Test Your Understanding

Multiple-Choice Questions

1 Which of the following technologies enables the creation of tokenised bonds with automated coupon payments?

A Robo-advisors
B DLT
C HFT
D Cloud Computing

2 In equity markets, what is the primary effect of algorithmic and HFT?
   A Eliminates regulatory oversight
   B Reduces market liquidity
   C Narrows bid-ask spreads and improves execution speed
   D Guarantees investor returns
3 Which of the following is an example of a DeFi application in capital markets?
   A MarketAxess electronic bond platform
   B Maple Finance for tokenised corporate credit
   C Traditional NYSE trading floor
   D Robo-advisory portfolio management
4 What is the main concern with integrating FinTech solutions into legacy T+2 settlement systems?
   A Reduced market transparency
   B Increased operational friction and potential failures
   C Elimination of intermediaries
   D Lower transaction costs
5 Hyper-personalisation in future capital markets primarily refers to:
   A Allowing investors to trade anonymously
   B AI-driven investment strategies tailored to individual goals and risk preferences
   C Blockchain-based cross-border settlements
   D DEX trading of synthetic assets

Short Questions

1 Define market fragmentation and explain how multiple electronic platforms can affect liquidity in capital markets.
2 List three key benefits of FinTech integration in debt markets, providing an example for each.
3 Explain the difference between weak-form, semi-strong-form, and strong-form market efficiency with an example of each.

Analytical Questions

1 Critically evaluate the risks and opportunities associated with the convergence of traditional capital markets and DeFi platforms. Include examples to support your answer.
2 Discuss how AI and big data are transforming credit risk assessment in bond markets. How do these innovations compare with traditional credit rating methods?
3 Examine the challenges of regulatory adaptation in the FinTech era. How can regulators balance innovation, financial inclusion, and systemic stability in increasingly decentralised markets?

Case Study: The Archegos Capital Collapse—Opacity and Systemic Risk in Modern Markets

In March 2021, Archegos Capital Management, a family office led by Bill Hwang, collapsed, causing losses exceeding $30 billion across its banking counterparties, including Credit Suisse and Nomura. Archegos accumulated highly leveraged, concentrated positions in a few equities, such as ViacomCBS and Discovery, using Total Return Swaps (TRS), which provide economic exposure without requiring direct ownership of the underlying assets. The firm dealt with multiple investment banks, each unaware of Archegos's total exposure due to the opaque nature of the OTC derivatives market. When the value of key positions declined, Archegos failed to meet margin calls, triggering forced liquidations by banks. This fire sale depressed stock prices further, creating a self-reinforcing market shock.

The episode underscores the systemic vulnerabilities of both traditional and technologically driven markets. Opacity in OTC trading obscured counterparty risk, a problem FinTech innovations like blockchain-based trade reporting could address by providing real-time, consolidated exposure data. Conversely, the highly electronic and interconnected infrastructure, including algorithmic risk management, may have accelerated the sell-off. Regulatory gaps, such as the limited oversight of family offices compared to hedge funds, exemplify the risks of regulatory lag and arbitrage. Archegos illustrates the critical need for transparency, enhanced risk monitoring, and coordinated oversight in environments where leverage, automation, and innovative instruments converge (SEC, 2022).

References

The Straits Times (2021) 'Archegos: how a little-known US investment firm shook global financial markets', *The Straits Times*. Available at: https://www.straitstimes.com/business/banking/archegos-how-a-little-known-us-investment-firm-shook-global-financial-markets (Accessed: 10 October 2025).

U.S. Securities and Exchange Commission (SEC). (2022). *Proposals on Enhancing Transparency and Stability in the Treasury and Swap Markets*. Washington, DC: U.S. Securities and Exchange Commission.

Case Study Questions

1 In what ways did the structure of the OTC derivatives market, combined with the use of TRS, amplify the scale and rapidity of the Archegos Capital collapse?
2 Evaluate how a specific FinTech solution, such as blockchain-based trade reporting or AI-driven counterparty risk assessment, might have either mitigated or inadvertently accelerated the Archegos crisis.
3 Considering the Archegos incident, what key lessons should regulators and financial institutions derive to manage risks associated with highly leveraged strategies and the integration of emerging financial technologies?

Further Reading

Arner, D.W., Barberis, J.N., & Buckley, R.P., (2020). *FinTech and the Future of Finance: Market and Regulatory Implications*. Cambridge: Cambridge University Press.

Bank for International Settlements (BIS). (2023). *The Crypto Ecosystem: Key Elements and Risks*. Basel: BIS.

Schär, F. (2021). Decentralised Finance: On Blockchain- and Smart Contract-based Financial Markets. *Federal Reserve Bank of St. Louis Review*, 103(2), 153–174.

References

Arner, D.W., Barberis, J., & Buckley, R.P. (2016). The Evolution of FinTech: A New Post-Crisis Paradigm? *Georgetown Journal of International Law*, 47(4), 1271–1319.

Arner, D.W., Barberis, J., & Buckley, R.P. (2020). The Future of FinTech and Finance: A Research Agenda. *University of Hong Kong Faculty of Law Research Paper No. 2020/017*.

Bank for International Settlements (BIS). (2019). The Future of Capital Markets: Digitalisation, Innovation and the Role of Regulation. *Committee on the Global Financial System Papers No. 63*.

Bank for International Settlements (BIS). (2023). FinTech Innovations in Fixed-Income Markets. *BIS Papers*.

Bavoso, V. (2020). The Promise and Perils of Alternative Market-Based Finance: The Case of P2P Lending in the UK. *Journal of Banking Regulation*, 21(4), 395–409. https://doi.org/10.1057/s41261-019-00118-9

Bodie, Z., Kane, A., & Marcus, A.J. (2021). *Investments* (12th ed.). New York: McGraw-Hill Education.

Chen, L., Pelger, M. and Zhu, J. (2023) Deep Learning in Asset Pricing. *Management Science*, 70(2), 714–750.

Claessens, S., Frost, J., Turner, G., & Zhu, F. (2018). FinTech Credit Markets Around the World: Size, Drivers and Policy Issues. *BIS Quarterly Review*, September, pp. 29–49. Basel: Bank for International Settlements.

D'Acunto, F., Prabhala, N., & Rossi, A.G. (2019). The Promises and Pitfalls of Robo-Advising. *The Review of Financial Studies*, 32(5), 1983–2020.

Demirgüç-Kunt, A., Klapper, L., & Singer, D. (2017). Financial Inclusion and Inclusive Growth: A Review of Recent Empirical Evidence. *World Bank Policy Research Working Paper No. 8040*.

European Investment Bank (EIB). (2021). EIB Issues Its First-Ever Digital Bond on a Public Blockchain [Press Release].

Financial Stability Board (FSB). (2022). *Assessment of Risks to Financial Stability from Cyber Incidents*. Basel: Financial Stability Board.

Financial Stability Board (FSB). (2023). *The Financial Stability Implications of Decentralised Finance*. Basel: Financial Stability Board.

Foley, S., & Putniņš, T.J. (2022). Meme Stocks and the Evolving Retail Investment Landscape. *Annual Review of Financial Economics*, 14, 167–187.

Gomber, P., Kauffman, R.J., Parker, C., & Weber, B.W. (2018). On the FinTech Revolution: Interpreting the Forces of Innovation, Disruption, and Transformation in Financial Services. *Journal of Management Information Systems*, 35(1), 220–265.

International Capital Market Association (ICMA). (2021). *The Green Bond Principles*. Zurich: International Capital Market Association.

Jagtiani, J., & Lemieux, C. (2021). The Roles of Alternative Data and Machine Learning in FinTech Lending: Evidence from the LendingClub Consumer Platform. *Financial Management*, 50(3), 803–832.

Kaplan, A., & Sauer, J. (2017). Robo-Advisors: Disrupting the Wealth Management Industry. *Harvard Business Review*, 95(4), 2–5.

Lewis, M. (2014). *Flash Boys: A Wall Street Revolt*. New York: W.W. Norton & Company.

Mazzocchi, J. (2021). The Electronification of the Corporate Bond Market. *Journal of Financial Markets*, 52, 100561.

McWaters, J., Galaski, R., & Chatterjee, S. (2017). *Beyond FinTech: A Pragmatic Assessment of Disruptive Potential in Financial Services*. Geneva: World Economic Forum.

Mishkin, F.S., & Eakins, S.G. (2018). *Financial Markets and Institutions* (9th ed.). Boston, MA: Pearson.

Morgan J.P.. (2020). *J.P. Morgan Creates Digital Coin for Payments* [Press Release].

Schär, F. (2021). Decentralised Finance: On Blockchain- and Smart Contract-Based Financial Markets. *Federal Reserve Bank of St. Louis Review*, 103(2), 153–174.

Securities and Exchange Commission (SEC). (2023). *Report on Algorithmic Trading and Market Structure*. Washington, DC: U.S. Securities and Exchange Commission.

Tapscott, D., & Tapscott, A. (2016). *Blockchain Revolution: How the Technology Behind Bitcoin Is Changing Money, Business, and the World*. New York: Penguin.

World Economic Forum (WEF). (2022). *The Future of Equity Markets in the Digital Age*.Geneva: World Economic Forum.

Zetzsche, D.A., Arner, D.W., & Buckley, R. P. (2020). Decentralised Finance (DeFi). *Journal of Financial Regulation*, 6(2), 172–203.

14 Technology in Commodities and Derivatives Markets

Chapter Overview

This chapter provides a comprehensive analysis of the disruption caused by Financial Technology (FinTech) in the commodities and derivatives markets, which underpin the global financial system. It discusses how these traditionally intricate, institution-centric, and opaque sectors are being transformed by technologies such as blockchain, smart contracts, artificial intelligence (AI), and decentralised finance (DeFi). The chapter first outlines the foundational structures of these markets, then examines the integration of FinTech innovations with existing systems. It contrasts established practices with digital advancements, critically evaluates both shared and unique risks, addresses the evolving regulatory landscape, and explores future trajectories. The analysis emphasises a transition towards greater efficiency, transparency, and accessibility.

Learning Objectives

By the end of this chapter, you should be able to:

1. Explain the structure, instruments, and economic functions of traditional commodities and derivatives markets.
2. Analyse how financial technologies, including blockchain, AI, and DeFi, are reshaping trading mechanisms, post-trade processes, and risk management practices.
3. Critically compare traditional market infrastructures with FinTech-enabled models in terms of transparency, efficiency, and market accessibility.
4. Evaluate the operational, systemic, and regulatory risks that emerge from the integration of FinTech into commodities and derivatives markets.
5. Assess real-world applications and case studies to determine the practical advantages, limitations, and future trajectory of technological innovation in these markets.

DOI: 10.4324/9781003775751-17

14.1 Introduction

The commodities market focuses on the exchange of physical raw materials, while the derivatives market manages risk through contracts linked to underlying assets. Both markets serve as essential components of global finance by enabling efficient price discovery, risk management, and capital allocation. Historically, these sectors were dominated by institutions and depended on manual processes. Structural opacity, particularly in high-volume over-the-counter (OTC) transactions, further characterised these markets—this traditional framework imposed barriers to entry and necessitated complex, multi-party manual settlement verification.

A significant transformation is underway as traditionally separate ecosystems converge, primarily driven by advancements in FinTech. FinTech is eliminating barriers between physical commodity trading and financial derivatives. According to Claessens, Frost, Turner, and Zhu (2018), new technologies are fundamentally reshaping financial services. These previously isolated markets are transitioning towards shared digital infrastructure and increased transparency. Technological innovation is driving both sectors away from legacy systems and towards integrated digital operations.

Digital advancements are transforming fundamental market functions, including accessibility, analytical capabilities, and settlement integrity. Digital platforms are broadening market access and facilitating higher volume execution. AI-driven analytics provide enhanced predictive modelling and risk assessment. Core settlement mechanisms are being redesigned, with blockchain-based solutions intended to improve security and streamline clearing processes, thereby reducing dependence on centralised ledgers (Tapscott & Tapscott, 2016). These innovations increase speed, accuracy, and regulatory compliance in trading, clearing, and risk management for both markets (Gomber, Kauffman, Parker, & Weber, 2018)

14.2 An Overview of the Markets

14.2.1 The Commodities Market

Definition and Objective: A commodity is a fundamental, standardised, and interchangeable good that serves as an input for the production of other goods or services. Commodities include raw materials such as crude oil, natural gas, metals, agricultural products, and energy resources. The commodities market provides a structured platform for the buying and selling of these goods, enabling producers, consumers, and investors to manage price risk and secure supply or demand commitments. It plays a critical role in price discovery, reflecting real-time supply-and-demand dynamics, and allows market participants to hedge against price volatility through instruments such as futures and options. Additionally, the commodities market contributes to efficient allocation of resources, guiding production, inventory management, and investment decisions across sectors. Beyond its functional role in commerce, the market acts as a macroeconomic indicator, offering insights into global economic trends, inflationary pressures, and sectoral performance, thereby influencing monetary policy and investment strategies (Geman, 2005).

Key Participants: The market involves commodity producers, traders, institutional investors such as banks and funds, organised exchanges such as Chicago Mercantile Exchange (CME) and Intercontinental Exchange, and regulators, including the Commodity Futures Trading Commission (CFTC) (Williams, 2001).

Market Instruments and Mechanisms: A commodity option is a financial contract that grants the holder the right, but not the obligation, to buy or sell a specified quantity of a commodity at a predetermined price, known as the strike price, on or before a specified expiration date. There are two primary types of commodity options: call options, which give the holder the right to purchase the commodity, and put options, which give the holder the right to sell it. Traders and businesses widely use these instruments to speculate on price movements, hedge against adverse price fluctuations, and manage risk in industries that rely heavily on commodities. By providing flexibility and risk management tools, commodity options play a crucial role in stabilising exposure and supporting strategic decision-making in commodity markets.

Spot Contracts: A spot contract involves the immediate payment and delivery of a commodity at the current market price. Immediate purchase and delivery at the current market price. For instance, an investor buys 100 barrels of crude oil at $70 per barrel, resulting in an immediate payment of 7,000. If the market price subsequently rises to 75 per barrel, giving the investor an unrealised capital gain of $500 {(75x100)–7000}.

Futures Contracts: Futures are standardised agreements to buy or sell an asset at a predetermined price on a specified future date. They are traded on regulated exchanges and commonly used for hedging or speculation. Standardised agreements to buy or sell at a future date and price, traded on regulated exchanges, used for hedging and speculation (Hull, 2022; Black, 1976). For instance, a farmer sells a futures contract for 1,000 bushels of wheat at $5 per bushel to lock in prices. If the market price falls to $4.50, the farmer avoids a $500 loss; if the price rises to $5.50, the farmer forgoes a $500 gain.

Forwards: Forwards are similar to futures but are customised OTC contracts. For example, a coffee importer may agree privately with a supplier to buy 500 kg of coffee at $10/kg in two months. Unlike futures, forwards are not standardised or exchange-traded and carry higher counterparty risk.

14.2.2 The Derivatives Market

Definition and Objective: A derivative is a financial instrument whose value is contingent on the performance of an underlying asset, such as a commodity, equity, bond, currency, interest rate, or market index. Derivatives function as contracts between two or more parties, specifying obligations to exchange cash flows or assets under predetermined conditions at present or in the future. The primary objectives of derivatives markets are risk management, price discovery, and the creation of speculative opportunities. They allow market participants, such as corporations, financial institutions, and investors, to hedge against fluctuations in asset prices, interest rates, or currency values, thereby mitigating exposure to market volatility. Derivatives also provide a mechanism for leveraged trading and arbitrage, enhancing liquidity and enabling efficient capital allocation. Furthermore, these instruments contribute to overall financial system stability by distributing risk across participants and facilitating the transfer of exposures to those best equipped to bear them. Through standardised exchange-traded contracts (like futures and options) and customised OTC agreements (such as forwards and swaps), derivatives underpin complex financial strategies and play a critical role in modern global finance (BIS, 2023).

Key Participants: Institutional investors, commercial banks, corporations, hedge funds, and Central Counterparties (CCPs) that mitigate counterparty risk by guaranteeing trades (Duffie & Zhu, 2011).

14.2.2.1 *Market Instruments and Mechanisms*

Futures and Forwards: Futures and forwards are derivative contracts that obligate parties to buy or sell an underlying asset at a predetermined price on a specified future date. Futures contracts are standardised, exchange-traded agreements with set contract sizes and settlement procedures, providing liquidity and reduced counterparty risk. Forwards are privately negotiated, customised contracts traded OTC, offering flexibility in terms but carrying higher counterparty risk (Hull, 2022). Both instruments are widely used for hedging against price fluctuations and for speculation.

Futures contract: A futures contract is a standardised, exchange-traded derivative agreement obligating parties to buy or sell an underlying asset at a predetermined price on a specified future date. For instance, a wheat farmer expects to harvest 1,000 bushels in three months. To lock in the current market price of $5 per bushel, the farmer sells a futures contract for 1,000 bushels at $5. If the market price at harvest drops to $4.50, the farmer avoids a $0.50 × 1,000 = $500 loss. Or if the price rises to $5.50, the farmer forgoes a gain of $0.50 × 1,000 = $500.

Forwards contract: A forward contract is a customised, OTC derivative agreement between two parties to buy or sell an underlying asset at a predetermined price on a specified future date. For instance, A coffee importer negotiates directly with a supplier to purchase 500 kg of coffee at $10/kg in two months. If the market price falls to $9/kg, the importer is still obligated to pay 10 per kilogram, resulting in an opportunity loss of 500 ([10 − 9] × 500). Conversely, if the price rises to $11/kg, the importer benefits by paying $10/kg instead of $11/kg.

Options: An option gives the holder the right, but not the obligation, to buy (call) or sell (put) an asset at a predetermined price (strike price) before or on a specific date. Contracts granting the right, but not the obligation, to buy (call) or sell (put) an asset at a strike price. For instance, buying a call option for 100 shares at $50 with a $2 premium: if the stock rises to $60, profit = (60 − 50 − 2) × 100 = $800; if the price is < $50, loss = premium ($200) (Black, Scholes & Merton, 1973).

Swaps: Swaps are agreements to exchange cash flows. Common types include interest rate swaps and credit default swaps. Interest rate swaps, for instance, Bank A pays 5% fixed on $1,000,000 to Bank B, receiving a London Interbank Offered Rate (LIBOR)-based floating rate. If LIBOR rises to 6%, net gain = $10,000. On the other hand, a credit default swap, for instance, protects a $1,000,000 corporate bond and provides compensation in the event of default (Hull, 2022; Li, 2000).

14.3 The FinTech Innovation in Commodities and Derivatives

14.3.1 *FinTech Innovation in Commodities and Derivatives Markets*

FinTech has emerged as a structural driver of change in both commodities and derivatives markets by digitising trading infrastructures, automating post-trade processes, and embedding advanced data analytics into pricing and risk management frameworks. Core innovations include electronic trading platforms, distributed ledger technology (DLT), smart contracts, AI, and DeFi architectures. These technologies enhance execution speed, reduce operational frictions, improve market transparency, and widen participation beyond traditional intermediaries, while simultaneously introducing new channels of operational, cyber, and model risk that require adaptive regulatory oversight (BIS, 2023; FSB, 2022) (Figure 14.1).

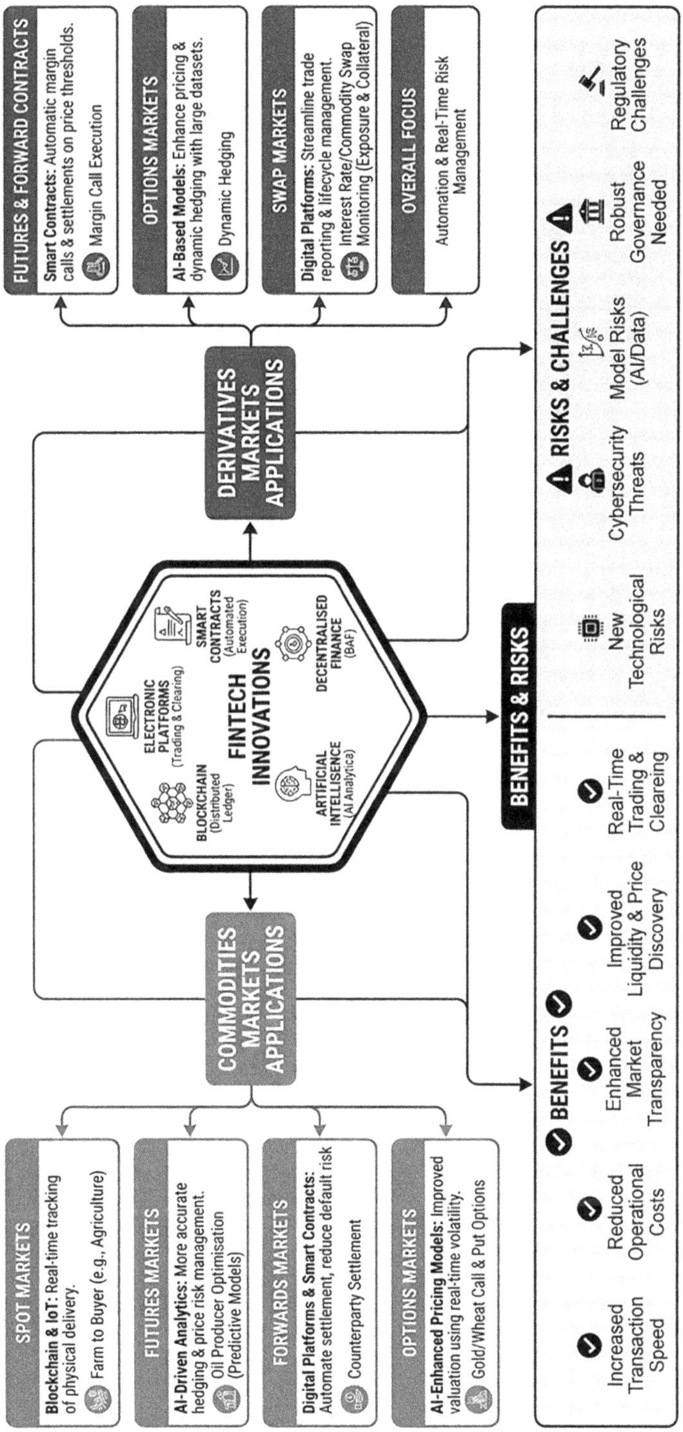

Figure 14.1 FinTech Innovation in Commodities and Derivatives Markets.

14.3.2 FinTech Applications in Commodities Markets

In commodity markets, FinTech enhances efficiency, traceability, and market access across spot, futures, forwards, and options. Blockchain and Internet of Things (IoT) systems improve verification of physical supply chains in spot markets by providing immutable records of origin, storage, and shipment, thereby supporting quality assurance and ESG compliance (OECD, 2020; World Economic Forum, 2021). In futures markets, electronic trading venues and AI-driven analytics enhance liquidity and price discovery while enabling producers and consumers to implement real-time hedging strategies (Gomber et al., 2018). Forward contracts benefit from digital documentation platforms and smart contract–enabled settlement mechanisms that reduce processing delays and counterparty risk in customised OTC agreements (ISDA, 2022). In commodity options markets, machine learning models improve volatility forecasting and pricing accuracy for call and put options written on assets such as crude oil, gold, or agricultural products (Heaton, Polson, & Witte, 2017).

14.3.3 FinTech Applications in Derivatives Markets

Within derivatives markets more broadly, FinTech innovations enhance lifecycle automation, valuation precision, and regulatory compliance across futures, forwards, options, and swaps. Smart contracts deployed on DLT platforms can automate margin calls, collateral adjustments, and settlement payments, reducing manual intervention and operational risk (Szabo, 1997; ISDA, 2022). AI-based models incorporate high-frequency market data and alternative information sources to refine volatility surfaces, correlation estimates, and scenario analysis, strengthening derivatives pricing and portfolio risk monitoring (IMF, 2023). In swap markets, including interest rate and commodity swaps, digital trading and RegTech systems streamline trade reporting, reconciliation, and compliance with clearing and margin requirements, thereby improving transparency and systemic risk oversight (Duffie & Zhu, 2011; BIS, 2023). While these developments increase efficiency and analytical capacity, they also introduce technology-driven vulnerabilities, including cyber risk, algorithmic model risk, and legal uncertainty regarding the enforceability of digital contracts.

14.4 A Comparison of Traditional and FinTech-Driven Markets

Table 14.1 compares traditional and FinTech-driven commodities and derivatives markets.

Table 14.1 The Main Changes That FinTech Has Brought to Traditional Markets and FinTech-Driven Markets

Feature	*Traditional Markets*	*FinTech-Driven Markets*
Market Access	Institutional dominance; high barriers for retail (Mishkin & Eakins, 2018)	Democratised via fractional ownership, mobile apps, and permissionless DeFi (Zetzsche et al., 2020)
Trading and Execution	Physical floors, voice brokers, opaque OTC deals	Digital platforms, algorithmic trading, and transparent on-chain order books (O'Hara, 2015)

(*Continued*)

Table 14.1 (Continued)

Feature	*Traditional Markets*	*FinTech-Driven Markets*
Settlement and clearing	Physical delivery, slow paper-based processes, T+1/T+2 via CCPs (Duffie & Zhu, 2011)	Tokenised assets, instant (T+0) settlement via smart contracts, reduced CCP reliance (ISDA, 2022)
Transparency	Limited price and supply chain transparency	Enhanced via blockchain-tracked provenance and live, on-chain transaction data (Yermack, 2017)
Risk Management	Manual hedging using standardised futures/options	AI-driven predictive analytics and dynamic, automated hedging tools (Heaton et al., 2017)
Product Innovation	Standardised contracts (e.g., monthly futures)	Customisable derivatives and tokenised assets via flexible smart contracts (Schär, 2021)
Regulation	Strict, established frameworks (e.g., CFTC, Financial Conduct Authority)	Evolving and uncertain regulations for digital assets and DeFi (e.g., MiCA) (Avgouleas & Kiayias, 2023)

14.5 Key Practical Issues of FinTech in Commodities and Derivatives Markets

The application of FinTech in commodities and derivatives markets improves efficiency and access but introduces significant risks. Algorithmic and high-frequency trading can intensify short-term volatility and contribute to flash crashes, particularly when many firms rely on similar models and shared cloud infrastructure, creating potential single points of failure (SEC, 2023; FSB, 2023). In DeFi-based derivatives markets, dependence on external price oracles adds vulnerability, as manipulated data feeds can trigger large, automated liquidations (Qin et al., 2021). At the same time, cybersecurity threats, including smart contract exploits and platform hacks, pose material risks to investor assets and market integrity (FSB, 2022).

Regulatory and operational challenges further complicate adoption. Blockchain systems operate across borders, raising jurisdictional issues and uncertainty regarding the legal enforceability of smart contracts (ISDA, 2022). Because innovation often outpaces regulation, firms may engage in regulatory arbitrage by operating in less restrictive environments (Avgouleas & Kiayias, 2023). Integrating new FinTech systems with legacy trading and settlement infrastructure is costly and complex, while limited interoperability across platforms can fragment liquidity and weaken price discovery (Gomber et al., 2018). Moreover, easier market access through digital platforms raises concerns about investor protection, as retail participants may lack the expertise to manage leveraged or complex derivative products (Foley & Putniņš, 2022).

Convergence between traditional finance and FinTech is nevertheless accelerating. Established institutions are adopting digital tools, illustrated by CME Group's Bitcoin futures and initiatives in gold tokenisation within traditional bullion markets (BIS, 2022). Hybrid models combine regulatory oversight with technological innovation, while policymakers are developing clearer frameworks, such as the EU's MiCA regulation and the CFTC's engagement with digital asset markets (European Union, 2023; CFTC, 2023). This convergence signals a gradual integration of digital innovation into the mainstream commodities and derivatives markets.

14.6 The Future of Commodities and Derivatives in the FinTech Era

The future of commodities and derivatives markets is expected to be shaped by greater automation, data integration, and digital infrastructure. AI-driven systems will enable real-time hedging, dynamic pricing, and more accurate forecasting of supply and demand.

At the same time, IoT-generated data from logistics and production networks will further improve pricing precision and risk management (Gro Intelligence, 2023). These developments point towards increasingly efficient and responsive markets.

Decentralisation will also expand, with wider use of decentralised exchanges (DEXs) and DeFi protocols for trading tokenised commodities and derivative instruments through smart contracts (Schär, 2021). At the same time, interoperability between traditional financial market infrastructures, such as CCPs, and blockchain-based systems may emerge, combining regulatory safeguards with technological efficiency.

Sustainable finance will grow in importance as AI-powered ESG analytics improve the measurement of environmental and social performance, supporting green commodity instruments and sustainability-linked derivatives (Flammer, 2021). In parallel, user-friendly FinTech tools are likely to enable more personalised hedging and investment products, allowing market participants to design contracts tailored to specific risk exposures and strategic objectives.

14.7 Conclusion

FinTech is reshaping commodities and derivatives markets by introducing a new operational paradigm that departs from traditional, intermediary-centric structures. Technologies such as blockchain enhance traceability and data integrity through immutable record-keeping, AI strengthens predictive analytics and risk modelling, and DeFi protocols expand access to trading and liquidity provision. Together, these innovations improve efficiency, reduce friction in post-trade processes, and lower barriers to participation, contributing to greater market transparency and inclusivity. As observed in the literature, the convergence of these technologies is fostering financial systems that are increasingly innovative, accessible, and operationally resilient (Arner et al., 2020; FSB, 2023).

Despite these benefits, the rapid integration of FinTech introduces substantial complexity and risk. Accelerated technological change heightens operational vulnerabilities, particularly in relation to cybersecurity, data integrity, and the resilience of digital market infrastructure. At the same time, the coexistence of regulated exchanges and decentralised platforms contributes to regulatory fragmentation and supervisory challenges. Addressing these issues requires more than technological adoption; it demands coordinated governance, adaptive regulatory frameworks, and robust risk management practices. The long-term sustainability of commodities and derivatives markets will therefore depend on the ability of market participants and regulators to balance innovation with systemic stability, ensuring that technological progress reinforces rather than undermines financial resilience.

Key Terms and Glossary

Spot Market A market where financial instruments or commodities are traded for immediate delivery.

Futures Contract A standardised legal agreement to buy or sell an asset at a predetermined price at a specified future date, traded on an exchange.

Derivative A financial contract whose value is dependent upon or derived from one or more underlying assets.

Smart Contract Self-executing contracts with the terms of the agreement directly written into code, which automatically execute upon predefined conditions.

Tokenisation The process of converting rights to a real-world asset into a digital token on a blockchain.

CCP (Central Counterparty) An entity that interposes itself between counterparties to contracts, becoming the buyer to every seller and the seller to every buyer to mitigate counterparty risk.

Oracle (in DeFi) A service that feeds external, real-world data onto a blockchain so that smart contracts can execute based on this information.

Test Your Understanding

Multiple-Choice Questions

1 Which of the following best describes a key benefit of blockchain technology in commodities and derivatives markets?

A Eliminates the need for regulators entirely
B Provides immutable provenance and enhances settlement security
C Ensures guaranteed profits for traders
D Replaces all traditional market participants

2 In derivatives markets, what is the primary difference between a futures contract and a forward contract?

A Futures are OTC and customised, and forwards are exchange-traded
B Futures are standardised and exchange-traded, and forwards are OTC and customised
C Both are standardised, but forwards settle immediately.
D Futures are only used by institutional investors

3 Which FinTech innovation allows the verification of transaction validity without exposing personal data?

A Smart contracts
B Zero-knowledge proofs
C Tokenisation
D High-frequency trading

4 One of the main risks introduced by FinTech integration into commodities and derivatives markets is:

A Reduced market transparency
B Systemic and operational risks, including cybersecurity threats
C Elimination of counterparty risk entirely
D Guaranteed market liquidity

5 How does DeFi impact traditional market accessibility?

A Restricts trading to institutional participants only
B Increases barriers due to complex regulations
C Broadens access via decentralised platforms and tokenised assets
D Removes all forms of risk management

Short Questions

1. Explain how AI improves risk management in commodities and derivatives markets.
2. Describe one way that smart contracts and DLT improve settlement efficiency in derivative transactions.
3. Identify two regulatory challenges that arise from FinTech adoption in these markets.

Analytical Questions

1. Compare and contrast traditional commodities and derivatives markets with FinTech-driven markets in terms of transparency, risk management, and market accessibility. Provide specific examples.
2. Discuss the operational and systemic risks associated with high-frequency trading and algorithmic models in FinTech-enabled derivatives markets. How can regulators mitigate these risks?
3. Evaluate the potential future impact of AI and DeFi on commodities and derivatives markets, considering both efficiency gains and systemic challenges. Use real-world examples to support your analysis.

Case Study: The dYdX Protocol and the Evolution of

dYdX is a leading decentralised exchange (DEX) specifically designed for trading perpetual contracts and other cryptocurrency derivatives without a central intermediary. Unlike traditional exchanges, users retain custody of their assets in their own wallets and interact directly with the protocol through smart contracts. Traders deposit cryptocurrency as collateral into these contracts and can open leveraged long or short positions on various tokenised assets. The smart contracts automate the entire trade lifecycle, including margin calculation, profit and loss updates, and automatic liquidation if collateral falls below the required maintenance margin.

The platform relies on external oracles to provide accurate, real-time price data for underlying assets. All transactions are recorded on a public blockchain, ensuring transparency and verifiability. By eliminating brokers and clearinghouses, dYdX achieves operational efficiency, global accessibility, and permissionless participation, allowing anyone with an internet connection and a compatible wallet to trade derivatives. Tokenised assets, such as wrapped Bitcoin, are commonly used as collateral, further bridging traditional finance and blockchain ecosystems.

dYdX exemplifies the convergence of FinTech trends, including disintermediation, automation via smart contracts, tokenisation, and global access. Its structure introduces both opportunities, such as lower barriers to entry and increased transparency, and risks, including counterparty exposure to smart contract vulnerabilities and reliance on the accuracy of oracles.

Reference

dYdX Foundation. (2023). *dYdX Protocol Documentation*. Available at: https://docs.dydx.exchange/ (Accessed: 1 March 2026).

Case Study Questions

1. How does dYdX's decentralised, non-custodial structure differ from a traditional centralised exchange like the CME with a CCP? Discuss the trade-offs in counterparty risk, access, and efficiency.
2. What is an oracle in a DeFi system, and what risks arise if it provides inaccurate or manipulated price data for dYdX?
3. How does dYdX's democratisation of derivatives trading create new investor protection challenges, and how can regulators address them without hindering innovation?

Further Reading

Bank for International Settlements (BIS). (2023). FinTech and the Digitalisation of Commodities and Derivatives Trading. *BIS Papers*.

Geman, H. (2005). *Commodities and Commodity Derivatives: Modelling and Pricing for Agricultural, Metals and Energy*. Chichester: John Wiley & Sons.

Hull, J.C. (2022). *Options, Futures, and Other Derivatives* (11th ed.). Harlow: Pearson.

Schär, F. (2021). Decentralised Finance: On Blockchain- and Smart Contract-based Financial Markets. *Federal Reserve Bank of St. Louis Review*, 103(2), 153–174.

References

Arner, D.W., Barberis, J., & Buckley, R.P. (2020). The Future of FinTech and Finance: A Research Agenda. *University of Hong Kong Faculty of Law Research Paper*.

Avgouleas, E. & Kiayias, A. (2023). The Regulation of Decentralised Finance: A Conceptual Framework. *European Banking Institute Working Paper Series*.

Bank for International Settlements (BIS). (2022). FinTech and the Digitalisation of Commodities Trading. *BIS Papers*.

Bank for International Settlements (BIS). (2023). *OTC Derivatives Statistics*. Basel: Bank for International Settlements.

Black, F. (1976). The Pricing of Commodity Contracts. *Journal of Financial Economics*, 3(1–2), 167–179.

Black, F., Scholes, M., & Merton, R.C. (1973). The Pricing of Options and Corporate Liabilities. *Journal of Political Economy*, 81(3), 637–654.

Claessens, S., Frost, J., Turner, G., & Zhu, F. (2018). FinTech Credit Markets Around the World: Size, Drivers and Policy Issues. *BIS Quarterly Review*, September, pp. 29–49.

Commodity Futures Trading Commission (CFTC). (2023). *CFTC Approves First DeFi Derivatives Platform* [Press Release].

Duffie, D., & Zhu, H. (2011). Does a Central Clearing Counterparty Reduce Counterparty Risk? *The Review of Asset Pricing Studies*, 1(1), pp. 74–95.

European Union. (2023). *Regulation (EU) 2023/1114 on Markets in Crypto Assets (MiCA)*. Brussels: European Union.

Financial Stability Board (FSB). (2022). *Assessment of Risks to Financial Stability from Cyber Incidents*. Basel: Financial Stability Board.

Financial Stability Board (FSB). (2023). *The Financial Stability Implications of Decentralised Finance*. Basel: Financial Stability Board.

Flammer, C. (2021). Corporate Green Bonds. *Journal of Financial Economics*, 142(2), 499–516.

Foley, S., & Putniņš, T.J. (2022). Meme Stocks and the Evolving Retail Investment Landscape. *Annual Review of Financial Economics*, 14, 129–151.

Geman, H. (2005). *Commodities and Commodity Derivatives: Modelling and Pricing for Agriculturals, Metals, and Energy*. Hoboken, NJ: John Wiley & Sons.

Gomber, P., Kauffman, R.J., Parker, C., & Weber, B.W. (2018). On the FinTech Revolution: Interpreting the Forces of Innovation, Disruption, and Transformation in Financial Services. *Journal of Management Information Systems*, 35(1), 220–265.

Gro Intelligence (2023) *2023 Performance Report on Gro Yield Forecast Models and Acreage Models.* Available at https://1926645.fs1.hubspotusercontent-na1.net/hubfs/1926645/2023%20Performance%20Report%20on%20Gro%20Yield%20Forecast%20Models%20and%20Acreage%20Models%20(2).pdf

Heaton, J.B., Polson, N.G., & Witte, J.H. (2017). Deep Learning for Finance: Deep Portfolios. *Applied Stochastic Models in Business and Industry*, 33(1), 3–12.

Hull, J.C. (2022). *Options, Futures, and Other Derivatives* (11th ed.). Harlow: Pearson Education.

International Monetary Fund (IMF). (2023). *Global Financial Stability Report*. Washington, DC: International Monetary Fund.

International Swaps and Derivatives Association (ISDA). (2022). *Smart Derivatives Contracts: From Concept to Construction*. New York: ISDA.

Li, D.X. (2000). On Default Correlation: A Copula Function Approach. *The Journal of Fixed Income*, 9(4), 43–54.

Mishkin, F.S., & Eakins, S.G. (2018). *Financial Markets and Institutions* (9th ed.). Boston, MA: Pearson.

O'Hara, M. (2015). High-Frequency Market Microstructure. *Journal of Financial Economics*, 116(2), 257–270.

Organisation for Economic Co-operation and Development (OECD). (2020). *Blockchain and the Commodities Sector*. Paris: OECD Publishing.

Qin, K., Zhou, L., Gamito, P., Jovanovic, P., & Gervais, A. (2021). *An Empirical Study of DeFi Liquidations. Proceedings of the 21st ACM Internet Measurement Conference*.pp. 336–350.

Schär, F. (2021). Decentralised Finance: On Blockchain- and Smart Contract-Based Financial Markets. *Federal Reserve Bank of St. Louis Review*, 103(2), 153–174.

Securities and Exchange Commission (SEC). (2023). *Report on Algorithmic Trading and Market Structure*.Washington, DC: SEC.

Szabo, N. (1997). Formalising and Securing Relationships on Public Networks. *First Monday*, 2(9).

Tapscott, D., & Tapscott, A. (2016). *Blockchain Revolution: How the Technology Behind Bitcoin Is Changing Money, Business, and the World*. New York: Penguin.

Williams, Jeffrey C. (2001) Commodity futures and options. In B. Gardner and G. Rausser (Eds.), *Handbook of Agricultural Economics*, Vol. 1. Amsterdam: Elsevier, pp. 745–791.

World Economic Forum. (2021). *Digital Transformation in Commodities Trading*. Geneva: World Economic Forum.

Yermack, D. (2017). Corporate Governance and Blockchains. *Review of Finance*, 21(1), 7–31.

Zetzsche, D.A., Arner, D.W., & Buckley, R.P. (2020). The Democratisation of Finance? The Rise of FinTech and Its Regulatory Implications. *European Business Organisation Law Review*, 21(1), 7–31.

15 Money Market and Financial Technology

Chapter Overview

This chapter examines the ongoing structural transformation of the global money market, a central mechanism for short-term funding and liquidity management, where established financial institutions and standardised instruments such as Treasury bills (T-Bills) and commercial paper (CP) have traditionally dominated. It focuses on how Financial Technology (FinTech), particularly artificial intelligence (AI), distributed ledger technology (DLT), and asset tokenisation, is reshaping market infrastructure by broadening access, enabling near real-time liquidity management, and strengthening risk monitoring and operational efficiency. These developments challenge conventional intermediation models while introducing new operational, technological, and regulatory risks, including cybersecurity, algorithmic governance, legal recognition of digital assets, and cross-border supervision. The chapter provides a comparative analysis of traditional and FinTech-enabled money market structures, evaluates how incumbent institutions are adapting their strategies and risk frameworks, and assesses the emerging role of programmable digital assets and smart contracts in transforming settlement, collateral management, and short-term funding dynamics.

Learning Objectives

By the end of this chapter, you should be able to:

1. Explain the structure, purpose, and key instruments of the traditional money market.
2. Analyse how FinTech innovations such as AI, blockchain, and tokenisation are transforming short-term financing and liquidity management.
3. Compare traditional money market mechanisms with FinTech-enabled and digital money market structures.
4. Evaluate the opportunities and risks associated with FinTech adoption in money markets, including regulatory and systemic implications.
5. Assess the future role of programmable digital assets, Central Bank Digital Currencies (CBDCs), and smart contracts in money market operations.

DOI: 10.4324/9781003775751-18

15.1 Introduction

The money market constitutes the core mechanism for global short-term financing and provides critical infrastructure for liquidity management among sovereign borrowers, financial institutions and multinational corporations. High-volume, low-margin transactions characterise it and rely on instruments such as T-Bills, CP, and repurchase agreements to satisfy immediate funding needs and support efficient cash allocation. Historically, participation has been concentrated among large institutions, resulting in a centralised market structure with significant barriers to entry. Settlement has often depended on complex bilateral over-the-counter arrangements that limit transparency and reduce overall operational efficiency (BIS, 2023).

FinTech is reshaping this established structure by addressing persistent inefficiencies and broadening market access. Digital platforms enhance transparency, reduce transaction costs, and enable a wider range of participants to engage in short-term funding activities. AI supports advanced treasury functions through predictive liquidity modelling and automated trading execution, which improves cash flow forecasting and portfolio optimisation. At the same time, distributed ledger technologies facilitate rapid and verifiable settlement of short-term debt instruments that previously required manual processing and reconciliation. These innovations collectively improve the speed, reliability and auditability of money market operations (IMF, 2025).

Such developments are redefining benchmarks for short-term financing efficiency and accelerating structural change in liquidity management practices. The expansion of digital money market funds (MMFs) and ledger-based settlement systems increases accessibility for a broader spectrum of corporate and institutional users while also strengthening operational resilience. Technological integration, therefore, supports a transition towards a more inclusive and technologically robust liquidity ecosystem that may also reduce certain forms of systemic vulnerability (FSB, 2023). As innovation continues to transform market infrastructure, both intermediaries and end users must adapt their governance, risk management, and compliance frameworks to ensure the effective and secure adoption of these evolving financial technologies (BIS, 2023; IMF, 2025).

15.2 Overview of the Money Market

15.2.1 Definition and Purpose of the Money Market

The money market is a specialised segment of the financial system where highly liquid, short-term debt instruments with maturities of one year or less are traded. It plays a critical role in maintaining liquidity for banks and corporations, supporting corporate cash management, and enabling central banks to implement monetary policy and influence short-term interest rates (Mishkin & Eakins, 2018). By efficiently allocating short-term capital, the money market channels surplus funds from lenders to borrowers with immediate financing needs, ensuring the smooth functioning of the financial system (Federal Reserve, 2023). For instance, A commercial bank with $50 million in excess reserves invests $20 million in a 3-month T-Bill yielding 2% annualised interest. At maturity, the investment returns $20,100,000, generating $100,000 in interest while maintaining liquidity. {Interest = $20,000,000 × 2% × (90/360)}.

15.2.2 Key Instruments

Treasury Bills (T-Bills): Short-term government securities issued at a discount and redeemed at face value. T-Bills are considered virtually risk-free and serve as benchmarks for other money market instruments. For instance, a 6-month T-Bill with a face value of $100,000 is sold at $98,500. At maturity, the investor receives $100,000, earning $1,500 in effective interest.

Commercial Paper (CP): Unsecured, short-term promissory notes issued by high-credit-quality corporations to finance working capital. For instance, a corporation issues $1,000,000 of CP at 99% of face value for 90 days. At maturity, the investor receives $1,000,000 and earns $10,000 in interest. (Issue price = 1,000,000 × 0.99 = $990,000; at maturity, the investor receives $1,000,000; interest earned = 1,000,000 − 990,000 = $10,000).

Certificates of Deposit (CDs): Bank-issued time deposits with fixed interest rates. They offer higher yields than savings accounts but impose penalties for early withdrawal. For instance, an investor deposits $50,000 in a 3-month CD at an annualised rate of 3%. Interest over three months is $375. {=50,000 × 0.03 × (90/360)}.

Repurchase Agreements (Repos): Short-term collateralised loans in which securities are sold with an agreement to repurchase them at a slightly higher price. Central banks use repos for liquidity management, and financial institutions use them for short-term funding. For instance, Bank A sells $5 million in securities to Bank B under a 7-day repo at an annualised rate of 0.5%. At maturity, Bank A repurchases the securities for approximately $5,000,486, paying about $486 in interest. {Interest = 5,000,000 × 0.005 × (7/360) = 486.11}.

Bankers' Acceptances (BAs): Bank-guaranteed promissory notes used mainly in international trade, reducing counterparty risk and facilitating financing. For instance, a firm issues a $500,000 BA to pay an exporter. The exporter sells it at a 1% discount, receiving $498,750 immediately. {Discount = 500,000 × 0.01 × (90/360); Proceeds = 500,000 − 1,250 = $498,750}.

Call and Notice Money: Short-term interbank loans, with call money for overnight borrowing and notice money for periods of 2–14 days. For instance, Bank X lends $10 million to Bank Y overnight at an annualised rate of 4% earns $1111.11. {Interest = $10,000,000 × 4% × (1/360) ≈ $1,111}.

Other Instruments: Eurodollar deposits, money market deposit accounts, and MMFs provide additional avenues for investors seeking short-term, low-risk returns. For instance, an investor places $100,000 in an MMF yielding 1.2% annualised. After one month, the interest earned $100. {= $100,000 × 1.2% × (30/360) = $100}.

15.2.3 Key Participants in the Money Market

Central Banks: Central banks are the primary regulators and liquidity providers in the money market. They implement monetary policy by conducting open market operations, adjusting short-term interest rates, and supplying or absorbing liquidity to maintain financial stability (Mishkin & Eakins, 2018). For instance, the Federal Reserve may purchase $1 billion in T-Bills from commercial banks to inject liquidity into the banking system, lowering short-term interest rates and encouraging lending.

Commercial Banks: Commercial banks act as intermediaries, borrowing and lending in the money market to meet their reserve requirements, manage liquidity positions, and address short-term funding needs. They also invest surplus funds in short-term instruments to earn returns. For instance, A commercial bank with excess reserves of $50 million might invest $20 million in a 3-month T-Bill to earn interest while maintaining liquidity.

Large Corporations: Large firms participate in the money market by issuing CP to finance working capital and operational expenses, and by investing idle cash in money market instruments to optimise returns. For instance, a corporation issues $10 million of 90-day CP at 99% of face value to fund payroll. The corporation receives $9.9 million upfront (10,000,000 × 0.99) and repays $10 million at maturity, incurring an interest cost of $100,000.

MMFs: MMFs pool funds from individual and institutional investors to invest in a diversified portfolio of short-term, low-risk instruments such as T-Bills, CP, and repos. They provide liquidity and maintain a stable net asset value (NAV), offering a safe investment avenue for participants. For instance, an investor deposits $100,000 in an MMF with an annualised yield of 1.2%. After one month, the investor earns approximately $100 in interest. {Interest = $100,000 × 1.2% × (30/360)}.

Government Agencies: Government agencies participate in the money market by issuing short-term debt instruments, such as T-Bills and government securities, to finance fiscal obligations. They also interact with the market to indirectly implement monetary policy. For instance, the U.S. Treasury issues $5 billion in 6-month T-Bills to fund short-term budgetary needs. Investors and banks purchase these bills, providing the government with liquidity.

15.3 The Role of FinTech in Money Market Transformation

15.3.1 Digital Money Market Platforms

FinTech has fundamentally enhanced access to the money market through digital platforms, enabling real-time rate comparison, rapid execution, and more efficient settlement processes. Digital platforms allow retail and institutional investors to engage directly with money market instruments, bypassing traditional intermediaries. For example, U.S. TreasuryDirect enables retail investors to purchase T-Bills directly, streamlining access and reducing transaction costs (World Bank, 2023). Similarly, CP issuance has been digitised, and money market application programming interfaces (APIs) integrated into neobanks enable instant subscription and settlement of short-term corporate debt (Figure 15.1).

Tokenisation of money market instruments, such as T-Bills, CP, and repurchase agreements, enables real-time auditing, immediate settlement, and lower counterparty and clearing risks. J.P. Morgan's Onyx platform exemplifies this innovation, processing tokenised intraday repo transactions with improved liquidity management and operational efficiency (J.P. Morgan, 2023).

15.3.2 Digital MMFs and Retail Access

FinTech has also transformed MMFs, expanding access to retail participants through mobile applications and online investment platforms. Alipay's Yu'e Bao, once the world's largest MMF, attracted millions of users by providing returns on idle cash while maintaining liquidity and ease of access. Platforms such as Robinhood and Wealthfront integrate cash-sweep accounts linked to MMFs, blending banking and investment functionalities and

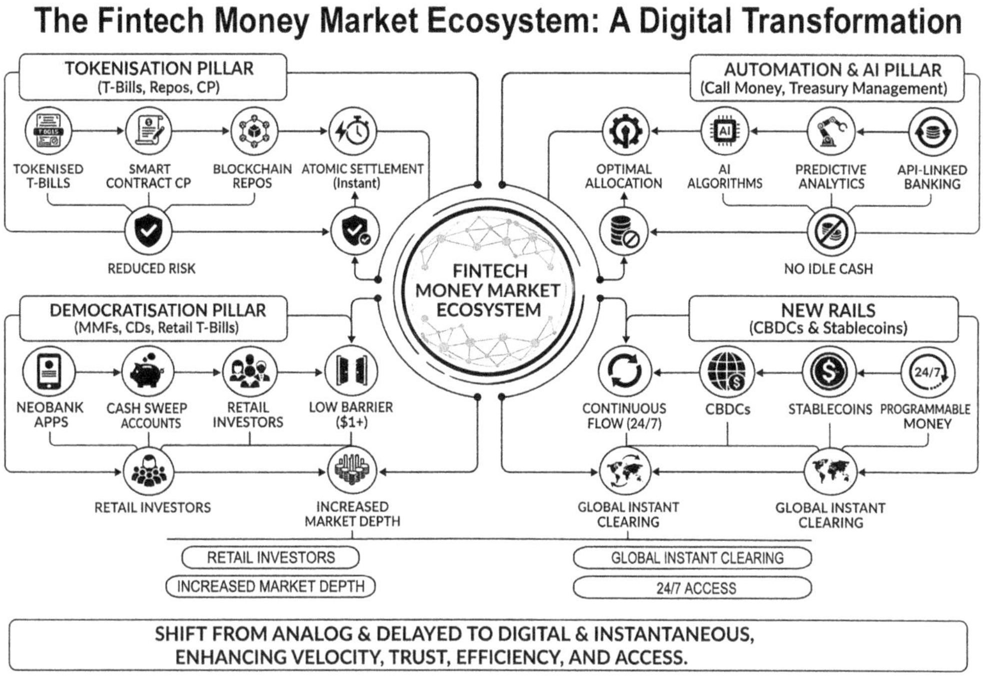

Figure 15.1 FinTech: Digital Transformation in Money Market.

enabling automated, low-friction allocation of short-term funds. This has broadened market participation and reduced reliance on traditional financial intermediaries.

15.3.3 AI, Automation, and Treasury Management

AI and automation are increasingly employed in corporate treasury management. Advanced systems use predictive algorithms to optimise cash holdings across multiple accounts, forecast short-term liquidity requirements, and automate investments into money market instruments such as T-Bills, CP, and repos (IMF, 2023). For instance, a multinational corporation may use AI-driven treasury software to allocate surplus funds daily into overnight call money markets or 7-day repos, maximising returns while maintaining sufficient liquidity for operational needs.

15.3.4 Digital Currencies and Money Market Impacts

The emergence of CBDCs and stablecoins represents a structural shift in short-term finance. CBDCs introduce programmable features such as conditional transfers or auto-expiry, potentially enhancing the precision and speed of monetary policy transmission (BIS, 2023). For example, a CBDC could automatically transfer idle government funds into short-term T-Bills or the repo market, thereby increasing market efficiency. Stablecoins, such as USD Coin and USD Tether, are increasingly used as collateral or settlement instruments in decentralised finance (DeFi) money market platforms, supporting continuous short-term liquidity and enabling immediate settlement of CP or repo-like transactions in a global, digital environment.

Table 15.1 Traditional vs Digital Money Markets

Characteristics	*Traditional Money Markets*	*Digital Money Markets*
Primary Participants	Banks, institutional investors, and mutual funds	Retail investors, algorithmic protocols, and decentralised autonomous organisations
Core Instruments	T-Bills, CP, and repurchase agreements (repos)	Tokenised bills/notes, yield-bearing stablecoins, DeFi lending/ borrowing pools
Access and Denomination	High minimums (e.g., $100,000+ per instrument)	Fractional, permissionless ownership (from $1 or less)
Trading Hours	Limited to business hours (e.g., 8 am–5 pm local time)	Continuous, 24 hours a day, 365 days a year
Settlement Cycle	Typically, T+1 or T+2 (trade date plus 1 or 2 days)	Near real-time settlement via blockchain
Regulatory Oversight	Established frameworks (e.g., Securities and Exchange Commission (SEC) Rule 2a-7 for funds, Federal Reserve)	Evolving, jurisdiction-specific crypto asset frameworks
Liquidity Mechanism	Intermediated by primary dealers, it relies on bid-ask spreads	Automated Market Makers and decentralised liquidity pools

15.4 A Comparison of Traditional and FinTech Money Markets

Table 15.1 delineates the fundamental differences between the traditional and digital market paradigms.

15.5 Opportunity, Challenges, and Key Practical Issues

15.5.1 Opportunities of FinTech and Traditional Money Markets

The integration of FinTech into the money market ecosystem is generating novel short-term instruments and institutional engagement that bridge FinTech innovations with established market infrastructure. Tokenisation of traditional instruments exemplifies this trend; for instance, Franklin Templeton's FOBXX tokenised T-Bill fund digitally represents T-Bill ownership on distributed ledgers, enabling near-real-time transferability of a historically settlement-bound asset (FSB, 2023). Similarly, major asset managers have launched digital funds that mirror conventional MMFs while leveraging blockchain for operational efficiency. BlackRock's tokenised short-term fund and J.P. Morgan's blockchain-enabled repurchase (repo) platform illustrate mainstream adoption by incumbents seeking the liquidity and transparency benefits of DLT (IMF, 2025). Hybrid platforms such as WisdomTree's Prime solution combine features of traditional MMFs with on-chain settlement capabilities, indicating functional interoperability between legacy and FinTech systems. These developments align with evolving liquidity management practices, including 24/7 lending markets and enhanced intraday liquidity mechanisms that transcend traditional operating hours (BIS, 2023).

15.5.2 Risks and Challenges of FinTech Adoption in the Money Market

Despite gains in efficiency and access, FinTech adoption in the money market introduces material regulatory, operational, and systemic risks. Supervisory frameworks often lag technological change, leaving automated RegTech systems to interpret complex and evolving rules governing CP, repo markets, and MMF liquidity and NAV requirements, which can create compliance gaps and legal exposure (IMF, 2023). At the operational level, digital infrastructure is vulnerable to cyber intrusions, data breaches, denial-of-service attacks, and fraud, while system outages can cause direct financial losses and reputational damage. Market fragmentation further constrains scalability, as differing token standards, smart contract architectures, and national legal regimes limit interoperability and increase transaction costs. These vulnerabilities intersect with financial stability concerns: the immediate redeemability of digital MMFs and stablecoins may intensify run dynamics during stress events, and DeFi-based short-term lending, operating beyond traditional regulatory perimeters, can foster opaque leverage and interconnected exposures that heighten systemic risk (BIS, 2023).

15.5.3 Key Practical Issues in FinTech-Enabled Money Markets

FinTech integration into money markets faces several practical challenges. The legal enforceability of smart contracts remains uncertain in many jurisdictions, creating ambiguity in payments, interest calculations, and dispute resolution. DeFi protocols rely on oracles to provide off-chain data, and any inaccuracies or manipulation can lead to mispricing or erroneous liquidations. Collateral volatility is another risk: unlike traditional repos with high-quality debt, DeFi often accepts volatile crypto assets, which can trigger cascading liquidations during price drops. Technical interoperability between legacy treasury systems, bank rails (e.g., Society for Worldwide Interbank Financial Telecommunication), and blockchain platforms complicates straight-through processing and institutional adoption. Finally, the borderless nature of digital platforms enables regulatory arbitrage, making cross-border compliance with securities, tax, and Anti-Money Laundering rules challenging.

15.6 Future of FinTech in the Money Market

The future of the money market is increasingly defined by digital transformation, with FinTech reshaping its structure, participants, and instruments rather than merely optimising existing processes. Tokenisation of short-term instruments such as T-Bills and CP will democratise access through fractional ownership and automate settlement, enhancing liquidity in secondary markets. AI- and API-driven systems are expected to enable real-time, 24/7 liquidity markets in which interest rates adjust dynamically, and surplus cash is matched with borrowers instantaneously across borders. Integration with open banking and enterprise systems will embed money market functionalities into payroll platforms, Enterprise Resource Planning software, and mobile banking applications, making short-term investment a seamless component of personal and corporate cash flow management. While these innovations promise greater efficiency, transparency, and inclusion, they also introduce complex challenges, including cybersecurity risks, regulatory arbitrage, and systemic vulnerabilities. Ensuring the stability and effectiveness of the evolving money market will require coordinated efforts among regulators, traditional financial institutions, and FinTech innovators to balance innovation with financial stability and consumer protection (IMF, 2025; BIS, 2023).

15.7 Conclusion

The global money market is undergoing a fundamental structural transformation driven by the widespread adoption of FinTech. Traditional reliance on standardised institutional instruments is increasingly complemented by innovations in AI, blockchain, and asset tokenisation, which are redefining the mechanisms of short-term finance. These technologies enhance operational efficiency, broaden market access, and enable real-time liquidity management, offering greater speed, precision, and flexibility than legacy systems allow. The market is therefore evolving beyond conventional operational constraints towards a more agile, technologically integrated framework.

Nonetheless, this digitalisation introduces complex governance challenges, requiring a reassessment of existing risk management frameworks to address emerging issues in operational security, cyber resilience, and cross-border settlement. The capacity of market participants to reconcile the pace of technological innovation with regulatory oversight will be critical in ensuring a stable transition. Coordinated global efforts are necessary to establish clear and scalable regulatory frameworks that balance innovation with systemic stability and investor protection. The trajectory of short-term finance is increasingly digital and programmable, necessitating collaboration among FinTech innovators, financial institutions, and regulators to realise a transparent, resilient, and efficient global money market (BIS, 2023; IMF, 2025).

Key Terms and Glossary

CP (Commercial Paper) An unsecured, short-term debt instrument issued by a corporation, typically for the financing of accounts receivable, inventories, and meeting short-term liabilities.

Repurchase Agreement (Repo) A form of short-term borrowing for dealers in government securities, involving the sale of securities with an agreement to repurchase them at a higher price at a later date.

MMF (Money Market Fund) A type of mutual fund that invests in high-quality, short-term debt instruments and cash equivalents, offering high liquidity with a very low level of risk.

Stablecoin A type of cryptocurrency whose value is pegged to a stable asset, like a fiat currency (e.g., USD) or gold.

Tokenised Intraday Repo The representation of a repurchase agreement as a digital token on a blockchain, enabling near-instantaneous settlement.

Test Your Understanding

Multiple-Choice Questions

1 Which of the following instruments is considered virtually risk-free and serves as a benchmark in the money market?

A CP
B BAs
C T-Bills
D CDs

2 A repurchase agreement (repo) is best described as:

A An unsecured short-term corporate loan
B A long-term government bond transaction
C A collateralised short-term loan involving securities
D A CBDC transaction

3 Which FinTech innovation primarily enables near real-time settlement and transparent record-keeping in money markets?

A AI
B DLT
C Open banking APIs
D Robo-advisory platforms

4 One major risk associated with digital MMFs and stablecoins is:

A Reduced liquidity
B Increased settlement delays
C Intensified run dynamics during market stress
D Elimination of regulatory oversight

5 Compared to traditional money markets, digital money markets typically offer:

A Higher minimum investment thresholds
B Limited trading hours
C Near real-time, continuous trading
D Exclusive access for banks only

Short Questions

1 Define the money market and explain its role in liquidity management.
2 Briefly explain how tokenisation can improve efficiency in money market instruments such as T-Bills or repos.
3 Identify two ways AI is used in modern corporate treasury and money market operations.

Analytical Questions

1 Critically analyse how FinTech is reshaping the traditional intermediation model in money markets. In your answer, consider both efficiency gains and emerging risks.
2 Evaluate the implications of digital MMFs and stablecoins for financial stability, particularly during periods of market stress.
3 Discuss the future role of CBDCs in money markets. How might programmable money affect monetary policy transmission and short-term funding dynamics?

Case Study: Franklin Templeton's On-Chain U.S. Government Money Fund

Franklin Templeton, one of the world's largest and most established asset management firms, has pioneered a significant innovation in the money market by launching a U.S.-registered government MMF that operates on a public blockchain. Rather than relying solely on traditional transfer agents and legacy record-keeping systems, the fund uses blockchain technology, specifically the Stellar network, to process transactions and record share ownership.

In this structure, each unit of the MMF is represented digitally by a blockchain-based token, the BENJI token. Investors who purchase shares in the fund receive BENJI tokens, which function as a digital representation of their ownership interest in the underlying portfolio of U.S. government securities. Transactions involving subscriptions, redemptions, and transfers are recorded on the blockchain, enabling near-instant settlement, improved transparency, and continuous availability beyond standard market hours.

Importantly, the fund remains fully compliant with U.S. securities regulations and is registered with the SEC. Franklin Templeton continues to perform traditional functions such as portfolio management, custody, valuation, and compliance, while the blockchain serves as an additional layer for transfer and record-keeping. This approach allows the firm to enhance operational efficiency and investor experience without compromising regulatory oversight, illustrating how traditional finance and blockchain technology can converge within a regulated framework.

References

Franklin Templeton. (2024). *Franklin Templeton Enables USDC Conversions on Benji Investments Platform*, 6 June 2024. Available at: https://www.franklintempleton.com/press-releases/news-room/2024/franklin-templeton-enables-usdc-conversions-on-benji-investments-platform (Accessed: 1 March 2026).

Franklin Templeton Trust. (2021). *Form N-1A – Franklin OnChain U.S. Government Money Fund*, Registration Statement, Securities and Exchange Commission, 15 March 2021. Available at: https://www.sec.gov/Archives/edgar/data/1786958/000137949121000981/filing212607593.htm (Accessed: 1 March 2026).

Case Study Questions

1 How does tokenisation improve the efficiency and functionality of a traditional MMF for both the issuer and investors?

2 What key regulatory challenges did Franklin Templeton face in obtaining SEC approval to operate a registered MMF on a public blockchain, and what does this suggest about the evolving regulatory environment?

3 How does Franklin Templeton's on-chain MMF demonstrate the convergence of traditional financial institutions and blockchain technology?

Further Reading

Bank for International Settlements (BIS). (2023). *The Crypto Ecosystem: Key Elements and Risks*. Basel: BIS.

International Monetary Fund (IMF). (2024). *Digital Money and Payments: Legal and Regulatory Considerations*. Washington, DC: IMF.

Mishkin, F.S., & Eakins, S.G. (2018). *Financial Markets and Institutions* (9th ed.). Harlow: Pearson.

References

Bank for International Settlements (2023) *OTC Derivatives Statistics*. Basel: Bank for International Settlements.

Federal Reserve. (2023). *Money Market Instruments and Operations*. Washington, DC: Federal Reserve Bank Publications.

International Monetary Fund (2023) *Global Financial Stability Report*. Washington, DC: International Monetary Fund.

International Monetary Fund (2025) *Global Financial Stability Report*. Washington, DC: International Monetary Fund.

International Monetary Fund (IMF). (2025). *Tokenisation and Financial Market Inefficiencies. FinTech Notes 2025/001*. Available at: https://www.imf.org/en/publications/fintech-notes/issues/2025/01/29/tokenization-and-financial-market-inefficiencies-561256

JPMorgan Chase & Co. (2023) *Onyx Digital Assets Platform*. New York: JPMorgan Chase & Co.

Mishkin, F.S., & Eakins, S.G. (2018). *Financial Markets and Institutions* (9th ed.). Boston, MA: Pearson.

World Bank (2023) *World Bank Data and Research Publications*. Washington, DC: World Bank.

16 Foreign Exchange (Forex) Market and Financial Technology

Chapter Overview

This chapter critically examines the impact of Financial Technology (FinTech) on the global foreign exchange (FX) market, the world's largest and most liquid financial marketplace. Traditionally dominated by major banks and multinational corporations, the FX market is undergoing significant structural change driven by technological innovation. The chapter analyses how decentralised trading platforms, algorithmic and artificial intelligence (AI)-driven trading systems, social trading networks, and blockchain-based settlement solutions are reshaping currency trading by improving execution efficiency, reducing transaction costs, enhancing transparency, and broadening market access. It also outlines the structure of the FX market, key participants, major currency pairs, and the characteristics of spot, forward, futures, and options contracts. A comparison of traditional FX models with FinTech-enabled approaches highlights increased automation, reduced intermediation, and faster settlement, alongside growing institutional adoption. Finally, the chapter addresses emerging challenges, including cybersecurity risks, heightened leverage, and regulatory uncertainty surrounding decentralised finance (DeFi)-based FX trading, underscoring the need for adaptive regulatory frameworks to maintain market integrity and financial stability (BIS, 2022).

Learning Objectives

By the end of this chapter, you should be able to:

1 Understand the structure, participants, and key instruments of the global FX market.
2 Analyse the role of FinTech in transforming FX trading, execution, and settlement.
3 Compare traditional FX market models with FinTech-driven approaches in terms of efficiency, transparency, and accessibility.
4 Identify the challenges and risks associated with FinTech adoption in FX, including cybersecurity, leverage, and regulatory uncertainty.
5 Evaluate future trends in FX markets, including AI-driven personalised trading, interoperable infrastructures, and decentralised institutional adoption.

DOI: 10.4324/9781003775751-19

16.1 Introduction

The FX market represents the largest and most liquid financial market globally, with a daily trading volume exceeding $7.5 trillion. This substantial scale underscores its essential role in supporting global economic activities, including international trade, investment, and central bank operations (BIS, 2022). Historically, participation was limited to major financial institutions, multinational corporations, and sovereign entities, as high barriers to entry and complex operational structures characterised the market.

Currently, the FX market is experiencing significant transformation, primarily driven by the rapid advancement of FinTech. These innovations are fundamentally altering the forex ecosystem by democratising access through intuitive platforms, automating trade execution and risk management, and reducing transaction costs. FinTech has also transformed cross-border payments, rendering them nearly instantaneous and transparent, thereby enhancing efficiency and minimising friction in global capital flows.

Technological advancements have increased market efficiency and broadened participation, enabling entry for a wider range of smaller participants. Previously, access was restricted to a select group. This chapter examines how FinTech is reshaping the FX landscape, with particular attention to its effects on market accessibility, operational paradigms, and the future trajectory of global currency markets.

16.2 Overview of the Forex Market

The Forex or FX market is a global, decentralised marketplace for the trading of currencies. It represents the world's largest and most liquid financial market, with an average daily turnover of approximately $6.6 trillion, according to the Bank for International Settlements (BIS, 2022). The Forex market plays a critical role in international trade, investment, and the implementation of monetary policy, facilitating currency conversion, risk management, and speculative activity.

16.2.1 Key Characteristics of the Forex Market

Decentralisation and Over-the-Counter (OTC) Trading: Unlike centralised stock exchanges, the FX market operates OTC primarily via a network of commercial banks, brokers, and electronic communication networks (ECNs). This decentralised structure allows continuous trading across major financial centres such as London, New York, Tokyo, and Singapore, enabling 24-hour price discovery from Sunday evening to Friday evening (Mishkin & Eakins, 2018).

High Liquidity: The market's enormous scale ensures significant liquidity, particularly in major currency pairs, allowing large transactions to be executed with minimal price impact or slippage. For example, a multinational corporation may convert $50 million into euros at the EUR/USD spot rate of 1.1000, receiving €45.45 million, with minimal deviation from the quoted rate. (=$50,000,000 USD÷1.1000 = €45,454,545.45).

Leverage: Leverage is widely available, permitting traders to control large positions with relatively small capital. While leverage can magnify gains, it can also amplify losses, and regulators such as the Financial Conduct Authority (FCA) and the European Securities and Markets Authority (ESMA) impose strict limits on retail leverage to manage systemic risk (FCA, 2018). For instance, a retail trader using 20:1 leverage can control $100,000 with a $5,000 margin; a 1% adverse movement in the exchange rate results in a $1,000 loss, equivalent to 20% of the initial margin (1%×$100,000=$1,000; $ 1,000÷$5,000=0.20=20% loss).

16.2.2 *Types of Forex Markets*

Spot Market: The spot market is the largest segment of the FX market. It involves the immediate exchange of one currency for another at the current market rate, with settlements typically occurring within two business days (T+2). Transactions in this market are straightforward and are often used by traders, businesses, and financial institutions for immediate currency needs. For example, selling €90,909 for USD at a rate of 1.1000 would yield $100,000, with payment and currency delivery completed within 2 days. The spot market offers high liquidity and reflects real-time market sentiment, making it a key indicator of global exchange rates. ($100,000÷ 1.10= €90,909)

Forwards: Forward contracts are customised, OTC agreements between two parties to exchange a specific amount of currency at a predetermined rate on a future date. These contracts are flexible in terms of size, settlement date, and currency pair. For instance, a US importer who needs to pay €500,000 in three months could enter a forward contract at EUR/USD 1.1050, fixing the USD payment at $552,500. Forward contracts are primarily used by corporations and financial institutions to manage FX risk. (€500,000×1.1050=$552,500).

Futures: Futures contracts are standardised agreements traded on regulated exchanges, such as the Chicago Mercantile Exchange (CME) Group. These contracts specify a fixed currency amount, rate, and maturity date and are centrally cleared, reducing counterparty risk. For example, a EUR/USD futures contract for €125,000 at a rate of 1.1000 obligates the delivery of $137,500 at maturity. Futures are often used by speculators and investors seeking exposure to currency movements with defined risk parameters. (€125,000×1.1000=$137,500).

Options Market: Currency options provide the right, but not the obligation, to buy (call) or sell (put) a currency at a specified strike price before a set expiration date. Options are widely used for hedging against adverse currency movements or for speculative purposes. For example, purchasing a EUR/USD call option with a strike price of 1.1200 for a premium of $1,000 gives the holder the right to buy €100,000 for $112,000, regardless of the spot rate at expiration. This flexibility makes options a valuable tool for managing currency risk while limiting potential losses. (€100,000×1.1200=$112,000). If the Euro falls below 1.1200, the holder lets the option expire. They lose only the $1,000 premium, not the full downside of holding the currency. If the Euro rises to 1.2000, the holder can still exercise the right to buy at 1.1200, capturing the profit.

16.2.3 *Key Participants in the Forex Market*

The FX market is highly diverse, with participants ranging from large institutions to individual traders:

Commercial and Central Banks: Commercial banks act as intermediaries, providing liquidity and facilitating currency transactions for clients. Central banks participate in stabilising their national currencies, managing foreign reserves, and implementing monetary policy. Their interventions can significantly influence exchange rates. Corporations and Multinational Companies: Businesses use the FX market to conduct international trade and hedge against currency risk. For example, a UK exporter receiving $1 million from U.S. clients might sell USD forward to lock in Great British Pound (GBP) proceeds and protect against exchange rate fluctuations.

Institutional Investors and Hedge Funds: These entities engage in currency trading for portfolio diversification, risk management, and speculative profit. They often use leverage and sophisticated strategies to maximise returns.

Retail Traders: Individual traders participate through online brokerages and trading platforms. The rise of FinTech has expanded access to the FX market, allowing retail participants to trade with lower costs and advanced tools.

FinTech Companies and Liquidity Providers: FinTech firms offer platforms, application programming interfaces (APIs), and automated trading tools that enable fast, efficient trade execution. Liquidity providers continuously quote bid and ask prices, ensuring market depth and smooth transactions.

16.2.4 Major Currency Pairs

Currencies are always quoted in pairs, reflecting the value of one currency relative to another. The most liquid and widely traded major pairs include EUR/USD, USD/JPY, GBP/USD, USD/CHF, AUD/USD, and USD/CAD. These pairs tend to have lower spreads and higher trading volumes. Cross-currency pairs, such as EUR/GBP, and exotic pairs, like USD/TRY, typically exhibit higher volatility and lower liquidity. For example, converting $50,000 to Japanese Yen at a spot rate of USD/JPY 135.50 would instantly yield ¥6,775,000.

16.3 The Role of FinTech in Forex Trading

FinTech has transformed the structure and accessibility of the global FX market, introducing innovations that enhance efficiency, reduce costs, and broaden participation. Key technological innovations in FX trading include online trading platforms, social and copy trading networks, automated and algorithmic execution, DeFi solutions, and business-to-business (B2B) or institutional API-driven services. These innovations have impacted the major segments of the FX market, including spot, forward, futures, and options markets (Figure 16.1).

16.3.1 Key FinTech Innovations in Forex Trading

Online FX Brokers and Trading Platforms: Platforms such as MetaTrader 4/5, cTrader, and TradingView have democratised FX trading. They provide retail and institutional traders with real-time pricing, advanced charting, one-click execution, algorithmic trading capabilities, and integrated risk management tools (King & Rime, 2020). For example, a retail trader can use MetaTrader 5 to execute a EUR/USD spot trade with automated stop-loss and take-profit parameters, previously available only to professional institutions.

Social and Copy Trading: Platforms like eToro, ZuluTrade, and NAGA allow less experienced traders to follow or automatically replicate the trades of expert investors. These networks leverage collective intelligence, sentiment analysis, and performance metrics to guide trading decisions. For instance, a novice trader can mirror the strategies of a top-performing GBP/USD trader, effectively gaining exposure to professional-level decision-making without deep market knowledge (Pelster & Hofmann, 2018).

Automated Trading and Smart Order Routing: Algorithmic trading, including Expert Advisors and high-frequency trading (HFT), executes orders based on predefined criteria with speeds beyond human capability. Smart order routing technology further optimises trade execution by directing orders to liquidity pools offering the best prices, reducing slippage and improving cost efficiency (Aldridge, 2013). For example, an

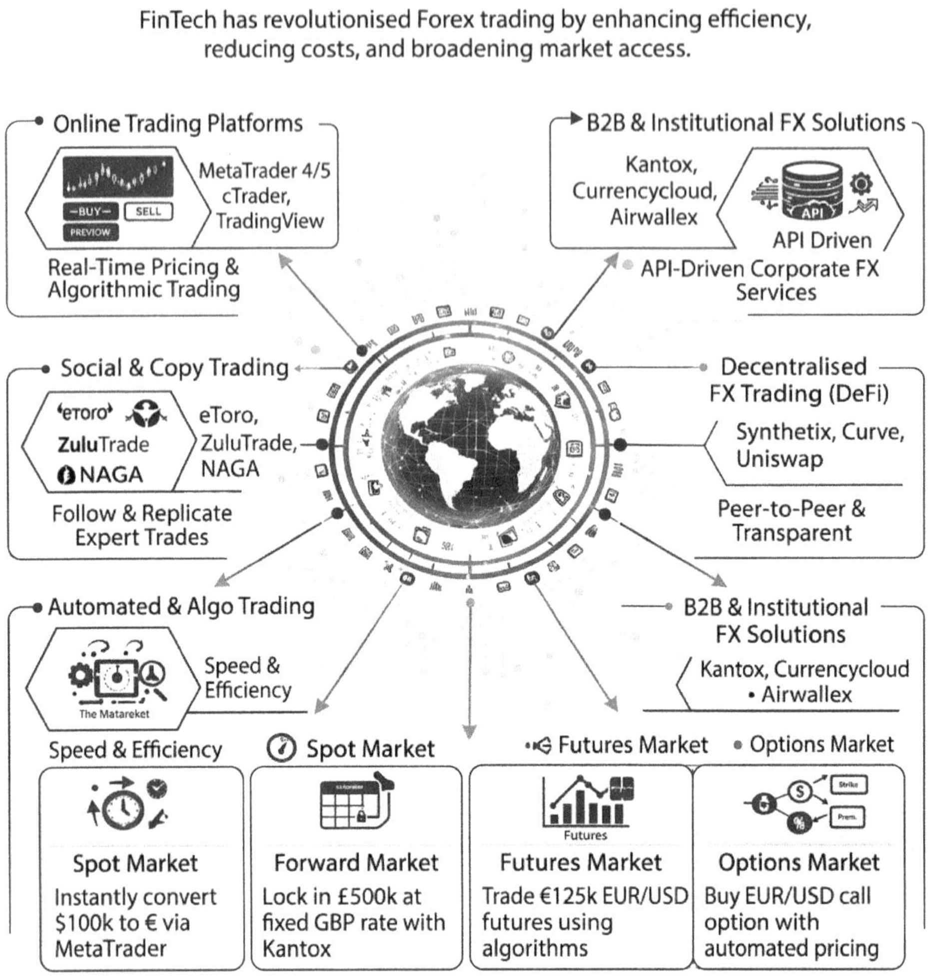

Figure 16.1 The Role of FinTech in Forex Trading.

institutional investor executing a USD/JPY futures position can use algorithmic trading to split a large order across multiple venues to achieve optimal execution.

Decentralised FX Trading (DeFi): DeFi protocols such as Synthetix, Curve, and Uniswap enable peer-to-peer trading of synthetic forex pairs and derivatives without central intermediaries. These platforms provide continuous market access, on-chain transparency, and reduced dependence on centralised systems, creating new avenues for trading currencies and hedging risks in a decentralised manner (Schär, 2021). For example, a trader can swap synthetic EUR/USD tokens on Synthetix at any time, bypassing traditional broker fees.

B2B and Institutional FX Solutions: FinTech companies such as Kantox, Currencycloud, and Airwallex offer API-driven FX services for corporate clients. These solutions facilitate automated currency conversion, multi-currency invoice settlement, and advanced treasury management, enabling firms to manage FX risk efficiently. For instance, a multinational company can use Airwallex APIs to automate EUR/USD payments for overseas suppliers while hedging exposure through forward contracts.

16.3.2 FinTech Applications in Different Forex Markets

Spot Market: In the spot FX market, FinTech platforms enable instant trade execution and access to deep liquidity pools. Retail traders can execute real-time EUR/USD spot transactions using online brokers such as MetaTrader, while institutions can employ smart order routing to minimise trading costs. For example, a trader converting $100,000 to EUR via a digital broker receives immediate settlement with optimised pricing.

Forward Market: FinTech innovations streamline the execution and management of forward contracts. Corporate clients can use platforms like Kantox to enter forward contracts automatically, locking in exchange rates for future currency obligations. For instance, a UK importer expecting a €500,000 payment in three months can enter into a EUR/GBP forward contract with Kantox, locking in a fixed GBP amount regardless of market fluctuations.

Futures Market: Algorithmic trading and smart order routing are extensively applied in currency futures markets. Institutions can use automated systems to manage large EUR/USD futures positions on exchanges like the CME, splitting orders across venues to reduce slippage and execution risk. For example, a hedge fund trading €125,000 EUR/USD futures may use an HFT algorithm to execute trades in milliseconds, optimising entry and exit prices.

Options Market: In FX options, FinTech solutions support automated pricing, risk analysis, and execution. Online platforms and algorithmic trading tools allow traders to purchase or sell currency options with precise strike prices and expiration dates. For example, a corporate treasurer can acquire a EUR/USD call option via an online platform, with the platform automatically calculating the premium and potential payoff scenarios to hedge against adverse currency movements.

16.4 A Comparison of Traditional and FinTech FX Markets

Table 16.1 explains the fundamental contrasts between the traditional and FinTech-driven FX paradigms.

Table 16.1 Key Differences: Traditional vs FinTech-Driven FX Markets

Feature	*Traditional FX Market*	*FinTech-Driven FX Market*
Market Structure	Interbank network via ECNs	Digital platforms and apps (e.g., Revolut, Wise)
Primary Participants	Banks, hedge funds, large corporations, and institutional investors	Retail traders, small and medium-sized enterprises, and crypto investors
Access Requirements	High minimums (often $1 million or more per transaction)	Low or no minimums; accessible with small amounts
Trading Hours	24 hours a day, 5 days a week (closes weekends)	24/7 trading, including cryptocurrency pairs
Transaction Speed	T+2 standard settlement cycle	Instant or same-day settlement
Pricing Transparency	Often opaque with bank markups and hidden fees	Real-time pricing with fully disclosed fees and margins
Cost Structure	Higher spreads (e.g., 50–100 pips for exotic pairs)	Competitive, low spreads (e.g., 0.1–1 pip for major pairs)
Technology and Execution	Phone/voice brokers, legacy banking systems, and manual processes	AI-powered execution, automated platforms, blockchain integration
Regulatory Environment	Strict, well-established frameworks (e.g., NFA, CFTC, MiFID II)	Evolving regulations vary significantly by jurisdiction

16.5 Opportunities, Challenges, and Key Practical Issues in the FinTech-Enabled FX Market

16.5.1 Opportunities Arising from Convergence in FinTech FX Markets

A defining development in contemporary FX markets is the convergence of traditional financial institutions and FinTech innovation, which is reshaping FX trading, settlement, and liquidity management. Hybrid trading platforms illustrate this integration, as established systems such as the Bloomberg Terminal now incorporate crypto-asset and digital FX data. At the same time, major financial institutions, including JPMorgan, have introduced blockchain-based FX settlement solutions through platforms such as Onyx. Institutional adoption of FinTech tools further underscores this convergence; for example, Goldman Sachs has explored distributed ledger technology for FX settlement efficiency, and State Street employs AI to enhance liquidity forecasting and treasury operations. At the infrastructure level, blockchain-based networks such as RippleNet and Continuous Linked Settlement initiatives aim to reduce the costs and settlement times of cross-border FX transactions. Simultaneously, the retail FX market has been transformed by neobanks and digital platforms such as Revolut and Wise, which offer near-interbank exchange rates and low-cost international transfers. In contrast, social trading platforms have democratised access to FX strategies and market participation.

16.5.2 Challenges in FinTech Adoption Within the FX Market

Despite these opportunities, adopting FinTech in FX markets poses significant challenges. One major concern is cybersecurity and platform resilience, as the digital architecture of FinTech FX platforms increases exposure to cyber threats such as hacking, phishing, and ransomware. Successful breaches can result in direct financial losses and long-term erosion of market confidence, requiring continuous investment in advanced security and operational safeguards. Another challenge arises from the widespread availability of high leverage on retail-focused FX platforms, which can expose inexperienced traders to rapid and substantial losses. This has prompted regulatory authorities to impose leverage caps, risk disclosure requirements, and investor education obligations to mitigate consumer harm. In addition, DeFi-based FX trading operates within an uncertain regulatory environment, where issues of jurisdiction, enforcement of KYC and Anti-Money Laundering (AML) standards, and the stability of collateral backing synthetic FX instruments remain unresolved, raising concerns about financial stability and regulatory arbitrage.

16.5.3 Key Practical Issues in FinTech FX Markets

Several practical issues further complicate the integration of FinTech into FX markets. In DeFi-based FX protocols, smart contract risk is a critical concern, as coding errors or security vulnerabilities can be exploited, leading to irreversible losses, as demonstrated by numerous high-profile DeFi failures. The legal enforceability of smart contracts in cross-border FX disputes also remains largely untested. Liquidity fragmentation represents another operational challenge, as the proliferation of centralised and decentralised trading venues can disperse liquidity across platforms, resulting in wider effective spreads and complicating best-execution requirements for institutional investors. DeFi FX systems are also highly dependent on price oracles to supply accurate off-chain exchange rate data; failures or manipulation of these oracles can trigger erroneous liquidations and destabilise trading protocols. Furthermore, integrating FinTech FX solutions, such as API-based trading or blockchain settlement systems, into existing treasury management systems and enterprise resource planning platforms presents substantial technical and organisational hurdles for large institutions. Finally, the borderless nature of digital FX platforms creates complex cross-jurisdictional compliance challenges, as firms must simultaneously adhere to differing regulatory, tax, and AML requirements across multiple legal regimes.

16.6 The Future of the FX Market

The future of the FX market will be increasingly shaped by advanced digital technologies that enhance efficiency, accessibility, and integration. AI and machine learning are expected to enable hyper-personalised FX trading, with platforms delivering customised strategies, real-time insights, and adaptive risk management tools based on individual user profiles and behaviour, improving decision-making and execution quality (BIS, 2022; IMF, 2023). At the infrastructure level, greater interoperability driven by blockchain technology and standardised APIs will facilitate seamless multi-currency transactions and near real-time cross-border settlement, reducing operational frictions and lowering barriers to market participation (FSB, 2022). In parallel, institutional adoption of decentralised FX mechanisms is likely to expand, as banks and asset managers selectively integrate smart contracts and decentralised liquidity pools for hedging and arbitrage, seeking enhanced transparency, efficiency, and access to new sources of liquidity within an evolving hybrid market structure (BIS, 2023; FSB, 2022).

16.7 Conclusion

FinTech has emerged as a transformative force in the FX market, reshaping its operational structure through automation, AI, and data-driven analytics. By lowering transaction costs and barriers to entry, FinTech has broadened market access and improved execution efficiency. At the same time, blockchain and other decentralised technologies have enhanced transparency and enabled faster, more secure settlement processes. These innovations are driving a shift towards more accessible, efficient, and technologically integrated FX markets.

At the same time, rapid technological adoption introduces systemic risks, including cybersecurity vulnerabilities, operational fragility, and regulatory uncertainty, particularly in DeFi-based FX activities. Ensuring market stability requires adaptive governance, robust risk management frameworks, and coordinated oversight that align innovation with regulatory compliance. The future FX market will likely feature greater institutional adoption of decentralised mechanisms, intelligent automation, and cross-platform interoperability, necessitating collaboration between FinTech innovators, traditional market participants, and regulators to maintain a resilient, secure, and inclusive trading ecosystem.

Key Terms and Glossary

Forex (FX) Market The global decentralised marketplace for the trading of currencies.

Spot Market The segment of the forex market where currencies are traded for immediate delivery.

Leverage The use of borrowed capital to increase the potential return of an investment, amplifying both gains and losses.

Algorithmic Trading The use of computer algorithms to automatically execute trading orders based on predefined criteria.

DeFi (Decentralised Finance) A blockchain-based financial infrastructure that aims to disintermediate traditional financial institutions.

Test Your Understanding

Multiple-Choice Questions

1 Which of the following best describes the FX market?
A Centralised stock exchange
B Decentralised OTC market
C Retail-only trading platform
D Regulated futures-only market

2 What is the primary function of algorithmic trading in FX markets?
A Manual order processing
B Executing trades automatically based on predefined strategies
C Eliminating regulatory compliance requirements
D Restricting retail participation

3 Which technology enables near-instant FX settlement and transparent record-keeping?
A HFT
B Blockchain
C Social trading networks
D Futures contracts

4 Retail FX traders are increasingly accessing interbank rates through:
A Traditional ECNs only
B Neobanks and FinTech platforms
C Central bank auctions
D Futures exchanges

5 One major risk of DeFi-based FX trading is:
A Low liquidity
B Regulatory uncertainty and smart contract vulnerabilities
C High entry barriers for retail traders
D Slow trade execution

Short Questions

1 Explain how FinTech has improved accessibility and efficiency in the FX market for retail traders.
2 Identify two major risks associated with decentralised FX trading platforms.
3 Distinguish between spot, forward, and futures FX markets in terms of settlement and purpose.

Analytical Questions

1 Evaluate the advantages and limitations of AI-driven trading strategies in both retail and institutional FX markets.
2 Analyse how blockchain and smart contract technology can transform cross-border FX settlement while considering operational and regulatory challenges.
3 Discuss the potential impact of FinTech convergence on the future structure of FX markets, focusing on hybrid platforms and institutional adoption of decentralised mechanisms.

Case Study: The Rise and Regulation of Retail FX Trading Platforms

The emergence of FinTech-enabled retail trading platforms such as MetaTrader and eToro, and neobank applications like Revolut, has significantly broadened access to the FX market. These platforms allow individual investors to trade currencies with low capital requirements and high leverage, features previously restricted to institutional participants. While this democratisation increases market participation, it has also exposed inexperienced traders to substantial financial risk, sometimes resulting in catastrophic losses. In response, the ESMA introduced regulatory safeguards in 2018, including leverage caps of 30:1 for major currency pairs and 20:1 for non-major pairs, as well as mandatory risk disclosures and educational requirements to improve consumer protection (ESMA, 2018).

Simultaneously, DeFi protocols such as Uniswap and Synthetix offer peer-to-peer FX trading without intermediaries, operate continuously, and are outside traditional regulatory oversight. While these platforms offer greater flexibility and accessibility, they introduce novel risks, including smart contract vulnerabilities, price-oracle manipulation, and limited investor recourse in the event of loss (Schär, 2021). This dual landscape, regulated retail platforms and unregulated DeFi FX protocols, illustrates the trade-offs between accessibility, innovation, and investor protection, highlighting the ongoing challenge for regulators seeking to balance market growth with systemic stability.

References

ESMA. (2018). *ESMA Agrees to Prohibit Binary Options and Restrict CFDs to Protect Retail Investors*. Paris: ESMA

Schär, F. (2021). Decentralised Finance: On Blockchain- and Smart Contract-Based Financial Markets. *SSRN*, 103(2), pp. 153–174.

Case Study Questions

1 What are the key risks for retail traders on regulated platforms like eToro versus decentralised protocols like Synthetix?
2 Are strict leverage limits effective for consumer protection, or do they unfairly restrict experienced traders? Explain.
3 How can regulators apply traditional FX rules, such as KYC and leverage limits, to DeFi trading platforms?

Further Reading

King, M. R., & Rime, D. (2020). *The Future of Foreign Exchange Markets. Bank for International Settlements Papers*, No. 106. Basel: Bank for International.

Ranaldo, A., & Somogyi, F. (2021) The Effects of FinTech on the Forex Market. In D. L. K. Chuen & R. H. Deng (Eds.), *The Palgrave Handbook of FinTech and Blockchain*. Cham: Palgrave Macmillan.

Schär, F. (2021). Decentralised Finance: On Blockchain- and Smart Contract-Based Financial Markets. *Federal Reserve Bank of St. Louis Review*, 103(2), 153–174.

References

Aldridge, Irene (2013) *High-Frequency Trading: a Practical Guide to Algorithmic Strategies and Trading Systems*. Hoboken, NJ: John Wiley & Sons.

Bank for International Settlements (2022) *Triennial Central Bank Survey of Foreign Exchange and OTC Derivatives Markets*. Basel: Bank for International Settlements.

Bank for International Settlements (2023) *OTC Derivatives Statistics at End-June 2023*. Basel: Bank for International Settlements.

European Securities and Markets Authority (ESMA). (2018). ESMA Agrees to Prohibit Binary Options and Restrict CFDs to Protect Retail Investors. [Press Release].

Financial Conduct Authority (FCA). (2018). CP18/38: Restricting Contract for Different Products Sold to Retail Clients. Available at: https://www.fca.org.uk/publications/consultation-papers/cp18-38-restricting-contract-difference-products-sold-retail-clients

Financial Stability Board (FSB). (2022). *Assessment of Risks to Financial Stability from Crypto Assets*. Available at: https://www.fsb.org/2022/02/assessment-of-risks-to-financial-stability-from-crypto-assets/

International Monetary Fund. (2023) *Global Financial Stability Report: Safeguarding Financial Stability amid High Inflation and Geopolitical Risks*. Washington, DC: International Monetary Fund. Available at: https://www.imf.org/en/Publications/GFSR/Issues/2023/04/11/global-financial-stability-report-april-2023

King, M. R., & Rime, D. (2020). The FX Market: Evolution and Future Prospects. *BIS Quarterly Review*, December, pp. 67–82.

Mishkin, F. S., & Eakins, S. G. (2018) *Financial Markets and Institutions* 9thGlobal edn. Harlow: Pearson.

Pelster, M., & Hofmann, A. (2018) About the Fear of Reputational Loss: Social Trading and the Disposition Effect. *Journal of Banking and Finance*, 94, 75–88. https://doi.org/10.1016/j.jbankfin.2018.07.003

Schär, F (2021) 'Decentralised Finance: On Blockchain- and Smart Contract-Based Financial Markets', *Federal Reserve Bank of St. Louis Review*, 103(2), 153–174.

17 Capital Market Infrastructure, Regulation, and Financial Technology

Chapter Overview

This chapter offers a detailed analysis of the major digital transformations driven by Financial Technology (FinTech) within the capital market infrastructure (CMI). Key components such as exchanges, clearinghouses, settlement systems, and custody services are undergoing significant redesign, mainly through the adoption of distributed ledger technology (DLT) (blockchain), artificial intelligence (AI), and cloud computing. These technological advancements are enabling a shift from centralised, hierarchical structures to more open, networked systems, which require corresponding regulatory changes, including the development of Regulatory Technology (RegTech) and Supervisory Technology (SupTech). The chapter also considers emerging risks and management challenges in this evolving environment and examines the trend towards a more interconnected, efficient, and resilient global financial system.

Learning Objectives

By the end of this chapter, you should be able to:

1. Identify the core components of traditional CMI and explain their respective functions.
2. Analyse how specific FinTech innovations (DLT, AI, cloud) are disrupting and reshaping each component of the CMI value chain.
3. Differentiate between RegTech and SupTech, providing concrete examples of their application in modern financial markets.
4. Evaluate the key challenges, including legal, operational, and regulatory, associated with the transition to a FinTech-enabled CMI.
5. Critically assess the potential future states of CMI, including the implications of concepts like Embedded Supervision and decentralised finance (DeFi).

DOI: 10.4324/9781003775751-20

17.1 Introduction

CMI forms the backbone of the global financial system, encompassing the organisational frameworks, technological systems, and regulatory mechanisms that support the full lifecycle of securities, from issuance and trading to settlement. Traditionally, CMI relied on centralised institutional processes, which often resulted in operational inefficiencies, protracted settlement cycles, and elevated operational risk. In recent years, however, the landscape has shifted markedly due to the convergence of market functions and the rapid adoption of FinTech, which is driving a fundamental transformation of established operational paradigms (Arner, Barberis & Buckley, 2020).

FinTech innovations are reshaping core components of CMI by replacing slow, opaque processes with highly automated, transparent, and efficient digital workflows. Technologies such as DLT and advanced automation tools directly address long-standing post-trade challenges, significantly reducing operational risk, settlement latency, and the reliance on multiple intermediaries (Claessens et al., 2018). These technological advancements necessitate a re-evaluation of conventional intermediation models, as digital solutions increasingly facilitate functions that were historically managed manually or via centralised entities.

Concurrently, regulatory bodies are evolving their oversight frameworks to address the growing complexity and digitalisation of capital markets. The strategic deployment of RegTech and SupTech enhances systemic risk monitoring, compliance enforcement, and market surveillance. The overarching policy objective is to balance the efficiency and accessibility gains offered by technological innovation with the need to preserve financial stability and investor protection. The combined evolution of modernised infrastructure and adaptive, technology-enabled regulation is therefore reshaping the architecture of global capital markets (Arner, Barberis & Buckley, 2020; Claessens et al., 2018).

17.2 An Overview of CMI and Regulation

17.2.1 Core Components of CMI

CMI comprises the institutions, systems, and processes that support the issuance, trading, clearing, and settlement of financial instruments. The smooth operation of CMI is critical for ensuring liquidity, reducing systemic risk, and maintaining market confidence. At the centre of this ecosystem are Financial Market Infrastructures (FMIs), as defined by international standards (CPMI-IOSCO, 2012). The main components include:

Trading Venues: Trading platforms facilitate price discovery and the execution of financial transactions. Examples include regulated exchanges such as the New York Stock Exchange, where equities like Apple Inc. shares are traded, and the London Stock Exchange, which lists companies like British Petroleum and The Hongkong and Shanghai Banking Corporation. Alternative trading platforms, including Multilateral Trading Facilities (MTFs) such as Cboe Europe, provide competitive venues that improve liquidity and reduce transaction costs.

Central Counterparties (CCPs): CCPs interpose themselves between buyers and sellers in derivatives and securities markets, effectively becoming the counterparty to both sides of a trade. This reduces counterparty credit risk and helps stabilise markets. For instance,

LCH Ltd. clears interest rate swaps for global banks. At the same time, CME Clearing manages futures and options on commodities and currencies, ensuring that obligations are met even if a participant defaults.

Central Securities Depositories (CSDs): CSDs provide safekeeping of securities and facilitate electronic transfers of ownership through book-entry systems. The Depository Trust and Clearing Corporation (DTCC) in the United States processes equities and corporate bonds, settling billions of dollars daily. In contrast, Euroclear in Europe settles cross-border securities, including government bonds and corporate debt, enabling efficient and secure transfers. Many securities are fully dematerialised or immobilised, allowing settlement without physical certificates.

Payment Systems: Payment infrastructures ensure the secure transfer of funds, which is the final step in securities settlement. Systems such as Fedwire in the US and TARGET2 in the Eurozone enable real-time gross settlement of large-value transactions, ensuring that payments and securities settle simultaneously, thereby reducing settlement risk.

17.2.2 The Traditional Regulatory Landscape

Regulation of CMI aims to maintain financial stability, protect investors, and foster transparent and efficient markets. Post-Global Financial Crisis reforms have strengthened oversight and introduced new requirements for clearing, reporting, and operational resilience:

Dodd-Frank Act (US, 2010): Following the 2008 crisis, Dodd-Frank mandated central clearing for standardised over-the-counter (OTC) derivatives to reduce counterparty risk. It also introduced Swap Execution Facilities (SEFs), which allow transparent trading of swaps. For example, interest rate swap contracts between major banks are now executed via SEFs such as Tradeweb, thereby improving market transparency.

European Market Infrastructure Regulation (EMIR, EU, 2012): EMIR requires central clearing of eligible OTC derivatives and establishes risk mitigation techniques, including daily margining and timely reporting. Major banks like Deutsche Bank and BNP Paribas comply with EMIR requirements by clearing euro-denominated interest rate swaps through LCH SA, thereby reducing systemic risk.

Markets in Financial Instruments Directive II (MiFID II, EU, 2018): MiFID II enhanced pre- and post-trade transparency and reshaped European trading markets. Platforms like BATS Europe and Chi-X Europe emerged to provide alternative venues for trading equities and derivatives, offering investors better pricing and execution quality.

Principles for FMIs (PFMIs): Developed jointly by Committee on Payments and Market Infrastructures and International Organization of Securities Commissions, the PFMIs provide comprehensive standards for risk management, governance, and operational resilience of FMIs (CPMI-IOSCO, 2012). For example, CCPs such as LCH Ltd. implement margining and default management frameworks in line with PFMI standards to mitigate counterparty and liquidity risks. Similarly, CSDs like DTCC maintain robust business continuity plans and cybersecurity protocols to comply with these principles (Figure 17.1).

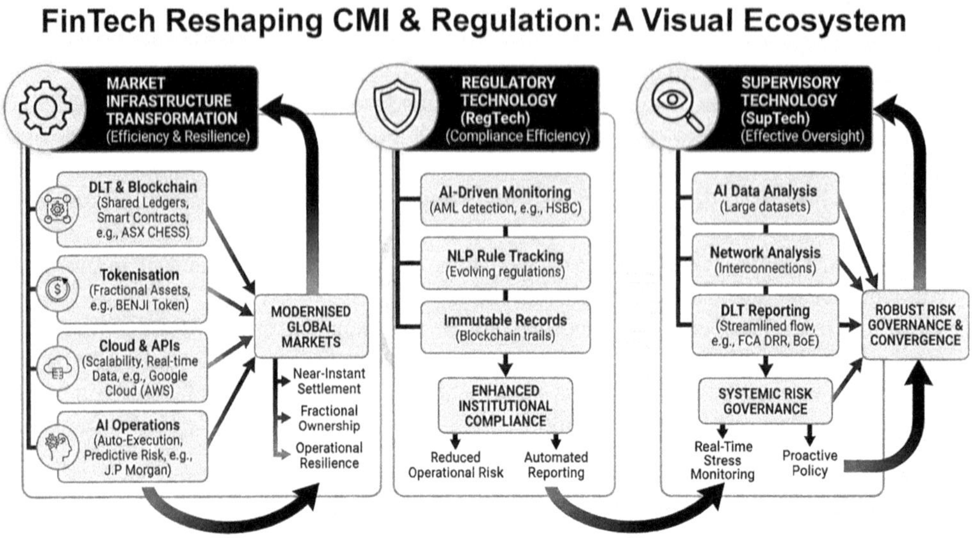

Figure 17.1 FinTech Innovation in CMI and Regulation.

17.3 The Role of FinTech in Reshaping CMI and Regulation

17.3.1 Market Infrastructure Transformation

FinTech is transforming CMI by introducing digital, automated, and highly efficient systems across trading, clearing, and settlement. Blockchain and DLT enable a shared ledger to record ownership, automate settlement, and embed smart contracts that implement risk controls similar to those performed by CCPs (BIS, 2023; Tapscott & Tapscott, 2016). Notable examples include the Australian Securities Exchange (ASX), which is integrating DLT into its Clearing House Electronic Sub-Register System (CHESS) settlement system, and the European Investment Bank's digital bonds, demonstrating how tokenised debt instruments streamline post-trade operations. Similarly, the tokenisation of assets, such as Franklin Templeton's BENJI token representing money market fund shares, enables fractional ownership, continuous trading, and near-instant settlement, reducing dependence on traditional intermediaries (BIS, 2022).

Other FinTech innovations include cloud computing and Application Programming Interfaces, which enhance scalability, integration, and operational efficiency. Global trading venues increasingly rely on platforms such as Google Cloud and Amazon Web Services to host data and analytics, enabling real-time risk monitoring and faster service deployment (McKinsey & Company, 2022). AI further optimises market operations through automated trade execution, market surveillance, predictive risk management, and CCP asset management. For example, J.P. Morgan applies AI in derivatives risk management, detecting anomalies, forecasting liquidity gaps, and improving margin allocation (BIS, 2023). Collectively, these technologies are modernising CMI, increasing efficiency, transparency, and resilience across global financial markets

17.3.2 RegTech and SupTech

FinTech is also transforming regulatory compliance through RegTech, which enables financial institutions to meet regulatory obligations more efficiently. Tools such as AI-driven transaction monitoring, natural language processing for tracking evolving rules, and blockchain-based immutable record-keeping reduce operational risk and enhance transparency (Arner, Barberis & Buckley, 2016). For instance, HSBC and Standard Chartered employ AI systems to detect suspicious transactions and automate anti-money laundering reporting, thereby improving speed and accuracy while reducing human error.

SupTech allows supervisory authorities to leverage technology for more effective oversight and systemic risk monitoring. Regulators use AI to analyse large transaction datasets, network analysis to assess interconnections among institutions, and DLT to streamline reporting. Notable examples include the UK Financial Conduct Authority's Digital Regulatory Reporting initiative, which employs blockchain and machine-readable formats to enhance reporting efficiency, and the Bank of England's SupTech projects, which monitor stress in payment and settlement systems in real time (FSB, 2020). Collectively, RegTech and SupTech support a resilient, transparent, and efficient CMI, demonstrating the convergence of operational efficiency and robust risk governance in modern financial markets.

17.4 A Comparison of Traditional and FinTech-Enabled CMI and Regulation

Table 17.1 compares traditional and FinTech-enabled CMI.

Table 17.1 A Contrast of Traditional and FinTech-Enabled CMI and Regulation

Aspect	*Traditional CMI and Regulation*	*FinTech-Enabled CMI and Regulation*
Infrastructure Structure	Centralised, hierarchical (Exchanges, CCPs, CSDs)	Decentralised, networked (DLT, peer-to-peer protocols)
Settlement Cycle	T+2 or longer, requiring extensive post-trade reconciliation	Near-instant (T+0) atomic settlement via DLT
Data and Reporting	Siloed, batch-based systems with delayed post-trade reporting	Unified, real-time data ledgers enabling granular, continuous regulatory access
Compliance Process	Manual, periodic, and rule-based	Automated, continuous, and embedded in protocol logic (e.g., smart contracts)
Risk Management	Centralised in clearinghouses (CCPs) and custodians	Distributed across the network via cryptographic and algorithmic mechanisms
System Interoperability	Achieved through industry standards and complex legal agreements	A major technical and governance challenge across diverse DLT protocols and legacy systems
Governance and Regulation	Clear, entity-based regulation with established accountability	Often unclear, facing jurisdictional ambiguity, especially for decentralised networks

Note: CCP, Central Counterparty; CMI, Capital Market Infrastructure; CSD, Central Securities Depository; DLT, Distributed Ledger Technology.

17.5 Key Practical Issues and Challenges

The integration of FinTech into CMI introduces several critical practical challenges. Interoperability remains a significant concern, as achieving seamless interaction between multiple DLT networks and between these networks and legacy systems involves complex technical and governance considerations. Failure to resolve these issues risks increased market fragmentation and operational inefficiencies (BIS, 2023).

Legal certainty and finality are also unresolved in many jurisdictions. The recognition of tokenised securities and the enforceability of smart contracts are essential to ensure that settlement on DLT platforms is legally binding and irrevocable, a prerequisite for maintaining financial stability (ISDA, 2022). Cybersecurity and concentration risks are heightened in a FinTech-enabled environment. While DLT can reduce single points of failure, vulnerabilities such as smart contract flaws, 51% attacks, and reliance on a limited number of major cloud providers pose systemic threats.

Regulatory arbitrage and governance of decentralisation present further challenges. DeFi protocols often operate across borders, using pseudonymous participants to circumvent traditional regulatory frameworks designed for identifiable legal entities. Ensuring accountability and establishing compliance mechanisms for decentralised autonomous organisations remains a complex task. Finally, data privacy and governance concerns arise from SupTech's capacity to monitor granular, real-time data, necessitating careful management of privacy rights, data ownership, and the potential for excessive surveillance.

17.6 The Future of CMI and Regulation in the FinTech Era

FinTech is reshaping the structure and governance of CMI, with significant implications for the future. The unbundling and rebundling of CMI functions are a key trend, as FinTech and DeFi protocols increasingly disaggregate traditional functions such as trading, clearing, and settlement from CSDs. Over time, these functions are expected to be recombined in innovative, technology-driven models that enhance efficiency and reduce reliance on legacy intermediaries.

Embedded supervision represents a transformative regulatory paradigm in which compliance is automatically monitored through access to shared ledgers, reducing the need for firms to submit traditional reporting data (Auer et al., 2021). The adoption of regulated stablecoins and Central Bank Digital Currencies (CBDCs) as settlement assets could further integrate payments and securities settlement, facilitating faster, more secure, and globally harmonised transactions (BIS, 2023). Finally, AI-driven predictive regulation will enable regulators to transition from reactive oversight to proactive monitoring, leveraging machine learning and predictive analytics to model market dynamics, anticipate systemic stress points, and enhance the resilience of financial markets.

17.7 Conclusion

The evolution of CMI, driven by FinTech, necessitates a parallel transformation in regulatory philosophy. This transition extends beyond superficial adoption of digital tools, representing a fundamental shift from centralised architectures towards more agile, decentralised networks. To fully realise the potential for greater efficiency, transparency, and market inclusivity, regulatory frameworks must be fundamentally redesigned rather than merely digitised. This involves a progressive evolution from RegTech solutions that automate compliance, to SupTech applications that enhance supervisory oversight, and ultimately towards embedded supervision, in which regulatory monitoring is seamlessly integrated into the operational fabric of digital market infrastructures. As industry analysts observe, the future of regulation is not merely digital; it is native to the new technological environment (Auer et al., 2021).

The ultimate measure of this transformation lies not in technological sophistication alone, but in its tangible outcomes. Effective modernisation should produce a financial system that delivers enhanced services, demonstrates robust resilience against systemic risks, and, critically, sustains the confidence of all market participants. Achieving a capital market ecosystem that is simultaneously innovative, secure, and equitable constitutes the central objective driving contemporary global efforts to redefine CMI for the digital era (BIS, 2023; Arner, Barberis & Buckley, 2020).

Key Terms and Glossary

FMI (Financial Market Infrastructure) A multilateral system among participating institutions, including the operator of the system, used for the purposes of clearing, settling, or recording payments, securities, derivatives, or other financial transactions.

CCP (Central Counterparty) An entity that interposes itself between counterparties to contracts traded in one or more financial markets, becoming the buyer to every seller and the seller to every buyer.

Tokenisation The process of converting rights to an asset into a digital representation, or token, on a distributed ledger.

RegTech The use of technology, particularly information technology, in the context of regulatory monitoring, reporting, and compliance.

SupTech The use of technology by supervisory agencies to improve the efficiency and effectiveness of supervision.

Legal Finality The point in time at which a transfer of securities or funds becomes irrevocable and unconditional under the law applicable to that transfer.

Test Your Understanding

Multiple-Choice Questions

1 Which of the following is NOT considered a core component of CMI?

A Trading Venues
B CCPs
C Commercial Banks' Retail Branches
D CSDs

2 The PFMIs primarily aim to:

A Increase trading volumes on exchanges
B Ensure operational resilience, risk management, and governance of FMIs
C Replace central banks in settlement operations
D Introduce tokenised securities globally

3 Which FinTech innovation allows near-instant settlement of securities and embedded risk management through smart contracts?

   A Cloud computing
   B DLT
   C MTFs
   D Traditional CSDs

4 RegTech differs from SupTech in that:

   A RegTech is used by regulators; SupTech is used by banks
   B RegTech automates compliance for institutions; SupTech enhances regulatory oversight
   C Both focus solely on cybersecurity.
   D SupTech is only applicable to blockchain-based markets

5 One key challenge in FinTech-enabled CMI is interoperability, which refers to:

   A Banks sharing customer data with regulators
   B Seamless integration between multiple DLT networks and legacy systems
   C Increased trading volumes on multiple exchanges
   D Ensuring all investors have equal access to financial education

Short Questions

1 Explain the difference between a CCP and a CSD in CMI.
2 Identify two practical challenges associated with integrating FinTech innovations into traditional CMI.
3 What is the concept of embedded supervision, and how does it change traditional regulatory reporting?

Analytical Questions

1 Discuss how DLT and tokenisation can reduce operational risk in post-trade settlement while introducing new legal and cybersecurity challenges.
2 Evaluate the potential implications of adopting CBDCs and regulated stablecoins as settlement assets on cross-border securities transactions.
3 Critically analyse the role of RegTech and SupTech in creating a more resilient and transparent financial system. How might embedded supervision further transform market oversight?

Case Study: The ASX CHESS Replacement Project

The ASX operates CHESS, a combined CCP and CSD system that clears and settles equity transactions in Australia. In 2016, ASX announced plans to replace CHESS with a new DLT-based system, developed with Digital Asset Holdings, aiming to modernise settlement processes, enhance transparency, and enable future innovations such as tokenised assets. The system was designed to provide a single source of truth for shareholdings, achieve near-instant (T+0) settlement, and use smart contracts and Digital Asset Modeling Language to automate corporate actions and other processes.

Despite its potential, the project experienced significant delays and a major reset in 2022 due to several challenges. Technical complexity raised concerns about system performance and resilience under stress. Governance issues emerged from ASX's dual role as both operator and market participant, leading to limited transparency and stakeholder confidence. Market participants, including brokers and custodians, reported high integration costs and operational burdens, raising questions about the feasibility of replicating all legacy functionalities. These setbacks underscore the challenges of transitioning critical market infrastructure to new technologies while balancing innovation, operational reliability, and stakeholder trust.

Reference

Australian Securities Exchange (ASX). (2022). *CHESS Replacement: Project Updates and Announcements*. Available at: https://www.asx.com.au/markets/clearing-and-settlement-services/chess-project (Accessed: 24 May 2026).

Henri Dodolfing (2023) *Case Study 21: The Australian Securities Exchange (ASX) $250 Million CHESS Blunder*. Zurich: Henri Dodolfing Consultancy. Available at: https://www.henricodolfing.ch/en/case-study-21-the-australian-securities-exchange-asx-250-million-chess-blunder/

Case Study Questions

1 What operational and financial challenges would a large broker face when connecting to a DLT-based settlement system like ASX CHESS?
2 Why is strong governance critical for a DLT-based FMI, and how can exchanges design governance to build trust among participants?
3 What lessons can other exchanges learn from ASX, and how could they adopt a phased approach to modernise infrastructure safely?

Further Reading

Auer, R., Cornelli, G. & Frost, J. (2021). Embedded Supervision: How to Build Regulation into Decentralised Finance. *Cryptoeconomic Systems*, 2(1), 1–30.

Zetzsche, D.A., Arner, D.W., & Buckley, R.P. (2020). Decentralised Finance (DeFi). *Journal of Financial Regulation*, 6(2), 172–203.

References

Auer, R., Cornelli, G.. & Frost, J. (2021). Embedded Supervision: How to Build Regulation into Decentralised Finance. *Cryptoeconomic Systems*, 2(1), 1–30.

Arner, D.W., Barberis, J., & Buckley, R.P. (2016). The Evolution of FinTech: A New Post-Crisis Paradigm? *Georgetown Journal of International Law*, 47(4), 1271–1319.

Arner, D.W., Barberis, J., & Buckley, R.P. (2020). The Future of FinTech and Finance: A Research Agenda. *University of Hong Kong Faculty of Law Research Paper No. 2020/017*.

Australian Securities Exchange (ASX). (2022). *CHESS Replacement*. [Project Updates and Announcements]. Available at: https://www.asx.com.au/markets/clearing-and-settlement-services/chess-project

Bank for International Settlements (BIS). (2022). FinTech and the Digitalisation of Commodities Trading. *BIS Papers No. 128*.

Bank for International Settlements (BIS). (2023). Blueprint for the Future Monetary System: Improving the Old, Enabling the New. *Annual Economic Report*.

Claessens, S., Frost, J., Turner, G., & Zhu, F. (2018). FinTech Credit Markets Around the World: Size, Drivers and Policy Issues. *BIS Quarterly Review*, September, pp. 29–49.

Committee on Payments and Market Infrastructures (CPMI) and International Organisation of Securities Commissions (IOSCO) (2012) *Principles for financial market infrastructures*. Basel: Bank for International Settlements.

Financial Stability Board (FSB). (2020). *The Use of Supervisory and Regulatory Technology by Authorities and Regulated Institutions*. Available at: https://www.fsb.org/uploads/P091020.pdf

International Swaps and Derivatives Association (ISDA). (2022). *Smart Derivatives Contracts: From Concept to Construction*. New York: ISDA.

McKinsey & Company. (2022). *The Future of Capital Markets: Digital, Decentralised, and Direct*. New York: McKinsey & Company.

Tapscott, D., & Tapscott, A. (2016). *Blockchain Revolution: How the Technology Behind Bitcoin Is Changing Money, Business, and the World*. New York: Penguin.

Part 4

Technology and Innovation in Finance and Banking

18 Money and Financial Technology

Chapter Overview

This chapter offers a thorough analysis of the development of money, tracing its evolution from early barter systems to the rise of complex digital currencies that define modern finance. It critically explores the transformative influence of Financial Technology (FinTech) on contemporary financial systems, examining the core functions and main features of money, as well as the rise of digital and decentralised currencies. The discussion assesses disruptive innovations such as blockchain technology, mobile payment systems, and Central Bank Digital Currencies (CBDCs). The chapter concludes with a forward-looking view on the future of money, highlighting themes such as greater financial inclusion, improved programmability of financial assets, and emerging regulatory and security concerns.

Learning Objectives:

By the end of this chapter, you should be able to:

1. Explain how money has evolved from traditional forms to modern digital systems and why innovations were needed.
2. Understand how scarcity, trust, and control work in fiat money, cryptocurrencies, and CBDCs, and their impact on monetary stability.
3. Evaluate FinTech innovations (mobile money, stablecoins, blockchain) for opportunities in inclusion, efficiency, and innovation, as well as related risks.
4. Compare traditional and digital monetary systems, noting differences, similarities, and challenges like interoperability and systemic risk.
5. Anticipate future trends in money, including CBDCs, embedded finance, and new technologies, while weighing trade-offs between programmability, privacy, and autonomy.

DOI: 10.4324/9781003775751-22

18.1 Introduction

The evolution of money has been substantial, progressing from basic commodity-based barter systems to advanced digital tokens. Despite these changes, the fundamental functions of money remain consistent: facilitating the exchange of goods and services, fostering trust in economic interactions, and enabling the organisation of economies, as Mishkin (2019) observes. In the twenty-first century, rapid technological advancements are not only refining monetary transactions but also redefining the very nature and utility of money.

This transformation is propelled by the rapidly expanding field of FinTech. FinTech encompasses a range of innovations that are transforming how individuals and organisations manage, transfer, and store wealth. Examples include digital payment systems, online lending platforms, blockchain-based currencies, and algorithmic trading. These developments reduce reliance on traditional financial institutions and provide greater efficiency, accessibility, and transparency in financial operations.

A comprehensive understanding of the relationship between money and FinTech is essential for navigating the contemporary financial landscape. This chapter examines this evolving dynamic in detail, demonstrating how technological innovation is reshaping financial instruments and processes, as well as transforming global financial practices and infrastructure. The chapter offers a thorough analysis of the challenges and opportunities arising from these developments.

18.2 The Fundamentals of Money

Money serves three main purposes: a medium of exchange, a store of value, and a unit of account (Mishkin, 2019). In the past, systems used commodity money, such as gold and silver. Later, state-issued fiat currency became the norm. Fiat money has value because governments and institutions support it, not because of its own worth. Today, digital forms of money are common and driven by technology. Together, these functions of money solve the problems of barter, such as the need for matching wants. As a result, they help trade, drive economic growth, and keep economies stable.

18.2.1 The Functions of Money

Medium of Exchange: Money serves as a critical medium of exchange by eliminating the inefficiencies inherent in barter systems, where transactions require a double coincidence of wants. By providing a generally accepted means of payment, money significantly lowers transaction costs, facilitates specialisation, and enables the expansion of markets (Mishkin, 2019). This role enhances economic efficiency by simplifying trade and enabling the smooth exchange of goods and services among diverse participants. For example, a farmer who produces wheat does not need to find a shoemaker who specifically wants wheat; instead, the farmer can sell wheat for money and then use that money to purchase shoes from any seller. In this way, money supports consistent price comparisons and is essential for the functioning of complex, modern economies.

Store of Value: Money serves as a store of value by allowing individuals and institutions to transfer purchasing power from the present into the future. By holding money rather than immediately spending income, economic agents can defer consumption and plan for future expenditures. This function depends on money maintaining a relatively stable value over time. When inflation is high or unpredictable, the purchasing power of money declines, eroding the real value of savings and undermining long-term financial planning (Bernanke, 2020). For example, if a household saves $5,000 for future education expenses but inflation rises sharply, that same amount may cover significantly fewer tuition costs than originally expected. In such circumstances, money becomes a less reliable store of value, creating uncertainty for both individuals and businesses.

Unit of Account: Money serves as a critical unit of account by providing a standardised measure for assigning value to goods, services, assets, and liabilities, thereby enabling precise economic comparison and decision-making. Money allows us to compare the values of items that are quite different (Mankiw, 2021). This common denominator underpins financial reporting, facilitates contractual agreements, and enhances market efficiency by ensuring consistency and transparency in valuation across diverse economic activities. For example, a consumer can decide between a laptop priced at $1,000 and a smartphone priced at $800 because both values are stated in the same unit of money, making comparison straightforward.

18.2.2 Key Characteristics of Money

For money to effectively perform its core functions, it must exhibit several key characteristics:

Durability: An essential characteristic of any effective form of money, it must withstand physical wear and remain usable over time. Physical currencies such as coins and banknotes are designed to be resilient, but they can still deteriorate with extensive handling. By contrast, digital money does not suffer physical damage and therefore avoids loss of value due to material decay (Dwyer, 2014). For example, a paper banknote may become torn or faded after years of circulation and eventually need to be replaced. In contrast, money held in a bank account retains its form and usability without physical deterioration.

Portability: A critical feature in modern finance, ensuring that financial assets can be easily transferred. As the Bank for International Settlements (BIS, 2020) notes, digital wallets and mobile banking have significantly enhanced monetary portability, enabling seamless cross-border transactions. These innovations improve efficiency, accessibility, and convenience for professionals and consumers alike, aligning with the demands of a globalised economy. For example, a business traveller can pay for services abroad using a mobile payment app without carrying large amounts of physical cash, completing the transaction instantly and securely.

Divisibility: A fundamental characteristic of effective money, allowing it to be broken into smaller units to support transactions of varying sizes. This ensures that money can be used efficiently for both large purchases and very small payments. Digital currencies illustrate this feature clearly; for instance, one Bitcoin can be divided into 100 million smaller units known as satoshis (Nakamoto, 2008), enabling highly precise transactions. Such fine granularity increases flexibility, supports liquidity, and facilitates broader usage across different economic contexts. For example, instead of needing to spend an entire Bitcoin, a user can pay a small online fee with only a fraction, making the currency practical for everyday microtransactions as well as high-value transfers.

Uniformity: Uniformity in currency ensures that each unit is interchangeable and identical in value, fostering trust and streamlining transactions. Money must be standardised so that everyone values each unit the same way, a principle essential for efficient economic exchange among professionals (Mankiw, 2021). For example, when someone deposits five

$20 bills into a bank account, the bank does not treat each bill differently; each one is counted as having the same value, which simplifies accounting and everyday transactions.

Scarcity: Limited supply, or scarcity, is a fundamental principle for maintaining the value of money. In fiat currency systems, central banks control the money supply to prevent inflation and preserve stability, while cryptocurrencies like Bitcoin enforce scarcity through algorithmic caps, ensuring a fixed and predictable supply (Böhme et al., 2015). This controlled scarcity helps sustain demand and long-term value. For example, central banks may limit the issuance of new banknotes or adjust interest rates to control the circulation of money, preventing excessive inflation and maintaining public confidence in the currency, similar in principle to Bitcoin's fixed 21-million-coin limit but managed through policy rather than an algorithm.

Acceptability: Acceptability refers to money being widely recognised and trusted as a valid form of payment. For fiat currencies, this trust is typically supported by government backing, which helps ensure people and businesses are willing to use them in everyday transactions. In the case of digital currencies like Bitcoin, acceptability relies on the credibility of decentralised networks and the security of the blockchain system (Gorton & Zhang, 2021). For example, the US dollar is universally accepted for goods and services within the United States because it is legal tender guaranteed by the government. In contrast, Bitcoin is increasingly accepted by online retailers and payment platforms, allowing users to pay for products digitally even without traditional banking intermediaries.

Stability of Value: Stability of value refers to money's ability to maintain its purchasing power over time, which is essential for economic confidence and planning. In fiat systems, central banks use monetary policy tools, such as interest rate adjustments and money supply management, to control inflation and maintain currency value stability (Bernanke, 2020). Digital currencies, however, often experience greater volatility, as their value is determined by market demand rather than government policy. For example, the US dollar remains relatively stable, allowing households to plan budgets and businesses to set prices with confidence. In contrast, Bitcoin's value can fluctuate sharply within days, making it less reliable for everyday transactions.

18.3 The Rise of FinTech and the Evolution of Money

FinTech leverages digital technology to enhance and automate financial services. Although technology has historically influenced finance, contemporary FinTech is disrupting traditional institutions and expanding access to financial services (Figure 18.1).

18.3.1 FinTech and Money Evolution

Cryptocurrencies and Blockchain: The evolution of money through FinTech has been significantly shaped by cryptocurrencies and blockchain technology. Bitcoin, introduced as a decentralised peer-to-peer cash system, disrupted traditional financial intermediaries by leveraging blockchain (Nakamoto, 2008). Today, the ecosystem includes stablecoins, cryptocurrencies pegged to fiat currencies to reduce volatility, offering a bridge between digital and traditional finance (Gorton & Zhang, 2021). Concurrently, CBDCs are being explored globally to modernise payment systems while preserving monetary sovereignty, as noted by the Bank for International Settlements (2022), which stated that CBDCs could enhance efficiency and financial inclusion. This shift highlights the transformative potential of digital assets in redefining monetary systems.

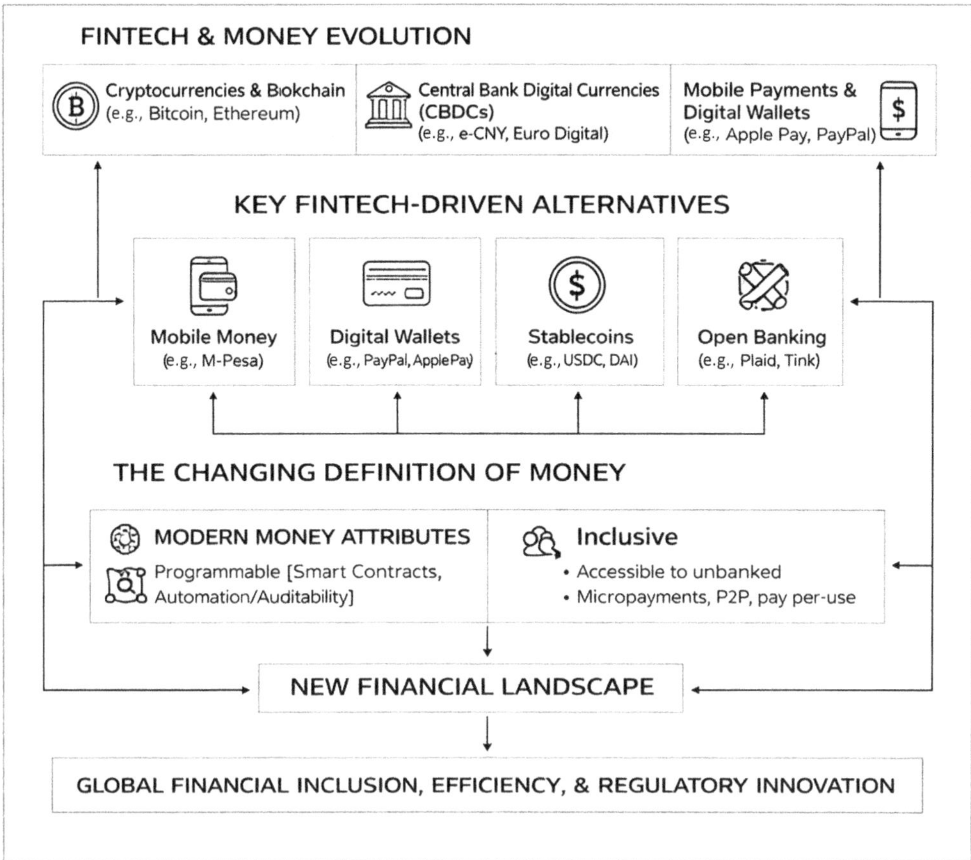

Figure 18.1 The Rise of FinTech and the Evolution of Money.

Mobile Payments and Digital Wallets: The evolution of FinTech has significantly transformed the way money is managed, particularly through mobile payments and digital wallets. Platforms like M-Pesa, Alipay, and PayPal have revolutionised financial accessibility, especially in underserved regions with limited traditional banking infrastructure. These services leverage mobile technology to facilitate seamless, secure transactions, empowering users with convenient payment and transfer solutions (Demirgüç-Kunt et al., 2022). By reducing reliance on physical cash and traditional banking systems, such innovations promote financial inclusion and efficiency, marking a pivotal shift in the global monetary landscape. The increasing adoption of these tools underscores their role in driving the digitisation of financial services worldwide.

18.3.2 Key FinTech-Driven Alternatives to Traditional Money

Mobile Money: FinTech-driven alternatives to traditional money, such as mobile money systems like M-Pesa, are transforming financial inclusion by enabling unbanked populations to store and transfer value via mobile devices. Operated by telecommunications firms, these platforms provide accessible, efficient, and secure financial services.

Digital Wallets: Digital wallets, such as Apple Pay and Google Pay, are key FinTech alternatives that are revolutionising payments. Digital wallets enable secure, contactless, peer-to-peer transactions, effectively consolidating multiple payment methods into a single, streamlined platform for users.

Stablecoins: Stablecoins such as USD Tether and USD Coin offer a FinTech-driven alternative to traditional money by merging blockchain efficiency with fiat-backed stability. Stablecoins provide liquidity and reduce volatility risk in digital transactions, making them instrumental in remittances and decentralised finance (DeFi) ecosystems.

CBDCs: CBDCs represent a transformative shift in monetary systems, offering digital sovereign currency solutions like China's e-CNY. As the Bank for International Settlements notes, CBDCs enhance payment efficiency, foster financial inclusion, and mitigate risks posed by private digital currencies. These state-backed innovations aim to modernise financial infrastructure while maintaining regulatory oversight.

Open Banking: Open Banking represents a transformative shift in financial services, leveraging API technology to enable secure data sharing between institutions and third-party providers. The Open Banking Implementation Entity empowers consumers by giving them greater control over their financial data, driving innovation and competition in the sector.

18.3.3 The Transforming Feature of Money

Money's definition is growing to include new features:

Programmable: The integration of smart contracts is fundamentally reshaping money, transforming it into a programmable tool. This innovation enables value to execute transactions automatically upon meeting pre-defined conditions, a shift some herald as moving money from a static asset to a dynamic agent of commerce.

Traceable: The evolution of money is significantly advanced by blockchain technology, which provides an immutable and transparent transaction ledger. This traceability offers unparalleled auditability, yet as critics note, it inherently raises significant privacy concerns for users by creating a permanent, public financial record.

Inclusive: The definition of money is evolving, driven by FinTech innovations that enhance financial inclusion. Digital financial services can reach the unbanked faster than traditional infrastructure (Demirgüç-Kunt et al., 2022). These advancements redefine accessibility, ensuring underserved populations gain equitable access to financial tools and systems.

Dynamic: Modern digital money is evolving beyond static value storage, becoming dynamic by design. Programmable money can autonomously adjust to economic indicators or policy shifts, enabling real-time financial responsiveness (IMF, 2024). This adaptability enhances the efficiency of monetary policy and financial stability, redefining the role of money in a digital economy. Professionals must assess the implications of these innovations for liquidity, regulation, and systemic risk.

18.4 Contrast and Convergence of Traditional and Digital Money

The fundamental contrast lies in tangibility, as sovereign states physically issue traditional money, while digital currencies exist as decentralised cryptographic entries. However, a notable convergence is emerging as central banks develop their own digital currencies (CBDCs), blurring these once-distinct boundaries and forging a new monetary paradigm.

Table 18.1 A Comparison Between Fiat and Digital Money

Feature	*Traditional Money (Fiat Currency)*	*Digital Money (Cryptocurrency/Token)*
Nature and Control	Centralised, issued and backed by sovereign states	Decentralised, often algorithmically governed or community-driven
Form	Physical (cash) and digital entries within traditional banking systems	Predominantly dematerialised, existing as digital entries on a distributed ledger
Regulation	Operates within well-established national and international regulatory frameworks	Faces significant regulatory uncertainty; jurisdictionally varied and evolving
Transaction Efficiency	Reliant on intermediaries; can be slower and more costly, especially cross-border	Often enables faster, cheaper transactions with reduced dependence on intermediaries

18.4.1 Fundamental Contrasts

Table 18.1 shows a comparison between Fiat and Digital Money

18.4.2 Key Areas of Convergence

Traditional and digital financial systems are increasingly converging.

Digital Payments: The convergence of fiat and digital money is most evident in digital payments, where platforms like digital wallets and real-time systems such as Faster Payments are transforming how we use traditional currency. As the Bank for International Settlements notes, the line between physical cash and electronic money is rapidly blurring, underscoring a fundamental shift in global financial infrastructure.

CBDCs: CBDCs represent the most direct fusion of state-backed trust and FinTech innovation, epitomising the convergence of fiat and digital money. They embody the next evolution in money, combining sovereign guarantee with the efficiency of a digital asset.

Cross-Border Payments: Cross-border payments represent a critical area of convergence between fiat and digital money, with FinTech firms such as Wise and Revolut utilising technology to deliver faster, more cost-effective remittance solutions. The integration of digital infrastructure into traditional finance is reshaping global transaction efficiency.

Regulatory Integration: Regulatory integration represents a pivotal area of convergence between fiat and digital money, exemplified by initiatives such as the EU's PSD2, which fosters innovation while ensuring consumer protection and financial stability. This framework enables secure collaboration between traditional institutions and FinTechs, bridging legacy systems with digital advancements under a unified regulatory umbrella.

18.5 Opportunities, Challenges, and Key Practical Issues

18.5.1 Opportunities

FinTech presents substantial opportunities to improve financial systems and expand access to financial services. A key contribution of FinTech is advancing financial inclusion, as exemplified by platforms like M-PESA, which have enabled millions of previously unbanked individuals to access essential financial services, thereby promoting broader economic participation and social mobility globally (Demirgüç-Kunt et al., 2022). In addition, FinTech drives service innovation by democratising access to sophisticated financial tools; technologies such as robo-advisors, micro-investing applications, and DeFi platforms lower traditional barriers to entry and empower a wider range of individuals to engage in investment and wealth management activities (Arner, Barberis & Buckley, 2020). FinTech further enhances efficiency and transaction speed, with blockchain-based payment systems like Ripple's XRP enabling near-instantaneous, low-cost settlements that challenge legacy infrastructures and point towards a more integrated and streamlined global financial ecosystem (Catalini & Gans, 2016). The ongoing convergence of traditional and digital financial systems, including CBDCs and stablecoins, underscores the sector's potential to deliver seamless, interoperable financial services that bridge the gap between conventional banking and innovative digital platforms (BIS, 2022).

18.5.2 Risk and Challenges

Despite the opportunities offered by FinTech, several challenges hinder its widespread adoption and integration. Regulatory uncertainty remains a significant obstacle, as the absence of a coordinated global framework constrains innovation and scalability, exemplified by the scrutiny faced by the Diem (formerly Libra) project (Financial Times, 2021). Cybersecurity and fraud risks are persistent concerns, with the digital infrastructure of FinTech platforms vulnerable to sophisticated attacks, as demonstrated by the 2014 collapse of the Mt. Gox cryptocurrency exchange, which highlighted the high stakes of safeguarding digital assets (Yermack, 2017). Moreover, the digital divide poses a major challenge, as unequal access to digital infrastructure and varying levels of digital literacy may exclude vulnerable populations, exacerbating existing inequalities and limiting the societal benefits of financial innovation (Demirgüç-Kunt et al., 2022). Together, these challenges underscore the need for robust regulatory frameworks, improved cybersecurity measures, and inclusive digital infrastructure to ensure that FinTech development remains sustainable, secure, and equitable.

18.5.3 Key Practical Issues of Digital Money

The integration of FinTech into the monetary system presents several practical issues that require careful consideration. Regulatory arbitrage and fragmentation emerge as major concerns, as the borderless nature of digital currencies contrasts with fragmented national regulations, allowing firms to exploit jurisdictional differences and potentially increasing systemic risk (BIS, 2022). Interoperability is another critical issue, as ensuring seamless transactions across CBDCs, stablecoins, and traditional banking infrastructures remains technically and commercially challenging, necessitating standardised protocols and cross-industry collaboration (ECB, 2021). Additionally, the rapid evolution of digital financial products highlights the importance of consumer protection and financial literacy, as informed and empowered users are essential for trust and inclusive adoption of new technologies (Demirgüç-Kunt et al., 2022). The convergence of traditional finance with DeFi and Big Tech platforms introduces systemic risk, creating new pathways for financial contagion that require coordinated regulatory oversight to maintain global financial stability (FSB, 2024). Finally, energy consumption and environmental concerns, particularly associated with Proof-of-Work blockchain systems such as Bitcoin, pose significant ESG challenges, underscoring the need for sustainable innovation in digital finance (International Energy Agency, 2021).

18.6 Future Innovation of FinTech Money

CBDCs Going Mainstream: CBDCs are poised to transform global finance, with over 130 countries currently exploring or developing them. Initiatives such as the Bank for International Settlements' mBridge project aim to enable seamless cross-border transactions, signalling a shift towards integrated digital monetary systems. However, these advancements raise critical questions about privacy and financial surveillance (IMF, 2024), underscoring the need for balanced regulatory frameworks. The mainstream adoption of CBDCs will depend not only on technological innovation but also on public trust and the protection of individual rights in an increasingly digital financial ecosystem.

Embedded Finance and Invisible Money: The future of FinTech lies in embedded finance and invisible money, where financial services seamlessly integrate into non-financial platforms, like ride-hailing or retail apps, making transactions effortless. Ambient finance will redefine convenience, turning everyday interactions into frictionless financial moments. This shift prioritises user experience, embedding payments, lending, and insurance into daily activities, eliminating the need for traditional banking touchpoints.

Quantum Computing and Cryptography: The emergence of quantum computing poses a significant threat to current cryptographic frameworks underpinning FinTech. The National Institute of Standards and Technology suggest that post-quantum cryptography is essential to safeguarding digital assets. Financial institutions must proactively adopt quantum-resistant algorithms to ensure long-term data integrity and system security.

18.7 Conclusion

The evolution of money from tangible artefacts to complex digital representations reflects a profound transformation in the financial landscape. At the same time, its fundamental economic functions, as a medium of exchange, unit of account, and store of value, remain intact. FinTech has emerged as a central driver of this transformation, catalysing innovation across mobile payments, digital assets, and open banking. However, the rapid pace of technological advancement presents a dual-edged challenge. While FinTech has the potential to enhance financial inclusion, operational efficiency, and service innovation, it also introduces significant risks, including regulatory frameworks that struggle to keep pace, heightened cybersecurity vulnerabilities, and the persistent need to ensure equitable access to prevent the deepening of existing inequalities (Demirgüç-Kunt et al., 2022; Yermack, 2017).

Looking ahead, the convergence of traditional finance with emerging digital constructs, such as CBDCs, signals a future in which money becomes increasingly programmable, traceable, and dynamic. Successfully navigating this paradigm shift requires a holistic, coordinated approach that integrates technological expertise with enduring economic principles. Policymakers, regulators, and financial institutions must collaboratively develop strategies that balance innovation with security, privacy, and inclusivity, thereby fostering a resilient and adaptable financial ecosystem capable of meeting the evolving needs of a digital economy (BIS, 2022; FSB, 2024).

Key Terms and Glossary

Fiat Money Government-issued currency that is not backed by a physical commodity but by the trust in the issuing government.

Cryptocurrency A digital or virtual currency that uses cryptography for security and operates on a decentralised network.

Stablecoin A type of cryptocurrency designed to maintain a stable value by being pegged to a reserve asset like a fiat currency.

CBDC A digital form of a country's sovereign currency, issued and regulated by the central bank.

Programmable Money Digital money that can be designed with rules and conditions (e.g., via smart contracts) that govern its use.

Mobile Money Financial services delivered via mobile devices, often targeting unbanked populations.

Digital Wallet A software-based system that stores payment information and enables electronic transactions.

Test Your Understanding

Multiple-Choice Questions

1 Which of the following is NOT considered a core function of money?

A Medium of exchange
B Store of value
C Unit of account
D Source of unlimited credit

2 What is the primary feature of stablecoins in the digital financial ecosystem?

A They are fully decentralised with unlimited supply
B They merge blockchain efficiency with fiat-backed stability
C They are issued exclusively by central banks
D They operate only within mobile wallets

3 Which of the following represents a key challenge in the adoption of FinTech?

A Financial inclusion
B Regulatory uncertainty
C Programmable money
D Faster transactions

4 CBDCs are designed primarily to:

A Replace all cryptocurrencies
B Preserve monetary sovereignty while enhancing efficiency and inclusion
C Operate independently of government oversight
D Function only for international remittances

5 Which attribute of modern digital money allows transactions to occur automatically when pre-defined conditions are met?

   A Traceability
   B Programmability
   C Portability
   D Acceptability

Short Questions

1 Explain how FinTech innovations such as mobile money and digital wallets enhance financial inclusion.
2 Identify and briefly describe three key characteristics of money that ensure its effective functioning in an economy.
3 What are the main risks associated with integrating traditional finance with DeFi platforms?

Analytical Questions

1 Compare and contrast fiat currency and cryptocurrencies in terms of control, regulation, and value stability. Use examples to support your answer.
2 Discuss the implications of programmable and traceable money for privacy, financial inclusion, and monetary policy. How can policymakers balance these competing concerns?
3 Evaluate the potential impact of CBDCs and embedded finance on the traditional banking sector and cross-border payment systems. What challenges might arise in terms of interoperability, regulation, and systemic risk?

Case Study: Nigeria's eNaira and the Challenge of Digital Currency Adoption

In October 2021, the Central Bank of Nigeria (CBN) launched the eNaira, becoming the first African country to introduce a CBDC. The initiative aimed to modernise Nigeria's payment system, lower the costs associated with cash usage, improve transaction efficiency, and expand financial inclusion among the country's large unbanked population. The eNaira was also expected to enhance monetary policy effectiveness and support Nigeria's broader digital transformation agenda.

Despite these objectives, adoption of the eNaira has remained limited. Nigeria already has a well-developed digital payments landscape, with widespread use of private-sector mobile money services, FinTech platforms, and bank-based electronic payment systems. Many consumers and businesses, therefore, perceive limited additional benefits from adopting a new state-issued digital currency. Moreover, structural constraints, such as uneven digital literacy, limited smartphone access, and unreliable internet connectivity, particularly in rural areas, have affected awareness and usability.

The rollout of the eNaira has raised broader questions about design, incentives, and public trust. While the CBN has emphasised coexistence with existing financial institutions, the introduction of a retail CBDC has implications for competition, innovation, and the balance between public and private roles in the financial system. The eNaira case illustrates the practical challenges of implementing digital sovereign money in an economy with diverse infrastructure capabilities and an already competitive payments ecosystem.

Reference

BIS (Bank for International Settlements) (2022). *CBDCs: An Opportunity for the Monetary System*. Basel: Bank for International Settlements.

Case Study Questions

1 Beyond the reasons stated, what other factors might be contributing to the slow public adoption of the eNaira?
2 How could the Nigerian Central Bank redesign its rollout strategy or the eNaira's features to better encourage use among both banked and unbanked populations?
3 What are the potential risks of a CBDC like the eNaira potentially crowding out private-sector financial innovations like mobile money?

Further Reading

Bank for International Settlements (BIS). (2022). CBDCs: An Opportunity for the Monetary System. *BIS Papers*.

Demirgüç-Kunt, A., Klapper, L., Singer, D. & Ansar, S. (2022) *The Global Findex Database 2021: Financial Inclusion, Digital Payments, and Resilience in the Age of COVID-19*. Washington, DC: World Bank

Gorton, G., & Zhang, J. (2021). Taming Wildcat Stablecoins. *Yale Journal on Regulation*, 38(2), 1–45.

Nakamoto, S. (2008). *Bitcoin: A Peer-to-Peer Electronic Cash System*. Available at: https://bitcoin.org/bitcoin.pdf

References

Arner, D. W., Barberis, J., and Buckley, R. P. (2020). The evolution of FinTech: A new post-crisis paradigm?. *Georgetown Journal of International Law*, 47(4), 1271–1319.

Bernanke, B. (2020). *The Federal Reserve and the Financial Crisis*. Princeton, NJ: Princeton University Press.

Bank for International Settlements (2020). *Annual Economic Report 2020: Digital Currencies and the Future of the Monetary System*. Basel: Bank for International Settlements.

BIS (Bank for International Settlements). (2022). *CBDCs: An Opportunity for the Monetary System*. Basel: Bank for International Settlements. BIS Papers No. 125.

Böhme, R., Christin, N., Edelman, B., & Moore, T. (2015). Bitcoin: Economics, Technology, and Governance. *Journal of Economic Perspectives*, 29(2), 213–238.

Catalini, C. and Gans, J.S. (2016). *Some Simple Economics of the Blockchain* (Working Paper No. 22952). Cambridge, MA: National Bureau of Economic Research.

Demirgüç-Kunt, A, Klapper, L, Singer, D and Ansar, S (2022) *The Global Findex Database 2021: Financial Inclusion, Digital Payments, and Resilience in the Age of COVID-19*. Washington, DC: World Bank.

Dwyer, G.P. (2014). The Economics of Bitcoin and Similar Private Digital Currencies. *Journal of Financial Stability*, 17, 81–91.

European Central Bank (2021) International Aspects of CBDCs: Open Research Questions. *Speech by Fabio Panetta, Member of the Executive Board of the ECB, ECB–CEBRA Conference*. Frankfurt am Main: European Central Bank.

FSB (Financial Stability Board). (2024). *DeFi and Systemic Risk*. FSB report. Basel: Financial Stability Board.

Financial Times (2021) Facebook-Backed Digital Currency Project Narrows Focus to US. *Financial Times*, 12 May.

Gorton, G., & Zhang, J. (2021). Taming Wildcat Stablecoins. *Yale Journal on Regulation*.38(2), 1–45.

International Energy Agency (2021) *World Energy Outlook 2021*. Paris: International Energy Agency.

International Monetary Fund (2024) *Digital Money, Cross-Border Payments, International Reserves, and the Global Financial Safety Net: Preliminary Considerations*. IMF Notes. Washington, DC: International Monetary Fund.

Mankiw, N.G. (2021). *Principles of Economics* (9th ed.). Boston, MA: Cengage Learning.

Mishkin, F.S. (2019). *The Economics of Money, Banking, and Financial Markets* (12th ed.). Boston, MA: Pearson.

Nakamoto, S. (2008). *Bitcoin: A Peer-to-Peer Electronic Cash System*. Available at: https://bitcoin.org/bitcoin.pdf

Yermack, D (2017) Corporate Governance and Blockchains. *Review of Finance*, 21(1), 7–31.

19 Open Banking and the API Economy

Chapter Overview

This chapter offers a thorough examination of the transformative impact of Open Banking and the API Economy on the financial services sector. Open Banking requires data sharing between banks and authorised third-party providers (TPPs) through secure Application Programming Interfaces (APIs). This encourages transparency, competition, and customer-focused innovation. The analysis examines regulatory frameworks, key technical mechanisms, and the collaborative ecosystem among traditional banks, Financial Technology (FinTech) firms, and TPPs. It also evaluates the benefits and major challenges, including cybersecurity risks, complex regulatory compliance requirements, and legacy system integration. The chapter concludes by exploring future trends, including artificial intelligence (AI)-powered APIs, global standardisation, and the growth of Banking-as-a-Service (BaaS).

Learning Objectives:

By the end of this chapter, you should be able to:

1. Explain Open Banking and the API Economy, including their regulatory, technological, and economic foundations, and how they reshape the financial services ecosystem.
2. Analyse how APIs enable services like Account Information Services (AIS), Payment Initiation Services (PIS), and consent management, and their impact on customer empowerment, innovation, and efficiency.
3. Evaluate Open Banking regulations (e.g., Revised Payment Services Directive (PSD2), General Data Protection Regulation (GDPR)) for data security, consumer protection, and market innovation.
4. Identify key risks and challenges, such as cybersecurity, compliance, legacy system integration, and API performance, and strategies to address them.
5. Assess emerging trends like Open Finance, AI-driven APIs, global standards, and BaaS, and their implications for inclusion, business models, and stability.

DOI: 10.4324/9781003775751-23

19.1 Introduction

The financial services industry is undergoing a significant transformation, primarily driven by the interconnected rise of Open Banking and the API Economy. These developments are dismantling traditional banking monopolies and fostering a more competitive and collaborative environment in which services are integrated across established banks, FinTech firms, and TPPs (Zetzsche et al., 2020). Open Banking serves as both a regulatory and technological framework, enabling the secure sharing of customer financial data with authorised TPPs through APIs, contingent upon explicit customer consent.

This paradigm shift specifically empowers consumers by granting them unprecedented control over their financial data, thereby fostering the development of highly personalised and innovative financial solutions. As highlighted by the European Banking Authority (2019), this consumer-centric approach is fundamental to Open Banking's regulatory design, promoting greater transparency and choice. Concurrently, the API Economy operates as a dynamic marketplace for exchanging data and functional capabilities, enabling highly efficient service integration and paving the way for novel revenue models that extend beyond conventional offerings.

As a result, incumbent financial institutions must comply with new regulations, adapt to changing customer expectations, and manage complex relationships that involve both collaboration and competition with emerging FinTech companies. Basole and Patel (2018) observe that the API Economy is essential for creating a market for data and functionality, driving efficient service integration and the development of new business models, which compels incumbents to innovate. This chapter will define the concepts of Open Banking and APIs, review the relevant regulatory frameworks, and critically examine the key opportunities, challenges, and trends shaping the current financial ecosystem.

19.2 Understanding Open Banking and the API Economy

Open Banking is a framework that allows banks to securely share customer-approved financial data with authorised third parties through APIs. This shifts control of data to consumers and encourages competition and innovation in financial services. Within the API economy, APIs act as digital connectors, enabling banks, FinTech firms, and platforms to integrate services such as account aggregation, instant payments, and personalised financial tools. While Open Banking improves efficiency and customer choice, it also requires strong cybersecurity, data protection, and regulatory oversight to maintain trust and financial stability (Figure 19.1).

19.2.1 Definition of Open Banking

Open Banking is a regulatory and technological framework that requires banks to share customer-approved data with licensed TPPs through standardised, secure APIs (Zetzsche et al., 2020). This model shifts control of financial data from institutions to consumers, promoting transparency, competition, and innovation within the financial sector (European Banking Authority, 2019). Key regulatory initiatives, such as the European Union's PSD2, have driven this transformation by mandating secure data sharing. Open Banking facilitates services such as account aggregation, which allows consumers to view multiple accounts in a single interface, advanced budgeting tools that analyse spending patterns, and alternative lending models that leverage richer data sources for credit assessment. For example, apps like Yolt aggregate multiple bank accounts to provide users with a comprehensive overview of their finances.

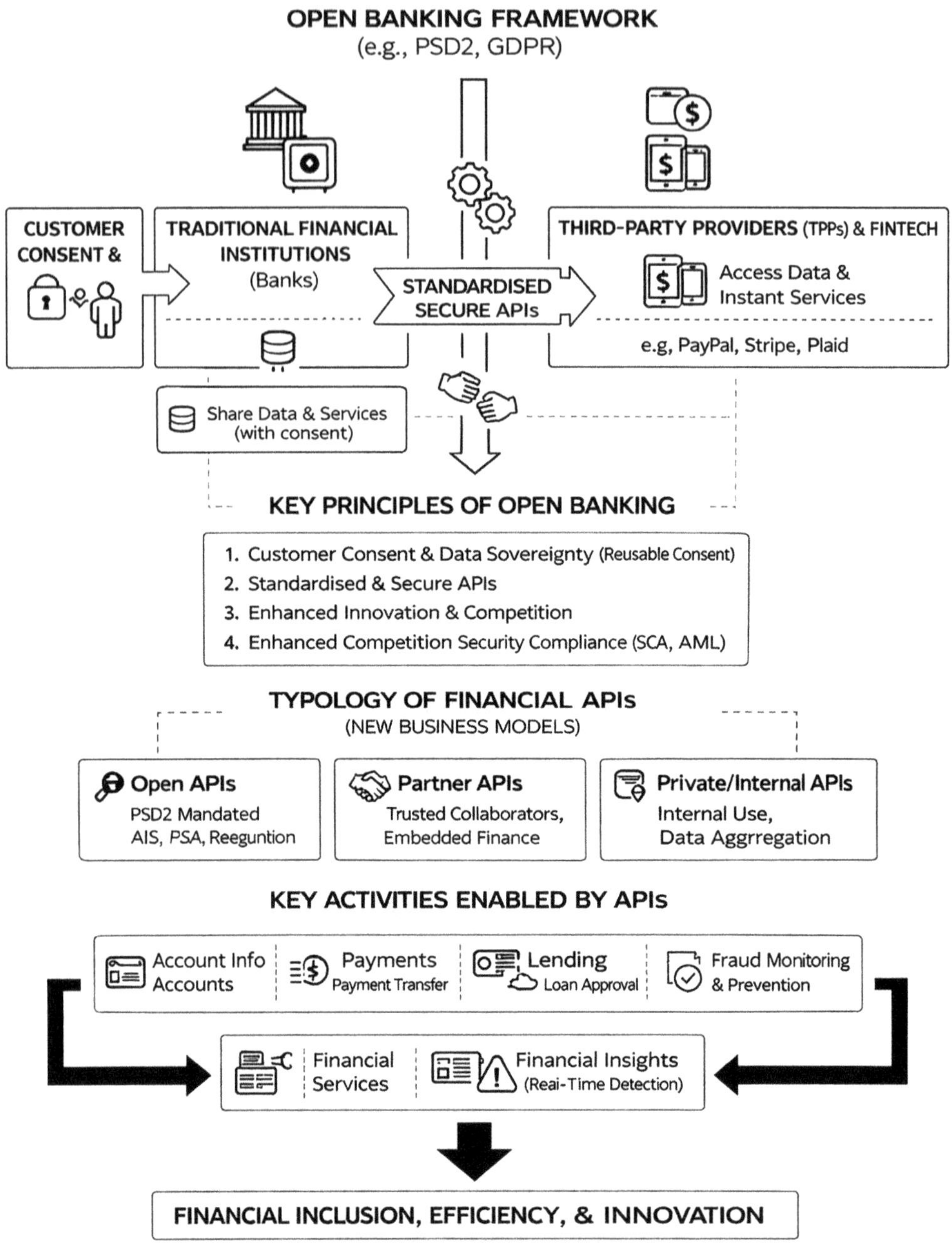

Figure 19.1 Understanding Open Banking and the API Economy.

19.2.2 Key Principles of Open Banking

Open Banking operates on several foundational principles:

Customer Consent and Data Sovereignty: A central tenet of Open Banking is that customers retain full control over their financial data, deciding who can access it and for what purpose. Consent must be informed, specific, and easily revocable (Open Banking Implementation Entity, 2021). For instance, a consumer may allow a budgeting app to access transaction data to provide personalised insights, but can revoke access at any time, maintaining control over their personal information.

Standardised APIs: Open Banking relies on standardised APIs to enable consistent, secure, and interoperable data exchange between banks and TPPs. This uniformity ensures seamless integration and a reliable user experience. For example, a personal finance app can connect multiple bank accounts and retrieve balances and transactions because all participating banks adhere to the same API standards (Basole & Patel, 2018).

Enhanced Competition: Open Banking fosters competition by enabling FinTech companies and TPPs to access financial data with customer consent. This levels the playing field, drives innovation, and offers consumers a broader range of financial services. For example, a customer could use a FinTech platform to compare loan offers across multiple banks in real time, helping secure the most favourable terms.

Security and Compliance: Strong security measures and regulatory compliance are essential to Open Banking. PSD2 and GDPR frameworks enforce practices such as Strong Customer Authentication (SCA) and multi-factor verification to protect sensitive data and maintain privacy (Zetzsche et al., 2020). For example, when linking a bank account to a third-party payment app, the user may authenticate via a password and one-time code, ensuring that only authorised parties can access their financial information.

19.2.3 The API Economy in Finance

The API Economy refers to a business model in which organisations expose data and services via APIs to generate new revenue streams, foster partnerships, and enable innovation (McKinsey & Company, 2020). In finance, APIs underpin Open Banking by providing standardised, secure channels for communication between diverse systems (Basole & Patel, 2018). APIs allow TPPs to embed core services such as payment initiation, identity verification, and real-time account access directly into their applications, improving both operational efficiency and customer convenience. For example, Klarna uses APIs to integrate payment and credit services directly into e-commerce platforms, streamlining the checkout process.

19.2.4 Key Activities Enabled by APIs

APIs enable a variety of essential financial services:

AIS: AIS APIs allow authorised TPPs to securely access and aggregate account data, including balances and transactions, in compliance with PSD2. This enables comprehensive dashboards, personalised budgeting tools, and enhanced credit assessments using real-time cash flow insights (European Banking Authority, 2019).

PIS: PIS APIs allow TPPs to initiate payments directly from a user's bank account, supporting features such as automated bill payments, peer-to-peer transfers, and pay-by-bank solutions. This reduces reliance on traditional card-based methods and improves transaction efficiency (Zetzsche et al., 2020).

Identity Verification and Consent Management: APIs implement standards such as OAuth 2.0 and SCA to manage identity verification and consent. Users can grant, monitor, or revoke access, ensuring secure and regulated data sharing. Companies like Affirm and Klarna use transactional data from APIs to perform real-time, behaviour-based credit assessments that extend beyond conventional credit bureau scoring methods.

Fraud Monitoring: APIs support real-time fraud detection by integrating multiple data sources, such as device ID and location, to identify anomalies. Financial institutions can then trigger alerts or block suspicious transactions immediately, enhancing security (Basole & Patel, 2018).

19.2.5 Typology of Financial APIs

Financial APIs can be categorised based on accessibility and purpose:

Open APIs: Publicly accessible APIs, often mandated by PSD2, enable licensed TPPs to securely access banking services and data. They enable AIS and PIS, promoting competition and innovation. For instance, a FinTech app can retrieve customer transaction data via an open API to provide personalised financial advice.

Partner APIs: Shared with trusted business partners, these APIs facilitate integrated services and operational efficiency. For example, the integration between eBay and PayPal allows seamless real-time payment processing (Smith, 2022).

Private APIs (Internal APIs): Restricted for internal organisational use, private APIs enable communication between internal systems, improving operational efficiency and supporting functions such as reporting and fraud detection. For example, a bank's loan management system may use internal APIs to access core account data securely.

Public APIs (Developer-Facing): Accessible to external developers, public APIs allow third-party applications to integrate with banking systems, expanding service offerings. These APIs require strong security and monitoring due to increased exposure to cyber threats. For example, payment service providers use public APIs to connect apps to multiple banks for transaction initiation, implementing strict authentication and encryption to prevent unauthorised access.

19.3 Challenges and Risks in Open Banking and the API Economy

19.3.1 Security and Fraud Risks

Open banking introduces significant security and fraud risks, particularly through API vulnerabilities and social engineering. As noted in the 2019 Capital One breach, weak API controls exposed over 100 million records, emphasising the need for rigorous security testing, strong authentication, and user education to safeguard sensitive financial data.

19.3.2 Regulatory Compliance

Navigating the multifaceted regulatory landscape presents a formidable challenge in Open Banking. Organisations must meticulously comply with a diverse array of international frameworks, from PSD2 to GDPR, as non-compliance risks severe financial and reputational damage. This necessitates a significant investment in legal expertise and agile compliance systems to operate successfully across borders.

19.3.3 Legacy System Integration

A fundamental challenge is the costly and complex integration of modern APIs with ageing core banking systems, such as Common Business-Oriented Language mainframes. Their inherent rigidity inhibits secure, real-time data sharing, significantly impeding banks' ability to adapt to the Open Banking ecosystem. This creates significant technical debt, slowing innovation.

19.3.4 Key Practical Issues and a Conceptual Framework

The successful implementation of Open Banking is challenged by several key practical issues, chief among them the economic sustainability of data providers. While TPPs rapidly derive value, banks shoulder the high costs of developing and maintaining secure, high-performance APIs, creating a fundamental imbalance. Furthermore, widespread consumer adoption depends on overcoming customer distrust and limited awareness, which requires transparent consent processes and clear communication of benefits. Finally, the ecosystem grapples with the technical dichotomy of ensuring API reliability while navigating the persistent tension between necessary standardisation and market-led fragmentation.

API Performance and Reliability: A critical challenge in open banking is ensuring API performance and reliability, as the ecosystem hinges on seamless connectivity. Poor uptime, latency, or outages disrupt transactions, degrade user experience, and erode trust in TPPs. Unreliable APIs stifle innovation, stressing the need for robust infrastructure to sustain ecosystem growth. Financial institutions and TPPs have to prioritise API stability to maintain operational efficiency and consumer confidence.

Standardisation vs Fragmentation: Despite initiatives like the Financial Data Exchange (FDX) promoting global standards, a key practical challenge in open banking is the significant regional fragmentation of API protocols. This considerable regional fragmentation forces FinTech operating internationally to integrate multiple, disparate standards, thereby substantially increasing development costs and operational complexity.

19.4 Future Trends in Open Banking and API

From Open Banking to Open Finance and Decentralised Finance (DeFi): Open Banking is evolving into Open Finance, extending data-sharing principles to investments, pensions, and insurance. Open Finance has the potential to deepen financial inclusion and innovation (World Bank, 2022). Integration with DeFi via APIs could seamlessly connect traditional finance to the blockchain, enabling smart contracts to securely leverage trusted, real-world financial data.

AI-Powered APIs: Integrating AI and machine learning with APIs is set to revolutionise open banking by enabling hyper-personalisation, predictive cash flow analytics, and advanced fraud detection. AI-driven APIs are transforming financial services by delivering real-time, data-driven insights, notes industry expert. These innovations will enhance efficiency, security, and customer-centric solutions, driving the next wave of FinTech evolution.

Global Standardisation: The push for global API standardisation, led by initiatives like the FDX, is transforming open banking by reducing integration costs and enabling seamless cross-border services. Common standards are the backbone of interoperability, fostering innovation and competition in financial ecosystems. This harmonisation is crucial for scaling secure, efficient open banking solutions worldwide.

BaaS: The rise of BaaS is redefining financial ecosystems by enabling non-banks, such as Uber or Amazon, to integrate banking products seamlessly via APIs. As banking becomes an embedded feature rather than a destination, BaaS fuels innovation, fostering a more interconnected, customer-centric financial landscape. This shift underscores the growing demand for frictionless, context-driven financial services within everyday digital experiences.

19.5 Conclusion

The advent of Open Banking and the rapidly expanding API economy is catalysing a profound transformation within the financial services sector, shifting the industry from a traditionally closed, siloed structure towards a more transparent, collaborative ecosystem centred on customer empowerment. Regulatory frameworks such as the European Union's PSD2, combined with advancements in secure data-sharing technologies, have facilitated this transition by enabling third-party developers to leverage financial institutions' infrastructure to create innovative applications and services. This paradigm fosters enhanced personalisation and integration of financial experiences, thereby promoting customer-centric value creation. Consequently, competition has intensified, entry barriers for FinTech firms have been reduced, and incumbent banks are increasingly compelled to evolve from conventional product-centric models towards platform-oriented, service-integrated approaches that extend the value chain.

Despite the potential benefits, the sustainability of this transformation depends on addressing critical challenges related to security, regulatory complexity, and technological legacy. The proliferation of data-sharing interfaces heightens cybersecurity risks, requiring robust encryption protocols, stringent identity verification, and real-time threat detection. Furthermore, the absence of regulatory harmonisation across jurisdictions constrains seamless cross-border operations, while outdated core banking infrastructures limit institutional scalability and operational agility. Looking ahead, the sector is likely to transition from Open Banking to a holistic Open Finance framework, encompassing insurance, investment, and wealth management services, underpinned by AI-driven insights and BaaS platforms. The long-term success of this evolving ecosystem will depend on striking an equilibrium between fostering innovation, safeguarding data privacy, ensuring regulatory compliance, and maintaining systemic resilience, with strategic emphasis on the responsible orchestration rather than mere ownership of financial data.

Key Terms and Glossary

AIS (Account Information Services) Services that aggregate a user's financial data from multiple accounts to provide a consolidated view.

API (Application Programming Interface) A set of rules and protocols that allows different software applications to communicate with each other.

BaaS (Banking as a Service) A model where licensed banks integrate their digital banking services directly into the products of non-bank businesses.

Open Banking A regulatory and technological framework that allows TPPs to access financial data from banks via APIs, with customer consent.

PIS (Payment Initiation Services) Services that allow a third party to initiate a payment directly from a user's bank account.

Test Your Understanding

Multiple-Choice Questions

1 Which of the following best defines Open Banking?

A Banks offering loans without regulatory oversight
B Sharing customer-approved data with licensed TPPs via secure APIs
C Selling financial data to third parties without consent
D Using blockchain exclusively for payment transactions

2 What is the primary purpose of PSD2 in the context of Open Banking?

A To allow banks to avoid sharing data with competitors
B To enforce secure, customer-consented data sharing between banks and TPPs
C To regulate cryptocurrency transactions
D To mandate AI implementation in all banking services

3 Which API type is restricted for internal organisational use only?

A Open API
B Public API
C Private API
D Partner API

4 A major challenge of Open Banking related to technology is:

A Over-reliance on cryptocurrency
B Integration of modern APIs with legacy banking systems
C Customer refusal to adopt mobile apps
D Excessive standardisation of services

5 Which emerging trend in Open Banking allows non-banks like Uber or Amazon to offer banking services via APIs?

A Open Finance
B BaaS
C DeFi
D AIS

Short Questions

1 Explain the principle of customer consent in Open Banking and why it is crucial.
2 Describe the difference between AIS and PIS.
3 List two key security measures implemented in Open Banking APIs to protect customer data.

Analytical Questions

1 Discuss the economic challenges that traditional banks face in implementing Open Banking APIs and how these might affect long-term sustainability.
2 Evaluate how AI-powered APIs could transform customer experience in financial services, giving examples of potential applications.
3 Assess the impact of regional API standard fragmentation on FinTech companies operating internationally and suggest strategies to mitigate these challenges.

Case Study: Monzo and Open Banking–Enabled Financial Management

Monzo, a UK-based digital challenger bank, has strategically embedded Open Banking into its core product offering rather than treating it solely as a regulatory obligation. Through its Connected Accounts feature, Monzo enables customers to link accounts held at competing banks, such as HSBC, Barclays, and Lloyds, directly within the Monzo app using Open Banking APIs and explicit customer consent. This allows users to view balances and transactions from multiple institutions in a single, unified interface.

By aggregating data across accounts, Monzo delivers a consolidated view of customers' financial lives. This holistic dataset supports advanced budgeting tools, real-time spending insights, and personalised savings recommendations that are difficult to replicate using data from a single account. As a result, Monzo positions itself as the customer's primary financial control centre, even when it is not the main account provider.

From a strategic perspective, this approach deepens customer engagement, increases app usage frequency, strengthens customer loyalty, and reduces switching risk. At the same time, reliance on Open Banking raises important concerns about data security, privacy, and consumer trust. Monzo must therefore ensure robust authentication, transparent consent management, and clear communication about how customer data is accessed, used, and protected.

Reference

Zetzsche, D.A., Buckley, R.P., Arner, D.W., & Barberis, J.N. (2020). The Evolution of FinTech: A New Post-crisis Paradigm. *Georgetown Journal of International Law*, 47(4), 1271–1319.

Case Study Questions

1 What are the key strategic advantages for Monzo in offering a service that aggregates data from its competitors?
2 What security and privacy concerns might a customer have when using the Connected Accounts feature, and how can Monzo mitigate them?
3 How does this use of Open Banking create a more compelling value proposition for customers compared to traditional banking apps?

Further Reading

European Banking Authority (EBA). (2019). *Final report on guidelines on open banking. Available at: https://www.eba.europa.eu*

McKinsey & Company. (2020). *The API Economy: Unlocking the Power of APIs in Financial Services.* Available at: https://www.mckinsey.com

Zetzsche, D.A., Buckley, R.P., Barberis, J.N., & Arner, D.W. (2020). *The Evolution of FinTech: A New Post-Crisis Paradigm. University of Illinois Law Review*, (5), 1471–1554.

References

Basole, R.C., & Patel, A. (2018). *Transformation through Unbundling: Visualising the API Economy. Proceedings of the 51st Hawaii International Conference on System Sciences.*

European Banking Authority (EBA). (2019). *Final Report on Guidelines on the Conditions to be Met to Benefit from an Exemption from the Contingency Mechanism under Article 33(6) of RTS on SCA and CSC.* Available at: https://www.eba.europa.eu

McKinsey & Company. (2020). *The API Economy: Unlocking the Power of APIs in Financial Services*. Available at: https://www.mckinsey.com

Open Banking Implementation Entity Standards (2021) *Consent dashboard and revocation*. Available at: https://standards.openbanking.org.uk/customer-experience-guidelines/account-information-services/consent-dashboard-revocation/v3-1-8/ (Accessed: 25 May 2026).

Smith, J. (2022) *API Integration and Digital Payment Ecosystems*. London: Routledge.

World Bank. (2022). The Role of APIs in Financial Inclusion. *Global Financial Development Report*. Washington, DC: World Bank.

Zetzsche, D.A., Buckley, R.P., Barberis, J.N., & Arner, D.W. (2020). The Evolution of FinTech: A New Post-Crisis Paradigm. *University of Illinois Law Review*, (2), 547–618.

20 Digital Lending and Credit Innovation

Chapter Overview

This chapter examines the significant transformation occurring in the lending industry driven by Financial Technology (FinTech). FinTech creates a clear distinction between traditional institutional methods and emerging digital models, such as peer-to-peer (P2P) lending, proprietary online platforms, and embedded finance. Several technological drivers support this change, including artificial intelligence (AI) for detailed credit assessment, blockchain for enhanced securitisation, and Open Banking Application Programming Interfaces (APIs) for seamless data exchange. These innovations are transforming credit risk assessment, improving loan accessibility, and enabling personalised borrower experiences. The analysis highlights the strategic intersection of conventional institutions and FinTech solutions, resulting in both significant opportunities, such as increased financial inclusion and customised product offerings, and notable challenges, such as complex regulatory compliance and the need for robust cybersecurity. These factors are poised to shape the industry's future development.

Learning Objectives

By the end of this chapter, you should be able to:

1. Explain the role of lending in financial institutions and how FinTech is transforming traditional lending processes and business models.
2. Analyse how technologies like AI, machine learning (ML), blockchain, and Open Banking APIs impact credit assessment, loan access, and personalised lending.
3. Compare traditional lending with FinTech approaches, P2P, online platforms, and embedded credit, highlighting disruption and convergence.
4. Evaluate opportunities and challenges in digital lending, including financial inclusion, efficiency, compliance, cybersecurity, and algorithmic bias.
5. Assess emerging trends, decentralised finance (DeFi), AI-driven hyper-personalisation, cross-border, and embedded lending, and their effects on market stability and consumer protection.

DOI: 10.4324/9781003775751-24

20.1 Introduction

Lending is a core function of financial institutions and a critical foundation for economic activity, providing essential capital to individuals, businesses, and governments (Mishkin, 2015). Borrowers utilise these funds for personal consumption, business growth, and strategic investments, while lenders earn returns through interest. This mutually beneficial relationship supports the efficient allocation of capital and promotes economic development.

The traditional lending model, once characterised by in-person interactions, manual processing, and extensive paperwork, is experiencing rapid transformation. This change is largely driven by the widespread adoption of FinTech, which is reshaping established financial practices. FinTech innovations expand credit access, improve operational efficiency, and democratise lending services, as noted by Arner et al. (2016).

This chapter provides a comprehensive analysis of the evolving lending landscape, focusing on several key areas. It examines the central role of lending in modern financial institutions, evaluates the transformative effects of technology on traditional lending processes, and assesses the various strategies by which FinTech is reshaping borrowing and lending paradigms.

20.2 Understanding Lending as a Financial Institution

20.2.1 Definition and Purpose of Lending

Lending refers to the provision of funds to a borrower under a formal agreement, in which the borrower is obliged to repay the principal amount, along with interest, over a specified period (Rose & Hudgins, 2013). Financial institutions, including commercial banks, credit unions, and specialised lenders, act as intermediaries, setting loan terms and assessing borrowers' creditworthiness. Interest serves both as compensation for the risk the lender undertakes and as an incentive to allocate capital (World Bank, 2022a).

The act of lending plays a critical role in stimulating economic growth by meeting consumer and business funding needs, ensuring liquidity, and generating profits for financial institutions. For businesses, access to credit facilitates expansion, innovation, and job creation. For individuals, loans enable major life expenditures such as purchasing homes or funding education, thereby improving quality of life and promoting social mobility (World Bank, 2022b). Additionally, lending supports cash flow management and addresses working capital requirements, while providing lenders with interest and fee-based income, forming a mutually beneficial economic relationship.

20.2.2 Lending Process

Lending is the provision of funds to a borrower under a contractual agreement, with repayment of the principal plus interest over a specified period, facilitated by financial institutions such as banks, credit unions, P2P platforms, online lenders, and microfinance institutions (MFIs) (Rose & Hudgins, 2013; World Bank, 2022b). These institutions assess the borrower's creditworthiness, including credit history, income, and debt-to-income ratio, to determine repayment feasibility. The loan process begins with an application in which the borrower provides necessary details, followed by evaluation, approval or denial, and, if approved, the execution of a contract outlining the loan amount, interest rate, repayment schedule, collateral requirements, and other covenants (Morduch, 1999). Upon disbursement of funds, the borrower is obligated to repay in accordance with the agreed terms, while the lender earns interest and fees as compensation for the risk. Lending serves as a catalyst for economic growth by enabling business expansion, entrepreneurship, and social mobility, while simultaneously providing financial institutions with a primary source of revenue. In practice, a borrower may obtain a personal loan from HSBC or an online lender like Social Finance, Inc. (SoFi), with approval based on credit assessment, followed by contractual agreement and scheduled repayments, exemplifying how modern lending combines financial intermediation, risk management, and economic facilitation.

20.2.3 Types of Lending Institutions

Commercial Banks: Commercial banks are traditional financial institutions that provide a broad range of lending services, including personal loans, mortgages, and business financing. They offer stability through established infrastructure, regulatory compliance, and professional customer support, positioning them as central pillars of the financial system (Rose & Hudgins, 2013). For instance, a customer may obtain a mortgage from Wells Fargo or HSBC, benefiting from structured repayment plans and advisory support.

In contrast, digital-first lenders such as SoFi and LendingClub offer fully online loan services, leveraging technology to streamline applications, automate approvals, and reach clients without physical branches. While both traditional and digital lenders facilitate access to credit, the delivery methods, speed, and customer experiences differ significantly.

Credit Unions: Credit unions are member-owned, not-for-profit cooperatives that prioritise their members' financial interests over profit generation. They generally offer lower fees, competitive interest rates, and personalised services, making them attractive for community-focused lending (Rosenberg et al., 2009). For example, a local credit union may provide affordable auto loans with flexible repayment terms. Digital credit unions, such as Self Lender, extend these benefits online, allowing members to access loans and savings products via mobile platforms while maintaining cooperative principles.

P2P Lenders: P2P lending platforms connect borrowers directly with individual or institutional investors, bypassing traditional banking intermediaries. P2P lenders use algorithmic credit assessments to offer competitive interest rates to borrowers and attractive returns to investors (Balyuk, 2019). LendingClub, for example, enables individuals to obtain personal loans funded by other users, whereas Funding Circle facilitates small business loans backed by online investors. These platforms demonstrate how technology can enhance credit accessibility and efficiency, contrasting with conventional in-branch underwriting processes used by banks.

Online Lenders: Non-bank institutions that deliver loans entirely through digital platforms. They often use alternative data, such as employment history or utility payments, to assess creditworthiness, enabling them to serve underserved populations (McIntosh et al., 2017). SoFi, for instance, offers student loan refinancing and personal loans through its mobile application, while Avant provides unsecured personal loans to applicants who may not qualify for traditional bank financing. These platforms highlight the growing shift towards technology-driven, accessible lending solutions.

MFIs: MFIs specialise in providing small loans, savings, and insurance services to low-income individuals in communities underserved by traditional banks. They play a key role in promoting financial inclusion and entrepreneurship, especially among women and small-scale business owners (Morduch, 1999). The Grameen Bank in Bangladesh, for example, offers microloans to rural entrepreneurs to start or expand businesses, lifting families out of poverty. Digitally enabled MFIs such as Kiva and Tala extend these services via mobile platforms, providing rapid, remote access to credit without requiring physical branch visits.

20.2.4 Types of Loans

Personal Loans: Personal loans are unsecured financial products extended to individuals based on income and credit history, without requiring collateral. They are typically repaid in fixed monthly instalments and carry higher interest rates than secured loans. For example, an individual may obtain a personal loan from HSBC to finance home renovations or consolidate credit card debt, benefiting from predictable repayment schedules (Rose & Hudgins, 2013).

Mortgages: Long-term, secured loans used to purchase real estate, with the property serving as collateral. They generally have lower interest rates than unsecured loans and are repaid over extended periods, facilitating homeownership and property investment. A practical example is a 30-year mortgage from Bank of America, which allows a family to purchase a home. At the same time, the bank retains a security interest in the property until full repayment (World Bank, 2022b).

Business Loans: Business loans provide capital to enterprises of all sizes, supporting activities such as equipment acquisition, working capital management, expansion, or mergers and acquisitions. These loans can be secured or unsecured and are tailored to the borrower's financial health, risk profile, and intended use. For instance, a small manufacturing firm may secure a business loan from JPMorgan Chase to purchase machinery, enabling production expansion while adhering to structured repayment terms (Rose & Hudgins, 2013).

20.3 The Evolution of FinTech in Lending

The rise of FinTech in lending represents a paradigm shift in credit accessibility, moving beyond traditional banking constraints. By leveraging sophisticated algorithms and alternative data analytics, these digital platforms expedite application processes and enable tailored loan solutions, thereby democratising finance for underserved demographics, including those with limited credit histories (EY , 2021). This data-driven approach fosters greater financial inclusion while optimising risk assessment and operational efficiency for lenders (Figure 20.1).

20.3.1 Key FinTech Innovations

Digital Lending Platforms: The rise of FinTech in lending has been driven by key innovations such as digital lending platforms, which streamline borrowing through automation and competitive rates. Marketplaces like LendingClub and Prosper eliminate traditional intermediaries, enabling faster, more efficient loan processing. These platforms leverage advanced algorithms and big data to assess creditworthiness, reducing costs and expanding access to credit. By connecting borrowers directly with lenders, FinTech firms are reshaping the lending landscape, offering transparency and convenience while challenging traditional banking models.

AI and ML: The rise of FinTech in lending has been driven by key innovations, particularly AI and ML. These technologies enhance credit assessment by analysing transaction and behavioural data, offering a more nuanced approach than traditional scoring methods (Fuster et al., 2019). Additionally, AI-powered chatbots improve efficiency and customer service, streamlining the lending process for both borrowers and lenders. These advancements support FinTech's transformative potential in reshaping financial services.

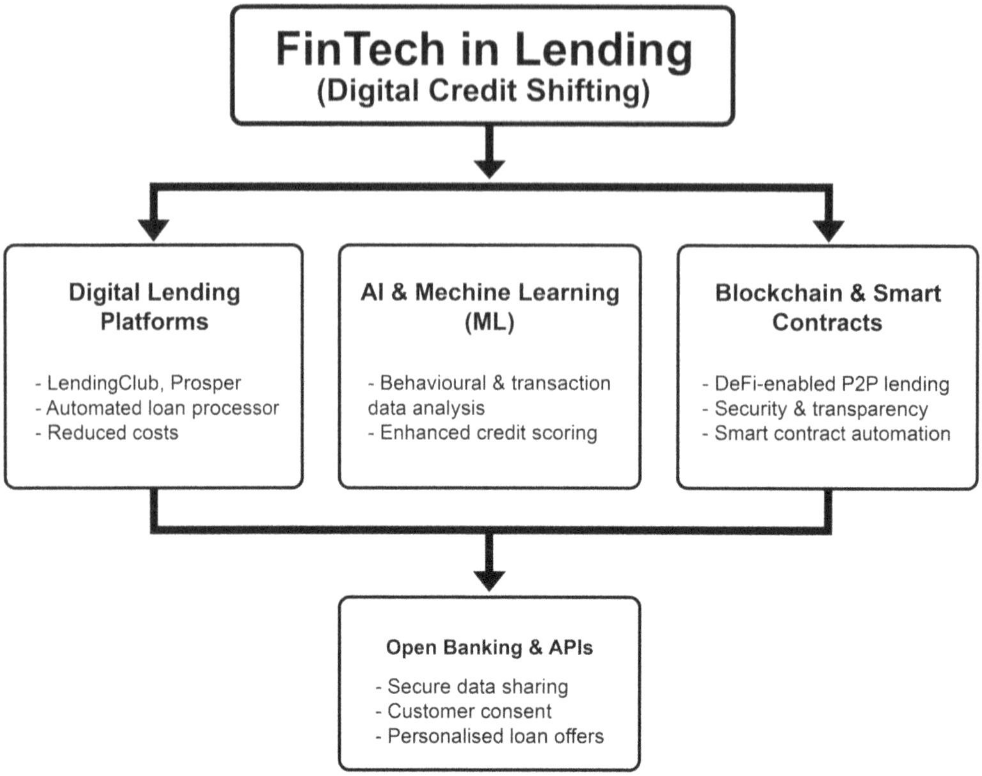

Figure 20.1 FinTech Transformation in Lending.

Blockchain Technology: The Rise of FinTech in lending is significantly propelled by key innovations, such as blockchain, which enable automated smart contracts for loan execution. This technology underpins DeFi platforms, facilitating P2P lending with greater security and transparency (Chen & Bellavitis, 2020).

Open Banking and APIs: The rise of FinTech in lending has been driven by key innovations such as Open Banking and APIs, which enable secure data sharing between institutions and third-party providers with customer consent. According to Zachariadis and Ozcan (2017), this approach provides lenders with a comprehensive view of an applicant's financial health, leading to more accurate risk assessments and personalised loan offers. These advancements enhance efficiency, transparency, and accessibility in the lending process.

20.3.2 Mechanism of FinTech Lending

FinTech lending uses digital platforms, automation, AI, and alternative data to streamline borrowing, bypassing traditional paperwork and enabling faster, more convenient access to credit. Borrowers can complete the entire loan lifecycle, from application to approval and disbursement, through a contactless, paperless, mobile-first process. Automated underwriting evaluates applications in real time, with funds disbursed directly to the borrower's account.

Credit assessment goes beyond balance sheets, leveraging turnover, cash flow, and digitally verified and alternative data. Segment-specific risk scorecards target existing,

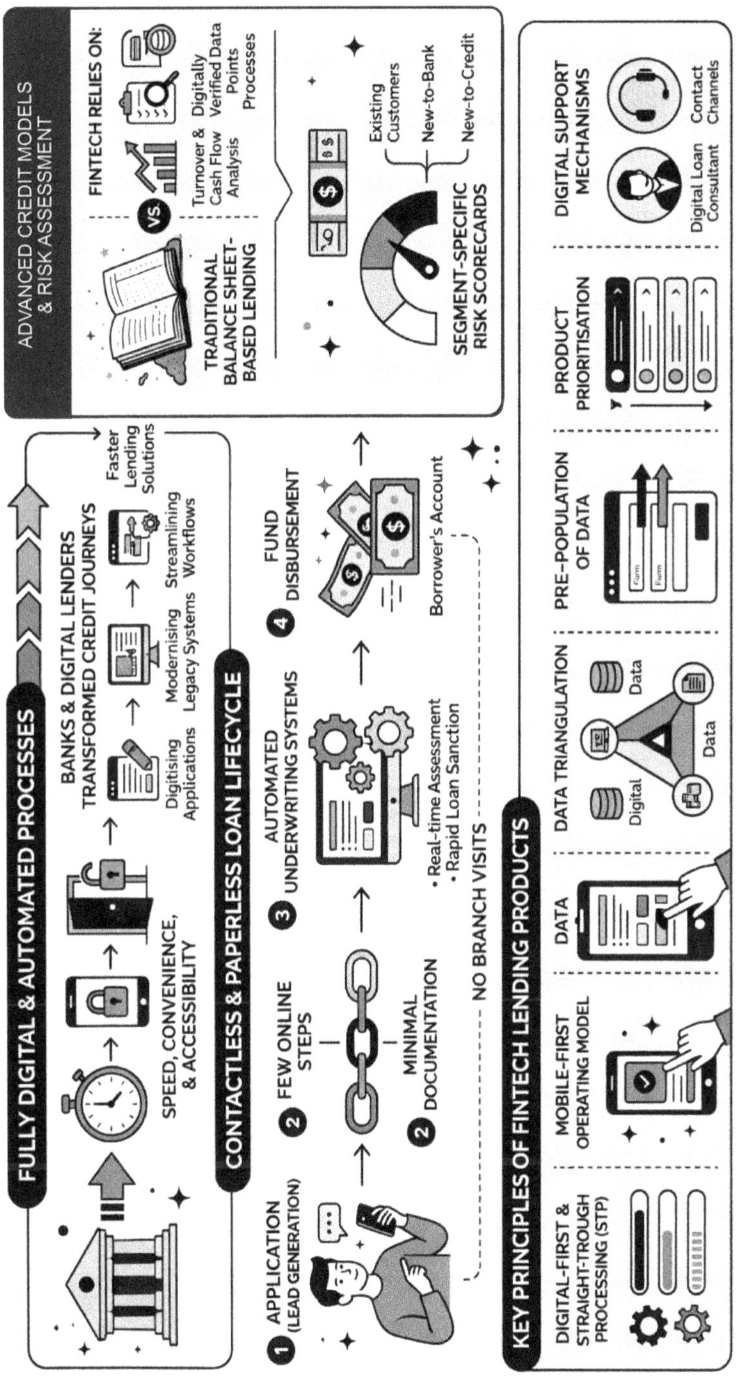

Figure 20.2 Mechanism of FinTech Lending.

new-to-bank, and new-to-credit customers. Funding models may include P2P lending or balance sheet lending.

Key principles of FinTech lending include:

- Straight-Through Processing and fully digital workflows
- Mobile-first design for seamless access
- Data triangulation through verified digital sources
- Pre-population of applicant information to reduce friction
- Product prioritisation based on business potential
- Digital support mechanisms such as online loan consultants, contact centres, and assisted digital channels

The result is a scalable, efficient, and highly personalised digital lending ecosystem that improves financial inclusion, reduces turnaround times, and enhances customer experience (Figure 20.2).

Step-by-Step key processes of FinTech lending are as follows.

Digital Application: Borrowers complete an online form and upload documents; bank account linking enables instant verification.

AI-Powered Risk Assessment: Algorithms analyse alternative data, such as cash flow, transaction history, and utility payments, to assess creditworthiness.

Automated Decisioning and Funding: Loans are approved in minutes or hours, with funds disbursed directly to the borrower's account.

Alternative Lending Models: Loans may be funded via P2P platforms or the lender's own balance sheet.

Servicing: Repayment management, account updates, and customer support are handled entirely online.

20.4 Contrast and Convergence of Traditional and FinTech Lending

Traditional lending, characterised by rigorous credit assessments and physical intermediaries, contrasts sharply with FinTech lending, which leverages digital platforms and algorithms for faster approvals. FinTech is reshaping finance by merging efficiency with accessibility. However, both models increasingly converge as banks adopt digital tools and FinTech firms incorporate risk-mitigation practices, blending innovation with tradition to meet evolving borrower needs.

20.4.1 A Comparative Analysis of Traditional and Digital Lending

Table 20.1 explains the fundamental differences between traditional and FinTech lending models.

20.4.2 Convergence of Models

A significant trend reshaping the financial services landscape is the convergence of traditional banking and FinTech lending models, fostering a hybrid ecosystem that leverages the strengths of both domains. Incumbent financial institutions are increasingly integrating advanced technologies such as AI, ML, and blockchain into their lending operations to

Table 20.1 Traditional vs FinTech Lending Models

Feature	*Traditional Lending Model*	*FinTech Lending Model*
Primary Institutions	Banks, Credit Unions	P2P Platforms, Neobanks
Application Process	In-person, paper-based, and often time-consuming	Fully online, digital, and highly automated
Approval Timeline	Days to weeks	Minutes to days
Credit Evaluation	Primarily, traditional credit scores and documented income	Utilises alternative data (e.g., cash flow, behaviour) and AI/ML models
Customer Experience	Formal, slower, and typically branch-dependent	User-friendly, fast, and entirely app/online-based
Financial Inclusion	Primarily serves creditworthy, traditionally banked individuals	Often targets underbanked populations and those with thin-file credit histories

Source: Adapted from chapter content and industry analysis (Deloitte, 2018).

refine credit risk assessment, streamline underwriting processes, and enhance operational efficiency, a transformation underscored by Deloitte (2018), which noted that technology adoption is no longer optional for traditional banks seeking competitiveness. Simultaneously, strategic alliances between established banks and agile FinTech firms are becoming more prevalent, creating synergistic collaborations in which traditional players contribute regulatory compliance expertise, substantial capital reserves, and long-standing customer trust. At the same time, FinTechs offer innovative, data-driven lending platforms and superior digital customer experiences. The future of lending lies not in disruption, but in partnership, highlighting the shift from competition to cooperation. These joint ventures enable faster loan approvals, broader financial inclusion, and personalised product offerings, all while maintaining the stability and oversight essential to the financial system.

20.5 Opportunities, Challenges, and Key Practical Issues

The integration of FinTech into lending generates both substantial opportunities and considerable challenges. Key practical issues contribute to a complex ecosystem characterised by multiple interdependencies.

20.5.1 Opportunities of FinTech Lending

FinTech lending offers significant opportunities to expand credit access, particularly for underbanked and underserved populations. By leveraging alternative data sources, such as transaction histories, social behaviour, and mobile usage patterns, FinTech platforms can assess creditworthiness in ways that traditional banks often overlook (Balyuk, 2019). Mobile-based and online lending solutions further enhance financial inclusion, especially in developing regions where physical banking infrastructure is limited. For instance, Tala in East Africa uses smartphone data to provide microloans to individuals without formal credit histories, enabling entrepreneurship and improving household income. Beyond inclusion, FinTech lending also drives efficiency and cost reduction. Automated loan processing, AI-driven credit assessments, and algorithmic decision-making reduce operational costs, improve risk-prediction accuracy, and enable more personalised loan products, ultimately lowering default rates and increasing scalability (McIntosh et al., 2017).

20.5.2 Risk and Challenges in FinTech Lending

Despite these advantages, FinTech lending faces considerable challenges, particularly in compliance, data protection, and cybersecurity. The rapid evolution of FinTech often outpaces regulatory frameworks, creating gaps that are exacerbated in cross-border lending where rules differ across jurisdictions (Arner et al., 2016). Reliance on personal and alternative data heightens privacy risks and ethical concerns over informed consent, while AI-driven credit models may inadvertently perpetuate historical biases, leading to discriminatory outcomes (Speckenmeyer, et al., 2025). Moreover, predictive models may fail under economic stress, increasing default risks, and digital platforms are prime targets for cybercrime, necessitating robust cybersecurity measures to protect sensitive financial information. For example, LendingClub and other P2P platforms invest heavily in encryption, real-time fraud monitoring, and regulatory reporting to maintain trust and operational resilience.

20.5.3 Key Practical Issues and a Conceptual Framework of FinTech Lending

Key practical issues in FinTech lending include integrating complex technologies, effective data governance, interoperability, and dynamic regulatory compliance. The growing use of ML has raised concerns about the "black box" nature of credit algorithms, prompting a demand for explainable AI (XAI) to ensure transparency, fairness, and compliance with regulations such as the Equal Credit Opportunity Act (Fuster et al., 2019). Ethical data governance and consumer consent are equally critical; FinTech firms must secure and process personal and alternative data responsibly, aligning with General Data Protection Regulation and Open Banking standards while maintaining innovative service delivery. Interoperability poses additional challenges in a fragmented ecosystem comprising banks, P2P lenders, Banking-as-a-Service providers, and data aggregators. Secure and standardised APIs are essential to enable seamless data exchange and frictionless customer experiences, yet competing technical standards complicate implementation. Finally, FinTech lenders must maintain regulatory compliance agility, continuously monitoring and adapting to evolving rules on lending limits, data privacy, and consumer protection across multiple jurisdictions. Establishing a structured conceptual framework that prioritises security, transparency, and scalability is critical to balancing innovation with operational stability and long-term sustainability.

20.6 The Future Development of Lending and FinTech

The lending landscape will continue to evolve, shaped by several key trends:

DeFi: The future of lending and FinTech is poised for transformation with the rise of DeFi, which leverages blockchain to enable P2P lending via smart contracts, reducing reliance on traditional intermediaries. DeFi's "trustless" protocols could further disintermediate financial institutions, offering greater efficiency and transparency (Chen & Bellavitis, 2020). This shift underscores the growing potential for blockchain-driven solutions to redefine global lending ecosystems, though regulatory and scalability challenges remain key considerations for widespread adoption.

AI-Powered Hyper-Personalisation: The future of lending lies in AI-driven hyper-personalisation, where loan terms dynamically adjust based on real-time financial behaviour. Lending is shifting from static assessments to continuous, data-driven evaluation, enabling institutions to offer tailored products that enhance risk management and customer satisfaction in an evolving FinTech landscape.

Cross-Border Lending: The future of lending will be increasingly shaped by FinTech platforms enabling seamless cross-border financing, offering borrowers global capital access and lenders diversified opportunities. Regulatory harmonisation is essential to unlocking the full potential of international FinTech lending in this evolving landscape.

Embedded Lending: The future of lending and FinTech will be shaped by embedded lending, in which credit services are seamlessly integrated into non-financial platforms such as e-commerce checkouts and Software as a Serviceapplications. This trend democratises access to credit by making it contextual and frictionless. By eliminating traditional barriers, embedded lending enhances user experience while driving financial inclusion. Professionals must adapt to this shift, as it redefines how businesses and consumers access capital efficiently. The convergence of technology and finance will continue to blur industry boundaries, fostering innovation in lending ecosystems.

20.7 Conclusion

The global lending ecosystem is undergoing a structural transformation driven by FinTech, marking a decisive shift towards digital credit innovation. The integration of advanced platforms, AI, and distributed ledger technologies has enhanced operational efficiency, redefined credit risk assessment, and fostered greater transparency in lending processes. These technological advancements have expanded financial inclusion, enabling underserved populations to access credit while creating more personalised and data-driven lending solutions. However, alongside these opportunities come complex strategic risks, including regulatory uncertainty, cybersecurity threats, and potential algorithmic bias. As industry analysts have noted, the success of digital lending depends not only on efficiency and speed but also on the strength of governance frameworks that guide innovation, ensure ethical data use, and maintain market integrity.

The sustainable development of the FinTech lending sector hinges on regulators and industry stakeholders striking a delicate balance between fostering innovation and safeguarding stability. Effective regulatory frameworks must support agile product development and competitive markets while enforcing robust consumer protection, transparent governance, and equitable credit access. Achieving this equilibrium is critical for maintaining trust, mitigating systemic risks, and unlocking the full potential of digital lending as a transformative force in global finance. Ultimately, the future of the lending ecosystem will depend on harmonising technological advancement with ethical, legal, and operational safeguards to ensure both innovation and sustainability.

Key Terms and Glossary

P2P Lending A method of debt financing that enables individuals to borrow and lend money directly without using a traditional financial institution.

Credit Scoring A statistical analysis performed by lenders to determine a borrower's creditworthiness.

Alternative Data Non-traditional data (e.g., utility payments, social media activity) used to assess credit risk for individuals with limited credit history.

DeFi Lending Lending and borrowing activities conducted on DeFi platforms using smart contracts and cryptocurrencies as collateral.

Embedded Lending The integration of loan offerings directly into non-financial platforms (e.g., at an e-commerce checkout).

Test Your Understanding

Multiple-Choice Questions

1 Which of the following best describes FinTech's impact on traditional lending?

A It replaces all banks with digital platforms.
B It enhances credit assessment, loan accessibility, and personalisation.
C It eliminates the need for regulatory compliance.
D It restricts loans to only high-income borrowers.

2 P2P lending platforms are distinct from traditional banks because they:

A Require borrowers to visit physical branches.
B Connect borrowers directly with individual or institutional investors.
C Offer only secured loans with collateral.
D Do not assess creditworthiness.

3 What is a key advantage of AI and ML in digital lending?

A Reduces operational efficiency
B Allows real-time, data-driven credit assessment
C Removes the need for cybersecurity
D Eliminates all default risk

4 Which of the following is an example of embedded lending?

A Borrowing from a local credit union branch
B Taking a loan directly within an e-commerce checkout process
C Obtaining a mortgage from a bank
D Crowdfunding on a P2P platform

5 A major challenge of digital lending includes:

A Fast approval timelines
B Lack of regulatory compliance and cybersecurity risks
C Expanded financial inclusion
D Improved operational efficiency

Short Questions

1 Explain the difference between traditional lending and FinTech lending models in terms of credit assessment and customer experience.
2 What role do Open Banking and APIs play in modern lending?
3 Identify two ways in which digital lending platforms enhance financial inclusion.

Analytical Questions

1 Evaluate the potential benefits and risks of integrating AI-driven credit scoring into traditional bank lending. Consider both operational efficiency and ethical concerns.
2 Discuss how the convergence of FinTech and traditional banking models can create a hybrid lending ecosystem. Include examples of how collaboration can improve credit access and operational efficiency.
3 Analyse the implications of DeFi for global lending. How might DeFi disrupt traditional intermediaries, and what regulatory challenges could arise?

Case Study: Upstart and AI-Driven Credit Underwriting

Upstart is a US-based FinTech lender that has redefined consumer lending by embedding AI and ML into its core underwriting process. Rather than relying primarily on traditional credit metrics such as Fair Isaac Corporation scores, Upstart's models incorporate a wide range of alternative data points, including educational attainment, field of study, employment history, and income patterns. By analysing thousands of variables simultaneously, the platform aims to produce a more granular, predictive assessment of borrower risk.

This data-driven approach has allowed Upstart to approve a higher proportion of applicants, particularly those with limited or thin-file credit histories, while maintaining, and in some cases improving, loan performance metrics compared to conventional underwriting models. As a result, the company positions itself as both a growth-oriented lender and a facilitator of financial inclusion.

However, the use of non-traditional data has attracted regulatory scrutiny and public debate. Critics argue that variables such as education or employment characteristics may act as proxies for protected attributes, potentially leading to unintended discrimination. Regulators, therefore, require assurance that AI-driven decisions are transparent, explainable, and compliant with fair lending laws.

Upstart's model illustrates both the transformative potential and governance challenges of AI-driven lending, raising important questions about fairness, accountability, and competitive pressure on traditional banks.

Reference

Upstart Holdings, Inc. (2021). *Form S-1 Registration Statement (IPO Prospectus)*. U.S. Securities and Exchange Commission. Available at: https://www.sec.gov/Archives/edgar/data/1647639/000119312520218380/d76767ds1.htm (Accessed: 1 March 2026).

Case Study Questions

1 What are the potential benefits and risks of using alternative data (like the education and employment field) for credit scoring?
2 How can a company like Upstart proactively demonstrate the fairness and lack of bias in its AI models to regulators and the public?
3 If you were a traditional bank, how would you respond to the competitive threat posed by AI-driven lenders like Upstart?

Further Reading

Chen, Y., & Bellavitis, C. (2020) Blockchain Disruption and Decentralised Finance: The Rise of Decentralised Business Models. *Journal of Business Venturing Insights*, 13, e00151.

EY (2021) *Global FinTech Adoption Index*. Available at: https://www.ey.com

Fuster, A., Goldsmith-Pinkham, P., Ramadorai, T., & Walther, A. (2019) Predictably Unequal? The Effects of Machine Learning on Credit Markets. *Journal of Finance*, 74(5), 2583–2621.

References

Arner, D.W., Barberis, J., & Buckley, R.P. (2016). The Evolution of FinTech: A New Post-Crisis Paradigm? *University of Hong Kong Faculty of Law Research Paper, No. 2016/047.*

Balyuk, T. (2019). Financial Technology and the Future of Lending. *Foundations and Trends in Finance*, 12(1–2), pp. 1–122.

Chen, Y., & Bellavitis, C. (2020). Blockchain Disruption and Decentralised Finance: The Rise of Decentralised Business Models. *Journal of Business Venturing Insights*, 13, e00151.

Deloitte (2018) *The Convergence of Banks and FinTech*. Available at: https://www.deloitte.com

EY (2021) *Global FinTech Adoption Index*. Available at: https://www.ey.com

Fuster, A., Plosser, M., Schnabl, P., & Vickery, J. (2019). The Role of Technology in Mortgage Lending. *The Review of Financial Studies*, 32(5), 1854–1899.

McIntosh, C., Sarang, A. and Sadoulet, E. (2017). Using Alternative Data to Predict Creditworthiness for the Unbanked. *Journal of Development Economics*, 127(1), 102–117.

Mishkin, F.S. (2015). *The Economics of Money, Banking, and Financial Markets* (11th ed.). Harlow: Pearson Education.

Morduch, J. (1999). The Microfinance Promise. *Journal of Economic Literature*, 37(4), 1569–1614.

Rose, P.S., & Hudgins, S.C. (2013). *Bank Management & Financial Services* (9th ed.). New York: McGraw-Hill Education.

Rosenberg, R., Gonzalez, A., & Narain, S. (2009). *The New Moneylenders: Are the Poor Being Exploited by High Microcredit Interest Rates?*, Washington, DC: Consultative Group to Assist the Poor (CGAP), Occasional Paper No. 15.

Speckenmeyer, P., Hilmer, C., Rauchecker, G., & Schryen, G. (2025) Parallel Branch-and-Price Algorithms for the Single Machine Total Weighted Tardiness Scheduling Problem with Sequence-Dependent Setup Times. *Computers & Operations Research*, 173, 106804. https://doi.org/10.1016/j.cor.2024.106804

World Bank. (2022a). *FinTech and the Future of Finance*: Washington, DC: World Bank Group.

World Bank. (2022b). *FinTech and the Future of Lending: Prospects and Challenges*. Washington, DC: World Bank Group.

Zachariadis, M., & Ozcan, P. (2017). The API Economy and Digital Transformation in Financial Services: The Case of Open Banking. *SWIFT Institute Working Paper, No. 2016-001.*

21 Payment, Remittances, and Digital Settlement

Chapter Overview

This chapter offers a thorough analysis of how Financial Technology (FinTech) innovation has transformed payment processing and remittances. In the past, these financial systems were slow, costly, and heavily reliant on extensive infrastructure (World Bank, 2021). Today, they are experiencing rapid digitisation. The chapter explores the main elements of modern payment systems, including merchant acquirers, payment gateways, card networks, and remittance platforms. It evaluates how FinTech facilitates faster, more affordable, and more inclusive transactions. It also considers the impact of technologies such as blockchain, mobile payments, and biometric authentication, and discusses ongoing challenges related to regulation, market fragmentation, and the digital divide.

Learning Objectives

By the end of this chapter, you should be able to:

1. Explain the structure, key components, and stakeholders of both traditional and modern payment ecosystems.
2. Analyse how FinTech innovations are transforming payment and remittance systems, including the roles of digital wallets, peer-to-peer (P2P) platforms, and real-time payments (RTP).
3. Evaluate the convergence between traditional banking infrastructure and emerging FinTech technologies, including blockchain-based payment solutions.
4. Critically assess the risks and challenges associated with digital payments, with particular emphasis on regulatory compliance, cybersecurity, and user adoption.
5. Examine emerging trends in the payments landscape, such as Central Bank Digital Currencies (CBDCs) and biometric authentication, and apply real-world case studies to contextualise theoretical concepts.

DOI: 10.4324/9781003775751-25

21.1 Introduction

In recent decades, payment processing has experienced a profound transformation, shifting from a landscape dominated by established banks and physical transactional methods. Payment processing and remittances, which include both domestic and cross-border fund transfers, are essential components of the global financial infrastructure. Historically, these systems exhibited inherent slowness, high operational costs, and significant limitations due to geographical boundaries and infrastructural disparities, as documented by the Bank for International Settlements in 2020. This context provides a foundation for examining the radical shifts currently redefining these fundamental financial operations.

The payment landscape is currently undergoing a significant transformation, primarily driven by the emergence of FinTech innovations. According to Arner et al. (2020), FinTech is fundamentally altering traditional payment paradigms. The integration of advanced technology with financial services is fostering unprecedented innovation, enabling faster, more cost-effective, and globally efficient transactions. This technological advancement is dismantling previous geographical and infrastructural barriers, allowing seamless financial flows across various scales.

Consequently, the once-cumbersome fund transfer processes are evolving into streamlined digital settlements, affecting both individual consumer payments and large-scale corporate remittances. This shift enhances operational efficiency and expands financial inclusion, particularly in regions that were previously underserved by conventional banking systems. The ongoing digital revolution in payments and remittances represents a pivotal moment in global finance, indicating continued innovation and deeper integration of digital solutions into routine financial transactions.

21.2 Understanding Payment Processing and Remittances

21.2.1 Definition and Purpose

Payment processing contains the comprehensive infrastructure and procedural framework that facilitates the secure, authorised, cleared, and settled transfer of funds between a payer and a payee. This system involves a network of key stakeholders, including the payer's financial institution (issuer), the payee's bank (acquirer), payment networks such as Visa or Mastercard, payment gateways, and central clearing and settlement mechanisms, that collectively ensure the seamless execution of transactions across diverse payment instruments like credit and debit cards, bank transfers, digital wallets, and RTP systems. Payment processing is the transfer of funds between parties through a system (BIS, 2020, p. 3), a function that is indispensable to the integrity and efficiency of modern financial ecosystems. The overarching purpose of this process is to enable accurate, timely, and secure financial exchanges that support commercial activity, minimise counterparty risk, and reinforce trust in the financial system, serving as a cornerstone for both domestic and international economic transactions.

In parallel, remittances represent a distinct yet integral component of the global payment landscape, specifically cross-border transfers sent by migrant workers to family members in their home countries. These flows play a pivotal socio-economic role by directly boosting household incomes, alleviating poverty, and strengthening foreign exchange reserves in recipient nations, particularly developing economies. Remittances not only serve as a stable and countercyclical source of external financing but also promote financial inclusion by

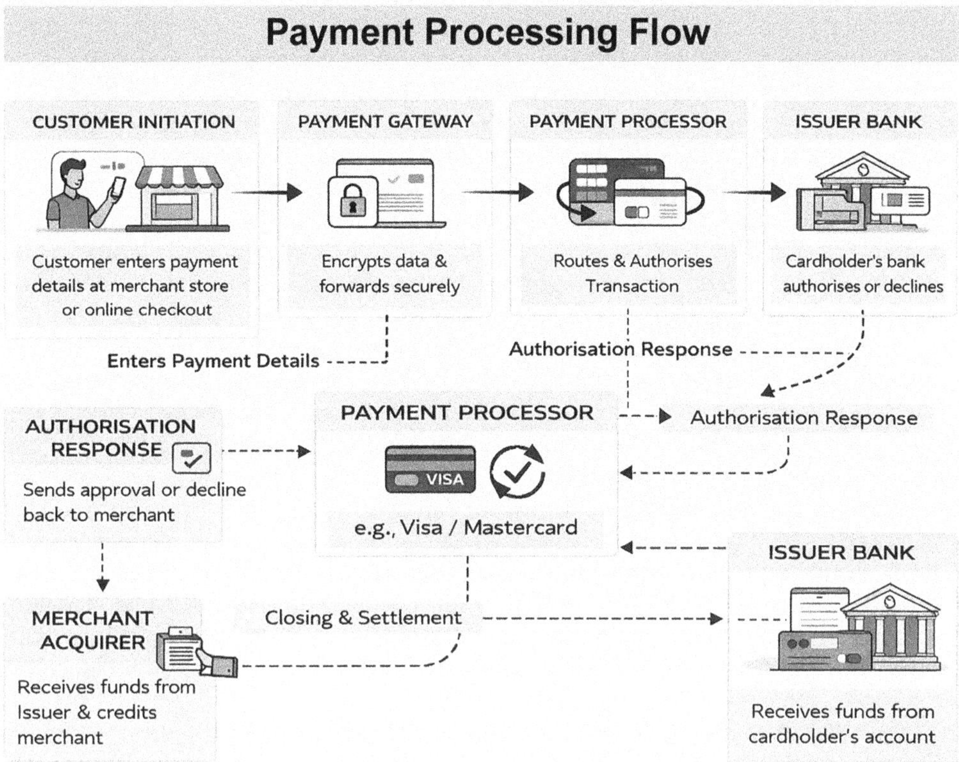

Figure 21.1 Flow of Digital Payment Processing.

integrating underserved populations into formal banking systems (World Bank, 2021). While payment processing broadly supports commercial and digital transactional efficiency, remittances focus on human and developmental impact, collectively reinforcing the dual mandate of modern financial systems: to drive economic activity and to foster inclusive growth. Together, these mechanisms form the backbone of global financial connectivity, underpinning both macroeconomic stability and individual financial well-being.

21.2.2 Key Elements of Payment Processing

The payment ecosystem comprises a complex network of interdependent participants. The following diagram depicts the principal stakeholders and the standard flow of a card-not-present (online) transaction.

Figure 21.1 shows payment processing flows.

Key Stakeholders in Payment Processing:

Merchant Acquirer: In payment processing, the merchant acquirer is a critical stakeholder, a financial institution that facilitates card transactions for merchants by providing payment infrastructure, managing fraud risks, and ensuring regulatory compliance (e.g.,

PCI DSS). The acquirer also settles funds by transferring them from the cardholder's bank to the merchant's account, ensuring seamless digital settlements (Chishti & Barberis, 2016). This role underscores the acquirer's importance in maintaining secure, efficient, and compliant payment ecosystems for businesses and consumers alike.

Payment Gateway: In payment processing, key stakeholders include the payment gateway, a critical technology service that securely transmits transaction data between merchants and processors. Payment gateways encrypt data, send authorisation requests, and support fraud screening (Gomber et al., 2018). These intermediaries ensure secure, efficient digital settlements by facilitating seamless transactions while mitigating risks for merchants and consumers alike. Their role is vital in maintaining trust and reliability in modern financial ecosystems.

Payment Processor: In payment processing, the payment processor serves as a critical intermediary, facilitating secure communication between merchants, card networks, and financial institutions. The processor ensures transaction integrity by verifying fund availability and authorisation in real time, enabling efficient, reliable digital settlements across global commerce ecosystems.

Issuer Bank: In payment processing, the issuer bank plays a critical role as the consumer's (buyer's) financial institution. It issues payment cards, authorises transactions based on available funds or credit limits, and ensures security through fraud detection. Issuer banks act as the first line of protection in safeguarding transactions while facilitating seamless payments. Additionally, they provide customer support, resolving disputes and enhancing user trust in digital settlements. Their involvement ensures compliance, efficiency, and reliability in the payment ecosystem.

Card Networks: Card networks, including Visa and Mastercard, play a pivotal role in payment processing by establishing operational standards, facilitating communication between issuers and acquirers, and ensuring global interoperability. These networks are the backbone of secure and efficient digital transactions, emphasising their critical function in security and dispute resolution (Zhao et al., 2022).

21.2.3 Key Players in Remittance Processing

Money Transfer Operators (MTOs): MTOs such as Western Union and MoneyGram play a pivotal role in global remittance flows, leveraging extensive agent networks to facilitate cross-border transfers. While their services are recognised for reliability, they often entail higher fees, costing migrants an average of 6.3% per transaction (Ratha, 2016).

Banks and Financial Institutions: Banks and financial institutions remain central to remittance processing, primarily utilising the SWIFT network for secure cross-border transfers. While reliable, these traditional systems are often criticised for slow transaction speeds and high fees, prompting scrutiny and competition. The cost and inefficiency of traditional remittance channels have created fertile ground for FinTech innovation (Arner et al., 2020), underlining the growing demand for faster, more affordable alternatives in global payment ecosystems.

Digital Remittance Platforms: FinTech firms such as Wise and Revolut have transformed remittance processing by leveraging technology to offer lower fees, real-time transaction tracking, and mid-market exchange rates. These platforms prioritise transparency and efficiency, challenging traditional banking models and enhancing users' access to global fund transfers (Morse, 2022).

21.3 The Rise of FinTech in Payment Processing and Remittances

FinTech has revolutionised these domains by leveraging digital technologies to create faster, more cost-effective, and accessible solutions.

21.3.1 Digital Payment Systems

The rise of FinTech has revolutionised payment processing and remittances through digital payment systems. Platforms such as Apple Pay, Google Pay, and Alipay leverage digital wallets and NFC technology to enable secure, contactless transactions, both online and in-store. These innovations enhance convenience and efficiency, transforming traditional payment ecosystems (Gomber et al., 2018). This shift underscores the growing reliance on FinTech solutions for seamless financial transactions in a digitally driven economy.

21.3.2 P2P Payments

P2P payment platforms like Venmo, Cash App, and Zelle have revolutionised digital transactions by enabling instantaneous fund transfers directly from bank accounts. These systems bypass traditional intermediaries, reducing settlement times to mere seconds (Zhao et al., 2022), enhancing efficiency and user convenience in modern payment ecosystems.

21.3.3 Cryptocurrencies and Blockchain Technology

Cryptocurrencies such as Bitcoin, supported by blockchain technology, offer transformative potential for cross-border payments by enabling secure, rapid, and low-cost transactions without intermediaries (Tapscott & Tapscott, 2016). However, challenges such as price volatility and regulatory ambiguity hinder widespread adoption, necessitating further innovation and policy clarity to facilitate FinTech integration.

21.3.4 Cross-Border

FinTech firms like Wise and WorldRemit have transformed cross-border payments through innovative currency-matching systems that significantly reduce exchange costs and transfer times. These platforms enhance transparency and affordability, challenging traditional banks' dominance in remittances (Morse, 2022).

21.3.5 Buy Now, Pay Later (BNPL)

BNPL is a short-term financing solution enabling consumers to defer payments into interest-free instalments, boosting e-commerce sales. However, critics warn of rising debt risks, prompting regulatory scrutiny. While BNPL services like Klarna and Afterpay enhance convenience, they may also heighten users' financial vulnerability (ASIC, 2020). Businesses and regulators must balance innovation with consumer protection.

21.4 Contrast and Convergence of FinTech in Payment Processing

The rapid evolution of FinTech in payment processing and remittances has introduced agile, cost-effective solutions that contrast sharply with traditional banking's slower, higher-fee structures. However, convergence is emerging as banks adopt blockchain and digital wallets to enhance efficiency. The future lies in hybrid models that merge FinTech innovation with institutional trust. This synergy is reshaping cross-border settlements, reducing delays, and improving financial inclusion.

21.4.1 A Comparison of Traditional and FinTech Systems

Table 21.1 shows the distinction between traditional and FinTech payments and remittances.

21.4.2 Convergence of Traditional and FinTech Payment Systems

The convergence of traditional and FinTech payment systems is generating a hybrid model that enhances efficiency, speed and interoperability across financial services. Legacy infrastructures such as the SWIFT Global Payments Innovation system now compete with blockchain-enabled networks like RippleNet, offering faster settlement times while established banks also adopt RTP rails such as the U.S. FedNow service (Arner, Barberis & Buckley, 2020). Institutional adoption illustrates this integration: Western Union, historically reliant on correspondent banking, has incorporated the Stellar blockchain for USDC-based settlements to reduce cost and latency, and JPMorgan's Liink platform utilises distributed ledger technology to streamline cross-border messaging and settlement (Tapscott & Tapscott, 2016). Embedded finance further blurs boundaries between FinTech and traditional payments by integrating financial capabilities into non-financial

Table 21.1 Differences Between Traditional and FinTech Payment and Remittances

Feature	*Traditional Systems*	*FinTech Systems*	*Impact/Implication*
Transaction Speed	1–5 business days (via SWIFT, ACH)	Instant to minutes (via Blockchain, RTP)	Dramatic reduction in settlement time, enabling real-time cash flow
Cost Structure	High fees (e.g., 3–10% for cross-border remittances)	Low fees (0.5–2% or fixed micro-fees)	Greatly improves affordability, especially for low-value transactions
Accessibility	Requires a formal bank account	Mobile-first, often account-free (e.g., M-Pesa)	Drives financial inclusion for the unbanked/underbanked
Core Technology	Legacy systems (mainframes, batch processing)	Cloud-native, Application Programming Interface, Blockchain, artificial intelligence (AI)/machine learning	Enables scalability, agility, and integration (Open Banking)
Transparency	Opaque; fees and tracking often unclear	Real-time tracking with clear fee breakdowns	Builds user trust and allows for better financial planning
Regulatory Environment	Heavy, established (anti-money laundering (AML)/know-your-customer (KYC), Financial Action Task Force, Basel III)	Evolving and adapting (Virtual Asset Service Provider licensing, Travel Rule, sandboxes)	Presents both a compliance challenge and an innovation opportunity

ecosystems. For example, Shopify's Balance accounts for merchants and Uber's instant payout feature for drivers embed banking functions directly into operational workflows (Gomber et al., 2018). Regulatory frameworks such as the FATF's Travel Rule, now applied to certain crypto transactions, create compliance bridges that align digital assets with conventional financial standards, promoting transparency and mitigating risk (FATF, 2021). Finally, cross-pollination of technology, including the adoption of AI-driven fraud detection by incumbent banks and the proliferation of peer-to-peer services like Zelle within traditional banking apps, underscores the shift toward hybrid financial ecosystems where collaboration enhances efficiency, security, and accessibility for businesses and consumers (Zetzsche et al., 2020).

21.5 Risks, Challenges, and Key Practical Issues of FinTech-Driven Payment and Remittance

21.5.1 Risk and Challenges

FinTech-driven payment and remittance systems face several structural risks and regulatory challenges that shape their development. Foremost among these is regulatory compliance, as firms must navigate overlapping frameworks covering data protection, AML, counter-terrorist financing, and KYC requirements. Regulations such as the GDPR impose strict data governance standards, while AML/KYC rules demand robust transaction monitoring and reporting systems. These obligations increase operational costs and can slow innovation, particularly for smaller firms with limited compliance resources, thereby creating friction between technological advancement and regulatory oversight (Zetzsche et al., 2017).

A second set of risks concerns security vulnerabilities and unequal adoption. The expansion of digital payment channels enlarges the attack surface for cybercrime, exposing platforms to fraud, phishing, identity theft, and system intrusions that can rapidly erode user trust. At the same time, market fragmentation, caused by the proliferation of closed-loop wallets and proprietary platforms, reduces interoperability and undermines the seamless experience FinTech seeks to provide. In addition, digital literacy gaps persist among elderly, rural, and low-income populations, limiting their ability or willingness to adopt digital financial services and reinforcing financial exclusion (Ozili, 2021).

21.5.2 Key Practical Issues

Key practical issues arise when implementing and scaling these systems. Interoperability remains a major technical barrier, as the lack of universal standards across payment platforms restricts seamless transactions and weakens network effects. Blockchain-based infrastructures face the scalability trilemma, in which trade-offs among speed, security, and decentralisation limit their suitability for high-volume retail payments. Furthermore, RTP environments require equally real-time compliance and fraud-detection systems, often powered by AI, that must balance effective risk monitoring with minimal disruption to legitimate users. Finally, the economic sustainability of some FinTech models, such as Buy-Now-Pay-Later services, remains uncertain due to reliance on merchant fees and favourable credit conditions, raising concerns about long-term resilience during periods of economic stress (BIS, 2022).

21.6 The Future of Payment Processing and Remittances

The future of payment processing and remittances will be strongly influenced by the development of CBDCs and the deeper integration of blockchain-based infrastructures. CBDCs, as digital representations of sovereign currency, have the potential to enhance settlement efficiency, reduce counterparty and liquidity risk, and strengthen the resilience of national and cross-border payment systems (BIS, 2020). They may also promote financial inclusion by enabling broader access to digital payment instruments. However, their design raises important policy considerations: CBDCs must be structured to complement rather than displace commercial banks and private payment providers, requiring careful choices around access, privacy, and the role of intermediaries. At the same time, distributed ledger technologies are moving beyond cryptocurrencies into institutional payment environments, enabling faster, more transparent, and auditable cross-border transactions. By streamlining reconciliation and reducing reliance on correspondent banking chains, blockchain-based systems offer cost and efficiency gains, although challenges related to scalability, regulation, and legacy integration persist (Tapscott & Tapscott, 2016).

Alongside infrastructural change, authentication technologies are reshaping how users authorise transactions. Biometric and voice-based payment methods, such as fingerprint scanning, facial recognition, and voice authentication, are increasingly positioned as secure and user-friendly alternatives to passwords and Personal Identification Numbers. These technologies can reduce fraud linked to stolen or reused credentials while supporting frictionless digital payment experiences, particularly in mobile and remote contexts. Nevertheless, the use of biometric identifiers introduces heightened privacy and cybersecurity risks, as compromised biometric data cannot easily be replaced. Effective implementation, therefore, depends on strong encryption, secure storage architectures, and advanced liveness detection to prevent spoofing, ensuring that improvements in convenience do not undermine system integrity.

21.7 Conclusion

FinTech has significantly reconfigured the global architecture of payments, remittances, and digital settlements by improving transaction speed, reducing costs, and broadening financial inclusion. Through mobile platforms, digital wallets, and RTP infrastructures, FinTech has streamlined cross-border transfers and expanded access to formal financial services for previously underserved and unbanked populations. Digital remittance channels, in particular, have been associated with substantially lower transaction costs compared to traditional MTOs, illustrating the efficiency gains enabled by platform-based models (World Bank, 2023). Contemporary financial systems are increasingly characterised by hybridisation, where established banking infrastructure coexists with agile digital solutions. This convergence combines the institutional trust, liquidity provision, and regulatory integration of traditional banks with the scalability and user-centric design of FinTech platforms, resulting in more seamless, accessible financial interactions for both consumers and institutions.

Despite these gains, the acceleration of digital finance introduces complex regulatory and security challenges. The expansion of data-intensive financial services heightens exposure to cyber threats, fraud, and operational disruptions, necessitating robust cybersecurity governance alongside compliance with AML, KYC, and data protection frameworks. International standard-setting bodies emphasise that financial innovation must be aligned with the preservation of financial integrity, consumer protection, and systemic stability (FSB, 2022). Looking ahead, emerging technologies such as CBDCs, distributed ledger–based settlement systems, and biometric authentication are expected to further transform the payments landscape. These innovations have the potential to enhance transparency, resilience, and efficiency, but their successful integration will depend on a balanced regulatory design, a secure technological architecture, and sustained public trust.

Key Terms and Glossary

Payment Gateway A technology service that authorises and processes payments for online retailers, acting as an intermediary between the merchant and the acquiring bank.

BNPL (Buy Now, Pay Later) A point-of-sale financing option that allows consumers to defer payment or pay in instalments.

RTP (Real-Time Payments) Payment systems that enable immediate or near-immediate transfer of funds between bank accounts.

Card Networks Global infrastructures (e.g., Visa, Mastercard) that govern the rules and facilitate communication between acquirers and issuers for card payments.

Remittances Cross-border transfers of money, typically by migrant workers to their families in their home countries.

Test Your Understanding

Multiple-Choice Questions

1 The financial institution that processes card payments on behalf of a merchant is called the:

A Issuer Bank
B Card Network
C Merchant Acquirer
D Payment Gateway

2 A FinTech solution that allows consumers to split a purchase into interest-free instalments at the point of sale is known as:

A A digital wallet
B BNPL
C A wire transfer
D A chargeback

3 A key advantage of blockchain technology in cross-border payments is its potential to:

A Increase transaction fees
B Slow down settlement times
C Reduce costs and increase transparency
D Require more intermediaries

4 The scalability trilemma in blockchain refers to the trade-off between:

A Speed, cost, and customer service
B Security, scalability, and decentralisation
C Regulation, innovation, and marketing
D Hardware, software, and wetware

5 A significant challenge for digital payment systems is ensuring:

A The complete elimination of cash
B Interoperability between different platforms and wallets
C Making all transactions reversible
D Slowing down transaction speeds for security

Short Questions

1 Briefly explain the difference between a payment gateway and a payment processor in digital transactions.
2 Why is interoperability important in modern digital payment ecosystems?
3 What is one key difference between traditional remittance systems (e.g., SWIFT) and modern digital remittance platforms (e.g., Wise)?

Analytical Questions

1 Critically assess the integration of traditional banking and FinTech in payment processing, considering the advantages of hybrid models and the regulatory or operational challenges they introduce.
2 Examine the main risks of the rapid expansion of digital payment systems, with emphasis on cybersecurity, regulatory compliance, and digital exclusion. How can regulators and firms ensure innovation while maintaining financial stability and protecting consumers?
3 Propose a competitive strategy for a traditional bank facing disruption in cross-border payments by FinTech firms, highlighting how it can leverage its existing strengths while incorporating FinTech capabilities.

Case Study: Wise and the Transformation of Cross-Border Payments

Wise (formerly TransferWise) is a FinTech firm that has reshaped the cross-border payments market by challenging the traditional economics of international money transfers. Historically, international transfers were dominated by banks and MTOs that relied on correspondent banking networks, opaque foreign exchange markups, and complex fee structures. Wise introduced an alternative model designed to reduce both cost and complexity for consumers.

Rather than sending money across borders, Wise operates a system of local bank accounts in multiple countries. When a customer initiates an international transfer, Wise matches the payment with a corresponding transfer moving in the opposite direction. Funds, therefore, remain largely within domestic banking systems, significantly reducing reliance on correspondent banks and associated fees. Customers are charged a clearly disclosed, low service fee and receive the real mid-market exchange rate, rather than a marked-up rate.

This approach has enabled Wise to offer faster, cheaper, and more transparent international transfers than many incumbents. As a result, it has attracted a large retail and small-business customer base and placed competitive pressure on traditional banks and MTOs to reconsider pricing and disclosure practices. However, Wise's model also raises questions about scalability, regulatory constraints, and suitability for high-value or complex international transactions, where customers may still prioritise the perceived security and guarantees of traditional banking institutions.

Reference

Morse, A. (2022). *The Remittance Revolution: How Low-Cost Transfers Are Changing the World*. Cambridge, MA: Harvard University Press.

Case Study Questions

1. Why were traditional banks and MTOs able to maintain high fees on cross-border payments for so long before the emergence of competitors like Wise?
2. What are the limitations of Wise's business model? In which scenarios might a customer still choose a traditional bank for a large international wire?
3. How does the transparency of Wise's pricing model build trust with consumers?

Further Reading

Arner, D. W., Barberis, J. N. and Buckley, R. P. (2020). The evolution of FinTech: A new post-crisis paradigm. in R. P. Buckley, D. W. Arner, & Veidt, R. (Eds.), *The Cambridge Handbook of FinTech*. Cambridge: Cambridge University Press.

BIS (Bank for International Settlements). (2020). *Payment and Settlement Systems in the CPSS Countries*. Basel: Bank for International Settlements.

Tapscott, D. and Tapscott, A. (2016). *Blockchain Revolution: How the Technology Behind Bitcoin Is Changing Money, Business, and the World*. New York: Portfolio/Penguin.

References

Arner, D.W., Barberis, J.N., & Buckley, R.P. (2020). The Evolution of FinTech: A New Post-Crisis Paradigm? In *The Cambridge Handbook of FinTech*. Cambridge: Cambridge University Press.

Australian Securities and Investments Commission (2020). *Report 672: Buy Now Pay Later: An Industry Review*. Canberra: ASIC.

Bank for International Settlements (BIS). (2020). *Annual Economic Report: Digital Currencies and the Future of the Monetary System*. Basel: BIS.

BIS (Bank for International Settlements). (2020). *Payment and Settlement Systems in the CPSS Countries*. Basel: Bank for International Settlements.

Bank for International Settlements (2022). *Buy Now, Pay Later: A Cross-Country Analysis*. Basel: Bank for International Settlements.

Chishti, S., & Barberis, J. (2016). *The FinTech Book: The Financial Technology Handbook for Investors, Entrepreneurs and Visionaries*. Chichester: Wiley.

Financial Action Task Force (FATF). (2021). *Updated Guidance for a Risk-Based Approach to Virtual Assets and Virtual Asset Service Providers*. Paris: FATF.

Financial Stability Board (2022). *Promoting Global Financial Stability: 2022 FSB Annual Report*. Basel: Financial Stability Board.

Gomber, P., Kauffman, R.J., Parker, C., & Weber, B.W. (2018). On the FinTech Revolution: Interpreting the Forces of Innovation, Disruption, and Transformation in Financial Services. *Journal of Management Information Systems*, 35(1), 220–265.

Morse, A. (2022). *The Remittance Revolution: How Low-Cost Transfers Are Changing the World.* London: The Economist Intelligence Unit.

Ozili, P.K. (2021). Digital Finance, Green Finance and Social Finance: Is There a Link? *Financial Internet Quarterly*, 17(1), 1–7.

Ratha, D. (2016). *The Hidden Force in Global Economics: Sending Money Home*. Washington, D.C.: World Bank.

Tapscott, D. and Tapscott, A. (2016). *Blockchain Revolution: How the Technology Behind Bitcoin Is changing Money, Business, and the World.* New York: Portfolio/Penguin.

World Bank. (2021). *Migration and Development Brief 35*. Washington, D.C.: World Bank Group.

World Bank. (2023). *Global Findex Database 2021: Financial Inclusion, Digital Payments, and Resilience in the Age of COVID-19*. Washington, DC: World Bank Group.

Zetzsche, D.A., Buckley, R.P., Arner, D.W., & Barberis, J.N. (2017). The RegTech Universe in Evolution. *SSRN Electronic Journal*. doi:10.2139/ssrn.3049244

Zetzsche, D.A., Buckley, R.P., Arner, D.W., & Barberis, J.N. (2020) Fintech and the Future of Finance: From Disruption to Orchestration. *European Business Organization Law Review*, 21(4), 835–873.

Zhao, J., Fan, S., & Yan, J. (2022). A Review of FinTech Research and the Way Forward. *Sustainability*, 14(19), 12417.

22 Wealth Management and Financial Technology (WealthTech)

Chapter Overview

This chapter examines the transformative influence of financial technology (FinTech) on wealth management, a sector traditionally centred on affluent clients and reliant on human advisors. Technological innovations, including robo-advisors, artificial intelligence (AI), and digital onboarding tools, are expanding access to these services (Arner et al., 2020). The chapter reviews key services such as portfolio management, estate planning, and tax strategies, and introduces the concept of Wealth Technology (WealthTech). It contrasts traditional and digital methods, explores the growing adoption of hybrid models, and considers challenges related to regulatory compliance, data security, and algorithmic bias. The chapter concludes with a perspective on future developments, including hyper-personalised services, embedded financial tools, Environmental, Social, and Governance (ESG) investment options, and advancements in predictive technology.

Learning Objectives

By the end of this chapter, you should be able to:

1. Explain the structure, objectives, and core services of the wealth management industry and identify its key institutional participants.
2. Analyse how FinTech innovations, such as robo-advisors, AI, and digital onboarding, are transforming traditional wealth management models.
3. Compare and contrast traditional, digital, and hybrid advisory models, assessing their respective advantages and limitations.
4. Evaluate the benefits and challenges of digital transformation in wealth management, including regulatory compliance, cybersecurity, and algorithmic risk.
5. Assess emerging trends in wealth management, particularly hyper-personalisation and ESG investing, and their implications for future industry development.

DOI: 10.4324/9781003775751-26

22.1 Introduction

Wealth management represents a specialised segment within financial services that focuses on advanced planning and investment advisory solutions. While the industry has historically served high-net-worth (HNW) and ultra-high-net-worth(UHNW) individuals, its scope has expanded to include the mass affluent segment. The core value proposition of wealth management has traditionally centred on interpersonal relationships and fiduciary trust. As noted by Cumming and Schweizer (2016), the sector relied on personal trust and human expertise, fostering a competitive environment based on reputation and customised service.

The contemporary landscape is undergoing a significant transformation due to the influence of FinTech, which has led to the emergence of WealthTech as a specialised subset. This technological evolution is fundamentally reshaping operational efficiency and the processes by which financial advice is generated and delivered. FinTech solutions now play a pivotal role in supporting data-driven decision-making, moving the industry standard from subjective judgement to quantifiable, analytical rigour. Additionally, integrating technology improves the speed, consistency, and scalability of advanced service offerings.

Importantly, technological integration serves not only as an internal efficiency driver but also as a strategic instrument for market expansion. By automating routine advisory tasks and reducing the costs of personalised planning, WealthTech platforms are democratising access to services once exclusive to elite clients. This enables firms to provide highly customised advice at scale, creating a competitive environment in which long-term success relies on using technological analytics to enhance, rather than supplant, the critical personal expertise of wealth managers.

22.2 Understanding Wealth Management

22.2.1 Definition and Purpose of Wealth Management

Wealth management is a specialised financial advisory discipline that integrates investment strategy, tax planning, estate planning, and risk management to support high-net-worth individuals (HNWIs) and families in achieving long-term financial objectives (Ariff, 2017). Unlike conventional financial advice, wealth management adopts a holistic, client-centric approach that encompasses retirement planning, cash-flow optimisation, philanthropic strategies, and insurance analysis to create a comprehensive financial roadmap. The emergence of WealthTech solutions further enhances this process by leveraging AI, automation, and data analytics to deliver more precise and efficient planning. The overarching goal of wealth management extends beyond asset growth to secure financial stability and facilitate intergenerational wealth transfer.

Wealth management encompasses four principal objectives:

Capital Growth: Wealth managers prioritise strategic asset allocation to align investment decisions with clients' risk tolerance and long-term goals. For example, a client with $5 million in investable assets might adopt a portfolio composed of 60% equities, 30% bonds, and 10% alternative investments. By rebalancing annually, the portfolio seeks to optimise growth while mitigating exposure to market volatility (Bodie et al., 2021).

Wealth Preservation: Protecting capital from risks such as inflation, taxation, and market downturns remains central. The first rule of investment is not to lose money, which exemplifies this principle. Modern WealthTech solutions enhance preservation by using predictive analytics and algorithm-driven strategies to anticipate risks and adjust investment allocations.

Intergenerational Transfer: Estate planning and succession strategies are designed to facilitate efficient transfer of assets across generations while maintaining tax efficiency. For instance, structured trusts can allow a family of four to transfer $10 million in assets while reducing inheritance tax exposure and preserving both wealth and the family legacy.

Holistic Financial Planning: Wealth management integrates all elements of a client's financial ecosystem, ensuring that investment, taxation, retirement, insurance, and estate considerations form a unified strategy. This comprehensive approach aligns financial decisions with clients' life goals and values (Ariff, 2017).

22.2.2 *Key Services in Wealth Management*

Wealth management services are designed to address the complex financial needs of affluent clients. These services include.

Investment Portfolio Management: Investment Portfolio management refers to allocating assets across stocks, bonds, and alternative investments to achieve desired returns while controlling risk. For example, a $2 million portfolio allocated 50% to equities, 40% to bonds, and 10% to real estate may be rebalanced quarterly to maintain a risk-adjusted illustrative target return of 6% per annum. Digital platforms like Betterment or Wealthfront automate this process, adjusting asset allocations based on risk profiles.

Financial and Retirement Planning: Financial and Retirement Planning evaluates clients' financial positions to design strategies that ensure long-term stability and retirement readiness. For instance, a client aiming for a $3 million retirement fund in 25 years might contribute $50,000 annually to a diversified portfolio, with assuming projections showing compound growth of 5–6% annually. Digital tools such as Personal Capital offer automated tracking and scenario analysis for similar planning.

Tax Optimisation: Maximising after-tax returns through methods such as tax-loss harvesting and utilising tax-advantaged accounts. For example, a client can use Individual Savings Accounts and pensions to reduce taxable income suppose by £50,000 annually, thereby preserving wealth.

Estate and Succession Planning: Estate and Succession Planning ensure efficient wealth transfer while minimising taxes. For instance, structured wills and trusts allow UHNW families to pass $20 million in assets to heirs with reduced inheritance tax liabilities (RBC Wealth Management 2024). Digital platforms such as Farewill facilitate online will creation and estate planning.

Risk Management and Insurance: Risk Management and Insurance entail identifying and mitigating financial risks through tailored insurance and strategic diversification. For instance, a $10 million portfolio may be safeguarded by life, property, and liability insurance coverage proportional to its potential exposure (.

Philanthropic Advisory: Philanthropic Advisory supports clients in aligning wealth with charitable goals using instruments such as donor-advised funds. For instance, a client donating $500,000 annually through a charitable trust can receive tax deductions while achieving targeted social impact.

22.2.3 *Types of Wealth Management Institutions*

The wealth management industry comprises diverse institutions that serve different client segments based on wealth level, financial needs complexity, and desired level of service (Capgemini, 2023). Each type of institution offers distinct functions tailored to its client base.

Private Banks: Private banks, such as Credit Suisse and UBS, primarily serve ultra-high-net-worth individuals by offering bespoke financial solutions and access to exclusive asset classes. Functions typically include customised portfolio management, tax optimisation, estate planning, and access to alternative investments such as private equity or hedge funds. For example, a client with $50 million in assets might receive a fully tailored investment strategy including direct equity investments, structured products, and international tax planning.

Independent Wealth Management Firms: Independent, fee-only firms, such as Edelman Financial Engines, provide objective financial advice without being constrained by proprietary products, thereby minimising conflicts of interest. Functions often include retirement planning, investment portfolio construction, risk assessment, and fiduciary advisory services. For instance, a client with $3 million in investable assets may receive a diversified portfolio recommendation alongside a tax-efficient retirement strategy, with the firm's fee linked solely to assets under management (AUM).

Financial Advisors and Planners: Services such as Vanguard Personal Advisor Services (VPAS) target the mass affluent, combining human expertise with digital tools to deliver personalised solutions. Functions include automated portfolio rebalancing, goal-based investment advice, and retirement projections. For example, a client saving for a $1 million retirement goal over 20 years might receive algorithmically optimised asset allocation recommendations and ongoing progress tracking, integrating both human consultation and technology.

Family Offices: Family offices are dedicated entities providing comprehensive, integrated management for UHNW families, addressing both financial and personal affairs. Functions include wealth preservation, succession planning, philanthropy management, and lifestyle oversight, such as property management or concierge services. For example, a family office managing $200 million may coordinate investments across multiple asset classes, administer trusts for intergenerational transfer, and manage charitable foundations aligned with the family's values.

22.3 FinTech in Wealth Management: The Rise of WealthTech

FinTech has transformed wealth management by leveraging automation, AI, machine learning (ML), and data analytics to deliver personalised advisory services, streamline operations, and reduce costs. The integration of these technologies in wealth management, often referred to as WealthTech, enhances the accessibility, efficiency, and data-driven quality of financial advice (Deloitte, 2022) (Figure 22.1).

22.3.1 *Key FinTech Innovations in Wealth Management*

Robo-Advisors: Robo-advisors are automated investment platforms that construct and manage low-cost, diversified portfolios based on clients' risk profiles and financial goals. Platforms such as Betterment and Wealthfront utilise algorithmic portfolio

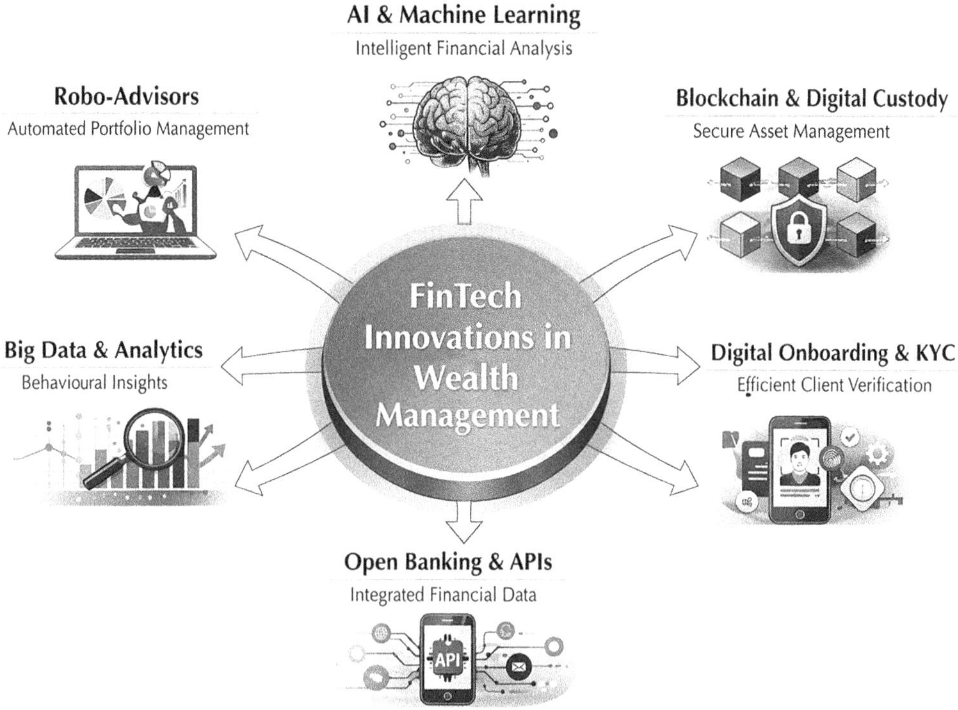

Figure 22.1 FinTech Innovations in Wealth Management.

allocation to optimise returns while minimising costs and effort for clients (D'Acunto & Rossi, 2021). For example, a client with a moderate risk tolerance investing $100,000 might receive a portfolio of 70% equities and 30% bonds, with automatic rebalancing executed quarterly.

AI and ML: AI and ML have become central to WealthTech, enhancing risk assessment, behavioural analysis, and personalised financial recommendations. Platforms like Schwab Intelligent Portfolios Premium employ AI to optimise asset allocation, monitor portfolio risk, and provide predictive financial planning (FSB, 2022). For instance, AI can analyse market conditions and client behaviour to recommend portfolio adjustments that align with long-term goals.

Big Data and Behavioural Analytics: Wealth managers increasingly use Big Data and behavioural analytics to analyse client spending, investment patterns, and market trends. Understanding behavioural biases, such as loss aversion or overconfidence, allows advisors to design personalised interventions and improve portfolio performance (Barber & Odean, 2013). For example, an advisor may use real-time analytics to suggest reducing equity exposure during periods of market over-optimism.

Blockchain and Digital Custody: Blockchain technology and smart contracts enhance transparency, security, and efficiency in wealth management. Decentralised ledgers facilitate secure digital custody of assets, while smart contracts automate processes like estate transfers or trust disbursements, reducing disputes and administrative costs (Tapscott & Tapscott, 2016).

Digital Onboarding and KYC: Digital onboarding, including biometric verification and AI-driven Know Your Customer (KYC) processes, streamlines compliance with anti-money laundering (AML) regulations. Platforms such as IDnow enable rapid client verification, reducing onboarding time from several days to minutes and improving overall client experience.

Open Banking and API Integration: Open Banking, enabled by APIs from providers such as Plaid, aggregates client financial data from multiple institutions, offering a consolidated view of assets and liabilities. This facilitates highly personalised advisory services and integrated financial planning (Zetzsche et al., 2020).

22.3.2 FinTech Innovations in Wealth Management Functions

WealthTech innovations extend beyond operational efficiency and data analytics, transforming core wealth management functions:

Investment Advice: Robo-advisors and AI platforms automate portfolio construction, rebalancing, and risk assessment. For example, a $500,000 portfolio managed through an AI-enabled platform can dynamically adjust allocations between equities, bonds, and alternatives based on real-time market trends and client-defined risk tolerance.

Tax Planning: Big Data and predictive analytics enable the identification of tax-loss harvesting opportunities and optimal utilisation of tax-advantaged accounts. A client with $1 million in equities can leverage AI-driven strategies to minimise capital gains taxes while maintaining desired exposure.

Risk Management: ML algorithms assess portfolio risk, market volatility, and client-specific exposures. For instance, predictive models can identify potential 10% drawdowns under stressed market scenarios, allowing the advisor to implement hedging or insurance strategies proactively.

Retirement Planning: AI-driven retirement planning tools forecast income requirements, project investment growth, and simulate various withdrawal strategies. For example, a client targeting a $2 million retirement corpus in 25 years could use AI-enabled simulations to determine annual contributions and an optimal asset allocation to achieve their goal.

Estate Planning: Blockchain and smart contracts enable secure, transparent, and automated asset transfers. WealthTech platforms can implement digital trusts or automated inheritance disbursements, reducing administrative delays and minimising legal risks.

Business Planning: For entrepreneur clients, FinTech tools provide integrated cash-flow forecasting, succession modelling, and tax optimisation strategies. A business owner with $10 million in company equity can simulate exit strategies, succession scenarios, and associated tax liabilities using AI-powered platforms.

22.4 A Comparison Between Traditional and FinTech Wealth Management

Following Table 22.1, the review of key technological innovations in wealth management, this section compares traditional and FinTech-based models and identifies areas of convergence within the industry.

Table 22.1 A Comparison Between Traditional and FinTech Wealth Management

Feature	*Traditional Wealth Management*	*FinTech Wealth Management*	*Industry Trend / Convergence*
Target Client	HNWIs (~$1M+ assets)	Mass affluent and retail investors	Hybridisation: Traditional firms target mass affluent digitally; FinTechs add services for HNWIs
Service Model	Human advisors (high-touch, 1:1 relationships)	Digital-first (robo-advisors, self-service apps)	Bionic Advice: Digital tools augment human advisors; hybrid models blend AI with human oversight
Account Minimums	High ($250K–$1M+)	Low to none ($0–$5K)	Democratisation: Lowering barriers to entry is now a market standard, pressuring traditional firms
Fee Structure	High (1–2% of AUM + product commissions)	Low (0.25–0.5% AUM) or subscription models	Fee Compression: Transparency and low-cost passive investing drive down fees across the industry
Investment Approach	Primarily active management & stock picking	Primarily passive/indexing + smart algorithms	Core-Satellite: Passive/indexing as the core, with active or thematic strategies as a satellite
Core Technology	Basic client portals, legacy back-office systems	AI-driven tax optimisation (tax-loss harvesting), APIs, cloud-native platforms	Tech-Enablement: Traditional firms invest in/acquire FinTech to modernise infrastructure and offerings
Personalisation	Custom, holistic financial plans (estate, tax)	Algorithm-based portfolio suggestions and automated rebalancing	Hyper-Personalisation at Scale: Using AI/Data to offer tailored insights to a broader client base

22.5 Opportunities, Challenges, and Key Practical Issues WealthTech

22.5.1 Opportunities in FinTech-Enabled Wealth Management

WealthTech offers several significant opportunities that are reshaping the wealth management landscape:

Accessibility and Democratisation: WealthTech platforms have reduced barriers to entry, enabling broader access to professional investment advice. For instance, Wealthfront allows clients to begin investing with as little as $500, expanding access beyond traditional HNWIs (D'Acunto & Rossi, 2021). This democratisation supports financial inclusion and provides emerging investors with opportunities previously limited to affluent clients.

Cost Efficiency: Automation in WealthTech reduces operational costs, allowing firms to offer lower fees while maintaining high-quality advisory services. For example, Betterment charges a 0.25% annual management fee compared with traditional advisory fees exceeding 1% of AUM, directly passing cost savings to clients and improving investment outcomes (Deloitte, 2022).

Enhanced Personalisation and Data-Driven Advice: WealthTech platforms leverage AI and Big Data to provide personalised investment strategies and predictive analytics. For example, Schwab Intelligent Portfolios Premium uses AI to recommend portfolio adjustments based on market trends and client-specific goals, providing a level of customisation that would be cost-prohibitive in traditional advisory models (FSB, 2022).

22.5.2 Convergence of Traditional and Digital Wealth Management

The hybrid WealthTech model represents a convergence of digital efficiency and human expertise, offering scalable yet personalised solutions.

Hybrid Advisory Models: Firms such as UBS SmartWealth and VPAS combine algorithmic portfolio management with access to certified financial planners (CFPs). A client investing $200,000 through these platforms might receive automated portfolio rebalancing alongside personalised retirement or tax planning consultations. This hybrid approach balances automation efficiency with human oversight, addressing diverse client needs and maintaining trust (Deloitte, 2022).

Institutional Adoption: Large wealth management institutions, including BlackRock and Morgan Stanley, increasingly integrate FinTech solutions into their advisory frameworks. AI-driven analytics, automated tax optimisation, and predictive risk management tools now complement traditional client interactions, making technology central to value creation rather than a supporting function (Deloitte, 2022).

Tech-Enabled Services: Hybrid WealthTech empowers advisors with smarter tools. For example, an advisor can use AI software to generate scenario-based retirement projections for a client while providing personalised guidance on spending patterns, estate planning, or investment timing. This approach enhances precision, scalability, and client outcomes without eliminating the critical human element required for complex financial decisions.

22.5.3 Risks, Challenges, and Key Practical Issues in WealthTech

Despite its advantages, WealthTech adoption presents several risks and practical challenges:

Cybersecurity Threats: Digital platforms storing sensitive client data are vulnerable to cyberattacks. The 2020 Robinhood breach, where user data and trading capabilities were compromised, illustrates the high stakes involved (Gai et al., 2018). Wealth management firms must continually invest in robust security protocols, multi-factor authentication, and encryption to mitigate these threats.

Regulatory Compliance: Automated platforms must adhere to fiduciary obligations, AML standards, and data protection laws. Ensuring compliance in algorithm-driven client interactions is complex, particularly when AI-based recommendations cross jurisdictional regulatory boundaries (Zetzsche et al., 2017). For example, a robo-advisor offering international portfolio management must comply with tax and securities regulations in multiple countries.

Algorithmic Bias and Over-Reliance: AI models may perpetuate biases inherent in training data, while over-reliance on automation can overlook nuanced client needs, such as family dynamics, business succession, or philanthropic goals (Bodie et al., 2021). A client relying solely on algorithmic advice may receive investment strategies unsuitable for long-term family wealth planning. Human oversight remains essential to address these complexities.

Digital Literacy and Trust: Clients with limited familiarity with digital platforms may be hesitant to adopt fully automated wealth management solutions (Ozili, 2021). For instance, older clients or those with lower technological proficiency may prefer hybrid models combining AI tools with human advisors to maintain confidence in financial decision-making.

22.6 The Future of FinTech Wealth Management

The future of FinTech in wealth management is likely to be characterised by hyper-personalisation and predictive, data-driven advisory services. Advances in AI enable platforms to dynamically adapt to clients' financial behaviours and life events, generating bespoke investment recommendations in real time. Morgan Stanley's 'Next Best Action' system exemplifies this trend, providing advisors with AI-driven insights to tailor portfolio strategies, optimise risk exposure, and align investments with evolving client objectives (Deloitte, 2022). Alongside hyper-personalisation, embedded wealth services are expected to integrate sophisticated financial guidance into everyday digital platforms, making investment advice more accessible and seamlessly embedded within non-financial applications. This evolution supports the democratisation of wealth management, allowing a broader spectrum of clients to engage with professional-grade financial planning tools (D'Acunto & Rossi, 2021).

Sustainability and values-based investing will also shape WealthTech's trajectory, with ESG tools becoming integral to advisory services. Platforms such as Betterment's ESG portfolios provide real-time tracking of social and environmental impact alongside financial performance, reflecting the growing demand for conscientious investment strategies (FSB, 2022). Predictive analytics will further enhance advisory capabilities by anticipating major life events, enabling proactive, rather than reactive, financial planning. The continued adoption of hybrid advisory models, which combine algorithmic precision with human judgement, ensures that WealthTech delivers scalable, efficient services while preserving personalised guidance for complex or emotionally sensitive decisions. Together, these innovations signal a shift towards a technologically augmented, client-centric wealth management ecosystem that aligns financial outcomes with individual goals and broader societal values (Deloitte, 2022; Tapscott & Tapscott, 2016).

22.7 Conclusion

The wealth management industry is undergoing a fundamental transformation as it shifts from a traditionally exclusive, advisor-centric model towards a technology-enabled, increasingly inclusive ecosystem. WealthTech innovations, including AI, automated investment platforms, and integrated digital infrastructures, have expanded access to sophisticated financial planning and enhanced the scalability and efficiency of advisory services. This transition has redefined the client–advisor relationship by enabling data-driven, personalised solutions to be delivered at scale, while lowering barriers to entry for a broader range of investors. As a result, FinTech has become a central driver in modernising wealth management and extending the reach of high-quality financial advice beyond its historical confines.

Looking ahead, the hybrid advisory model is widely recognised as the most sustainable framework for the future of wealth management. By combining algorithmic efficiency and analytical precision with human judgement, behavioural insight, and relationship management, this model allows advisors to focus on complex strategic decisions, long-term planning, and client engagement. However, the long-term viability of this approach depends on effectively addressing critical challenges, including cybersecurity risks, regulatory compliance, and ethical concerns surrounding algorithmic transparency and bias. A sustained commitment to robust governance, technological resilience, and regulatory alignment will be essential to preserving trust and ensuring that WealthTech contributes to a secure, equitable, and resilient wealth management ecosystem.

Key Terms and Glossary

Wealth Management A holistic financial service that combines investment advice, financial planning, and other services for affluent clients.

Robo-Advisor A digital platform that provides automated, algorithm-driven financial planning and investment services with minimal human supervision.

HNWI (High-Net-Worth Individual) A person with investable assets above a certain threshold, typically $1 million.

ESG Investing An investment strategy that considers ESG factors alongside financial returns.

Hybrid Advisory Model A service model that combines automated robo-advisory tools with access to human financial advisors.

Test Your Understanding

Multiple-Choice Questions

1 Which of the following best defines WealthTech?

A A replacement of human advisors with automated trading systems
B The use of blockchain exclusively for asset custody
C The application of FinTech innovations to enhance wealth management services
D A subset of retail banking focused on mass-market clients

2 Which FinTech innovation primarily enables automated portfolio construction and rebalancing based on client risk profiles?

A Open Banking APIs
B Robo-advisors
C Digital KYC systems
D Blockchain smart contracts

3 A key advantage of hybrid advisory models is that they:

A Eliminate the need for regulatory oversight
B Replace personalised advice with algorithms
C Combine algorithmic efficiency with human judgement
D Focus exclusively on ultra-HNWIs

4 Which of the following is a major risk associated with WealthTech adoption?

A Increased account minimums
B Algorithmic bias in automated decision-making
C Reduced access to financial data
D Declining use of data analytics

5 ESG-focused WealthTech platforms primarily enable investors to:

A Maximise short-term speculative returns
B Avoid regulatory compliance requirements
C Track financial performance alongside social and environmental impact
D Eliminate investment risk entirely

Short Questions

1 Explain how robo-advisors use client risk profiles to construct investment portfolios.
2 Briefly describe the role of Open Banking and APIs in enhancing personalised wealth management services.
3 Identify two key differences between traditional wealth management and FinTech-based wealth management models.

Analytical Questions

1 Critically evaluate the extent to which WealthTech has democratised access to wealth management services. In your answer, consider both opportunities and limitations.
2 Analyse the risks associated with over-reliance on AI in wealth management. How can hybrid advisory models mitigate these risks?
3 Discuss how predictive analytics and hyper-personalisation may reshape the future role of wealth managers. What implications does this have for client trust and regulatory oversight?

Case Study: Vanguard's Hybrid Advice Model

Vanguard, widely recognised for its leadership in low-cost index investing, has expanded its value proposition through VPAS. This hybrid wealth management model combines automated investment management with human financial advice. For an advisory fee of approximately 0.30% of AUM, clients receive portfolios constructed and monitored using algorithm-driven asset allocation, primarily invested in Vanguard exchange-traded funds. These portfolios are complemented by access to a CFP who provides personalised guidance.

The hybrid structure allows Vanguard to deliver scalable, rules-based investment discipline while also addressing more complex client needs that extend beyond portfolio construction. Human advisors play a key role in areas such as retirement planning, tax-aware decision-making, and behavioural coaching during periods of market volatility. This integration is particularly valuable for clients who seek reassurance, accountability, and contextual judgement, elements that fully automated platforms often struggle to provide.

The success of VPAS is reflected in its rapid asset growth, with hundreds of billions of dollars entrusted to the platform. This growth indicates strong investor demand for advice models that balance cost efficiency with personal interaction. Vanguard's approach illustrates how traditional asset managers can leverage FinTech without abandoning human expertise, positioning the firm competitively between pure robo-advisors and traditional high-cost advisory models.

Reference

Deloitte (2022). *The Future of Wealth Management: From Analogue to Digital*. London: Deloitte Insights.

Case Study Questions

1 What specific client needs does a hybrid model address that a pure robo-advisor (like Betterment) or a traditional human-only advisor might not?
2 How does Vanguard's brand reputation help it succeed in the hybrid advice space?
3 What are the operational challenges in scaling a service that relies on both technology and a large staff of human advisors?

Further Reading

Capgemini. (2023). *World Wealth Report 2023*. Paris: Capgemini Research Institute.
D'Acunto, F., Rossi, A.G. (2021). Robo-Advising. In: R. Rau, R. Wardrop, L. Zingales (Eds.), *The Palgrave Handbook of Technological Finance*. Cham: Palgrave Macmillan.
Deloitte (2022). *The Future of Wealth Management: From Analogue to Digital*. London: Deloitte Insights.

References

Ariff, M. (2017). Wealth Management, its Definition, Purpose, Structure and Practices. In M. Ariff, S. Mohamad (Eds.), *Islamic Wealth Management: Theory and Practice* (pp. 25–52). Cheltenham: Edward Elgar Publishing.
Arner, D. W., Barberis, J. N., & Buckley, R. P. (2020). The Evolution of FinTech: A New Post-Crisis Paradigm? In *The Cambridge Handbook of FinTech*. Cambridge: Cambridge University Press.
Barber, B. M., & Odean, T. (2013). The Behaviour of Individual Investors. In *Handbook of the Economics of Finance* (Vol. 2, pp. 1533–1570). Amsterdam: Elsevier.
Bodie, Z., Kane, A., & Marcus, A. J. (2021). *Investments* (12th ed.). New York: McGraw-Hill Education.
Capgemini. (2023). *World Wealth Report 2023*. Paris: Capgemini Research Institute.
Cumming, D., & Schweizer, D. (2016). *The FinTech Book: The Financial Technology Handbook for Investors, Entrepreneurs and Visionaries*. Chichester: Wiley.
D'Acunto, F., Rossi, A.G. (2021). Robo-Advising. In R. Rau, R. Wardrop, L. Zingales (Eds.), *The Palgrave Handbook of Technological Finance*. Palgrave Macmillan.
Deloitte. (2022). *The Future of Wealth Management: From Analogue to Digital*. London: Deloitte Insights.
Financial Stability Board (FSB). (2022). *Artificial Intelligence and Machine Learning in Financial Services*. Basel: FSB.
Gai, K., Qiu, M., & Sun, X. (2018). A Survey on FinTech. *Journal of Network and Computer Applications*, 103, 1–15.

Ozili, P. K. (2021). Digital Finance, Green Finance and Social Finance: Is There a Link? *Financial Internet Quarterly*, 17(1), 1–7.

RBC Wealth Management. (2024). Setting Up a Trust for a Global Family. Available at: https://www.rbcwealthmanagement.com/en-uk/insights/setting-up-a-trust-for-a-global-family

Tapscott, D., & Tapscott, A. (2016). *Blockchain Revolution: How the Technology Behind Bitcoin is Changing Money, Business, and the World*. New York: Penguin.

Zetzsche, D. A., Buckley, R. P., Arner, D. W., & Barberis, J. N. (2017). The RegTech Universe in Evolution. *SSRN Electronic Journal*. doi: 10.2139/ssrn.3049244

Zetzsche, D. A., Buckley, R. P., Arner, D. W., & Barberis, J. N. (2020). The Future of Open Banking. *SSSRN Electronic Journal*. doi: 10.2139

23 Blockchain and Cryptocurrency

Chapter Overview

This chapter examines the transformative influence of blockchain and cryptocurrency on contemporary finance and banking. It explains how blockchain technology, through distributed ledger technology (DLT), enables the decentralised and immutable recording of transactions, thereby enhancing transparency, security, and operational efficiency within financial systems (Tapscott & Tapscott, 2016). The chapter traces the evolution of cryptocurrencies from foundational assets such as Bitcoin (BTC) and Ethereum (ETH) to the emergence of stablecoins, highlighting their disruptive implications for payments, lending, and asset management. Particular attention is given to smart contracts and decentralisation as core mechanisms underpinning decentralised finance (DeFi), positioning it as an alternative to traditional financial services. The discussion further considers growing institutional adoption, associated opportunities, and regulatory challenges, and analyses the convergence of TradFi and DeFi as a significant structural shift in monetary and banking frameworks.

Learning Objectives

By the end of this chapter, you should be able to:

1. Understand and explain blockchain technology and cryptocurrencies, including the principles of decentralisation, transparency, and immutability.
2. Differentiate and analyse major crypto-assets such as BTC, ETH, and stablecoins in terms of design and economic function.
3. Explain and evaluate key blockchain applications in financial services, including payments, remittances, lending, and asset tokenisation, across both retail and institutional contexts.
4. Critically analyse the implications of DeFi for traditional banking and financial intermediation.
5. Evaluate institutional adoption and analyse regulatory, technological, and security challenges, including the role of central bank digital currencies (CBDCs).

DOI: 10.4324/9781003775751-27

23.1 Introduction

The financial sector is undergoing a significant and lasting transformation driven by blockchain technology and cryptocurrencies. While initially regarded by established institutions as a disruptive threat, blockchain has quickly been recognised as a vital infrastructural advancement because of its decentralisation, immutability, and transparency. These characteristics are intended to address persistent systemic issues in TradFi, especially those related to trust, efficiency, and security in systems reliant on intermediaries. Recent scholarship now identifies blockchain as a foundational innovation with the potential to redefine operational models across multiple sectors (Arner, Barberis, & Buckley, 2020).

In parallel, cryptocurrencies have evolved from being primarily speculative retail assets to becoming integral elements of institutional investment portfolios. This evolution requires established financial firms to reassess and formulate comprehensive strategies for managing and utilising digital assets. Institutional interest is reflected in the actions of global regulatory bodies and central banks, which are actively exploring ways to incorporate the benefits of digital currencies while preserving monetary stability. CBDCs have become a major area of research, aiming to combine the efficiency of digital ledger technology with necessary regulatory oversight and control (BIS, 2020).

However, this transition is marked by considerable market friction and significant challenges. Stakeholders face ongoing regulatory uncertainty that limits scalable institutional adoption, increased cybersecurity risks associated with decentralised networks, and technological obstacles such as interoperability and energy consumption. Addressing these challenges is essential for ensuring future financial stability. This chapter provides a rigorous analysis of how these technologies are transforming finance, emphasising both the disruptive forces they introduce and the strategic opportunities they offer for modernisation.

23.2 Understanding Blockchain and Cryptocurrencies

23.2.1 Definition and Architecture of Blockchain

Blockchain is a revolutionary DLT designed to record transactions securely, transparently, and immutably across a decentralised network of computers. A blockchain is a shared, immutable ledger that facilitates recording transactions and tracking assets within a business network. Each transaction is grouped into a block, cryptographically linked to the preceding one, forming an unbroken chain that ensures data integrity. Decentralisation eliminates single points of control, fostering a trustless system where transactions are validated through consensus mechanisms, such as Proof-of-Work (PoW) or Proof-of-Stake. This structure ensures that no single entity can alter historical records without network-wide agreement, making manipulation computationally impractical. The blockchain's resilience stems from its cryptographic underpinnings and decentralised validation process, which collectively prevent unauthorised modifications (Narayanan, Bonneau, Felten, Miller, & Goldfeder, 2016). By removing intermediaries, blockchain enhances efficiency, reduces fraud, and enables verifiable transparency, key attributes that underpin its applications in finance, supply chains, and digital identity. Its transformative potential lies in creating a tamper-proof system where trust is algorithmically enforced rather than institutionally mandated, reshaping how industries manage and authenticate data (Figure 23.1).

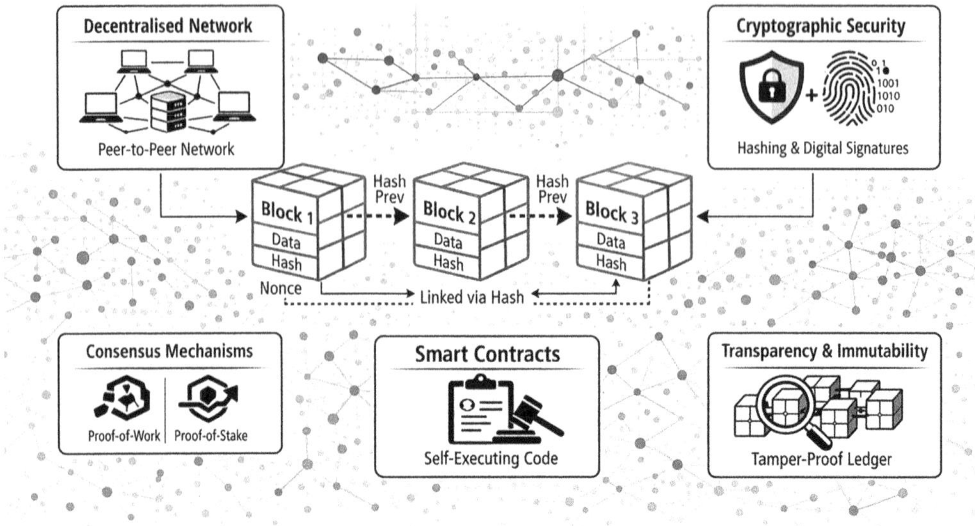

Figure 23.1 Blockchain Architecture.

23.2.2 Key Features of Blockchain

Decentralisation: A core feature of blockchain is the distribution of data and control across a peer-to-peer network rather than relying on a single central authority. This structure increases resilience, strengthens security, and reduces the risk of system failure or attacks (Yaga, Mell, Roby, & Scarfone, 2018). By sharing data across multiple nodes, blockchain ensures transparency and immutability, creating a tamper-proof record of transactions. For example, in the cryptocurrency BTC, no single institution controls the ledger; instead, every network participant maintains a copy, making it resistant to fraud and censorship while enabling secure, trustless transactions.

Immutability: A fundamental feature of blockchain, ensuring that once a transaction is recorded on the ledger, it cannot be changed or deleted. This is achieved through cryptographic hashing and consensus mechanisms, which create a secure, tamper-evident record (Narayanan et al., 2016). This feature enhances trust and transparency, making blockchain ideal for applications that require data integrity. For example, in supply chain management, a blockchain can record every step of a product's journey, from manufacturing to delivery, so that stakeholders can verify the product's origin and handling history without fear of data manipulation.

Transparency: A key feature of blockchain technology, it allows all transaction histories to be visible to participants on the network while maintaining user pseudonymity. This open and auditable ledger enables independent verification of transactions, fostering trust and accountability in a decentralised system (Catalini & Gans, 2016). For example, in cryptocurrency networks like ETH, every token transfer is recorded on the blockchain, allowing users and auditors to track and verify transactions without compromising individual identities, thereby helping prevent fraud and ensuring the integrity of the network.

Security: Security is a fundamental feature of blockchain, achieved through advanced cryptographic techniques such as hashing and digital signatures, as well as consensus mechanisms like PoW and Proof-of-Stake. These systems validate transactions immutably and protect the network against tampering or fraud, creating a resilient, trustless environment. For example, in BTC, each transaction is cryptographically verified by multiple nodes before being added to the blockchain, ensuring that records cannot be altered and preventing double-spending or unauthorised access.

Smart Contracts: Smart contracts are self-executing programmes that automatically enforce the terms of an agreement without intermediaries, reducing transaction costs and delays. They encode rules and penalties directly into the contract, ensuring impartial, automated execution that enhances trust and efficiency within blockchain networks (Szabo, 1997). For example, on the ETH blockchain, a smart contract can automatically release payment to a freelancer once a completed project is uploaded and verified, eliminating the need for a middleman and ensuring both parties fulfil their obligations.

23.2.3 Definition and Purpose of Cryptocurrency

Cryptocurrency is a form of digital or virtual currency that leverages cryptographic techniques and blockchain technology to facilitate secure, decentralised transactions without reliance on traditional financial intermediaries such as banks or governments (WEF, 2021). Cryptocurrencies are digital tokens that operate on blockchain networks, ensuring transparency, immutability, and resistance to fraud (IMF, 2022). These digital assets serve multiple purposes, including acting as a medium of exchange, a store of value, and a foundation for programmable financial applications, such as smart contracts and DeFi protocols. BTC, the first and most prominent cryptocurrency, was introduced in 2008 by the pseudonymous Satoshi Nakamoto as a response to the financial crisis, proposing a peer-to-peer electronic cash system that eliminates the need for central authority (Nakamoto, 2008). By enabling direct value transfers between parties, cryptocurrencies can reduce transaction costs, accelerate settlement times, and enhance financial inclusion, particularly for unbanked populations. Their decentralised nature, however, also presents regulatory challenges, as governments and institutions seek to balance innovation with concerns over security, volatility, and illicit use. Despite these complexities, cryptocurrencies continue to reshape global financial systems, driving discussions on the future of money and digital economies.

Figure 23.2 shows the purpose and features of cryptocurrencies.

23.2.3.1 Types of Cryptocurrencies

BTC: BTC, the pioneering cryptocurrency introduced in 2009, is often referred to as *digital gold* due to its decentralised nature, fixed supply of 21 million coins, and role as a store of value and medium of exchange. Designed by the pseudonymous Satoshi Nakamoto, BTC operates on a PoW blockchain, ensuring security and transparency. Its scarcity and widespread adoption have cemented its status as the benchmark for other cryptocurrencies. As the first mover in the space, BTC remains a foundational asset in the evolving digital economy, though its volatility and scalability challenges continue to spark debate among professionals.

ETH: ETH is a programmable blockchain platform that supports smart contracts and decentralised applications (dApps), serving as a cornerstone for the DeFi ecosystem. ETH enables developers to build and deploy applications that operate without downtime or third-party interference, underscoring its transformative role in blockchain innovation (Buterin, 2014).

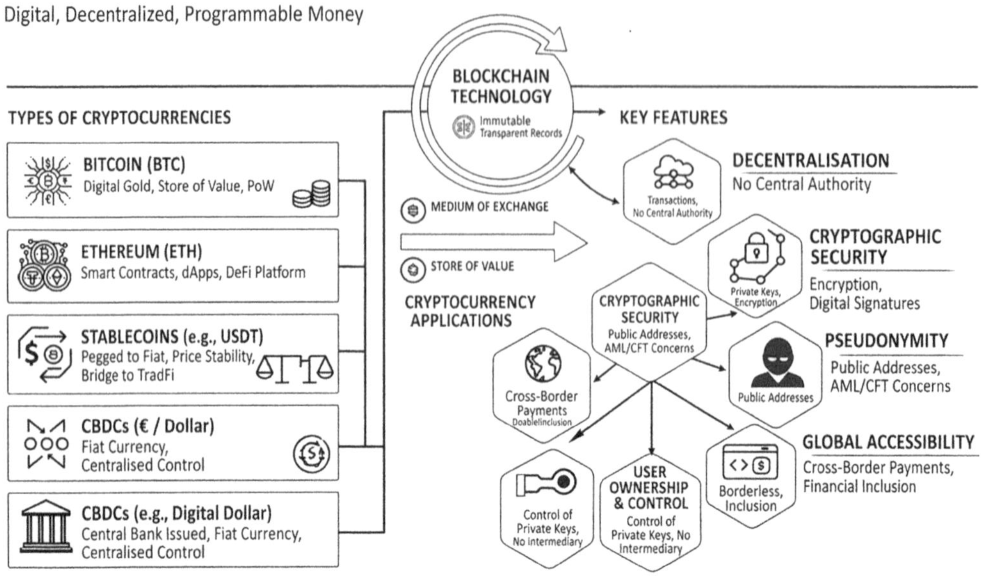

Figure 23.2 Cryptocurrency: Purpose and Features.

Stablecoins (e.g., USD Tether, USD Coin): Stablecoins, such as USDT and USDC, are digital assets pegged to stable reserves, such as the US dollar, offering price stability amid volatile markets. Stablecoins serve as a critical bridge between TradFi and the crypto ecosystem, enabling efficient transactions and liquidity management in DeFi environments (Bullmann, Klemm, & Pinna, 2019).

CBDCs: CBDCs are digital versions of a nation's fiat currency, issued and regulated by the central bank. CBDCs are a direct liability of the central bank, distinguishing them from decentralised cryptocurrencies through their centralised control and sovereign backing (BIS, 2020).

23.2.3.2 Key Features of Cryptocurrencies

Decentralisation: Cryptocurrencies are inherently decentralised, eliminating reliance on a central authority by distributing control across a peer-to-peer network. Traditional currencies depend heavily on trust in central institutions, which can create vulnerabilities (Nakamoto, 2008). In contrast, decentralisation enhances transparency and reduces systemic risk.

Blockchain Technology: Cryptocurrencies utilise blockchain, a form of DLT, to maintain secure, transparent, and immutable transaction records. By addressing the trust-based limitations of conventional currencies, blockchain enables tamper-resistant records accessible to all network participants, promoting accountability and strengthening the resilience of digital financial systems (Nakamoto, 2008).

Cryptographic Security: Cryptocurrencies use cryptography to ensure transaction integrity and confidentiality, protecting digital assets, wallets, and user identities. Through hashing and digital signatures, the network maintains a tamper-resistant and trustworthy financial system (Nakamoto, 2008).

Pseudonymity: Cryptocurrencies offer pseudonymity, allowing users to transact through public addresses rather than personal identities, providing a layer of privacy without complete anonymity. However, this raises concerns regarding Anti-Money Laundering (AML) and Counter-Terrorist Financing (CFT) compliance. At the same time, cryptocurrency transactions are not fully anonymous; pseudonymity complicates regulatory efforts to trace illicit activities (FATF, 2021). Consequently, financial institutions and regulators emphasise stronger identity verification measures to mitigate risks while preserving transactional efficiency.

Global Accessibility: A defining feature of cryptocurrencies is their global accessibility, enabling seamless, cross-border transactions for any user with internet access. By removing geographical constraints, cryptocurrencies promote financial inclusion and operational efficiency. Their decentralised structure enables individuals and businesses worldwide to transact directly, minimising costs and delays while expanding economic participation. This capability is particularly transformative in regions with limited or underdeveloped banking infrastructure.

User Ownership and Control: A fundamental aspect of cryptocurrency is user ownership and control, whereby individuals retain their private keys, granting them direct and exclusive custody of their digital assets without dependence on centralised intermediaries.

Programmability: A highly transformative feature of cryptocurrencies is their programmability. On platforms such as ETH, this capability supports the creation of self-executing smart contracts, enabling complex, automated financial agreements and dApps that extend beyond simple value transfer. This innovation allows sophisticated financial logic to operate autonomously, without intermediaries, fundamentally reshaping transactional trust and automation.

23.3 The Blockchain and Crypto in TradFi

23.3.1 FinTech Innovation: Blockchain and Cryptocurrency in Finance

The integration of blockchain and cryptocurrency into financial systems has generated several major technological innovations that are reshaping TradFi and banking.

23.3.1.1 Zero-Knowledge Proofs (ZKPs)

ZKPs are cryptographic techniques that enable one party to verify the validity of information without revealing the underlying data. In financial services, ZKPs enhance privacy while maintaining transactional integrity. For example, privacy-oriented blockchain networks such as Zcash utilise ZKPs to validate transactions without disclosing the sender, receiver, or transaction value, thereby protecting user confidentiality (Ben-Sasson et al., 2014). Zero-knowledge proofs (ZKPs) are increasingly explored in banking applications for know-your-customer (KYC) and identity verification processes. These techniques allow financial institutions to confirm customer compliance without directly accessing or storing sensitive personal information, which reduces the risk of data breaches (Deloitte, 2022).

23.3.1.2 Cross-Chain Interoperability

Cross-chain interoperability enables the transfer of assets and information across different blockchain networks, addressing fragmentation within decentralised ecosystems. Platforms such as Polkadot and Cosmos provide architectural frameworks that allow multiple blockchains to communicate securely . A notable example is Chainlink's Cross-Chain

Interoperability Protocol, which facilitates secure cross-chain transfers of tokenised assets and data between decentralised and institutional blockchain systems. This interoperability improves liquidity and capital efficiency in DeFi markets by enabling assets to be deployed across multiple blockchain environments (Chainlink, 2023).

23.3.1.3 AI-Driven Smart Contracts

AI-driven smart contracts integrate artificial intelligence with blockchain-based automation to enable dynamic contract execution. In decentralised lending and derivatives markets, AI-powered smart contracts can automatically adjust interest rates, collateral requirements, or margin thresholds in response to real-time market volatility. For example, algorithmic lending protocols use machine learning models to optimise risk assessment and pricing mechanisms, reducing default risk and enhancing capital allocation efficiency (Cong and He, 2019). This approach significantly reduces the need for manual intervention while improving scalability and responsiveness in financial markets.

23.3.1.4 Tokenisation of Real-World Assets

Tokenisation involves converting real-world assets into digital tokens recorded on a blockchain, enabling fractional ownership and improved liquidity. A prominent example is the tokenisation of real estate assets, in which blockchain platforms issue tokens representing proportional ownership of properties, allowing investors to trade them on secondary markets (Abreu, Mendes, & Santos, 2023). Similarly, tokenisation has been applied to fine art and private equity, reducing entry barriers and settlement times while broadening investor participation in traditionally illiquid markets (OECD, 2020).

23.3.2 Blockchain and Cryptocurrency Applications in Finance

Blockchain and cryptocurrency technologies have been widely adopted across financial services, leading to practical applications that transform core financial functions.

23.3.2.1 Smart Contracts

Smart contracts are self-executing agreements embedded on a blockchain that automatically enforce contractual conditions. In decentralised lending, platforms such as Aave rely on smart contracts to manage loan origination, collateral liquidation, and interest payments without bank intermediation (Schär, 2021). In the insurance sector, blockchain-based smart contracts have been deployed to automate claims processing, such as flight-delay insurance products that trigger payouts automatically when predefined conditions are met, thereby reducing administrative costs and settlement delays (Swiss Re, 2021).

23.3.2.2 Digital Currencies

Cryptocurrencies such as BTC and ETH function as decentralised digital currencies that enable peer-to-peer transactions without central authority oversight. BTC has been widely used for cross-border remittances, particularly in regions with limited banking infrastructure, due to its ability to facilitate low-cost, borderless transfers (Böhme et al., 2015). ETH extends this functionality by enabling programmable money through smart contracts, supporting DeFi applications such as lending, trading, and payments (Buterin, 2014).

23.3.2.3 *Cross-Border Payments*

Blockchain technology has significantly improved cross-border payment systems by reducing settlement times and transaction costs. For example, RippleNet enables financial institutions to process international payments in near real time using DLT, offering greater transparency and efficiency compared to traditional correspondent banking networks such as the Society for Worldwide Interbank Financial Telecommunication (Hayes, 2019). This capability improves liquidity management and reduces counterparty risk for banks engaged in international transactions.

23.3.2.4 *Decentralised Finance*

DeFi refers to blockchain-based financial services that operate without centralised intermediaries. Platforms such as Uniswap facilitate decentralised trading through automated market-making mechanisms, while Aave enables decentralised lending and borrowing via smart contracts (Schär, 2021). These platforms allow users to access financial services without traditional banking relationships, thereby promoting financial inclusion, particularly in underbanked regions (World Economic Forum, 2022).

23.3.2.5 *Fraud Prevention and Transparency*

Blockchain's immutable, transparent ledger enhances fraud prevention by enabling traceable, verifiable transaction records. In trade finance, blockchain platforms are used to track goods and payments across supply chains, reducing the risks of invoice fraud and duplicate financing (Kouhizadeh et al., 2021). Financial institutions can leverage these immutable records to improve auditing and regulatory compliance, thereby strengthening trust and accountability in financial transactions (Dierksmeier & Seele, 2020).

23.3.3 Significance of Blockchain and Cryptocurrency in Finance and Banking

The economic significance of blockchain and cryptocurrency lies in their capacity to reshape financial market structures and redefine the role of intermediaries. Asset tokenisation exemplifies this transformation by enabling the fractional ownership and trading of traditionally illiquid assets such as real estate and private equity, thereby improving market liquidity and broadening investor participation (Abreu et al., 2023). Additionally, blockchain-based compliance and regulatory technologies enhance transparency and traceability, reducing compliance costs and improving the effectiveness of AML and know-your-customer (KYC) frameworks (Dierksmeier & Seele, 2020). While regulatory uncertainty and technological risks remain, the integration of blockchain and crypto-assets into TradFi signals a structural shift towards more efficient, inclusive, and technologically resilient banking systems.

23.4 Opportunities, Challenges, and Key Issues of Blockchain and Cryptocurrency

23.4.1 Opportunities and Convergence

Blockchain and cryptocurrency create significant opportunities for TradFi by improving efficiency, promoting financial inclusion, and accelerating convergence between decentralised and conventional financial systems. Blockchain-based distributed ledgers replace fragmented record-keeping with a single, immutable source of truth, reducing reconciliation costs and settlement times while increasing transparency (Tapscott & Tapscott, 2016). Smart contracts further enhance efficiency by automating processes such as payments, clearing, and asset transfers, thereby reducing reliance on intermediaries. At the same time, decentralised financial platforms extend access to financial services for unbanked and underbanked populations by enabling savings, lending, and remittances through digital wallets, bypassing traditional barriers such as geographic isolation and high transaction fees (=. These developments contribute to a growing convergence in which traditional financial institutions adopt blockchain-based solutions to complement existing infrastructures.

23.4.2 Risks and Challenges

Despite these opportunities, the adoption of blockchain and cryptocurrency within TradFi presents substantial risks and challenges. Regulatory uncertainty remains a major constraint, as inconsistent classification of crypto-assets across jurisdictions complicates compliance with taxation, disclosure, and investor protection requirements (Arner et al., 2020). Market volatility further undermines the suitability of cryptocurrencies as stable media of exchange or stores of value, introducing significant risk for both users and financial institutions (Baur, Hong, & Lee, 2023). In addition, cybersecurity and custody risks persist, particularly due to vulnerabilities in exchanges and wallet providers, as well as the irreversible nature of private key loss, which conflicts with traditional consumer protection and asset recovery standards.

23.4.3 Key Practical Issues in Implementation

Several practical issues also limit the seamless integration of blockchain and cryptocurrency into mainstream finance. Scalability remains a critical technical challenge, as early-generation blockchains such as BTC and ETH process far fewer transactions per second than conventional payment systems, leading to congestion and elevated fees during peak demand (Croman et al., 2016). Environmental concerns associated with the energy-intensive PoW consensus mechanism further attract regulatory and ESG scrutiny, raising questions about long-term sustainability (Truby, 2018). Moreover, the lack of mature, regulatory-compliant infrastructure, including custody solutions and interoperable systems, continues to hinder institutional adoption. Addressing these practical constraints is essential for blockchain and cryptocurrency to achieve sustainable, widespread integration into traditional financial systems.

23.5 The Future Trends of Blockchain and Cryptocurrency

The future of blockchain and cryptocurrency in TradFi is increasingly characterised by convergence rather than disruption, as traditional financial institutions and DeFi platforms evolve in tandem. Rather than being displaced, incumbent financial actors are selectively adopting blockchain-based technologies to improve efficiency, transparency, and settlement speed, particularly through applications such as asset tokenisation, real-time clearing, and enhanced auditability. Concurrently, DeFi platforms are adapting to institutional and regulatory expectations by incorporating identity verification, compliance mechanisms, and more robust risk management frameworks to support scalability and institutional participation (Aramonte, Huang, & Schrimpf, 2021). This mutual adaptation is fostering the emergence of a hybrid financial ecosystem that combines the automation, programmability, and transparency of DeFi with the stability, consumer protection, and regulatory oversight associated with TradFi. As a result, the interaction between TradFi and DeFi is likely to reshape financial infrastructure and governance structures, enhancing efficiency, resilience, and financial inclusion across the global financial system rather than resulting in a zero-sum competitive outcome (Aramonte et al., 2021).

23.6 Conclusion

Blockchain technology and cryptocurrencies constitute a profound structural shift in the global financial system, replacing reliance on centralised institutional intermediaries with decentralised, cryptographically secured trust mechanisms. Through immutable and transparent distributed ledgers, these technologies enable more efficient value transfer, enhance auditability, and reduce counterparty risk. Despite these advantages, their widespread adoption remains constrained by critical challenges, including scalability limitations, fragmented and evolving regulatory frameworks, and persistent security and governance risks. Overcoming these obstacles will require coordinated efforts to strengthen technical infrastructure, enhance regulatory clarity, and build institutional trust and operational resilience.

Looking forward, the gradual convergence of DeFi and TradFi appears both inevitable and necessary for the maturation of digital financial ecosystems. Traditional institutions are increasingly leveraging blockchain to improve efficiency and transparency, while DeFi platforms are adapting to regulatory and compliance expectations. This convergence underscores the importance of collaboration among regulators, financial institutions, and technology innovators to develop balanced frameworks that promote innovation without compromising financial stability or consumer protection. Ultimately, the future of finance will be shaped by the strategic alignment of algorithmic efficiency, distributed consensus, and regulatory oversight, laying the foundation for a more inclusive, resilient, and robust global financial system.

Key Terms and Glossary

Blockchain A distributed, immutable digital ledger that records transactions securely and transparently.

Smart Contract Self-executing contracts with the terms of the agreement directly written into code, which runs on a blockchain.

DLT (Distributed Ledger Technology) A digital system for recording asset transactions where the records and their details are stored across multiple locations.

Tokenisation The process of converting rights to an asset into a digital token on a blockchain.

PoW (Proof of Work) A consensus mechanism for blockchain networks that requires participants to perform computationally intensive work to validate transactions and create new blocks.

Test Your Understanding

Multiple-Choice Questions

1 Which of the following is a key feature of blockchain that ensures recorded transactions cannot be altered?

A Decentralisation
B Transparency
C Immutability
D Programmability

2 Which cryptocurrency platform is primarily known for enabling smart contracts and dApps?

A BTC
B ETH
C USDT
D Ripple (XRP)

3 What is a primary advantage of tokenising real-world assets using blockchain?

A Complete anonymity of transactions
B Fractional ownership and improved liquidity
C Elimination of regulatory compliance
D Guaranteed returns on investment

4 Which of the following represents a key challenge of integrating blockchain into TradFi?

A Increased transaction speed
B Regulatory uncertainty
C Reduced reconciliation costs
D Enhanced transparency

5 Which statement best describes the future convergence of TradFi and DeFi?

A DeFi will fully replace all traditional banks.
B TradFi will ignore blockchain technologies.
C A hybrid ecosystem will emerge, combining DeFi automation with TradFi oversight.
D Blockchain will remain only for speculative purposes.

Short Questions

1 Define blockchain and explain its core features that contribute to trust in financial systems.
2 What are stablecoins, and how do they facilitate the integration of cryptocurrency into traditional financial systems?
3 Identify two practical challenges that limit widespread blockchain adoption in mainstream finance.

Analytical Questions

1 Discuss how smart contracts and DeFi could alter the traditional lending and borrowing model in banking.
2 Evaluate the economic significance of asset tokenisation and its potential impact on market liquidity and investor participation.
3 Analyse the potential benefits and risks associated with the convergence of TradFi and DeFi for global financial stability.

Case Study: JPMorgan Chase and JPM Coin

JPMorgan Chase, one of the world's largest and most systemically important financial institutions, has embraced blockchain technology through its dedicated Onyx division. Rather than adopting public, permissionless networks such as BTC or ETH, JPMorgan has developed JPM Coin, a private, permissioned blockchain designed specifically for institutional use. JPM Coin facilitates the real-time transfer of U.S. dollars between approved JPMorgan client accounts and is primarily used for wholesale payment activities, including securities settlement, interbank transfers, and corporate treasury operations.

Unlike traditional payment infrastructure, which often relies on intermediaries and batch processing, JPM Coin enables near-instant settlement, reducing transaction times from days to seconds. This increased speed enhances liquidity management and lowers operational and counterparty risk for both the bank and its corporate clients. Access to the network is tightly controlled, with participation limited to verified institutional users, ensuring compliance with regulatory requirements such as AML and KYC standards.

This case illustrates how a traditional financial institution can integrate blockchain technology to improve efficiency and transparency without abandoning centralised governance or regulatory oversight. Rather than disrupting existing structures, JPM Coin demonstrates how blockchain can be adapted to support established financial systems, raising important questions about decentralisation, control, and the evolving role of blockchain within regulated banking environments (Baur et al., 2023).

Reference

Baur, D.G., Hong, K., & Lee, A.D. (2023). Bitcoin: A Haven and Diversifier for Traditional Assets? *Journal of International Financial Markets, Institutions and Money*, 82, 101708.

Case Study Questions

1 In what ways does a private, permissioned blockchain such as JPM Coin differ from public blockchains like BTC or ETH, and why is this model more appropriate for a highly regulated financial institution?
2 What advantages does the use of JPM Coin offer to JPMorgan's corporate clients when conducting large-scale or wholesale transactions?
3 Does JPM Coin reflect true blockchain decentralisation, or is it mainly a faster, more efficient centralised system? Explain your view.

Further Reading

BIS (Bank for International Settlements). (2020). *Central Bank Digital Currencies: Foundational Principles and Core Features*. Basel: BIS.

Narayanan, A., Bonneau, J., Felten, E., Miller, A., & Goldfeder, S. (2016). *Bitcoin and Cryptocurrency Technologies: A Comprehensive Introduction*. Princeton: Princeton University Press.

Schär, F. (2021). Decentralized Finance: On Blockchain- and Smart Contract-Based Financial Markets. *Federal Reserve Bank of St. Louis Review*, 103(2), 153–174.

References

Abreu, M., Mendes, V., & Santos, J. (2023). Tokenisation of Assets: A Review of the Literature and Future Research Agenda. *Journal of Financial Transformation*, 57, 1–12.

Aramonte, S., Huang, W., & Schrimpf, A. (2021). DeFi Risks and the Decentralisation Illusion. *BIS Quarterly Review*, September, pp. 1–14.

Arner, D.W., Barberis, J.N., & Buckley, R.P. (2020). The Evolution of FinTech: A New Post-Crisis Paradigm? In *The Cambridge Handbook of FinTech*. Cambridge: Cambridge University Press.

Baur, D.G., Hong, K., & Lee, A.D. (2023). Bitcoin: A Haven and Diversifier for Traditional Assets? *Journal of International Financial Markets, Institutions and Money*, 84, 1–14.

Ben-Sasson, E., Chiesa, A., Garman, C., Green, M., Miers, I., Tromer, E. and Virza, M. (2014) 'Zerocash: Decentralized anonymous payments from Bitcoin', *2014 IEEE Symposium on Security and Privacy*. San Jose, CA: IEEE, pp. 459–474. doi: 10.1109/SP.2014.36

BIS (Bank for International Settlements). (2020). *Central Bank Digital Currencies: Foundational Principles and Core Features*. Basel: BIS.

Böhme, R., Christin, N., Edelman, B. and Moore, T. (2015) 'Bitcoin: Economics, technology, and governance', *Journal of Economic Perspectives*, 29(2), pp. 213–238

Bullmann, D., Klemm, J., & Pinna, A. (2019). In Search for Stability in Crypto Assets: Are Stablecoins the Solution? *ECB Occasional Paper Series*.

Buterin, V. (2014). Ethereum: A Next-Generation Smart Contract and Decentralised Application Platform. *Ethereum White Paper*.

Catalini, C., & Gans, J.S. (2016). Some Simple Economics of the Blockchain. *NBER Working Paper*. No. 22952. Cambridge, MA: National Bureau of Economic Research.

Chainlink (2023) *Cross-Chain Interoperability Protocol (CCIP): Technical Overview and Documentation*. Chainlink Labs. Available at: https://chain.link/cross-chain

Croman, K., et al. (2016). On Scaling Decentralised Blockchains. In *Financial Cryptography and Data Security*. Berlin: Springer, pp. 106–125.

Cong, L. W. and He, Z. (2019) 'Blockchain disruption and smart contracts', *Review of Financial Studies*, 32(5), 1754–1797.

Dierksmeier, C., & Seele, P. (2020). Blockchain and Business Ethics. *Business Ethics: A European Review*, 29(2), 324–336.

Deloitte (2022) *The future of wealth management: From analogue to digital*. London: Deloitte Insights.

FATF (Financial Action Task Force). (2021). *Updated Guidance for a Risk-Based Approach to Virtual Assets and Virtual Asset Service Providers*. Paris: FATF.

Hayes, A. (2019). The Socio-Technological Impact of Blockchain Technology on the Future of Banking and Financial Services. *Journal of Risk and Financial Management*, 12(3), 1–20.

IMF (International Monetary Fund). (2022). *The Crypto Ecosystem and Financial Stability Challenges*. Washington, D.C.: International Monetary Fund.

Kouhizadeh, M., Sarkis, J. and Zhu, Q. (2021) 'At the nexus of blockchain technology and sustainable supply chain management: A literature review', *International Journal of Production Research*, 59(7), 2300–2325.

Nakamoto, S. (2008). *Bitcoin: A Peer-to-Peer Electronic Cash System*. Available at: https://bitcoin.org/bitcoin.pdf

Narayanan, A., Bonneau, J., Felten, E., Miller, A., & Goldfeder, S. (2016). *Bitcoin and Cryptocurrency Technologies: A Comprehensive Introduction*. Princeton, NJ: Princeton University Press.

OECD (2020) *The Tokenisation of Assets and Potential Implications for Financial Markets*. Paris: Organisation for Economic Co-operation and Development.

Schär, F. (2021). Decentralised Finance: On Blockchain- and Smart Contract-Based Financial Markets. *Federal Reserve Bank of St. Louis Review*, 103(2), 153–174.

Swiss Re Institute. (2021). *Blockchain and Smart Contracts in Insurance: A New Era of Automated Insurance Solutions*. Zurich: Swiss Re Institute. Available at: https://www.swissre.com/institute/

Szabo, N. (1997). Formalising and Securing Relationships on Public Networks. *First Monday*, 2(9). doi: 10.5210/fm.v2i9.548

Tapscott, D., & Tapscott, A. (2016). *Blockchain Revolution: How the Technology Behind Bitcoin is Changing Money, Business, and the World*. New York: Penguin.

Truby, J. (2018). Decarbonising Bitcoin: Law and Policy Choices for Reducing the Energy Consumption of Blockchain Technologies and Digital Currencies. *Energy Research & Social Science*, 44, 219–226.

WEF (World Economic Forum). (2021). *Crypto, What Is It Good For?* Geneva: World Economic Forum.

World Economic Forum (2022) *The Future of Financial Inclusion in the Digital Economy*. Geneva: World Economic Forum.

Yaga, D., Mell, P., Roby, N., & Scarfone, K. (2018). *Blockchain Technology Overview*. NIST Interagency/Internal Report 8202. Gaithersburg, MD: National Institute of Standards and Technology. doi: 10.6028/NIST.IR.8202

24 Artificial Intelligence (AI) in Finance and Banking

Chapter Overview

This chapter critically examines the transformative role of Artificial Intelligence (AI) in the finance and banking sectors. AI has shifted from a futuristic concept to an operational necessity. It enhances decision-making, optimises risk management, and deepens customer engagement (Varshney, 2022). The discussion details how core AI technologies, Machine Learning (ML), Natural Language Processing (NLP), and Robotic Process Automation (RPA), are applied in high-stakes functions. These include sophisticated fraud detection, dynamic credit scoring, and advanced algorithmic trading. Deploying these technologies requires careful consideration of ethical, regulatory, and operational challenges. The analysis concludes with a strategic roadmap for human-AI collaboration, autonomous finance systems, and robust standards for Explainable Artificial Intelligence (XAI).

Learning Objectives

By the end of this chapter, you should be able to:

1 Explain the fundamental concepts, technologies, and methods underpinning AI in finance.
2 Identify and evaluate key applications of AI in banking, including fraud detection, credit scoring, algorithmic trading, and customer service.
3 Assess the benefits and operational impact of AI on efficiency, decision-making, and personalised banking.
4 Critically examine the risks, challenges, and ethical considerations of AI, including algorithmic bias, data privacy, and transparency.
5 Explore emerging trends and real-world case studies, including XAI, autonomous finance, and human-AI collaboration in financial institutions.

DOI: 10.4324/9781003775751-28

24.1 Introduction

The integration of AI is fundamentally transforming operational and strategic paradigms in the banking and finance industries. This transformation is marked by the automation of complex processes, resulting in substantial efficiency gains and a redefined client experience. The effects are particularly apparent in customer-facing services, where chatbots and virtual assistants deliver continuous, around-the-clock support and facilitate prompt query resolution. The adoption of these AI technologies alters the nature of interactions between financial institutions and clients, fostering greater accessibility and responsiveness (Borges, Laurindo, Spínola, Gonçalves, & Mattos, 2021).

In addition to improving operational throughput, AI offers significant value through advanced data analysis capabilities. AI systems can efficiently process large datasets to identify subtle, non-obvious patterns and trends essential to effective oversight. This analytical capacity is critical for precise risk assessment and the deployment of real-time fraud detection systems. By proactively detecting anomalies and continuously refining security protocols, AI reduces financial losses and strengthens institutional security. This data-driven approach to security and risk management is essential for maintaining stability in the contemporary financial sector (Deloitte, 2023).

From a strategic perspective, AI is facilitating a significant shift towards highly personalised financial services. By analysing detailed client behaviour, institutions use AI to deliver tailored recommendations that enhance customer satisfaction and promote loyalty. In specialised domains such as investment and lending, AI-driven predictive analytics supports decision-making by enabling more accurate portfolio optimisation and improved decision quality. As AI applications continue to develop, strategic adoption is increasingly vital for institutions aiming to sustain competitiveness in a rapidly evolving, data-driven financial environment.

24.2 Understanding Artificial Intelligence

24.2.1 Definition and Purpose

AI in finance and banking refers to the application of advanced computational technologies, including ML, NLP, and computer vision, to automate processes, analyse large volumes of data, and generate actionable insights (Russell & Norvig, 2021). AI systems can learn from historical and real-time data, recognise patterns, and make predictions, enabling financial institutions to enhance operational efficiency, manage risks more effectively, and improve the customer experience (Brynjolfsson & McAfee, 2017). Key applications of AI in finance include fraud detection, credit risk assessment, regulatory compliance, algorithmic trading, and customer service automation. By leveraging AI, banks and financial firms can deliver services that are faster, more secure, and increasingly personalised, reflecting a broader shift towards data-driven, intelligent financial operations (Agrawal, Gans, & Goldfarb, 2018).

24.2.2 Key Characteristics of Artificial Intelligence

AI systems are defined by a set of traits that collectively enable machines to perform tasks traditionally associated with human intelligence, adapt to new data, and operate autonomously across complex domains (Goodfellow, Bengio, & Courville, 2016).

Feature Engineering: Feature engineering constitutes a core methodological component of AI, enabling systems to systematically identify, transform, and select the most informative variables from high-dimensional datasets to enhance predictive performance. By refining input features, AI models can reduce noise, mitigate multicollinearity, and improve generalisation capacity. Dimensionality reduction and orthogonalisation techniques, such as Principal Component Analysis and Gram–Schmidt orthogonalisation, are frequently employed to eliminate redundancy and construct uncorrelated feature sets, thereby strengthening computational efficiency and model accuracy (Hastie, Tibshirani, & Friedman, 2009).

Artificial Neural Networks (ANNs): ANNs emulate the structure of the human brain by connecting layers of neurons to process information. Variants include feedforward networks, which process information unidirectionally, and recurrent networks, which maintain memory of previous inputs. Optimisation methods, including pruning, quantisation, and knowledge distillation, are applied to improve efficiency without compromising accuracy (LeCun, Bengio, & Hinton, 2015).

Deep Learning: Deep Learning is an extension of ANNs with multiple hidden layers, enabling automatic feature extraction and achieving superior performance in tasks such as image recognition, speech processing, and autonomous systems. These models often rely on high-performance computing resources, particularly Graphics Processing Units, to manage computational complexity (Goodfellow et al., 2016).

NLP: NLP allows AI systems to interpret and generate human language, supporting applications such as chatbots, virtual assistants, automated translation, and sentiment analysis. NLP converts spoken or written language into structured machine-readable formats, facilitating communication and decision-making in financial contexts (Jurafsky & Martin, 2021).

Perception: The ability of AI to interpret sensory data from cameras, microphones, and other input devices. Applications include computer vision for facial recognition, object detection, and scene understanding, which are increasingly deployed in banking for identity verification and fraud prevention (Szeliski, 2020).

Automation: Automation of Repetitive Tasks is another core characteristic, exemplified by virtual assistants and RPA, which can manage scheduling, transaction processing, and routine inquiries, thereby reducing operational costs and human error.

Data Ingestion: Enables AI systems to collect, integrate, and process massive datasets in real time, generating actionable insights for decision-making in trading, risk management, and customer service. Emerging capabilities such as quantum computing, cloud-based AI deployment, and intelligent robotics further enhance the scale, speed, and autonomy of AI applications in finance (Arute et al., 2019; Chen, Kornblith, Norouzi, & Hinton, 2020) (Figure 24.1).

24.3 Key AI Technologies Driving Change in Finance and Banking

AI is driving a profound transformation in finance and banking by enabling intelligent automation, advanced data analytics, and predictive decision-making. Several AI subfields

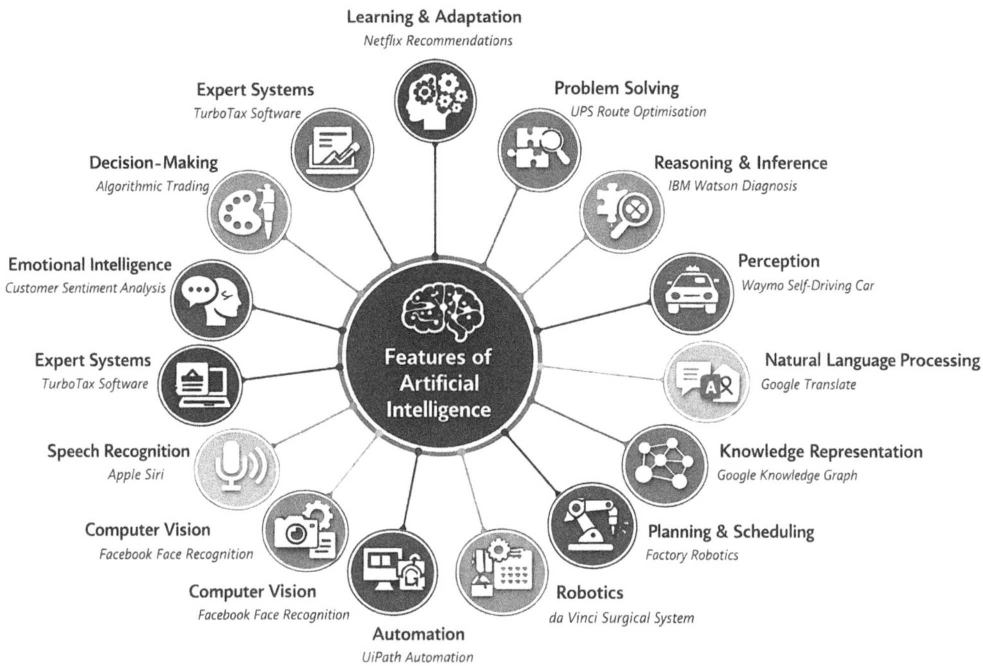

Figure 24.1 Key Feature of Artificial Intelligence.

contribute to a layered technology stack that converts raw data into actionable insights, supporting operational efficiency, risk management, and customer-centric services (Russell & Norvig, 2021).

24.3.1 Machine Learning

ML, a core branch of AI, allows systems to identify patterns in data and generate predictions or decisions without explicit programming (Bishop, 2006). In financial services, ML is widely used for credit risk assessment, fraud detection, and algorithmic trading. For instance, Lloyds Bank employs ML algorithms to monitor transactional behaviour in real time, detecting anomalies that may indicate fraudulent activity and enabling rapid intervention. Similarly, ML-based credit scoring models evaluate borrower risk more accurately than traditional methods, facilitating faster loan approvals and reducing default rates, thereby enhancing both efficiency and decision quality (West & Bhattacharya, 2016).

24.3.2 Natural Language Processing

NLP enables computers to interpret, process, and generate human language in a context-aware manner, supporting enhanced decision-making and customer interactions (Hirschberg & Manning, 2015). Financial institutions leverage NLP for chatbots, sentiment analysis, and compliance automation. For example, the Royal Bank of Scotland uses an NLP-powered virtual assistant to provide 24/7 customer support, handling account and transaction queries. Investment firms also employ NLP to analyse news and social media for market sentiment, guiding trading decisions. At the same time, compliance teams use NLP to automatically review contracts and regulatory documents, reducing human error and accelerating workflows.

24.3.3 Robotic Process Automation

RPA employs software robots to automate repetitive, rule-based tasks across financial operations, including data entry, transaction processing, report generation, and compliance monitoring (van der Aalst, Bichler, & Heinzl, 2018). By reducing manual intervention, RPA decreases operational costs and error rates while allowing employees to focus on strategic tasks. HSBC, for example, uses RPA to automate mortgage application processing, validate customer data, and generate reports efficiently, improving turnaround times and enhancing staff roles in risk assessment and customer advisory services.

24.3.4 Deep Learning

Deep learning, an advanced subset of ML, uses multi-layered neural networks to analyse complex, high-dimensional, and unstructured data (LeCun et al., 2015). In finance, deep learning underpins applications such as real-time fraud detection, predictive market analysis, and AI-powered virtual assistants. Citibank employs deep learning to monitor millions of daily transactions, identifying suspicious behaviour faster than conventional systems. Deep learning also enables personalised financial guidance through AI-driven assistants, improving both customer experience and security in banking services.

24.3.5 Algorithmic Trading

AI-driven algorithmic trading automates trade execution based on data-driven strategies that analyse historical and real-time market data, as well as sentiment from news and social media, to optimise trading decisions (Bodie, Kane, & Marcus, 2021). Hedge funds such as Renaissance Technologies utilise these AI algorithms to exploit market inefficiencies, executing thousands of trades per second with minimal human intervention. This integration of speed, adaptive learning, and predictive analytics enhances market efficiency, scalability, and overall trading performance.

24.3.6 Personalised Banking and Customer Service

AI has transformed customer engagement by enabling highly personalised banking services tailored to individual behaviours, financial goals, and preferences. Virtual assistants and predictive analytics allow banks to provide proactive guidance, transaction alerts, and budgeting advice. For example, Bank of America's Erica delivers personalised spending insights, while Capital One's Eno monitors accounts to detect unusual activity in real time. AI recommendation engines analyse customer data to suggest suitable financial products or investment strategies, shifting banking from reactive service to proactive financial partnership and strengthening client relationships (Kumar, Dixit, Javalgi, & Dass, 2019).

24.4 Artificial Intelligence in Finance and Banking

AI is increasingly transforming finance and banking by enabling automation, predictive analytics, and data-driven decision-making across a wide range of operations. AI applications improve efficiency, enhance customer experience, mitigate risk, and support regulatory compliance (Russell & Norvig, 2021). This section examines the key applications of AI, including credit scoring, regulatory compliance, algorithmic trading, workflow automation, fraud detection, and investment management, highlighting practical examples and their impacts (Figure 24.2).

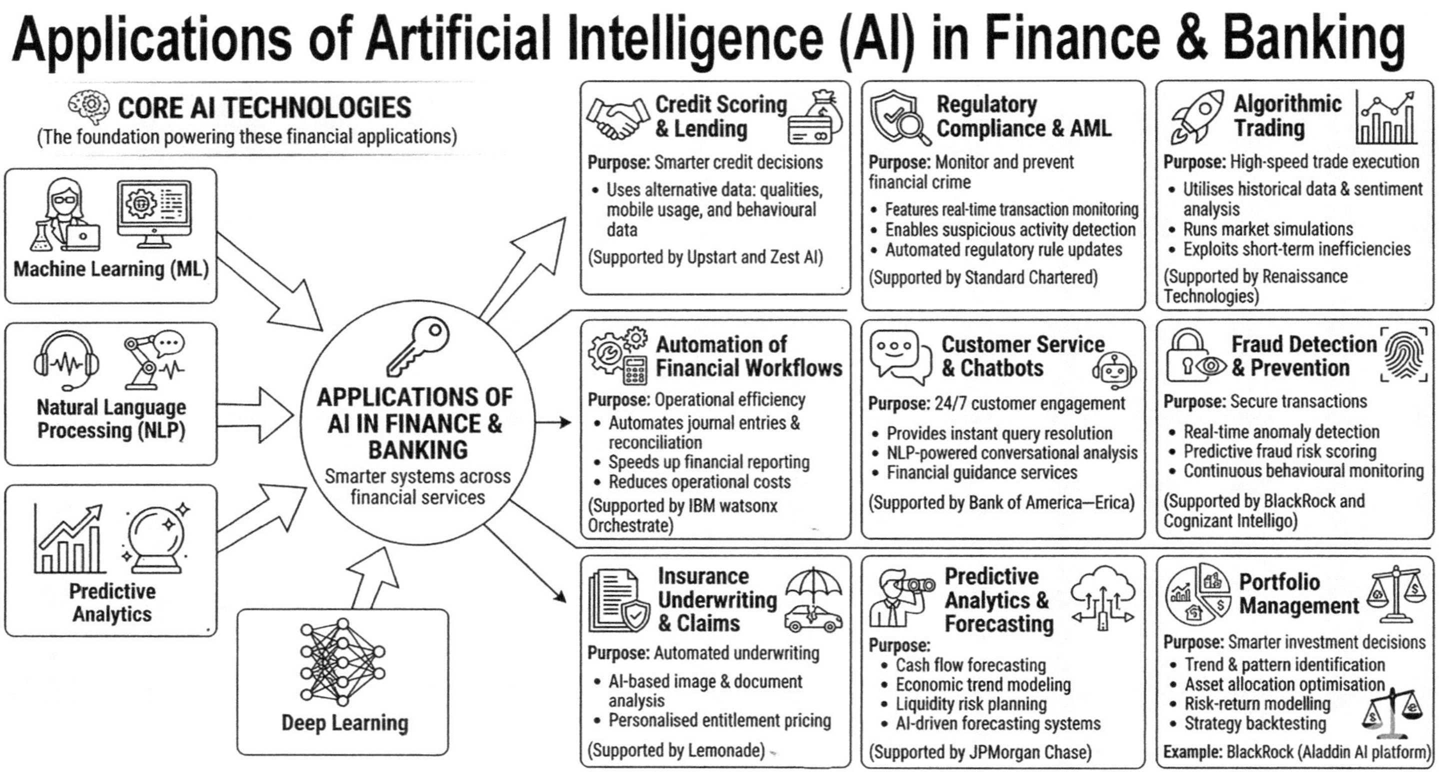

Figure 24.2 Artificial Intelligence in Finance and Banking.

24.4.1 Credit Scoring and Lending

AI enhances credit scoring and lending by expanding the scope of risk assessment beyond traditional financial data. ML algorithms can integrate alternative data, such as utility payments, mobile phone activity, and social media behaviour, to generate more comprehensive credit profiles (Bartram, Branke, & Motahari, 2023). For example, Upstart, a US-based lending platform, uses AI-driven models to assess borrower risk, enabling greater access to personal loans for individuals with limited credit histories. Similarly, Zest AI applies ML to reduce bias in lending decisions, promoting fairer credit allocation. Credit unions employing AI for underwriting have reported a 40% increase in approvals for women and minority applicants (Bartram et al., 2023). Such applications improve financial inclusion, lower default risks, and increase the efficiency of lending operations.

24.4.2 Regulatory Compliance and Anti-Money Laundering (AML)

AI significantly enhances regulatory compliance and AML efforts by automating the monitoring and detection of suspicious financial activities. ML and NLP algorithms can analyse millions of transactions in real time, identifying unusual patterns indicative of fraud or money laundering (Zetzsche et al., 2017). Standard Chartered, for instance, deploys AI systems to monitor daily transactions across its global accounts, automatically flagging suspicious activity and reducing false positives. Additionally, AI tools can scan and interpret regulatory texts to update internal compliance policies, ensuring institutions remain aligned with evolving legal frameworks (Kokina & Davenport, 2017). This reduces manual workload, enhances the accuracy of compliance operations, and enables faster responses to potential regulatory breaches.

24.4.3 Algorithmic Trading

Algorithmic trading leverages AI to automate trade execution, using historical market data, news sentiment, and real-time price movements to optimise strategies. Reinforcement learning models simulate market scenarios and dynamically adapt to changing conditions, improving decision-making speed and accuracy (Bodie et al., 2021). Hedge funds such as Renaissance Technologies employ AI-driven trading algorithms to execute thousands of trades per second, exploiting market inefficiencies and improving profitability while managing risk. By combining predictive analytics with high-speed execution, algorithmic trading significantly enhances market efficiency and supports sophisticated investment strategies.

24.4.4 Automation of Financial Workflows

AI-powered workflow automation optimises repetitive financial operations, such as expense management, journal entries, and reporting. For instance, IBM's Watsonx Orchestrate® automates journal entry processes, reducing cycle times by over 90% and generating annual savings of approximately USD 600,000 (IBM, 2023). This automation reduces operational costs, mitigates errors, and allows human employees to focus on higher-value analytical or strategic tasks, thereby improving organisational productivity and scalability.

24.4.5 Customer Service and Chatbots

AI-driven chatbots and virtual assistants enhance customer service by providing 24/7 support for routine inquiries and transactions. NLP enables these systems to interpret and respond to customer queries accurately. Bank of America's Erica chatbot, for example, has handled over two billion interactions, assisting customers with balance inquiries, bill payments, and financial advice (Kumar et al., 2019). Such systems improve response times, increase accessibility, and allow human agents to address complex cases, ultimately enhancing customer satisfaction and operational efficiency.

24.4.6 Fraud Detection and Prevention

AI improves fraud detection by using predictive analytics and deep learning algorithms to identify unusual transaction patterns in real time. Credit card companies, for instance, deploy AI to detect abnormal spending, such as unexpected purchases abroad, preventing unauthorised transactions (Bose & Mahapatra, 2022). Financial institutions using AI for fraud detection report higher accuracy, faster investigation times, and fewer false positives, thereby enhancing overall security and customer trust.

24.4.7 Insurance Underwriting and Claims Processing

AI transforms insurance operations by automating underwriting and claims workflows through NLP and image recognition. AI systems can analyse documents and photos rapidly, allowing faster risk assessment, personalised policy pricing, and quicker claims settlements. For example, AI-based platforms can evaluate car damage images or textual claim forms within seconds, accelerating approvals for routine claims such as windshield repairs (PwC, 2021). This improves operational efficiency, reduces human error, and strengthens fraud detection capabilities.

24.4.8 Portfolio Management and Investment Strategies

AI is increasingly employed in portfolio management to identify market trends, optimise asset allocation, and provide actionable investment insights. A 2025 survey indicates that 91% of asset managers are using or planning to use AI for portfolio construction and research, up from 55% in 2023 (CFA Institute, 2025). AI systems enable both institutional and retail investors to access advanced investment strategies previously available only to professional traders, promoting better-informed decisions and more efficient capital allocation.

24.4.9 Predictive Analytics and Forecasting

Predictive analytics applies AI models to historical financial data to anticipate future trends, support cash flow management, and optimise strategic decision-making. AI-driven forecasting tools analyse economic indicators and market patterns to provide actionable insights for investment and liquidity planning (Davenport & Ronanki, 2018). Financial institutions leveraging predictive analytics can enhance operational efficiency, mitigate risk, and improve the allocation of financial resources.

24.5 Opportunity, Challenges, and Key Practical Issues

24.5.1 Opportunities and Convergence of AI in Finance

AI is transforming finance by enabling faster, more accurate, and data-driven decision-making across risk management, investment, compliance, and customer engagement. By analysing large datasets in real time, AI generates actionable insights that enhance operational efficiency and mitigate risks (Financial Stability Board, 2022). For example, JPMorgan Chase uses AI to monitor millions of transactions and detect fraud in real time. ML also leverages historical patterns to forecast market trends and credit risk, as demonstrated by HSBC's predictive credit assessments (Brynjolfsson & McAfee, 2017).

AI automates repetitive processes such as transaction reconciliation, data entry, and regulatory reporting, reducing operational costs and errors while allowing staff to focus on high-value tasks (Bughin et al., 2017). Customer-facing AI, including chatbots and virtual assistants, provides personalised, 24/7 support. Bank of America's Erica virtual assistant exemplifies AI's role in improving customer experience through proactive financial guidance (Huang & Rust, 2021). Collectively, these applications highlight the convergence of AI with traditional finance, supporting efficiency, scalability, and enhanced client services.

24.5.2 Risks and Challenges in AI Adoption

Despite its benefits, AI introduces ethical, operational, and systemic risks. Algorithmic bias remains a key concern, as models trained on historical data may replicate discriminatory practices in credit scoring and lending (Mehrabi, Morstatter, Saxena, Lerman, & Galstyan, 2021). Lack of transparency in complex models ("black box" AI) complicates regulatory compliance and stakeholder trust (Adadi & Berrada, 2018). Data privacy is another critical issue, requiring strict safeguards to comply with GDPR and CCPA while protecting sensitive financial information (Finck, 2023). Over-reliance on AI can also create systemic risks, where model errors or adversarial attacks propagate across interconnected financial systems (Buchanan, 2019). Mitigation requires human oversight, ethical AI frameworks, and robust governance.

24.5.3 Key Practical Issues in AI Implementation

Practical AI deployment depends on systems' ability to learn, adapt, and handle complexity efficiently. AI must operate in uncertain environments, respond to dynamic environments, and interact effectively with users and other systems (Russell & Norvig, 2021). Context dependence and multi-disciplinary integration are essential to ensure relevance and robustness, while goal-oriented design aligns AI outputs with institutional objectives. Addressing these practical considerations ensures AI enhances risk management, operational efficiency, financial inclusion, and customer engagement, while maintaining ethical and regulatory standards.

24.6 The Road Ahead of Artificial Intelligence

The future of AI in finance will be shaped by the adoption of explainable models, autonomous systems, and enhanced human-AI collaboration. XAI aims to make AI decisions transparent, interpretable, and auditable, addressing the "black box" problem associated with complex ML models used in credit scoring, fraud detection, and algorithmic trading (Gunning et al., 2019). XAI enhances accountability, regulatory compliance, and stakeholder trust by enabling institutions to validate outcomes, support audits, and ensure adherence to frameworks such as the EU's right-to-explanation requirements. By demystifying AI processes, XAI fosters responsible deployment and strengthens customer confidence in automated financial decision-making.

Autonomous Finance represents the evolution towards hyper-personalised, fully automated financial management. In this paradigm, AI systems independently monitor and optimise clients' financial ecosystems, managing savings, payments, and investment portfolios in real time while adapting to market conditions and individual objectives (Davenport & Ronanki, 2018). Such autonomous systems are poised to enhance operational efficiency, improve financial outcomes, and transform the client-advisor dynamic by shifting from assisted decision-making to fully delegated, data-driven management.

Finally, Human-AI Collaboration, or augmented intelligence, emphasises the complementary strengths of AI and human expertise. While AI excels at large-scale data processing, predictive analytics, and pattern recognition, humans contribute contextual judgement, strategic insight, and ethical oversight (Raisch & Krakowski, 2021). This synergistic model enhances decision quality, promotes innovation, and mitigates ethical and operational risks, ensuring that AI amplifies rather than replaces human capabilities in financial services. Collectively, these trends indicate a future in which AI adoption is characterised by transparency, autonomy, and collaboration, reshaping operational models and client experiences across the financial sector.

24.7 Conclusion

In conclusion, AI has profoundly transformed the finance and banking sector, emerging as a central driver of digital innovation. Technologies such as ML, NLP, and deep learning are no longer futuristic concepts; they are essential tools that enhance operational efficiency, strengthen security measures, and enable highly personalised customer experiences. Beyond mere automation, AI serves as a critical enabler of advanced risk modelling, real-time fraud detection, and streamlined regulatory compliance. AI is not just an upgrade; it is a complete reinvention of how financial services are created and delivered.

Yet the rapid integration of AI also introduces complex governance and ethical challenges that require careful and proactive management. Financial institutions must address issues such as algorithmic bias, model explainability, data privacy, and systemic risks arising from interconnected automated systems. Neglecting these concerns risks eroding consumer trust, inviting regulatory scrutiny, and undermining AI's transformative potential. The institutions that will thrive are those that deploy AI not solely for efficiency or cost reduction but to cultivate intelligent, equitable, and resilient financial ecosystems. Achieving this requires a steadfast commitment to responsible innovation, embedding ethical principles, transparency, and accountability throughout the AI lifecycle. Finally, prioritising these values will not only safeguard public confidence but also lay the foundation for sustainable competitive advantage in the evolving financial landscape.

Key Terms and Glossary

ML (Machine Learning) A subset of AI that enables systems to learn and improve from experience without being explicitly programmed.

NLP (Natural Language Processing) A branch of AI that helps computers understand, interpret, and manipulate human language.

Algorithmic Bias Systematic and repeatable errors in a computer system that create unfair outcomes, such as privileging one arbitrary group of users over others.

XAI (Explainable Artificial Intelligence) Methods and techniques that make the outputs of AI models understandable to humans.

RPA (Robotic Process Automation) The use of software robots to automate highly repetitive, routine tasks typically performed by humans.

Test Your Understanding

Multiple-Choice Questions

1 Which AI technology is primarily used for analysing unstructured data and enabling applications like voice assistants and image recognition in finance?

A RPA
B ML
C Deep Learning
D Predictive Analytics

2 Which of the following is a key benefit of AI-driven credit scoring over traditional methods?

A Reduces all operational costs to zero
B Incorporates alternative data to improve accuracy and financial inclusion
C Eliminates the need for regulatory compliance
D Automatically guarantees loan approval

3 Which AI application is most closely associated with real-time detection of suspicious financial activity?

A Customer service chatbots
B Fraud detection and AML systems
C Algorithmic trading
D Portfolio management

4 What is the primary goal of XAI in the financial sector?

A Fully automate all banking operations without human oversight
B Make AI decision-making transparent, interpretable, and auditable
C Increase transaction speed without regulatory compliance
D Replace all financial analysts with AI.

5 Which of the following best describes the concept of "augmented intelligence" in finance?

A AI systems making decisions independently of humans
B Humans performing all decisions without AI support
C AI and humans collaborating, combining computational power with judgement and ethical oversight
D Replacing all human decision-makers with AI algorithms

Short Questions

1 Define RPA and provide one example of its application in banking.
2 Explain how AI improves predictive credit risk assessment compared to traditional scoring models.
3 Identify two ethical or operational challenges associated with AI adoption in finance.

Analytical Questions

1 Critically evaluate the impact of AI-driven algorithmic trading on market efficiency and systemic risk. Provide examples of real-world applications.

2 Discuss how XAI can enhance stakeholder trust and regulatory compliance in financial institutions. What challenges might institutions face in implementing XAI?
3 Analyse the role of AI in transforming customer service within banking. How does the integration of chatbots and virtual assistants balance efficiency, personalisation, and customer trust?

Case Study: DBS Bank's AI-Powered Transformation

Singapore's DBS Bank has embraced an ambitious "AI-first" strategy, implementing over 1,500 AI models across more than 370 business applications. These range from AI-powered chatbots that enhance customer service and engagement to AI-driven credit scoring systems, real-time fraud detection, and algorithmic trading platforms. By embedding AI into its operations, DBS has not only achieved substantial economic gains, reportedly exceeding SGD 370 million in 2023, but has also accelerated project deployment timelines, improved operational efficiency, and strengthened decision-making capabilities across the organisation.

To ensure responsible and sustainable AI usage, DBS has adopted the P-U-R-E ethical framework, which emphasises Proportionality, Understandability, Respect, and Explainability. This framework guides the design, deployment, and monitoring of AI systems, helping the bank balance innovation with compliance, risk management, and public trust.

By strategically leveraging AI, DBS gains more than cost savings; it strengthens customer engagement, enhances risk management, and fosters data-driven innovation. However, the reliance on AI also introduces risks. For instance, in fraud detection, a poorly performing or biased model could generate false positives or negatives, potentially harming customers, eroding trust, and exposing the bank to regulatory penalties. Ethical governance frameworks like P-U-R-E are therefore essential to mitigate such risks while maximising the benefits of AI.

Reference

Deloitte (2023). *The Future of AI in Banking.* Available at: https://www2.deloitte.com/ (Accessed: 1 March 2026).

Case Study Questions

1 Apart from cost reductions, what strategic benefits does DBS achieve by adopting an AI-first approach, particularly in terms of customer engagement, operational efficiency, and competitive advantage?
2 Why is implementing an ethical framework like P-U-R-E essential for the responsible and sustainable deployment of AI in a highly regulated and sensitive sector such as banking?
3 Choose one AI application at DBS (e.g., fraud detection or credit scoring) and analyse the potential consequences if the AI system were inaccurate, biased, or poorly performing.

Further Reading

Brynjolfsson, E., & McAfee, A. (2017). *Machine, Platform, Crowd: Harnessing Our Digital Future*. New York: W.W. Norton & Company.
Raisch, S., & Krakowski, S. (2021). Artificial Intelligence and Management: The Automation–Augmentation Paradox. *Academy of Management Review*, 46(1), 192–210.
Russell, S., & Norvig, P. (2021). *Artificial Intelligence: A Modern Approach* (4th ed.). Harlow: Pearson.

References

Adadi, A., & Berrada, M. (2018). Peeking Inside the Black Box: A Survey on Explainable Artificial Intelligence (XAI). *IEEE Access*, 6, 52138–52160.
Agrawal, A., Gans, J., & Goldfarb, A. (2018). *Prediction Machines: The Simple Economics of Artificial Intelligence*. Boston: Harvard Business Review Press.
Arute, F. et al. (2019). Quantum Supremacy using a Programmable Superconducting Processor. *Nature*, 574(7779), 505–510.
Bartram, S.M., Branke, J., & Motahari, S. (2023). Artificial Intelligence in Finance: Challenges, Benefits and Regulatory Implications. *Journal of Financial Stability*, 65, 101115.
Bishop, C.M. (2006). *Pattern Recognition and Machine Learning*. New York: Springer.
Bodie, Z., Kane, A., & Marcus, A.J. (2021). *Investments* (12th ed.). New York: McGraw-Hill Education.
Borges, A.F.S., Laurindo, F.J.B., Spínola, M.M., Gonçalves, R.F., & Mattos, C.A. (2021). The Strategic Use of Artificial Intelligence in the Digital Era: Systematic Literature Review and Future Research Directions. *International Journal of Information Management*, 57, 102225.
Bose, I., & Mahapatra, R.K. (2022). Business Data Analytics for Fraud Detection. *Decision Support Systems*, 50(1), 1–12.
Brynjolfsson, E., & McAfee, A. (2017). *Machine, Platform, Crowd: Harnessing Our Digital Future*. New York: W.W. Norton & Company.
Buchanan, B. (2019). *The Cybersecurity Dilemma: Hacking, Trust, and Fear Between Nations*. Oxford: Oxford University Press.
Bughin, J., Hazan, E., Ramaswamy, S., Chui, M., Allas, T., Dahlström, P., Henke, N. and Trench, M. (2017) *Artificial Intelligence: The Next Digital Frontier?* New York: McKinsey Global Institute.
CFA Institute. (2025). *AI in Investment Management Survey Report*. Charlottesville: CFA Institute.
Chen, T., Kornblith, S., Norouzi, M., & Hinton, G. (2020). *A Simple Framework for Contrastive Learning of Visual Representations. Proceedings of the 37th International Conference on Machine Learning*, 1597–1607.
Davenport, T.H., & Ronanki, R. (2018). Artificial Intelligence for the Real World. *Harvard Business Review*, 96(1), 108–116.
Deloitte. (2023). *AI in Financial Services: Risk, Regulation and Resilience*. London: Deloitte Insights.
Financial Stability Board. (2022). *Artificial Intelligence and Machine Learning in Financial Services*. Basel: FSB.
Finck, M. (2023). *Artificial Intelligence and Data Protection Law*. Cambridge: Cambridge University Press.
Goodfellow, I., Bengio, Y., & Courville, A. (2016). *Deep Learning*. Cambridge, MA: MIT Press.
Gunning, D., Stefik, M., Choi, J., Miller, T., Stumpf, S., & Yang, G.-Z. (2019). XAI—Explainable Artificial Intelligence. *Science Robotics*, 4(37), eaay7120.
Hastie, T., Tibshirani, R., & Friedman, J. (2009). *The Elements of Statistical Learning* (2nd ed.). New York: Springer.
Hirschberg, J., & Manning, C.D. (2015). Advances in Natural Language Processing. *Science*, 349(6245), 261–266.
Huang, M.-H., & Rust, R.T. (2021). Artificial Intelligence in Service. *Journal of Service Research*, 24(1), 3–18.
IBM (2023). *Watsonx Orchestrate: Automating Financial Workflows*. Armonk, NY: IBM.
Jurafsky, D., & Martin, J.H. (2021). *Speech and Language Processing* (3rd ed.). Upper Saddle River, NJ: Prentice Hall.
Kokina, J., & Davenport, T.H. (2017). The Emergence of Artificial Intelligence: How Automation Is Changing Auditing. *Journal of Emerging Technologies in Accounting*, 14(1), 115–122.

Kumar, V., Dixit, A., Javalgi, R., & Dass, M. (2019). Digital Transformation of Customer Experience: A Review and Research Agenda. *Journal of Business Research*, 99, 101–115.

LeCun, Y., Bengio, Y., & Hinton, G. (2015). Deep Learning. *Nature*, 521(7553), 436–444.

Mehrabi, N., Morstatter, F., Saxena, N., Lerman, K., & Galstyan, A. (2021). A Survey on Bias and Fairness in Machine Learning. *ACM Computing Surveys*, 54(6), 1–35.

PwC. (2021). *AI in Insurance: Smarter Risk, Faster Claims*. London: PwC.

Raisch, S., & Krakowski, S. (2021). Artificial Intelligence and Management: The Automation–Augmentation Paradox. *Academy of Management Review*, 46(1), 192–210.

Russell, S.J., & Norvig, P. (2021). *Artificial Intelligence: A Modern Approach* (4th ed.) Harlow: Pearson.

Szeliski, R. (2020). *Computer Vision: Algorithms and Applications* (2nd ed.). London: Springer.

van der Aalst, W., Bichler, M., & Heinzl, A. (2018). Robotic Process Automation. *Business & Information Systems Engineering*, 60(4), 269–272.

Varshney, K.R. (2022). *Trustworthy Machine Learning*. New York: Morgan & Claypool.

West, J., & Bhattacharya, M. (2016). Intelligent Financial Fraud Detection: A Comprehensive Review. *Computers & Security*, 57, 47–66.

Zetzsche, D.A., Buckley, R.P., Arner, D.W. & Barberis, J.N. (2017). The RegTech universe in evolution. *SSRN Electronic Journal*, doi: 10.2139/ssrn.3049244

25 Technology in Regulation (RegTech) and Compliance Innovation

Chapter Overview

This chapter explores the rise and significance of Regulatory Technology (RegTech) as a transformative force within the financial services sector. RegTech leverages advanced technologies, including Artificial Intelligence (AI), Machine Learning (ML), blockchain, and cloud computing, to enhance compliance processes, mitigate risk, and increase operational efficiency (Arner, Barberis, & Buckley, 2017). The chapter underscores the critical role of automating regulatory functions such as Know Your Customer (KYC), Anti-Money Laundering (AML), regulatory reporting, and risk monitoring in navigating the increasingly complex post-2008 financial regulatory environment. It provides a detailed examination of RegTech's core components, practical applications, implementation challenges, and anticipated future trajectories. Additionally, the chapter emphasises the need for collaboration between financial institutions and regulatory authorities to fully realise the benefits of RegTech innovations.

Learning Objectives

By the end of this chapter, you should be able to:

1. Explain how AI, ML, and blockchain enhance regulatory compliance in financial institutions.
2. Identify and describe the principal applications of RegTech, including KYC, AML, transaction monitoring, and regulatory reporting.
3. Analyse the challenges of implementing RegTech, particularly issues related to legacy system integration and data privacy.
4. Evaluate real-world RegTech use cases and assess their impact on compliance efficiency and risk management.
5. Predict and discuss future developments in RegTech, such as real-time compliance, regulatory innovation, and global harmonisation of standards.

DOI: 10.4324/9781003775751-29

25.1 Introduction

The intersection of rapid digital transformation and a more demanding regulatory environment has established RegTech as essential for advanced financial institutions. The expansion of regulatory frameworks following the 2008 financial crisis significantly increased compliance costs and operational complexity. As Arner, Barberis, and Buckley (2016) observed, the proliferation of regulations has imposed substantial burdens, requiring innovative solutions that surpass traditional, labour-intensive methods. RegTech addresses these challenges by leveraging advanced computational capabilities to efficiently manage complex compliance requirements.

RegTech employs advanced technologies, including AI, ML, and big data analytics, to automate essential and routine compliance functions. These technologies are applied across the compliance spectrum, enabling automated KYC processes, improving transaction monitoring to detect illicit activities, and producing dynamic, accurate regulatory reports. Automation of these high-volume tasks reduces human error, decreases both direct compliance costs and indirect risk-related expenses, and strengthens the overall resilience of institutional control frameworks.

A principal advantage of contemporary RegTech solutions is their scalability and adaptability, which benefit both large multinational banks and smaller, specialised financial institutions aiming to maintain strict regulatory compliance without high administrative costs. These solutions enable continuous monitoring of the regulatory landscape, allowing institutions to respond quickly and effectively to legislative changes. Additionally, RegTech capabilities are expected to advance through emerging trends such as blockchain for secure, transparent data sharing and smart contracts for automating complex, rules-based compliance activities, thereby improving the efficiency and security of future regulatory processes.

25.2 Understanding of RegTech

25.2.1 Nature and Functions of RegTech

RegTech refers to the use of advanced digital technologies to improve efficiency, accuracy, and cost-effectiveness in regulatory compliance within the financial sector. By leveraging AI, ML, blockchain, data analytics, and cloud computing, RegTech automates compliance processes, enables real-time monitoring, and supports predictive risk management, moving beyond traditional, manual, and fragmented approaches (IIF, 2016). Its primary functions include automating KYC procedures, AML monitoring, regulatory reporting, risk analytics, and regulatory change management. For example, KYC automation enables institutions to verify identities, assess risk, and screen against sanctions or watchlists efficiently, as demonstrated by Revolut, which uses AI-driven document verification and facial recognition for instant onboarding while checking global sanctions lists. Similarly, AML monitoring leverages AI-powered transaction surveillance to detect suspicious activity promptly. HSBC employs such systems to analyse large datasets, flag anomalies, and generate regulatory reports, thereby reducing errors and increasing transparency. Automated reporting further enhances compliance by standardising data aggregation for frameworks such as Markets in Financial Instruments Directive II and Basel III, improving accuracy, timeliness, and auditability (Arner et al., 2017). Additionally, predictive risk analytics allow institutions to identify emerging risks and implement proactive interventions, transforming compliance from a reactive obligation into a data-driven, preventative function.

25.2.2 The Regulatory Landscape in Finance and Banking

Since the 2008 global financial crisis, regulatory requirements for financial institutions have intensified, encompassing AML, Countering the Financing of Terrorism (CFT), KYC, data protection, and systemic risk management, including Basel III standards (Basel Committee on Banking Supervision, 2017). These obligations have driven the adoption of RegTech to enhance compliance efficiency and accuracy. AML and CFT regulations, for instance, require continuous monitoring of financial transactions to prevent illicit activity. RegTech solutions utilise AI and real-time analytics to automate transaction surveillance, improve risk detection, and generate alerts for compliance teams. Barclays in the UK applies AI-driven AML platforms to dynamically assess customer risk, flag suspicious transactions instantly, and consolidate data for standardised regulatory reporting, thereby reducing operational burden and increasing transparency (FATF, 2020).

KYC regulations mandate comprehensive customer due diligence (CDD) to mitigate financial crime risks. RegTech tools support these requirements through automated identity verification, AI-driven risk scoring, and real-time sanctions and watchlist screening, thereby improving accuracy and reducing operational costs. Revolut, for example, verifies customer identities using document uploads and facial recognition while automatically screening against global sanctions lists, with cloud-based systems enabling scalable processing and maintaining audit-ready records (Arner et al., 2017). Similarly, data protection laws such as General Data Protection Regulation (GDPR) in the European Union (EU) and California Consumer Privacy Act (CCPA) in the US impose strict obligations on the collection, storage, and processing of personal data. RegTech platforms assist in managing customer consent, detecting unusual access patterns, and ensuring compliance, while cloud infrastructure provides scalable, transparent frameworks for secure data governance (FSB, 2019).

Stress testing and capital adequacy have become essential components of regulatory compliance under Basel III, requiring robust scenario analysis and maintenance of sufficient capital buffers. RegTech solutions facilitate these processes by automating complex calculations and replacing manual spreadsheets with scalable, audit-ready platforms, enhancing predictive capabilities and regulatory adherence. Barclays, for example, employs RegTech systems to simulate adverse market conditions and calculate capital adequacy in real time, supporting faster decision-making and ensuring compliance with regulatory thresholds (Basel Committee on Banking Supervision, 2017). Overall, the integration of RegTech across AML/CFT, KYC, data protection, and risk management functions demonstrates its central role in efficiently and effectively addressing the increasing complexity of financial regulation.

25.2.3 RegTech Architecture

Data Analytics and Visualisation: RegTech platforms utilise advanced analytics to process large volumes of structured and unstructured data, transforming them into actionable compliance insights. Tools such as dashboards, heat maps, and interactive reports facilitate real-time monitoring of regulatory performance, track key risk indicators, and support informed decision-making. For example, Deloitte (2023) emphasises that visualisation tools allow compliance teams to communicate complex analytical findings clearly across organisational hierarchies, improving oversight and responsiveness.

AI and ML: AI and ML form the backbone of predictive and automated compliance. These technologies detect anomalies in transaction patterns, assess risk exposures, and support predictive monitoring of potential regulatory violations. Continuous learning algorithms enable institutions to improve detection accuracy over time, reduce false positives, and respond rapidly to emerging risks.

Blockchain and Distributed Ledger Technology: Blockchain provides tamper-proof, transparent records that strengthen data integrity and traceability. Applications include maintaining immutable audit trails, verifying identities during KYC processes, and securely recording transactional data. This ensures regulatory transparency and allows regulators and institutions to validate historical transactions with confidence.

Cloud Computing: Cloud-based architectures deliver scalable, flexible, and cost-efficient infrastructure for RegTech operations. Cloud solutions enable institutions to manage large datasets, dynamically adjust workloads, and integrate multiple compliance tools into a single platform. The Bank for International Settlements (BIS, 2022) highlights that cloud-based RegTech improves operational agility and reduces infrastructure costs. Standard Chartered, for instance, leverages cloud platforms to combine predictive analytics with transaction monitoring, enabling efficient real-time regulatory reporting across multiple jurisdictions (Figure 25.1).

25.3 RegTech in Finance and Banking

RegTech in the finance and banking sector is an integrated ecosystem of technology-driven solutions that efficiently, accurately, and at scale manage regulatory and compliance risks. These solutions shift institutions from manual, fragmented compliance models to cohesive, automated frameworks, enabling real-time monitoring, predictive risk management, and strategic governance.

25.3.1 Key RegTech Functions

Digital Identity and KYC: RegTech automates customer identification, verification, and ongoing due diligence, including document verification, biometric checks, and sanctions or watchlist screening. This ensures compliance with CDD regulations throughout the customer lifecycle. For example, Revolut employs AI-driven document verification and facial recognition to onboard customers instantly while cross-checking global sanctions lists, reducing manual intervention and accelerating the onboarding process (Arner et al., 2017).

AML Monitoring: AML platforms continuously monitor transactions and customer behaviour to detect suspicious activity associated with money laundering or terrorist financing. These systems use rules-based engines, ML algorithms, and network analysis to generate alerts for further investigation. Deutsche Bank, for instance, employs AI-powered AML monitoring systems to analyse millions of daily transactions, automatically flagging anomalies for compliance teams, thereby enhancing detection accuracy while reducing operational effort.

Transaction Monitoring and Fraud Detection: RegTech tools analyse payment flows and account activity in real time to identify fraudulent transactions, insider trading, market abuse, or other financial crimes. Barclays implements AI-driven transaction monitoring to detect unusual account patterns, such as sudden large transfers or atypical spending behaviour, enabling the bank to block suspicious activity immediately and alert the customer for verification.

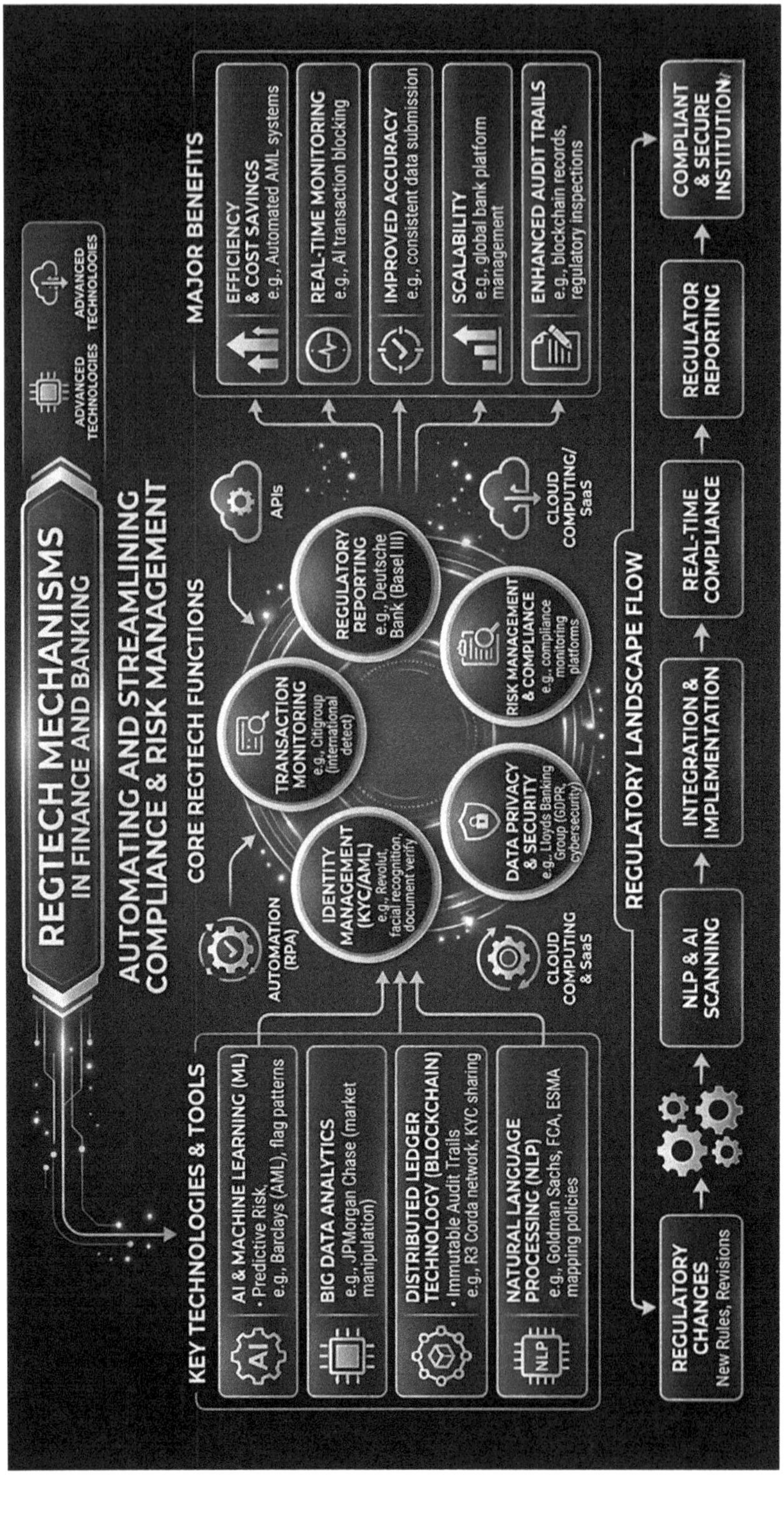

Figure 25.1 RegTech Ecosystem.

Automated Regulatory Reporting: These platforms gather, validate, reconcile, and format data from multiple internal systems to produce accurate, timely submissions to regulators. HSBC uses automated reporting systems to comply with Basel III capital requirements, reducing errors, expediting reporting, and ensuring adherence to international banking regulations (Deloitte, 2023).

Regulatory Change Management: RegTech solutions track updates to laws, regulations, and supervisory guidance across jurisdictions, enabling banks to interpret new requirements and integrate them into internal policies. Thomson Reuters Regulatory Intelligence, for example, provides real-time updates that allow compliance teams to adjust procedures promptly and maintain alignment with evolving regulations.

Risk Analytics and Predictive Monitoring: Advanced analytics evaluate historical and real-time data to identify emerging compliance and operational risks. Tools support stress testing, scenario analysis, and early-warning indicators. Standard Chartered uses predictive analytics to monitor transaction patterns and market exposures, flagging potential liquidity or compliance risks before escalation, enabling proactive intervention and risk mitigation.

Data Governance and Integrity Management: Ensures regulatory data is accurate, complete, and traceable. Platforms employ data quality controls, reconciliation systems, metadata management, and, in some cases, blockchain for tamper-evident records. Barclays uses these tools to validate and monitor reporting data, ensuring consistency, accuracy, and audit readiness across UK and EU financial regulations.

Cybersecurity and Data Privacy Compliance: Monitors system access, detects breaches, manages encryption, and ensures adherence to data privacy regulations, such as GDPR. Lloyds Banking Group utilises RegTech tools to secure network activity, detect cyber threats, and maintain regulatory compliance, thereby mitigating the risk of data breaches and regulatory penalties.

Workflow Automation and Case Management: Streamlines compliance processes, including alert handling, investigations, approvals, and regulatory filings. NatWest employs automated case management systems to manage suspicious transaction alerts efficiently, ensuring that investigations follow standardised workflows, maintain documentation, and are fully auditable.

25.3.2 Collaboration Between Regulators and Institutions

RegTech has significantly enhanced collaboration between financial institutions and regulators by creating mechanisms for testing and integrating innovative compliance technologies in a controlled environment. One notable initiative is the regulatory sandbox, pioneered by the Financial Conduct Authority (FCA, 2015), which enables banks and FinTech firms to trial new RegTech solutions under close regulatory supervision. This framework reduces the operational and compliance risks associated with innovation while allowing regulators to gain early insights into the functionality, benefits, and potential risks of emerging technologies.

In parallel, regulators are increasingly deploying their own technology-driven tools, commonly referred to as Supervisory Technology (SupTech), to monitor financial institutions in real time. SupTech solutions enable a more comprehensive, data-driven view of institutional and systemic risks, improve the accuracy and efficiency of compliance assessments, and support the development of more effective, evidence-based regulatory policies (BIS, 2020). Together, RegTech and SupTech create a dynamic, interactive ecosystem in which financial institutions can innovate responsibly, and regulators can enhance oversight with greater precision and responsiveness.

25.4 Opportunity, Challenges, and Key Issues of RegTech

25.4.1 Opportunities and Convergence of RegTech in Traditional Finance

RegTech offers significant opportunities for financial institutions by automating compliance, reducing costs, improving reporting accuracy, and enabling rapid adaptation to evolving regulations. The global RegTech market is projected to reach $60.7 billion by 2030, reflecting growing demand for technology-driven solutions (Fortune Business Insights, 2023). Key applications include KYC, AML monitoring, transaction surveillance, regulatory reporting, and risk management, supported by AI, ML, blockchain, and cloud computing. For example, HSBC uses AI-driven platforms to analyse transactions, detect anomalies, and produce automated regulatory reports, enhancing efficiency and transparency (Deloitte, 2023).

RegTech is increasingly integrated into the digital transformation of traditional banking operations, aligning regulatory compliance with strategic and operational objectives. For instance ,Standard Chartered leverages predictive analytics and transaction monitoring to provide real-time insights across jurisdictions, improving operational efficiency, customer experience, and return on regulatory investment. This convergence positions RegTech as a critical enabler of modern financial management.

25.4.2 Risks and Challenges of RegTech

Despite its potential, RegTech adoption comes with multiple risks and challenges. Technical complexity is a significant barrier, as standardising data, information technology (IT) infrastructure, and reporting concepts across jurisdictions is necessary for effective operation (Buchak, Matvos, Piskorski, & Seru, 2023). Integration with legacy systems is often costly and technically challenging due to outdated infrastructure, creating compatibility issues and potential disruption to ongoing operations. Cultural resistance within institutions also hinders adoption, as employees accustomed to traditional methods may perceive RegTech as a threat to job security or operational norms.

Additionally, data privacy and cybersecurity remain critical concerns. RegTech platforms consolidate sensitive financial and personal data, increasing vulnerability to cyber threats and necessitating robust security measures to comply with regulations such as GDPR and CCPA (Zetzsche, Buckley, Arner, & Barberis, 2017). Regulatory fragmentation and uncertainty further complicate adoption, as institutions must implement multiple, jurisdiction-specific systems to comply with varying local standards, increasing operational complexity and costs. Fraud monitoring systems are also inconsistent across institutions, underscoring the need for more coordinated industry approaches to AML/CTF compliance. Talent gaps represent another challenge, as specialised skills are required to operate and interpret advanced RegTech tools effectively.

25.4.3 Key Implementation Issues of RegTech

Successful RegTech implementation requires addressing integration, governance, and workforce readiness. Legacy IT systems must be aligned with modern platforms, while data governance ensures accuracy, traceability, and audit readiness. Workforce training is essential to equip compliance staff with the skills to manage AI, ML, and analytics tools effectively. Institutions must also conduct cost-benefit analyses to justify investment, given high upfront costs. For instance, NatWest uses workflow automation to standardise investigations of suspicious transactions, while Lloyds Banking Group continuously monitors networks to ensure cybersecurity and regulatory compliance. Effective adoption combines technology, governance, and human resources to maximise efficiency, reduce risk, and strengthen operational resilience.

25.5 The Future of RegTech in Finance and Banking

The future of RegTech in finance and banking is poised for significant growth, driven by ongoing digital transformation and the increasing complexity of regulatory requirements. A central trend is the expanded adoption of AI and automation, enabling institutions to shift compliance from a reactive, manual task to a proactive, strategic function. ML facilitates predictive risk assessments, allowing financial institutions to detect potential regulatory breaches before they occur, thereby reducing operational costs, improving decision-making, and enhancing regulatory trust. Concurrently, global regulatory harmonisation is expected to play a critical role in shaping RegTech adoption. Greater international coordination and standardisation of compliance rules would reduce fragmentation and inefficiency, enabling the development of scalable and interoperable RegTech solutions. By aligning regulatory frameworks, institutions can implement innovative technologies more efficiently, streamline reporting processes, optimise resource allocation, and ultimately enhance resilience across the financial sector (Arner et al., 2017; PwC, 2024).

Another significant trajectory for RegTech lies in its deeper integration with FinTech firms and enhanced cybersecurity capabilities. Collaboration between traditional banks and FinTech innovators will combine regulatory expertise with advanced technologies such as AI, data analytics, and cloud computing, producing smarter, scalable compliance solutions that improve operational efficiency and adaptability. Furthermore, cybersecurity is expected to become an intrinsic component of RegTech platforms, incorporating AI-driven threat detection, advanced encryption, and real-time monitoring to secure sensitive financial and customer data. This security-by-design approach ensures compliance while mitigating operational and reputational risks. Finally, the shift towards real-time compliance, enabled by continuous monitoring and advanced analytics, will transform regulatory oversight from periodic audits into an instantaneous, integrated operational function. This evolution positions RegTech not merely as a compliance tool but as a strategic asset that strengthens risk management, operational agility, and regulatory alignment across the financial ecosystem (Deloitte, 2023).

25.6 Conclusion

RegTech marks a transformative shift in the financial sector, fundamentally changing how institutions navigate increasingly complex regulatory landscapes. With rising demands for stringent AML compliance, data protection, and systemic risk management, AI-driven automation has become essential for achieving efficiency, accuracy, and scalability. By streamlining regulatory reporting, enhancing fraud detection, and optimising CDD, RegTech empowers institutions to fulfil compliance obligations while reducing operational friction. The integration of RegTech transforms compliance from a cost centre into a strategic advantage, enabling organisations to redirect resources towards innovation and growth. This evolution from reactive compliance to proactive governance not only mitigates risk but also strengthens overall organisational resilience in a dynamic regulatory environment.

Looking forward, the development of RegTech depends on continued collaboration among regulators, financial institutions, and technology providers to align innovation with compliance imperatives. Standardised data frameworks, jurisdiction-specific solutions, and scalable platforms will be critical in advancing the sector. Embracing digital transformation is no longer optional; it is central to maintaining both systemic stability and competitive advantage. RegTech isn't just about keeping pace with regulations; it's about future-proofing the financial ecosystem. Finally, the maturation of RegTech will play a pivotal role in reinforcing trust, enhancing operational robustness, and ensuring long-term sustainability within the global financial system.

Key Terms and Glossary

RegTech The use of technology, particularly AI and data analytics, to facilitate the delivery of regulatory requirements more efficiently and effectively.

SupTech The use of technology by regulatory authorities to enhance their supervision and monitoring of financial institutions.

KYC (Know Your Customer) The process of a business verifying the identity of its clients to assess risk and ensure compliance with AML laws.

AML (Anti-Money Laundering) A set of laws, regulations, and procedures intended to prevent criminals from disguising illegally obtained funds as legitimate income.

Regulatory Sandbox A framework set up by regulators that allows FinTech startups and other innovators to test their products in a controlled environment under supervision.

Test Your Understanding

Multiple-Choice Questions

1 Which of the following technologies is NOT typically associated with RegTech in finance?

A AI
B Blockchain
C Cloud Computing
D Hydraulic Engineering

2 What is a primary function of RegTech in financial institutions?

A Investment portfolio management
B Automating compliance processes and regulatory reporting
C Physical cash handling
D Customer loyalty programme management

3 Which financial institution uses AI-driven platforms for real-time AML transaction monitoring, as mentioned in the chapter?

A NatWest
B HSBC
C Lloyds Banking Group
D Standard Chartered

4 Which regulatory framework is frequently supported by RegTech for automated reporting?

   A GDPR
   B Basel III
   C International Organization for Standardization (ISO) 9001
   D Sarbanes–Oxley Act

5 The concept of SupTech refers to:

   A SupTech used by regulators to monitor institutions in real time
   B Superior technology for consumer banking apps
   C Supply chain management in finance
   D Security technology for personal devices

Short Questions

1 Define RegTech and explain its significance in financial compliance.
2 Identify two key challenges in implementing RegTech in traditional financial institutions.
3 Explain how predictive analytics and AI transform compliance from reactive to proactive processes.

Analytical Questions

1 Analyse how the convergence of RegTech with FinTech is reshaping operational efficiency and risk management in traditional banking.
2 Evaluate the role of cloud computing and blockchain in enhancing the scalability, transparency, and auditability of RegTech systems.
3 Discuss the potential impact of global regulatory harmonisation on the adoption and effectiveness of RegTech solutions across jurisdictions.

Case Study: ComplyAdvantage and AI-Powered Financial Crime Fighting

Compliance with AML regulations is a major operational and financial burden for banks. Traditional rule-based transaction monitoring systems often generate a high number of false positives, requiring extensive manual review by compliance teams and slowing the detection of genuine financial crime. ComplyAdvantage, a RegTech company, addresses these challenges by employing AI and ML to analyse transactional data in real time. Its platform screens transactions against global sanctions lists, watchlists, and other regulatory databases, while also detecting subtle, complex patterns indicative of suspicious or illicit activity.

By learning from historical data and continuously adapting to new typologies of financial crime, ComplyAdvantage's AI-driven system can reduce false positives by over 70%. This allows compliance teams to focus on legitimate threats, improving both the speed and accuracy of financial crime detection. The platform also provides audit-ready records and automated alerts, helping banks meet regulatory expectations more efficiently. However, relying on third-party AI solutions raises concerns about data security, model transparency, and reliance on external technology providers. Understanding these trade-offs is crucial for banks seeking to integrate AI-powered RegTech into their compliance frameworks.

Reference

Arner, D.W., Barberis, J.N. and Buckley, R.P., 2017. FinTech, RegTech, and the Reconceptualisation of Financial Regulation. *Northwestern Journal of International Law & Business*, 37(3), 371–413.

Case Study Questions

1. How does an AI-driven approach from a firm like ComplyAdvantage fundamentally improve upon traditional, rule-based transaction monitoring systems?
2. What new risks might a bank introduce by relying on a third-party AI platform for a critical function like AML compliance?
3. Why might regulators be initially cautious about approving AI-based compliance tools, and what could RegTech firms do to alleviate these concerns?

Further Reading

Arner, D.W., Barberis, J.N., & Buckley, R.P., 2017. FinTech, RegTech, and the Reconceptualisation of Financial Regulation. *Northwestern Journal of International Law & Business*, 37(3), 371–413.

Deloitte. (2023). *The Future of RegTech in Banking: From Compliance to Competitive Advantage*. London: Deloitte.

Financial Conduct Authority (FCA). (2015). *Call for Input: Supporting the Development and Adoption of RegTech*. London: FCA.

References

Arner, D.W., Barberis, J., & Buckley, R.P. (2016). The Evolution of FinTech: A New Post-Crisis Paradigm? *University of Hong Kong Faculty of Law Research Paper, No. 2016/035*.

Arner, D.W., Barberis, J., & Buckley, R.P. (2017). FinTech, RegTech, and the Reconceptualisation of Financial Regulation. *Northwestern Journal of International Law & Business*, 37(3), 371–413.

Basel Committee on Banking Supervision. (2017). *Basel III: Finalising Post-Crisis Reforms*. Basel: Bank for International Settlements.

BIS (Bank for International Settlements). (2020). *Suptech Tools for Market Conduct Supervision*. Basel: BIS Innovation Hub.

Bank for International Settlements (2022) *Big Tech Interdependencies: A Key Policy Blind Spot*. BIS Insights No. 44. Basel: Bank for International Settlements. Available at: https://www.bis.org/fsi/publ/insights44.htm

Buchak, G., Matvos, G., Piskorski, T., & Seru, A. (2023). FinTech, Regulatory Arbitrage, and the Rise of Shadow Banks. *Journal of Financial Economics*, 148(2), 255–282.

Deloitte. (2023). *The Future of RegTech in Banking: From Compliance to Competitive Advantage*. London: Deloitte Insights.

Financial Stability Board (2019) *Third-party Dependencies in Cloud Services: Considerations on Financial Stability Implications*. Basel: Financial Stability Board.

Financial Action Task Force (FATF) (2020) *Digital Transformation of AML/CFT*. Paris: FATF. Available at: https://www.fatf-gafi.org/en/publications/Digitaltransformation/Digital-transformation.html (Accessed: 10 Oct 2025).

Financial Conduct Authority (FCA). (2015). *Call for Input: Supporting the Development and Adoption of RegTech*. London: FCA.

Fortune Business Insights (2023) *Regtech Market Size to Surpass USD 60.77 Billion by 2030, exhibiting a CAGR of 24.9%*. Available at: https://www.globenewswire.com/news-release/2023/09/11/2740560/0/en/Regtech-Market-Size-to-Surpass-USD-60-77-billion-by-2030-exhibiting-a-CAGR-of-24-9.html (Accessed: 15 Oct 2025).

Institute of International Finance (IIF). (2016). *RegTech in Financial Services: Solutions for Compliance and Reporting*. Washington, D.C.: IIF.

PwC. (2024). Financial Services Technology 2024: Trends Shaping the Future of Financial Services. Available at: https://www.pwc.com

Zetzsche, D.A., Buckley, R.P., Arner, D.W., & Barberis, J.N. (2017). From FinTech to TechFin: The Regulatory Challenges of Data-Driven Finance. European Banking Institute Working Paper Series No. 6; University of Hong Kong Faculty of Law Research Paper No. 2017/007; University of Luxembourg Law Working Paper No. 2017-001. Available at: https://ssrn.com/abstract=2959925

26 Data Analytics in Banking and Finance

Chapter Overview

The development of the modern financial sector increasingly depends on the effective use of Big Data, which has become vital for fostering innovation and gaining a competitive advantage. Big Data is defined by the 5 Vs: volume, veracity, value and variety (McAfee & Brynjolfsson, 2012). This rapid, intricate data supports transformative applications across key financial functions, improving decision-making in risk management, customer analytics, and operational efficiency. Despite these strategic benefits, implementing robust Big Data frameworks poses practical challenges. Financial institutions need to establish strong data governance, handle privacy issues, and address a shortage of analytical talent. As a result, the industry's future lies in integrating advanced Artificial Intelligence (AI) analytics and creating secure, collaborative open banking ecosystems.

Chapter Learning Objectives

By the end of this chapter, you should be able to:

1. Explain Big Data and its core characteristics (i.e., 5 Vs) within the context of financial services.
2. Describe the architecture and components of a Big Data platform used by financial institutions.
3. Evaluate key applications of Big Data for risk management, customer insights, and operational efficiency.
4. Analyse challenges in implementing Big Data initiatives, including data governance, integration, privacy, and regulatory compliance.
5. Examine the impact of Open Banking, Application Programming Interfaces (APIs), ethical considerations, and emerging trends on Big Data strategies in finance.

26.1 Introduction

The banking and finance industry has long relied on extensive datasets, a dependence that has intensified in the digital era. This shift has led to the generation of Big Data at an unprecedented scale and complexity. Data now originates from diverse sources, including

DOI: 10.4324/9781003775751-30

transactional records, real-time market feeds, social media sentiment, mobile application interactions, and geolocation information (Marr, 2015). Consequently, the capacity to capture, store, and analyse these large and complex datasets has become a fundamental strategic requirement for financial institutions.

Big Data analytics represents a significant transformation within the industry, advancing beyond traditional retrospective reporting to enable the extraction of predictive insights. These capabilities facilitate personalised customer experiences, support real-time fraud detection, and enhance the accuracy of risk modelling frameworks. Such developments are essential for improving operational efficiency, increasing customer satisfaction, and mitigating financial risks in the current complex market environment.

This chapter examines the transformative impact of Big Data on the financial sector. It reviews the technological innovations that enable advanced data analytics, discusses the primary challenges financial institutions encounter during implementation, and considers emerging trends in data analytics for banking and finance. The objective is to provide a comprehensive overview of how data-driven strategies are reshaping the industry (Figure 26.1).

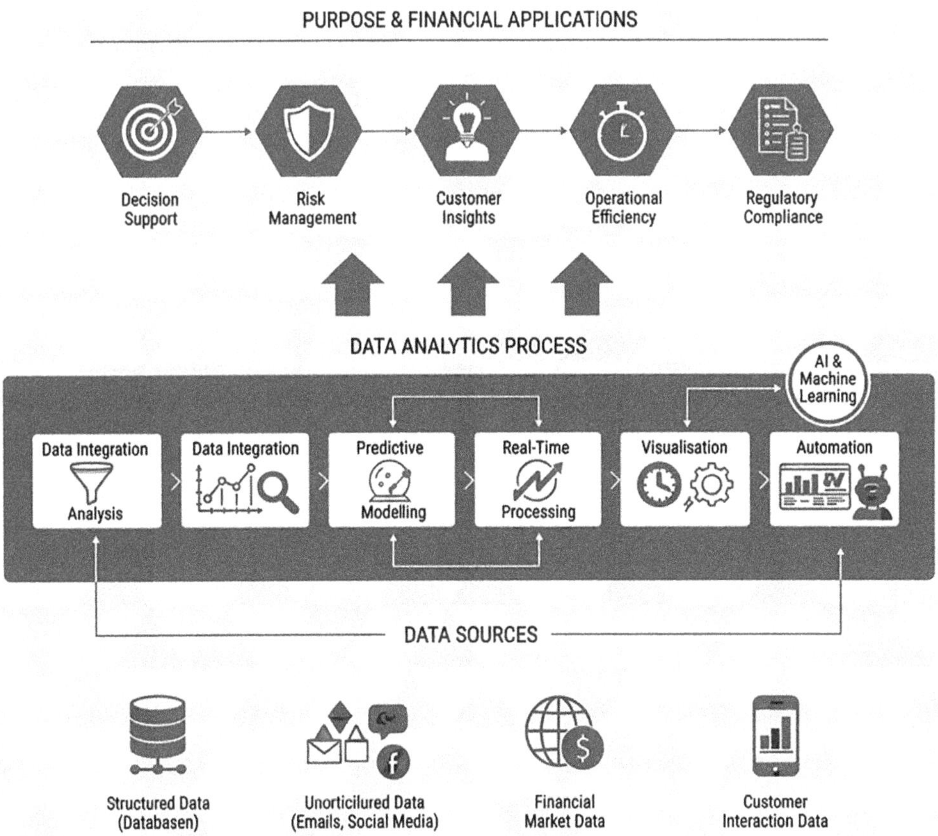

Figure 26.1 Big Data Analytics in Finance.

26.2 Understanding Big Data in a Financial Context

26.2.1 Define Data Analytics

Data analytics has become a cornerstone of modern banking and finance, enabling institutions to transform vast volumes of raw data into actionable intelligence. By systematically collecting, cleaning, and analysing data from diverse sources, ranging from transactional databases to social media feeds, financial organisations can uncover critical patterns and trends that inform strategic decisions. Companies that leverage data effectively have a significant competitive advantage (Davenport, 2013). In this context, data analytics not only enhances decision-making but also strengthens an institution's ability to anticipate market shifts, adapt to customer needs, and maintain regulatory compliance in an increasingly complex financial landscape.

26.2.2 Nature of Data Analytics

The application of data analytics in finance is characterised by several key features that collectively enhance its effectiveness. Data integration enables banks to consolidate structured and unstructured data, while statistical analysis and predictive modelling help identify risk factors and predict future behaviour. Real-time processing capabilities support instant fraud detection and high-frequency trading decisions, and data visualisation tools make complex findings accessible through intuitive dashboards and reports. Furthermore, automation powered by machine learning (ML) and AI improves analytical accuracy and operational speed. These capabilities are instrumental in fulfilling core financial objectives such as risk management, customer segmentation, and process optimisation, turning data into a strategic asset.

26.2.3 Purpose of Data Analytics

The primary purpose of data analytics in the financial sector is to support evidence-based decision-making across multiple domains. It strengthens risk management by identifying anomalous transactions and forecasting credit risks, thereby mitigating potential losses. Institutions leverage customer insights derived from behavioural analytics to personalise services and improve satisfaction, directly impacting retention and revenue. Operationally, analytics uncovers inefficiencies in workflows and resource allocation, driving cost reductions and performance improvements. Additionally, in an era of stringent regulatory demands, data analytics ensures accurate reporting and facilitates compliance with frameworks such as Basel III and General Data Protection Regulation (GDPR). As one industry executive remarked, in today's financial environment, data isn't just informative, it's foundational to resilience and innovation.

26.2.4 Big Data Characteristics

Big Data is often defined by a set of attributes known as the 5 Vs, each of which has particular significance in the financial sector.

Volume: The enormous scale of data generated and processed by financial institutions. For example, a global investment bank may handle terabytes of information daily, encompassing millions of transactions, client account records, market feeds, and derivative positions (Dijcks, 2013). Managing such volume requires scalable storage and processing systems, such as Hadoop clusters or cloud-based data lakes.

Velocity: Velocity captures the speed at which data is created, transmitted, and analysed. High-frequency trading, real-time fraud detection, and instant payment systems demand that data be processed within milliseconds. For instance, payment platforms like VisaNet must detect potential fraudulent transactions in real time to prevent losses and protect customers (Gandomi & Haider, 2015).

Variety: Highlights the range of data types, from structured datasets in relational databases (e.g., account balances and transaction logs) to unstructured data such as call centre transcripts, emailed statements, social media interactions, and news feeds. Banks increasingly combine these sources to generate comprehensive customer insights.

Veracity: Veracity addresses the accuracy, reliability, and trustworthiness of data. Erroneous or incomplete data can lead to flawed credit assessments, regulatory breaches, or trading mistakes. For example, inaccurate pricing data in a trading algorithm could trigger significant financial losses, making rigorous data validation and quality control essential (I).

Value: Value emphasises the ultimate goal of Big Data: generating actionable insights that create economic benefit. By analysing customer behaviour, market trends, and operational performance, financial institutions can enhance revenue, reduce costs, and mitigate risk. For example, predictive analytics in retail banking can identify customers likely to default on loans, enabling proactive risk management and portfolio optimisation.

26.3 The Big Data Architecture in Finance

A robust big data architecture is fundamental to modern banking and finance, enabling institutions to capture, process, and analyse large volumes of heterogeneous financial data for risk management, regulatory compliance, and strategic decision-making (Figure 26.2).

26.3.1 Financial Data Sources and Types

The foundation of financial big data architecture lies in the systematic acquisition of diverse data sources. Banks generate vast volumes of structured data from core systems such as transaction processing platforms, customer relationship management systems, and general ledgers, which support operational reporting and risk assessment. In parallel, regulatory requirements necessitate the collection of compliance-related datasets, including Know Your Customer and Anti-Money Laundering (AML) records. Increasingly, institutions also ingest market data, payment streams, and customer interaction data. To handle high-velocity data flows, technologies such as Apache Kafka enable real-time streaming and reliable data capture (Kreps, 2014). For example, retail banks stream card transaction data in real time to support fraud detection and regulatory monitoring.

26.3.2 Financial Data Ingestion Layer

The data ingestion layer acts as the entry point for all financial data, integrating both real-time and batch data from internal systems and external sources. Streaming platforms such as Kafka process market feeds and transaction events, while tools such as Apache NiFi and Apache Flink manage dataflows and enable real-time analytics. Standard financial messaging formats, including Society for Worldwide Interbank Financial Telecommunication and Financial Information eXchange protocols, are integrated alongside modern API gateways that support open banking. This layer ensures reliable data delivery to downstream Extract, Transform, Load and Extract, Load, Transform pipelines, enabling consistent and timely analytical processing (Deming, 2000).

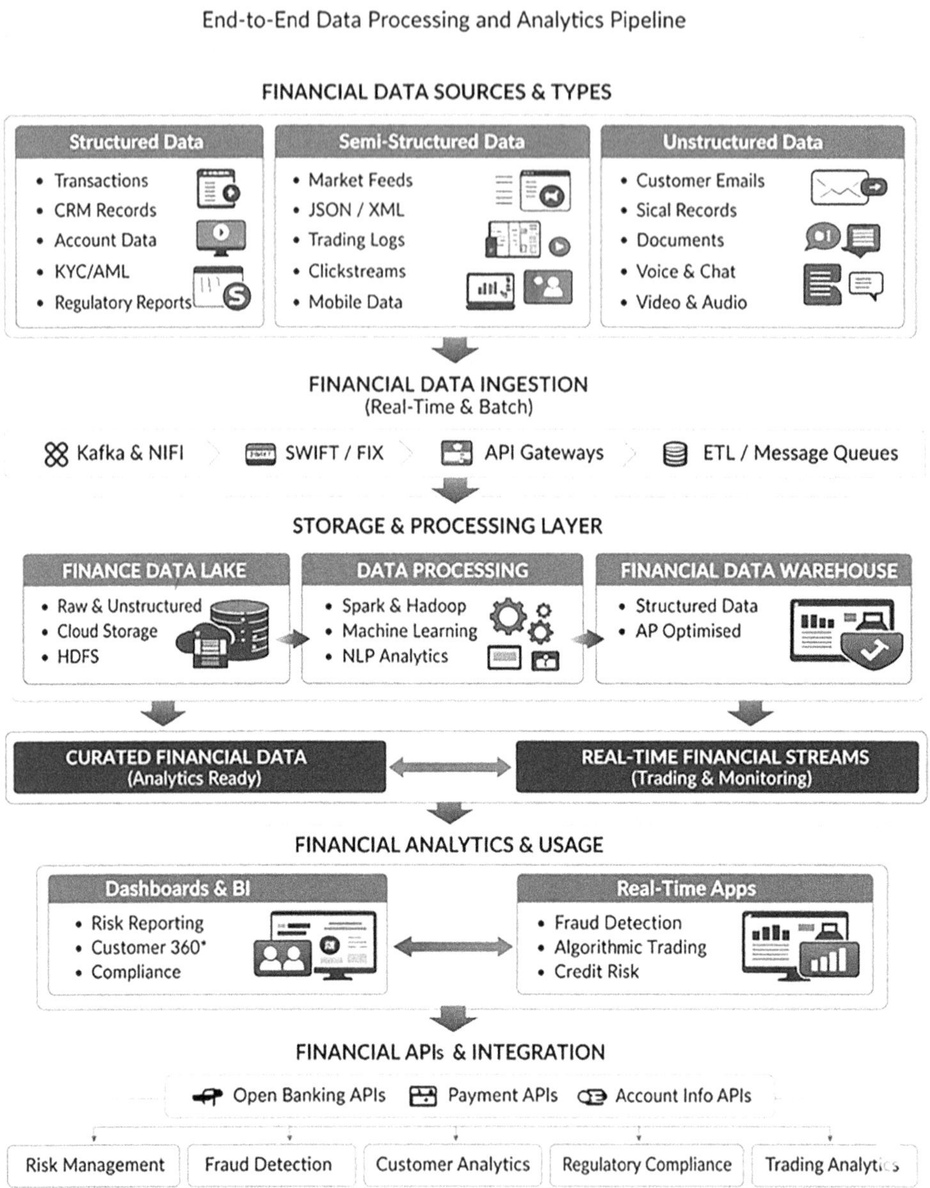

Figure 26.2 Big Data Architecture in Finance and Banking.

26.3.3 Storage and Processing Layer

Following ingestion, data is stored and processed within a multi-tier infrastructure comprising data lakes, processing engines, and data warehouses. Financial data lakes store raw, unstructured data using cloud platforms (e.g., Amazon S3, Azure Blob Storage) or HDFS, providing schema-on-read flexibility. Processing engines such as Apache Spark and Hadoop support batch and real-time analytics, including ML for credit scoring and fraud detection. In contrast, financial data warehouses store structured, curated data using schema-on-write designs and columnar storage (e.g., Snowflake, Redshift) to optimise reporting and business intelligence. This layered approach balances analytical agility with governance and performance.

26.3.4 Curated and Real-Time Data

Modern financial architectures support both curated datasets and real-time data streams. Curated data is cleaned, structured, and optimised for dashboards, regulatory reporting, and strategic analysis. Real-time data streams, by contrast, support time-sensitive applications such as trading systems, transaction authorisation, and fraud monitoring. For example, real-time payment streams allow banks to block suspicious transactions instantly, while curated datasets support periodic stress testing and regulatory submissions.

26.3.5 Financial Analytics and Usage Layer

The analytics and usage layer transforms processed data into actionable insights through business intelligence tools and advanced analytics. Dashboards built using platforms such as Tableau and Power BI enable institutions to monitor risk exposure, compliance metrics, portfolio performance, and customer behaviour. Beyond descriptive analytics, real-time applications support algorithmic trading, credit risk assessment, and AML monitoring. These capabilities enhance operational efficiency and enable faster, data-driven decision-making.

26.3.6 Financial APIs and Integration Layer

The APIs and integration layer facilitate secure, standardised data exchange between analytics platforms and internal or external systems. Driven by regulations such as PSD2, open banking APIs enable controlled data sharing with third-party providers, supporting payment initiation, account information services, and digital innovation (Zetzsche, Buckley, Arner, & Barberis, 2020). This layer ensures that insights generated by analytics engines are accessible across customer-facing applications, partner ecosystems, and regulatory reporting systems.

26.3.7 Finance-Specific Applications

At the application layer, big data architectures enable finance-specific use cases that deliver strategic value. Risk management systems apply advanced analytics to credit, market, and liquidity risk assessment, while machine-learning-based fraud-detection systems identify anomalous transactions in real time. Customer analytics applications support segmentation, churn prediction, and personalised product offerings. In regulatory compliance, automated reporting supports frameworks such as Basel III, IFRS 9, and AML requirements. In trading, data-driven analytics power algorithmic strategies and portfolio optimisation. As highlighted by the Basel Committee on Banking Supervision (BCBS 239), effective aggregation and use of diverse data sources are critical for responsive risk management and financial stability.

26.4 Big Data and Data Analytics in Finance

Big data and advanced analytics underpin FinTech innovation by enabling financial institutions to process large volumes of heterogeneous data for improved decision-making. The widespread use of digital transactions, mobile platforms, and alternative data has transformed how banks manage risk, analyse markets, and deliver personalised services. By integrating ML, high-frequency data processing, and real-time analytics, institutions enhance efficiency, accuracy, and competitiveness across financial systems.

Key applications include real-time market analysis, customer analytics, risk management, investment optimisation, fraud detection, and regulatory compliance.

26.4.1 Risk Management and Fraud Detection

Big data analytics has materially strengthened risk management and fraud detection by enabling the analysis of large-scale historical and real-time transactional data. ML models identify complex fraud patterns and adapt dynamically, outperforming static rule-based systems in accuracy and speed (West & Bhattacharya, 2016).

In credit risk assessment, lenders increasingly incorporate alternative data such as transaction histories, utility payments, and digital activity to develop more comprehensive borrower profiles. This improves default prediction while expanding responsible access to credit, supporting financial inclusion (Bartram, Branke, & Motahari, 2023). For example, real-time card fraud systems used by global banks detect anomalous spending behaviour and trigger immediate intervention.

26.4.2 Customer Analytics and Personalisation

Big data enables a "Customer 360" view by integrating transaction records, digital interactions, and service data into unified customer profiles. Advanced analytics and ML facilitate personalised product recommendations, targeted marketing, and risk-adjusted pricing. This data-driven personalisation improves customer engagement, loyalty, and lifetime value in competitive financial markets (Kumar, Rajan, Venkatesan, & Lecinski, 2019). Digital banks, for instance, tailor savings and credit products based on real-time spending and income patterns.

26.4.3 Algorithmic Trading and Market Analysis

Big data analytics is central to algorithmic trading and quantitative investment strategies. Institutions analyse high-frequency market data alongside alternative sources such as social media sentiment and consumer transactions to uncover predictive signals (Bodie, Kane, & Marcus, 2021). ML models enable rapid execution, minimise transaction costs, and exploit short-lived market inefficiencies. AI-driven execution engines used by major investment banks optimise trade timing and liquidity management, enhancing risk-adjusted returns.

26.4.4 Operational Efficiency and Regulatory Compliance

Data analytics improves operational efficiency by identifying process inefficiencies and optimising internal workflows. In regulatory compliance, RegTech solutions use ML and natural language processing to automate monitoring, reporting, and anomaly detection, supporting compliance with frameworks such as MiFID II and GDPR (Arner, Barberis, & Buckley, 2017). This reduces compliance risk and manual burden while strengthening governance.

26.4.5 ML for Loan Evaluation in Peer-to-Peer (P2P) Lending

ML has transformed credit risk assessment by enabling predictive models that capture non-linear relationships in large datasets. In P2P lending, platforms classify borrowers using behavioural, transactional, and alternative data. Common methods include logistic regression, random forests, gradient boosting, support vector machines, and neural networks. LendingClub, for example, employs gradient boosting models that outperform traditional credit scoring in predictive accuracy.

26.4.6 Survey of ML Approaches in P2P Lending

Research identifies several dominant ML approaches: supervised learning models for default prediction; ensemble methods that improve accuracy through bagging and boosting (Brown and Mues, 2012); feature selection techniques such as PCA and LASSO; deep learning models for sequential data; and explainable AI tools (e.g., SHAP, LIME) to enhance model transparency. Empirical studies show gradient boosting performs particularly well for mid-risk borrowers (Krainikov et al., 2022).

26.4.7 Financial Volatility Networks

Volatility networks model interconnectedness and spillovers across financial assets using graph-based frameworks (Billio et al., 2012). Volatility estimation relies on Generalised Autoregressive Conditional Heteroskedasticity (GARCH) and Dynamic Conditional Correlation (DCC)-GARCH models, as well as realised volatility from high-frequency data (Andersen et al., 2001). During the COVID-19 crisis, volatility networks revealed heightened cross-market spillovers, indicating increased systemic risk (Diebold and Yilmaz, 2014).

26.4.8 Risk-Based Trading and Deep Learning

Risk-based trading systems integrate risk measures such as VaR and CVaR with algorithmic execution strategies. Deep learning models, particularly Long Short-Term Memory and Transformer architectures, capture temporal price dependencies and improve signal generation (Sirignano & Cont, 2019). J.P. Morgan's LOXM system illustrates the application of reinforcement learning to optimise execution and reduce market impact (EDXTV (2025)).

26.4.9 Non-Linear ARDL Analysis

The Non-Linear Autoregressive Distributed Lag (NARDL) model captures asymmetric short- and long-run effects by decomposing explanatory variables into positive and negative shocks (Shin, Yu & Greenwood-Nimmo, 2014). In FinTech and big data analytics, NARDL is increasingly applied to large financial datasets to analyse non-linear market responses to interest rates, exchange rates, and commodity prices. Its integration with high-frequency and alternative data improves risk assessment and stress testing. Empirical evidence shows that oil price increases have stronger contractionary effects on financial conditions than price decreases, highlighting the importance of asymmetry in data-driven financial analysis (Apergis & Payne, 2014).

26.4.10 VAR and VECM Analysis

Vector Autoregression (VAR) and Vector Error Correction Model (VECM) frameworks are central to financial data analytics for modelling dynamic interrelationships among multiple financial variables. VAR models support forecasting and impulse-response analysis using large multivariate datasets of stationary series, while VECMs capture short-run dynamics and long-run equilibrium relationships among cointegrated variables. In FinTech applications, these models are embedded within big data platforms to analyse market interconnectedness and systemic risk. Empirical VAR studies show that volatility shocks, proxied by the VIX, have persistent negative effects on equity markets, informing algorithmic trading and portfolio risk management strategies (Bernanke, Gertler & Watson, 1997).

26.5 Opportunities, Challenges, and Key Practical Issues

26.5.1 Opportunities and Convergence of Big Data and Data Analytics

The convergence of big data, advanced analytics, and financial services has become central to FinTech innovation. Financial institutions increasingly leverage large-scale transactional, behavioural, and alternative data to improve decision-making, enhance customer experience, and strengthen competitiveness. This convergence enables a shift from rule-based systems to predictive and real-time analytics.

One key opportunity is predictive analytics, where big data supports forecasting of credit risk, market movements, and investment opportunities. For example, banks now use transaction-level and cash-flow data to improve default prediction beyond traditional credit scoring models (McAfee & Brynjolfsson, 2012).

Personalised banking represents another major opportunity. By integrating customer data across digital channels, banks can deliver tailored financial products and targeted services, increasing customer satisfaction and retention (Kumar et al., 2019). Digital banks commonly recommend customised savings or credit products based on individual spending behaviour.

Big data analytics also enhances fraud detection and risk management. Real-time transaction monitoring enables early identification of anomalous behaviour, reducing fraud losses and response times (West & Bhattacharya, 2016). In addition, advanced analytics improves customer segmentation, operational efficiency, and cost reduction through process automation.

26.5.2 Risks and Challenges of Big Data and Data Analytics

Despite its transformative potential, the use of big data analytics in banking and finance presents significant risks and challenges. A central issue is data integration, as financial institutions must combine data from heterogeneous sources, including legacy systems, external providers, and unstructured digital data. Achieving a unified and reliable data architecture is complex, costly, and time-consuming.

Cybersecurity and data privacy pose critical risks due to the sensitive nature of financial data. Large-scale data repositories and analytics platforms are attractive targets for cyber-attacks, increasing the potential for data breaches and financial crime. Ensuring robust security frameworks and compliance with data protection regulations is therefore essential (Arner et al., 2017).

Data quality remains another major challenge. Inaccurate, incomplete, or biased data can lead to flawed analytics and poor decision-making, particularly in credit risk and fraud detection models. Maintaining data accuracy and consistency across systems requires strong data governance structures.

Furthermore, skill shortages constrain effective adoption. The demand for data scientists, ML engineers, and domain experts exceeds supply, limiting many banks' ability to fully exploit advanced analytics (Bughin et al., 2018). Ethical concerns also arise regarding transparency, algorithmic bias, and responsible data usage, particularly when automated models influence lending or pricing decisions.

26.5.3 Key Practical Issues of Big Data Analytics

In practice, the adoption of big data analytics in banking and finance faces several structural and operational barriers. Legacy system integration is one of the most persistent challenges, as many banks operate on outdated IT infrastructures that are incompatible with modern analytics platforms. Upgrading these systems often requires substantial investment and organisational change.

Data quality management is another practical issue, as effective analytics depends on reliable, well-governed data. Without consistent standards and validation processes, analytical outputs may be unreliable. Closely related is the shortage of skilled professionals, which limits the effective design, implementation, and interpretation of analytics models.

Ethical and regulatory considerations further complicate adoption. Banks must ensure responsible data use, protect customer privacy, and comply with evolving regulatory requirements such as GDPR and financial conduct regulations. Regulatory compliance often increases implementation complexity and slows innovation (Arner et al., 2017).

26.6 The Future of Big Data in Finance

The convergence of advanced analytics, regulatory change, and ethical governance will drive the future of big data in finance. Increasing integration with AI and ML is enabling financial institutions to move from descriptive analysis towards predictive and prescriptive decision-making, improving risk management, customer insights, and operational efficiency (Varshney, 2022). At the same time, the expansion of open banking, supported by regulations such as PSD2, is reshaping data ownership by promoting secure data sharing through APIs, shifting competition from data hoarding to data collaboration and fostering innovation within financial ecosystems (Zetzsche et al., 2020). The growing adoption of synthetic data further supports this evolution by allowing institutions to develop and validate models while preserving privacy and regulatory compliance (Jordon et al., 2022). Finally, increasing reliance on complex AI models has heightened the need for explainable, ethical AI, ensuring transparency, fairness, and accountability in automated financial decision-making (Adadi & Berrada, 2018).

26.7 Conclusion

The adoption of Big Data analytics has fundamentally reshaped the banking and finance sector, shifting decision-making from intuition-driven to data-driven. Financial institutions increasingly view data as a strategic asset, critical for maintaining competitive advantage. Effectively analysing vast, diverse datasets enables innovation in product development, operational efficiency, and market positioning. Advanced analytics help optimise processes, customise financial offerings, and support strategic leadership, making data fluency central to modern financial strategy.

From fraud detection to personalised banking, Big Data applications are driving measurable improvements in risk management, compliance, and customer engagement. ML models facilitate real-time monitoring, anomaly detection, and more accurate credit risk assessments while enhancing regulatory adherence. Detailed customer segmentation enables hyper-personalised services, increasing satisfaction and lifetime value. Achieving these benefits, however, requires addressing challenges such as modernising legacy IT systems, establishing strong data governance, and ensuring ethical handling of customer information. Moving forward, investments in scalable infrastructure and transparent, fair algorithmic decision-making will be essential to creating a resilient, efficient, and trustworthy global financial ecosystem.

Key Terms and Glossary

Big Data Extremely large and complex datasets that cannot be easily managed or analysed with traditional data processing tools.

Customer 360 A comprehensive view of a customer by aggregating data from all available touchpoints and sources.

Data Governance The overall management of the availability, usability, integrity, and security of data in an organisation.

Data Lake A centralised repository that allows you to store all your structured and unstructured data at any scale.

Data Silos A situation where data is isolated in separate departments or systems within an organisation, preventing integration and a unified view.

Test Your Understanding

Multiple-Choice Questions

1 Which of the following best defines Big Data in finance?

A Small datasets processed manually for decision-making
B Large, high-velocity, and diverse datasets enabling analytics-driven insights
C Data only from social media platforms
D Transaction logs only

2 Which Big Data characteristic refers to the trustworthiness and accuracy of financial data?

A Volume
B Velocity
C Veracity
D Value

3 In financial big data architecture, which layer is primarily responsible for integrating data from internal and external sources?

A Storage and Processing Layer
B Data Ingestion Layer
C Financial Analytics Layer
D API Integration Layer

4 Which ML model is commonly used in P2P lending to predict loan default risk?

A Logistic Regression
B Gradient Boosting Machine
C Random Forest
D All of the above

5 Which regulatory initiative promotes secure data sharing and open banking APIs in Europe?

A Basel III
B GDPR
C PSD2
D MiFID II

Short Questions

1 Explain the five Vs of Big Data and provide one example of their relevance in banking.
2 Describe the role of ML in fraud detection and credit risk assessment.
3 What are the key challenges in adopting Big Data analytics in financial institutions?

Analytical Questions

1 A retail bank wants to improve its real-time fraud detection system using Big Data analytics. Discuss how data ingestion, storage, and real-time processing layers contribute to this objective.
2 Consider a scenario where interest rate increases affect loan default risk differently from decreases. Explain how a NARDL model could be applied using financial transaction data to analyse this asymmetry.
3 Compare and contrast VAR and VECM models in the context of algorithmic trading and market risk analysis, highlighting the role of high-frequency and alternative data.

Case Study: Ant Group's Sesame Credit

Ant Group, a subsidiary of Alibaba, created Sesame Credit, a digital credit scoring system designed to assess the creditworthiness of individuals with limited or no formal credit history. The system aggregates vast amounts of data from Alipay's ecosystem, including payment histories, bill settlement records, social connections, online purchases, and even non-financial behaviours such as completing video games or online activities. By leveraging this alternative data, Sesame Credit provides scores that enable access to microloans, insurance, and other financial services, extending financial inclusion to millions of previously underserved consumers in China.

While the system has expanded access to credit, it raises significant ethical and societal concerns. Using personal and behavioural data for financial evaluation blurs the line between financial assessment and social surveillance, posing risks to individual privacy and autonomy. Additionally, reliance on unconventional indicators such as social interactions or gaming behaviour may introduce algorithmic bias, disproportionately affecting certain demographic groups. The approach also prompts questions about its acceptability in other cultural and regulatory contexts. Implementing a similar model in Western countries, where privacy expectations and data protection laws are stricter, would require careful consideration of consent, transparency, fairness, and potential societal consequences to ensure ethical compliance while pursuing financial inclusion (World Bank, 2021).

References

Shu, C. (2015). Data from Alibaba's E-commerce Sites Is Now Powering a Credit-Scoring Service. *TechCrunch*, 27 January. Available at: https://techcrunch.com (Accessed: 3 March 2026).

Zhang, W. (2016). Exploring the Improved Personal Credit Scoring Model of Ant Financial Services in its Disruptive Innovation Process. *International Conference on Applied Social Science Research*. Atlantis Press. Available at: https://www.atlantis-press.com (Accessed: 3 March 2026).

Case Study Questions

1 Discuss the ethical dilemma between financial inclusion and data privacy in the context of Sesame Credit.
2 What potential for algorithmic bias exists in a scoring system that incorporates data like social networks and gaming habits?
3 Could a similar model be successfully and ethically implemented in a Western country with different cultural norms around privacy? Why or why not?

Further Reading

Bernard, Marr (2015) *Big Data: Using SMART Big Data, Analytics and Metrics to Make Better Decisions and Improve Performance*. Chichester: John Wiley & Sons.

DalleMule, L., & Davenport, T.H. (2017). What's Your Data Strategy? *Harvard Business Review*, 95(3), 112–121.

McAfee, A., & Brynjolfsson, E. (2012). Big Data: The Management Revolution. *Harvard Business Review*, 90(10), 60–68.

References

Adadi, A., & Berrada, M. (2018). Peeking Inside the Black Box: A Survey on Explainable Artificial Intelligence (XAI). *IEEE Access*, 6, 52138–52160.

Apergis, N., & Payne, J.E. (2014) The Oil Price–Stock Market Nexus in the US: Evidence from Nonlinear Causality in Mean and Variance. *Energy Economics*, 45, 199–207.

Andersen, T.G., Bollerslev, T., Diebold, F.X., & Labys, P. (2001). The Distribution of Realized Exchange Rate Volatility. *Journal of the American Statistical Association*, 96(453), 42–55.

Arner, D.W., Barberis, J. & Buckley, R.P. (2017). FinTech, RegTech, and the Reconceptualisation of Financial Regulation. *Northwestern Journal of International Law & Business*, 37(3), 371–413.

Bartram, S.M., Branke, J. & Motahari, M., 2023. Artificial Intelligence in Financial Services. *Annual Review of Financial Economics*, 15, 87–107.

Bernanke, B.S., Gertler, M., & Watson, M.W. (1997) Systematic Monetary Policy and the Effects of Oil Price Shocks. *Brookings Papers on Economic Activity*, 1997(1), 91–157

Billio, M., Getmansky, M., Lo, A.W., & Pelizzon, L. (2012) Econometric Measures of Connectedness and Systemic Risk in the Finance and Insurance Sectors. *Journal of Financial Economics*, 104(3), 535–559.

Bodie, Z., Kane, A. & Marcus, A.J., 2021. *Investments* (12th ed.). New York: McGraw-Hill Education.

Brown, I., & Mues, C. (2012). An Experimental Comparison of Classification Algorithms for Imbalanced Credit Scoring Data Sets. *Expert Systems with Applications*, 39(3), 3446–3453.

Bughin, J., Hazan, E., Ramaswamy, S., Chui, M., Allas, T., Dahlström, P., Henke, N., & Trench, M. (2018) *Notes from the AI Frontier: Modeling the Impact of AI on the World Economy*. McKinsey Global Institute. Available at: https://www.mckinsey.com/featured-insights/artificial-intelligence/notes-from-the-ai-frontier-modeling-the-impact-of-ai-on-the-world-economy (Accessed: 10 Oct 2025).

Davenport, T.H. (2013). *Analytics at Work: Smarter Decisions, Better Results*. Boston: Harvard Business Review Press.

Deming, W. E. (2000). *The New Economics for Industry, Government, Education* (2nd ed.). Cambridge, Mass: MIT Press.

Dijcks, J.P., 2013. Oracle: Big Data for the Enterprise. *Oracle White Paper*.

Diebold, F.X. and Yilmaz, K. (2014) On the Network Topology of Variance Decompositions: Measuring the Connectedness of Financial Firms. *Journal of Econometrics*, 182(1), pp. 119–134.

EDXTV (2025). JPMorgan's LOXM and Beyond: AI Systems Reducing Slippage in Trade Execution. Available at: https://edxtv.com/jpmorgans-loxm-and-beyond-ai-systems-reducing-slippage-in-trade-execution/ (Accessed: 15 Oct 2025).

Gandomi, A. & Haider, M. (2015). Beyond the Hype: Big Data Concepts, Methods, and Analytics. *International Journal of Information Management*, 35(2), 137–144.

Jordon, J., Szpruch, L., Houssiau, F., Bottarelli, M., Cherubin, G., Maple, C. et al. (2022). *Synthetic Data – What, Why and How?* London: The Alan Turing Institute. Available at: *arXiv*. Available at: https://arxiv.org/abs/2205.03257

Krainikov, K., Stöckli, E. & Incekara-Hafalir, E. (2022). Machine Learning Approaches in Consumer Credit Risk Assessment: Performance Across Borrower Risk Segments. *Journal of Risk and Financial Management*, 15(9), p. 402. doi:10.3390/jrfm15090402

Kreps, J. (2014). *Kafka: A Distributed Messaging System for Log Processing. Proceedings of the 6th International Workshop on Networking Meets Databases*, 1–7.

Kumar, V., Rajan, B., Venkatesan, R. & Lecinski, J. (2019). Understanding the Role of Artificial Intelligence in Personalised Engagement Marketing. *California Management Review*, 61(4), 135–155.

Marr, B. (2015). *Big Data: Using SMART Big Data, Analytics and Metrics to Make Better Decisions and Improve Performance*. Hoboken: John Wiley & Sons.

McAfee, A., & Brynjolfsson, E., (2012). Big Data: The Management Revolution. *Harvard Business Review*, 90(10), 60–68.

Shin, Y., Yu, B., & Greenwood-Nimmo, M. (2014) Modelling Asymmetric Cointegration and Dynamic Multipliers in a Nonlinear ARDL Framework. In R.C. Sickles & W.C. Horrace (Eds.), *Festschrift in Honor of Peter Schmidt: Econometric Methods and Applications*. New York: Springer, pp. 281–314.

Sirignano, J. and Cont, R. (2019) Universal Features of Price Formation in Financial Markets: Perspectives from Deep Learning. *Quantitative Finance*, 19(9), 1449–1459

Varshney, K.R. (2022). *Trustworthy Machine Learning*. Chappaqua, NY: Independently Published.

West, J. & Bhattacharya, M. (2016). Intelligent Financial Fraud Detection: A Comprehensive Review. *Computers & Security*, 57, 47–66.

World Bank. (2021). *The Global Findex Database 2021: Financial Inclusion, Digital Payments, and Resilience in the Age of COVID-19*. Washington, DC: World Bank

Zetzsche, D.A., Buckley, R.P., Arner, D.W. & Barberis, J.N. (2020). The Future of Open Banking. *SSRN Electronic Journal*.

27 Machine Learning in Banking and Finance

Chapter Overview

This chapter explores the significant and transformative impact of Machine Learning (ML) on banking and financial services. Unlike traditional statistical methods, ML algorithms learn from data independently, enabling the identification of complex, non-linear relationships that support automated decision-making, predictive analytics, and prescriptive advice (Bishop, 2006). The chapter systematically reviews key ML paradigms, supervised, unsupervised, and Reinforcement Learning (RL), and their strategic applications in areas such as credit risk evaluation, high-frequency trading, and fraud detection. It also discusses practical challenges in deploying ML, including data integrity, model transparency, and the shift to operational use. The chapter concludes by examining the future of ML, with emphasis on more advanced, ethical, and integrated frameworks.

Learning Objectives

By the end of this chapter, you should be able to:

1. Define ML and explain its main paradigms, including supervised, unsupervised, and RL.
2. Identify and assess key ML applications in finance, such as credit scoring, algorithmic trading, fraud detection, and customer service.
3. Describe the ML project lifecycle within financial institutions and the role of ML Operations (MLOps) and model governance in ensuring regulatory compliance.
4. Analyse challenges in ML implementation, including data quality, model risk, interpretability, and algorithmic bias.
5. Discuss ethical considerations, emerging trends, and the future impact of ML on the financial sector.

27.1 Introduction

The banking and finance sector is experiencing a fundamental methodological transformation, shifting rapidly from traditional data-driven analysis to advanced, algorithm-driven decision architectures powered by ML. In contrast to conventional quantitative models

DOI: 10.4324/9781003775751-31

that depend on predetermined linear relationships and fixed operational rules, ML algorithms autonomously learn complex, non-linear interactions and identify hidden patterns within extensive historical datasets (Hastie et al., 2009). This adaptive capability enables financial institutions to develop resilient modelling frameworks that dynamically respond to changes in market volatility and consumer behaviour, thereby offering a significant competitive advantage over static systems.

The adoption of ML technologies is having a significant impact across essential financial functions. In credit and lending, ML systems surpass the limitations of traditional Fair Isaac Corporation (FICO) scoring by enabling institutions to assess and underwrite risk for previously underserved or unscorable populations. This advancement expands financial inclusion and optimises portfolio health. In capital markets, ML enables the instantaneous execution of high-frequency trading strategies and complex algorithmic operations at speeds beyond human capabilities. Furthermore, the integration of ML transforms critical functions such as risk management, fraud detection, and operational oversight from reactive processes to highly predictive and proactively managed practices.

Given the strategic importance of this transition, the shift constitutes a comprehensive restructuring of competitive capabilities rather than a mere efficiency improvement. This chapter presents a structured examination of ML in the financial domain. The discussion delineates core theoretical ML paradigms and explores their practical applications across key sub-sectors, including lending, wealth management, and regulatory compliance. Additionally, the analysis addresses significant practical and ethical challenges encountered during system implementation and projects the future trajectory and potential of machine-driven finance.

27.2 Core Paradigms of Machine Learning

Taxonomy of Machine Learning in Finance' can be broadly categorised into three main paradigms, each suited to different problem types and applications. These paradigms use data in distinct ways to generate insights, automate decision-making, and optimise financial processes.

Supervised Learning: Supervised learning is the most widely used ML approach in finance. Algorithms are trained on labelled datasets, where input features, such as income, transaction history, or account activity, are linked to specific outcomes, such as credit default or fraud. The model learns these relationships to make predictions on new data. Common algorithms include Logistic Regression, Decision Trees, Random Forests, and Gradient Boosting Machines like XGBoost (Friedman, 2001). For instance, Upstart uses supervised learning to evaluate borrower creditworthiness beyond traditional FICO scores, predicting default risk by incorporating alternative data like education, employment history, and utility payments. Supervised learning is also widely applied in fraud detection and risk assessment.

Unsupervised Learning: Unsupervised learning works on unlabelled data, identifying hidden structures, clusters, or patterns without predefined outcomes. This approach is particularly useful for customer segmentation, anomaly detection, and the identification of emerging fraud patterns. Techniques include K-Means Clustering, Hierarchical Clustering, and Principal Component Analysis (Shlens, 2014). For instance, HSBC applies unsupervised learning to detect unusual transaction patterns in large datasets, identifying potential money laundering or insider trading activities without prior examples of suspicious behaviour. It is also used for segmenting clients for personalised financial offerings.

Reinforcement Learning (RL): An agent interacts with a dynamic environment, makes sequential decisions, and receives feedback in the form of rewards or penalties. Over time, the agent learns strategies that maximise cumulative rewards. In finance, RL is increasingly used in algorithmic trading, portfolio optimisation, and dynamic pricing, where agents adapt to changing market conditions. For instance, Citadel, a quantitative hedge fund, applies RL to its trading algorithms to dynamically adjust positions in response to real-time market movements, aiming to optimise returns while managing risk. RL is also applied in adaptive portfolio management to continuously improve strategy.

27.2.1 The Machine Learning Lifecycle

The ML lifecycle in finance and banking comprises structured stages that develop effective, reliable, and compliant models. Each stage addresses real-world business needs while navigating regulatory and operational challenges (Figure 27.1).

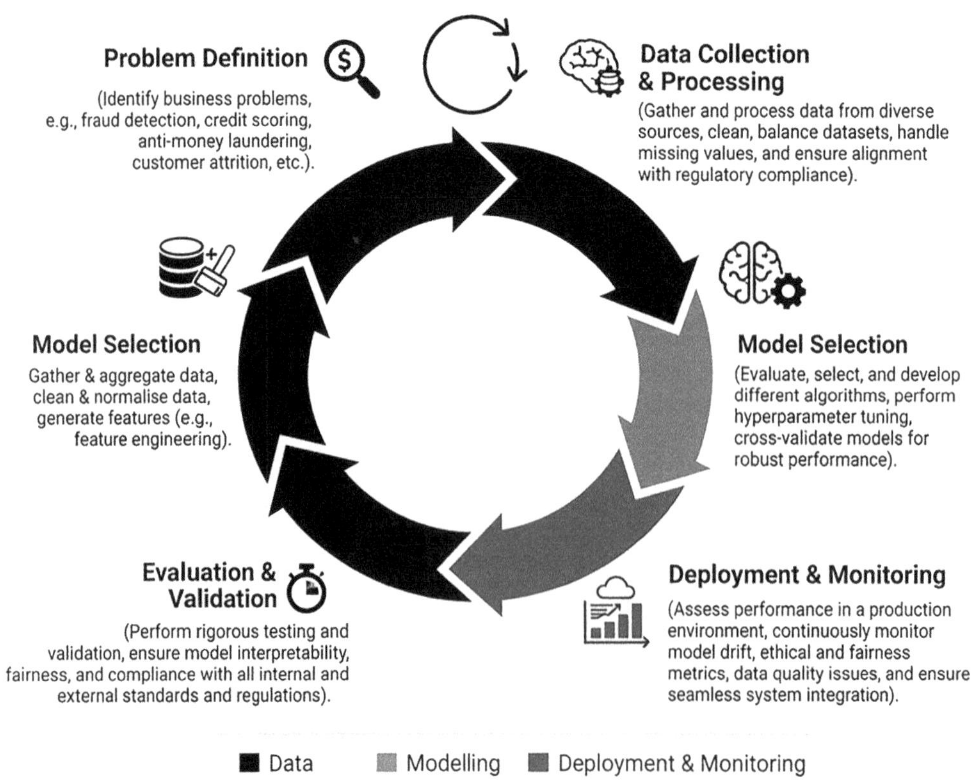

Figure 27.1 The Machine Learning Lifecycle in Finance and Banking.

Problem Definition: The first step is identifying a business problem suitable for ML. For example, a bank may aim to reduce credit card fraud by predicting suspicious transactions in real time. Clearly defining objectives ensures that the model aligns with institutional goals and compliance requirements.

Data Collection and Preprocessing: Financial institutions gather structured and unstructured data from sources such as transaction records, customer profiles, and market feeds. For instance, Lloyds Bank aggregates years of customer transaction histories to detect anomalous spending patterns. Preprocessing, including cleaning, normalisation, and feature engineering, ensures high-quality inputs for model training.

Model Selection and Training: Based on the problem, the bank selects an appropriate ML algorithm, such as supervised learning for credit scoring or RL for algorithmic trading. For example, Upstart uses supervised learning models to evaluate borrower creditworthiness beyond traditional FICO scores, leveraging alternative data like utility payments and employment history. Models are trained iteratively to optimise predictive accuracy.

Evaluation and Validation: Model performance is assessed using metrics appropriate to the financial task, such as precision, recall, or area under the Receiver Operating Characteristic curve. Backtesting is common in trading applications. For example, a hedge fund like Renaissance Technologies backtests algorithmic trading models against historical market data to ensure reliability before deployment.

Deployment and Monitoring: Once validated, models are integrated into production systems for real-time or batch decision-making. Continuous monitoring is essential to detect model drift or changing market conditions. For example, HSBC deploys artificial intelligence (AI) systems for Anti-Money Laundering (AML) transaction monitoring, automatically flagging suspicious activities while adjusting risk thresholds based on evolving customer behaviour.

27.3 Key Applications of Machine Learning in Finance

27.3.1 Credit Scoring and Underwriting

ML-based credit scoring extends beyond FICO-driven approaches by integrating alternative data such as cash flow transactions, rental and utility payments, and employment history to better assess borrowers with limited credit records. Models such as Gradient Boosting Machines capture complex, non-linear relationships across these features, improving risk prediction accuracy (Bartram et al., 2023). For example, a digital lender may evaluate income stability and consistent rent payments to approve a first-time borrower. Despite these benefits, lenders must ensure model transparency, fairness, and regulatory compliance to manage bias and ethical risks.

27.3.2 Algorithmic Trading and Portfolio Management

ML techniques, particularly deep learning and RL, are widely applied in algorithmic trading and portfolio management to process high-frequency market data, news sentiment, and macroeconomic indicators. These models adapt dynamically to changing market conditions and identify short-lived arbitrage opportunities (Bodie et al., 2021). For example, an RL-based trading agent can optimise execution strategies in equity markets by learning when to trade and how much to allocate. Similarly, robo-advisors apply ML to deliver automated, personalised portfolio allocations aligned with investor risk profiles.

27.3.3 Fraud Detection and AML

ML plays a critical role in fraud detection and AML by analysing large volumes of transactional data to identify suspicious behaviour. Supervised models leverage historical fraud cases to predict known risk patterns, while unsupervised and semi-supervised techniques detect novel or evolving fraud schemes. These approaches significantly reduce false positives compared to traditional rule-based systems (West & Bhattacharya, 2016). For example, anomaly detection models can flag unusual transaction sequences indicative of money laundering, enabling faster investigation and improved compliance effectiveness.

27.3.4 Customer Service and Sentiment Analysis

ML, particularly Natural Language Processing (NLP), enhances customer service and market analysis in financial institutions. NLP-driven chatbots and virtual assistants automate routine inquiries, improving response times and reducing operational costs. In parallel, sentiment analysis models process news articles, earnings calls, and social media to quantify market sentiment (Hirschberg & Manning, 2015). For example, a bank may deploy a chatbot to resolve account issues. At the same time, traders use sentiment indicators to adjust short-term trading strategies in response to shifts in public and investor perceptions.

27.4 Opportunity, Challenges, and Key Practical Issues

27.4.1 Opportunities and Convergence of Machine Learning

The integration of ML and AI in banking and finance presents significant opportunities for innovation while complementing traditional financial processes. These technologies enhance operational efficiency, decision-making, and customer engagement by processing vast volumes of structured and unstructured data.

Customer Experience: AI-driven chatbots and virtual assistants automate customer service, enabling rapid, personalised interactions while reducing reliance on manual processes. For example, digital banks like Monzo leverage ML to provide transaction categorisation, instant notifications, and tailored financial advice, enhancing user satisfaction.

Risk Management: ML models can identify complex patterns in historical and real-time data to improve risk assessment. Traditional credit scoring is augmented by alternative data sources, such as utility payments, social behaviour, and transaction histories, resulting in more comprehensive risk evaluation (Bartram et al., 2023).

Fraud Detection: AI and ML detect anomalies in transaction patterns more efficiently than rule-based systems. For instance, Lloyds Bank integrates card transactions, online banking activity, and Automated Teller Machine (ATM) usage into ML models to identify abnormal spending and prevent fraud in real time (West & Bhattacharya, 2016).

Credit Assessment: ML automates credit scoring, enabling faster, more accurate lending decisions while reducing human bias. Upstart, a US-based platform, uses supervised learning models that evaluate borrowers beyond traditional credit bureau scores, enabling faster loan approval with lower default rates (Fuster et al., 2019).

Operational Efficiency: AI-driven process automation reduces manual effort and improves productivity in areas such as compliance monitoring, report generation, and trade execution. Goldman Sachs, for example, integrates ML into algorithmic trading platforms to predict short-term price movements and execute trades at high speed, enhancing overall operational performance (Bodie et al., 2021).

Despite these advantages, convergence with traditional processes also presents challenges. Institutions must maintain transparency, ensure ethical deployment of ML models, and comply with data privacy regulations while leveraging ML to augment, not replace, established banking procedures.

27.4.2 Risks and Challenges of Machine Learning in Finance

The adoption of ML in financial institutions entails several inherent risks and challenges:

Data Quality and Availability: High-quality, representative data is crucial for model performance. Incomplete, siloed, or non-stationary datasets can lead to inaccurate predictions and systemic errors (Hashem et al., 2015). For example, ML models in fraud detection require continuous integration of transactional, online, and ATM data to ensure reliability.

Model Overfitting and Validation: Financial datasets are often noisy and non-stationary, which increases the risk of overfitting. Time-series cross-validation and out-of-sample testing are essential to ensure models generalise effectively to future market conditions (. Upstart applies time-based validation for credit models to avoid data leakage and maintain predictive accuracy.

Explainability and Transparency: Many advanced ML models, such as deep neural networks and gradient boosting machines, are opaque. Explainable AI (XAI) tools like Shapley Additive Explanations (SHAP) and Local Interpretable Model-agnostic Explanations (LIME) are increasingly used to interpret predictions and comply with regulatory requirements (Adadi & Berrada, 2018). Barclays, for instance, employs XAI to justify loan approvals under FCA regulations.

Regulatory Compliance: ML models must comply with financial regulations, including the Federal Reserve and Office of the Comptroller of the Currency Model Risk Management guidelines (SR 11-7), requiring independent validation, documentation, and continuous performance evaluation.

Cybersecurity and Privacy: ML systems process sensitive customer data, necessitating strong encryption, anonymisation, and secure pipelines to prevent breaches and ensure General Data Protection Regulation compliance. Revolut, for example, uses encrypted pipelines for ML applications in fraud detection and credit assessment while maintaining privacy standards.

27.4.3 Key Practical Issues in Implementing Machine Learning

Financial institutions face several operational and technical issues when deploying ML systems:

Data Acquisition and Feature Engineering: Transforming raw financial data into meaningful features requires substantial domain expertise. For example, in fraud detection, Lloyds Bank converts transactional patterns into features such as geographic anomalies and spending frequency to improve model accuracy.

Model Deployment and MLOps: Transitioning from development to production requires robust MLOps frameworks to handle versioning, monitoring, and retraining. HSBC applies MLOps pipelines to continuously monitor AI-driven AML transaction monitoring models, ensuring accuracy despite changing transaction patterns.

Scalability and Integration: ML models must integrate seamlessly with legacy systems and real-time transaction platforms. Goldman Sachs' trading systems demonstrate how ML can handle millions of high-frequency trades without latency, ensuring decisions are executed within milliseconds.

Ethical Use and Governance: Institutions must balance innovation with transparency, fairness, and accountability. Ethical considerations include preventing algorithmic bias in lending and ensuring models do not disadvantage vulnerable populations.

Model Risk Management: Regular model validation, documentation, and independent review are essential to mitigate risks arising from errors or unintended consequences. Barclays implements structured governance to ensure all models are auditable, interpretable, and regulatory-compliant.

27.5 The Future of Machine Learning

The future of ML in finance is expected to be shaped by several converging trends that enhance predictive accuracy, decision-making, and operational efficiency. Advances in deep learning and RL will enable sophisticated market simulations, stress testing, and highly personalised financial products, supporting adaptive strategies and automation across institutions. Causal ML will move beyond correlation to identify true cause-and-effect relationships, allowing banks to optimise interventions, assess marketing effectiveness, and improve resource allocation. Federated learning will facilitate collaborative model training across multiple banks without sharing raw data, preserving privacy while enhancing fraud detection, risk assessment, and other applications. Concurrently, ethical AI and bias mitigation will become essential, with standardised frameworks ensuring fairness, transparency, and regulatory compliance, ultimately providing both a risk management safeguard and a competitive advantage in the evolving financial landscape.

27.6 Conclusion

ML has transformed finance and banking by enabling data-driven decision-making, enhancing risk assessment, and improving operational efficiency. Key applications include credit scoring, fraud detection, algorithmic trading, and automated customer service, delivering faster processes, greater accuracy, and stronger security. Successful implementation requires high-quality data, robust governance, and adherence to regulatory standards, including transparency and bias mitigation.

Looking ahead, the future of ML in finance depends on strategic integration rather than technology alone. Institutions that embed models into core operations, prioritise ethical AI, maintain continuous oversight, and invest in explainable, risk-aware frameworks will gain a competitive advantage. When technical innovation aligns with governance and organisational strategy, ML can drive scalable, secure, and customer-centric solutions while sustaining trust and regulatory compliance in the global financial system.

Key Terms and Glossary

Feature Engineering The process of using domain knowledge to create input features that make ML algorithms work better.

MLOps (Machine Learning Operations) A set of practices that aims to deploy and maintain ML models in production reliably and efficiently.

Overfitting A modelling error that occurs when a function is too closely aligned to a limited set of data points, reducing its predictive power.

Supervised Learning A type of ML where the model is trained on a labelled dataset.

Unsupervised Learning A type of ML where the model finds patterns in an unlabelled dataset.

Test Your Understanding

Multiple-Choice Questions

1 Which of the following best describes supervised learning in finance?

A Discovering hidden patterns in unlabelled data
B Learning from feedback in dynamic trading environments
C Training models on labelled data to predict outcomes such as credit default
D Simulating financial markets using reinforcement strategies

2 Which ML paradigm is primarily used for portfolio optimisation and algorithmic trading?

A Supervised learning
B Unsupervised learning
C RL
D Semi-supervised learning

3 XAI tools such as SHAP and LIME are primarily used in finance to:

A Increase transaction speed in high-frequency trading
B Enhance model interpretability and regulatory compliance
C Automatically generate alternative data sources
D Train unsupervised clustering algorithms

4 A major challenge in deploying ML models in finance is:

A Excessive computing speed
B Data privacy and cybersecurity
C Overabundance of labelled datasets
D Low-dimensional data

5 Federated learning in financial ML primarily addresses:

A Reducing latency in algorithmic trading
B Training models collaboratively across institutions while preserving data privacy
C Automating customer service using chatbots
D Detecting high-frequency trading anomalies

Short Questions

1 What is the key difference between supervised and unsupervised ML?
2 Describe the role of RL in algorithmic trading.
3 Identify two key ethical or regulatory challenges associated with ML adoption in finance.

Analytical Question

1 A retail bank wants to implement ML for real-time fraud detection. Explain how data acquisition, feature engineering, model selection, and MLOps pipelines contribute to building an effective, compliant system.
2 Discuss how federated learning and causal ML could be applied to enhance cross-institutional risk assessment while ensuring data privacy and regulatory compliance.
3 Describe how a Model Risk Management framework, like SR 11-7, would need to change to handle the special risks of a self-learning RL trading algorithm, compared to a traditional static supervised learning model.

Case Study: Renaissance Technologies and Algorithmic Trading

Renaissance Technologies is a secretive quantitative hedge fund best known for its Medallion Fund, which has consistently delivered extraordinary returns for decades. The firm's success is largely due to its use of advanced ML and statistical models that detect subtle, non-linear patterns in vast amounts of market data. Unlike traditional financial firms, Renaissance hires mathematicians, physicists, and computer scientists rather than conventional finance professionals. This multidisciplinary team develops and refines highly sophisticated algorithms that can process large datasets, identify emerging market signals, and execute trades at high speed.

The reliance on ML provides a strong competitive advantage, but it also introduces unique risks. Models may behave unpredictably during extreme or unexpected market events, sometimes called *black swan* events, leading to significant losses if not properly managed. Additionally, many of the firm's algorithms operate as *black boxes*, making it difficult for internal teams to fully understand or explain how trading decisions are generated. This can create challenges for risk management and regulatory compliance, as decisions driven by complex ML models may lack transparency.

Renaissance Technologies illustrates both the transformative potential and the inherent complexities of fully algorithmic trading, highlighting the importance of expertise, robust oversight, and careful consideration of model limitations in financial innovation.

Reference

Bodie, Z., Kane, A., & Marcus, A. J. (2021). *Investments* (13th ed.).New York: McGraw-Hill Education.

Case Study Questions

1 Why is a multidisciplinary team of scientists often more successful in developing trading algorithms than a team of traditional financial experts?
2 What are the unique risks associated with relying entirely on ML-driven trading strategies, especially during black swan market events?
3 How might the black box nature of some complex ML models pose a challenge for internal risk management at a firm like Renaissance?

Further Reading

Hastie, T., Tibshirani, R., & Friedman, J. (2009). *The Elements of Statistical Learning*. New York: Springer.

Mehrabi, N., Morstatter, F., Saxena, N., Lerman, K., & Galstyan, A. (2021). A Survey on Bias and Fairness in Machine Learning. *ACM Computing Surveys (CSUR)*, 54(6), 1–35.

Sculley, D., Holt, G., Golovin, D., Davydov, E., Phillips, T., Ebner, D., Chaudhary, V., Young, M., Crespo, J.F., & Dennison, D. (2015). Hidden Technical Debt in Machine Learning Systems. *Advances in Neural Information Processing Systems*, 28, 2503–2511.

References

Adadi, A., & Berrada, M. (2018). Peeking Inside the Black-Box: A Survey on Explainable Artificial Intelligence (XAI). *IEEE Access*, 6, 52138–52160.

Bartram, S. M., Branke, J., & Motahari, M. (2023). Artificial Intelligence in Financial Services. *Annual Review of Financial Economics*, 15, 87–107.

Bishop, C. M. (2006). *Pattern Recognition and Machine Learning*. New York: Springer.

Bodie, Z., Kane, A., & Marcus, A. J. (2021). *Investments* (12th ed.). New York: McGraw-Hill Education.

Friedman, J. H. (2001). Greedy Function Approximation: A Gradient Boosting Machine. *Annals of Statistics*, 29(5), 1189–1232.

Fuster, A., Plosser, M., Schnabl, P. and Vickery, J. (2019) The Role of Technology in Mortgage Lending. *The Review of Financial Studies*, 32(5), pp. 1854–1899.

Hastie, T., Tibshirani, R., & Friedman, J. (2009). *The Elements of Statistical Learning: Data Mining, Inference, and Prediction* (2nd ed.). New York: Springer.

Hashem, I.A.T., Yaqoob, I., Anuar, N.B., Mokhtar, S., Gani, A. and Khan, S.U. (2015) The Rise of "big data" on Cloud Computing: Review and Open Research Issues. *Information Systems*, 47, 98–115

Hirschberg, J., & Manning, C. D. (2015). Advances in Natural Language Processing. *Science*, 349(6245), 261–266.

Shlens, J. (2014). A Tutorial on Principal Component Analysis. *arXiv preprint arXiv:1404.1100*.

West, J., & Bhattacharya, M. (2016). Intelligent Financial Fraud Detection: A Comprehensive Review. *Computers & Security*, 57, 47–66.

28 Cybersecurity and Digital Resilience

Chapter Overview

This chapter provides a comprehensive examination of cybersecurity and digital resilience in the financial services sector. Accelerated digital transformation and the proliferation of big data have intensified the complexity of cyber threats, posing risks to financial stability and undermining consumer confidence. The chapter analyses the evolving threat landscape, distinguishing the roles of cybersecurity in protecting assets and data from malicious activity, and digital resilience in ensuring operational continuity during disruptions. It further explores technological frameworks, regulatory mandates, and strategic measures essential for establishing secure and resilient financial infrastructures. Key focus areas include the integration of Artificial Intelligence (AI), cloud security, third-party risk management, and adherence to regulatory standards as fundamental components of an effective and sustainable digital defence strategy (BIS, 2023; FSB, 2022; NIST, 2023).

Learning Objectives

By the end of this chapter, you should be able to:

1. Explain the difference between cybersecurity and digital resilience and describe how they work together to protect financial institutions.
2. Identify and analyse major cyber threat vectors targeting banks and understand the motivations of various threat actors.
3. Evaluate the components of a modern cybersecurity framework, including basic controls and advanced technologies such as AI-driven security tools.
4. Design a digital resilience strategy, covering business continuity (BC), incident response, and disaster recovery (DR) planning.
5. Assess the challenges and emerging trends that are shaping the future of cybersecurity and digital resilience in the financial sector.

DOI: 10.4324/9781003775751-32

28.1 Introduction

The financial services industry occupies a pivotal position within the global cybersecurity landscape. It serves both as a primary target for malicious actors and as a crucial component in defending against systemic disruption. This dual responsibility has intensified as digital transformation accelerates. The sector has experienced widespread adoption of big data analytics, large-scale cloud migration, and the growth of application programming interface (API)-centric ecosystems. While these technological advancements have fostered significant innovation and efficiency, they have also substantially increased the sector's attack surface. This expansion has introduced complex interdependencies and novel vulnerabilities that require advanced protective strategies.

In this context, the threat landscape facing financial institutions has changed significantly. Both the sophistication and frequency of cyberattacks have increased at an alarming rate. Contemporary adversaries include opportunistic criminal organisations employing advanced ransomware, as well as well-funded state-sponsored groups. These threat actors utilise highly targeted, persistent tactics to compromise critical infrastructure, disrupt operations, and exfiltrate sensitive data. The scale and complexity of these threats require a proactive and adaptive security strategy. Financial institutions must transition from reactive incident response to predictive intelligence and comprehensive preventive frameworks.

In response to escalating risks, the financial services sector is undergoing a significant strategic transformation. The industry is shifting from traditional perimeter-based security models to a comprehensive, integrated framework. This new approach combines robust cybersecurity controls with proactive digital resilience strategies. It is designed to maintain uninterrupted operational continuity, protect proprietary and customer data, and preserve financial stability, even during severe cyber incidents (Lagioia, 2023; World Economic Forum, 2024). By embedding resilience across its digital infrastructure, the sector seeks not only to deter cyberattacks but also to enable rapid recovery and adaptation. This strategy strengthens trust and stability in an increasingly interconnected, high-risk digital environment.

28.2 The Cyber Threat Landscape

28.2.1 Key Threat Vectors in Cybersecurity

Financial institutions face a wide range of cyber threats due to their critical role in the economy and reliance on digital systems.

Ransomware-as-a-Service (RaaS): RaaS provides attack tools as a service, enabling even relatively inexperienced cybercriminals to launch ransomware attacks that can disrupt critical banking operations. For example, the 2021 Colonial Pipeline incident in the United States demonstrated how outsourced ransomware tools can cause significant operational and economic impact.

Supply Chain and Third-Party Attacks: Cyber adversaries frequently exploit vulnerabilities in less-secure vendors, software suppliers, or cloud service providers to gain unauthorised access to financial networks. The 2020 SolarWinds breach exemplifies this risk, as multiple organisations, including financial institutions, were compromised through a trusted vendor's software update.

API Security Vulnerabilities: The expansion of open banking and interconnected financial systems has increased the attack surface through APIs. Poorly secured APIs may expose sensitive customer information. For instance, a vulnerability in a European bank's API enabled unauthorised access to account data, illustrating the risks of FinTech integration.

AI-Powered Attacks: Malicious actors increasingly leverage generative AI to create deepfake identities, conduct sophisticated social engineering, and develop evasive malware. A notable example occurred in 2022, when an AI-generated voice scam deceived a UK company into transferring €220,000, highlighting the practical dangers of AI-enabled fraud.

Cloud Configuration Exploits: Misconfigurations in cloud infrastructure can result in unauthorised data access. Capital One's 2019 breach, which affected over 100 million customers due to a misconfigured Amazon Web Services firewall, underscores the critical importance of secure cloud configuration and monitoring.

28.2.2 Motivations and Actors in Cybersecurity

Financial Gain: One of the primary motivations driving cybercriminal activity is the pursuit of direct financial profit. This may be achieved through fraudulent transactions, the theft of sensitive financial data, or ransomware extortion. For instance, the 2017 WannaCry ransomware outbreak, which impacted numerous organisations worldwide, including financial institutions, illustrates how attackers exploit malware to demand payments in exchange for restoring access to critical systems.

Geopolitical Objectives: Nation-state actors may target financial institutions to achieve strategic objectives, such as destabilising national economies, acquiring sensitive information, or supporting proxy operations. For instance, the 2015 cyberattack on the Bangladesh Bank, attributed to state-sponsored hackers, resulted in the theft of $81 million, demonstrating how financial systems can be manipulated to serve geopolitical agendas.

Hacktivism: Ideologically motivated actors engage in cyberattacks to advance political or social causes. These attacks often seek to disrupt financial services or damage institutional reputations. For instance, anonymous-affiliated campaigns against major banks during the 2010–2011 global protests illustrate how hacktivist groups exploit financial infrastructure to convey political messages and influence public discourse.

Insider Threats: Employees or contractors with authorised access may intentionally or inadvertently compromise sensitive systems and data. For instance, in 2014, a rogue trader at a European bank manipulated internal systems, causing significant financial losses and reputational damage, highlighting the substantial risks posed by trusted insiders.

28.3 The Cybersecurity Defence Framework

The financial sector is increasingly reliant on digital infrastructure, making cybersecurity a critical component of operational resilience and regulatory compliance. Banks and financial institutions manage vast volumes of sensitive information and execute highly time-sensitive transactions. Any compromise of these systems can result in substantial financial losses, reputational damage, and legal penalties. To mitigate these risks, a robust cybersecurity framework is essential. Effective cybersecurity in finance requires a multi-layered approach that integrates foundational security controls, advanced technological solutions, and adherence to both national and international regulatory standards (Figure 28.1).

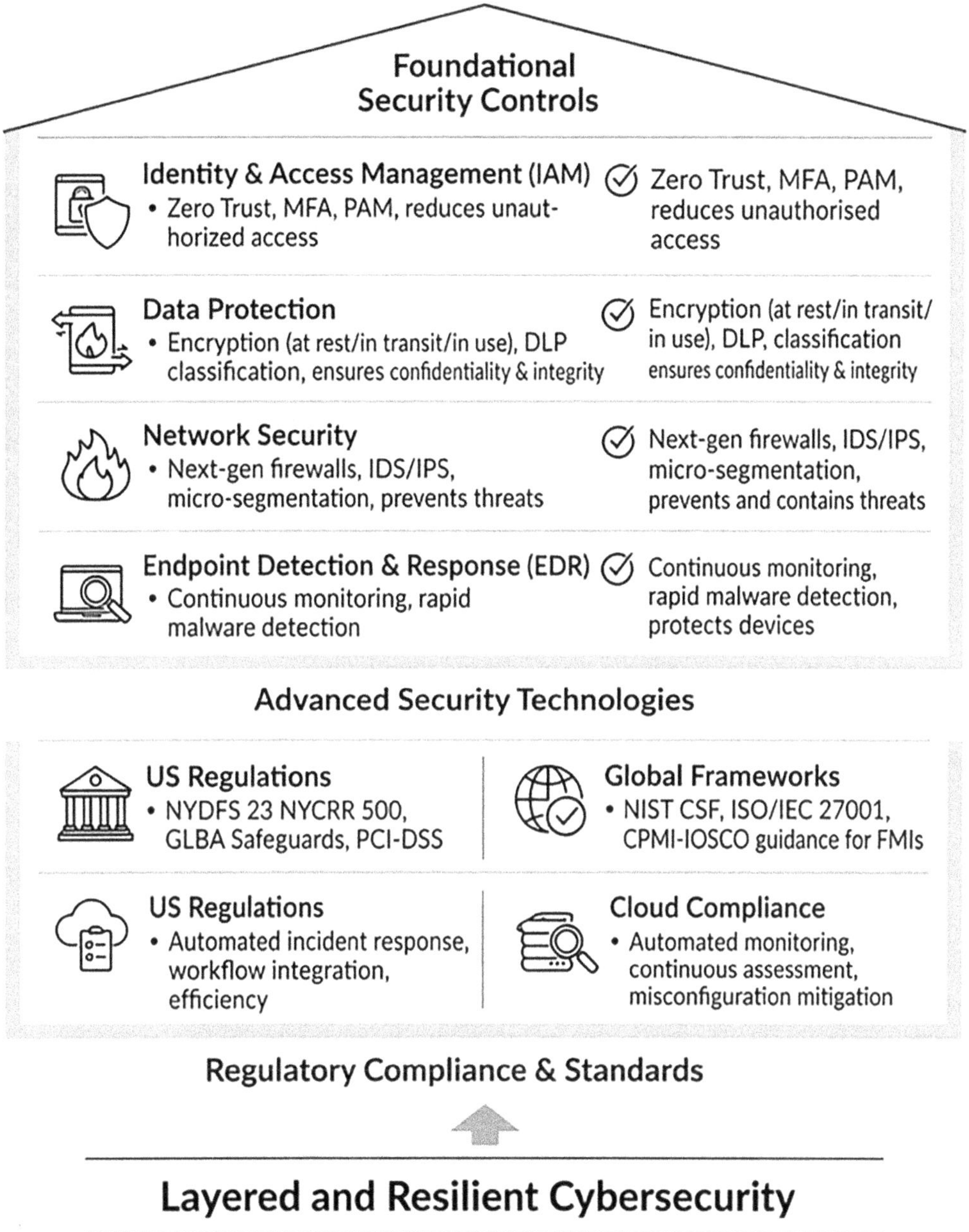

Figure 28.1 The Cybersecurity Defence Framework in Finance and Banking.

28.3.1 Foundational Security Controls

Identity and Access Management (IAM): Controlling access to financial systems is one of the most fundamental cybersecurity measures. Institutions increasingly implement Zero Trust principles, operating under the assumption of 'never trust, always verify'. Multi-factor authentication (MFA) strengthens identity verification, while privileged access management ensures high-level accounts are closely monitored and restricted to prevent misuse. By enforcing strict IAM protocols, financial institutions significantly reduce the risk of unauthorised access and minimise potential damage in the event of credential compromise (NIST, 2023).

Data Protection: Protecting sensitive financial data is central to cybersecurity efforts. Organisations deploy encryption techniques to secure data at rest, in transit, and even during processing. Data loss prevention tools monitor and prevent unauthorised data transfers, while data classification frameworks categorise information based on sensitivity and regulatory requirements. Collectively, these measures maintain the confidentiality, integrity, and availability of financial information, ensuring that both customer and institutional data are protected from unauthorised access or misuse.

Network Security: Network defences form a critical line of protection against external threats. Next-generation firewalls, intrusion detection and prevention systems (IDS/IPS), and micro-segmentation techniques are commonly employed to isolate network segments and contain potential breaches. By controlling network traffic and monitoring for anomalous activity, banks can detect early indicators of attacks and mitigate threats before they propagate across the network.

Endpoint Detection and Response (EDR): The proliferation of connected devices in financial operations increases exposure to cyber risks. EDR solutions continuously monitor endpoints for suspicious activity, enabling rapid detection and response to threats. This proactive approach prevents the spread of malware and minimises system compromise, ensuring operational continuity across the organisation.

28.3.2 Advanced Security Technologies

AI and machine learning (ML) for Threat Detection: AI and ML algorithms are increasingly leveraged to analyse large volumes of network traffic and user behaviour. These tools can identify anomalies and detect emerging threats more effectively than traditional monitoring methods, providing proactive defences against sophisticated attacks. By learning from patterns of normal activity, AI-driven systems can recognise deviations indicative of cyber intrusions, enabling a timely response (BIS, 2023).

Security Orchestration, Automation, and Response (SOAR): SOAR platforms automate incident response workflows, integrate threat intelligence, and reduce reliance on manual processes. By streamlining the detection, investigation, and mitigation of cyber threats, SOAR enhances operational efficiency and ensures faster remediation, minimising potential business disruption.

Deception Technology: Deception solutions deploy realistic decoy assets, such as honeypots, to attract potential attackers. These decoy systems allow security teams to observe malicious behaviour in a controlled environment, gaining insights into attack methods while protecting genuine operational assets. This proactive strategy improves threat intelligence and informs defensive measures.

Cloud Security Posture Management (CSPM): As financial services increasingly adopt cloud computing, CSPM tools provide continuous monitoring and automated assessment of cloud environments. These solutions detect misconfigurations, enforce security policies, and ensure regulatory compliance, reducing the risk of unauthorised access or data exposure in cloud-based infrastructure.

28.3.3 Regulatory Compliance and Standards

Financial institutions operate in highly regulated environments, necessitating adherence to both national and international standards. In the United States, key regulations include the New York Department of Financial Services Cybersecurity Regulation (23 New York Codes, Rules, and Regulations 500), the Gramm-Leach-Bliley Act (GLBA) Safeguards Rule, and the Payment Card Industry Data Security Standard, all of which provide specific guidance on safeguarding financial data and implementing robust cybersecurity controls.

Internationally, frameworks such as the National Institute of Standards and Technology (NIST) Cybersecurity Framework, ISO/IEC 27001, and Committee on Payments and Market Infrastructures – International Organisation of Securities Commissions guidance on cyber resilience for financial market infrastructures establish globally recognised best practices. Compliance with these standards ensures that financial institutions maintain comprehensive risk management processes, effective governance, and incident response capabilities, reducing exposure to cyber threats and enhancing stakeholder confidence.

28.3.4 Integrated Cybersecurity Approach

By integrating foundational controls, advanced technological solutions, and regulatory compliance measures, financial institutions can build a layered and resilient cybersecurity defence framework. This multi-pronged strategy not only mitigates the risk of cyberattacks but also supports operational continuity, regulatory compliance, and financial system stability. Furthermore, a robust cybersecurity posture fosters stakeholder trust, protects organisational reputation, and enables financial institutions to safely leverage digital transformation initiatives, including cloud services, AI analytics, and open banking platforms.

In conclusion, the dynamic and evolving cyber threat landscape requires financial institutions to implement comprehensive, multi-layered cybersecurity frameworks. Combining preventive controls, cutting-edge technologies, and strict compliance with regulatory standards enables banks to effectively defend against emerging threats while maintaining operational resilience and safeguarding sensitive financial data.

28.4 Digital Resilience: Beyond Prevention

28.4.1 The Resilience Mindset

Digital resilience represents a strategic shift in cybersecurity philosophy, recognising that no preventive measure can eliminate the risk of cyber incidents. Instead of relying solely on defensive controls, digital resilience emphasises the organisation's capacity to sustain essential operations under adverse conditions and to restore normal functionality promptly following disruptions. This mindset requires an adaptive approach that integrates proactive planning, real-time response capabilities, and continuous improvement to minimise the operational, financial, and reputational impacts of cyber events.

28.4.2 Core Components of Digital Resilience

A robust digital resilience framework comprises several interdependent elements designed to ensure organisational continuity and rapid recovery. BC/DR planning is a foundational component that involves developing and maintaining comprehensive strategies to restore critical systems and data. This includes implementing segregated, regularly tested backups and clearly defined recovery objectives, such as Recovery Time Objectives (RTOs) and Recovery Point Objectives (RPOs).

Incident Response Planning is another essential element, encompassing the establishment of formalised procedures, delineation of roles and responsibilities within a Computer Incident Response Team, and the execution of regular tabletop exercises. These measures enable organisations to respond to security incidents in a coordinated, efficient, and systematic manner.

System Redundancy and Failover Capabilities are critical for ensuring the availability of mission-critical systems, including financial transaction platforms and operational infrastructure. By architecting systems with redundancy and automatic failover mechanisms, organisations can maintain service continuity during outages or attacks.

Lastly, Cyber Crisis Management addresses the broader strategic implications of cyber incidents, providing executive-level protocols for managing legal considerations, stakeholder communications, and public relations. Together, these components form an integrated framework that extends beyond mere prevention, equipping organisations with the resilience required to navigate an increasingly complex and hostile digital environment.

28.5 Comparing and Contrasting Cybersecurity and Digital Resilience

Cybersecurity focuses on preventing cyber threats through protective measures like firewalls, encryption, and access controls. Digital resiliency, by contrast, accepts that some attacks will succeed and emphasises maintaining operations, rapid recovery, and adaptability. It integrates BC, DR, incident response, and system redundancy. In short, cybersecurity is about prevention, while digital resiliency ensures the organisation can withstand and recover from incidents. Together, they form a complementary framework for effectively managing cyber risk. Table 28.1 compares cybersecurity and digital resilience.

Table 28.1 A Comparison Between Cybersecurity and Digital Resiliency

Feature	*Cybersecurity*	*Digital Resilience*	*Key Takeaway*
Primary Focus	Prevent, Protect, Detect Keep threats out, secure assets, and identify breaches early	Respond, Recover, Adapt Maintain BC during and after an incident, minimising impact	*Cybersecurity* aims to prevent incidents; *Digital Resilience* ensures you can withstand and recover from them
Time Orientation	Proactive and Predictive Focused on stopping incidents *before* they occur	Reactive and Adaptive Focused on managing *ongoing* incidents and improving *future* readiness	They form a continuous lifecycle: before, during, and after an attack
Core Question	How do we keep the attackers out?	How do we keep the business running if they get in?	Cybersecurity is the locked door; Resilience is the plan to keep the lights on if the door is breached

(*Continued*)

Table 28.1 (Continued)

Feature	*Cybersecurity*	*Digital Resilience*	*Key Takeaway*
Key Metrics	• MTTD: Mean Time to Detect • MTTR: Mean Time to Respond • Threats Blocked/ Incident Count	• RTO (how fast to restore) • RPO (acceptable data loss) • Downtime Cost/ Impact Severity	Cybersecurity metrics track defensive performance; Resilience metrics track operational readiness and recovery
Key Technologies	Firewalls, IDS/IPS, EDR/ XDR, IAM, Encryption, SIEM, Vulnerability Scanners	Immutable Backups, DR Systems, Redundant Architectures, SOAR, Chaos Engineering Tools	Cybersecurity tech is the shield. Resilience tech is the safety net and repair kit
Organisational Mindset	Build an impenetrable fortress Emphasises Zero Trust, defence-in-depth, and robust perimeters	Assume breaches are inevitable Emphasises BC, graceful degradation, and adaptive recovery	The strategic shift is from absolute prevention to prepared endurance

28.6 Risks and Challenges in Cybersecurity and Digital Resilience

Financial institutions face significant risks due to the asymmetry of attack: defenders must secure all assets, while attackers need only exploit one vulnerability. The 2016 Bangladesh Bank cyber heist, which saw over US$100 million stolen via the Society for Worldwide Interbank Financial Telecommunication vulnerabilities, illustrates this risk (Balu, 2022).

Regulatory fragmentation adds complexity, as banks must comply with multiple, sometimes conflicting regimes such as GDPR, GLBA, and local cybersecurity laws, increasing operational costs and creating potential security gaps (Waliullah et al., 2025).

The innovation-security trade-off presents another challenge. Rapid deployment of digital services can introduce vulnerabilities if security testing is insufficient, particularly in open API and mobile banking platforms. Cyber insurance is also increasingly limited, with higher premiums and narrower coverage, making robust preventive measures essential.

Key practical issues include supply chain vulnerabilities, where third-party components may be compromised, as evidenced by the rising number of fintech breaches linked to vendors (Qodex, 2025). Emerging technologies such as AI, IoT, and blockchain enhance threat detection but introduce new risks, including adversarial attacks and privacy concerns (Department for Science, Innovation and Technology, 2025). Cyber threat awareness and continuous staff training are crucial to counter phishing, ransomware, and AI-driven attacks (Terranova Security, 2024). Finally, incident response planning with regular testing ensures operational continuity and rapid recovery from breaches.

28.7 Future Trends in Cybersecurity and Digital Resilience

The future of financial cybersecurity and digital resilience is increasingly shaped by technological innovation, regulatory evolution, and the growing sophistication of cyber threats. Quantum-resistant cryptography is emerging as a critical focus, as financial institutions prepare for the advent of quantum computing, which could compromise current encryption standards, prompting the adoption of post-quantum algorithms to safeguard sensitive data (BIS, 2023). Regulatory pressures are reinforcing resilience strategies, with authorities such as the U.S. Securities and Exchange Commission mandating comprehensive incident disclosure, penetration testing, and cyber war-gaming exercises to ensure preparedness and adaptive response capabilities (SEC, 2023). Technological advancements, particularly integrated AI-driven defence systems, allow institutions to predict, detect, and respond to threats autonomously and in real time, countering increasingly sophisticated attacks. Concurrently, the principle of resilience-by-design is gaining prominence, advocating for integrating security and continuity features into the architecture of new financial systems and products rather than treating them as post-deployment measures. Collectively, these developments indicate a strategic shift towards proactive, adaptive, and technology-enabled approaches to securing financial infrastructure while ensuring operational continuity and long-term organisational stability (FSB, 2022; NIST, 2023).

28.8 Conclusion

In today's financial sector, cybersecurity and digital resilience must be recognised as integrated strategic priorities rather than isolated operational functions. Effective protection relies not only on robust perimeter defences but also on an organisation's capacity to maintain critical operations and transactional integrity amid disruptions. Key measures, such as MFA, network segmentation, and proactive threat intelligence, are essential in fostering resilience while minimising downtime and enabling rapid recovery, mitigating financial and reputational losses that often exceed preventive expenditures. Leading institutions are moving from fragmented security approaches to comprehensive defence-in-depth frameworks, combining advanced preventive controls, including Zero Trust architectures and EDR systems, with agile incident response and recovery protocols.

Embedding resilience within governance structures and organisational culture is critical for sustaining cyber readiness. Executive leadership must ensure accountability through oversight and resource allocation, while fostering a security-aware workforce remains paramount, particularly as human error accounts for the majority of breaches. Continuous employee training reinforces individual responsibility and strengthens enterprise-wide defence. By treating cybersecurity and digital resilience as enduring strategic imperatives, financial organisations can protect stakeholder trust, maintain operational continuity, and achieve a competitive advantage in an increasingly complex and volatile digital environment.

Key Terms and Glossary

Penetration Testing An authorised simulated cyberattack on a computer system, performed to evaluate the security of the system.

Ransomware Malicious software that blocks access to a computer system or data until a sum of money is paid.

RPO (Recovery Point Objective) The maximum acceptable amount of data loss measured in time.

RTO (Recovery Time Objective) The target amount of time within which a business process must be restored after a disruption to avoid unacceptable consequences.

Security Orchestration, Automation and Response (SOAR) A suite of technologies that enable organisations to collect data about security threats from multiple sources and automate responses to low-level threats.

Zero Trust A security model based on the principle of "never trust, always verify", requiring strict identity verification for every person and device trying to access resources on a network, regardless of whether they are sitting within or outside of the network perimeter.

Test Your Understanding

Multiple-Choice Questions

1 Which of the following best describes the distinction between cybersecurity and digital resilience?

A. Cybersecurity prevents incidents; digital resilience ensures operational continuity and recovery
B. Cybersecurity focuses on system redundancy; digital resilience focuses on encryption
C. Cybersecurity ensures compliance; digital resilience prevents attacks entirely
D. Cybersecurity is reactive; digital resilience is proactive

2 What do supply chain vulnerabilities in financial institutions pose as a key risk?

A. Over-reliance on in-house cybersecurity teams
B. Exploitation of third-party software or vendor components to access financial systems
C. Failure to adopt cloud computing
D. Excessive regulatory oversight

3 Which of the following technologies is specifically used to automate and orchestrate incident response workflows in financial cybersecurity?

A. CSPM
B. Deception Technology
C. SOAR
D. EDR

4 The 2016 Bangladesh Bank cyber heist illustrates which cybersecurity challenge?

A. Insider threats
B. Regulatory fragmentation
C. Asymmetry of attack
D. Innovation-security trade-off

5 Which future trend in financial cybersecurity focuses on preparing institutions for threats posed by quantum computing?
A. AI-driven threat detection
B. Quantum-resistant cryptography
C. Resilience-by-design
D. Federated incident response

Short Questions

1 Explain the role of incident response planning in digital resilience within financial institutions.
2 What are the primary motivations of cyber threat actors targeting banks? Provide examples.
3 Describe how AI and ML enhance threat detection in financial cybersecurity.

Analytical Questions

1 Analyse the key cybersecurity and digital resilience risks of migrating a bank's core systems to the cloud and propose a framework to manage these risks.
2 Assess the cybersecurity challenges posed by blockchain and AI in finance and suggest strategies to mitigate them.
3 Evaluate the operational and strategic impacts of the SEC's four-day cyber incident reporting rule and outline how a bank should adapt its incident response and crisis management.

Case Study: The MOVEit Supply Chain Attack and Its Impact on Financial Services

In May 2023, the Clop ransomware group exploited a zero-day vulnerability in Progress Software's MOVEit Transfer, a widely used secure file transfer application. Rather than attacking financial institutions directly, the threat actors targeted this critical third-party tool, exemplifying a supply chain attack that indirectly compromised numerous banks and their service providers, including pension administrators and data analytics firms.

The consequences for financial organisations were significant. Direct data theft occurred, with sensitive customer information, financial documents, and internal reports exfiltrated. The attackers employed a double-extortion strategy, encrypting files while threatening to publish stolen data unless ransom demands were met. Operational disruption followed, as organisations were forced to take MOVEit servers offline, interrupting legitimate financial workflows and delaying critical data transfers. Additionally, the incident exposed widespread third-party risk, highlighting that the security posture of a single vendor can directly affect the confidentiality and integrity of data across hundreds of client organisations.

This case underscores the importance of proactive vendor risk management, continuous monitoring, and robust digital resilience strategies that anticipate and respond to incidents originating outside an institution's direct control. It also illustrates the necessity for comprehensive cyber incident planning, including supply chain-specific scenarios, to maintain operational continuity and safeguard sensitive financial information.

Reference

CISA. (2023). *Cyber Security Advisory (CSA) Exploitation of Progress MOVEit Transfer Vulnerability*. Available at: https://www.cisa.gov/news-events/cybersecurity-advisories/aa23-158a

Case Study Questions

1 The MOVEit incident highlights the risks associated with third-party vendors. What specific due diligence measures and continuous monitoring practices should a bank implement to mitigate such risks from critical software providers like Progress Software?

2 From a digital resilience standpoint, how should a bank structure its incident response plan to effectively manage a supply chain attack in which the root cause lies outside the organisation's direct control?
3 If you were the Chief Information Security Officer of a bank affected by the MOVEit attack, what key insights and recommendations would you present to the Board to enhance the organisation's overall cyber resilience posture?

Further Reading

Financial Stability Board (FSB). (2022). *Enhancing Third-Party Risk Management and Oversight*. Basel: Financial Stability Board.

Lagioia, M. (2023). Cyber Resilience in the Financial Sector. *Journal of Financial Compliance* 7(2), pp. 112–125.

National Institute of Standards and Technology (NIST). (2023). *Cybersecurity Framework (CSF) 2.0*. Gaithersburg, MD: NIST.

World Economic Forum. (2024). *The Global Cybersecurity Outlook*. Geneva: World Economic Forum.

References

Balu, R. (2022) *Bangladesh Bank Cyber Heist: Incident Analysis, Master's Project, College of Computing, School of Computer Science and School of Public Policy*, Georgia Institute of Technology. Available at: https://repository.gatech.edu/entities/publication/5298e3b1-1e01-415e-ac16-f7856e3d929a

Bank for International Settlements (BIS). (2023). *Project Leap: Quantum-Proofing the Financial System*. Basel: BIS Innovation Hub. Available at: https://www.bis.org/about/bisih/topics/cyber_security/leap.htm (Accessed: 2026).

Department for Science, Innovation and Technology. (2025). *AI Cyber Security: Protecting and Promoting the UK's AI Ecosystem*. London.

Financial Stability Board (FSB). (2022). Digital Resilience and Cyber Risk in Financial Institutions. *FSB Report*.

Lagioia, F. (2023) Cybersecurity and Digital Operational Resilience in Financial Services. *Journal of Financial Regulation and Compliance*, 31(4), pp. 567–582.

National Institute of Standards and Technology (NIST). (2023). *Framework for Improving Critical Infrastructure Cybersecurity*. Gaithersburg, MD: National Institute of Standards and Technology.

Qodex (2025) Cybersecurity Challenges Facing FinTech. *Qodex Blog*. Available at: https://qodex.ai/blog/cybersecurity-challenges-facing-fintech (Accessed: 10 Oct 2025).

Terranova Security (2024) Cybersecurity Concerns in the Finance Sector. *Terranova Security Blog*. Available at: https://www.terranovasecurity.com/blog/cybersecurity-concerns-finance-sector (Accessed: 15 Oct 2025).

United States Securities and Exchange Commission (2023) *Cybersecurity Risk Management, Strategy, Governance, and Incident Disclosure*. Washington, D.C.: Securities and Exchange Commission.

World Economic Forum. (2024). *Cyber Risk and Digital Resilience in Financial Services*. Geneva: World Economic Forum.

Waliullah, M., George, Z., Hasan, T., Alam, M., Sumaiya, M., Khatun, M.S.M., Noor, A. & Siddiqui, A. (2025) Assessing the Influence of Cybersecurity Threats and Risks on the Adoption and Growth of Digital Banking: A Systematic Literature Review. *American Journal of Advanced Technology and Engineering Solutions*, 1, 226–257

Part 5

Future Trends, Sustainability, and Frontiers

29 FinTech and Geopolitics

Chapter Overview

This chapter explores the convergence of Financial Technology (FinTech) and global geopolitics, emphasising their growing importance. It goes beyond technical and economic viewpoints to show how innovations like digital currencies, blockchain, and digital payment systems are increasingly used as tools of national power and foreign policy (Brunnermeier, James, & Landau, 2022). The chapter investigates the geopolitical motivations behind the rise of Central Bank Digital Currencies (CBDCs), the reshaping of digital trade routes by FinTech, and the substantial influence of these developments on existing financial sanctions. It also discusses the debate around digital sovereignty and its role in fragmenting the global financial system into competing domains. The analysis compares the potential for improved financial inclusion and efficiency with the major challenges, such as a possible *splinternet of finance*, where the global financial system could become divided into separate digital financial ecosystems due to regulatory divergence, differing technological standards, and emerging systemic risks (Carstens, 2021).

Learning Objectives

By the end of this chapter, students should be able to:

1. Analyse how FinTech is transforming the tools and levers of national power and global strategic competition.
2. Evaluate the geopolitical motivations driving the development of CBDCs and other sovereign digital payment systems.
3. Assess the impact of FinTech, particularly blockchain and cryptocurrencies, on the efficacy of international financial sanctions.
4. Explain the concept of digital sovereignty and its implications for the fragmentation of the global financial system.
5. Critically discuss the dual-use nature of FinTech as both a tool for financial inclusion and a potential instrument of state control and surveillance.

DOI: 10.4324/9781003775751-34

29.1 Introduction

FinTech has evolved beyond its initial disruptive role within Silicon Valley startups to become a central domain of geopolitical competition in the twenty-first century. Its strategic significance now extends into national security doctrines and the broader framework of international power relations. States increasingly recognise the need to control financial infrastructure. The capacity to establish technical standards for digital payments and to expand a currency's global reach has emerged as a critical component of contemporary statecraft.

Advanced technologies, including blockchain and digital currencies, are at the forefront of this transformation. These innovations fundamentally challenge the post-World War II financial order, which the US dollar and Western-controlled systems such as the Society for Worldwide Interbank Financial Telecommunication have dominated. Major powers, particularly China, are developing CBDC initiatives to enhance their global economic influence. Concurrently, the proliferation of cryptocurrencies allows non-state actors to conduct financial activities outside traditional state oversight. This development accelerates the formation of a new landscape referred to as 'geofinance' (Bremmer & Sams, 2022).

This evolving dynamic necessitates a comprehensive reassessment of economic statecraft, as it introduces new interdependencies and vulnerabilities within the global financial system. The characteristics of FinTech compel a revaluation of monetary sovereignty, a process accelerated by the rapid digitalisation of transactions and assets worldwide. This chapter examines how FinTech is transforming economic statecraft, analyses the associated risks and opportunities, and discusses the profound implications for both national and international monetary policy in the digital era.

29.2 The Geopolitical Drivers of FinTech Innovation

FinTech innovation is increasingly shaped by state policies and geopolitical strategies, reflecting objectives that extend beyond market dynamics. Governments now treat financial technologies as instruments to strengthen national power, strategic autonomy, and resilience in the global political economy (Auer, Cornelli, & Frost, 2020; Lee, 2021) (Figure 29.1).

The following key factors illustrate how these geopolitical considerations drive FinTech development.

29.2.1 Monetary Sovereignty and Control

CBDCs are a strategic tool for preserving monetary sovereignty. The rise of private stablecoins and foreign digital currencies threatens central banks' ability to manage money supply, domestic payments, and financial stability. By issuing CBDCs, states reinforce monetary control and secure the primacy of public institutions. For example, China's digital yuan (e-CNY) enables the government to regulate digital payments, maintain domestic financial authority, and counter the influence of private stablecoins, demonstrating a direct intersection between FinTech innovation and state-driven monetary objectives (Auer et al., 2020).

29.2.2 Strategic Competition and Influence

CBDCs are increasingly deployed as instruments of economic competition, with countries seeking leadership in technical standards and cross-border payment networks. The US and

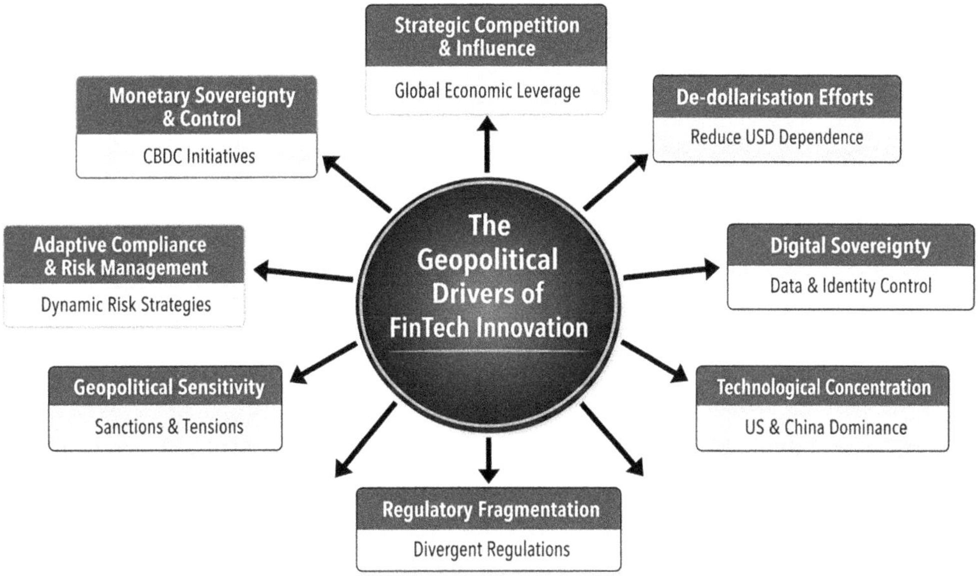

Figure 29.1 The Geopolitical Drivers of FinTech Innovation.

China exemplify this trend, investing in digital payment infrastructures to assert global economic leverage. This drives FinTech innovation as states incentivise domestic development of payment technologies and platforms, ensuring that national firms remain competitive in setting international standards (Lee, 2021).

29.2.3 *De-dollarisation Efforts*

FinTech and digital currencies are central to geopolitical strategies aimed at reducing dependency on the US dollar. Nations such as Russia and China utilise blockchain-based settlement systems to bypass US-dominated financial networks, mitigate sanction exposure, and strengthen financial sovereignty. These initiatives drive innovation in cross-border digital payment systems and encourage domestic adoption of alternative currency infrastructures, demonstrating FinTech's role in strategic economic autonomy (Zarate, 2022).

29.2.4 *Digital Sovereignty*

The pursuit of digital sovereignty motivates states to control national data, digital identities, and financial transaction flows. Regional FinTech initiatives, such as the European Union's (EU) promotion of indigenous payment systems and strict data governance frameworks, reflect this goal. By fostering secure and autonomous digital infrastructures, governments stimulate innovation in payment solutions, data protection technologies, and local FinTech ecosystems (Newman, 2020).

29.2.5 *Technological Concentration*

The concentration of advanced financial technologies in the US and China creates systemic risks for global financial stability and shapes competitive dynamics. Geopolitically, states drive domestic FinTech development to reduce dependency on foreign technology and secure critical infrastructure. This results in accelerated research, investment in FinTech startups, and national strategies for resilient digital financial ecosystems (Lee, 2021).

29.2.6 Regulatory Fragmentation

Divergent regulations across jurisdictions present both a challenge and a driver of FinTech innovation. Firms must develop adaptive compliance frameworks capable of navigating diverse legal environments, and incentivise technological solutions for regulatory reporting, cross-border compliance, and risk management. Regulatory divergence thus promotes innovation in automated compliance and governance tools (Newman, 2020).

29.2.7 Geopolitical Sensitivity

Cross-border FinTech operations must consider sanctions, political tensions, and regional laws. Initiatives like blockchain-based settlements in sanctioned countries illustrate the operational challenges firms face. These pressures drive the development of resilient, adaptive, and geopolitically aware FinTech solutions capable of operating under complex regulatory and strategic conditions (Zarate, 2022).

29.2.8 Adaptive Compliance and Risk Management

The evolving geopolitical landscape, coupled with cybersecurity and regulatory pressures, necessitates dynamic risk management and adaptive compliance platforms. Governments' strategic use of FinTech for economic security encourages the private sector to innovate in monitoring, threat detection, and risk mitigation technologies, making compliance systems both a defensive and growth-oriented driver of FinTech innovation (Lee, 2021).

29.3 Key Geopolitical Arenas in FinTech

29.3.1 The CBDC Race and the Digital Yuan (e-CNY)

China's advancement in the development and deployment of its CBDC, the digital yuan (e-CNY), marks a pivotal shift in the global FinTech landscape with profound geopolitical implications. Through extensive and systematic domestic trials, the People's Bank of China (PBOC) has demonstrated a strategic commitment to embedding the e-CNY within the nation's financial architecture. Domestically, the digital currency enhances the state's ability to monitor financial transactions with greater precision, streamline payment systems, and improve the efficacy of monetary and fiscal policy implementation. The increased traceability of financial flows strengthens regulatory oversight. It facilitates more robust enforcement of anti-money laundering and financial crime measures, thereby reinforcing centralised control over the country's financial ecosystem.

On the international front, the e-CNY is positioned as a key instrument in China's broader ambition to internationalise the renminbi (RMB) and reduce reliance on the US dollar-dominated financial infrastructure. By offering a secure, efficient, and scalable platform for cross-border transactions, China aims to encourage greater use of the RMB in global trade and finance. Moreover, by integrating e-CNY infrastructure into its overseas economic initiatives, particularly within Belt and Road Initiative (BRI) partner nations, China is laying the groundwork for a Digital Silk Road. This initiative not only promotes technological interoperability with Chinese standards but also fosters long-term financial dependencies, potentially reshaping global payment networks and advancing China's strategic influence in the digital financial order (Hillman, 2021; Kynge, Morris, & Zhen, 2021).

29.3.2 FinTech and the Future of Financial Sanctions

Financial sanctions have long been a cornerstone of Western geopolitical strategy, leveraging dominance over traditional banking and payment systems. However, the rise of FinTech introduces a paradoxical dynamic that could both undermine and enhance their efficacy. Decentralised technologies, such as cryptocurrencies and blockchain networks, enable sanctioned entities to bypass conventional financial channels, potentially diminishing the reach of sanctions (Farrell & Newman, 2019). Conversely, FinTech also provides states with new coercive instruments; by controlling critical digital infrastructures such as cloud services, payment platforms, and compliant digital wallets, the United States and its allies can implement more targeted and technologically sophisticated sanctions regimes. This evolving landscape suggests that while FinTech may erode traditional enforcement mechanisms, it simultaneously opens avenues for innovative, data-driven financial coercion, reshaping the geopolitical dimensions of economic statecraft.

29.3.3 The Battle for Digital Trade and Payment Standards

The governance of cross-border data flows and digital payment systems has emerged as a critical geopolitical arena, where the battle to set global standards is a proxy for broader competition between political-economic models. This contest is not merely technical but fundamentally ideological, pitting visions of digital sovereignty against one another. The United States champions a market-driven approach that prioritises innovation and private sector leadership, while China advocates for state-centric standards that integrate digital finance with national surveillance infrastructures. Conversely, the EU exerts its influence through a rigorous regulatory framework focused on data protection and consumer rights, as exemplified by the General Data Protection Regulation and Revised Payment Service Directive. As these divergent models are promoted internationally, the outcome of this standards war will profoundly shape the future architecture of global digital commerce; indeed, the actors that succeed are positioned to exert substantial influence over the future institutional and technological architecture of the entire digital economy (Brunnermeier et al., 2022).

29.4 Opportunities, Challenges, and Key Practical Issues

29.4.1 Opportunities of FinTech and Geopolitics

Expansion of Digital Public Infrastructure: FinTech-enabled digital public infrastructure can significantly enhance financial inclusion by integrating unbanked and underbanked populations into formal financial systems. India's Unified Payments Interface (UPI) exemplifies this potential, providing seamless, interoperable payment solutions that improve access to banking services, increase transaction efficiency, and strengthen domestic economic resilience (BIS Innovation Hub, 2022).

Efficiency in Cross-Border Transactions: Blockchain-based payment systems, including multi-CBDC platforms such as the mBridge project, demonstrate the potential to reduce transaction costs, shorten settlement times, and enhance transparency in cross-border financial flows. By improving interoperability between central banks, these systems can streamline international trade and enhance global financial efficiency (BIS Innovation Hub, 2022).

Monetary Policy Innovation: CBDCs offer novel tools for implementing monetary policy. By enabling direct interactions among central banks, financial institutions, and end users, CBDCs may improve policy transmission, facilitate liquidity management, and enable more agile responses to economic shocks, as observed in pilot CBDC initiatives in China and the Bahamas (Auer et al., 2020; IMF, 2021).

29.4.2 Risks and Challenges of FinTech and Geopolitics

Fragmentation of the Global Financial System: Rapid, uneven adoption of digital financial infrastructures risks creating incompatible technological and regulatory blocs. Such fragmentation can undermine interoperability, increase transaction frictions, and reduce the efficiency of international economic integration (Carstens, 2021).

Weaponisation of Interdependence: States with control over critical digital financial infrastructures can leverage this influence to exert political and economic pressure. Dependence on foreign payment systems, cloud services, or technical standards can transform economic interdependence into strategic vulnerability, as seen in sanctions-related restrictions affecting cross-border payments (Farrell & Newman, 2019).

Surveillance and Authoritarian Control: The integration of digital currencies with identity systems raises concerns about privacy and civil liberties. In authoritarian regimes, these technologies can enable pervasive state surveillance and control over individuals and firms, potentially undermining trust in digital financial ecosystems (Zarate, 2022).

Regulatory Fragmentation and Illicit Finance Risks: The absence of coordinated international regulatory frameworks creates compliance burdens for multinational FinTech firms while enabling regulatory arbitrage. This can be exploited for money laundering, terrorism financing, and other illicit activities (Newman, 2020).

29.4.3 Key Practical Issues for Geopolitical FinTech Strategy

Shift in Monetary Power: The growing adoption of national digital currencies is gradually reshaping global monetary influence. For example, China's e-CNY and Russia's digital ruble aim to establish regional significance, challenging the US dollar's historical predominance and contributing to a more multipolar monetary system (Zarate, 2022).

Emergence of Economic Statecraft via Digital Finance: Geopolitical competition increasingly occurs through digital financial channels. States can influence international finance by controlling digital currency networks, establishing cyber capabilities targeting financial infrastructures, and shaping global technical and governance standards (Lee, 2021).

Rise of Techno-Nationalism: Governments now frame FinTech capabilities as strategic national assets. Technologies such as artificial intelligence–driven regulatory tools, quantum-resistant cryptography, and advanced payment infrastructures are seen as essential for national security, technological sovereignty, and economic competitiveness (BIS, 2023).

Redefinition of Neutrality and Alliances: As digital payment ecosystems align with geopolitical blocs, countries may face pressures to choose between competing financial networks. These decisions can shape diplomatic alignments, trade partnerships, and access to global financial services, exemplified by regional adoption of alternative payment systems in response to sanctions (Farrell & Newman, 2019).

29.5 Conclusion

The convergence of FinTech and geopolitics is rapidly transforming the global financial landscape, as financial technologies evolve into strategic tools of statecraft. No longer confined to commercial disruption, innovations like CBDCs, blockchain networks, and cross-border payment platforms are being leveraged to advance national interests, reshape economic alliances, and circumvent traditional financial controls. As noted by economist Eswar Prasad (2021), digital currencies are not just about efficiency; they are becoming instruments of geopolitical influence. This shift challenges the dominance of established financial institutions and necessitates reevaluating enforcement mechanisms, such as sanctions, in a digitised economy. Meanwhile, the race for technological supremacy risks fragmenting the global financial system into competing blocs, as nations prioritise digital sovereignty over interoperability.

While FinTech promises greater financial inclusion and efficiency, its geopolitical dimensions introduce complex risks, including regulatory fragmentation and systemic instability. Policymakers must navigate this duality by fostering international cooperation while safeguarding national security interests. As Christine Lagarde (2022) has emphasised, the future of money must balance innovation with trust, both within and across borders. Achieving this equilibrium demands a collaborative, forward-looking approach that aligns technological progress with the principles of stability and equity in the digital financial era.

Key Terms and Glossary

Geopolitics The study of the effects of geography (human and physical) on international politics and international relations, now extended to include digital and economic spheres.

Digital Sovereignty The concept that a state has the authority to exercise control over its digital infrastructure, data, and governance, free from undue external influence.

CBDC (Central Bank Digital Currency) A digital form of a country's fiat currency that is a direct liability of the central bank, representing a potential new tool for monetary policy and payments.

De-Dollarisation The process of reducing the reliance on the US dollar as a primary reserve currency, medium of exchange, and unit of account in international trade and finance.

Financial Sanctions Commercial and financial penalties applied by one or more countries against a targeted state, group, or individual.

Technological Spheres of Influence Geopolitical blocs centred around a dominant technological power, characterised by shared standards, infrastructure, and regulatory models.

Splinternet/Financial Fragmentation The divergence of the global internet and financial system into separate, non-interoperable blocs due to differing national regulations, standards, and geopolitical agendas.

Test Your Understanding

Multiple-Choice Questions

1 Which of the following is a primary geopolitical driver for the development of CBDCs?

A Reducing transaction fees for retail customers
B Preserving monetary sovereignty and control over domestic payments
C Increasing venture capital funding for FinTech startups
D Enhancing cryptocurrency mining efficiency

2 The digital yuan (e-CNY) primarily aims to:

A Replace cash entirely in rural China
B Enhance cross-border privacy for citizens
C Strengthen China's domestic financial control and international influence
D Facilitate anonymous cryptocurrency trading

3 Which risk is associated with the fragmentation of global digital financial infrastructure?

A Enhanced cross-border interoperability
B Increased transaction frictions and reduced efficiency
C Reduction of sanctions exposure
D Faster CBDC adoption in all countries

4 FinTech technologies can undermine traditional financial sanctions because:

A They reduce transaction fees for banks
B Decentralised networks allow sanctioned entities to bypass conventional systems
C CBDCs eliminate cross-border payments
D They guarantee full compliance with all national regulations

5 Digital sovereignty in the context of FinTech refers to:

A National control over data, financial transactions, and digital identity systems
B The global adoption of cryptocurrencies by individuals
C Corporate control of cross-border payments
D Private sector leadership in setting all technical standards

Short Questions

1 Explain how CBDCs can be used as instruments of strategic economic competition between major powers.
2 Identify two key opportunities that FinTech-enabled digital public infrastructure provides for financial inclusion.
3 Describe one practical risk associated with integrating digital currencies and identity systems in authoritarian regimes.

Analytical Questions

1 Evaluate the dual role of FinTech as both a tool for financial inclusion and a potential instrument of state control. Use examples such as India's UPI and China's e-CNY to support your argument.
2 Analyse the geopolitical implications of de-dollarisation efforts through digital currencies and blockchain-based settlement systems. How might these initiatives affect global financial stability and alliances?
3 Discuss the challenges and opportunities posed by regulatory fragmentation and divergent technological standards on cross-border FinTech adoption. How should multinational FinTech firms adapt strategically?

Case Study: The Digital Yuan (e-CNY) and China's Geostrategy

The PBOC began developing a CBDC in 2014, resulting in the e-CNY, the world's largest and most advanced digital currency pilot. Unlike decentralised cryptocurrencies, the e-CNY is state-controlled, designed to complement physical cash, and provides the government with unprecedented oversight of domestic financial transactions (Kynge et al., 2021).

The e-CNY enhances financial system monitoring, supports anti-fraud and anti-money laundering efforts, and strengthens the transmission of monetary policy. It also challenges private payment platforms, such as Alipay and WeChat Pay, by reasserting state control over digital payments. Its "controllable anonymity" balances user privacy with the government's ability to trace transactions for regulatory and law enforcement purposes, reflecting China's dual goal of fostering innovation while maintaining social and financial control (Lee, 2021).

Globally, the e-CNY serves as a tool for RMB internationalisation and strategic influence, particularly among BRI countries. By offering faster, cheaper cross-border payments, it could encourage RMB trade settlement, foster financial dependencies, and provide alternatives to US dollar–dominated channels, potentially circumventing sanctions for countries like Iran and Russia.

The e-CNY faces international scepticism over China's data governance and surveillance. In response, the US and EU are accelerating CBDC development and coordinating digital payment standards, creating cautious competition rather than outright rejection. The e-CNY exemplifies how state-backed digital currencies combine domestic control, economic strategy, and geopolitical ambition, reshaping the future of global finance.

Case Study Questions

1 How does the e-CNY's design, particularly its controllable anonymity, balance China's goals of promoting innovation while retaining social and financial control?
2 To what extent could the e-CNY, through integration with the BRI, challenge the US dollar's dominance in global trade? What factors will influence its success or limitations?
3 As an advisor to the European Central Bank, what recommendations would you make for the development of a digital euro in response to the geopolitical and competitive implications of the e-CNY?

Further Reading

Auer, R., Cornelli, G., & Frost, J., 2020. Rise of the Central Bank Digital Currencies: Drivers, Approaches and Implications. *BIS Working Papers, No. 880*. Basel: Bank for International Settlements.

Brunnermeier, M.K., James, H., & Landau, J.P., 2022. *The Digitalisation of Money and the Future of the Global Financial System*. Princeton: Princeton University Press.

Prasad, E., 2021. *The Future of Money: How the Digital Revolution Is Transforming Currencies and Finance*. Cambridge, MA: Harvard University Press.

References

Auer, R., Cornelli, G., & Frost, J. (2020). *Rise of the Central Bank Digital Currencies: Drivers, Approaches and Technologies*. Basel: Bank for International Settlements.

BIS. (2023). *Technological Innovation in Financial Markets: Policy Considerations for Central Banks*. Basel: Bank for International Settlements.

BIS Innovation Hub. (2022). *Cross-Border Payments and Digital Public Infrastructure: mBridge and Other Multi-CBDC Initiatives*. Basel: Bank for International Settlements.

Bremmer, I., & Sams, P. (2022). *Geofinance: How Technology Is Reshaping Global Economic Power*. New York: Portfolio Penguin.

Brunnermeier, M.K., James, H., & Landau, J-P. (2022). *Digital Currencies, Digital Trade, and the Future of Financial Governance*. Princeton: Princeton University Press.

Carstens, A. (2021). *Digital Currencies and the Global Financial System: Risks and Opportunities. Speech at the IMF–BIS Annual Conference*, Basel, 15 March.

Farrell, H., & Newman, A.L. (2019). Weaponised Interdependence: How Global Economic Networks Shape State Coercion. *International Security*, 44(1), 42–79.

Hillman, J.E. (2021). *China's Digital Silk Road: Implications for Global Financial Influence*. Washington, DC: Centre for Strategic and International Studies.

IMF. (2021). *Central Bank Digital Currencies: Foundational Principles and Pilot Experiences*. Washington, DC: International Monetary Fund.

Kynge, J., Morris, I., & Zhen, H. (2021). China's e-CNY and the Internationalisation of the Renminbi. *Financial Times Special Report*, 12 October.

Lagarde, C. (2022). The Future of Money: Innovation and Trust in the Digital Age. *Speech at the European Central Bank Forum, Frankfurt*, 22 June.

Lee, D.K.C. (2021). Financial Technology and State Power: Geopolitics of Digital Finance. *Journal of International Economic Policy*, 8(2), 105–128.

Newman, A.L. (2020). Digital Sovereignty and Regulatory Divergence in Global FinTech. *Journal of European Public Policy*, 27(7), 1010–1029.

Prasad, E. (2021). *The Future of Money: How the Digital Revolution Is Transforming Currencies and Finance*. Cambridge, MA: Harvard University Press.

Zarate, J.C. (2022). De-dollarisation and Digital Currencies: Strategic Responses to US Financial Dominance. *Journal of Strategic Studies*, 45(3), 467–490.

30 FinTech in Emerging Economies

Chapter Overview

This chapter offers a thorough analysis of the transformative role of Financial Technology (FinTech) in emerging economies. In these settings, FinTech bypasses traditional banking infrastructure to improve financial inclusion and boost economic development (Demirgüç-Kunt, Klapper, Singer, & van Oudheusden, 2018). The discussion considers unique market conditions, such as large unbanked populations, widespread mobile adoption, and changing regulatory frameworks, which together support a lively FinTech ecosystem. The chapter explores key innovations, including mobile money, digital microlending, and blockchain-based remittances, assessing their influence on poverty alleviation, Small- and Medium-sized Enterprise (SME) financing, and women's economic empowerment (Suri & Jack, 2016). It also critically appraises ongoing challenges, such as digital divides, regulatory limitations, and consumer protection risks, and outlines future trends and implications for policymakers, investors, and the global financial system.

Learning Objectives

By the end of this chapter, you should be able to:

1. Identify the unique drivers and enabling conditions for FinTech growth in emerging economies.
2. Analyse the impact of key FinTech innovations, such as mobile money, on financial inclusion and socio-economic development.
3. Evaluate the role of regulatory approaches, including sandboxes, in balancing innovation and risk.
4. Assess the persistent challenges, including infrastructure gaps and consumer vulnerability, that hinder FinTech's potential.
5. Discuss the future outlook and strategic implications of FinTech for sustainable development in emerging markets.

DOI: 10.4324/9781003775751-35

30.1 Introduction

FinTech represents a global movement, yet its transformative potential is particularly significant in emerging economies. Dynamic, youthful populations and rapid urbanisation characterise these regions. Importantly, traditional banking infrastructures in these areas have often been inadequate or inaccessible. Consequently, FinTech serves as a fundamentally disruptive force rather than a mere incremental innovation, substantially reshaping the financial landscape across diverse markets (Gomber, Koch, & Siering, 2018).

Digital finance in these contexts advances through a process of *leapfrogging*, enabling the rapid adoption of digital financial services. Such technologies eliminate reliance on centralised bank branches and legacy systems. The proliferation of mobile communications has facilitated this transition, transforming mobile devices into access points for formal financial services for millions (GSMA, 2023). Notable examples include the success of M-Pesa in Kenya and the rapid expansion of digital payment ecosystems in countries such as India and China.

The primary function of FinTech in emerging markets is to address significant gaps in financial inclusion, such as access to formal credit, secure savings, tailored insurance products, and reliable payment infrastructure. A comprehensive analysis requires a structured approach. This overview will identify the catalysts for digital adoption, examine principal FinTech models, assess socio-economic impacts, and evaluate the challenges associated with achieving inclusive digital finance.

30.2 The Unique FinTech Landscape in Emerging Economies

The FinTech landscape in emerging economies has undergone rapid expansion, driven by rising mobile phone penetration, improved internet connectivity, and growing demand for accessible and efficient financial services. Unlike developed economies, where FinTech often enhances existing banking infrastructure, emerging markets exhibit structural gaps in traditional financial service provision, including limited branch networks and high transaction costs. These constraints, combined with large, underserved populations, create both significant challenges and opportunities for FinTech adoption. The interaction between technological diffusion, demographic characteristics, and institutional deficiencies has created a conducive environment for FinTech innovation, positioning digital financial services as a key driver of financial inclusion and broader economic development (World Bank, 2022).

30.2.1 Nature and Characteristics of FinTech in Emerging Economies

Mobile-first financial infrastructure: FinTech ecosystems in emerging economies are fundamentally mobile-centric, reflecting the fact that mobile phone penetration often exceeds access to formal banking services. Mobile devices, therefore, constitute the primary infrastructure for delivering payments, savings, credit, and remittance services in a cost-effective and scalable manner (Aker & Mbiti, 2010; World Bank, 2022). A prominent example is M-Pesa in Kenya, which enables users without bank accounts to transfer money, pay bills, and store value using basic mobile phones, significantly expanding financial access in rural and low-income communities (Suri & Jack, 2016).

Large unbanked and underbanked populations: A defining characteristic of emerging economies is the substantial proportion of unbanked and underbanked individuals, driven by high account maintenance costs, geographic barriers, and documentation requirements

(Demirgüç-Kunt et al., 2018). FinTech firms target these segments by offering simplified, low-cost digital financial products that lower entry barriers to formal financial systems. Evidence from the Global Findex Database demonstrates that access to digital financial services is positively associated with increased savings, borrowing, and remittance activity among previously excluded populations (Demirgüç-Kunt et al., 2018). In India, Paytm has facilitated the integration of millions of first-time users into digital payments through mobile wallets and QR-code-based transactions, particularly following policy initiatives such as demonetisation and Unified Payments Interface (UPI) expansion (Reserve Bank of India, 2021).

Informality and reliance on alternative data: High levels of informal employment in emerging economies reduce the applicability of traditional credit assessment models based on formal income documentation and credit histories (La Porta & Shleifer, 2014). In response, FinTech providers increasingly rely on alternative data sources, such as mobile phone usage, transaction records, social media activity, and utility payments, to assess creditworthiness. These data are often analysed using machine learning algorithms to mitigate information asymmetries and improve risk prediction (Berg, Burg, Gombović, & Puri, 2020). Digital lenders in Southeast Asia, for example, use mobile transaction histories to extend microloans to informal workers and small enterprises with no prior banking relationships.

Leapfrogging traditional banking systems: Consumers in emerging economies frequently bypass conventional banking infrastructure, transitioning directly from cash-based transactions to mobile and digital financial solutions. This leapfrogging dynamic accelerates FinTech adoption and enables rapid scaling without the need for extensive investment in physical banking infrastructure (Aker et al., 2016). Mobile wallets and QR-code payment systems across Sub-Saharan Africa and parts of Asia illustrate how digital platforms can effectively substitute for traditional banking channels at scale (World Bank, 2022).

Evolving regulatory frameworks: FinTech development in many emerging markets initially occurred in relatively permissive regulatory environments, enabling rapid innovation. However, regulators are increasingly adopting adaptive and innovation-friendly frameworks to balance technological advancement with consumer protection and financial stability. Regulatory sandboxes, proportional licensing, and risk-based supervision are now widely used to facilitate experimentation while mitigating systemic risk (BIS, 2021; World Bank, 2020). Brazil's central bank-led implementation of the PIX instant payment system demonstrates how coordinated regulatory oversight can support secure, efficient, and widespread adoption of digital financial infrastructure (Banco Central do Brasil, 2022).

30.2.2 FinTech Transformation in Emerging Economies

Expansion of financial inclusion: FinTech plays a central role in integrating unbanked populations into formal financial systems by reducing transaction costs, simplifying onboarding processes, and improving geographic accessibility. Digital payments and mobile money services enable households and micro-enterprises to participate more fully in formal economic activity, which is associated with enhanced financial resilience and improved welfare outcomes (Demirgüç-Kunt et al., 2018; Suri & Jack, 2016).

Transformation of credit access: By leveraging alternative data and artificial intelligence (AI)-driven credit assessment models, FinTech firms expand access to credit for individuals and SMEs traditionally excluded from formal lending markets. Digital lending platforms and buy now, pay later services provide short-term liquidity and working capital, supporting entrepreneurship and consumption (Berg et al., 2020). Nubank in Brazil exemplifies this transformation by offering mobile-based credit products characterised by simplified approval processes, lower fees, and rapid scaling relative to incumbent banks (Nubank, 2023).

Formalisation of economic activity: Digital financial transactions generate verifiable data trails that gradually formalise economic activity, increasing transparency and improving access to financial products such as credit, insurance, and savings instruments (Klapper, Lusardi, & van Oudheusden, 2016). Embedded finance solutions within e-commerce and ride-hailing platforms further integrate financial services into everyday economic interactions, reinforcing participation in formal markets.

Improved efficiency in financial intermediation: FinTech reduces inefficiencies inherent in traditional banking systems, including high transaction costs, slow settlement times, and limited geographic reach. Instant payment infrastructures, such as Brazil's PIX, facilitate real-time, low-cost transfers and enhance competition within payment markets, substantially improving the efficiency and inclusiveness of domestic financial systems (Banco Central do Brasil, 2022; World Bank, 2022).

30.2.3 Economic Significance of FinTech in Emerging Markets

SME productivity and growth: Improved access to digital payments and credit enhances productivity by alleviating liquidity constraints, improving cash flow management, and facilitating market expansion. Digital lending and embedded finance solutions are particularly important in underserved regions, where access to traditional finance remains limited (Beck, Chen, Lin, & Song, 2018).

Poverty reduction and household resilience: Mobile money and digital financial services enable households to smooth consumption through savings, remittances, and emergency credit, thereby reducing vulnerability to economic shocks. Empirical evidence suggests that access to mobile financial services improves household welfare, resilience, and labour market outcomes, especially among low-income and rural populations (Demirgüç-Kunt et al., 2018; Suri & Jack, 2016).

Financial sector competition and innovation: FinTech intensifies competition within financial sectors traditionally dominated by incumbent banks, exerting downward pressure on fees and incentivising service innovation. Neobanks and digital platforms enhance consumer welfare by offering more transparent, efficient, and user-oriented financial services, while also encouraging incumbents to modernise their offerings (Philippon, 2019).

Regulatory and macroeconomic benefits: The adoption of Regulatory Technology (RegTech) and Supervisory Technology tools strengthens regulatory capacity by enabling real-time monitoring of transactions, compliance, and systemic risk. These technologies enhance financial stability, improve supervisory effectiveness, and support innovation-led growth and better governance in emerging economies (BIS, 2021; World Bank, 2020).

30.3 Key FinTech Innovations in Emerging Economies

FinTech innovation in emerging economies is increasingly characterised by integration, automation, and platform-based delivery, fundamentally transforming how financial services are accessed and consumed. These innovations reduce reliance on traditional financial intermediaries and embed financial services seamlessly into everyday economic activities, thereby accelerating financial inclusion, lowering transaction costs, and improving allocative efficiency (Philippon, 2019; World Bank, 2022) (Figure 30.1).

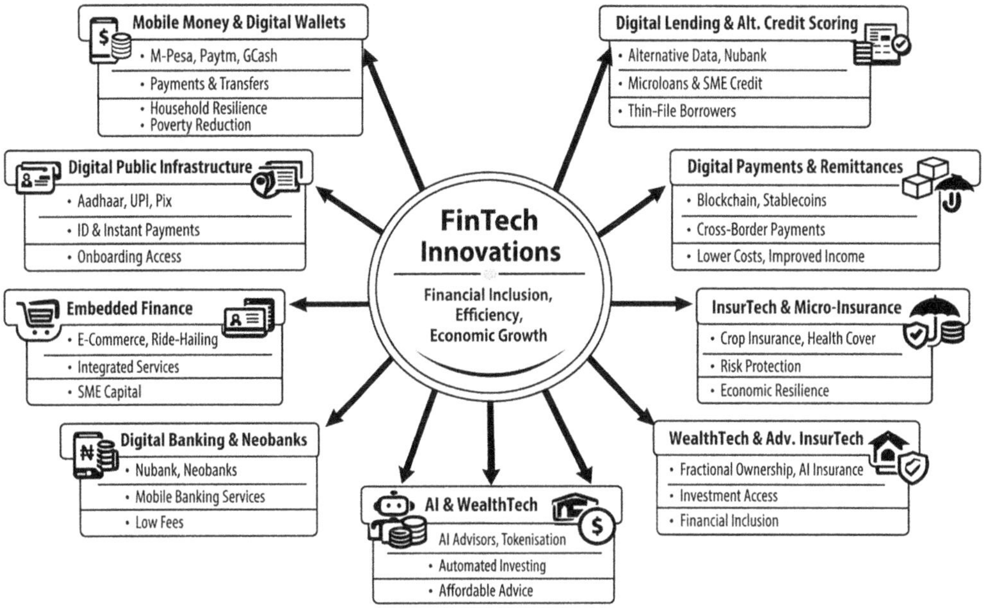

Figure 30.1 FinTech Innovations in Emerging Economies.

30.3.1 Mobile Money and Digital Wallets

Mobile money and digital wallet platforms represent the most pervasive FinTech innovation in emerging economies. These systems enable users to store value, transfer funds, pay bills, and receive wages via mobile devices, often without requiring a formal bank account. This delivery model is particularly effective in rural and low-income contexts where traditional banking infrastructure is limited or absent (Aker & Mbiti, 2010; World Bank, 2022). Empirical evidence from Kenya shows that mobile money adoption through M-Pesa has enhanced household consumption smoothing, increased remittance flows, and contributed to poverty reduction, with particularly strong welfare effects for female-headed households (Suri & Jack, 2016). Comparable platforms, such as Paytm in India and GCash in the Philippines, demonstrate the scalability and adaptability of mobile wallets across diverse emerging market contexts (Demirgüç-Kunt et al., 2018).

30.3.2 Digital Lending and Alternative Credit Scoring

Digital lending platforms in emerging economies leverage alternative data sources, such as mobile phone usage, airtime purchases, transaction histories, and utility payments, to build credit profiles for individuals and small enterprises without formal credit records. The application of machine learning and big data analytics enables lenders to mitigate information asymmetries and expand access to microloans and short-term emergency financing (Berg et al., 2020). Empirical evidence suggests that alternative data-based credit scoring models can outperform traditional credit bureau information in predicting default risk, particularly for thin-file borrowers (Berg et al., 2020). However, the rapid growth of digital credit also raises concerns regarding data privacy, algorithmic opacity, consumer protection, and the risk of over-indebtedness among vulnerable borrowers, especially in lightly regulated environments (BIS, 2021; World Bank, 2020).

30.3.3 Digital Payments and Remittances

Digital payment systems and blockchain-enabled platforms are transforming domestic and cross-border remittance markets, which constitute a vital source of income for households in many emerging economies. By reducing transaction costs and settlement times, digital remittance solutions increase the effective income beneficiaries receive (World Bank, 2023). The World Bank reports that digital channels typically offer significantly lower remittance fees than traditional money transfer operators, particularly in South–South corridors (World Bank, 2023). In this context, stablecoins are increasingly being explored as programmable money that enable near-instant, low-cost international transfers by bypassing correspondent banking networks (Arner, Barberis, & Buckley, 2022). These innovations contribute to poverty reduction, household financial resilience, and local economic development.

30.3.4 Insurance Technology (InsurTech) and Micro-Insurance

InsurTech innovations in emerging markets primarily focus on providing micro-insurance products covering health, agriculture, life, and asset-related risks. Delivered through mobile platforms, these products feature simplified underwriting, low premiums, and flexible payment schedules, making insurance more accessible to low-income and vulnerable populations (Churchill & Matul, 2012). For example, index-based crop insurance schemes delivered via mobile platforms in East Africa enable smallholder farmers to manage climate-related risks more effectively by automatically triggering payouts based on weather data (World Bank, 2021). By lowering entry barriers, InsurTech enhances economic resilience, strengthens social protection mechanisms, and encourages participation in formal financial systems.

30.3.5 Digital Public Infrastructure

Digital public infrastructure constitutes a foundational enabler of FinTech ecosystems in emerging economies. National digital identity systems, such as India's Aadhaar, combined with real-time payment platforms like India's UPI and Brazil's PIX, provide secure identification, authentication, and instant transaction capabilities at scale (Gelb & Metz, 2018; World Bank, 2022). These systems significantly reduce onboarding costs, enhance trust, and create interoperable platforms that enable private FinTech firms to innovate. Empirical evidence indicates that robust digital public infrastructure accelerates financial inclusion and improves access to formal financial services for underserved populations (World Bank, 2022).

30.3.6 Embedded Finance and Invisible Banking

FinTech services in emerging economies are increasingly embedded within non-financial digital platforms, giving rise to *invisible banking*, where financial transactions occur seamlessly in the background of everyday activities. Payments, credit, and insurance are integrated into e-commerce, ride-hailing, and gig-economy applications, reducing friction and improving user experience (BIS, 2021). For example, embedded lending within e-commerce platforms enables SMEs to access working capital based on real-time sales data, illustrating how financial services are becoming integral components of broader digital ecosystems rather than standalone products (Klapper et al., 2016).

30.3.7 *Digital Banking and Neobanks*

Digital-only banks, commonly known as neobanks, are expanding rapidly in emerging markets by offering full-service banking without physical branches. These institutions rely on mobile applications to deliver payments, savings, and credit products at lower operational costs than traditional banks (Philippon, 2019). Nubank in Brazil, with over 90 million customers, exemplifies how neobanks can scale rapidly by prioritising user experience, transparency, and fee reduction (Nubank, 2023). The growth of neobanks intensifies competition in financial sectors traditionally dominated by incumbent banks, generating efficiency gains and improvements in consumer welfare.

30.3.8 *Advanced AI-Driven Financial Services*

AI increasingly underpins FinTech innovation in emerging economies. AI-powered chatbots provide personalised financial guidance and customer support, while more advanced agentic AI systems automate financial decision-making processes such as bill payments, budgeting, and portfolio rebalancing (BIS, 2021). These technologies improve operational efficiency and expand access to financial advice at low marginal cost. However, their deployment also raises governance challenges related to transparency, explainability, accountability, and ethical use, particularly in regulatory environments with limited supervisory capacity (OECD, 2021).

30.3.9 *Wealth Technology (WealthTech) and Advanced InsurTech*

WealthTech innovations are expanding access to investment opportunities through fractional ownership and the tokenisation of real-world assets, allowing retail investors to acquire small shares of high-value assets such as real estate, commodities, or art (Catalini & Gans, 2020). In parallel, AI-driven underwriting enables instant approval of micro-insurance products without extensive documentation or medical examinations. Together, these developments democratise access to wealth accumulation and risk management tools that have traditionally been accessible only to higher-income groups, contributing to broader financial inclusion and long-term economic participation.

30.4 Opportunities, Challenges, and Key Practical Issues in Emerging Economies

30.4.1 *Opportunities, Convergence, and Transformative Potential*

FinTech offers transformative opportunities in emerging economies by expanding financial inclusion, improving efficiency, and fostering economic formalisation. Digital financial services allow unbanked populations to save, transfer funds, access credit, and manage risk, enhancing household welfare and small-business growth. Empirical studies show that mobile money adoption in Kenya through M-Pesa improved consumption smoothing, increased remittance flows, and reduced poverty, with particularly strong benefits for female-headed households (Suri & Jack, 2016). Platforms such as Paytm in India and GCash in the Philippines illustrate how mobile wallets can scale across diverse contexts, integrating previously excluded users into formal financial systems (Demirgüç-Kunt et al., 2018).

The convergence of FinTech with AI, real-time payments, and digital platforms amplifies its impact. AI-driven credit scoring models utilise alternative data to provide loans to thin-file borrowers, while blockchain-based stablecoins and instant settlement rails lower the cost and time of cross-border remittances (Berg et al., 2020; World Bank, 2023). Embedded finance integrates payments, credit, and insurance into e-commerce and gig-economy platforms, creating invisible banking that reduces friction and encourages formal economic participation. Tokenisation of assets enables fractional investments, broadening access to previously restricted opportunities, and collectively these innovations enhance transparency, improve governance, and support sustainable economic development (Catalini & Gans, 2020; World Bank, 2022).

30.4.2 Risks and Challenges

Despite its promise, FinTech adoption in emerging markets faces structural and regulatory obstacles. A persistent digital divide, driven by limited smartphone access, unreliable internet, and low digital literacy, can exclude marginalised populations, undermining the goal of inclusive financial systems (BFA Global, 2022). Consumer protection issues are also significant, as opaque digital lending terms, high interest rates, and aggressive marketing have contributed to over-indebtedness among vulnerable users. Weak data privacy frameworks further increase the risk of misuse of personal information, eroding trust in digital financial platforms (World Bank, 2020).

Technological and regulatory challenges compound these risks. Financial services are frequent targets of AI-enabled cyberattacks, including identity fraud, phishing, and synthetic identities (BIS, 2023). Regulatory fragmentation and localisation create a complex compliance landscape for firms operating across borders, while limited interoperability among payment systems reduces network effects and constrains scale (Arner et al., 2022; World Bank, 2023). Collectively, these issues highlight the need for coordinated strategies to mitigate both technological and institutional vulnerabilities in FinTech ecosystems.

30.4.3 Key Practical Issues in FinTech Adoption

Practical adoption of FinTech increasingly depends on embedding compliance, governance, and operational readiness into core systems. Compliance-as-infrastructure is now common, with agentic AI programmed to block transactions that violate anti-money laundering or sanctions rules, reducing reliance on post-hoc regulatory enforcement (OECD, 2021). Real-time data integrity is critical, requiring unified, auditable data systems that can explain AI-driven decisions and ensure accountability to supervisors (BIS, 2021).

Institutional dynamics also shape adoption. Sponsor banks now require independent audits and continuous monitoring before engaging with FinTech partners, shifting compliance responsibility onto the firms themselves. Workforce transformation presents an additional challenge, as automation and AI are projected to replace substantial routine financial functions by 2030. Firms must retrain staff for specialised roles in AI oversight, regulatory compliance, and model governance to prevent operational and governance failures, ensuring that FinTech adoption is sustainable and inclusive (OECD, 2021).

30.5 Conclusion

FinTech has emerged as a transformative force in emerging economies, revolutionising financial inclusion by overcoming traditional infrastructure barriers through mobile technology and digital innovation. Services such as mobile money and digital lending have empowered unbanked populations, fostered economic participation and reduced poverty.

As noted by the World Bank, Digital financial services have the potential to reach over 1.7 billion adults globally who remain excluded from formal banking. However, challenges such as unequal digital access, regulatory fragmentation, and weak consumer safeguards threaten to widen disparities, necessitating robust governance to balance innovation with stability.

To unlock FinTech's full potential, a collaborative approach involving policymakers, industry leaders, and global institutions is imperative. Financial services inclusion also facilitates reducing inequality. This stresses the need for coordinated strategies that promote equitable access while mitigating risks. By addressing these challenges, FinTech can catalyse resilient, inclusive financial ecosystems that align technological progress with broader socio-economic development goals in emerging markets.

Key Terms and Glossary

Financial Inclusion The provision of affordable and accessible financial services to disadvantaged and low-income segments of society.

Leapfrogging The ability of developing economies to bypass older, inferior technologies and directly adopt advanced, more efficient systems (e.g., skipping landlines for mobile phones).

Mobile Money A service that allows users to store, send, and receive money using a mobile phone.

Unbanked/Underbanked Populations that have no access (unbanked) or insufficient access (underbanked) to formal financial services from regulated institutions.

Agent Banking A model where retail agents (e.g., shopkeepers) act as intermediaries, providing basic banking services on behalf of a financial institution.

Regulatory Sandbox A framework set up by a regulator that allows FinTech startups and other innovators to conduct live experiments in a controlled environment under a regulator's supervision.

Digital Identity A unique electronic representation of an individual used for authentication in online transactions.

Test Your Understanding

Multiple-Choice Questions

1 Which of the following is the primary driver of FinTech adoption in emerging economies?

A High branch density of traditional banks
B Mobile-first infrastructure and widespread smartphone adoption
C Low population growth
D Strict regulatory environments

2 M-Pesa in Kenya primarily demonstrates which aspect of FinTech in emerging economies?

A AI-driven credit scoring
B Mobile money and financial inclusion
C Blockchain-based asset tokenisation
D Embedded finance in e-commerce

3 Which challenge is most directly associated with digital lending in emerging markets?

   A Overstaffing in banks
   B Consumer over-indebtedness and data privacy concerns
   C Excessive interoperability of payment platforms
   D Lack of demand for digital payments

4 The term "leapfrogging" in the context of emerging market FinTech refers to:

   A Skipping traditional banking infrastructure and adopting digital financial solutions directly
   B Gradually building branch networks before mobile services
   C Using blockchain for micro-insurance exclusively
   D Expanding regulatory oversight before technological adoption

5 Which of the following innovations integrates financial services directly into non-financial platforms, often referred to as "invisible banking"?

   A Neobanks
   B Embedded finance
   C Micro-insurance
   D RegTech

Short Questions

1 Explain how alternative data is used in FinTech to extend credit to previously unbanked populations in emerging economies.
2 Identify two ways in which digital public infrastructure, such as Aadhaar or UPI, supports FinTech innovation.
3 Describe the role of FinTech in promoting SME productivity and growth in emerging markets.

Analytical Questions

1 Critically evaluate the risks and challenges associated with rapid FinTech adoption in emerging economies, considering both technological and regulatory dimensions.
2 Analyse how mobile money and digital wallet platforms can contribute to poverty reduction and financial resilience, providing empirical examples.
3 Discuss the convergence of advanced technologies such as AI, blockchain, and embedded finance in emerging markets, and assess their potential impact on financial inclusion and economic development.

Case Study: India's Digital Public Infrastructure—The 'India Stack'

India has developed a comprehensive digital public infrastructure known as the India Stack, comprising interoperable Application Programming Interfaces that enable identity verification, digital payments, document storage, and consented data sharing. Its key components include Aadhaar, a biometric digital identity system covering over 1.3 billion people; the UPI, a real-time interbank and person-to-merchant payment platform; DigiLocker, a secure cloud-based document storage system; and the Account Aggregator framework, which facilitates consent-based access to financial data.

The India Stack has catalysed a FinTech revolution by addressing fundamental barriers to financial inclusion. Aadhaar provides a verifiable, unique identity, solving the problem of identity verification for banking and credit services. UPI reduces transaction costs and enables seamless digital payments, extending access from low-income individuals and street vendors to formal businesses. The Account Aggregator framework has supported innovative lending models, allowing lenders to access comprehensive financial data and improve credit assessment for individuals and Micro, Small, and Medium Enterprises.

The platform has advanced financial inclusion, formalised economic activity, and driven competition and innovation in India's FinTech sector. Nevertheless, challenges remain, including ensuring digital literacy for rural and elderly populations, safeguarding privacy and security amid centralised data collection, and addressing infrastructure gaps such as uneven internet connectivity. India Stack is now regarded as a replicable model for emerging economies seeking inclusive digital financial systems.

Case Study Questions

1. How did Aadhaar and UPI address the barriers of identity verification and high transaction costs that limit financial inclusion?
2. What are the trade-offs between efficiency and inclusion versus privacy and data security in a centralised digital identity system like Aadhaar?
3. For another emerging economy aiming to replicate India's success, what two factors are most critical, and what is one key pitfall to avoid?

Further Reading

Arner, D.W., Barberis, J., & Buckley, R.P. (2022). *FinTech and the Future of Finance: Market and Policy Implications*. Cambridge: Cambridge University Press.

Demirgüç-Kunt, A., Klapper, L., Singer, D., Ansar, S., & Hess, J. (2018). *The Global Findex Database 2017: Measuring Financial Inclusion and the FinTech Revolution*. Washington, DC: World Bank.

Philippon, T. (2019). *The Great Reversal: How America Gave Up on Free Markets*. Cambridge, MA: Harvard University Press.

References

Aker, J.C., & Mbiti, I.M. (2010). Mobile Phones and Economic Development in Africa. *Journal of Economic Perspectives*, 24(3), 207–232.

Aker, J.C., Boumnijel, R., McClelland, A., & Tierney, N. (2016) Payment Mechanisms and Anti-Poverty Programs: Evidence from a Mobile Money Cash Transfer Experiment in Niger. *Economic Development and Cultural Change*, 65(1), pp. 1–37.

Arner, D.W., Barberis, J., & Buckley, R.P. (2022). The Evolution of Fintech: A New Post-Crisis Paradigm? *Georgetown Journal of International Law*, 53, 1–55.

Banco Central do Brasil. (2022). *PIX: Instant Payment System Overview*. Available at: https://www.bcb.gov.br/en

Bank for International Settlements (BIS). (2021). *RegTech and SupTech: Implications for Regulatory and Supervisory Practices*. Basel: BIS.

Bank for International Settlements (BIS). (2023). *Cybersecurity in Financial Services: Emerging Risks and Mitigation*. Basel: BIS.

Beck, T., Chen, T., Lin, C., & Song, F.M. (2018). Financial Innovation: The Bright and the Dark Sides. *Journal of Banking & Finance*, 93, 1–17.

Berg, T., Burg, V., Gombović, A., & Puri, M. (2020). On the Rise of Fintechs: Credit Scoring Using Digital Footprints. *Review of Financial Studies*, 33(7), 2845–2897.

BFA Global. (2022). *The Digital Divide and Financial Inclusion in Emerging Markets*. Available at: https://www.bfaglobal.com

Catalini, C., & Gans, J.S. (2020). Some Simple Economics of the Blockchain. *Communications of the ACM*, 63(7), 80–90.

Churchill, C., & Matul, M. (2012). *Protecting People with Low Incomes: A Microinsurance Compendium*. Geneva: International Labour Organisation.

Demirgüç-Kunt, A., Klapper, L., Singer, D., & van Oudheusden, P. (2018). *The Global Findex Database 2017: Measuring Financial Inclusion and the Fintech Revolution*. Washington, DC: World Bank.

Gelb, A., & Metz, A. (2018). *Identification for Development: The Biometrics Revolution*. Washington, DC: Centre for Global Development (Policy Paper 113).

Gomber, P., Koch, J.A., & Siering, M. (2018). Digital Finance and Fintech: Current Research and Future Research Directions. *Journal of Business Economics*, 88, 537–580.

GSMA (2023). *Mobile Money: State of the Industry Report*. London: GSMA.

Klapper, L., Lusardi, A., & van Oudheusden, P. (2016). *Financial Literacy around the World: Insights from the Standard & Poor's Ratings Services Global Financial Literacy Survey*. Washington, DC: World Bank.

La Porta, R., & Shleifer, A. (2014). Informality and Development. *Journal of Economic Perspectives*, 28(3), 109–126.

Nubank. (2023). *Annual Report 2023*. Available at: https://www.nubank.com.br/en/

OECD. (2021). *AI in Financial Services: Governance, Accountability, and Transparency*. Paris: OECD Publishing.

Philippon, T. (2019). The Fintech Opportunity. *NBER Working Paper No. 26495*.

Reserve Bank of India. (2021). *Digital Payments in India: Growth and Policy Initiatives*. Mumbai: RBI.

Suri, T., & Jack, W. (2016). The Long-Run Poverty and Gender Impacts of Mobile Money. *Science*, 354(6317), 1288–1292.

World Bank. (2020). *Fintech and Financial Inclusion in Emerging Markets*. Washington, DC: World Bank.

World Bank. (2021). *Index-Based Insurance for Agriculture: Lessons from East Africa*. Washington, DC: World Bank.

World Bank (2022). *Digital Financial Services and Inclusion: Emerging Market Trends*. Washington, DC: World Bank.

World Bank (2023). *Remittance Costs and Cross-Border Payments in Developing Countries*. Washington, DC: World Bank.

31 Embedded Finance

Chapter Overview

This chapter examines the rapid rise of embedded finance, a crucial trend in Financial Technology (FinTech). Embedded finance involves seamlessly integrating financial services into digital platforms and customer experiences that were previously non-financial. It covers industries such as e-commerce, healthcare, and gig economy apps. These integrations provide payments, credit, insurance, and investment tools, enhancing convenience. Platform operators benefit from new revenue streams, and financial inclusion grows. This shift is driven by robust Application Programming Interface (API) infrastructure, open banking regulations, and scalable cloud computing, all of which boost transaction speed. The chapter considers the impact on stakeholders, businesses gaining a competitive edge, consumers seeking easier access, and regulators maintaining oversight. It also discusses the key challenges, prominent applications, and future trends of this rapidly evolving market.

Learning Objectives

By the end of this chapter, you should be able to:

1. Define embedded finance and explain its role and strategic significance within the broader FinTech ecosystem, including how it reshapes the delivery of financial services.
2. Describe the technological foundations of embedded finance, particularly the role of APIs, cloud infrastructure, and platform architectures in enabling financial capabilities to be integrated into non-financial products.
3. Identify and explain the main components and use cases of embedded finance, including payments, lending, insurance, and other financial services embedded across industries such as e-commerce, gig platforms, and healthcare.
4. Analyse the business and user impact of embedded finance, including how it improves customer experience, increases engagement, and creates new revenue and monetisation models for platforms and service providers.
5. Evaluate the risks, regulatory considerations, and outlook of embedded finance, including privacy, compliance, ethical concerns, and the evolving opportunities and challenges for organisations adopting these models.

DOI: 10.4324/9781003775751-36

31.1 Introduction

Embedded finance represents a significant transformation in the delivery of financial services. It involves the seamless integration of financial products such as payments, lending, and insurance into non-financial business platforms. According to McKinsey & Company (2021), this development is rapidly reshaping the industry by converting traditional services into unified, user-centric experiences. By eliminating conventional barriers to accessing capital or insurance, embedded finance repositions core financial functions from supplementary offerings to integral components of the customer journey. As a result, it has become a primary catalyst for digital commerce.

The implementation of embedded finance relies on advanced technological infrastructure, particularly robust APIs and sophisticated data analytics. These technologies allow non-financial organisations to offer highly personalised financial products precisely when needed. The primary advantages include enhanced transactional convenience, increased customer engagement, and a strengthened value proposition for host platforms. For instance, major e-commerce platforms offer instant loans at checkout, while ride-hailing services extend targeted credit facilities to their drivers (Accenture, 2021).

The advantages of embedded finance go beyond operational efficiency, offering strategic market benefits such as enhanced customer loyalty and increased revenue. By providing a seamless, integrated process from product discovery through purchase and financing, businesses reinforce their competitiveness within the digital ecosystem. The growing demand for integrated digital experiences positions embedded finance as central to future financial strategies. Therefore, a thorough professional analysis of its technological foundations, regulatory environment, and long-term implications for the financial services sector is warranted.

31.2 An Understanding of Embedded Finance

31.2.1 Define Embedded Finance

Embedded finance refers to the direct integration of financial services, such as payments, lending, insurance or investment products, into the digital interfaces of non-financial platforms and applications. Rather than requiring users to navigate to traditional financial institutions, these services are delivered in situ at the point of need, often within the workflow of a host application (Bain & Company, 2022). Technological enablers such as APIs, cloud computing and open banking infrastructures have facilitated this integration, enabling real-time, seamless interactions that align with consumer expectations for instant digital services.

31.2.2 Nature and Characteristics

Embedded finance is defined by several interrelated characteristics that enable financial services to operate invisibly, contextually, and efficiently within non-financial platforms.

Invisibility and Contextual Integration: Invisibility and Contextual Integration mean that financial services are embedded so seamlessly that users barely perceive them as separate functions, and they appear exactly when relevant within the user's workflow. For instance, ride-hailing apps automatically offer in-app driver insurance and instant payment options, allowing users to complete transactions without leaving the platform (Accenture, 2021).

API-Driven Architecture: the use of APIs to connect the host platform with regulated financial service providers. This enables modular, real-time, and interoperable service delivery. For example, e-commerce platforms integrate Buy Now, Pay Later (BNPL) options at checkout via APIs, allowing customers to split payments instantly without redirecting to third-party sites (Accenture, 2021).

Decoupled Regulatory Model: The Decoupled Regulatory Model describes the separation of operational control from regulatory responsibility. Non-financial platforms manage the customer experience and data, while licensed banks or Bank-as-a-Service providers handle compliance, reporting, and risk management. An example is payroll software that offers early wage access, where the financial partner ensures regulatory compliance while the platform maintains user engagement (Bain & Company, 2022).

Data Intensity and Predictive Analytics: The collection of high-frequency behavioural and transactional data to inform real-time decision-making. This often replaces traditional credit scoring with more accurate, context-driven models. For instance, e-commerce platforms can approve BNPL offers instantly by analysing a user's purchase history and app engagement (Bain & Company, 2022).

Seamless Financial Service: Financial Service Delivery seamlessly is the outcome of combining invisibility, APIs, decoupled compliance, and data-driven insights. Financial services are delivered in a frictionless manner aligned with user intent, enhancing adoption and satisfaction. Subscription apps exemplify this by allowing users to top up wallets, make payments, or obtain microloans directly within the platform, without interruption (Accenture, 2021).

31.2.3 Purpose of Embedded Finance

The primary objective of embedded finance is to reduce friction in customer journeys and to contextualise financial offerings. By eliminating unnecessary redirects and interruptions, embedded services can reduce abandonment rates and accelerate key decision points, such as loan approvals or payment authorisations (World Economic Forum, 2021). Contextual delivery ensures that financial products are presented when and where they are most relevant to user intent, enhancing both utility and uptake. For non-financial firms, embedded finance also serves as a monetisation strategy, generating revenue through mechanisms such as transaction fees, lending spreads, and referral commissions.

31.2.4 Significance and Benefits

Embedded finance is increasingly recognised as a strategic imperative in digital commerce, with implications for financial inclusion, business performance and customer loyalty. In emerging economies, embedded platforms often become the first formal financial contact for previously 'thin-file' individuals and small enterprises, extending credit through alternative data sources when traditional banking reach is limited. Firms that embed financial services often realise higher customer lifetime value and lower acquisition costs, thereby contributing to competitive advantage. Moreover, integrating financial tools into core digital experiences increases customer 'stickiness', as users are less inclined to migrate away from platforms that host essential financial functions.

31.3 The Role of Embedded Finance in FinTech

Embedded finance has become a foundational element of the FinTech domain, marked by the strategic integration of financial services into non-financial digital platforms. By

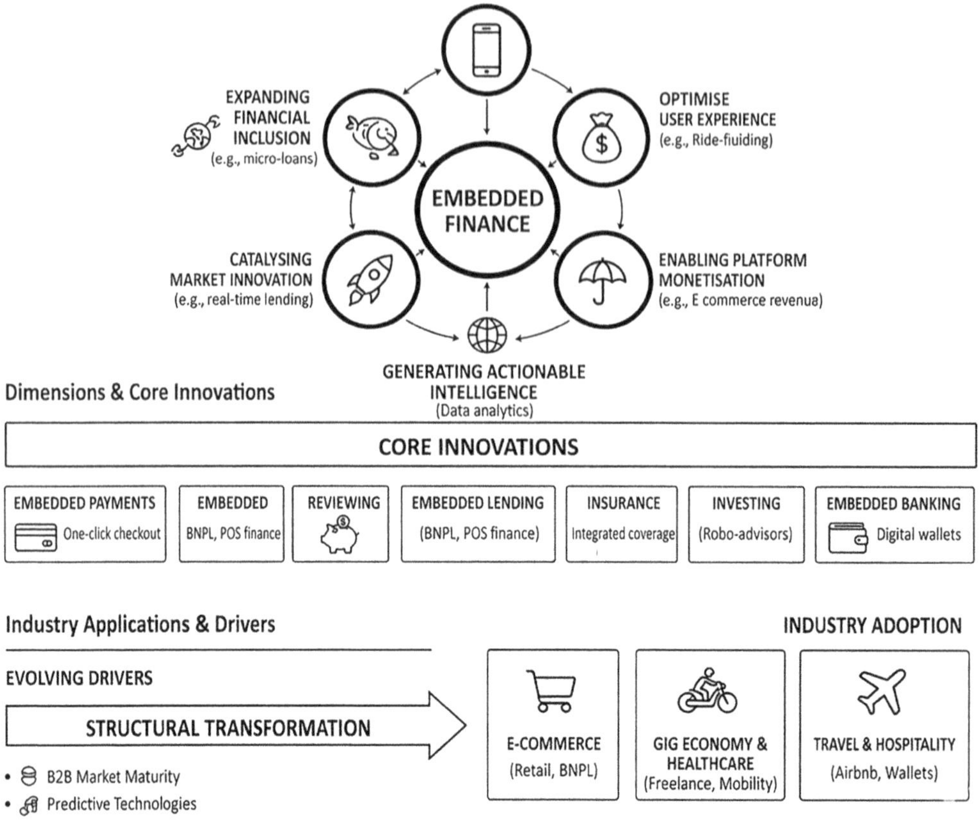

Figure 31.1 Embedded Finance in FinTech: Transforming Financial Services Across Industries.

dissolving traditional boundaries between financial and non-financial systems, embedded finance reconfigures how financial services are accessed, delivered, and monetised in the digital economy (Figure 31.1).

31.3.1 Dimensions of Embedded Finance's Role in FinTech

Embedded finance's significance in FinTech can be conceptualised across five interconnected dimensions:

Expanding Financial Inclusion: Embedded finance removes structural barriers to financial access by integrating core services, such as payments and credit, into widely used digital platforms. This architectural embedding reduces geographic and procedural frictions that traditionally exclude unbanked or underserved populations, particularly in emerging markets where formal banking penetration is low. For example, mobile commerce platforms offering in-app microloans enable users without formal bank accounts to complete purchases and build transactional histories (World Economic Forum, 2021).

Optimising User Experience: By situating financial transactions within native digital interfaces, embedded finance eliminates context-switching between disparate applications. Conducting payments or accessing credit without redirecting to external services reduces friction, improves convenience, and enhances user trust and loyalty. An illustrative case is ride-hailing services that integrate in-app payments, loyalty rewards, and driver financing into a single interface, creating a cohesive user journey that strengthens platform engagement.

Catalysing Market Innovation: Embedded finance decouples financial service delivery from traditional banking charters, allowing agile FinTech startups and non-financial brands to introduce novel financial solutions. This diffusion of innovation pressures incumbent financial institutions to modernise and adopt digital practices more rapidly. For instance, fintech platforms that embed real-time lending and risk-scoring capabilities challenge legacy banks to develop competitive digital credit products (McKinsey & Company, 2021).

Enabling Platform Monetisation. Embedded finance enables non-financial platforms to generate new revenue streams by facilitating third-party financial product offerings without bearing the full regulatory capital burden of a licensed institution. Platforms can earn commissions on transactions, referral fees for credit products, or margins on embedded insurance. For example, e-commerce marketplaces that embed insurance at checkout generate ancillary revenue while enhancing product value for consumers.

Generating Actionable Intelligence: The integrated nature of embedded finance yields rich behavioural and transactional data that supports advanced analytics. This data enables granular credit risk modelling, real-time fraud detection, and the customisation of financial products, forming a feedback loop that improves risk management and user engagement. For example, platforms can use purchasing patterns and app usage metrics to tailor credit limits or offer dynamic pricing models that reflect individual risk profiles.

31.3.2 Core Innovations Underpinning Embedded Finance

Embedded finance is operationalised through technological innovations and strategic partnerships, enabling seamless integration within non-financial platforms. These components collectively enhance accessibility, convenience, and value creation.

Embedded Payments: Embedded payments integrate payment gateways directly into merchant systems, enabling one-click transactions that reduce complexity and lower cart abandonment rates. For instance, travel booking platforms provide instant payments integrated with airline and hotel systems, streamlining the checkout process and improving conversion rates (Mendoza-Tello et al., 2019).

Embedded Lending: Delivered through mechanisms such as BNPL or point-of-sale financing APIs, embedded lending offers context-specific credit to consumers and working capital solutions to businesses. For example, online retailers embed BNPL options at checkout, enabling customers to finance purchases in instalments without a separate credit application, thereby increasing sales volume (Marlin, 2021).

Embedded Insurance: Embedded insurance integrates coverage products directly within relevant purchasing contexts, reducing perceived risk and strengthening the overall value proposition of the primary transaction. For example, electronics retailers may offer extended warranty coverage at the point of sale, embedding insurance decisions into the purchase experience (Capgemini, 2022).

Embedded Investing: Through partnerships with regulated brokerages, platforms offer functionalities such as fractional investing and automated portfolio management. This lowers traditional barriers, such as high minimum investment thresholds, promoting broader participation in financial markets. For instance, social trading platforms embed investment functionality that allows users to allocate small amounts into diversified portfolios directly through social apps (Chen et al., 2021).

Embedded Banking: Leveraging Banking-as-a-Service (BaaS) infrastructure, embedded banking enables non-financial platforms to offer core banking services, such as digital wallets and branded deposit accounts, via licensed APIs. This integration consolidates financial needs within a single digital ecosystem. For example, a retail app might host a branded wallet that supports loyalty points, instant payments, and savings features (Moser et al., 2022).

31.3.3 Structural Transformations in FinTech

Expected that embedded finance is going to shift from a disruptive innovation to a structural backbone of the FinTech sector, fundamentally transforming how financial services are distributed, consumed, and monetised. FinTech is no longer delivered through standalone applications. Still, it operates as invisible, embedded layers within daily digital experiences, seamlessly integrating payments, lending, and insurance into e-commerce, ride-hailing, and enterprise software workflows. This invisible integration reduces friction, eliminates redirects, and lowers customer drop-off rates, resulting in higher customer lifetime value and lower acquisition costs. At the same time, the competitive landscape increasingly rewards either deep vertical specialisation or large-scale infrastructural capabilities, with success concentrated among platforms that focus on industry-specific solutions, such as logistics or construction lending, or achieve extensive digital scale, thereby combining efficiency, contextual relevance, and operational depth to strengthen both user engagement and platform monetisation.

31.3.4 Evolving Drivers of Embedded Finance Adoption

The maturity of the Business-to-Business (B2B) market increasingly drives the adoption of embedded finance, advances in predictive technologies, and the integration of compliance into core infrastructure. Embedded finance has permeated multiple industries, transforming how financial services are delivered and consumed by integrating them directly into sector-specific platforms.

In the e-commerce sector, platforms such as Amazon and Shopify embed financial solutions, including BNPL, merchant lending, and loyalty-point conversion into currency. These integrations streamline the checkout process, reduce cart abandonment, and create additional revenue streams for merchants (Bain & Company, 2022). For example, Shopify Capital provides small businesses with immediate access to financing, enabling inventory expansion and operational growth without reliance on traditional bank loans.

Within the gig economy and freelance platforms, embedded finance mitigates the financial volatility experienced by independent workers. Platforms such as Uber and DoorDash offer instant payment options, real-time income tracking, and integrated tax management tools, enhancing cash-flow stability for drivers and freelancers while reinforcing platform engagement and loyalty (KPMG, 2021).

In the healthcare sector, embedded financial services improve affordability and accessibility. Telehealth and medical service platforms integrate billing, BNPL options, and insurance processing directly into their interfaces, simplifying payment workflows and enabling patients to manage costs better. For instance, CareCredit provides point-of-service financing for elective medical procedures, allowing patients to access care without upfront financial strain.

The travel and hospitality sector also benefits from embedded finance, with platforms such as Airbnb incorporating dynamic travel insurance, digital wallets, and multi-currency exchange capabilities. These embedded solutions enhance convenience, increase transactional security, and create a seamless booking experience, ultimately improving customer satisfaction and encouraging repeat usage (World Travel & Tourism Council, 2022).

31.4 Opportunities, Challenges, and Key Practical Issues of Embedded Finance

Embedded finance has evolved into a strategic imperative within the FinTech landscape, offering significant opportunities for innovation, financial inclusion, and operational efficiency, while simultaneously introducing complex risks and implementation challenges.

31.4.1 Opportunities for Embedded Finance

Embedded finance fundamentally reshapes the creation and distribution of financial value by embedding services directly into non-financial platforms. Deep vertical integration allows sector-specific platforms, such as logistics, construction, and healthcare, to offer contextual lending, automated insurance, and other tailored financial products, enhancing relevance and utility for users. For example, procurement platforms can provide automated invoice financing, enabling small- and medium-sized enterprises to access working capital precisely when materials are ordered, alleviating cash-flow constraints. Enhanced customer loyalty is another key benefit; firms report 2–5 times higher customer lifetime value and up to a 30% reduction in acquisition costs by invisibly embedding financial services into the user journey. The B2B market has emerged as a critical growth segment, estimated at $4.1 trillion, in which integrated tools, such as automated working capital or embedded credit within enterprise software, solve essential financial and operational challenges. Finally, AI-driven hyper-personalisation enables real-time, context-aware financial offers, for instance, dynamically providing project-specific insurance when a contractor books materials, optimising both the customer experience and revenue potential (Bain & Company, 2022; McKinsey & Company, 2021).

31.4.2 Risks and Challenges of Embedded Finance

The decoupling of financial services from traditional banks to non-financial platforms introduces a range of complex risk vectors. AI-powered fraud has become increasingly sophisticated, with generative AI enabling synthetic identities and deepfakes that can bypass conventional Know Your Customer or biometric verification, making adaptive, real-time fraud prevention essential (Arner et al., 2020). Operational resilience is another concern; as financial services become deeply interconnected, failures in third-party cloud services or API infrastructures can propagate systemic disruptions. Regulators now treat cyber resilience as a principal concern for embedded finance platforms. Regulatory fragmentation poses further challenges, as firms must navigate diverse local mandates, such as the UK's Consumer Duty and the EU AI Act, leading to potential compliance debt and operational complexity. Additionally, adverse selection risks arise when traditional banks retain only highly regulated, capital-intensive functions, losing direct access to high-margin customer relationships to platform providers (Zachariadis & Ozcan, 2017).

31.4.3 Key Practical Issues in Embedded Finance

Successful implementation of embedded finance requires addressing operational, technical, and economic challenges. Integration complexity arises from connecting non-financial platforms to financial service providers via APIs; poorly designed or unreliable integrations can result in transaction errors, security breaches, and poor user experiences. For example, e-commerce platforms embedding BNPL and digital wallets must ensure consistent, low-latency connectivity across multiple providers to maintain seamless checkout processes (Möhlmann et al., 2021). Partnership management is critical, as platforms typically rely on multiple financial partners for lending, payments, and card issuance. Effective orchestration demands clear service-level agreements, co-developed risk frameworks, and alignment on customer experience (Bain & Company, 2022). Finally, economic and risk management considerations require platforms to manage credit risk, revenue-sharing arrangements, and operational costs, including compliance, technology maintenance, and cybersecurity, to safeguard profitability and financial sustainability. For example, embedded lending providers must maintain robust credit underwriting and monitoring systems to prevent losses while scaling operations efficiently (Drasch et al., 2018).

31.5 Conclusion

Embedded finance constitutes a transformative development in the digital economy, fundamentally altering how financial services are accessed and delivered through non-financial platforms. By integrating financial functionalities, including payments, lending, and insurance, directly into digital experiences such as e-commerce checkouts or software-as-a-service applications, this model enables finance to become invisible yet ever-present within the user journey (McKinsey & Company, 2023a). Supported by advanced FinTech infrastructure, embedded finance shifts service delivery from traditional banking channels to real-time, context-aware touchpoints, enhancing operational efficiency and improving user convenience. The resulting experience is characterised by higher conversion rates, personalised interactions, and increased customer lifetime value, facilitated by scalable system architectures that integrate modern APIs with legacy core systems and manage high-volume transactional flows.

The continued expansion of embedded finance relies not only on technological capability but also on governance, trust, and regulatory alignment. Ethicality, data integrity, and inclusive access are critical to ensuring equitable participation and long-term ecosystem resilience. Strategic collaboration is essential: financial institutions must partner with FinTech innovators, regulators need to adapt frameworks to accommodate borderless digital finance, and platform operators must safeguard consumer data while ensuring compliance. As observed in industry analyses, the future of finance will be defined not by banks or technology companies alone but by ecosystems governed through transparency, shared accountability, and coordinated oversight, shaping a stable, inclusive, and user-centric financial landscape.

Key Terms and Glossary

Embedded Finance The integration of financial services (e.g., payments, lending) into non-financial platforms and customer journeys.

BNPL An embedded lending product that allows consumers to split purchases into instalments.

BaaS The underlying model that enables non-banks to offer embedded financial services by leveraging the licensed infrastructure of traditional banks.

Embedded Insurance The integration of insurance offerings (e.g., travel insurance) directly into the sales process of a related product or service.

Contextual Banking Providing financial services at the precise moment they are needed within a user's current activity or platform.

Test Your Understanding

Multiple-Choice Questions

1 Which of the following best defines embedded finance?

A Traditional banking services delivered via branch networks
B Integration of financial services into non-financial platforms
C Cryptocurrency trading platforms
D Standalone FinTech applications

2 What technological component is most critical for enabling embedded finance?

A Blockchain ledgers
B APIs
C Physical point-of-sale terminals
D Traditional credit scoring systems

3 Which of the following is NOT a key component of embedded finance?

A Embedded Payments
B Embedded Lending
C Embedded Insurance
D Physical bank branch expansion

4 How does embedded finance contribute to financial inclusion?

A By offering high-interest loans to wealthy customers
B By integrating core financial services into widely used platforms
C By reducing the number of financial apps available
D By replacing digital wallets with cash payments

5 Which challenge is associated with the decoupling of financial services from banks?

A Simplified regulatory compliance
B AI-powered fraud and operational risk
C Increased physical branch access
D Reduced data collection requirements

Short Questions

1 Explain the concept of "seamless financial service delivery" in embedded finance.
2 List three industries where embedded finance has had a significant impact and give one example in each.
3 What are the primary risks associated with embedded finance for non-financial platforms?

Analytical Questions

1 Critically analyse how embedded finance transforms customer experience compared to traditional banking. Include examples of integrated payments and lending in your discussion.
2 Evaluate the strategic benefits for non-financial platforms adopting embedded finance. Consider monetisation, customer engagement, and competitive advantage.
3 Discuss the regulatory and operational challenges of embedded finance. How can partnerships with licensed financial institutions mitigate these risks?

Case Study: Uber's Embedded Financial Ecosystem

Uber has strategically integrated financial services into its platform to address operational challenges and enhance its overall ecosystem. Central to this strategy is Uber Wallet, which enables drivers and couriers to manage earnings efficiently, and the Uber Debit Card, which allows instant access to funds, mitigating the cash-flow volatility inherent in gig work. Through Uber Money, the company provides additional financial services, including savings and transaction management, as well as vehicle loans and lease options to support driver mobility and operational continuity.

This embedded financial ecosystem aligns closely with Uber's strategic objectives. By improving driver financial stability and convenience, Uber enhances retention and loyalty, reducing churn and maintaining a reliable supply of active drivers. Simultaneously, these services create new monetisation opportunities, from transaction fees to interest on lending products, while deepening the engagement of drivers within the platform, effectively transforming Uber from a ride-hailing app into a comprehensive financial hub for the gig economy.

However, venturing into financial services introduces regulatory, operational, and reputational risks, as Uber is not a licensed bank. Compliance with financial regulations, safeguarding sensitive customer data, and managing credit or liquidity risks are critical. For drivers, the ecosystem offers convenience and faster access to earnings but may also create dependency, potentially limiting flexibility to use alternative financial providers or services.

References

McKinsey & Company. (2023b). *The Next Wave of Disruption in Payments*. Available at: https://www.mckinsey.com.br/industries/financial-services/our-insights/the-2023-mckinsey-global-payments-report (Accessed: 3 March 2026).

Wiles, K., & Sweeney, K. (2019) How Uber Makes Its Drivers Pay. *Wall Street Journal (Eastern Edition)*. Available at: https://www.researchgate.net/publication/336371201_How_Uber_Makes_Its_Drivers_Pay

Case Study Questions

1 How does Uber's adoption of embedded finance strategically enhance its core ride-hailing and delivery business beyond merely creating a new income stream?
2 As a non-bank entity, what specific risks does Uber face by offering embedded financial services, and how might it manage them?
3 For an Uber driver, what are the advantages and disadvantages of relying primarily on the platform's embedded financial ecosystem for their banking and financial needs?

Further Reading

Accenture. (2021). *Embedded Finance: The Future of Financial Services Is Here*. Dublin: Accenture.

McKinsey & Company. (2021). *The Next Wave of Disruption in Payments*. New York: McKinsey & Company.

World Economic Forum. (2021). *The Future of Embedded Finance*. Geneva: World Economic Forum.

References

Accenture. (2021). *Embedded Finance: Transforming the Customer Experience*. Dublin: Accenture. Available at: https://bankingblog.accenture.com/tag/embedded-finance (Accessed: 8 February 2026).

Arner, D.W., Barberis, J., & Buckley, R.P. (2020) The Evolution of Fintech: A New Post-Crisis Paradigm?, *Georgetown Journal of International Law*, 47(4), 1271–1319.

Bain & Company (2022). *The Rise of Embedded Finance and its Implications for Non-Financial Platforms*. Boston, MA: Bain & Company.

Capgemini (2022) *World Insurance Report 2022*. Paris: Capgemini.

Chen, Y., Gozman, D., & Zhang, X. (2021) Embedded Investing in Digital Platforms: Opportunities and Challenges. *Journal of Financial Innovation*, 7(2), 45–62.

Drasch, B.J., Schweizer, A., & Urbach, N. (2018) The Risks of Embedded Finance for Platform Operators. *Business & Information Systems Engineering*, 60(4), 291–304.

KPMG. (2021). *Embedded Finance in the Gig Economy*. London: KPMG Insights.

Marlin, R. (2021) Buy Now, Pay Later: Market Dynamics and Embedded Finance Applications. *Financial Services Review*, 30(3), 221–236.

McKinsey & Company. (2021) *Global Banking Annual Review: The Rise of Embedded Finance*. New York: McKinsey & Company. Available at https://www.mckinsey.com/industries/financial-services/our-insights/global-banking-annual-review-archive

McKinsey & Company. (2023a). Embedded Finance: How Banks and Fintechs Can Win in the Next Era of Financial Services. Available at: https://www.mckinsey.com/industries/financial-services/our-insights

McKinsey & Company. (2023b). *The Next Wave of Disruption in Payments*. Available at: https://www.mckinsey.com.br/industries/financial-services/our-insights/the-2023-mckinsey-global-payments-report (Accessed: 3 March 2026).

Mendoza Tello, J.E., de la Cruz, E., & Ruiz, E. (2019) Digital Wallets and Payment Integration. *International Journal of Digital Banking*, 1(1), 23–35.

Möhlmann, M., et al. (2021) API Integration and Operational Risk in Embedded Finance. *Journal of Banking Technology*, 14(2), 112–129.

Moser, T., Reiner, R., & Schubert, S. (2022) Embedded Banking: Opportunities and Platform Design. *FinTech Journal*, 8(1), 55–78.

World Economic Forum. (2021). *FinTech and Financial Inclusion: Embedded Finance Insights*. Geneva: World Economic Forum.

World Travel & Tourism Council. (2022). *Embedded Finance Applications in Travel and Hospitality*. London: WTTC.

Zachariadis, M., & Ozcan, P. (2017) The API Economy and Digital Platforms: Disruptive Innovation in Financial Services. *Information Systems Research*, 28(2), 276–290.

32 Sustainable and Ethical Finance

Chapter Overview

This chapter critically examines the evolving convergence of sustainable finance, ethical investing, and Financial Technology (FinTech). This influential nexus is fundamentally transforming global financial markets (Arner, Barberis, & Buckley, 2020). The chapter thoroughly explores a variety of sustainable finance products, including green bonds, Environmental, Social, and Governance (ESG) funds, and Sustainability-Linked Loans (SLLs). Simultaneously, it outlines the core principles of ethical investing. The analysis shows how FinTech innovations, such as Artificial Intelligence (AI), blockchain, and robo-advisors, are improving transparency, accessibility, and data integrity within responsible investing (Dorfleitner & Braun, 2019). Despite these progressions, the chapter also discusses significant challenges. These include widespread greenwashing, regulatory gaps, and the ongoing lack of standardisation in ethics. The chapter ends with a review of global trends and policy initiatives that drive the movement towards a more sustainable and equitable financial future.

Learning Objectives

By the end of this chapter, you should be able to:

1 Define sustainable finance and ethical investment and distinguish between their underlying principles and objectives.
2 Evaluate how FinTech innovations, such as AI and blockchain, are enhancing transparency, accessibility, and impact measurement in sustainable investing.
3 Critically examine the potential benefits and inherent limitations of incorporating ESG criteria into investment decisions.
4 Identify and discuss key challenges in the sustainable finance ecosystem, including greenwashing, data quality issues, and the lack of standardised ethical metrics.
5 Assess the influence of evolving global regulations and the opportunities presented by democratising access to sustainable investment products.

DOI: 10.4324/9781003775751-37

32.1 Introduction

The global financial landscape is experiencing a systemic transformation, driven by increased recognition of macro-level risks, including climate change, social inequality, and weaknesses in corporate governance. This shift requires the financial industry to actively support the achievement of the Sustainable Development Goals. Investment strategies are therefore evolving to incorporate comprehensive environmental and social risk assessments alongside traditional financial metrics. In response, the market has rapidly introduced advanced sustainable finance products, such as green bonds, ESG-integrated funds, and specialised impact investment vehicles. This development indicates a fundamental repositioning of the industry towards long-term value creation.

Ethical investing represents a closely related paradigm, emphasising the integration of moral values and social impact objectives into capital allocation decisions. This approach requires investors to apply rigorous non-financial criteria when assessing long-term risks and opportunities. The objective is to achieve verifiable positive societal outcomes in addition to competitive financial returns (Sandberg, Juravle, Hedesström, & Hamilton, 2022). Growing investor demand for responsible and principled capital deployment has driven innovation in asset management products. This evolution necessitates increased transparency, standardisation, and accountability in the reporting of measurable social and environmental performance.

The rapid expansion and credibility of sustainable and ethical investment mandates are supported by advances in FinTech. Technologies such as AI and distributed ledger systems, including blockchain, address data challenges related to transparency, accuracy, and standardisation in ESG reporting and risk assessment. Serving as critical enablers, these technologies enhance the efficiency and effectiveness of accessing, analysing, and managing responsible investments (Macpherson & Zwick, 2022). They offer scalable, innovative solutions essential to maintaining integrity and meeting the growing global demand for responsible investment products.

32.2 Understanding Sustainable Finance and Ethical Investment

32.2.1 Defining the Purposes

32.2.1.1 Sustainable Finance

Sustainable finance refers to the integration of ESG factors into financial decision-making, to promote long-term economic activities that benefit both society and the environment (European Commission, 2021). This approach extends beyond traditional financial analysis by embedding sustainability considerations into capital allocation, risk assessment, and financing decisions. According to United Nations Environment Programme (UNEP) (2020), the growth of digital finance and FinTech innovations has accelerated access to green finance, improved transparency in ESG reporting, and mobilised resources for sustainable projects. For instance, green bonds issued by governments and corporations now fund renewable energy infrastructure, water management systems, and climate-resilient urban development, demonstrating how capital allocation can advance environmental objectives.

32.2.1.2 Ethical Investment

Ethical investment, often referred to as Socially Responsible Investing (SRI), prioritises moral and ethical criteria alongside financial returns. Investors may select companies based on positive ethical attributes, such as strong labour standards or leadership in renewable energy, or exclude firms operating in industries considered harmful, such as tobacco, weapons, or fossil fuels (Cowton, 1999). Ethical investors also engage in shareholder activism, using their voting rights to influence corporate practices related to human rights, environmental impact, and governance standards (Renneboog, ter Horst, & Zhang, 2008). FinTech platforms have facilitated this approach, allowing retail investors to align portfolios with personal values, for example, by selecting funds that invest exclusively in renewable energy or fair-trade companies.

32.2.2 Characteristics of Sustainable Finance and Ethical Investment

32.2.2.1 Sustainable Finance

Sustainable finance has evolved from a regulatory-focused framework to a practical, outcome-oriented approach that prioritises measurable social, environmental, and economic impacts. By 2026, it is characterised by maturity, with global sustainable bond issuance exceeding $6 trillion, positioning these instruments as central to fixed-income markets and a critical mechanism for directing capital towards sustainable development (European Commission, 2021).

Outcome-Oriented Integration: Investment decisions are assessed based on tangible sustainability results rather than solely on disclosure or compliance. Capital is directed to projects that demonstrably mitigate climate change, improve social welfare, or enhance corporate governance. For example, banks may prioritise loans to renewable energy developers with measurable carbon reduction outcomes, such as solar or wind farm projects, ensuring investments deliver verifiable environmental impact (European Commission, 2021).

Pragmatic Transition Finance: Capital is increasingly provided to high-carbon or legacy companies that implement credible, science-based decarbonisation strategies. For instance, automotive firms investing in electrification or steel producers adopting carbon capture technology can access SLLs with terms contingent on achieving emission-reduction targets (UNEP, 2020). This approach supports a gradual transition to low-carbon operations without penalising companies immediately for historical emissions.

Risk-Based Foundation: Climate, environmental, and policy-related risks are now embedded into financial models and portfolio stress tests alongside traditional metrics such as interest rate, duration, and foreign exchange exposure. This integration accounts for systemic ESG-related risks and enhances long-term resilience and financial stability (European Commission, 2021).

Sharpened Labelling and Credibility: Regulatory standards require that terms such as sustainable or green be verifiable, backed by concrete allocations, and aligned with strict benchmarks, such as the EU Climate Benchmarks. This ensures transparency and prevents misleading claims, enhancing investor confidence (European Commission, 2021).

Focus on Adaptation and Resilience: Sustainable finance increasingly supports projects designed to address physical climate risks, such as flood defences, drought-resistant agriculture, climate-resilient infrastructure, and urban planning initiatives. For example, climate-resilient urban drainage systems have been financed to reduce flood risk in European cities (UNEP, 2020).

Double Materiality: Companies disclose both the effects of sustainability factors on financial performance and their own environmental and social impacts. For instance, an energy utility might report the financial impact of carbon pricing on profits while simultaneously quantifying greenhouse gas emissions and social effects on local communities (European Commission, 2021).

Digital Resilience and AI Integration: AI-driven analytics are applied to assess energy- and water-intensive projects, including industrial facilities and large data centres, allowing investors to model operational efficiency, environmental impact, and climate risks in real time. Digital tools also enhance monitoring, reporting, and compliance, enabling more precise allocation of sustainable capital (UNEP, 2020).

Standardised Reporting: Voluntary ESG disclosures are increasingly replaced by mandatory, audited frameworks such as the International Sustainability Standards Board (ISSB)–aligned standards. These frameworks provide comparable, decision-ready data, reducing information asymmetry and mitigating the risk of *greenwashing* by firms claiming sustainability without evidence (European Commission, 2021).

32.2.2.2 Ethical Investment

Ethical investment, also known as SRI, is a value-driven investment approach that prioritises moral and ethical principles alongside financial performance. Unlike sustainable finance, which addresses broad ESG risks and systemic impacts, ethical investing focuses on the investor's ethical compass, guiding decisions on 'what to own' and 'what to exclude' in accordance with personal, institutional, or faith-based values (Cowton, 1999; Renneboog et al., 2008).

Moral Alignment: Ethical investments are screened to exclude activities that violate human dignity or social responsibility, such as arms manufacturing, exploitative labour practices, tobacco, gambling, adult entertainment, and high-carbon fossil fuels. This ensures capital allocation aligns with ethical principles and societal norms (Cowton, 1999).

Active Stewardship: Ethical investors actively engage with companies in their portfolios, influencing governance, environmental policies, and labour standards, rather than relying solely on exclusionary measures. For instance, shareholders may vote to enforce supply chain transparency or improved corporate climate practices (Renneboog et al., 2008).

Faith and Value-Based Roots: Many ethical investment frameworks originate from religious or philosophical traditions. Sharia-compliant finance prohibits interest-based lending and speculative investments, while Quaker-led funds historically avoid companies associated with exploitation or social harm (Renneboog et al., 2008).

Negative and Positive Screening: Ethical funds systematically exclude *sin stocks* through negative screening while employing positive screening to identify best-in-class companies with superior ethical performance. Examples include firms demonstrating gender pay equity, high supply chain transparency, or leadership in renewable energy adoption.

AI-Driven Ethical Audits: Modern ethical investing integrates technology, using AI tools to scan corporate operations and algorithms to ensure compliance with ethical standards. For example, automated audits can detect bias in hiring or lending algorithms, preventing unethical practices from being indirectly financed (Cowton, 1999).

Transparency of Intent: Ethical funds provide detailed ethical lineage reports, clarifying why each company was selected and preventing ethical washing. These reports allow investors to verify that capital is deployed strictly in accordance with stated ethical boundaries (Renneboog et al., 2008).

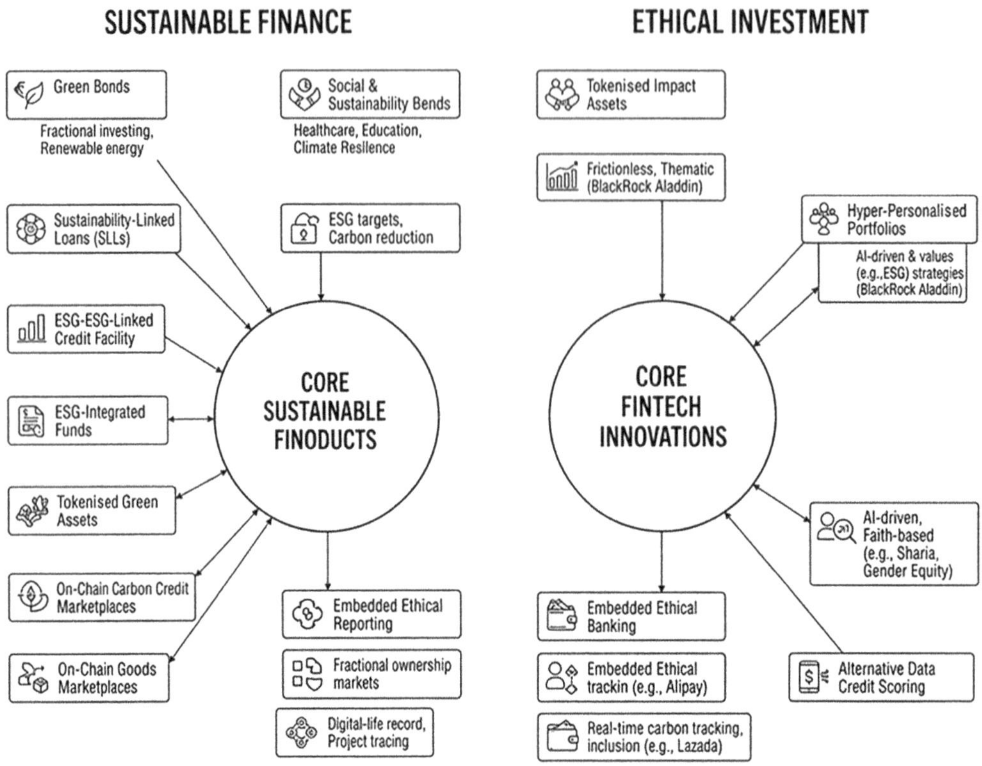

Figure 32.1 FinTech Innovation: Sustainable and Ethical Finance.

Impact Focus: Ethical investments emphasise tangible real-world outcomes over market index performance. Capital is allocated to projects that deliver measurable societal or environmental benefits, such as renewable energy, social housing, or community development initiatives (Cowton, 1999; Renneboog et al., 2008) (Figure 32.1).

32.3 Products and Services with FinTech Innovation

32.3.1 Sustainable Finance

Sustainable finance has transitioned from a niche market to a central component of global capital allocation, driven by technological innovation that aligns investments with ESG objectives. FinTech has played a pivotal role in broadening access, enhancing transparency, and enabling automated compliance with increasingly stringent regulatory mandates (European Commission, 2021; ICMA, 2021).

Core Sustainable FinTech Products and Innovations:

Green Bonds: Debt instruments dedicated exclusively to projects with verified environmental benefits, guided by frameworks such as the Green Bond Principles, which emphasise use-of-proceeds reporting and independent project evaluation (ICMA, 2021). For example, the European Union's sovereign green bonds under the NextGenerationEU recovery plan fund renewable energy infrastructure and energy-efficient building renovations.

FinTech platforms now enable fractional investments in green bonds, allowing retail investors to participate in large-scale climate initiatives.

Social and Sustainability Bonds: Social bonds finance projects addressing defined social challenges, such as healthcare or education, while sustainability bonds combine social and environmental objectives. The World Bank's gender equality and climate resilience bonds exemplify this dual-purpose model, attracting ESG-focused capital from institutional and retail investors alike (ICMA, 2021).

SLLs: These loans tie financial terms to predefined Sustainability Performance Targets (SPTs), incentivising ESG improvements across the borrower's operations. Interest rates adjust in line with the achievement of targets, such as reductions in carbon intensity or enhanced board diversity, thereby linking financial costs directly to environmental and social performance (Loan Market Association, 2023).

ESG-Integrated Funds: Investment funds systematically incorporate ESG factors into portfolio construction through negative screening, positive selection, or thematic strategies. BlackRock's iShares ESG-aware exchange-traded funds (ETFs), for instance, overweight high-rated ESG companies while excluding firms exposed to controversial activities, reflecting material ESG factors in long-term risk-adjusted returns (Amel-Zadeh & Serafeim, 2018).

Automated Sustainability Reporting Platforms: Platforms such as Gprnt employ AI to scrape utility, logistics, and operational data, generating audit-ready ESG reports compliant with Scope 3 emissions and mandatory reporting requirements. This automation reduces reporting burdens and ensures regulatory alignment.

Tokenised Green Assets and Renewable Energy: Blockchain technology enables fractional ownership of real-world assets, including solar farms and other renewable energy infrastructure, democratising access to previously illiquid green investment markets.

On-Chain Carbon Credit Marketplaces: Carbon credits are now issued and traded as digital tokens, ensuring provenance and preventing double-counting. Hybrid products, such as tokenised carbon baskets, allow investors to participate in verifiable, structured carbon markets.

Digital Green Bonds: Distributed ledger technology enables the issuance of bonds with immutable records, tracing investor funds directly to the financed renewable energy projects, enhancing transparency and accountability.

32.3.2 Ethical Investment in FinTech

The rise of FinTech has transformed ethical investment, making high-conviction strategies and real-time monitoring accessible to retail investors. Digital platforms now support fractional ownership, hyper-personalised portfolios, and automated compliance with moral and ethical frameworks, thereby democratising access to markets historically restricted to institutional investors (Cowton, 1999; Renneboog et al., 2008).

Tokenised Impact Assets: Blockchain platforms enable fractional ownership of real-world ethical projects, such as community solar installations or biodiversity-rich land. This innovation allows retail investors to participate directly in socially and environmentally impactful initiatives that were previously illiquid or reserved for institutions.

Hyper-Personalised Ethical Portfolios: WealthTech platforms use AI to construct portfolios aligned with an investor's moral map, accommodating faith-based strategies (e.g., Sharia-compliant investing) or theme-based approaches (e.g., modern slavery prevention, gender equity). These portfolios allow investors to align capital deployment with deeply held ethical principles.

Embedded Ethical Banking: FinTech apps like Algbra and Aspiration integrate ethical features into daily financial interactions, including real-time carbon footprint tracking and guarantees that deposits are not used to finance fossil fuel or other harmful industries.

Alternative-Data Credit Scoring: Platforms such as Lenddo leverage non-traditional data, including mobile transaction histories, to provide credit access to thin-file or unbanked individuals, promoting financial inclusion and equitable access to capital (Renneboog et al., 2008).

32.4 Challenges and Key Practical Issues in Sustainable and Ethical Finance

32.4.1 Risks and Challenges

32.4.1.1 Challenges in Sustainable Finance

Sustainable finance will operate under strict regulatory frameworks that directly influence system design and operational practices. The EU Corporate Sustainability Reporting Directive (CSRD) requires large firms to report on double materiality, disclosing both how sustainability factors affect their business and how their operations impact society and the environment (European Commission, 2021). Similarly, the EU AI Act classifies financial AI systems, used for credit scoring, fraud detection, and anti-money laundering, as high-risk, mandating fully auditable and defensible decision-making processes (European Commission, 2021). Fragmented regulatory requirements, such as California's SB 253 and SB 261 climate disclosure mandates, create cross-border compliance complexities (de Freitas Netto, Sobral, Ribeiro, & Freire, 2020). Operational risks are compounded by AI-driven cyberattacks, deepfake-enabled fraud, and the high computational energy demands of blockchain and AI systems, which can paradoxically undermine environmental objectives (Arner et al., 2020). A practical illustration is the European Investment Bank's green bonds, which finance renewable energy and industrial transition projects. These instruments must comply with diverse reporting standards and verify measurable environmental impacts across multiple jurisdictions, highlighting both regulatory and operational challenges (ICMA, 2021)

32.4.1.2 Challenges in Ethical Investment

Ethical investment within FinTech faces analogous technological, operational, and regulatory challenges. AI-dependent systems introduce risks such as algorithmic bias, opaque decision-making, and potential misallocation of capital when autonomous agentic platforms operate without human oversight (Cowton, 1999; Renneboog et al., 2008). Maintaining ethical credibility is critical, as misleading claims or social-washing practices can incur penalties from regulators such as BaFin (Khan, Serafeim, & Yoon, 2016). Security and identity risks, including synthetic identities and deepfake impersonation, threaten digital trust, while extensive alternative-data collection amplifies privacy concerns. Regulatory fragmentation further complicates operations, as the EU AI Act imposes high-risk obligations on AI-driven investment decisions and the UK Sustainability Disclosure Requirements establish first-time sustainability reporting for smaller asset managers (European Commission, 2021). Platforms such as Triodos Sustainable Investment Fund demonstrate practical compliance, as AI-driven monitoring ensures that portfolio companies adhere to strict ethical and ESG standards while delivering measurable social and environmental outcomes (Cowton, 1999; Renneboog et al., 2008).

32.4.2 Key Practical Issues

32.4.2.1 Key Practical Issues on Implementing Sustainable Finance

Regulatory, technological, and operational constraints heavily influence the practical implementation of sustainable finance. Mandatory frameworks such as the EU CSRD and the Corporate Sustainability Due Diligence Directive require audited, comprehensive sustainability reporting. At the same time, AI-enabled systems must maintain immutable audit trails to ensure transparency and compliance with the EU AI Act and the Digital Operational Resilience Act (European Commission, 2021). Data integrity and standardisation remain critical challenges, as fragmented ESG datasets, particularly from SMEs supplying larger corporations, must be consolidated to ensure accurate Scope 3 emissions reporting and reliable ESG performance measurement. Additionally, technological and ethical risks persist, including algorithmic bias in green lending, synthetic identity fraud enabled by generative AI, and the environmental paradox of high energy and water consumption in blockchain and AI systems, which may undermine the sustainability objectives they are intended to support (Arner et al., 2020). Operationally, firms are adopting structured, outcome-focused programmes with compliance hard-coded into AI systems, a shortage of hybrid talent combining technical, regulatory, and sustainability expertise, and real-time monitoring systems to detect greenwashing or fraud as it occurs (Khan et al., 2016).

32.4.2.2 Key Practical Issues on Ethical Investment

Ethical investment faces comparable practical challenges, particularly regarding AI explainability, compliance, and data integrity. High-risk AI systems must provide defensible, transparent decisions under the EU AI Act, while compliance-as-infrastructure embeds ethical and regulatory constraints directly into system architecture to prevent violations (Cowton, 1999; Renneboog et al., 2008). Reliable ethical investing also depends on high-quality, real-time ESG data; fragmented enterprise datasets must be consolidated into actionable data products, and SMEs are increasingly required to provide automated data to meet compliance standards. Fraud prevention and digital trust are central concerns, with platforms implementing zero-trust architectures and behavioural biometrics to mitigate risks of synthetic identity and deepfake-enabled attacks. Strategic challenges in sustainable and ethical finance include greenwashing, regulatory fragmentation, inconsistent ethical metrics, data integrity issues, and barriers to financial inclusion stemming from the digital divide (Arner et al., 2020; de Freitas Netto et al., 2020). An illustrative example is the blockchain-based auditing platform Gprnt, which automates verification of renewable energy and social impact projects, ensuring compliance with CSRD reporting requirements and preventing greenwashing in both sustainable and ethical investment products (ICMA, 2021).

32.5 Conclusion

The convergence of sustainable finance, ethical investing, and FinTech marks a defining evolution in the global financial landscape. Heightened awareness of climate change, social inequity, and corporate governance failures has catalysed a shift from profit-centric models towards investment strategies focused on long-term, inclusive value creation. Finance is not just a tool for economic growth; it is a lever for systemic transformation (World Economic Forum, 2020). This reimagined role positions financial institutions as key enablers of sustainable development, channelling capital towards initiatives that support a resilient, low-carbon, and equitable global economy. Investors are increasingly demanding accountability, prompting asset managers and banks to embed ESG criteria into their decision-making frameworks.

FinTech significantly amplifies this transition by enhancing transparency, scalability, and access to sustainable investment opportunities. Tools such as blockchain ensure supply chain traceability, while AI enables real-time ESG risk assessment and performance monitoring, empowering stakeholders with actionable insights. However, obstacles persist, including inconsistent sustainability metrics, regulatory fragmentation, and the growing concern of greenwashing. Without standardised reporting and enforceable disclosures, the integrity of sustainable finance is at risk. Addressing these challenges demands robust regulatory oversight, harmonised global standards, and cross-sector cooperation. Achieving a truly sustainable financial system will require governments to implement binding ESG regulations, financial institutions to internalise sustainability into their core strategies, and technology innovators to uphold ethical principles in product development.

Key Terms and Glossary

ESG A set of criteria used to evaluate a company's operations and its ethical and sustainable impact.

Green Bond A fixed-income instrument specifically earmarked to raise money for climate and environmental projects.

Impact Investing Investments made with the intention to generate positive, measurable social and environmental impact alongside a financial return.

Greenwashing The process of conveying a false impression or providing misleading information about how a company's products are more environmentally sound.

SLLs (Sustainability-Linked Loan) Loan instruments that incentivise the borrower's achievement of predetermined SPTs (Sustainability Performance Targets).

Test Your Understanding

Multiple-Choice Questions

1 Which of the following best describes sustainable finance?

A Investments focused solely on short-term financial returns.
B Integration of ESG factors into financial decision-making to promote long-term societal and environmental benefits.
C Investment in high-risk technology startups only.
D Excluding all traditional financial analysis from investment decisions.

2 Ethical investment differs from sustainable finance primarily because:

A It ignores ESG risks.
B It prioritises the investor's moral and ethical values, guiding "what to own" and "what to exclude".
C It relies only on government mandates.

D It focuses exclusively on financial returns.

3 Which FinTech innovation enables fractional ownership of green bonds and renewable energy infrastructure?

A Robo-advisors
B Blockchain technology
C AI-based portfolio optimisation
D Crowdfunding via social media

4 Which of the following is an example of regulatory-driven reporting in sustainable finance?

A ISSB voluntary guidelines
B EU CSRD
C ESG blogs and opinion polls
D Internal corporate ESG newsletters

5 Which of the following risks is associated with ethical investment using AI systems?

A Algorithmic bias and explainability gaps
B Inflation rate fluctuations
C Foreign exchange risk
D Short-term interest rate volatility

Short Questions

1 Explain the concept of *double materiality* in sustainable finance and provide an example.
2 Describe how AI and blockchain technologies enhance transparency and accessibility in ethical investing.
3 Identify two key operational or data challenges facing sustainable finance and provide examples.

Analytical Questions

1 Critically evaluate the potential conflict between profit maximisation and maintaining ethical integrity in AI-driven investment platforms. Use examples from ethical FinTech applications.
2 Discuss how regulatory fragmentation (e.g., differing EU, US, and regional ESG requirements) affects the implementation of global sustainable finance products such as green bonds.
3 Analyse the role of FinTech in democratising access to sustainable and ethical investments, and assess the potential risks related to fraud, data privacy, and the digital divide.

Case Study: The Rise and Scrutiny of ESG ETFs

Asset managers have expanded the market for ESG-focused ETFs, offering products that claim to integrate ESG considerations into portfolio construction. These ETFs are marketed to both retail and institutional investors who want exposure to capital markets while supporting sustainability objectives. Strong investor demand has led to rapid asset growth, positioning ESG ETFs as a major segment of modern portfolio strategies.

However, this growth has attracted increasing scrutiny. Critics argue that some ESG ETFs hold companies similar to those in conventional index funds, casting doubt on whether sustainability criteria meaningfully influence investment decisions. Others point to vague screening methodologies, inconsistent ESG ratings across providers, and limited disclosure about how ESG factors affect security selection and portfolio weighting. These issues have led to concerns about *greenwashing*, where funds overstate their sustainability credentials.

Regulators have begun responding. Frameworks such as the EU's Sustainable Finance Disclosure Regulation now require asset managers to explain how ESG risks are integrated into investment processes and to provide more standardised sustainability reporting. At the same time, advances in FinTech and AI are creating new tools to gather, analyse, and verify ESG data from diverse sources. As a result, ESG ETFs sit at the intersection of investor demand, regulatory oversight, and technological innovation, highlighting both the promise and the practical challenges of sustainable finance.

Reference

Amel-Zadeh, A., & Serafeim, G. (2018). Why and How Investors Use ESG Information: Evidence from a Global Survey. *Financial Analysts Journal*, 74(3), 87–103.

Case Study Questions

1 What specific actions can an asset manager take to prove that its ESG fund is genuinely sustainable and avoid accusations of greenwashing?
2 How can FinTech and AI be used to improve the quality and verification of ESG data for investors?
3 Should the primary goal of an ESG fund be to maximise risk-adjusted returns or to maximise positive social/environmental impact? Can it achieve both?

Further Reading

Amel-Zadeh, A., & Serafeim, G. (2018). Why and How Investors Use ESG Information. *Financial Analysts Journal*, 74(3), 87–103.
Fink, L. (2021). *Larry Fink's 2021 letter to CEOs*. New York: BlackRock. Available at: https://www.blackrock.com/corporate/investor-relations/larry-fink-ceo-letter (Accessed: 3 March 2026).
Khan, M., Serafeim, G., & Yoon, A. (2016). Corporate Sustainability: First Evidence on Materiality. *The Accounting Review*, 91(6), 1697–1724.

References

Amel-Zadeh, A., & Serafeim, G. (2018). Why and How Investors Use ESG Information: Evidence from a Global Survey. *Financial Analysts Journal*, 74(3), 87–103.
Arner, D.W., Barberis, J., & Buckley, R.P. (2020). FinTech and RegTech: Impact on Regulators and Banks. *Journal of Banking Regulation*, 21, 1–14.
Cowton, C.J. (1999). The Development of Ethical Investment Products. *Business Ethics: A European Review*, 8(1), 13–24.
de Freitas Netto, S.V., Sobral, M.F.F., Ribeiro, A.R., & Freire, F.M. (2020). Concepts and Practices of Greenwashing: A Systematic Review. *Environmental Sciences Europe*, 32, 19.

Dorfleitner, G., & Braun, S. (2019). *Sustainable Finance: Concepts, Tools, and Practices*. Cham: Springer.

European Commission (2021). *Corporate Sustainability Reporting Directive (CSRD)*. Brussels: European Commission.

International Capital Market Association (ICMA). (2021). *Green Bond Principles: Voluntary Process Guidelines for Issuing Green Bonds*. London: ICMA.

Khan, M., Serafeim, G., & Yoon, A. (2016). Corporate Sustainability: First Evidence on Materiality. *The Accounting Review*, 91(6), 1697–1724.

Loan Market Association (2023). *Sustainability-linked Loans: Guidance and Market Practice*. London: LMA.

Macpherson, A., & Zwick, A. (2022). The Role of FinTech in Sustainable and Ethical Investing. *Journal of Sustainable Finance & Investment*, 12(4), 345–367.

Renneboog, L., ter Horst, J., & Zhang, C. (2008). Socially Responsible Investments: Institutional Aspects, Performance, and Investor Behaviour. *Journal of Banking & Finance*, 32(9), 1723–1742.

Sandberg, J., Juravle, C., Hedesström, T., & Hamilton, I. (2022). Ethical and Sustainable Investing: Challenges and Opportunities. *Sustainable Finance Review*, 5(2), 101–120.

United Nations Environment Programme (UNEP). (2020). *Financing Sustainable Development: Global Trends in Green Finance*. Nairobi: UNEP.

World Economic Forum (2020). *Sustainable Finance in the Age of Climate Risk*. Geneva: World Economic Forum.

33 Quantum Finance

Chapter Overview

This chapter explores Quantum Finance as an emerging interdisciplinary field that combines quantum computing with financial technology to address complex financial problems beyond the practical limits of classical computation (Orús, Mugel, & Lizaso, 2019). By exploiting quantum mechanical principles such as superposition and entanglement, Quantum Finance enhances key financial activities, including risk assessment, portfolio optimisation, derivative pricing, and cybersecurity. Recent advances include the use of Quantum Machine Learning (QML) for improved predictive analytics, quantum cryptography for secure data transmission, and quantum algorithms for more efficient fraud detection. Despite its transformative potential, the field remains constrained by current hardware limitations, challenges in developing scalable and reliable algorithms, and unresolved ethical and regulatory issues. Nonetheless, increasing investment and collaboration among technology companies, financial institutions, and research organisations indicate a sustained global effort to overcome these barriers and integrate quantum solutions into mainstream financial systems.

Learning Objectives

By the end of this chapter, you should be able to:

1. Define quantum finance and explain its foundational concepts.
2. Identify applications of quantum computing in finance, including risk assessment, portfolio optimisation, and derivative pricing.
3. Explain how QML enhances financial modelling and decision-making.
4. Evaluate the role of quantum cryptography in strengthening cybersecurity within financial systems.
5. Examine how the integration of quantum technologies with financial technology (FinTech) is transforming areas such as trading, fraud detection, and data security.

DOI: 10.4324/9781003775751-38

33.1 Introduction

Quantum finance represents a significant advancement in the field, leveraging the computational capabilities of quantum computers (Baaquie, 2004). As financial technology continues to evolve rapidly, quantum finance introduces novel methods for processing information that surpass the limitations of classical computing. By utilising principles such as superposition and entanglement, quantum computers can solve complex mathematical problems more efficiently, which is expected to transform key areas including risk assessment, investment selection, and data security (Coyle, Delaney, Keane, & Orrell, 2020).

Quantum finance is anticipated to have substantial impacts, offering increased computational speed and enhanced analytical accuracy. Quantum algorithms can rapidly analyse large volumes of financial data, facilitating improved investment decisions and the identification of patterns that traditional methods may overlook. Additionally, quantum cryptography is expected to strengthen the protection of financial data against emerging cyber threats (Gyongyosi & Imre, 2019). The adoption of these quantum technologies can improve operational efficiency and security, but may also require financial institutions to adapt their existing processes.

Above all, the transition to quantum finance represents more than an upgrade in computational technology; it signifies a fundamental shift in the conceptualisation and management of financial systems. The integration of quantum physics principles with traditional banking practices is poised to significantly transform the financial sector (Orrell, 2018). Rather than merely enhancing existing processes, quantum finance establishes new boundaries for financial innovation, requiring professionals to prepare for these forthcoming changes.

33.2 Understanding Quantum Finance

33.2.1 Defining Quantum Finance

Quantum finance is an interdisciplinary field that applies mathematical formalisms and computational principles derived from quantum mechanics to the modelling of financial markets and economic decision-making processes. It moves beyond metaphorical interpretations by formally employing quantum probability theory, Hilbert space representations, and quantum stochastic processes to model contextuality, interference effects, and non-classical correlations observed in financial behaviour (Haven & Khrennikov, 2013). In contrast to classical probabilistic frameworks, which assume stable preferences and additive probabilities, quantum probability allows outcomes to depend on context and information ordering. For example, investor decision-making during periods of market stress can be represented as a superposition of competing expectations, providing a structured explanation for abrupt shifts in risk appetite, herding behaviour, and sudden changes in market sentiment that classical expected utility models do not adequately capture (Figure 33.1).

33.2.2 Nature of Quantum Finance

The nature of quantum finance is both theoretical and computational. From a theoretical perspective, it extends quantitative finance by incorporating quantum-inspired mathematical structures, such as operator theory and quantum stochastic calculus, to describe asset price dynamics and market interactions. From a computational perspective, it explores how quantum computing technologies can enhance financial analytics through significant speedups in simulation and optimisation. Quantum algorithms, including Quantum Monte

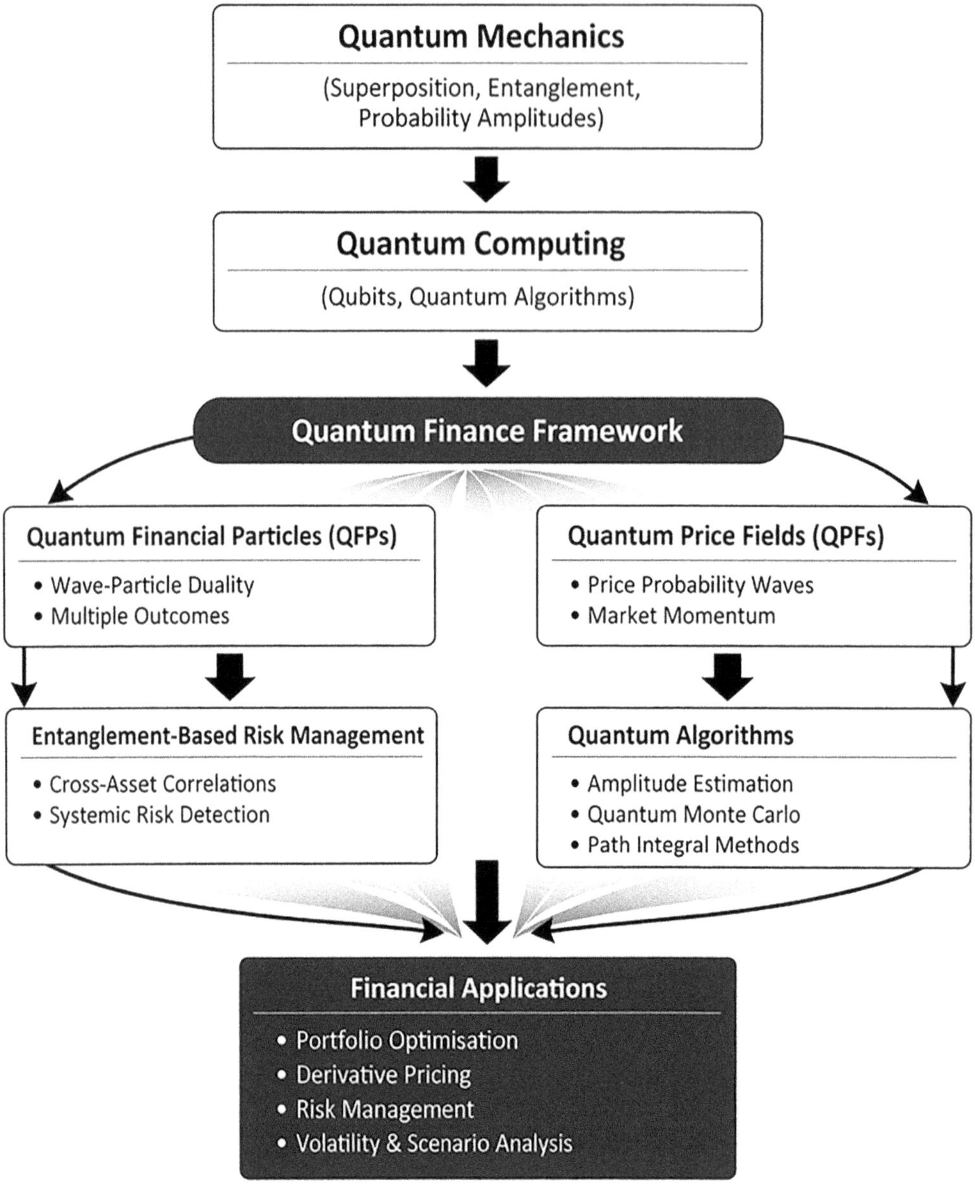

Figure 33.1 Quantum Finance Framework.

Carlo methods and Grover's search algorithm, have demonstrated the potential to accelerate computationally intensive tasks, such as portfolio optimisation and risk analysis, that are challenging for classical systems. In parallel, quantum-inspired models rooted in quantum field theory have been proposed for derivative pricing, particularly for complex options and interest rate products characterised by nonlinear and path-dependent payoffs (Baaquie, 2004). For instance, the valuation of a multi-asset exotic option with barriers and stochastic volatility may be approximated more efficiently using quantum-inspired pricing frameworks than with traditional tree-based or lattice models.

33.2.3 Mechanisms of Quantum Finance

Quantum finance integrates quantum computing with financial modelling by exploiting core quantum mechanical principles, such as superposition and entanglement, to analyse complex financial systems. Its central objective is to utilise the capacity of quantum information processing to manage high-dimensional and uncertain data more efficiently than classical methods, thereby improving risk management, portfolio optimisation, and derivative pricing (Orús et al., 2019). Within this framework, financial instruments can be represented as quantum states, enabling the simultaneous evaluation of multiple potential market outcomes. For example, through superposition, a quantum optimisation algorithm can encode a vast number of portfolio allocations within a single computational state, allowing an institutional investor to identify an optimal risk–return configuration across thousands of assets more rapidly than classical optimisation techniques (Rebentrost, Gupt, & Bromley, 2018). Asset prices may also be modelled as quantum probability fields, in which wave functions describe the distribution and momentum of price movements, providing a richer representation of volatility and collective market dynamics. Furthermore, entanglement enables the modelling of complex, nonlinear interdependencies between assets, improving the detection and management of systemic risk during periods of financial stress, such as when equity, currency, and commodity markets become tightly coupled. From a computational standpoint, quantum algorithms such as quantum amplitude estimation offer quadratic speedups over classical Monte Carlo simulations, significantly reducing the computational time required to price complex, path-dependent derivatives. In addition, path integral methods adapted from quantum physics allow for more accurate simulation of asset price trajectories over time, capturing volatility clustering and nonlinear behaviour observed in real financial markets (Baaquie, 2004; Woerner & Egger, 2019).

33.2.4 Functions and Purpose of Quantum Finance

The primary function and purpose of quantum finance is to address financial problems that are computationally infeasible or inefficient under classical approaches, particularly those characterised by high dimensionality, uncertainty, and real-time data processing. In pricing and optimisation, quantum algorithms may evaluate vast combinations of asset allocations simultaneously, enabling faster identification of optimal portfolios. For example, a global asset manager allocating capital across thousands of securities under regulatory and risk constraints could employ a quantum optimisation routine to explore feasible portfolio configurations, rather than classical solvers efficiently. In modelling market uncertainty, quantum concepts such as superposition allow multiple potential market states to be represented within a single framework; for instance, an interest rate risk model could encode several yield-curve scenarios concurrently, facilitating more integrated stress testing. In addition, QML seeks to improve forecasting by identifying subtle nonlinear patterns in large, heterogeneous datasets. A practical illustration is the integration of satellite imagery with financial and macroeconomic data to anticipate supply-chain disruptions before they are reflected in asset prices, thereby supporting more informed investment decisions.

33.2.5 Significance of Quantum Finance

The economic and strategic significance of quantum finance lies in its potential to overcome the structural limitations of many classical financial models, which often rely on simplifying assumptions such as normally distributed returns, constant volatility, and linear correlations. These assumptions frequently fail to capture the nonlinear, path-dependent, and regime-switching behaviour observed in real markets (Rebentrost et al., 2018). Quantum-based probabilistic and computational frameworks offer greater flexibility in modelling complex dependencies and dynamic uncertainty. Moreover, as contemporary financial systems generate massive volumes of high-frequency, heterogeneous data, quantum algorithms are designed to process high-dimensional data spaces more efficiently, potentially improving large-scale risk analysis, scenario simulation, and the extraction of trading signals (Woerner & Egger, 2019). From an industry perspective, major financial institutions such as Goldman Sachs and JPMorgan Chase have established research collaborations with technology firms, including IBM and D-Wave, to explore quantum applications in optimisation, simulation, and cryptography. These initiatives reflect the expectation that quantum capabilities may deliver long-term competitive advantages in pricing accuracy, risk management, and financial innovation (Brennan & Maroney, 2022).

33.3 Quantum Finance in Financial Technology

33.3.1 Portfolio Optimisation

Portfolio optimisation becomes computationally demanding when large asset universes, transaction costs, and regulatory constraints are included. Quantum optimisation algorithms are designed to explore many feasible portfolio configurations simultaneously, potentially improving solution speed and quality (Bouland, Fefferman, Nirkhe, & Vazirani, 2020). For example, a pension fund allocating capital across global equities, bonds, and alternative assets could use a quantum-enhanced optimiser to rebalance its portfolio under climate risk limits and liquidity constraints, identifying efficient allocations more rapidly than with classical solvers.

33.3.2 Derivative Pricing

Valuing complex derivatives, particularly path-dependent or exotic options, requires intensive simulation. Quantum techniques such as Quantum Amplitude Estimation can accelerate Monte Carlo methods used in pricing and risk measurement (Rebentrost et al., 2018). For instance, an investment bank pricing a basket option linked to multiple equity indices could run a large number of correlated market scenarios more efficiently, enabling faster recalibration of hedging strategies during volatile periods.

33.3.3 Fraud Detection and Anomaly Detection

QML models offer new approaches to analysing high-volume transaction data to detect irregular patterns. A retail bank, for example, could apply quantum-enhanced anomaly detection to millions of daily card transactions, identifying subtle behavioural deviations that signal emerging fraud schemes in near real time.

33.3.4 Credit Scoring and Risk Assessment

QML may also improve credit risk modelling by capturing complex, nonlinear relationships in borrower data (Moll et al., 2022). For example, a digital lender could combine income history, spending behaviour, and alternative data sources to generate more granular credit scores, allowing more accurate risk-based pricing while potentially expanding access to credit.

33.4 Opportunity, Challenges, and Key Practical Issues

33.4.1 Quantum Synergy

Quantum computing is increasingly recognised as a transformative technology within the FinTech sector, offering new opportunities to enhance data analytics, artificial intelligence, and cybersecurity, while enabling more sophisticated financial modelling. One of the most significant opportunities lies in QML, which allows financial institutions to detect complex patterns and anomalies in high-dimensional time-series data more efficiently than classical methods (Biamonte et al., 2017). For example, a trading firm could apply QML to analyse intraday price fluctuations across multiple asset classes, enabling rapid adjustments to algorithmic strategies and improving early detection of fraudulent or anomalous transactions. Similarly, quantum-enhanced models can improve real-time risk assessment: quantum algorithms can simulate thousands of market scenarios simultaneously, facilitating accurate estimation of Value-at-Risk under diverse economic conditions (Eggers, Gravett, Kaye, & Orrell, 2021). In cryptography and cybersecurity, quantum computing also creates both opportunities and challenges. Current public-key cryptosystems, such as Rivest–Shamir–Adleman (RSA) and Elliptic Curve Cryptography, are vulnerable to Shor's algorithm, motivating the adoption of post-quantum cryptography (PQC) to safeguard sensitive financial data. For instance, banks implementing PQC protocols can ensure secure client communications and transactions, preserving confidentiality in a quantum-enabled threat landscape (Gyongyosi & Imre, 2019). Additionally, quantum algorithms offer potential improvements in high-speed trading optimisation, as superposition allows simultaneous evaluation of numerous trade scenarios, reducing latency and enhancing the capture of short-lived arbitrage opportunities (Rosenberg, 2020). Collectively, these innovations demonstrate the convergence of quantum computing with traditional financial processes, extending the capabilities of established analytics, trading, and risk management frameworks.

33.4.2 Risk and Challenges of Quantum Finance

Despite these opportunities, quantum finance also entails substantial risks and challenges. A central concern is the current hardware limitation: most quantum processors are Noisy Intermediate-Scale Quantum (NISQ) devices, characterised by limited qubit counts, high error rates, and susceptibility to decoherence, which restricts reliable execution of large-scale financial algorithms (Preskill, 2018). Algorithmically, many quantum models remain at an experimental stage and require extensive validation before deployment in production environments, presenting both technical and operational uncertainty (Bouland et al., 2020). Regulatory uncertainty further complicates adoption, as existing frameworks do not adequately address quantum-specific issues in cybersecurity, risk reporting, and market oversight. Initiatives such as the NIST PQC Standardisation project highlight the emerging need for governance structures capable of mitigating these risks (Brennan & Maroney, 2022). Ethical and societal considerations also arise, particularly regarding equitable access to advanced computational resources. Without careful oversight, quantum technologies could be concentrated among well-capitalised institutions, exacerbating inequalities and creating a quantum divide within financial markets (Brennan & Maroney, 2022).

33.4.3 Key Practical Issues of Quantum Finance

The key practical issues in adopting quantum finance reflect the intersection of hardware, algorithmic, and talent constraints. First, hardware fidelity and scalability remain critical bottlenecks: NISQ devices cannot yet support fault-tolerant execution of complex portfolio optimisation or derivative pricing algorithms, limiting their use for mission-critical applications (Preskill, 2018). Second, algorithmic maturity and hybrid integration represent ongoing challenges. Hybrid quantum-classical approaches, in which quantum processors handle computationally intensive sub-tasks while classical systems manage overall workflows, are currently the most feasible approach, but require significant development and optimisation for domain-specific financial tasks (Cerezo et al., 2021). Finally, the talent and knowledge gap poses a barrier to implementation, as the financial sector lacks sufficient professionals with expertise spanning quantum mechanics, computational methods, and financial modelling. Addressing this skills shortage is essential for the design, validation, and deployment of effective quantum solutions in practice (Brennan & Maroney, 2022). Together, these practical considerations define the current frontier of quantum finance adoption, highlighting both the transformative potential and the significant operational hurdles that must be overcome.

33.5 Conclusion

Quantum FinTech represents a transformative intersection of quantum computing and financial technology, with the potential to fundamentally reshape traditional financial models. By harnessing the computational advantages of quantum algorithms, financial institutions can perform complex risk assessments, optimise portfolios, and price derivatives with a speed and precision unattainable through classical systems. This technological shift, however, requires close collaboration among quantum scientists, finance professionals, and regulators to ensure that innovation is both effective and responsible.

The evolution of quantum finance depends on balancing advanced research with ethical and regulatory considerations. While the potential applications, including accelerated portfolio optimisation, enhanced fraud detection, and real-time risk modelling, are substantial, challenges such as cybersecurity vulnerabilities, regulatory uncertainty, and equitable access must be addressed. Successful adoption will demand sustained investment, interdisciplinary expertise, and governance frameworks that align quantum innovation with financial stability and integrity, ensuring that the benefits of this emerging technology are realised responsibly across the financial sector.

Key Terms and Glossary

Quantum Computing A type of computation that harnesses the collective properties of quantum states, such as superposition and entanglement, to perform calculations.

Qubit The basic unit of quantum information, which can exist in a superposition of 0 and 1 states, unlike a classical bit.

Quantum Supremacy The point at which a quantum computer can solve a problem that is practically impossible for a classical computer.

NISQ (Noisy Intermediate-Scale Quantum) The current era of quantum computing is characterised by quantum processors with 50-100 qubits that are prone to errors.

PQC (Post-Quantum Cryptography) Classical cryptographic algorithms that are thought to be secure against an attack by a quantum computer.

Test Your Understanding

Multiple-Choice Questions

1 Which principle of quantum mechanics allows quantum finance to evaluate multiple portfolio configurations simultaneously?

A Decoherence
B Superposition
C Entropy
D Classical probability

2 What is a key advantage of QML in financial applications?

A Eliminates all market risk
B Improves pattern recognition in high-dimensional datasets
C Guarantees higher returns in trading
D Replaces the need for portfolio managers

3 Why are traditional cryptosystems such as RSA vulnerable in a quantum-enabled financial ecosystem?

A They cannot encrypt large datasets
B Quantum algorithms like Shor's algorithm can break them
C They are incompatible with high-frequency trading
D They rely on Monte Carlo simulations

4 Which of the following represents a practical challenge in adopting quantum finance?

A Faster Monte Carlo simulations
B NISQ hardware limitations
C Improved credit scoring
D Multi-asset portfolio optimisation

5 Quantum finance improves risk modelling by using entanglement to:

A Reduce trading latency
B Capture complex, nonlinear correlations between assets
C Replace human decision-making entirely
D Simplify regulatory reporting

Short Questions

1 Define quantum finance and explain its difference from classical financial modelling.
2 Describe how quantum algorithms, such as Quantum Amplitude Estimation, enhance derivative pricing.
3 Explain the role of PQC in securing financial systems against quantum threats.

Analytical Questions

1 Evaluate the potential impact of QML on high-frequency trading strategies. Use examples to illustrate advantages and limitations.

2 Discuss the regulatory and ethical challenges posed by the adoption of quantum finance. How might these influence the equitable distribution of technological benefits?
3 Consider a pension fund managing a large multi-asset portfolio. Analyse how quantum optimisation could change the fund's risk–return profile compared to classical optimisation approaches.

Case Study: Goldman Sachs' Quantum Research for Derivative Pricing

Goldman Sachs has been at the forefront of exploring the applications of quantum computing in finance, with a particular focus on derivative pricing. Pricing complex derivatives often requires extensive Monte Carlo simulations to model a wide range of potential market scenarios. These simulations are computationally demanding on classical systems, especially when high accuracy or real-time updates are required. Goldman Sachs' research teams are developing quantum algorithms to accelerate Monte Carlo methods, leveraging principles of superposition and entanglement to evaluate many market outcomes simultaneously.

To advance this work, Goldman Sachs has partnered with quantum technology firms such as QC Ware and IBM. These collaborations aim to test and refine quantum algorithms on emerging hardware, with the long-term goal of achieving a practical 'quantum advantage'—performing derivative pricing calculations significantly faster than classical methods. Beyond computational speed, quantum models may also improve financial risk assessment by capturing complex correlations, nonlinear dependencies, and rare-event scenarios that traditional models struggle with.

However, moving these innovations from research to production involves substantial challenges. Current quantum processors, known as NISQ devices, are limited in qubit count and prone to errors, making reliable, large-scale implementation difficult. Goldman Sachs must therefore develop hybrid quantum-classical workflows, rigorously validate results, and ensure that these emerging technologies integrate securely and effectively into existing financial systems (Brennan & Maroney, 2022).

Reference

Brennan, C., & Maroney, O. (2022). *The Quantum Future of Financial Services*. Available at: https://www.ibm.com/thought-leadership/institute-business-value/report/quantum-financial-services (Accessed: 3 March 2026).

Case Study Questions

1 Why is derivative pricing, and Monte Carlo simulation in particular, a 'killer app' for early quantum computing in finance?
2 Beyond speed, what qualitative improvements might quantum models bring to financial risk assessment?
3 Given the current NISQ era of hardware, what are the practical challenges Goldman Sachs faces in moving its research from theory to production?

Further Reading

Coyle, B., Henderson, M., Leipold, J.C., Kashefi, E., & Kumar, N. (2020). Quantum Machine Learning for Finance. *IEEE Computer*. 53(10), 70–79

Orús, R., Mugel, S., & Lizaso, E. (2019) Quantum Computing for Finance: Overview and Prospects. *Reviews in Physics*, 4, 100028.

Preskill, J. (2018) Quantum Computing in the NISQ Era and Beyond. *Quantum*, 2, 79.

References

Baaquie, B.E. (2004). *Quantum Finance: Path Integrals and Hamiltonians for Options and Interest Rates*. Cambridge: Cambridge University Press.

Biamonte, J., Wittek, P., Pancotti, N., Rebentrost, P., Wiebe, N., & Lloyd, S. (2017). Quantum Machine Learning. *Nature*, 549(7671), 195–202.

Bouland, A., Fefferman, B., Nirkhe, C., & Vazirani, U. (2020). On the Complexity and Verification of Quantum Random Circuit Sampling. *Nature Physics*, 15(2), 159–163.

Brennan, T., & Maroney, O. (2022). Quantum Computing and Finance: Opportunities, risks, and regulation. *Journal of Financial Technology*, 6(1), 45–63.

Cerezo, M., Arrasmith, A., Babbush, R., Benjamin, S., Endo, S., Fujii, K., McClean, J., Mitarai, K., Yuan, X., Cincio, L., & Coles, P. (2021). Variational Quantum Algorithms. *Nature Reviews Physics*, 3(9), 625–644.

Coyle, B., Delaney, J., Keane, M., & Orrell, D. (2020). Applications of Quantum Computing in Financial Systems. *Journal of Computational Finance*, 23(2), 1–28.

Eggers, J., Gravett, T., Kaye, P., & Orrell, D. (2021). Quantum Computing for Financial Risk Management. *Quantum Finance Review*, 2(1), 30–49.

Gyongyosi, L., & Imre, S. (2019). Quantum Computing Approaches in the Finance Sector. *IEEE Access*, 7, 1815–1834.

Haven, E., & Khrennikov, A. (2013). *Quantum Social Science*. Cambridge: Cambridge University Press.

Moll, J., Barkoutsos, P., Bishop, L., Chow, J.M., Cross, A., Egger, D.J., Filipp, S., Fuhrer, A., Gambetta, J., Ganzhorn, M., & Ganzhorn, M. (2022). Quantum-Enhanced Machine Learning for Credit Risk Analysis. *npj Quantum Information*, 8(1), 1–12.

Orrell, D. (2018). *Quantum Economics*. London: Icon Books.

Orús, R., Mugel, S., & Lizaso, E. (2019). Quantum Computing for Finance: Overview and Prospects. *Reviews in Physics*, 4, 100028.

Preskill, J. (2018). Quantum Computing in the NISQ Era and Beyond. *Quantum*, 2, 79.

Rebentrost, P., Gupt, B., & Bromley, T.R. (2018). Quantum Computational Finance: Monte Carlo Pricing of Financial Derivatives. *Physical Review A*, 98(2), 022321.

Rosenberg, G. (2020). High-Frequency trading and Quantum Computing: A Review. *Journal of Computational Finance*, 24(3), 1–25.

Woerner, S., & Egger, D.J. (2019). Quantum Risk Analysis. *npj Quantum Information*, 5(1), 1–8.

34 Metaverse and Web3 Finance

Chapter Overview

This chapter explores the convergence of Metaverse and Web3 technologies, signalling a transformative shift in financial services. Core elements such as blockchain, smart contracts, Non-Fungible Tokens (NFTs), and Decentralised Autonomous Organisations (DAOs) are examined for their roles in enabling decentralised, user-focused virtual economies (Wong et al., 2023). The discussion extends to emerging financial constructs, including virtual real estate, play-to-earn (P2E) models, and Metaverse-native banking systems. The chapter offers a critical evaluation of opportunities for financial innovation and inclusion, as well as challenges posed by regulatory uncertainty, emerging technologies, and cybersecurity threats (Deloitte, 2022). It concludes with a forward-looking analysis of the key implications for financial institutions, consumers, and regulators.

Learning Objectives

By the end of this chapter, you should be able to:

1. Define the Metaverse and Web3 and explain their symbiotic relationship in shaping the future of finance.
2. Identify and describe the key technological components that underpin the Web3-enabled Metaverse.
3. Analyse the new financial models and asset classes emerging within the Metaverse, such as virtual real estate and P2E economies.
4. Evaluate the opportunities for financial institutions and the challenges related to regulation, security, and accessibility.
5. Critically assess the long-term implications of a mature Metaverse economy on global financial systems.

DOI: 10.4324/9781003775751-39

34.1 Introduction

The digital landscape is undergoing a fundamental transformation, shifting from the two-dimensional, platform-focused Web2 model to the immersive, user-focused ecosystem of the Metaverse. This notable transition is based on the decentralised principles of Web3 (Ball, 2022). Instead of merely being a technological advancement, it represents a significant socio-economic revolution. The combination of these elements creates persistent, shared virtual environments where users interact, transact, and generate verifiable digital value. This development lays the groundwork for new forms of digital existence and commerce.

Web3 Finance is crucial for the sustainability of the emerging digital economy. This infrastructure is built on distributed ledger technology, which enables verifiable digital ownership and permissionless, peer-to-peer value exchange. By using smart contracts, as outlined by Voshmgir (2020), programmable money can be enabled and complex financial transactions automated without relying on traditional centralised intermediaries. This strong foundation addresses the specific financial needs of virtual worlds and ensures both transparency and security in transactions.

This emerging financial framework already drives significant economic activity by fostering dynamic in-world economies that create real-world income and tangible value (Nadini et al., 2021). Activities include high-value virtual real estate transactions, asset securitisation, and digital asset trading within complex, decentralised marketplaces. Given its scale and the early stage of development, this chapter systematically examines the evolving financial architecture, scrutinises initial operational systems, and critically evaluates both the major opportunities and the regulatory and technological challenges involved in integrating it into the global financial system.

34.2. Understanding the Foundations: Metaverse and Web3

34.2.1. The Metaverse

The Metaverse refers to a persistent, shared digital universe that integrates aspects of physical reality with immersive virtual environments. It enables multiple users to interact simultaneously with virtual worlds, digital objects, and other participants through technologies such as Virtual Reality (VR), Augmented Reality (AR), and the internet (Mystakidis, 2022). Key characteristics of the Metaverse include interoperability, which allows assets, identities, and data to move seamlessly across platforms, and persistence, meaning the virtual environment continues to evolve and persist even when individual users are offline. This continuous, multisensory environment supports social interaction, digital commerce, gaming, education, and professional collaboration, representing a convergence of digital and physical experiences.

34.2.2. Web3: The Decentralised Backbone

Web3, often described as the third generation of the internet, represents a paradigm shift from centralised control towards individual user empowerment, underpinned by blockchain technology. This decentralised ledger system enables secure recording and verification of transactions, ensuring that users maintain ownership of their data, digital assets, and online identities (Zheng, et.al.,, 2018). The foundational principles of Web3 include decentralisation, trustlessness, and user ownership. Decentralisation distributes data and governance across multiple nodes rather than relying on a single controlling entity. At the same time,

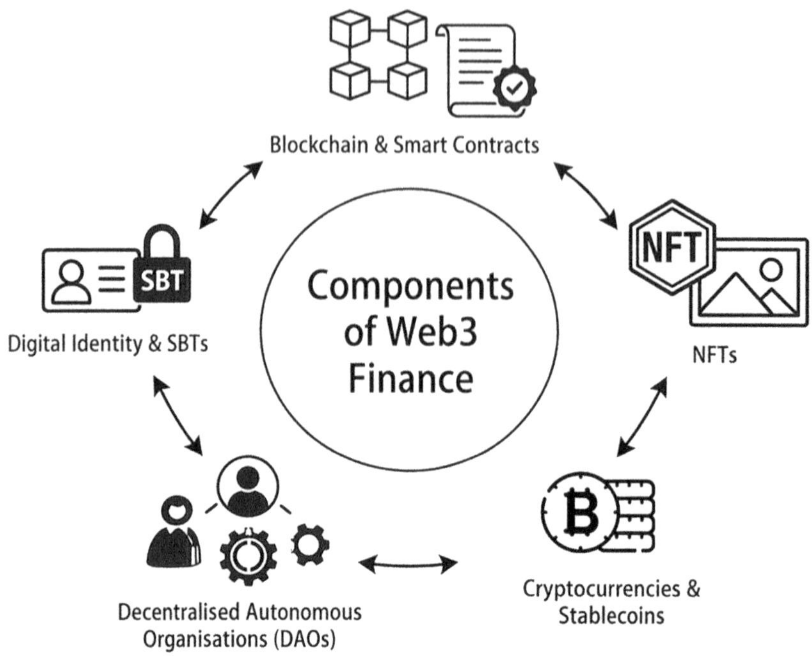

Figure 34.1 Components of Web3 Finance in the Metaverse.

trustlessness allows participants to engage in transactions and interactions without intermediaries, relying on cryptographic protocols and smart contracts for verification and execution (Wood, 2014). User ownership ensures individuals retain control over their personal information and virtual assets, fostering greater participation in digital economies. The integration of Web3 with the Metaverse amplifies these capabilities, as immersive virtual environments provide spaces for social, professional, and recreational interaction. At the same time, the decentralised infrastructure of Web3 supports secure economic activity, governance, and digital asset management within these platforms, creating novel opportunities for engagement, collaboration, and value creation (Dionisio, Burns, & Gilbert, 2013) (Figure 34.1).

34.2.3. Technological Framework of Web3 Finance in the Metaverse

34.2.3.1 Blockchain and Smart Contracts

Blockchain functions as a decentralised, immutable ledger that records all transactions transparently and securely. Smart contracts are self-executing programmes stored on the blockchain, which automatically enforce the terms of agreements, ranging from simple transactions to complex financial arrangements (Szabo, 1997).

34.2.3.2 Non-Fungible Tokens (NFTs)

NFTs are unique digital assets recorded on a blockchain that represent verifiable ownership of items such as virtual land, digital apparel, characters, or artwork. By establishing provable digital property rights, NFTs enable secure exchange and monetisation of assets within Metaverse environments (Wang, Li, Jiang, Wang, & Li, 2021).

34.2.3.3 Cryptocurrencies and Stablecoins

Digital currencies serve as mediums of exchange within online economies. While cryptocurrencies exhibit volatile market values, stablecoins are designed to maintain a stable price by being pegged to fiat currencies, facilitating predictable economic transactions in decentralised environments (G7 Working Group, 2022).

34.2.3.4 Decentralised Autonomous Organisations

DAOs are member-governed digital collectives in which decisions are made collaboratively rather than by a single controlling entity. They provide frameworks for managing shared resources, virtual environments, and community-led initiatives in transparent, democratic ways (Hassan & De Filippi, 2021).

34.2.3.5 Digital Identity and Soulbound Tokens (SBTs)

Digital identity systems enable the management of personal information and credentials within virtual environments. SBTs are non-transferable digital tokens that represent achievements, memberships, or affiliations, providing verifiable proof of an individual's participation or status in online ecosystems (Buterin et al., 2022).

34.3 Innovation in Finance: Metaverse and Web3

34.3.1 Key Innovations in Metaverse Finance

Financial institutions are increasingly leveraging the Metaverse to deliver immersive, interactive services. Virtual banking branches enable customers' avatars to interact with digital agents, offering a novel way to access financial services. Examples include JPMorgan's Onyx Lounge in Decentraland, HSBC's virtual land presence in The Sandbox, and BPI's 3D branch, which facilitates mortgage and loan simulations. In addition, banks are developing virtual asset management and lending services, offering meta-mortgages for virtual land and custody solutions for NFTs and other digital collectables. AI-powered avatars function as 24/7 financial advisors, analysing user behaviour to deliver personalised recommendations on investments and products. Gamified financial literacy initiatives, such as interactive VR games, are being used to educate younger audiences, including Gen Z, on budgeting and financial planning. Moreover, workforce training and collaboration are migrating to immersive environments, with institutions such as Bank of America employing VR simulations to train employees on client engagement and empathy in customer interactions.

34.3.2 Key Innovations in Web3 Finance and Banking

Web3 finance is enabling decentralised, programmable financial systems that operate independently of traditional intermediaries. Institutions are adopting Decentralised Finance (DeFi) protocols to offer lending, borrowing, and trading services without conventional banks, including mechanisms such as 'self-repaying loans' that leverage high-yield DeFi platforms. Tokenisation of real-world assets is creating liquid markets for previously illiquid assets such as real estate, artwork, and securities, enabling fractional ownership. For example, a commercial building can be represented as blockchain tokens and sold to multiple investors. Blockchain-powered systems, such as Stellar and Ripple, are enabling instant, low-cost cross-border payments and replacing legacy settlement systems. Web3 also promotes self-sovereign digital identities, allowing users to control personal data and perform Know Your Customer/Anti-Money Laundering (AML) verification directly via cryptographic wallets. Finally, stablecoins like USD Tether and USD Coin are increasingly used for everyday transactions, while central banks are exploring Central Bank Digital Currencies (CBDCs) to provide secure, rapid, and regulated digital payment solutions.

34.4 Opportunity, Challenges, and Key Practical Issues Web3 in Finance

34.4.1 Opportunities

The convergence of Web3 technologies and the Metaverse has created a transformative financial ecosystem, generating new opportunities for innovation, economic inclusion, and immersive digital commerce. Virtual real estate, traded as NFTs on platforms such as Decentraland and The Sandbox, derives value from factors analogous to the physical world, including location, user traffic, and development potential (Ficca, 2022). P2E gaming platforms, exemplified by Axie Infinity, enable users to generate tradable NFTs and cryptocurrencies through gameplay, offering alternative income streams, particularly in emerging markets (Zheng et al., 2018). The integration of metaverse-native DeFi protocols further enhances these ecosystems by providing financial services such as lending against virtual land and insurance for digital assets. At the same time, tokenised commerce and advertising allow brands to monetise virtual spaces and sell NFT-based products. Blockchain's decentralised, programmable, and composable characteristics facilitate the creation of highly customisable financial instruments within these immersive environments, supporting novel business models that were previously unfeasible. For example, a virtual real estate developer could offer NFT-backed leases incorporating revenue-sharing from virtual events or advertising, illustrating how Web3 finance converges with metaverse platforms to enable new markets, revenue streams, and enhanced user empowerment through data sovereignty and asset ownership.

34.4.2 Risk and Challenges

Despite these opportunities, Web3 and Metaverse financial ecosystems face several challenges. Regulatory uncertainty remains a key concern, with the legal status of virtual assets, taxation frameworks, consumer protection, and cross-jurisdictional compliance often ambiguous or inconsistent (FSB, 2022). Technical limitations, including network congestion, high transaction fees, and low throughput on current blockchain networks, impede scalability and widespread adoption. Security risks are pronounced, encompassing smart contract vulnerabilities, phishing attacks, and NFT theft, all of which threaten users' digital assets. Access barriers, such as the requirement for advanced hardware and reliable internet connectivity, may exacerbate digital inequalities. Additionally, the high volatility of virtual assets and cryptocurrencies introduces significant financial risk, requiring participants and institutions to develop effective risk management strategies tailored to these emerging digital markets.

34.4.3 Key Practical Issues of Web3 and Metaverse

The integration of Web3 and Metaverse technologies is set to transform finance by blurring the boundaries between the physical and digital economies, giving rise to phygital assets with both tangible and digital twin representations recorded on blockchain networks (Ficca, 2022).

Traditional financial institutions, including banks and payment providers, must adapt to operate across these hybrid economies, facilitating transactions and bridging value between physical and virtual domains. This evolution also necessitates the development of new regulatory frameworks to address the unique challenges of borderless digital markets, including taxation, consumer protection, AML, and systemic risk management. For example, financial regulators may need to establish protocols for auditing NFT-backed financial instruments to ensure transparency, mitigate fraud, and foster innovation in digital asset markets.

34.5 Conclusion

The integration of the Metaverse and Web3 finance represents a paradigm shift in digital interaction, social engagement, and economic activity, enabling open and interoperable ecosystems in which user-governed economies can emerge. This development redefines value creation by aligning incentives with user ownership and participation, signalling a departure from centralised models towards more equitable digital structures. However, the realisation of this potential is constrained by significant challenges, including technological scalability, regulatory uncertainty, and cybersecurity vulnerabilities, all of which require coordinated innovation and comprehensive policy frameworks to ensure sustainable growth.

Establishing a responsible and inclusive Metaverse economy demands proactive collaboration among technologists, policymakers, and financial institutions. Developers must design immersive, secure, and resilient infrastructures, while regulators must implement adaptable guidelines that protect stakeholders without hindering innovation. As highlighted by the World Economic Forum (WEF, 2022), the future of digital economies hinges on balancing innovation with trust and accountability. Strategic and ethical decision-making today will determine whether these virtual environments expand global economic participation or exacerbate existing inequalities. Only through deliberate governance and stewardship can the Metaverse and Web3 achieve their promise as equitable and enduring components of the digital economy.

Key Terms and Glossary

Metaverse A collective virtual shared space, created by the convergence of virtually enhanced physical reality and physically persistent virtual space, including the sum of all virtual worlds, AR, and the internet.

Web3 A proposed next generation of the internet that is decentralised, based on blockchain technology, and emphasises user ownership and control of data and digital assets.

NFT (Non-Fungible Token) A unique cryptographic token on a blockchain that represents ownership of a specific digital or physical asset and is not interchangeable with other tokens.

DAO (Decentralised Autonomous Organisation) An organisation represented by rules encoded as a transparent computer program, controlled by the organisation's members, and not influenced by a central government.

P2E (Play-to-Earn) A video game business model that allows players to earn real-world financial value, typically in the form of cryptocurrency or NFTs, through their in-game activities and achievements.

Virtual Real Estate Plots of land or property that exist in a virtual world, often purchased as NFTs, which can be developed, leased, or sold.

Interoperability The ability of different Metaverse platforms and systems to connect and interact seamlessly, allowing users to transfer assets and identity across them.

Test Your Understanding

Multiple-Choice Questions

1 Which of the following best describes the principle of Web3?

A Centralised control of data and assets
B Individual user empowerment via decentralisation
C Proprietary virtual marketplaces controlled by corporations
D Exclusive reliance on fiat currencies

2 What is the primary function of NFTs in the Metaverse?

A To stabilise cryptocurrency prices
B To provide verifiable ownership of unique digital assets
C To facilitate anonymous peer-to-peer messaging
D To replace blockchain as a ledger

3 Which innovation allows financial institutions to interact with customers in immersive virtual environments?

A CBDCs
B Virtual banking branches and AI-powered avatars
C DeFi self-repaying loans
D Tokenised securities trading

4 What is a key challenge in Web3 and Metaverse finance adoption?

A Excessive liquidity in virtual real estate
B Regulatory uncertainty and cybersecurity risks
C Over-reliance on paper-based transactions
D Lack of NFTs for identity verification

5 How does the convergence of Web3 and the Metaverse facilitate financial innovation?

A By restricting asset ownership to central authorities
B By enabling programmable, decentralised, and composable financial instruments
C By replacing blockchain with traditional databases
D By eliminating the need for digital identity verification

Short Questions

1 Explain the role of smart contracts in Web3 finance.
2 Identify two examples of Metaverse-based financial services and briefly describe their function.
3 What are "phygital" assets, and why are they significant in Web3 finance?

Analytical Questions

1 Critically analyse how virtual real estate in platforms like Decentraland and The Sandbox can create new revenue streams for financial institutions. Include potential risks and rewards.
2 Evaluate the challenges of integrating traditional banking operations into immersive Metaverse environments. How might institutions address technological, regulatory, and security concerns?

3 Discuss the implications of decentralised digital identity systems and SBTs for financial inclusion, privacy, and regulatory compliance in virtual economies.

Case Study: The Rise and Re-Calibration of Axie Infinity

Axie Infinity, developed by Sky Mavis, became an early emblem of blockchain-based P2E gaming, enabling players to collect, breed, and battle NFT creatures called Axies and earn tradable in-game tokens. Participants acquired Axies to begin play, earned Smooth Love Potion (SLP) through victories, and could convert these rewards into cryptocurrency, while Axie Infinity Shards served as a governance token. At its 2021 peak, the game attracted millions of daily users, particularly in Southeast Asia, where token earnings served as significant income for many players, illustrating the potential of Web3 finance to generate real-world economic value within virtual environments.

Nevertheless, the underlying economic model proved unsustainable because its tokenomics relied on continuous new-user growth to sustain demand for Axies and SLP, leading to inflation and declining utility as player inflows slowed. In March 2022, this fragility was exacerbated by a major security breach: attackers exploited vulnerabilities in the Ronin Network sidechain infrastructure, gaining control of sufficient validator keys to drain approximately 173,600 Ether and 25.5 million USDC, over $600 million, from the Ronin bridge. The exploit highlighted significant systemic risks in nascent Web3 infrastructure, paused bridge operations, and undermined confidence in decentralised gaming ecosystems.

In response, Sky Mavis paused critical functions, reimbursed affected users, and strengthened security protocols. The project also shifted away from a purely extractive P2E model towards a more sustainable Play-and-Earn framework designed to support long-term engagement and economic balance. This evolution underscores the importance of resilient economic design, robust security, and adaptive tokenomics for sustainable Metaverse economies.

References

FINMA. (2022). *Annual Report 2022: Focus on Digital Assets*. Bern:Swiss Financial Market Supervisory Authority.

Kampakis, S. (2022). The Sustainability of Play-to-Earn Economies: A Tokenomics Perspective. *Journal of Web3 Studies*, 1(2), 45–67.

Case Study Questions

1 Identify the primary factors that contributed to the early success of Axie Infinity's P2E model and explain why the economic design ultimately proved unsustainable.
2 Evaluate how the 2022 Ronin Bridge hack revealed systemic vulnerabilities, not only within Axie Infinity but across the broader Metaverse and Web3 finance ecosystem.
3 Based on Axie Infinity's experience, propose strategies that other Metaverse projects could adopt to design more resilient and sustainable virtual economies

Further Reading

Ball, M. (2022). *The Metaverse: And How It Will Revolutionise Everything*. New York: Liveright Publishing.

Buterin, V., Weyl, E.G. and Oh, J. (2022) *Decentralized society: finding Web3's soul*. Microsoft Research. Available at: https://papers.ssrn.com/sol3/papers.cfm?abstract_id=4105763 (Accessed: 27 May 2026).

Voshmgir, S. (2020). *Token Economy: How the Web3 Reinvents the Internet* (2nd ed.). Berlin: Token Kitchen.

References

Ball, M. (2022). *The Metaverse and Web3: Decentralisation of the Digital Economy*. London: Routledge.

Deloitte (2022). *Emerging Financial Ecosystems in the Metaverse and Web3*. Deloitte Insights. Available at: https://www.deloitte.com/uk/en/Industries/consumer/blogs/2022/web3-and-metaverse.html

Dionisio, J.D.N., Burns, W.G., & Gilbert, R. (2013). '3D Virtual Worlds and the Metaverse: Status and Future Possibilities. *ACM Computing Surveys*, 45(3), 1–38.

Ficca, M. (2022). 'Virtual Real Estate in the Metaverse: Economic Models and Investment Opportunities. *Journal of Digital Finance*, 4(2), 45–60.

Financial Stability Board (2022) *Assessment of risks to financial stability from crypto-assets*. Basel: Financial Stability Board. Available at: https://www.fsb.org/2022/02/assessment-of-risks-to-financial-stability-from-crypto-assets/

G7 Working Group on Stablecoins (2022) *G7 public policy principles for retail central bank digital currencies (CBDCs)*. London: HM Treasury. Available at https://www.gov.uk/government/publications/g7-public-policy-principles-for-retail-central-bank-digital-currencies-and-g7-finance-ministers-and-central-bank-governors-statement-on-central-bank

Hassan, S., & De Filippi, P. (2021). Decentralised Autonomous Organisations and Blockchain Governance. *Journal of Blockchain Studies*, 2(1), 15–28.

Mystakidis, S. (2022). The Metaverse Is a Digital Ecosystem. *Multimedia Tools and Applications*, 81, 31797–31833.

Nadini, M., Alessandretti, L., Di Giacinto, F., Martino, M., Parini, S., Aiello, L.M., & Baronchelli, A. (2021). Mapping the Metaverse: DeFi, NFTs, and Virtual Economies. *Scientific Reports*, 11(1), 1–14.

Szabo, N. (1997). Formalising and Securing Relationships on Public Networks. *First Monday*, 2(9). DOI: https://doi.org/10.5210/fm.v2i9.548

Voshmgir, S. (2020). *Token Economy: How Blockchains and Smart Contracts Revolutionise the Economy*. Berlin: Token Kitchen.

Wang, Q., Li, R., Jiang, J., Wang, H., & Li, X. (2021). NFTs as Digital Assets in Virtual Worlds: Ownership, Trade, and Economic Implications. *Journal of Digital Economy*, 3(1), 12–27.

Wong, K. W., Ng, K. K. H., Chiu, W. K., & Ho, G. T. S. (2023). A Comprehensive Review of the Metaverse: Fundamentals, Technologies and Applications. *Internet of Things*, 23, 100885.

Wood, G. (2014). *Ethereum: A Secure, Decentralised Generalised Transaction Ledger*. Ethereum Project Yellow Paper.

World Economic Forum (WEF). (2022). *Shaping the Metaverse: Bridging Innovation and Trust in Digital Economies*. Available at: https://www.weforum.org/reports/shaping-the-metaverse

Zheng, Z., Xie, S., Dai, H., Chen, X. and Wang, H. (2018) 'Blockchain challenges and opportunities: a survey', *International Journal of Web and Grid Services*, 14(4), pp. 352–375

35 The Road Ahead

Human-Centric and Inclusive FinTech

Chapter Overview

This concluding chapter traces the evolution of Financial Technology (FinTech) and outlines a clear path for its future. It advocates a shift towards a Human-Centric and Inclusive FinTech ecosystem. The chapter argues that the next phase of FinTech must be guided by ethics, equity, and empowerment (Arner, Zetzsche, & Buckley, 2020). Achieving this requires addressing algorithmic bias and ensuring digital financial services are accessible to older people, people with disabilities, and those with limited digital literacy. Prioritising consumer data rights is also vital. The chapter explores frameworks such as Explainable Artificial Intelligence (XAI), Privacy-Enhancing Technologies (PETs), and Universal Design as essential for a sustainable and trustworthy financial future. Finally, it describes the roles and shared responsibilities of stakeholders, emphasising the importance of collaboration to build a FinTech landscape that genuinely benefits humanity.

Learning Objectives

By the end of this chapter, students should be able to:

1. Define human-centric FinTech and articulate its core principles, distinguishing it from purely profit-driven technological deployment.
2. Analyse the ethical challenges in modern FinTech, including algorithmic bias, data privacy erosion, and digital exclusion.
3. Evaluate technological and regulatory tools, such as XAI, Universal Design, and ethics-by-design frameworks, for building more equitable financial systems.
4. Assess the role of digital and financial literacy as a critical enabler of genuine inclusion and consumer protection.
5. Propose strategies for different stakeholders (regulators, firms, educators) to foster a human-centric FinTech future collaboratively.

DOI: 10.4324/9781003775751-40

35.1 Introduction

The evolution of FinTech has been driven by swift disruption, broader financial access, and enhanced operational efficiency. Today, as the industry matures, it reaches a crucial turning point that demands careful consideration. Rapid innovation was once guided by the philosophy of move fast and break things. However, this approach now prompts important questions about who truly benefits from disruption and what its societal consequences are. Discriminatory algorithms, exploitative lending practices, persistent digital divides, and significant privacy concerns highlight the risks of an advanced yet socially disconnected financial ecosystem. These issues echo Zuboff's (2019) concerns about systems that fail to respond adequately.

This chapter contends that FinTech's enduring success is not solely measured by financial value or quick transactions. Its true impact lies in its ability to enhance financial well-being, safeguard individual rights, and include those who have been excluded from mainstream services. The future of FinTech must emphasise human needs. It should design technology to serve people, rather than merely automate processes. This transition requires prioritising social benefits over technological progress.

Creating a human-centred and inclusive FinTech requires concerted effort from all stakeholders. Ethical standards, inclusivity, and transparent practices must be incorporated from the outset of any innovation. Only through this approach can FinTech address current challenges and genuinely empower people worldwide.

35.2 The Imperative for a Human-Centric Approach

Several critical factors underscore the need to adopt a human-centric orientation in FinTech. First, the limitations of techno-solutionism are increasingly apparent. The assumption that technology alone can resolve complex socio-economic challenges has proven inadequate; without careful attention to human contexts, technological interventions risk exacerbating existing inequalities (Morozov, 2013). Second, public trust in financial technologies has been undermined by high-profile data breaches, opaque algorithmic processes, and unethical data practices. Integrating human-centred considerations is therefore essential for restoring and sustaining the social licence required for FinTech operations (World Economic Forum, 2021). Third, regulatory and consumer pressures are intensifying. Emerging frameworks such as the General Data Protection Regulation and AI-specific legislation, alongside heightened consumer activism, compel firms to prioritise fairness, accountability, and transparency.

Organisations that proactively identify and mitigate ethical risks in the design of inclusive products are better positioned to achieve sustainable growth. Such firms are likely to cultivate stronger customer loyalty and exhibit greater resilience in the face of reputational challenges and regulatory scrutiny (Figure 35.1).

35.3 Pillars of Human-Centric and Inclusive FinTech

35.3.1 Ethical AI and Mitigating Algorithmic Bias

AI underpins many FinTech services, including credit scoring, insurance underwriting, and targeted marketing. However, algorithmic decision-making can inadvertently perpetuate societal biases. For instance, AI models trained on historical credit data may systematically disadvantage certain demographic groups, such as racial minorities or women, by reflecting

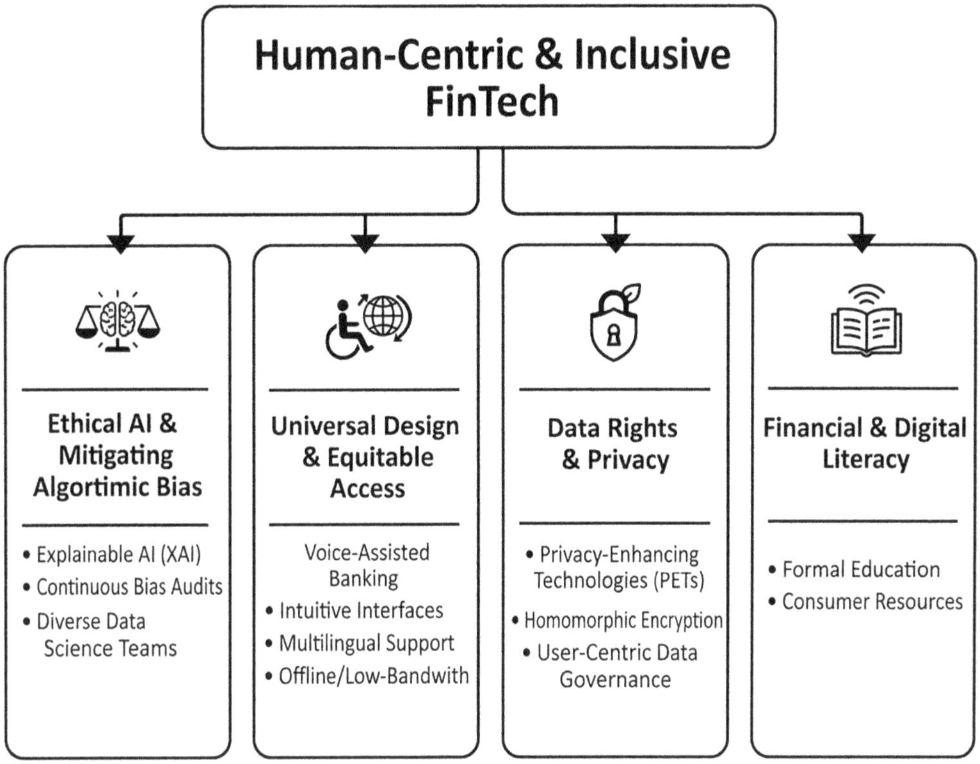

Figure 35.1 Pillars of Human-Centric and Inclusive FinTech.

entrenched patterns of inequality (Mehrabi, Morstatter, Saxena, Lerman, & Galstyan, 2021). To mitigate these risks, FinTech firms must adopt XAI, which enables the interpretability and transparency of algorithmic decisions, allowing stakeholders to scrutinise and contest outcomes (Adadi & Berrada, 2018). Continuous bias auditing is also critical; regular algorithmic evaluation can identify discriminatory patterns, prompting corrective measures. Furthermore, assembling diverse data science teams ensures that multiple perspectives inform system design, reducing the likelihood of unconscious bias influencing decision-making. For example, Zest AI uses explainable machine learning to improve fairness in credit underwriting while maintaining predictive accuracy.

35.3.2 Universal Design and Equitable Access

Inclusive FinTech requires products designed to serve users with diverse abilities, socio-economic backgrounds, and levels of digital literacy. Many platforms neglect the needs of elderly individuals, people with disabilities, or those in low-connectivity regions. Applying universal design principles ensures that services are inherently accessible, without requiring adaptation. Features such as voice-assisted banking, intuitive interfaces, multilingual support, and offline-first functionality expand accessibility. For example, the mobile banking platform Tala offers low-bandwidth, offline-compatible services in emerging markets, enabling individuals without consistent internet access to participate in digital financial systems.

35.3.3 Data Rights and Privacy as a Fundamental Right

In the era of data-driven finance, protecting personal information is both an ethical and legal necessity. Business models based on surveillance capitalism, which commodify user data, conflict with the principles of privacy and individual autonomy (Zuboff, 2019). To safeguard users, FinTech firms should deploy PETs, such as differential privacy, homomorphic encryption, and federated learning, that enable data analysis while protecting sensitive information. Establishing user-centric data governance frameworks further ensures that individuals retain meaningful control over their data, including the ability to grant, restrict, or revoke consent. An example is the FinTech company Truelayer, which provides APIs that enable users to control and share financial data with third-party applications securely.

35.3.4 Financial and Digital Literacy as an Enabler

Technological innovation benefits users only when they possess the knowledge to use it effectively. Individuals lacking digital financial literacy are more susceptible to poor financial decisions, higher debt, and exposure to fraud. Addressing this gap requires coordinated efforts among governments, educational institutions, and FinTech providers. Integrating digital financial literacy into school curricula and providing accessible consumer education resources can equip users to navigate complex digital financial ecosystems. For instance, 'Junior Achievement', an international non-profit organisation focused on youth financial and entrepreneurial education, collaborates with financial institutions to deliver interactive digital learning programmes that improve understanding of personal finance and digital banking tools.

35.4 Opportunities, Challenges, and Key Practical Issues: Human-Centric FinTech

35.4.1 Opportunities

Adopting a human-centric and inclusive approach in FinTech offers multiple strategic and societal opportunities. Firms that demonstrate ethical practices can enhance public trust, creating a competitive advantage through strengthened, long-term customer relationships (Gomber et al., 2017). By designing financial products that address the needs of underserved or marginalised populations, such as low-income communities, individuals with disabilities, or digitally excluded groups, organisations can access previously untapped markets, supporting inclusive economic growth. For example, Tala, a mobile lending platform, leverages alternative data sources to extend microloans to users in emerging markets who lack formal credit histories, simultaneously promoting financial inclusion and business growth. Moreover, embedding ethical and inclusive considerations into product development and innovation processes can foster creative problem-solving, producing more robust and resilient technological solutions (Brennen & Kreiss, 2016). Collectively, these practices not only strengthen the social fabric by promoting fairness and equity but also help reduce systemic financial inequalities.

35.4.2 Challenges

Implementing ethical safeguards and PETs presents substantial operational and financial challenges. Conducting continuous algorithmic bias audits, integrating XAI frameworks, and complying with evolving data protection standards increase development costs and extend time-to-market, creating an *ethics tax* for organisations (Mehrabi et al., 2021). Translating broad ethical principles into concrete engineering and design specifications is technically and organisationally complex, particularly when navigating fragmented regulatory environments with inconsistent national and international rules governing AI, data privacy, and consumer protection (Zuboff, 2019). The tension between short-term profitability and long-term ethical commitments further complicates adoption, as firms under pressure to scale rapidly may deprioritise responsible innovation. For instance, digital credit scoring systems that neglect fairness considerations have at times led to discriminatory lending practices, undermining trust and exposing firms to regulatory scrutiny.

35.4.3 Key Implications for the Future

Looking ahead, ethics must be recognised as a strategic competency within FinTech organisations, integrated into both decision-making and innovation processes rather than relegated solely to compliance functions (Adadi & Berrada, 2018). The rise of values-driven consumers, who increasingly consider ethical practices, data stewardship, and social impact in their financial decisions, will influence market dynamics, incentivising firms to prioritise transparency, fairness, and accountability. Traditional success metrics should evolve to include impact-oriented indicators assessing financial well-being, inclusion, and consumer trust alongside conventional financial performance measures. Addressing these complex challenges will require collaborative governance models that coordinate engagement among industry actors, regulatory authorities, academic institutions, and civil society. Such collaboration can help establish accountable, inclusive, and trustworthy FinTech ecosystems that balance innovation with societal responsibility. For example, the Partnership on AI convenes multiple stakeholders, including FinTech firms, academics, and regulators, to develop frameworks for the ethical and responsible deployment of AI.

35.5 Conclusion

The development of FinTech presents a critical juncture for stakeholders, in which prioritising algorithmic efficiency risks reinforcing exclusion and exacerbating social and economic inequalities. In contrast, a human-centric approach foregrounds dignity, agency, and financial resilience. As industry leaders have observed, FinTech must bridge gaps, not widen them, underscoring the ethical obligation to design systems that effectively serve marginalised populations. Realising this vision necessitates a fundamental operational shift, moving beyond profit-oriented metrics toward design processes informed by empathy, robust governance structures, and mechanisms for mitigating bias. With approximately 1.7 billion adults remaining unbanked globally, the evaluation of FinTech's success must extend beyond innovation to encompass inclusivity and equitable access.

Achieving such outcomes requires coordinated, multi-stakeholder engagement, including regulatory harmonisation, financial literacy initiatives, and rigorous ethical accountability frameworks. As the World Bank highlights, financial inclusion catalyses equitable economic growth. Accordingly, the sector must advance beyond technical sophistication to ensure that technology serves as a democratising instrument, expanding access while safeguarding fairness. Ultimately, the enduring impact of FinTech will be determined not solely by market performance but by its contribution to human well-being, demonstrating that innovation and inclusivity are not mutually exclusive but inherently interconnected.

Key Terms and Glossary

Human-Centric Design A design philosophy that prioritises the needs, wants, and limitations of the end-user at every stage of the design process.

Algorithmic Bias Systematic and repeatable errors in a computer system that create unfair outcomes, such as privileging one arbitrary group of users over others.

XAI A set of processes and methods that allows human users to comprehend and trust the results and output created by machine learning algorithms.

Universal Design The design of products and environments to be usable by all people, to the greatest extent possible, without the need for adaptation or specialised design.

PETs (Privacy-Enhancing Technologies) A range of technologies that allow for the extraction of valuable insights from data while protecting the underlying sensitive information.

Ethics-by-Design The integration of ethical considerations into the design and architecture of technology and business practices from the very beginning.

Digital Literacy The ability to use information and communication technologies to find, evaluate, create, and communicate information, requiring both cognitive and technical skills.

Test Your Understanding

Multiple-Choice Questions

1 Which of the following best defines human-centric FinTech?

A Technology designed solely to maximise profit
B FinTech prioritising ethical, inclusive, and user-focused design
C Platforms using AI exclusively for algorithmic trading
D Any FinTech product operating in emerging markets

2 XAI in FinTech primarily serves to:

A Increase the processing speed of AI algorithms
B Make algorithmic decisions interpretable and transparent
C Reduce the need for human oversight entirely
D Enable automatic credit scoring without compliance checks

3 Which principle ensures that FinTech products are accessible to users of varying abilities, socio-economic status, and digital literacy?

A Algorithmic bias mitigation
B PETs
C Universal design
D Digital asset tokenisation

4 PETs in FinTech are used to:

A Facilitate high-frequency trading
B Allow data analysis without exposing raw personal information
C Reduce AI model training time
D Replace all regulatory compliance requirements

5 A significant challenge of adopting human-centric FinTech is:

A Lower adoption of digital payments in emerging markets
B Increased development costs and extended time-to-market due to ethical safeguards
C Limited blockchain interoperability
D Decline in cryptocurrency usage

Short Questions

1 Explain how algorithmic bias in AI-based FinTech services can affect marginalised groups. Provide an example.
2 Describe two ways in which universal design principles can improve financial inclusion.
3 Identify and explain one regulatory or technological tool that FinTech firms can use to enhance data privacy for users.

Analytical Questions

1 Critically assess how a human-centric approach in FinTech can balance ethical responsibilities with business profitability. Use examples from platforms like Tala or Zest AI.
2 Evaluate the potential impact of values-driven consumers on FinTech product development and organisational decision-making.
3 Discuss the implications of integrating XAI and PETs in FinTech on global financial inclusion and trust.

Case Study: The Dutch Bank, Bunq, and Its Fairness Algorithm

Bunq, a Dutch challenger bank, has positioned itself as a user-centric, ethically oriented alternative to traditional financial institutions, emphasising transparency and fairness as core values of its brand. Central to this strategy is the development of the Fairness algorithm, a publicly disclosed model for determining personal loan interest rates. Unlike conventional black-box credit scoring systems, Bunq's algorithm relies on a simple, transparent set of criteria: the loan amount, loan duration, and the user's relationship with the bank, including account tenure and average balance. Notably, the model excludes factors such as postal code, education, or employment history, which are commonly used in other scoring systems but may introduce discriminatory bias. This approach aligns with the principles of XAI and demonstrates a deliberate effort to mitigate algorithmic bias while enhancing consumer trust.

The strategy has proven effective as a marketing differentiator, attracting customers who prioritise ethical and transparent financial practices. However, it also entails commercial and operational challenges. By omitting traditional risk indicators, Bunq may face higher credit risk relative to competitors. Furthermore, reliance on customer relationship metrics may inadvertently advantage wealthier clients, introducing an alternative form of bias. Finally, questions remain regarding the scalability of this simplified model in larger, more diverse markets. Overall, Bunq's initiative exemplifies the complexities and trade-offs inherent in operationalising human-centric, ethical design in FinTech.

Reference

Bunq. (2023). *Fair and Transparent Lending: How Bunq Determines Personal Loan Interest Rates*. Amsterdam: Bunq. Available at: https://www.bunq.com (Accessed: 3 March 2026).

Case Study Questions

1. In what ways does Bunq's Fairness algorithm reflect human-centric FinTech principles, particularly regarding bias mitigation and model explainability?
2. Does Bunq's exclusion of traditional data points, such as postal code, enhance fairness, or could it produce unintended adverse effects? Provide a reasoned justification.
3. If Bunq were to implement this lending model in an emerging market with a largely unbanked population lacking prior customer relationships, what alternative data sources or model adaptations would you recommend to preserve its human-centric approach while effectively managing credit risk?

Further Reading

Arner, D.W., Zetzsche, D.A., & Buckley, R.P. (2020). *FinTech and the Future of Finance*. Cambridge: Cambridge University Press.

World Economic Forum. (2021). *Global Future Council on Financial and Monetary Systems: The Future of Responsible Finance*. Geneva: World Economic Forum.

Zuboff, S. (2019). *The Age of Surveillance Capitalism: The Fight for a Human Future at the New Frontier of Power*. London: Profile Books.

References

Adadi, A., & Berrada, M. (2018). Peeking Inside the Black-Box: A Survey on Explainable Artificial Intelligence (XAI). *IEEE Access*, 6, 52138–52160.

Arner, D.W., Zetzsche, D.A., & Buckley, R.P. (2020). The Future of FinTech and Financial Inclusion: A Human-Centric Approach. R.P. Buckley, D.W. Arner & J.N. Barberis (Eds.), *The Cambridge Handbook of Fintech*. Cambridge: Cambridge University Press.

Brennen, J.S. and Kreiss, D. (2016) Digitalization. In K.B. Jensen & R.T. Craig (Eds.), *The International Encyclopedia of Communication Theory and Philosophy*. Chichester: John Wiley & Sons, pp. 1–11.

Gomber, P., Koch, J.A., Siering, M. and Weber, P. (2017). Digital Finance and Fintech: Current Research and Future Research Directions. *Journal of Business Economics*, 87(5), 537–580.

Mehrabi, N., Morstatter, F., Saxena, N., Lerman, K., & Galstyan, A. (2021). A Survey on Bias and Fairness in Machine Learning. *ACM Computing Surveys*, 54(6), 1–35.

Morozov, E. (2013). *To Save Everything, Click Here: The Folly of Technological Solutionism*. New York: PublicAffairs.

World Economic Forum. (2021). *The global FinTech Ecosystem: Designing a More Inclusive Financial System*. Geneva: World Economic Forum.

Zuboff, S. (2019). *The Age of Surveillance Capitalism: The Fight for a Human Future at the New Frontier of Power*. New York: PublicAffairs.

Multiple-Choice Questions and Answers

Chapter	*Q1*	*Q2*	*Q3*	*Q3*	*Q5*	*Chapter*	*Q1*	*Q2*	*Q3*	*Q3*	*Q5*
Chapter 1	B	C	B	B	B	Chapter 18	D	B	B	B	B
Chapter 2	B	B	D	B	C	Chapter 19	B	B	C	B	B
Chapter 3	B	B	B	B	B	Chapter 20	B	B	B	B	B
Chapter 4	B	C	B	C	C	Chapter 21	C	B	C	B	B
Chapter 5	B	C	B	D	B	Chapter 22	C	B	C	B	C
Chapter 6	C	B	C	C	B	Chapter 23	C	B	B	B	C
Chapter 7	B	B	C	A	B	Chapter 24	C	B	B	B	C
Chapter 8	B	C	C	B	C	Chapter 25	D	B	D	B	A
Chapter 9	B	B	C	C	B	Chapter 26	B	C	B	D	C
Chapter 10	B	B	C	C	B	Chapter 27	C	A	B	B	B
Chapter 11	B	B	C	B	C	Chapter 28	A	B	C	C	B
Chapter 12	B	B	B	A	B	Chapter 29	B	C	B	B	A
Chapter 13	B	C	B	B	B	Chapter 30	B	B	B	A	B
Chapter 14	B	B	B	B	C	Chapter 31	B	B	D	B	B
Chapter 15	C	C	B	C	C	Chapter 32	B	B	B	B	A
Chapter 16	B	B	B	B	B	Chapter 33	B	B	B	B	B
Chapter 17	C	B	B	B	B	Chapter 34	B	B	B	B	B
						Chapter 35	B	B	C	B	B

Glossary

Automated Clearing House (ACH) An electronic network for processing transactions, such as direct deposits and bill payments, in batches.

Artificial Intelligence (AI) The simulation of human intelligence in machines to perform tasks like learning, problem-solving, and decision-making. FinTech is used for credit scoring, fraud detection, and customer service.

Anti-Money Laundering (AML) A set of laws, regulations, and procedures intended to prevent criminals from disguising illegally obtained funds as legitimate income.

Application Programming Interface (API) A set of defined rules that enable different applications to communicate and share data. The backbone of Open Banking and embedded finance.

Authorised Push Payment Fraud (APP Fraud) A scam where a customer is tricked into voluntarily and authoritatively sending a payment to a fraudster-controlled account.

Account Takeover (ATO) A type of fraud where criminals gain unauthorised access to a user's financial accounts using stolen credentials.

Automated Teller Machine (ATM) An electronic banking outlet that allows customers to complete basic transactions without the aid of a branch representative.

Banking-as-a-Service (BaaS) A model where licensed banks integrate their digital banking services directly into the products of non-bank third parties via APIs.

Business Email Compromise (BEC) A sophisticated scam targeting businesses working with foreign suppliers and/or companies that regularly perform wire transfer payments.

Buy Now, Pay Later (BNPL) A type of short-term financing that allows consumers to make purchases and pay for them over time, often in instalments with zero interest.

Central Bank Digital Currency (CBDC) A digital form of a country's fiat currency that is a direct liability of the central bank.

Central Counterparty (CCP) A clearing house that interposes itself between counterparties to contracts traded in financial markets, becoming the buyer to every seller and the seller to every buyer.

Customer Due Diligence (CDD) The process of a business verifying the identity of its clients and assessing their suitability and potential risks.

Counter-Financing of Terrorism (CFT) Measures and regulations aimed at preventing and detecting the flow of funds to terrorist organisations.

Card-Not-Present Fraud (CNP Fraud) Fraud occurs when a stolen payment card is used to purchase without the physical card being presented (e.g., online or over the phone).

Deutscher Aktienindex (DAX) A German blue-chip stock market index consisting of the 40 major companies trading on the Frankfurt Stock Exchange.

Decentralised Finance (DeFi) An emerging financial technology based on secure distributed ledgers that removes control from banks and institutions over money and financial products.

Distributed Ledger Technology (DLT) A digital system for recording the transactions of assets, in which the transactions and their details are recorded in multiple places at the same time. Blockchain is a type of DLT.

European Central Bank (ECB) The European Central Bank administers monetary policy within the Eurozone.

Electronic Communication Network (ECN) A computerised system that automatically matches buy and sell orders for securities in the market.

Electronic Know Your Customer (e-KYC) The digital process of verifying the identity of clients remotely, using documents, biometrics, and databases.

Environmental, Social, and Governance (ESG) A set of standards for a company's operations that socially conscious investors use to screen potential investments.

Financial Action Task Force (FATF) An intergovernmental organisation that designs and promotes policies and standards to combat money laundering and terrorist financing.

Financial Conduct Authority (FCA) A financial regulatory body in the United Kingdom that operates independently of the UK government.

Financial Data Exchange (FDX) A US-based consortium working to develop a common standard for secure and convenient consumer and business access to their financial data.

Financial Technology (FinTech) The integration of technology into financial services companies' offerings aims to improve their use and delivery to consumers.

Foreign Exchange (FX/Forex) The global marketplace for trading national currencies against one another.

General Data Protection Regulation (GDPR) A regulation in EU law on data protection and privacy in the European Union and the European Economic Area.

High-Frequency Trading (HFT) A type of algorithmic trading characterised by high speeds, high turnover rates, and high order-to-trade ratios.

Initial Coin Offering (ICO) A type of funding using cryptocurrencies, in which new projects sell their underlying crypto tokens in exchange for bitcoin or ether.

International Monetary Fund (IMF) An international financial institution that works to achieve sustainable growth and prosperity for its 190 member countries.

Insurance Technology (InsurTech) The use of technology innovations is designed to squeeze out savings and efficiency from the current insurance industry model.

Internet of Things (IoT) The network of physical objects ("things") embedded with sensors, software, and other technologies for the purpose of connecting and exchanging data with other devices and systems over the internet.

Initial Public Offering (IPO) The process of offering shares of a private corporation to the public in a new stock issuance for the first time.

Know Your Customer (KYC) The process of a business verifying the identity of its clients to assess risk and ensure legitimacy.

Mergers and Acquisitions (M&A) A general term that refers to the consolidation of companies or assets through various types of financial transactions.

Machine Learning (ML) A subset of AI that enables systems to learn and improve from experience without being explicitly programmed.

Markets in Crypto-Assets (MiCA) A regulatory framework for crypto-assets in the European Union.

Natural Language Processing (NLP) A branch of AI that helps computers understand, interpret, and manipulate human language.

Non-Fungible Token (NFT) A unique digital identifier that cannot be copied, substituted, or subdivided, recorded in a blockchain, and used to certify authenticity and ownership.

Neobank (Neobank) A type of direct bank that operates exclusively online without traditional physical branch networks.

Over The Counter (OTC) Trading of securities between two counterparties is executed outside of formal exchanges and without the supervision of an exchange regulator.

Peer-to-Peer (P2P) A decentralised platform whereby two individuals interact directly with each other, without intermediation by a third party (e.g., P2P lending).

Revised Payment Service Directive (PSD2) A European regulation that mandates banks to open their payment infrastructure and customer data to third-party providers via APIs.

Post-Quantum Cryptography (PQC) Also known as quantum-resistant cryptography, it refers to cryptographic algorithms believed to be secure against attacks by quantum computers.

Regulatory Technology (RegTech) The management of regulatory processes within the financial industry through technology is often used to facilitate compliance, monitoring, and reporting.

Robotic Process Automation (RPA) A software technology that makes it easy to build, deploy, and manage software robots that emulate human actions, interacting with digital systems and software.

Real-Time Gross Settlement (RTGS) A funds transfer system where transfer of money or securities takes place from one bank to another on a real-time and gross basis.

Suspicious Activity Report (SAR) A document that financial institutions must file with the Financial Crimes Enforcement Network (FinCEN) following a suspected incident of money laundering or fraud.

Securities and Exchange Commission (SEC) An independent agency of the US federal government, responsible for protecting investors and maintaining the fair and orderly functioning of the securities markets.

Small and Medium-Sized Enterprises (SME) Businesses that maintain revenues, assets, or several employees below a certain threshold.

Security Token Offering (STO) A type of public offering in which tokenised digital securities, known as security tokens, are sold in cryptocurrency exchanges.

Supervisory Technology (SupTech) The use of technology by regulatory bodies to supervise and monitor the financial industry more effectively and efficiently.

Society for Worldwide Interbank Financial Telecommunication (SWIFT) A global member-owned cooperative that provides a secure messaging system for financial transactions between banks.

Third-Party Provider (TPP) In Open Banking, a provider that uses APIs to access a bank's data (with customer consent) to offer financial services.

Third-Party Risk Management (TPRM) The process of identifying, assessing, and mitigating risks presented by using external vendors and service providers.

Total Value Locked (TVL) A metric used in the DeFi space to measure the total amount of assets deposited in a protocol or across a set of protocols.

Usage-Based Insurance (UBI) A type of vehicle insurance that calculates premiums based primarily on the driving behaviour of the insured, monitored via telematics.

Unified Payments Interface (UPI) An instant real-time payment system developed by the National Payments Corporation of India to facilitate inter-bank transactions.

Virtual Asset Service Provider (VASP) A business that conducts activities like exchanging between virtual assets and fiat currencies, transferring virtual assets, and safekeeping/administering virtual assets.

Verified Carbon Unit (VCU) A tradable certificate representing one tonne of carbon dioxide equivalent that has been reduced or removed from the atmosphere.

Wealth Technology (WealthTech) The use of technology to disrupt and improve the wealth and asset management industry (e.g., robo-advisors).

Explainable AI (XAI) Methods and techniques for applying artificial intelligence so that humans can understand the results of the solution.

Index

Pages in *italics* refer to figures, pages in ***bold-italics*** refer to boxes.